In the Words of
Nelson Mandela

In the Words of Nelson Mandela

Compiled and edited by
Jennifer Crwys-Williams

PROFILE BOOKS

First published in Great Britain in 2010 by
PROFILE BOOKS LTD
3A Exmouth House
Pine Street
London EC1R 0JH
www.profilebooks.com

First published in South Africa by
Penguin Books Ltd

10 9 8 7 6 5 4 3 2 1

Printed and bound in Great Britain by
Clays, Bungay, Suffolk

A CIP catalogue record for this book is available from the
British Library.

ISBN 978 1 84668 447 0

FSC
Mixed Sources
Product group from well-managed
forests and other controlled sources

Cert no. SGS-COC-2061
www.fsc.org
© 1996 Forest Stewardship Council

The paper this book is printed on
is certified by the © 1996 Forest
Stewardship Council A.C. (FSC). It is
ancient-forest friendly. The printer holds
FSC chain of custody SGS-COC-2061

This book is dedicated to the children of South Africa in the hope that as they grow they may find inspiration from the thoughts of Nelson Rolihlahla Mandela – and that, in his words on receiving the Nobel Peace Prize, they and other children the world over, may 'play in the open veld, no longer tortured by the pangs of hunger or ravaged by disease or threatened with the scourge of ignorance, molestation and abuse ... children are the greatest of our treasures.' In particular, I hope this little book inspires the children in my own family, living in both the old and the new worlds: Amber, Cassandra, Sebastian, Phoebe and Blaise.

Acknowledgements

My special thanks to the journalists who, over the years, have interviewed Nelson Mandela and who have provided me with much of the material used in this book. It is no exaggeration to say that without their help this book would not have been possible.

I received substantial amounts of help for the first edition of this book from Susan Segar, then political correspondent of *The Natal Witness*.

Thanks too to Carole Blake of Blake Friedmann & Associates, who has been generous with her support and interest.

Introduction

Nelson Mandela is the world's role model. He has been described as 'the world's last great super-hero', 'an icon of forgiveness, compassion, mag-nanimity and reconciliation for the entire globe', 'a myth', 'an icon of righteousness', and, by Bill Clinton when celebrating his eighty-fifth birthday in July 2003, 'You have taught us the freedom of forgiveness, the futility of coercive power ... and the joy of service.' His wife, Graça Machel, has said pointedly that 'he is a symbol but not a saint'.

However he is described, he has become a towering symbol of reconciliation and sacrifice. Above all, he is perceived as a man who did his duty.

With the reach and might of twenty-first-century communications, the myth of the man some-times conceals the very real human being who exists beneath the hyperbole. How better, then, to let Nelson Mandela speak for himself in his own unembellished words?

Perhaps his thoughts, reproduced on these pages, and honed over many years of tribulation, will inspire people, young and old, monied and impov-erished, the world over.

In particular, I hope it will inspire people who have had few role models in their lives, and who have suffered their own apartheids in their own countries.

Jennifer Crwys-Williams

'I will continue fighting for freedom until the end of my days.'

on abortion

Women have the right to decide what they want to do with their bodies.

on his achievements

Don't tempt me to beat my chest and to say this is what I have done!

In spite of interviewers the world over hoping for intimate revelations, Nelson Mandela dislikes speaking about himself and invariably refers to the 'collective' – meaning, of course, the African National Congress

I must not be isolated from the collective who are responsible for the success.

When I make a mistake, I normally say: 'It's these young chaps,' and when they do something good, I say: 'This is the man.'

To illustrate his point, Madiba beat his chest – this was in an internationally televised interview, December 1997: Mandela Meets the Media

on Africa

For centuries, an ancient continent has bled from many gaping sword wounds.

No doubt Africa's renaissance is at hand – and our challenge is to steer the continent through the tide of history.

The people of the continent are eager and willing to be among the very best in all areas of endeavour.

The peoples of resurgent Africa are perfectly capable of deciding upon their own future form of government and discovering and themselves dealing with any dangers which might arise.

We need to exert ourselves that much more, and break out of the vicious cycle of dependence imposed on us by the financially powerful; those in command of immense market power and those who dare to fashion the world in their own image.

Africa, more than any other continent, has had to contend with the consequences of conquest in a denial of its own role in history, including the denial that its people had the capacity to bring about change and progress.

It would be a cruel irony of history if Africa's actions to regenerate the continent were to unleash a new scramble for Africa which, like that of the nineteenth century, plundered the continent's wealth and left it once more the poorer.

Conflict threatens not only the gains we have made but also our collective future.

The African rebirth is now more than an idea – its seeds are being sown in the regional communities we are busy building and in the continent as a whole.

Can we continue to tolerate our ancestors being shown as people locked in time?

Africa yearns and deserves to redeem her glory, to reassert her centuries-old contribution to economics, politics, culture and the arts; and once more to be a pioneer in the many fields of human endeavour.

One destabilising conflict anywhere on the continent is one too many.

For as long as the majority of people anywhere on the continent feel oppressed, are not allowed democratic participation in decision-making processes, and cannot elect their own leaders in free and fair elections, there will always be tension and conflict.

A continent which, while it led in the very evolution of human life and was a leading centre of learning, technology and the arts in ancient times, has experienced various traumatic epochs, each one of which has pushed her peoples deeper into poverty and backwardness.

We cannot abuse the concept of national sovereignty to deny the rest of the continent the right and duty to intervene when, behind those sovereign boundaries, people are being slaughtered to protect tyranny.

He said this in June 1998 in his address to the Organisation of African Unity

We should treat the question of peace and stability on our continent as a common challenge.

Africa has long traversed past a mindset that seeks to heap all blame on the past and on others.

on being an African

Teach the children that Africans are not one iota inferior to Europeans.

From his seminal 'No Easy Walk to Freedom' speech, 21 August 1953

The lack of human dignity experienced by Africans is the direct result of the policy of white supremacy.

Spoken from the dock at the Rivonia Treason Trial, 20 April 1964, which sent him to prison for 27 long years

All of us, descendants of Africa, know only too well that racism demeans the victims and dehumanizes its perpetrators.

We are rising from the ashes of war.

He said this while presenting the Africa Peace Award to the war-torn country of Mozambique in November 1997. Madiba's wife, Graça Machel, is the widow of the former president of that country and he feels a great bond with it

---

on the African National Congress

As no man is an island, so too are we not men of stone who are unmoved by the noble passions of love, friendship and human compassion.

He was referring to the formation of the ANC Youth League on Easter Sunday, 1944. Mandela and his lifelong friends Oliver Tambo and Walter Sisulu, were prominent among its founding fathers – the young Turks of their day. This

*quotation was from a speech made in Uppsala
Cathedral, Sweden, in March 1990*

We must move from the position of a resistance
movement to one of builders.

For us the struggle against racism has assumed
the proportions of a crusade.

The African National Congress is the greatest
achievement of the twentieth century.

*From an interview in 1997, the year he
relinquished his presidency of the party*

I have always been a member of the African
National Congress and I will remain a member of
the African National Congress until I die.

---

on the African Renaissance

As we dream and work for the regeneration of our
continent, we remain conscious that the African
Renaissance can only succeed as part of the development of a new and equitable world order in
which all the formerly colonised and marginalised
take their rightful place, makers of history rather
than the possessions of others.

As we stand on the threshold of a new African
era characterised by democracy, sustainable economic development and a re-awakening of our

rich cultural values and heritage, African unity remains our watchword and the Organisation of African Unity our guide.

----

on Afrikaners

As those who drew benefits from a previous programme of affirmative action, they should realise better than anyone else how such a programme can contribute towards making the community more productive.

I have often noticed Afrikaans people remark that the new South Africa gives them a feeling of freedom now that they have entered a wider world of relationships with fellow South Africans.

Maybe it was out of fear that they themselves would one day become the oppressed once again.

On possible reasons for the Afrikaners oppressing fellow South Africans during apartheid, and spoken in the tense run-up to South Africa's first democratic election in 1994

When you speak Afrikaans, you go straight to their hearts.

When an Afrikaner changes, he changes completely.

Many Afrikaners, who once acted with great cruelty and insensitivity towards the majority in our country, to an extent you have to go to jail to understand, have changed completely and become loyal South Africans in whom one can trust.

---

on age

What nature has decreed should not generate undue insecurity.

I am nearing my end. I want to be able to sleep until eternity with a broad smile on my face, knowing that the youth, opinion-makers and everybody is stretched across the divide, trying to unite the nation.

From a speech to students at the University of Potchefstroom, February 1996. He was then 77. Nelson Mandela was born in the tiny Transkei village of Mvezo on 18 July 1918

I will be 81 when I finally retire, and I never thought a man in his 70s should take over an organisation like the ANC.

The autumn of our lives presages the African spring.

He said this in Ouagadougou, Burkina Faso, addressing the Organisation of African Unity.

*He celebrated his 80th birthday at home in
Johannesburg with his family on 18 July 1998*

One of the advantages of old age is that people respect you because of your grey hair and say all manner of nice things about you that are not based on who you really are.

I only keep myself busy so that I can prove that although I'm a has-been, I've still got some work to do.

*Said in 2002, when he was 84 and as busy
as ever*

To be an old man is very nice because, as a young man, I didn't get the support I am getting now.

*He recounted the $10 million given to him
by TV talk-show host Oprah Winfrey, and a
number of banks whom he phoned at intervals
of 15 minutes, raising enough money to send
20 young people to university. The occasion was
the launch in Johannesburg, July 2003, of the
Mindset Network educational project. Nelson
Mandela joked that the first thing he would do
when he reached the 'next world' would be to
ferret out the billionaires. 'I am going to say to
them "raise money" because I know the poor
are everywhere and these children need to go to
school.'*

on aids

Aids is clearly a disaster, effectively wiping out the development gains of the past decades and sabotaging the future.

Nelson Mandela was closing the 13th
International Aids conference in Durban, July
2000, and drew a standing ovation

The challenge is to move from rhetoric to action, and action at an unprecedented intensity and scale.

There is no shame to disclose a terminal disease from which you are suffering.

He said this in 2002, after making a deliberate
gesture by publicly embracing HIV-infected Aids
activist Zackie Achmat; he also disclosed that
three members of his own family had died of
Aids. He was criticised by a prominent gay HIV-
positive South African judge, Edwin Cameron,
for failing to give a message on Aids when he was
president. 'In 199 ways, he was our country's
saviour. In the 200th way, he was not.'

Those who are infected with this terrible disease do not want stigma, they want love.

On the fifth anniversary of the death of Britain's
Princess Diana (31 August 2002), he paid
special tribute to her work in smashing the

*superstitions surrounding the disease. He noted
that she had gone to hospitals with Aids patients,
sitting on their beds and shaking hands. 'We have
to continue to break that stigma,' he noted at the
time*

We must not continue to be debating, to be arguing, when people are dying.

This is a global injustice. It is a travesty of human rights on a global scale.

*Nelson Mandela in Paris, July 2003. He was
speaking about the cost of life-saving medicine
for poor Aids sufferers*

I was just a number. Millions of people today infected with Aids are classified as just a number. They too are serving a prison sentence for life.

*Nelson Mandela launched his 46664 Give One
Minute of Your Life to Aids campaign in October
2003. The culmination of the campaign was the
46664 concert at Green Point Stadium, Cape
Town, on 29 November 2003*

A tragedy of unprecedented proportions is unfolding in Africa.

*This statement was a precursor to the 46664
concert for Aids. People worldwide were urged
to phone 082 1 46664 to listen to music –
and raise money for the fight against the dread
disease*

Aids today in Africa is claiming more lives than the sum total of all wars, famines and floods and the ravages of such deadly diseases as malaria.

I had no idea when I started this campaign that it would affect a member of my family ... I have called you here today to announce that my son has died of Aids.

A visibly saddened Nelson Mandela said this on 6 January 2004 at his Houghton home, telling the world about the death of his 54 year-old son, Makgatho Mandela. Makgatho's second wife, Joyce Zondi, also died in 2004, of pneumonia

The only way to make it appear like a normal illness like TB and cancer is to come out and say somebody died because of HIV/Aids, and people will stop regarding it as an extraordinary illness reserved for people who go to hell instead of heaven.

Madiba, explaining why he had made public the cause of his son's death

I would love to enjoy the peace and quiet of retirement but I know that, like many of you, I cannot rest while our beloved continent is ravaged by a deadly epidemic.

Nelson Mandela at his second 46664 concert for Aids relief. It was held in Cape Town in March 2005

For every woman infected by HIV, we destroy a generation.

---

on alliances

No true alliance can be built on the shifting sands of evasions, illusions, and opportunism.

---

on anger

Anger is a temporary feeling – you soon forget it, particularly if you are involved in positive activities and attitudes.

---

on apartheid

Apartheid is the rule of the gun and the hangman.

The universal struggle against apartheid was not an act of charity arising out of pity for our people, but an affirmation of our common humanity.

Out of the experience of an extraordinary human disaster that lasted too long, must be born a society of which all humanity will be proud.

At his inauguration as President of South Africa,
10 May 1994

It would have been immoral to keep quiet while a racist tyranny sought to reduce an entire people into a status worse than that of beasts of the forest.

The millions of graves strewn across Europe which are the result of the tyranny of Nazism, the decimation of the native peoples of the Americas and Australia, the destructive trail of the apartheid regime against humanity – all these are like a haunting question that floats in the wind: why did we allow these to happen?

Apartheid continues to live with us in the leaking roofs and corrugated walls of shacks; in the bulging stomachs of hungry children; in the darkness of homes without electricity; and in the heavy pails of dirty water that rural women carry for long distances to cook and to quench their thirst.

He said this in November 1997, one month
before stepping down as president of the ANC

At each turn of history, apartheid was bound to spawn resistance; it was destined to bring to life the forces that would guarantee its death.

With the exception of the atrocities against the Jews during World War II, there is no evil that has been as condemned by the entire world as apartheid.

He was speaking in December 1998, his last full year as President of South Africa

The struggle against apartheid can be typified as the pitting of remembering against forgetting.

---

on appearances

Appearances constitute reality.

---

on a Bill of Rights

A Bill of Rights is an important statement about the nature of power relations in any society.

The ANC has had a Bill of Rights since 1923

A Bill of Rights cannot be associated with the political or economic subordination of either the majority or the minority.

A Bill of Rights is a living thing.

---

on being a black man in a white man's court (1962)

I hate race discrimination most intensely and in all its manifestations. Even though I now happen to be tried by one whose opinion I hold in high esteem, I detest most violently the set-up that surrounds me here. It makes me feel that I am a black man in a white man's court.

Nelson Mandela appeared in the Old Synagogue in Pretoria from 15 October–7 November 1962 following his arrest in August after being on the run for 17 months. Hand-written first drafts of many of his political speeches written before he went to prison exist – but not the most famous one of all, spoken at the Rivonia Trial, because his 'I am prepared to die' speech was a collaborative effort

When my sentence has been completed I will still be moved, as men are always moved, by their consciences; I will still be moved by my dislike of the race discrimination against my people when I come out from serving my sentence, to take up again, as best I can, the struggle for the removal of those injustices until they are finally abolished once and for all.

Spoken in court, on 7 November 1962, at the end of his 'Synagogue' trial when he was convicted and sentenced to three years' imprisonment on charges of incitement and two years' imprisonment for leaving South Africa without valid travel documents

on black consciousness

In various forms and under various labels, this attitude of mind and way of life have coursed through the veins of all the motive forces of struggle.

Black consciousness has fired the determination of leaders and the masses alike.

The driving thrust of black consciousness was to forge pride and unity amongst all the oppressed, to foil the strategy of divide-and-rule, to engender pride among the mass of our people and confidence in their ability to throw off their oppression.

Above all, the liberation movement asserted that the people would most readily develop consciousness of their proud being, of their equality with everyone else, of their capacity to make history.

The value that black consciousness placed on culture reverberated across our land; in our prisons; and amongst the communities in exile – and our people, who were once enjoined to look to Europe and America for creative sustenance, turned their eyes to Africa.

Nelson Mandela was commemorating the death of black consciousness leader Steve Biko

on black South Africans

The blacks think this transformation was brought about by military victory, and they have defeated the whites. They think the whites are lying on the floor and begging for mercy.

From an interview during his July 1996 state visit to Britain

on his 80th birthday

Life will go on as normal.

But Nelson Mandela was being disingenuous. He had made plans to marry the former wife of the late president of Mozambique, Graça Machel. Only a handful of people knew and they kept the secret until the marriage was announced on Mandela's birthday

I feel very well. I feel on top of the world.

Madiba was speaking to journalists from the Sowetan just before his birthday. He told them he had been late for his meeting because he had been exercising: 'Of course, I am not as vigorous as some of you young men, but I do my exercises every morning.'

If you live until 80 you have the respect of everybody, including those who used to despise you.

*Nelson Mandela celebrated his 80th birthday
at his home in Houghton, Johannesburg,
South Africa, by quietly marrying Graça
Machel, the former wife of the late President of
Mozambique, Samora Machel. Their marriage
delighted the world*

If I could be given another 80 years.

*This was said in response to a journalist's
question: What would you like for your
birthday?*

I have been quite overwhelmed by the expressions of good wishes. There is so much to be thankful for.

---

on his 90th birthday

After nearly 90 years of life, it is time for new hands to lift the burdens. It is in your hands now.

*Nelson Mandela had just made his slow way to
the podium for the 46664 concert in London's
Hyde Park in June 2008 in celebration of his
90th birthday on 18 July. Organised by actor
Will Smith, the stars included Johnny Clegg,
the Soweto Gospel Choir and Congolese singer
Papa Wemba. A slugfest of stars, including
Bill Clinton and Oprah Winfrey, attended a*

*separate dinner in his honour. Five years earlier,
at Mandela's 85th birthday celebration, Bill
Clinton attended his party and paying tribute
to his friend, he said: 'You have taught us the
freedom of forgiveness, the futility of coercive
power... and the joy of service.'*

Your voices carried across the water to inspire us
in our prison cells far away. Tonight, we can stand
before you free.

In front of cheering fans at the 46664 concert

I would be nothing without the ANC. The struggle
has been my life and the ANC led that struggle.

*Nelson Mandela's opening words at the ANC
rally at Loftus Versfeld Stadium, Pretoria, in
celebration of his 90th birthday. He went on to
say: 'I thank the ANC for having given meaning
to my 90 years on this planet, in this country we
all love so dearly.'*

As you know, I am not a speaker at all, and I'm
not going to make any exception on this occasion,
except to say thank you all for what you have done
for me. Thank you.

*Speaking from his family home in Qunu on
his birthday. There was a feast of traditional
dishes, together with crayfish, tiger prawn
tails, calamari and wines. Thousands of local
wellwishers, who affectionately call him 'Tata
Mkhulu', gathered outside the homestead so*

loved by him. Struggle heroes Ahmed Kathrada and George Bizos were with him, as were many others especially invited to celebrate his birthday. The event was made even more special by his grandson, the newly installed Chief Mandla Mandela, who drove three cattle from the rural outpost of Mvezo, the birthplace of Nelson Mandela in the Eastern Cape, to Qunu, some 25 km away. The cattle were a tribute to his grandfather. Joined by five of his senior councillors, the journey took eight hours. The Chief wore a royal Xhosa blanket and carried a knobkerrie. As he approached his grandfather's house, he and his men, with the cattle in front, passed between crowds of ululating villagers. 'We knew we had to make this journey,' he said. He is formally known as Nkosi Zwelivelile Mandela

on Bosnia

They [the leaders] thought through their blood and not through their brains.

on boxing

I did not enjoy the violence of boxing as much as the science of it.

In the ring, rank, age, colour and wealth are irrelevant.

Nelson Mandela was a heavyweight boxer himself, training every evening at Jerry Moloi's boxing gymnasium, Soweto

on boycotts

By and large, boycotts are recognised and accepted by the people as an effective and powerful weapon of political struggle.

on the British

I regard the British parliament as the most democratic institution in the world, and the independence and impartiality of its judiciary never fail to arouse my admiration.

on Cairo

Africa's greatest city.

on Cape Town

It was here, three centuries ago, that sailors from Europe triggered off the chain of the dispossession whose consequences we are still grappling with today.

In Cape Town resides part of the souls of many nations and cultures, priceless threads in the rich diversity of our African nation.

The city hosted me and my colleagues for over 26 years.

Robben Island lies off the coast of Cape Town and can be clearly seen from Table Mountain. Cape Town, of course, was also the city which welcomed him on his first day of freedom

on the Caribbean

[The Caribbean] has, in song and verse, in political philosophy and action, long been a source for the articulation of both the lamentations and aspirations of black people everywhere.

When Africans were wrenched from their continent, they carried Africa with them and made the Caribbean a part of Africa.

on change

Belief in the possibility of change and renewal is perhaps one of the defining characteristics of politics and of religions.

_____

on charity

Cash handouts might sustain you for a few months, at the end of which your problems remain.

_____

on his childhood

When I was a boy brought up in my village in the Transkei, I listened to the elders of the tribe telling stories about the good old days, before the arrival of the white man.

In his autobiography, Long Walk to Freedom, *Mandela writes touchingly about his childhood. His collaborator on the book was* Time *contributor Richard Stengel; it took 18 months to write, starting with a manuscript Mandela had begun secretly in his prison cell. They began work daily at 6.45 am – Mandela is an early riser to this day*

I hoped and vowed then that, among the treasures that life might offer me, would be the opportunity to serve my people and make my own humble contribution to the freedom struggle.

on children

Children are the most vulnerable citizens in any society and the greatest of our treasures.

Nobel Peace Prize ceremony, Oslo, Norway
1993

The children must, at last, play in the open veld, no longer tortured by the pangs of hunger or ravaged by disease or threatened with the scourge of ignorance, molestation and abuse, and no longer required to engage in deeds whose gravity exceeds the demands of their tender years.

The children who sleep in the streets, reduced to begging to make a living, are testimony to an unfinished job.

There can be no keener revelation of a society's soul than the way in which it treats its children.

Taken from his summary of the first year of the
Nelson Mandela Children's Fund, 1996 (on
the Worldwide Web at http://www.web.co.za/
mandela/children)

The true character of a society is revealed in how it treats its children.

When you see the children, the way they are dressed, completely emaciated, you are really moved.

He was speaking about children in general, and
about the children who live around the Transkei
villages he calls home, in particular

on circumcision

The pain went into the marrow of my bones.

I was not as forthright and strong as the other boys that preceded me.

The fact that courage is expected of you in the face of the unbearable gives you strength for the rest of your life.

on clothes

My father gave me his riding breeches and he cut them, and they had twine which I used as a belt, and that is how I went to school for the first time. I had a pair of shorts, sandals but no socks, a sleeveless shirt and no underwear, which is very humiliating.

Talking to the then editor of French Vogue,
December 1993, and referring to the early
days of his imprisonment – a far cry from the
'Madiba style' shirts he has made famous. They
are generally made of silk and lined with silk –

*and the pattern is perfectly aligned, making them
costly in terms of fabric to make*

There isn't a single article I wear that I have
bought – people just generously give me clothes.

1994, after seven months as president

Every time I put on a bow tie I am so uncomfortable I can hardly talk.

Everybody just looks at my face – not at my clothes.

---

on colonialism

The resistance of the black man to white colonial
intrusion was crushed by the gun.

*Taken from Mandela's letter, smuggled out of
Robben Island after the 1976 Soweto uprising,
and published internationally by the ANC in
1980*

The nineteenth-century colonisation of the
African continent was in many respects the culmination of the Renaissance-initiated expansion
of European dominion over the planet.

---

on communication

One of our strongest weapons is dialogue.

on communism

For many decades communists were the only political group in South Africa who were prepared to
treat Africans as human beings and their equals;
who were prepared to eat with us; talk with us, live
with us and work with us.

Spoken from the dock at the Rivonia Treason
Trial, 20 April 1964

There is so much hypocrisy behind some of this
red-baiting that it sickens me, and I feel like saying
to the culprits: 'How dare you say to me, a man
of 75, that I must denounce my friends, and for
whom?'

on compromise

That is the nature of compromising: you can compromise on fundamental issues.

At one of his first interviews after his release
from 27 years' imprisonment, 15 February
1990. He was released on 11 February 1990

If you are not prepared to compromise, then you
must not enter into, or think about, the process of
negotiation at all.

Compromise must not undermine your own position.

Insignificant things, peripheral issues, don't need any compromise.

-----

on conciliation

No organisation whose interests are identical with those of the toiling masses will advocate conciliation to win its demands.

-----

on conflict

One effect of sustained conflict is to narrow our vision of what is possible.

From the 2000 Independent News & Media lecture at Trinity College, Dublin

All enduring conflicts, even if they start with right on one or other side, reach a point at which neither side is wholly right or wrong.

-----

on the Congressional Gold Medal, USA

The award with which you honour me is an expression of the common humanity that binds us, one person to another, nation to nation, and people of the north to people of the south.

He received the medal at the Rotunda on Capitol Hill, Washington, on 23 September 1998, his last visit to the USA as President of South Africa

I receive it with pride, as a symbol of the partnership for peace, prosperity and equity as we enter the new millennium.

The medal has also been received by Mother Teresa, Winston Churchill, Thomas Edison, Walt Disney and Joe Louis among roughly 100 others

---

on the South African constitution

We give life to our nation's prayer for freedom regained and a continent reborn.

On signing the new South African constitution into law at Sharpeville, 10 December 1996

Let us now, drawing strength from the unity which we have forged, together grasp the opportunities and realise the vision enshrined in this constitution.

Respect for human life, liberty and well-being must be enshrined as rights beyond the power of any force to diminish.

on criticism

If the criticism is valid, it must be made.

on culture

Like truth, culture and creativity are enduring.

on his culture

In my culture we don't discuss personal questions with young people.

Our families are far larger than those of whites and it is always a pleasure to be fully accepted throughout a village, district, or even several districts, accompanied by your clan, and be a beloved household member, where you can call at any time, completely relaxed, sleep at ease and freely take part in the discussion of all problems, where you can even be given livestock and land to build, free of charge.

From an undated letter to his cousin Sisi, written from Robben Island

on the dead

In eulogies to the departed, the works of the living sometimes bear little relation to reality.

The names of only very few people are remembered beyond their lives.

on his death

It would be very egotistical of me to say how I would like to be remembered. I'd leave that entirely to South Africans. I would just like a simple stone on which is written, 'Mandela'.

Taken from a moving article for The New York Times *magazine by Anthony Lewis, 23 March 1997*

There will be life after Mandela.

On my last day I want to know that those who remain behind will say: 'The man who lies here has done his duty for his country and his people.'

He said this in 1999, in Qunu, where he was warmly welcomed shortly after his retirement

on the death sentence

The death sentence is a reflection of the animal instinct still in human beings.

on democracy

What is important is not only to attain victory for democracy, it is to retain democracy.

Democracy and human rights are inseparable.

A democratic political order must be based on the majority principle, especially in a country where the vast majority have been systematically denied their rights.

Let us never be unmindful of the terrible past from which we come – that memory not as a means to keep us shackled to the past in a negative manner, but rather as a joyous reminder of how far we have come and how much we have achieved.

He was speaking to a joint sitting of parliament, held to mark 10 years of democracy in South Africa

A guiding principle in our search for and establishment of a non-racial, inclusive democracy in our country has been that there are good men and women to be found in all groups and from all sectors of society; and that in an open and free society those South Africans will come together to jointly and cooperatively realise the common good.

To a joint sitting of parliament on 10 May 2004

Let us refrain from chauvinistic breast-beating; but let us also not underrate what we have achieved in establishing a stable and progressive democracy where we take freedoms seriously; in building national unity in spite of decades and centuries of apartheid and colonial rule; in creating a culture in which we increasingly respect the dignity of all.

---

on demonstrations

Mass action is a peaceful form of channelling the anger of the people.

---

on detention without trial

The detention without trial of political opponents is contrary to the basic principles of a democratic polity.

on determination

As long as you have an iron will you can turn misfortune into advantage.

From a letter to his daughter, Zindzi Mandela, September 1990

on what he would die for

I have fought against white domination, and I have fought against black domination. I have cherished the ideal of a democratic and free society in which all persons live together in harmony and with equal opportunities. It is an ideal which I hope to live for and to achieve. But if needs be, it is an ideal for which I am prepared to die.

Delivered from the dock at the Rivonia Treason Trial, April 1964

on discipline

Discipline is the most powerful weapon to get liberation.

An organisation can only carry out its mandate if there is discipline, and where there is no discipline there can be no real progress.

on domesticity

I make my own bed every day. I don't allow the ladies who look after me to do it. I can cook a decent meal ... I can polish a floor.

on education

Parents have the right to choose the kind of education that shall be given to their children.

Make every home, every shack or rickety structure a centre of learning.

on election day (27 April 1994)

It was as though we were a nation reborn.

Nelson Mandela was 75 when he cast his first vote at Ohlange High School, Inanda, KwaZulu-Natal

We can loudly proclaim from the rooftops – Free at last! Free at last!

After Martin Luther King, Jnr (the closing words from his 'I Have a Dream' speech, Washington 28 August 1963). Nelson Mandela spoke the words on the first day of the first democratic South African elections, 27 April 1994

I stand before you humbled by your courage with a heart full of love for all of you.

---

on emigration

To this day we continue to lose some of the best among ourselves because the lights in the developed world shine brighter.

---

on enemies

If a man fights back he is likely to get more respect than he would if he capitulated.

At his Bishopscourt, Cape Town, press conference on 15 February 1990, his first after his release from 27 years' imprisonment

I wanted South Africa to see that I loved even my enemies while I hated the system that turned us against one another.

Mandela's presidency was notable for the efforts he made towards reconciliation – including taking tea in the all-white Boer enclave of Oranje with the widow of the architect of apartheid, Dr Hendrik Verwoerd, and meeting Dr Percy Yutar, prosecuting attorney at the Rivonia Treason Trial

on his family

I have had to separate myself from my dear wife and children, from my mother and sisters, to live as an outlaw in my own land.

I am convinced that your pain and suffering was far greater than my own.

Said during his first speech as a free man, at a rally in Cape Town, 11 February 1990

I did not in the beginning choose to place my people above my family, but in attempting to serve my people, I found I was prevented from fulfilling my obligations as a son, a brother, a father and a husband.

He has said this frequently, and might have added 'and as a grandfather'. In 1997 he had 21 grandchildren

Our political activities have just destroyed our family.

Spoken after two and a half years as president of South Africa and referring to his retirement, which he expected to be spent largely as a global statesman

To see your family, your children being persecuted when you are absolutely helpless in jail, that is one of the most bitter experiences, most painful experiences, I have had.

Playing with [my] grandchildren makes me forget about the troubles of the world.

on fear

Our deepest fear is not that we are inadequate. Our deepest fear is that we are powerful beyond measure. As we are liberated from our own fear, our presence automatically liberates others.

on his favourite things

My favourite animal is the impala because it is alert, curious, rapid and able to get out of difficult conditions easily – and with grace.

Taken from French Vogue *December 1993/ January 1994. It was a historic issue – edited by Nelson Mandela himself – and now a collector's item*

Koeksisters are my favourite: in 1941 I was paid £2 a month and I reserved 10/- each weekend for koeksisters.

Koeksisters are a sticky Afrikaans sweet: plaited dough, deep fried and dunked in cold syrup. He was talking to satirist Pieter-Dirk Uys

My favourite pastime: reading.

on the football World Cup, 2010

Our time has come.

Nelson Mandela had travelled with other South African leaders to Zurich, Switzerland in May 2004, to make final representations to Fifa in anticipation of South Africa's successful bid to win the rights to the Football World Cup in 2010. Mandela was there with two South African Nobel Peace Prize laureates: FW de Klerk and Archbishop Desmond Tutu. Everyone united as South Africa's 29-minute presentation was shown

My friends, it is 28 years since Fifa took its step against racial inequality and helped inspire the final struggle against apartheid.

Nelson Mandela, of course, was South Africa's trump card

I felt like a young man of 15!

Nelson Mandela after Fifa president Sepp Blatter revealed that South Africa had won the 2010 World Cup: 'Fifa World Cup 2010: South Africa.' Desmond Tutu told a reporter: 'I want to go outside and dance, man!'

The beauty of this victory is that we were dealing with highly capable competitors who made it difficult for us to forecast what the result would be.

*Madiba turned to the dismayed Moroccan
delegation after it had lost out on the 2010
World Cup to comfort them*

---

on freedom

There is no easy walk to freedom.

*He was 35 when he made that statement in his
famous 'No Easy Walk to Freedom' speech. The
words were originally spoken by India's first
prime minister after independence, Jawaharlal
Nehru*

Too many have suffered for the love of freedom.

*Still imprisoned, this was from his first speech in
almost 25 years. It was read in Johannesburg to
wildly cheering crowds by his youngest daughter,
Zindzi, on 10 February 1985*

Only free men can negotiate.

*He spoke about this frequently: 'Only free men
can negotiate; prisoners cannot enter into
contracts.'*

No power on earth can stop an oppressed people
determined to win their freedom.

*From 'The Struggle is My Life' press statement,
26 June 1961*

There is no such thing as part freedom.

Only through hardship, sacrifice and militant action can freedom be won.

No South African should rest and wallow in the joy of freedom.

To men, freedom in their own land is the pinnacle of their ambitions, from which nothing can turn men of conviction aside.

We do not want freedom without bread, nor do we want bread without freedom.

To overthrow oppression is the highest aspiration of every free man.

From Mandela's 'Black Man in a White Court' statement at his trial held in the Old Synagogue, Pretoria, from 15 October to 7 November 1962

A man who takes away another man's freedom is a prisoner of hatred.

After 27 years' imprisonment, Nelson Mandela walked to freedom through the gates of Victor Verster Prison, Paarl, at 4.16 pm on 11 February 1990. He was 71

Freedom cannot be achieved unless women have been emancipated from all forms of oppression.

To be free is not merely to cast off one's chains, but to live in a way that respects and enhances the lives of others.

Our freedom is incomplete without the freedom of the Palestinians; without the resolution of conflicts in East Timor, the Sudan and other parts of the world.

The choice is not between freedom and justice on the one hand, and their opposite, on the other.

For as long as legitimate bodies of opinion feel stifled, vile minds will take advantage of justifiable grievances to destroy, to kill and to maim.

---

on the Freedom Charter (1955)

It has received international acclaim as an outstanding human rights document.

The Charter is more than a mere list of demands for democratic reforms.

---

on friendship

Friendship and support from friends is something which is a source of tremendous inspiration always and to everyone.

Those who are ready to join hands can overcome the greatest challenges.

on the future

The fall of our century will carry away the foliage of bitterness which has accumulated in our hearts, and to which colonialism, neo-colonialism and white minority domination gave birth.

You are responsible for your own future, and with hard work you can accomplish anything and make your dreams come true.

Nelson Mandela was referring to South African
Idols winner Karin Kortje, whose rise from a
Grabouw apple picker to the nation's songster
was embraced by everyone. He was speaking in
December 2005

on goals

The ways in which we will achieve our goals are bound by context, changing with circumstances even while remaining steadfast in our commitment to our vision.

Chris Hani Award at 10th National Congress of
SACP, Johannesburg, 1 July 1998

on government

When a government seeks to suppress a peaceful demonstration of an unarmed people by mobilising the entire reserves of the state, military and police, it concedes powerful mass support for such a demonstration.

Said in 1961, when he was living in hiding, and was referred to as the Black Pimpernel in the nation's press. A small monument has now been erected close to the spot where he was finally arrested on the night of 5 July 1962 outside the small KwaZulu-Natal town of Howick

There is always a danger that when there is no opposition, the governing party can become too arrogant – too confident of itself.

There is nothing which makes people more appreciative of a government than that it should be able to deliver services.

on government corruption

Corruption in government – that is a plague that must be erased from every regime in every place in the world.

on Harlem, New York

Harlem symbolizes the strength and beauty in resistance and you have taught us that out of resistance to injustice comes renaissance, renewal and rebirth.

on hate

No one is born hating another person because of the colour of his skin, or his background, or his religion.

on health

The wounds that cannot be seen are more painful than those that can be treated by a doctor.

on heroes

No single individual can assume the role of hero or Messiah.

There are men and women chosen to bring happiness into the hearts of people – those are the real heroes.

on his heroes

Muhammed Ali was an inspiration to me even in prison because I thought of his courage and commitment. He used mind and body in unison and achieved success.

I would never miss a movie with Sophia Loren in it.

Kobie Coetsee – I have immense respect for that man because when no member of the National Party wanted to hear about the ANC, he was working systematically with me. He is one of my heroes.

Kobie Coetsee was Minister of Justice under PW Botha prior to Nelson Mandela's release on 11 February 1990

My heroes are men and women, black and white, who are worried about socio-economic questions: people like Mother Theresa and many others – these are my heroes.

He said this in a television interview with talk-show host Tim Modise on Carte Blanche in July 2003. The interview, mostly done at Shambala game lodge, was in celebration of Nelson Mandela's 85th birthday

on himself

I have always regarded myself, in the first place, as an African patriot.

From the dock at the Rivonia Treason Trial, 20 April 1964. It took him two weeks, working in his cell at night, to write the speech

I don't think there is much history can say about me.

I wanted to be able to stand and fight with my people and to share the hazards of war with them.

From the Rivonia Treason Trial, 20 April 1964

I was made, by the law, a criminal, not because of what I had done, but because of what I stood for, because of what I thought, because of my conscience.

Spoken at the Old Synagogue Trial, Pretoria, 7 November 1962

I'm an ordinary person, I have made serious mistakes, I have serious weaknesses.

I am what I am, both as a result of people who respected me and helped me, and of those who did not respect me and treated me badly.

I will pass through this world but once, and I do not want to divert my attention from my task, which is to unite the nation.

Spoken in February 1996 when he was 77 years old

Rather than being an asset, I'm more of a decoration.

Referring to himself as President of South Africa

In prison I had been worried by people depicting me as a superhuman being who could achieve the impossible.

Nelson Mandela, reflecting in 1999 on a long life

People expect me to do more than is humanly possible.

I carry with me the frailties of my age and the fetters of prejudice that are a privilege of my years.

He said this in 1997 in front of the International Olympic Committee, Lausanne, in a fruitless bid to persuade them to bring the Olympics to Cape Town in 2004

I haven't suffered to the same extent other people have whilst I was relaxing in prison.

Any man or institution that tries to rob me of my dignity will lose.

I was not a messiah, but an ordinary man who became a leader because of extraordinary circumstances.

This was a frequent refrain: 'That was one of the things that worried me – to be raised to the position of a semi-god – because then you are no longer a human being.'

I seem to arrive more firmly at the conclusion that my own life struggle has had meaning only because, dimly and perhaps incoherently, it has sought to achieve the supreme objective of ensuring that each, without regard to race, colour, gender or social status, could have the possibility to reach for the skies.

Judge me not on how I have risen, but on how many times I have fallen and risen.

Whatever my wishes might be, I cannot bind future generations to remember me in the particular way I would like.

If you come across as a saint, people can be very discouraged.

He said this in a reflective mood in February 2000

I wanted to be known as Mandela, a man with weaknesses, some of which are fundamental, and a man who is committed, but, nevertheless, sometimes fails to live up to expectations.

August 2004

---

on history

History shows that penalties do not deter men when their conscience is aroused.

Ordinary South Africans are determined that the past be known, the better to ensure that it is not repeated.

From a speech launching the Truth and Reconciliation Commission in February 1996

Blaming things on the past does not make them better.

The past is a rich resource on which we can draw in order to make decisions for the future.

The purpose of studying history is not to deride human action, nor to weep over it or to hate it, but to understand it – and then to learn from it as we contemplate our future.

It is the dictate of history to bring to the fore the kind of leaders who seize the moment, who cohere the wishes and aspirations of the oppressed.

He could have been speaking about himself; he was, in fact, speaking about the murdered black consciousness leader, Steve Bantu Biko, on the commemoration of the 20th anniversary of his death (1997)

---

on home

I long to see the little stones on which I played as a child, the little rivers, where I swam – but I am stationed in Johannesburg.

Spoken with longing just after his release in 1990. When Nelson Mandela built his house in the village of Qunu, Transkei, where he was brought up, he built the house identically to the one he had lived in at Victor Verster Prison, Paarl. He says he 'became friendly with the walls of the house'. To this day, he says he was happiest there, between the years 1988 and 1990

Everybody comes back to where they were born.

He was spending Christmas 1996 at Qunu

It becomes important, the older you get, to return to places where you have wonderful recollections.

For the years of his imprisonment, it was the modest Sowetan house he shared with his then wife, Winnie – No 8115, Orlando West – which he dreamt about. In May 1997, together with

his third wife, Graça Machel, he bought a new
home in Houghton, Johannesburg, specifically
to make space for his 21 grandchildren, some of
whom live with him for extended periods

---

on homosexuality

There was a time when I reacted with revulsion
against the whole system of being gay.

I was ashamed of my initial views, coming from
a society which did not know this type of thing.

I understand their position, and I think they are
entitled to carry on with what pleases them.

---

on honour

Which man of honour will desert a lifelong friend
at the insistence of a common opponent and still
retain a measure of credibility with his people?

From an open letter to PW Botha, State
President of South Africa, March 1989, who
had offered him a conditional freedom. Mandela's
youngest daughter, Zindzi, read it to a rapt crowd
at the Jabulani Stadium, Soweto, on 10 February
1985

on his hopes

As I sit in Qunu and grow as ancient as its hills, I will continue to entertain the hope that there has emerged a cadre of leaders in my own country and region, on my continent and in the world, which will not allow that any should be denied their freedom, as we were, that any should be turned into refugees, as we were, that any should be condemned to go hungry, as we were, that any should be stripped of their human dignity, as we were.

He was speaking, for the last time as South African Head of State, to the United Nations' General Assembly, New York, 21 September 1998

on housing

Every man should have a house near where he was born.

He said this to Richard Stengel, who worked with him on Long Walk to Freedom *in April 1993, when he visited the modest house he built himself in the Transkei*

A man is not a man until he has a house of his own.

Nelson Mandela now has several houses: one is in Houghton, Johannesburg, which he shares with his wife, Graça Machel, as he does their home in Maputo, Mozambique; he has a home in Cape Town, and one is in Qunu, South Africa, the village where he spent his childhood. The Qunu house has been considerably enlarged to accommodate Nelson Mandela's large family and friends

The families who live in shacks with no running water, sanitation, and electricity are a reminder that the past continues to haunt the present.

---

on humanity

Many of us will have to pass through the valley of the shadow of death again and again before we reach the mountaintops of our desires.

This was a powerful sentence in Nelson Mandela's seminal 'No Easy Walk to Freedom' speech, delivered in September 1953

It is a fact of the human condition that each shall, like a meteor – a mere brief passing moment in time and space – flit across the human stage and pass out of existence.

From his Address to the Joint Session of the Houses of Congress of the USA, 26 June 1990,

where he was rapturously received only months
after his release

To deny any person their human rights is to challenge their very humanity.

Let the strivings of us all prove Martin Luther King Jnr to have been correct when he said that humanity can no longer be tragically bound to the starless midnight of racism and war.

The key to the protection of any minority is to put core civil and political rights beyond the reach of temporary majorities by guaranteeing them as fundamental human rights, enshrined in a democratic constitution.

None of us can be described as having virtues or qualities that raise him or her above others.

After climbing a great hill, one only finds that there are many more hills to climb.

The universe we inhabit as human beings is becoming a common home that shows growing disrespect for the rigidities imposed on humanity by national boundaries.

Deep down in every human heart, there is mercy and generosity.

As long as poverty, injustice and gross inequality persist in our world, none of us can truly rest.

on imperialism

Imperialism means the denial of political and economic rights and the perpetual subjugation of the people by a foreign power.

Imperialism has been weighed and found wanting.

on being impetuous

It's very important not to shoot from the hip.

on important things

The important thing is to give happiness to people.

Nelson Mandela said this in a television interview to mark his 85th birthday (and the fifth anniversary of his marriage to Graça Machel)

on Inauguration Day, 10 May 1994

One of the outstanding human victories of the century.

I was overwhelmed with a sense of history.

The time for the healing of the wounds has come. The moment to bridge the chasms that divide us has come. The time to build is upon us.

Taken from his Inaugural speech. His inauguration as President of South Africa was held at the Union Buildings in Pretoria, a day no South African who watched it will ever forget

---

on India

India's independence was a victory for all people under colonial rule.

A part of India's soul resides in South Africa as a revered part of our national life.

He was referring to Mahatma Gandhi

---

on Islam

Islam has enriched and become part of Africa; in turn, Islam was transformed and Africa became part of it.

---

on jellybeans

What are jellybeans? Are they something that is eaten?

on June 16 (Freedom Day)

June 16 is the day on which we South Africans commemorate the contribution of our youth to the achievement of democracy, and rededicate ourselves to creating a just society. Celebrated in South Africa as Freedom Day, June 16 1976 was the day on which the youth of Soweto rose in anger against the use of Afrikaans in schools. This escalated into what is known as the Soweto Uprising. It led directly to the end of apartheid and to the exile of many thousands of young South Africans who left the country illegally to join resistance movements such as the ANC.

on justice

In our country and throughout the British world, as far as I know, and in the jurisprudence of many civilised countries, a person is regarded as innocent until he is convicted.

on his last day

On my last day I want to know that those who remain behind will say: 'The man who lies here has done his duty for his country and his people.'

On being welcomed home to Qunu on his retirement in 1999

on leadership

It is a mistake to think that a single individual can unite the country.

When you want to get the cattle to move in a certain direction, you stand at the back with a stick, and then you get a few of the cleverer cattle to go to the front and move in the direction that you want them to go. The rest of the cattle follow the few more energetic cattle in the front, but you are really guiding them from the back.

Nelson Mandela then added: 'That is how a leader should do his work'

I never choose between stars or teams – it's a tactless thing for a leader to do.

Mandela's reasoning was that if you put a team or a star above others you immediately forfeit their support

There are times when a leader can show sorrow, in public, and that it will not diminish him in the eyes of his people.

As when he comforted Nomboniso Gasa, who was raped on Robben Island in January 1997. He openly showed his distress and anger

Many in positions of power and privilege pursue cold-hearted philosophies which terrifyingly proclaim: I am not your brother's keeper!

He was speaking to the United Nations in October 1995

A leadership commits a crime against its own people if it hesitates to sharpen its political weapons which have become less effective.

A leader who relies on authority to solve problems is bound to come to grief.

We have the high salaries and we are living in luxury: that destroys your capacity to speak in a forthright manner and tell people to tighten their belts.

From a September 1994 interview some four months after he was inaugurated as President of South Africa

It is important to surround yourself with strong and independent personalities, who will tell you when you are getting old.

Nelson Mandela said this in 1996 when there was speculation about his health, and queries were being raised in South Africa as to whether he would be able to complete his term of office

It is the fate of leadership to be misunderstood; for historians, academics, writers and journalists to reflect great lives according to their own subjective canon.

The mark of great leaders is the ability to understand the context in which they are operating and act accordingly.

---

on liberation

The people are their own liberators.

---

on Libya

The people of Libya shared the trenches with us in our struggle for freedom.

This was said at a banquet in Tripoli, Libya, in October 1997. Nelson Mandela went to great lengths to get to the pariah country, and was staunch – and even angry – in the face of American disapproval. One of his mottoes is never to forget a friend – even if they are held in opprobrium by many

---

on life

Life is like a big wheel: the one who's at the top, tomorrow is at the bottom.

on literature

We could not have made an acquaintance through literature with human giants such as George Washington, Abraham Lincoln and Thomas Jefferson and not been moved to act as they were moved to act.

He said this in a speech to the US Congress in June 1990, shortly after his release from incarceration. One of Nelson Mandela's favourite poems was William Ernest Henley's Invictus; Irish poet Seamus Heaney's work was also important to him, and he has quoted South African poet Ingrid Jonker on several occasions

When we read we are able to travel to many places, meet many people and understand the world.

Whilst on Robben Island, Mandela and his fellow prisoners avidly read Shakespeare: Coriolanus, Henry V and Julius Caesar being favourites. The prisoners staged Sophocles' Antigone, in which Mandela played the part of the tyrant Creon

on longevity

If your attitude is to do things which are going to please the community and human beings, then of course you are likely to live a long life. To go to bed feeling that you have done some service to the community is very important.

———

on love

The world is truly round and seems to start and end with those we love.

From a letter to Winnie, 1 July 1979

I am not nervous of love for love is very inspiring.

Spoken on his State visit to the UK, July 1996. Only a few people at that time knew of his love for Graça Machel, widow of Samora Machel, President of Mozambique

To be in love is an experience that every man must go through.

One should be so grateful at being involved in such an experience.

It is such a wonderful period for me.

Spoken in April 1997, and referring to his relationship with Graça Machel

I'm in love with a remarkable lady. She has changed my life.

This was said with a broad smile in a South African television interview in February 1998. The remarkable lady was, of course, Graça

Machel, whom he married on his 80th birthday,
18 July 1998

I don't regret the setbacks I have had before and, late in my life, I am blooming like a flower because of her support.

Again, referring to Graça Machel

Holding Graça's hand is the one thing I love most in the world.

People must learn to hate, and if they can learn to hate, they can be taught to love, for love comes more naturally to the human heart than its opposite.

---

on marriage

The whole purpose of a husband and wife is that when hard times knock at the door you should be able to embrace each other.

According to our custom, you marry the village and not the human being.

A man and wife usually discuss their most intimate problems in the bedroom.

Spoken in March 1996, in public, at his divorce
hearing from his second wife, Winnie

Ladies don't want to be marrying an old man like me.

On being asked towards the end of 1996
whether he would marry Graça Machel

---

his marriage to Graça Machel, 18 July 1998

Now you won't shout at me and say I am setting a bad example.

Nelson Mandela said this to fellow Nobel
Peace Prize holder, Archbishop Desmond Tutu,
immediately after his marriage. Tutu had
criticised him for living with Graça and setting a
bad example

My wife has put a spring in me and made me full of hope.

He said this in May 2002 after nearly four years
of marriage to Graça

Evelyn Mase, his first wife

She was a quiet, pretty girl from the countryside who did not seem over-awed by the comings and goings.

He met his first wife in the lounge of Walter and Albertina Sisulu's home. He asked her to marry him within a few months and married in a civil ceremony at the Native Commissioner's Court in Johannesburg. They had four children (Thembikile, 1946; Makaziwe, 1947, who died at nine months; Makgatho, 1951; and Makaziwe, 1954) and divorced in 1958

Winnie Madikizela-Mandela, his second wife

She was dazzling, and even the fact that she had never before tasted curry and drank glass after glass of water to cool her palate only added to her charm.

The couple's first date was at an Indian restaurant near his Johannesburg offices. He says he asked her to marry him on their first date, but Winnie always claimed he didn't propose to her at all. They were married in a local church in Bizana on 14 June 1958 and divorced only in March 1996. They had two daughters

I had hoped to build you a refuge, no matter how small, so that we would have a place for rest and sustenance before the arrival of the sad, dry days.

From a letter to Winnie from Robben Island, 26 June 1977

Had it not been for your visits, wonderful letters and your love, I would have fallen apart many years ago.

From a letter to Winnie, 6 May 1979

I have often wondered whether any kind of commitment can ever be sufficient excuse for abandoning a young and inexperienced woman in a pitiless desert.

Letter to Winnie after her 1986 'Boxes and Matches' speech

I cannot say for certain if there is such a thing as love at first sight, but I do know that the moment I first glimpsed Winnie Nomzamo, I knew that I wanted to have her as my wife.

She married a man who soon left her; that man became a myth; and then that myth returned home and proved to be just a man after all.

In a curiously similar turn of phrase, Graça Machel, widow of President Samora Machel of Mozambique, and Nelson Mandela's third wife, said of him in an interview at the beginning of 1998: 'I found this very simple man who appeared so humble, so soft, so common. It was a conflict between myth and the reality.'

I embrace her with all the love and affection I have nursed for her inside and outside prison from the moment I first met her.

Announcing his separation from Winnie,
13 April 1992

My love for her remains undiminished.

Part of his poignant separation announcement

I was the loneliest man during the period I stayed with her.

During his divorce trial, March 1996

---

on memory

In the life of any individual, family, community or society, memory is of fundamental importance.

Memory is the fabric of identity.

At the heart of every oppressive tool developed by the apartheid regime was a determination to control, distort, weaken, even erase people's memories.

---

on men

Men must follow the dictates of their conscience irrespective of the consequences which might overtake them for it.

This was part of his 'Black Man in a White
Court' statement in the Old Synagogue, Pretoria,

on 15 October 1962. The Rivonia Treason Trial
still lay ahead

---

on the Middle East peace process

The spurning of agreements reached in good faith
and the forceful occupation of land can only fan
the flames of conflict.

Extremists on all sides thrive, fed by the blood lust
of centuries gone by.

Palestinian and Israeli campaigners for peace
know that security for any nation is not abstract;
neither is it exclusive.

At the end of a century which has seen a desert
of devastation caused by horrific wars, a century
which has at last gained much experience in the
peaceful resolution of conflicts, we must ask: is
this a time for war; is this a time for sending young
men to their death?

This was said on his being awarded an Honorary
Doctorate by Ben-Gurion University of the
Negev, 19 September 1997

on misfortunes

There are few misfortunes in this world that you cannot turn into a personal triumph if you have the iron will and the necessary skill.

on morality

A movement without a vision is a movement without moral foundation.

on the National Party

We are hopeful that, in their role, they will add another brick into the edifice of our young democracy.

Nelson Mandela was speaking in parliament in June 1996

For people that had to invoke the name of God as they made our people suffer? For people who warped the concept of Christianity to cloak the abomination of apartheid in it?

He was incredulously referring to the National Party, the bulwark of apartheid until 1994, versus the South African Communist Party

on negotiation

Concessions are inherent in negotiations.

When you negotiate you have to accept the integrity of another man.

When you negotiate you must be prepared to compromise.

Negotiated solutions can be found even to conflicts that have come to seem intractable and that such solutions emerge when those who have been divided reach out to find the common ground.

Only free men can negotiate.

He wrote this in a letter to then State President PW Botha, dismissing with contempt Botha's offer of conditional release. And although it was illegal for Mandela's words to be repeated in South Africa at that time, his letter was defiantly read out to the crowds by his youngest daughter, Zindzi, at Jabulani Stadium, Soweto, on 10 February 1985. He had another five years of imprisonment to go

If successful negotiations lead to talk of miracles, then it is in part because they achieve what pain too long endured had made to seem impossible.

This was part of a lecture he gave at Trinity College, Dublin, in April 2000

on the new world order

Can we say with confidence that it is within our reach to declare that never again shall continents, countries or communities be reduced to the smoking battlefields of contending forces of nationality, religion, race or language?

Intervention only works when the people concerned seem to be keen for peace.

If I have any moral authority – and I say if – moral authority doesn't solve world problems.

The reality can no longer be ignored that we live in an interdependent world which is bound together to a common destiny.

As the world frees itself from the dominance of bi-polar power the stark division of the world's people into rich and poor comes all the more clearly into view.

We operate in a world which is searching for a better life – without the imprisonment of dogma.

Let us join hands to ensure that as we enter the new millennium, the political rights that the twentieth century has recognised, and the independence that nations have gained, shall be translated into peace, prosperity and equity for all.

As consciousness grows about the inter-dependence of the nations on our planet, so do all major decisions that derive from the system of governance become subject to international review and become dependent for their success on approval and support by an international constituency.

As the process of globalisation grows apace, so does the system of international governance also grow stronger.

The problems are such that for anybody with a conscience who can use whatever influence he may have to try to bring about peace, it's difficult to say no.

He was asked if, in spite of his retirement,
he would help to bring about peace in Iraq
(September 2002)

---

on the Nobel Peace Prize

Let it never be said by future generations that indifference, cynicism or selfishness made us fail to live up to the ideals of humanism which the Nobel Peace Prize encapsulates.

Nobel Peace Prize ceremony, Norway,
10 December 1993. He received the award
jointly with FW de Klerk, at that time still State
President of South Africa. The Nobel Peace Prize
had a special meaning for him, because his award

*was preceded by two other South Africans: Chief
Albert Luthuli, former president of the ANC was
a Nobel Peace Prize winner, as was Archbishop
Desmond Tutu*

I assumed the Nobel Committee would never consider for the peace prize the man who had started
Umkhonto we Sizwe.

*Spear of the Nation, the military wing of the
ANC, formed by Nelson Mandela in June 1961.
Arguing his case, he said: 'Sebatana ha se bokwe
ka diatla.' ('The attacks of the wild beast cannot
be averted with only bare hands.')*

---

on old ANC comrades

In the last few years we have walked this road with
greater frequency, marching in the procession to
bid farewell to the veterans of our movement,
paying our last respects to the fallen spears of the
nation from a generation now reaching the end of
a long and heroic struggle.

*He was speaking at the funeral of his friend of
60 years, the self-effacing Walter Sisulu (May
2003).*

Those of us from that generation, who are singled
out to stay the longest, have to bear the pain of
seeing our comrades go.

They fought a noble battle and lived their lives in pursuit of a better life for all who follow.

The democracy in which we bury them and honour them is the sweet fruit of their lives of struggle and sacrifice.

---

on Olympians

The difference between Olympians and the rest of us is: they behave as long-time friends who occasionally compete, while we behave as long-time adversaries who occasionally get along.

---

on oppression

To overthrow oppression has been sanctioned by humanity and is the highest aspiration of every free man.

From his famous 'No Easy Walk to Freedom' speech, 1954

For as long as legitimate bodies of opinion feel stifled, vile minds will take advantage of justifiable grievances to destroy, to kill and to maim.

For as long as the majority of people anywhere on the continent [of Africa] feel oppressed, are not allowed democratic participation in decision-making process, and cannot elect their own leaders in free and fair elections, there will always be tension and conflict.

Never and never again shall the laws of our land rend our people apart or legalise their oppression and repression.

on Orania

The way in which we were received by everybody in Orania was as if I was in Soweto.

Nelson Mandela visited the diehard all-white dorp of Orania in the Northern Cape to visit the 94-year-old widow of the architect of apartheid, Hendrik Verwoerd(August 1995). When she died at 98 he noted that 'She and her husband are part of South Africa's history even though we sharply condemned their policies.'

on the Organisation of African Unity (OAU)

[It is] the midwife of our freedom.

Nelson Mandela made this comment towards the end of his presidency. He was speaking at the Summit Meeting of OAU Heads of State and Government, Ouagadougou, Burkina Faso, 8 June 1998

on his parents

My father was a polygamist with four wives and nine children.

My mother was my first friend in the proper sense of the word.

The graves mean a great deal to me because my beloved parents are here and it arouses a great deal of emotion in me because part of myself lies buried here.

He was standing next to his parents' simple graves in Qunu. His mother died while he was on Robben Island and the authorities denied him permission to attend her funeral. The first time he was able to pay his respects to her was after his release from prison in 1990

on peace

Peace and democracy go hand in hand.

It is not easy to talk about peace to people who are mourning every day.

I will go down on my knees to beg those who want to drag our country into bloodshed and persuade them not to do so.

Peace and prosperity, tranquillity and security are only possible if these are enjoyed by all without discrimination.

We live in a world and in times in which it is recognized that peace is the most powerful weapon any community or people has to bring about stability and progress through development.

This was part of the Independent News and Media lecture he delivered at Trinity College, Dublin, in April 2000

---

on people

I love you. You are my own flesh and blood. You are my brothers, sisters, children and grandchildren.

Speaking to the people of South Africa

I surely wish the pockets of my shirt were big enough to fit all of you in.

To his compatriots in the Transkei

Language, culture and religion are important indicators of identity.

Justice and liberty must be our tool, prosperity and happiness our weapon.

It is in the character of growth that we should learn from both pleasant and unpleasant experiences.

The suffering of the people of any single country affects all of us no matter where we find ourselves.

[I am] an old man who loves you all from the bottom of his heart.

You must accept the integrity of everyone and let bygones be bygones.

on personalities

Steve Biko, murdered black consciousness activist

There can be no doubt that he was one of the most talented and colourful freedom fighters South Africa has produced.

[He was] one of the greatest sons of our nation.

He said this in East London on 12 September 1997, the 20th anniversary of Steve Biko's death

That he was indeed a great man who stood head and shoulders above his peers is borne out not only by the testimony of those who knew him and worked with him, but by the fruit of his endeavours.

A fitting product of his time; a proud representative of the re-awakening of a people.

George Bush, former president of the USA

I am aware that he is surrounded by dinosaurs who offer him all sorts of advice.

He said this as US war drums were attempting to muster support for unilateral action against Iraq, September 2002. He further separated Bush from the actions of his administration by describing Deputy President Dick Cheney as 'an arch-conservative' and George Bush as 'a man with whom you can do business.'

Mangosuthu Buthelezi, IFP president and politician

When we are together, he is very, very courteous. But when he is away from you, he behaves totally differently, because he does not know if he is still your friend or not.

The problem is when he leaves the cabinet and appears on public platforms. Then he behaves like any other politician.

Prince Charles

This is a real king, not the Lion King.

Nelson Mandela's grandchildren were being introduced to Prince Charles during his historic official visit to South Africa, October 1997. The Prince of Wales was accompanied by his younger son, Prince Harry

Bill Clinton, former US president

There is a vow of goodwill between us.

President Clinton has been my friend even before he became president. I respect him very much.

I will support my friend even if he has been deserted by the entire world.

He said this at a press conference in Washington on his last official visit to the USA as President of South Africa, September 1998

Hansie Cronje, disgraced captain of the Proteas

I am saying without excusing what he has done if the allegations are proven right, that he can be a role model and turn this tragedy into triumph.

*Alas, in his confession to evangelist Ray
McCauley, placed before the King Commission
of Inquiry in 2002, Hansie said: 'In a moment
of stupidity and weakness, I allowed Satan and
the world to dictate terms to me, rather than the
Lord.'*

His untimely death is one of those pieces of
human tragedy that leaves us so shocked.

*Hansie Cronje was killed in a plane crash on 1
June 2002*

FW de Klerk, former state president

He had the courage to admit that a terrible wrong
had been done to our country and people through
the imposition of the system of apartheid.

Nobel Peace Prize Address

If there is anything that has cooled relations
between me and Mr de Klerk, it is his paralysis as
far as violence is concerned.

*This was said in September 1992, with reference
to the Boipatong massacre and the increasingly
inexplicable 'third force' violence in South Africa*

Dis goed om te sien hoe ons saam oud word (It's
good to see us growing old together).

*Nelson Mandela at FW de Klerk's 70th birthday
party on 17 March 2006. Three South African*

Nobel Peace Laureates were at the party, held
at the Mount Nelson, Cape Town: De Klerk,
Mandela and Desmond Tutu

Diana, Princess of Wales

I found her very graceful, highly intelligent, and committed to worthy causes, and I was tremendously impressed by her warmness.

[She] became a citizen of the world through her care for people everywhere.

He said this at the State Banquet for Prince
Charles held in Cape Town, South Africa, on 4
November 1997

Queen Elizabeth II

The Queen is a very gracious lady and I'm sure she'll put a country boy at ease.

On the eve of his historic – and jubilant – state
visit to Britain, July 1996

Muammar Gaddafi, president of Libya

He helped us at a time when we were all alone, when those who are now saying we should not come here were helping our enemies.

Said at the start of his controversial October 1997 visit to Libya, in the face of UN and US disapproval

My brother leader.

Mahatma Gandhi

It would not be right to compare me to Gandhi. None of us could equal his dedication or his humility.

He showed us that it was necessary to brave imprisonment if truth and justice were to triumph over evil.

Nelson Mandela was speaking at the conferral of the Freedom of Pietermaritzburg on Mahatma Gandhi in April 1997

We must never lose sight of the fact that the Gandhian philosophy may be a key to human survival in the twenty-first century.

Opening of the Gandhi Hall, Lenasia
27 September 1992

Chris Hani, assassinated leader of the South African Communist Party

A white man, full of prejudice and hate, came to our country and committed a deed so foul that our whole nation now teeters on the brink of disaster. A white woman, of Afrikaner origin, risked her life so that we might know, and bring to justice, this assassin.

Speech to all South Africans, calming the angry youth after Hani's assassination at the hands of a white man (10 April 1993) The 'white woman' was Hani's neighbour, who witnessed the murder, and alerted the police

---

Archbishop Trevor Huddleston

His sacrifices for our freedom told us that the true relationship between our people was not one between poor citizens on the one hand and good patricians on the other, but one underwritten by our common humanity and our human capacity to touch one another's hearts across the oceans.

Ernest Urban Trevor Huddleston died in Britain in 1998 at the age of 84. At his request, his

ashes were brought back to South Africa, to lie in
his old church in the razed suburb of Sophiatown
where he worked and lived as an Anglican priest
in the 1950s. Joint Houses of Parliament speech
11 July 1996

Michael Jackson, entertainer

He will be missed and memories cherished of him
for a long time. Be strong.

Jackson died at 2.26 pm in Los Angeles on 25
June 2009.

Tony Leon, former Leader of the Opposition, South Africa

[He is] a leader whose dynamism and capacity for
analysis keeps everyone on their toes.

You have far more support for all that you have
done than you might read about.

Nelson Mandela in December 2006, after the
Democratic Alliance leader announced he would
be standing down

Martin Luther King, Jnr

He grappled with and died in the effort to make a contribution to the just solution of the same great issues of the day which we have had to face as South Africans.

From his Nobel Peace Prize Address, 10 December 1993

Patricia de Lille, politician

Patricia de Lille is one of that rare breed of politician of whom it can be said that no matter what political party she would belong to, one cannot help liking and admiring her.

Thabo Mbeki, former President of South Africa

He is polite but he is not a yes-man. He will always stand his ground.

He is a man of exceptional quality, very respectful, very warm.

He was speaking in December 1997

He is a modest man and I know he would prefer that I do not sing his personal praises, but his achievement as president and national leader is the embodiment of what our nation is capable of.

Nelson Mandela addressing the joint session of the two houses of parliament on 10 May 2004 and celebrating a decade of democracy in the country

Whether I'm alive or gone, he will respect the constitution.

Nelson Mandela, during his 85th birthday celebrations in 2003

Robert Mugabe, politician

[There has been] a tragic failure of leadership in our neighbouring Zimbabwe.

Mandela has always been discreet regarding his northern neighbour. In a brief but pointed speech at a dinner for his 90th birthday in London he mentioned not only Robert Mugabe but Darfur ('We watch with sadness the continuing tragedy in Darfur')

Beyers Naude, cleric

He inspired us – that's the value of Oom Bey.

Nelson Mandela, after visiting Naudé's 91-year-old widow, Ilse, on 8 September 2004, following her husband's death the previous day

If someone asks me what kind of a person a New South African should be, I will say: 'Take a look at Beyers and his wife Ilse.'

Oom Bey's life was one of contribution, a true humanitarian and a true son of Africa.

General Colin Powell, US politician

I won't wash this hand you have shaken.

It was a mutual admiration session: Colin Powell had just said: 'This is truly a very great honour for me.'

Cyril Ramaphosa, businessman

He is a son to me.

A young man of considerable ability destined to occupy a very important position in our political life.

Anton Rupert, businessman

Mooi loop, Anton.

Anton Rupert died in his sleep on 18 January 2006. He was one of South Africa's greatest philanthropists

---

Walter Sisulu, politician and lifelong friend

We walked side by side through the valley of death, nursing each other's bruises, holding each other up when our steps faltered. And together we were priviledged to savour the taste of freedom.

Nelson Mandela met Walter Sisulu in 1941. Sisulu, who died in 2003, was a singular influence on him for the rest of his life. They went to Robben Island together. The release of Sisulu ahead of his old friend was a sure sign that the unthinkable was about to happen: the release of Nelson Mandela from prison

While many of us have been honoured by countries in every continent with awards, including Nobel peace prizes, there is one man who has not received some of these, but nonetheless he stands head and shoulders above us all because of his humility and simplicity.

Nelson Mandela, in the foreword to the biography of Walter and Albertina Sisulu In Our Lifetime *by Elinor Sisulu*

I now know that when my time comes, Walter will be there to meet me, and I am almost certain he will hold out an enrolment form to register me into the ANC in that world, cajoling me with one of his favourite songs we sang when mobilizing people behind the Freedom Charter:

Libhaliwe ma oGama lakho kuloMqulu weNkululeko
Vuma silibhale kuloMqulu weNkululeko.

(Has your name been enrolled in the struggle for freedom
Permit us to register you in the struggle for freedom.)

Nelson Mandela, in a statement to SAPA late
at night on 5 May 2003. His dearest friend,
Walter Sisulu, had just died

Xhamela is no more. May he live forever. His absence has carved a void. A part of me is gone.

From the moment we first met, he has been my friend, my brother, my keeper, my comrade.

Nelson Mandela, from a tribute he wrote and
which was published on 7 May 2003

In a sense I feel cheated by Walter. If there be another life beyond this physical world, I would have loved to be there first so that I could welcome him. Life has determined otherwise.

'Don't get involved with that man Walter Sisulu,' I was warned when I first arrived in Johannesburg.

'If you do, you will end up spending the rest of your life in jail.' Of course, I ignored this advice.

Those of us from that generation, who are singled out to stay the longest, have to bear the pain of seeing our comrades go.

How can we speak about this great unifier to people without recognizing and honouring that great unity in his own life: that of Walter and Albertina as a marital couple, a unity of such deep friendship and mutual respect, a personal and political partnership that transcended and survived all hardships, separations and persecution.

He knew how to throw a left hook, but never below the belt.

Nelson Mandela, at the unveiling of the
tombstone of his old friend in December 2003

Adelaide Tambo

A life dedicated to service and freedom.

He had been asked to describe Adelaide Tambo's
life. She died of a heart attack on 1 February
2007, 14 years after her husband, Oliver. She
was 77

Oliver Tambo, former President of the ANC

When I looked at him in his coffin, it was as if a part of myself had died.

Oliver Tambo was Nelson Mandela's lifelong friend. They were in law practice together. Later on the head of the ANC, Tambo lived most of his life in exile. He returned to South Africa, but died shortly afterwards, not living long enough to see his dream of a democratic South Africa realised

He is my greatest friend and comrade for 50 years.

I am not prepared to sell the birthright of the People – open letter to PW Botha, read by Zindzi at Jabulani Stadium, 10 February 1985

He enriched my own life and intellect, and neither I nor indeed this country (South Africa) can forget this colossus of our history.

Address to the closing session of the 50th National Conference of the ANC, Mafikeng 20 December 1997

Nobel Laureate Archbishop Desmond Tutu

He's a terrific fellow.

He has been a blessing and inspiration to count-less people through his ministry; his acts of com-passion; his prophetic witness; and his political engagement.

Said at the thanksgiving service for the ministry of Archbishop Tutu in Cape Town, June 1996

Jacob Zuma, politician and President of South Africa, May 2009

We wish him well as he considers his future and want to reassure him of our continued friendship.

While we are naturally deeply saddened that a person who had made such a major contribution to our liberation and democracy had to come to this point in his life and career, we fully support the president in this difficult time in the life of our government, nation and organisation.

Nelson Mandela in a statement which supported former President Thabo Mbeki's sacking of Jacob Zuma from his position of Deputy President in June 2005. Later, Zuma resigned as an MP

on his statue, Parliament Square, London

When Oliver Tambo and I visited Westminster Abbey and Parliament Square in 1962, we half-joked that we hoped that one day a statue of a black person would be erected here alongside General Smuts. Oliver would have been proud today.

Nelson Mandela after his statue was unveiled

The history of the struggle in South Africa is rich with the story of heroes and heroines, some of them leaders, some of them followers. All of them deserve to be remembered.

Nelson Mandela, in Parliament Square, London, 29 August 2007, after his 2.7m bronze statue was unveiled, making him the second South African, after Jan Smuts, to be given the rare recognition of a place opposite the Houses of Parliament. British Prime Minister Gordon Brown, in his speech, said: 'From this day forward, this statue will stand here, in sight of this ancient forum of democracy, to commemorate and celebrate for the ages triumph in the greatest of causes and the most inspiring and greatest leader of our generation – and one of the most courageous and best-loved men of all time.'

Though this statue is of one man, in actual fact it symbolises all those who have resisted oppression, especially in my country.

---

on the art of persuasion

Don't address their brains. Address their hearts.

---

on stealing pigs

We had a method as young chaps of about 16 or 17 of stealing pigs. We had very clever ways of doing so. We would take the remains of kaffir beer, as they called it, and then we'd go to the direction of the wind, so that the wind would blow it from us to the village where the pigs were. And then we'd leave a little bit of the remains of the beer, and then the pigs come out ... Then we put the stuff further away ... and they will follow us. When they are far away ... we stab it ... the owners will not hear its shouts, and then we roast it and eat it.

Nelson Mandela was talking with the Oscar-winning Tsotsi *stars Presley Chweneyagae, Terry Pheto and director Gavin Hood after they returned triumphantly from Hollywood in March 2006* _on_ photography

Good use of photography will give even poverty with all its rags, filth and vermin a measure of divineness rarely noticeable in real life.

Letter to his daughter Zindzi, 6 August 1979

_on_ politics

Political division, based on colour, is entirely artificial and, when it disappears, so will the domination of one colour group by another.

From the dock at the Rivonia Treason Trial, 20 April 1964

We should not allow South African politics to be relegated to trivialities chosen precisely because they salve the consciences of the rich and powerful, and conceal the plight of the poor and powerless.

75th anniversary of the SACP, 28 July 1996

If you are a politician you must be prepared to suffer for your principles.

---

on poverty

It should never be that the anger of the poor should be the finger of accusation pointed at all of us because we failed to respond to the cries of the people for food, for shelter, for the dignity of the individual.

Address to US Congress, 28 June 1990

We can neither heal nor build, if on the one hand, the rich in our society see the poor as hordes of irritants; or if, on the other hand, the poor sit back, expecting charity.

None can be at peace while others wallow in poverty and insecurity.

International Day of Solidarity with the Palestinians, 4 December 1997

Poverty still grips our people. If you're poor, you're not likely to live for long.

Said in a 90th birthday interview with CNN

Poverty and deprivation in our midst demean all of us.

This was part of a short speech made at the ANC rally at Loftus Versfeld, Pretoria, to celebrate his 90th birthday in July 2008

In this new century, millions of people in the world's poorest countries remain imprisoned, enslaved and in chains. They are trapped in the prison of poverty. It is time to set them free.

He was speaking to an audience of thousands in Trafalgar Square, London, on 3 February 2005, the eve of a meeting by the finance ministers of the Group of Seven industrialised nations. When he heard after he became President of South Africa in May 1994 what his salary would be (R700 000pa) he said: 'No, this is too high. I would like you to cut it down', which was promptly done

Poverty is man-made and can be overcome and eradicated by the actions of human beings.

---

on praise

I think the accolades that one gets are more because of old age.

He was 80 when he said this

---

on being president (of South Africa)

This has placed a great responsibility on my shoulders.

We enter into a covenant that we shall build a society in which all South Africans, both black and white, will be able to walk tall, without any fear in their hearts, assured of their inalienable right to human dignity – a rainbow nation at peace with itself and the world.

From his Inaugural speech, 10 May 1994

At the end of my term I'll be 81. I don't think it's wise that a robust country like South Africa should be led by a septuagenarian.

Spoken in 1996 when there were rumours about his health

It is a way of life in which it's hard to dedicate time to the things that are really close to your heart.

My present life, even if it's not the easiest way of life, is very rewarding.

Spoken in mid-1997, one of his busiest years

---

on the press

A critical, independent and investigative press is the lifeblood of any democracy.

It was the press who never forgot us.

Spoken just after his February 1990 release

A press conference is not a place to discuss rumours.

The press is one of the pillars of democracy.

A bad free press is preferable to a technically good, subservient one.

None of our irritations with the perceived inadequacies of the media should ever allow us to suggest even faintly that the independence of the press could be compromised or coerced.

---

on prison

Nothing is more dehumanising than isolation from human companionship.

Nelson Mandela saw Robben Island for the first time from Table Mountain, Cape Town, in 1947. Less than 20 years later, he was incarcerated there

The long, lonely wasted years.

He was prisoner 466/64

I believe the way in which you are treated by the prison authorities depends on your demeanour and you must fight that battle and win it on the very first day.

There I had time, just to sit for hours and think.

The advantage of prison life is that you can sit and think and see yourself and your work from a distance.

In prison I had been worried by people depicting me as a superhuman being who could achieve the impossible.

He was reflecting on a long life in 1999

What always worried me in prison was [that I could acquire] the image of someone who is always 100 per cent correct and can never do any wrong.

He was speaking at the launch of a book about him in November 1999

I realised that they could take it all except my mind and heart. And I just made a decision not to give them away.

Nelson Mandela, as quoted by Bill Clinton in November 2000. Mandela was referring to his jailers and to the people who had put him in prison

---

on racism

I detest racialism, because I regard it as a barbaric thing, whether it comes from a black man or a white man.

*'Black Man in a White Court' statement, Old
Synagogue, 15 October 1962*

Racism pollutes the atmosphere of human relations and poisons the minds of the backward, the bigoted and the prejudiced.

Harlem speech, 21 June 1990

Our struggle is the struggle to erase the colour line that all too often determines who is rich and who is poor.

Harlem speech, 21 June 1990

As we enter the last decade of the twentieth century, it is intolerable and unacceptable that the cancer of racism is still eating away at the fabric of societies in different parts of our planet.

Harlem speech, 21 June 1990

We must ensure that colour, race and gender become only a God-given gift to each one of us and not an indelible mark or attribute that accords a special status to any.

Address to UN, 3 October 1994

Racism is a blight on the human conscience.

*Joint Houses of Parliament speech, 11 July
1996*

We shall never again allow our country to play host to racism. Nor shall our voices be stilted if we see that another, elsewhere in the world, is victim to racial tyranny.

Joint Houses of Parliament speech, 11 July 1996

Racism must be consciously combated and not discreetly tolerated.

Clark University Investiture, 10 July 1993

The very fact that racism degrades both the perpetrator and the victim commands that, if we are true to our commitment to protect human dignity, we fight on until victory is achieved.

Address to UK parliament, 11 July 1996

All of us know how stubbornly racism can cling to the mind and how deeply it can infect the human soul.

Address to UN General Assembly, 3 October 1994

It will perhaps come to be that we who have harboured in our country the worst example of racism since the defeat of Nazism, will make a contribution to human civilisation by ordering our affairs in such a manner that we strike an effective and lasting blow against racism everywhere.

Address to UK parliament, 11 July 1996

I hate the practice of race discrimination, and in my hatred I am sustained by the fact that the overwhelming majority of mankind hate it equally.

'Black Man in a White Court' statement, Old Synagogue, 15 October 1962

Death to racism.

Harlem speech, 21 June 1990

When the secretaries-general [of the UN] were white, we never had the question of any country ignoring the UN. But now that we have black secretaries-general, certain countries that believe in white supremacy are ignoring the UN. We have to combat that without reservation.

Nelson Mandela, in Jakarta, Indonesia, September 2002. He repeated that statement, in regard to the Iraq crisis, in February 2003, when he said: 'Both US President Bush as well as Tony Blair are undermining an idea which was sponsored by their predecessors. Is this because the secretary-general of the UN is now a black man? They never did that when secretaries-general were white.'

Social problems don't just change because you have made a law – it takes a great deal of time.

Nelson Mandela said this in February 2004 when he was presented with an honorary doctorate from Britain's Open University by

the former Speaker of the House of Commons,
Baroness Betty Boothroyd

---

on reaching heaven

I will look for a branch of the ANC and join it.

---

on reconciliation

The mission of reconciliation is underpinned by what I have dedicated my life to: uplifting the most down-trodden sections of our population and all round transformation of society.

Above all the healing process involves the nation, because it is the nation itself that needs to redeem and reconstruct itself.

Interfaith Commissioning Service for the TRC,
13 February 1996

Reconstruction goes hand in hand with reconciliation.

Thanksgiving Service for Archbishop Tutu, 23
June 1996

We can easily be enticed to read reconciliation and fairness as meaning parity between justice and injustice.

International Day of Solidarity with the
Palestinian People, 4 December 1997

---

on Regina Mundi

A church that refused to allow God's name to be
used to justify discrimination and repression.

Regina Mundi Day, 30 November 1997. Regina
Mundi is a cathedral in Soweto, frequently
the focus of defiance during the struggle, and
symbolic to many of the fight for freedom

A literal battlefield between forces of democracy
and those who did not hesitate to violate a place
of religion with teargas, dogs and guns.

Regina Mundi Day, 30 November 1997

Regina Mundi became a worldwide symbol of the
determination of our people to free themselves.

Regina Mundi Day, 30 November 1997

---

on regrets

My greatest regret in life is that I never became the
heavyweight boxing champion of the world.

on relaxing

When I have no visitors over weekends, I remain the whole day in my pyjamas and eat samp.

You must find your own garden.

For Nelson Mandela, the garden was not a place of retreat but of renewal. His first garden was on Robben Island (there are now no traces of it) although he used to grow enough spinach to feed fellow political prisoners on Sunday after Sunday. When he was transferred to Pollsmoor Prison in 1982, he had an garden using thirty-two, sliced in half, 44-gallon oil drums. According to his biographer, Richard Stengel, he grew tomatoes, onions, aubergines, strawberries, spinach and other vegetables, working on the garden for two hours every morning and again later in the day

on his release from prison

I greet you all in the name of peace, democracy and freedom for all.

Historic words indeed; he said them to the wildly excited crowd as he walked out of Victor Verster Prison, Paarl, holding the hand of his then wife Winnie on 11 February 1990. He was 71

I would be merely rationalising if I told you that I am able to describe my own feelings. It was breathtaking, that is all I can say.

Along the route [from Paarl to Cape Town] I was surprised to see the number of whites who seemed to identify themselves with what is happening to the country today amongst blacks.

I was completely overwhelmed by the enthusiasm.

---

on religion

Without the church, without religious institutions, I would never have been here today.

The simple lesson of religions, of all philosophies and of life itself is that, although evil may be on the rampage temporarily, the good must win the laurels in the end.

*From a letter to his friend, Fatima Meer, 1
January 1976. Less than six months later,
the Soweto uprising broke out, signalling the
eventual end of apartheid*

The strength of inter-religious solidarity in action against apartheid, rather than mere harmony or co-existence, was critical in bringing that evil system to an end.

*'Renewal & Renaissance – Towards a New World
Order'; lecture at the Oxford Centre for Islamic
Studies, 11 July 1997*

[African traditional religion] is no longer seen as
despised superstition which had to be superseded
by superior forms of belief; today its enrichment
of humanity's spiritual heritage is acknowledged.

*'Renewal & Renaissance' lecture at the Oxford
Centre for Islamic Studies, 11 July 1997*

We need religious institutions to continue to be
the conscience of society, a moral custodian and
a fearless champion of the interests of the weak
and downtrodden.

Regina Mundi Day, 30 November 1997

Whether you are a Christian, a Muslim, a Bud-
dhist, a Jew or a Hindu, religion is a great force
and it can help one have command of one's own
morality, one's own behaviour and one's own
attitude.

---

on preparing for his retirement

I must step down while there are one or two people
who admire me.

November 1996, when he was 77

I intend to do a bit of farming when I step down. I will be without a job and I don't want to find myself standing at the side of the road with a placard saying: unemployed.

There is no reason whatsoever for anyone to think there will be dislocation in South Africa as a result of the stepping down of an individual.

I look forward to the period when I will be able to wake up with the sun, to walk the hills and valleys of Qunu in peace and tranquillity.

Nelson Mandela has often spoken of Qunu with longing. On this occasion it was especially so. This was the final sentence in his 'private' (as opposed to his controversial five-hour 'political') speech at the historic 50th ANC conference held in Mafikeng in December 1997, when he relinquished his presidency of the ANC, and clearly looked ahead towards his retirement in 1999

I will be able to have that opportunity in my last years to spoil my grandchildren and try in various ways to assist all South African children, especially those who have been the hapless victims of a system that did not care.

ANC Conference speech, 20 December 1997

My retirement will give me the opportunity to sit down with my children and grandchildren and listen to their dreams and to help them as much as possible.

I will still go into Shell House on Mondays and carry out whatever instructions my president gives me.

Shell House, the former ANC headquarters, is in the heart of Johannesburg. The president of the ANC in December 1997 was Thabo Mbeki

Born as World War I came to a close and departing from public life as the world marks half a century of the Universal Declaration of Human Rights, I have reached that part of the long walk when the opportunity is granted, as it should be to all men and women, to retire to some rest and tranquillity in the village of my birth.

Mandela was speaking to the United Nations' General Assembly in September 1998. It was his last address as South African head of State. Many in the audience had tears in their eyes

It is as a peaceful and equitable world takes shape that I and the legions across the globe who dedicated their lives in striving for a better life for all will be able to retire in contentment and at peace.

Part of his address to the World Council of Churches, 1998

I'll get a board that says 'Unemployed' and stand on street corners.

This was his standard joke for some time before his retirement

I'm a part of the world. I will work with the UN, which does sterling work – if I am needed.

If there's anything that would kill me it is to wake up in the morning not knowing what to do.

He said this in 2002, when he was 84

---

on his retirement as president of the African National Congress (ANC)

The time has come to hand over the baton in a relay that started more than 85 years ago in Mangaung; nay more, centuries ago when the warriors of the Autshumanyo, Makhanda, Mzilikazi, Moshweshwe, Khama, Sekkukkuni, Lobatsibeni, Cetshwayo, Nghunghunyane, Uithalder and Rambulana, laid down their lives to defend the dignity and integrity of their being as a people.

Here are the reins of the movement – protect and guard its precious legacy.

I will remember this experience fondly for as long as I live.

I know that the love and respect that I have enjoyed is love and respect for the ANC and its ideals.

The time has come for me to take leave.

All the above quotations were taken from Nelson Mandela's valedictory address to the closing session of the historic 50th national conference of the ANC on 20 December 1997. As the speech drew to its conclusion, he had tears in his eyes

---

on his retirement as MP and president of South Africa (1999)

I step down with a clear conscience, feeling that I have in a small way done my duty to my people and my country.

I would like to rest. I welcome the prospect of revelling in obscurity.

I have 27 grandchildren and more are coming ... it tears my heart when I get home and my youngest grandchild asks: 'Grandpa are you going out again?'

Whatever regrets I have are irrelevant.

Nelson Mandela, at a farewell breakfast for the media at the Presidential Guest House, Pretoria, on 10 May 1999

And yet another retirement (2004)

When I told one of my advisers that I wanted to retire, he growled at me. 'You *are* retired'. If that is really the case, then I should say I now announce that I am retiring from retirement.

Mandela was speaking at the offices of the Nelson Mandela Foundation on 1 June 2004. He left a R1 billion endowment to be raised by the three charitable organisations that bear his name (the NelsonMandela Foundation, the Nelson Mandela Children's Fund and the Nelson Mandela Rhodes Foundation), to be used to improve the lives of South Africans

I am confident that nobody present here today will accuse me of selfishness if I ask to spend time, while I am still in good health, with my family, my friends – and also with myself.

I do not intend to hide away totally from the public, but henceforth I want to be in the position of calling you to ask whether I would be welcome, rather than being called upon to do things and participate in events.

The appeal therefore is: don't call me, I'll call you.

At the end of his speech, Mandela received a five minute standing ovation. His response: 'Thank you, it's nice to have billionaires clapping for me.'

on revenge

You can't build a united nation on the basis of revenge.

In an interview with the New York Times in March 1997: he was referring to the Truth and Reconciliation Commission

on the South African right wing

There are still powerful elements among whites who are not reconciled with the present transformation and who want to use every excuse to drown the country in bloodshed.

If you want to mobilise every section of the population, you can't do it with feelings of hatred and revenge.

on Robben Island

Siqithini – **the Island** – a place of pain and banishment for centuries, and now of triumph.

Heritage Day, Robben Island, 24 September 1997

Without question the harshest, most iron-fisted outpost in the South African penal system.

Robben Island, nine kilometres off the Cape coast and set in the tumultuous Atlantic Ocean, has been used as a prison for hundreds of years – the first prisoner was Harry the Strandloper, confined there by the Dutch in 1658. But Robben Island is no longer a prison – it has been turned into a museum and can be visited by anyone. Mandela revisited his old prison on 11 February 1994, posing in his old cell in B Section, and showing the world the limestone quarry which he and his associates had worked in year after year

A symbol of the victory of the human spirit over political oppression; and of reconciliation over enforced division.

Heritage Day, Robben Island, 24 September 1997

The Island has become a monument of the struggle for democracy, part of a heritage that will always inspire our children and our friends from other lands.

Freedom of the City of Cape Town, 27 November 1997

---

on Rwanda

Rwanda stands out as a stern and severe rebuke to all of us.

The louder and more piercing the cries of despair – even when that despair results in half-a-million dead in Rwanda – the more these cries seem to encourage an instinctive reaction to raise our hands so as to close our eyes and ears.

Address to UK parliament, 11 July 1996

None of us can insulate ourselves from so cata-strophic a scale of human suffering.

Address to UK parliament, 11 July 1996

---

on the rugby World Cup, South Africa, 1995

Our whole nation stood behind a sport which was once a symbol of apartheid.

None more so than Nelson Mandela himself. He appeared at the final wearing captain Francois Pienaar's No 6 shirt – and brought the entire country along with him, surely one of the most successful efforts at reconciliation in South Africa

When it was 12/12 I almost collapsed. I was abso-lutely tense.

When I left the stadium my nerves were com-pletely shattered.

I'm still recovering.

In an interview with The New York Times,
1997

And the rugby World Cup, Paris, 2007

You have put us **on the map** of the world because of your performance.

The team visited Nelson Mandela at his Houghton home; coach Jake White and Bok captain John Smit held the Webb Ellis Trophy over Mandela's head in a replay of the 1995 World Cup. And, as in 1995, Mandela was wearing Springbok colours. There was another link with the Rugby World Cup of 1995: Captain John Smit noted shortly after the historic 15-6 Bok win, 'We had 45 million South Africans and the rest of the world shouting for us,' more or less echoing Francois Pienaar's words 12 years before

on sabotage

I planned it as a result of a calm and sober assessment of the situation, after many years of oppression and tyranny of my people by the whites.

*From the Rivonia Treason Trial, 20 April 1964
– the trial which sent him to prison for 27 years*

on self-respect

If you are in harmony with yourself, you may meet a lion without fear, because he respects anyone with self-confidence.

on soccer

Soccer is one of the sporting disciplines in which Africa is rising to demonstrate her excellence, for too long latent in her womb.

African Cup of Nations Tournament opening,
January 1996

on society

The great lesson of our time is that no regime can survive if it acts above the heads of the ordinary citizens of the country.

A society that does not value its older people denies its roots and endangers its future.

At the launch of the SA leg of the International
Year of Older Persons

Social problems don't just change because you have made a law – it takes a great deal of time.

Nelson Mandela said this in February 2004
when he was presented with an honorary
doctorate from Britain's Open University by
the former Speaker of the House of Commons,
Baroness Betty Boothroyd

on South Africa

We are marching to a new future based on a sound basis of respect.

It is in the deep interests of our country to ensure that the same principles of freedom and democracy that we hold to be true find resonance in other parts of the world.

Chris Hani Award, 10th National Congress of
the SACP, Johannesburg, 1 July 1998

We live with the hope that as she battles to remake herself, South Africa will be like a microcosm of the new world that is striving to be born.

From his Nobel Peace Prize Address,
10 December 1993

Each time one of us touches the soil of this land, we feel a sense of personal renewal.

Inaugural speech, 10 May 1994

Never and never again shall it be that this beautiful land will again experience the oppression of one by another and suffer the indignity of being the skunk of the world.

From his moving Inaugural speech, 10 May 1994

No society emerging out of the grand disaster of the apartheid system could avoid carrying the blemishes of its past.

Address to Joint Houses of Parliament, 11 July 1996

If we are able today to speak proudly of a 'rainbow nation', it is in part because the world set us a moral example which we dared to follow.

Had the new South Africa emerged out of nothing, it would not exist.

Address to Joint Houses of Parliament, 11 July 1996

The first founding stone of our new country is national reconciliation and national unity. The fact that it has settled in its mortar needs no advertising.

Address to UK parliament, 11 July 1997

We do face major challenges, but none are as daunting as those we have already surmounted.

On receiving the Freedom of the City of London, July 1996

Never and never again shall the laws of our land rend our people apart or legalise their oppression and repression.

Inauguration speech, 10 May 1994

We must work for the day when we, as South Africans, see one another and interact with one another as equal human beings and as part of one nation united, rather than torn asunder, by its diversity.

Address to 49th session of UN, 3 October 1994

Being latecomers to freedom and democracy, we have the benefit of the experience of others.

'Renewal & Renaissance – Towards a New World Order', lecture at Oxford Centre for Islamic Studies, 11 July 1997

In the same way that the liberation of South Africa from apartheid was an achievement of Africa, the reconstruction and development of our country is part of the rebirth of the continent.

'Renewal & Renaissance – Towards a New World Order' lecture, 11 July 1997

The hard slog of reconstruction and development is as exciting as the tremors of conflict.

South Africa is a worldwide icon of the universality of human rights; of hope, peace and reconciliation.

Heritage Day, Robben Island, 24 September
1997

In time, we must bestow on South Africa the greatest gift – a more humane society.

20th anniversary of Steve Biko's death,
12 September 1997

What we have achieved will serve as a symbol of peace and reconciliation, and of hope, wherever communities and societies are in the grip of conflict.

Hon Doctorate by Ben-Gurion University of the
Negev, Cape Town, 19 September 1997

We can never be complacent, because the legacies of our past still run very deeply through our society.

Sowetan Nation Building 10th Anniversary
speech, 30 June 1998

We are regarded as a pioneering nation when it comes to reaching a peaceful settlement.

South Africa has a special responsibility to work for peace, democracy and development everywhere.

Nelson Mandela, on the 10th anniversary of his
11 February 1990 release from prison

Our nation comes from a history of deep division and strife; let us never through our deeds or words take our people back down that road.

Nelson Mandela was addressing the ANC and a 5 000-strong crowd at Loftus Versfeld Stadium, Pretoria, at a rally to celebrate his 90th birthday in July 2008

on South Africans

We are all one nation in one country.

Each one of us is as intimately attached to the soil of this beautiful country as are the famous jacaranda trees of Pretoria and the mimosa trees of the bushveld.

From his Inaugural speech, 10 May 1994

My country is rich in the minerals and gems that lie beneath its soil, but I have always known that its greatest wealth is its people, finer and truer than the purest diamonds.

It is our privilege as South Africans to be living at a time when our nation is emerging from the darkest night into the bright dawn of freedom and democracy.

Unveiling of mural celebrating the adoption of the new constitution, 8 August 1996

Pride in our country is a common bond between us all. It is the essence of our new patriotism.

Farewell for SA representatives to the Olympic Games, Atlanta, 28 June 1996

The onus is on us, through hard work, honesty and integrity, to reach for the stars.

With all our colours and races combined in one nation, we are an African people.

Address to UK parliament, 11 July 1997

Having achieved our own freedom, we can fall into the trap of washing our hands of difficulties that others face.

International Day of Solidarity with the Palestinian People, 4 December 1997

A society for centuries trampled upon by the jack-boot of inhumanity.

20th anniversary of Steve Biko's death, 12 September 1997

By joining hands South Africans have overcome problems others thought would forever haunt us.

Sowetan Nation Building 10th Anniversary speech, Johannesburg, 30 June 1998

There is no more fascinating story today than how South Africans who were enemies now work together to confound the prophets of doom who expected rivers of blood to flow across the country.

He said this shortly after returning from
his valedictory tour of the US and Canada,
September 1998

South Africans are conscious of their obligations to do whatever they can to contribute to the advancement of peace, democracy and justice whenever possible.

My wish is that South Africans never give up on the belief in goodness, that they cherish that faith in human beings as a cornerstone of our democracy.

Let us never be unmindful of the terrible past from which we come – that memory not as a means to keep us shackled to the past in a negative manner, but rather as a joyous reminder of how far we have come and how much we have achieved.

Nelson Mandela to a joint sitting of parliament
on 10 May 2004, celebrating the 10th
anniversary of democracy in South Africa

on sport

Sport can reach out to people in a way which politicians can't.

I have always believed that sport is a right, not a privilege.

---

on the struggle

The Struggle is my life.

From his famous press statement of 26 June 1961, whilst living underground as the Black Pimpernel

Struggle that does not strengthen organisation can lead to a blind alley.

Struggle without discipline can lead to anarchy.

Struggle without unity enables the other side to pick us off one by one.

Harlem speech 21 July 1990

No organisation whose interests are identical with those of the toiling masses will advocate conciliation to win its demands.

From Liberation, June 1953

[South Africans] displayed heroism, an incredible sense of discipline and a capacity for selflessness, as well as a quiet determination not to bend the knee to the dictates of tyrants.

The success or failure of all the campaigns against apartheid, from the 1946 African miners' strike to the resistance campaigns of the 80s, depended on a willingness to give up the comforts of life.

Running through the struggle like a golden thread is one motif – the indomitable human spirit and a moving capacity for self-sacrifice and discipline.

A willingness to make sacrifices for a loftier purpose was the unwritten code of the struggle.

No struggle can be waged effectively in isolation.

Chris Hani Award, 10th National Congress of the SACP, 1 July 1998

---

on survival

For me, survival is the ability to cope with difficulties, with circumstances, and to overcome them.

---

on talk

Rhetoric is not important. Actions are.

---

on thoughts

Thinking is one of the most important weapons in dealing with problems.

------

on time

Lack of punctuality is something which shows lack of respect for the organisation and those appointed into positions, and a lack of self respect.

More often than not, an epoch creates and nurtures the individuals which are associated with its twists and turns.

ANC Conference, 20 December 1997

One minute can change the world.

------

on the Truth and Reconciliation Commission

Above all the healing process involved the nation, because it is the nation itself that needs to redeem and reconstruct itself.

*The Truth and Reconciliation Commission
started its work in February 1996. It heard
of atrocities from the right and the left, heard
testimony from murderers and torturers – and
also from victims and the families of dead
victims. It was intended to be an instrument of
reconciliation and not revenge*

All South Africans face the challenge of coming to terms with the past in ways which will enable us to face the future as a united nation at peace with itself.

Some criticise us when we say that whilst we can forgive, we can never forget.

Ordinary South Africans are determined that the past be known, the better to ensure that it is not repeated.

Incomplete and imperfect as the process may be, it shall leave us less burdened by the past and unshackled to pursue a glorious future.

This was said in his New Year's message to South Africa, 1998; it followed a harrowing year at the Truth and Reconciliation Commission, where the country's brutal past was opened for all to see. One of the last people called to give evidence before the Commission in 1997 was Winnie Madikizela-Mandela, the President's second (and former) wife

We are all bound to agonise over the price in terms of justice that the victims have to pay.

20th anniversary of Steve Biko's Death, 12 September 1997

The half-truths of a lowly interrogator cannot and should not hide the culpability of the commanders and the political leaders who gave the orders.

20th anniversary of Steve Biko's Death,
12 September 1997

_____

on ubuntu

The spirit of *ubuntu*, that profound African sense that we are human only through the humanity of other human beings – is not a parochial phenomenon, but has added globally to our common search for a better world.

There are numerous definitions of ubuntu –
kindness towards human beings is perhaps too
mild; as Mandela says, it is to do with one's
humanity being enriched by another's.

(Ubuntu means) that if we are to accomplish anything in this world, it will in equal measure be due to the work and achievement of others.

Nelson Mandela wrote this in 1998 as part of
the preface to Richard Stengel's book Mandela's
Way

_____

on unilateral decisions

We are really appalled by any country, whether it be a superpower or a small country, that goes outside the United Nations and attacks independent countries.

He said this on 2 September 2002 as the USA looked increasingly unlikely to go through the United Nations in its pursuit of weapons of mass destruction in Iraq. He had also tried to phone George Bush himself (and failed), but had phoned George Bush Snr instead: 'I asked him to speak to his son. I have already spoken to General Colin Powell and I am waiting to speak to Condoleezza Rice. I have not given up trying to persuade President Bush not to attack Iraq.' It was also the day he awarded Nelson Mandela scholarships to 11 post-graduate students, met French President Jacques Chirac at his home, telephoned US Security Adviser Condoleezza Rice and (at 6 pm) launched the Fifth World Parks Congress at the Nedcor building in Sandton

I resent any country, be it a superpower or not, that takes a unilateral decision to attack another country.

Nelson Mandela was speaking on 5 September 2002, stating at the same time that there was every reason to support the US if it attacked Iraq, providing the action had been ratified by the United Nations

on the United Kingdom

I regard the British parliament as the most demo-cratic institution in the world, and the independence and impartiality of its judiciary never fail to arouse my admiration.

From the Rivonia Treason Trial, 20 April 1964

Your right to determine your own destiny was used to deny us to determine our own.

From his speech to the House of Commons,
5 May 1993

This country has produced men and women whose names are well known in South Africa, because they, together with thousands of others of your citizens, stood up to oppose this evil system and helped to bring us to where we are today.

Speech to House of Commons, 5 May 1993

We return to this honoured place neither with pikes nor a desire for revenge nor even a plea to your distinguished selves to assuage our hunger for bread. We come to you as friends.

From his historic speech to both Houses of
Parliament, London, July 1996

In a sense, I leave a part of my being here.

Receiving the Freedom of the City of London,
July 1996

The UK, as one of the bastions of democracy, has an obligation to ensure that we have all the material needs to entrench democracy in our country.

I love every one of you. You must understand that the people of South Africa are very grateful to you.

Addressing a crowd of 10 000 from the balcony
of South Africa House, Trafalgar Square,
London, July 1996

---

on the USA

We are linked by nature, but proud of each other by choice.

Of New York, which he visited with Winnie on
his first trip abroad after his February 1990
release, he said: 'To see it from the bottom of its
great glass-and-concrete canyons while millions
upon millions of pieces of ticker tape came
floating down was a breathtaking experience.'

Let us keep our arms locked together so that we form a solid phalanx against racism.

Address to US Congress, 28 June 1990

The stand you took established the understanding among the millions of our people that here we have friends, here we have fighters against racism who feel hurt because we are hurt, who seek our success because they too seek the victory of democracy over tyranny.

Address to the joint Houses of Congress of the USA, September 1994

Who are they now to pretend they are the police-men of the world, the ones who should decide for the people of Iraq what should be done with their government and their leadership?

Nelson Mandela was speaking about the USA and UK's plans to invade Iraq in 1993. He accused the US of seeking Iraqi oil and accused US President George Bush and UK Prime Minister Tony Blair of undermining the UN and its Secretary-General, Kofi Annan. 'Is it because the Secretary-General of the United Nations is a black man?' he angrily asked

How can they have the arrogance to dictate to us where we should go or who our friends should be?

A heated comment made at a dinner in Johannesburg in October 1997 on the eve of his controversial visit to Libya. The USA had expressed its disapproval of the visit

on violence

Government violence can do only one thing, and that is to breed counter-violence.

'Black Man in a White Court' statement, Old Synagogue, 15 October 1962

Take your guns, your knives and your pangas, and throw them into the sea.

His first speech in the troubled province of KwaZulu-Natal after his release from prison, 25 February 1990

People who kill children are no better than animals.

Use violence only in self-defence.

In the end, the cries of the infant who dies because of hunger or because a machete has slit open its stomach, will penetrate the noises of the modern city and its sealed windows to say: am I not human too!

From his historic speech to the Joint Houses of Parliament of the United Kingdom, 11 July 1996

We hope the world will reach a stage when it realises that the use of violence against any community is something that puts us next to animals.

Violence and non-violence are not mutually exclusive; it is the predominance of the one or the other that labels a struggle.

_____

on the vote

The question of education has nothing to do with the question of the vote.

As in Zimbabwe, there was a vocal section of white voters who maintained that the vote should not be given to uneducated or barely literate people. Some form of qualification, resulting in a limited franchise, was suggested. This was rejected – as it had been in Zimbabwe – in favour of one man, one vote

A vote without food, shelter and health care would be to create the appearance of equality while actual inequality is entrenched.

Clark University Investiture, 10 July 1993

_____

on white South Africans

The majority of white men regard it as the destiny of the white race to dominate the man of colour.

From the ANC Youth League Manifesto of 1944, largely written by him

White supremacy implies black inferiority.

*From the dock at the Rivonia Treason Trial, 20
April 1964*

Just as many whites have killed just as many
blacks.

*Asked about deaths of white civilians in ANC
attacks, 1990*

Whites fear the reality of democracy.

As long as whites think in terms of group rights
they are talking the language of apartheid.

Spoken before the April 1994 elections

Whites are fellow South Africans and we want
them to feel safe, and we appreciate the contribution they have made towards the development of
this country.

They have had education, they have got the
knowledge, skills and expertise. We want that
knowledge and expertise now that we are building our country.

The whites still think as if there were no blacks, or
coloureds, or Indians.

*Said on his wildly successful state visit to the
United Kingdom, July 1996*

Our blood did not want to deal with such people ...
but our brains said something else.

He was speaking in March 1999, referring
to the ANC's decision to go for a negotiated
settlement with the Nationalist government;
this led to the April 1994 general election which
brought him to his presidency

---

on women

The beauty of a woman lies as much in her face
as in her body.

From a letter to his daughter Zindzi, 5 March
1978

If a pretty woman walks by, I don't want to be out
of the running.

He was talking to foreign correspondent Patti
Waldmeir at the time

Women today are very sensitive to men expressing
opinions without consulting them.

It's a unique woman who can turn the whole
world around and make it the best living place to
experience.

Nelson Mandela said this in May 2002, some
four years after his marriage to Graça Machel

For every woman and girl violently attacked, we
reduce our humanity.

on work

Job, jobs and jobs are the dividing line in many families between a decent life and a wretched existence.

Workers need a living wage – and the right to join unions of their own choice and to participate in determining policies that affect their lives.

Soweto rally, 13 February 1990

on the world

The problems are such that for anybody with a conscience who can use whatever influence he may have to try to bring about peace, it's difficult to say no.

on writing

Writing is a prestigious profession which puts one right into the centre of the world and, to remain on top, one has to work really hard, the aim being a good and original theme, simplicity in expression and the use of the irreplaceable word.

From a letter to his daughter Zindzi,
4 September 1977

on xenophobia

Never forget the greatness of a nation that has overcome its division. Let us never descend into destructive divisiveness.

Nelson Mandela wrote this on 13 May 2008 as South Africa struggled with xenophobic riots countrywide. This was the headline to an advertisement in the Sunday Times of 1 June 2008 supported by hundreds of South Africans from Archbishop Emeritus Desmond Tutu to Leon Geffen

on youth

I admire young people who are concerned with the affairs of their community and nation perhaps because I also became involved in struggle whist I was still at school.

Bastille Day, Paris speech, 14 July 1996

Young people are capable, when aroused, of bringing down the towers of oppression and raising the banners of freedom.

Bastille Day, 14 July Paris speech, 1996

I appeal to the youth and all those on the ground: start talking to each other across divisions of race and political organisations.

I pay tribute to the endless heroism of youth.

Address to rally in Cape Town, 11 February 1990

Whenever I am with energetic young people, I feel like a recharged battery.

Speech at the Food for Life Festival, Durban, 23 April 1997

---

on Zulus

No people can boast more proudly of having ploughed a significant field in the struggle.

Rally in Durban, 25 February 1990

Zulus have fought a long struggle against oppression.

Rally in Durban, 25 February 1990

The Battle of Isandlwana in 1879 has been an inspiration for those of us engaged in the struggle for justice and freedom in South Africa.

The battle took place under the shadow of a midday eclipse on 22 January 1879

Sources

ANC Youth League Manifesto, 1944; BBC News; *Leadership*; *Liberation* (June 1953); M-Net (*Funigalore*); *Saturday Star*; *The Star*; *Sunday Times*; *Mail & Guardian*; *Sowetan*; *The Argus*; *Cape Times*; SAPA; AP; *Business Day*; *The New York Times*; *Newsweek*; Reuters; *RSA Review* 1995; *The Natal Witness*; *Vogue* (French edition), Dec 1993/Jan 1994; *Time*; *The Financial Times*; *The Daily Telegraph*; *The Sunday Telegraph*; *The Sunday Independent*; *ThisDay*

The Struggle is My Life (Pathfinder, New York); *Nelson Mandela: The Man and the Movement* by Mary Benson (Penguin); *Higher than Hope* by Fatima Meer (Madiba); *The Historic Speech of Nelson Rolihlahla Mandela at the Rivonia Trial* (Learn & Teach Publications); *Rivonia – Operation Mayibuye: A Review of the Rivonia Trial* by HHW de Villiers (Afrikaanse Pers-Boekhandel); *Anatomy of a Miracle* by Patti Waldmeir (WW Norton & Company, 1997); *Madiba* (Martin Schneider), 1997; *Beyond the Miracle* by Allister Sparks (Jonathan Ball Publishers); *A Prisoner in the Garden* (Penguin/Nelson Mandela Foundation), 2005

Radio Good Hope; Radio 702; SABC; SATV (Allister Sparks' interview) 1998; Carte Blanche (M-Net)

2004; ANC Youth League Manifesto, 1944; Nelson Mandela Foundation. 'No Easy Walk to Freedom' speech, 21 September 1953; 'A New Menace in Africa' speech, March 1958; Verwoerd's Tribalism speech, May 1959; 'The Struggle is My Life' press statement, 26 June 1961; Letter to the Prime Minister, Dr HF Verwoerd, 26 June 1961; Address to the Conference of the Pan-African Freedom Movement of East and South Africa, Addis Ababa, January 1962; 'Black Man in a White Court' Trial speech, the Old Synagogue, Pretoria, 7 November 1962; Rivonia Treason Trial speech, 20 April 1964; Letter to his daughter Zindzi Mandela, 4 September 1977; Mandela's Call to the Youth of South Africa smuggled speech, 1980; 'Whilst Still in Prison', his first speech in almost 25 years, defiantly read by Zindzi Mandela, 10 February 1985; Release from Victor Verster Prison speech, Cape Town, 11 February 1990; Bishopscourt press conference, 12 February 1990; FNB Stadium (Soccer City) speech, Johannesburg 13 February 1990; Bloemfontein speech, 25 February 1990; Durban Rally speech, 25 February 1990; Address to the Swedish Parliament, 13 March 1990; Harlem speech, New York, 21 June 1990; Address to the Joint Session of the Houses of Congress of the USA, 26 June 1990; Announcement of his separation from Winnie, 13 April 1992; Gandhi Hall, Lenasia, speech, 27 September 1992; Speech to the House of Commons, United Kingdom, 5 May 1993; Acceptance Address at the Clark University Investiture, Atlanta, 10 July 1993; Nobel Peace Prize Award Ceremony speech, Oslo, Norway, 10 December 1993; ANC

Election Victory speech, 2 May 1994; Inauguration speech, 10 May 1994; Address to the 49th Session of the General Assembly, United Nations, 3 October 1994; Business Leaders speech, New Delhi, India, 26 January 1995; African Cup of Nations Tournament speech, 13 January 1996; Opening address to third session of Parliament, 9 February 1996; Interfaith Commissioning Service for the Truth & Reconciliation Commission speech, 13 February 1996; University of Potchefstroom speech, 19 February 1996; Opening of SA Parliament speech, 9 February 1996; Thanksgiving Service for the Ministry of Archbishop Tutu, Cape Town, 23 June 1996; SA Representatives to Olympic & Paralympic Games, Atlanta, speech, 28 June 1996; Joint Houses of Parliament Speech, London, 11 July 1996; Freedom of the City of London, Guildhall speech, 10 July 1996; Bastille Day speech, Paris, 14 July 1996; OAU Summit speech, Yaounde, 8 July 1996; 75th Anniversary of the South African Communist Party speech, 28 July 1996; Warrenton Presidential School Project speech, 30 August 1996; Signing of the SA Constitution speech, Sharpeville 10 December 1996; Food for Life, Pietermaritzburg speech, 23 April 1997; Freedom of Pietermaritzburg speech, 25 April 1997; State Banquet speech for President Museveni of Uganda, 27 May 1997; Lecture at the Oxford Centre for Islamic Studies, 11 July 1997; Commemoration of the 20th Anniversary of Steve Biko's Death speech, East London 12 September 1997; Honourary Doctorate by Ben-Gurion University of the Negev, Cape Town, 19 September 1997; Heritage Day speech, Robben Island, 24 September 1997; State

Banquet for Prime Minister Gujral of India, Cape Town 7 October 1997; Collar of the Nile Speech, Cairo, 21 October 1997; Colonel Qadhafi speech, Tripoli, 22 October 1997; Presentation of the Africa Peace Award to Mozambique, Durban, 1 November 1997; State Banquet for Prince Charles speech, Cape Town, 4 November 1997; Foreign Correspondents Association speech, Johannesburg, 21 November 1997; Freedom of the City of Cape Town speech, 27 November 1997; Regina Mundi Day speech, Soweto, 30 November 1997; Bram Fischer Memorial Trust speech, Bloemfontein, 28 November 1997; International Day of Solidarity with the Palestinian People speech, Pretoria, 4 December 1997; Farewell as President of the ANC speech, Mafikeng, 20 December 1997; OAU Heads of State & Government speech, Ouagadougou, Burkina Faso, 8 June 1998; Freedom of the City of Cardiff, speech, Cardiff, Wales, 16 June 1998; Sowetan Nation Building 10th Anniversary speech, Johannesburg, 30 June 1998; Chris Hani Award speech, 10th National Congress of the South African Communist Party, Johannesburg, 1 July 1998; Closing ceremony speech at the 19th Meeting of Heads of Government of the Caribbean Community, St Lucia, 4 July 1998; State banquet for President Rawlings of Ghana speech, Pretoria, 9 July 1998; Aids Speech, Paris, 14 July 2003; International Year of Older Persons speech, Cape Town, 17 July 2003; '46664 Give One Minute of Your Life to Aids' speech, 21 October 2003

NEW

ATKINS

FOR A NEW

YOU

NEW
ATKINS
FOR A NEW
YOU

The **ULTIMATE DIET** for **SHEDDING WEIGHT**
and **FEELING GREAT**

Drs Eric Westman,
Stephen Phinney
and Jeff Volek

Vermilion
LONDON

3 5 7 9 10 8 6 4 2

Published in the UK in 2010 by Vermilion, an imprint of Ebury Publishing
First published in the USA by Fireside, a division of Simon & Schuster, Inc., in 2010

Ebury Publishing is a Random House Group company

The Random House Group Limited Reg. No. 954009

Addresses for companies within the Random House Group can be found at

www.rbooks.co.uk

A CIP catalogue record for this book is available from the British Library

The Random House Group Limited supports The Forest Stewardship Council
(FSC), the leading international forest certification organisation. All our titles that
are printed on Greenpeace-approved FSC certified paper carry the FSC logo.
Our paper procurement policy can be found at
www.rbooks.co.uk/environment

Mixed Sources
Product group from well-managed
forests and other controlled sources
www.fsc.org Cert no. TT-COC-2139
© 1996 Forest Stewardship Council
FSC

Printed in the UK by CPI Cox & Wyman, Reading, RG1 8EX

ISBN 9780091935573

Copies are available at special rates for bulk orders. Contact the sales
development team on 020 7840 8487 for more information.

To buy books by your favourite authors and register for offers, visit
www.rbooks.co.uk

The late Dr Robert C Atkins established the nutritional principles that remain the core of the Atkins Diet. This innovative thinker worked tirelessly to help people understand how to improve their health by implementing these principles. With every passing year, independent research continues to confirm the wisdom of his ideas. We are proud to carry on Dr Atkins's legacy as we explore new frontiers in the low-carbohydrate dietary approach.

Contents

PART IV: A DIET FOR LIFE: THE SCIENCE OF GOOD HEALTH

Foreword

> That which seems the height of absurdity in one
> generation often becomes the height of wisdom in
> another.
>
> —*John Stuart Mill*

When does a treatment once considered alternative become mainstream? Is it when thousands of overweight people shrink themselves and improve their diabetes control with a low-carbohydrate way of eating? Does it require years of an obesity epidemic in the setting of a lifestyle increasingly reliant on high-carbohydrate and processed foods? Possibly, but for physicians deciding whether to recommend a low-carbohydrate diet instead of a low-fat diet to their patients, it comes down to one thing: *science*.

Books, newspaper articles and websites are wonderful ways to share new information; however, the ultimate way to change minds on a large scale is to do research. When study after study shows the same startling proof, physicians start to realise that what they previously regarded as unjustified is now scientifically verified.

In my work as a paediatric neurologist at Johns Hopkins Hospital in Baltimore, Maryland, in the US, caring for children with uncontrolled seizures, I have had the pleasure of witnessing a similar revolution in thinking over the past fifteen years. The ketogenic diet, similar to a low-carbohydrate diet, was created in 1921 as a treatment for epilepsy. Before the 1990s, even at major teaching hospitals in the United States, this dietary approach was often discarded as 'voodoo', unpalatable and less effective than medications. Today, it is a widely used and universally accepted treatment worldwide. Scepticism is now rare, and almost all doctors acknowledge the effectiveness of the ketogenic diet. How did the perception of this treatment undergo such a radical change in just a decade and a half? Was it lectures at national meetings, parent support groups or television coverage? They all certainly helped, but, again and even more important, research and hard scientific proof transformed disbelievers into advocates.

In *New Atkins for a New You*, you will discover how in the same time frame science has similarly transformed the Atkins Diet from what was once considered a 'fad' into an established, medically validated, safe and effective treatment. This book also offers a wealth of new advice and insights into doing the Atkins Diet correctly, including numerous simplifications, making it easier for people everywhere to achieve the benefits of a low-carbohydrate lifestyle than ever before. As you will soon see, the volume you hold in your hands is far more than a typical how-to diet book. Not only have Dr Eric C Westman, Dr Jeff S Volek and Dr Stephen D Phinney summarised the hundreds of research studies published in top medical journals, they have also authored many of them. In more than 150 articles these three international experts on the use of low-carbohydrate diets to combat obesity, high cholesterol and type-2 diabetes have led the way in repeatedly proving how a low-carbohydrate approach is superior to a low-fat one.

As a member of the Atkins Scientific Advisory Board, I have admired the work of these three clinician-scientists. It has been helpful to be able to call on each of them for their willing advice, and in a way now you can too, through this book. Their common-sense approach to starting and maintaining a low-carbohydrate diet is evident throughout the book, and their vast knowledge is especially evident in Part IV, 'A Diet for Life: The Science of Good Health'. I know that I will often refer my patients to this section.

I find it sad that Dr Robert C Atkins did not live to see his diet so strongly validated both in scientific research and in this new book, which so heavily bases its recommendations on that research. Many of his ideas, personal observations based on thousands of patients and philosophy, which appear in *Dr Atkins' Diet Revolution* and his other books, have been validated in this book with science to back them up. When the first edition of *Diet Revolution* was published in 1972, the low-carbohydrate concept was not one that doctors embraced, nor did they think that it would prevail. In Dr Atkins's lifetime his dietary approach was subject to scepticism and disbelief by much of the nutritional community. Perhaps there is no greater tribute to his memory than that this is typically no longer the case today.

I foresee exciting times ahead for the Atkins Diet. Already in my field of neurology, low-carbohydrate diets, researchers are studying its application for epilepsy in adults, as well as for Alzheimer's disease, autism, brain tumours and amyotrophic lateral sclerosis (ALS). There is published evidence from Dr Westman and others that these diets help not only obesity and type-2 diabetes, but possibly even schizophrenia, polycystic ovarian disease, irritable bowel disease, narcolepsy and gastro-oesophageal reflux disease (GORD). Obviously, there is growing evidence that low-carbohydrate diets are good for more than just your waistline! I am also personally hopeful that the Atkins Diet will become an accepted tool to combat the growing worldwide epidemic of childhood obesity. With its new content and firm underpinning of research, *New Atkins for a New You* will also enable researchers to use it as a 'bible' to develop correct protocols in low-carbohydrate studies.

I urge you to use this book not only as a guide to a healthier lifestyle but also as a scientific reference for your bookshelf. Friends and family may question why you are following the Atkins Diet, and even some doctors who have not read the latest research could discourage you from trying this approach. Although your personal results in your appearance and laboratory tests may change their minds within a few weeks, even before that, please let this book help you to enlighten them. Drs Phinney, Volek and Westman suggest at the beginning of Chapter 11 that 'You may want to share these chapters with your healthcare professional'. I could not agree more. Be sure to also point out the more than a hundred references at the end.

So I ask again, when does a treatment believed to be 'fad' science turn into an accepted fact? When does one man's 'diet revolution' become the status quo for people committed to leading a healthier lifestyle? The answer is . . . now. Enjoy all the advice, meal plans, recipes, success stories and – most important – science this book has to offer our generation and our children's generation.

Eric H Kossoff, MD
Medical Director, Ketogenic Diet Center
Departments of Neurology and Pediatrics
Johns Hopkins Hospital
Baltimore, Maryland, USA

Introduction

Welcome to the new Atkins.

You have a lot on your plate. Between holding down a job and/or raising a family and other activities, you're probably long on responsibilities and commitments and short on time. No doubt your to-do list grows with every passing day. So the last thing you need is a dietary approach that's complicated or time-consuming. Instead, you want an easy-to-follow way of eating that allows you to slim down quickly and stay there, address certain health problems and boost your energy.

Atkins is the programme you've been looking for.

Maybe you've heard about Atkins before. Maybe you've even tried it before. If so, this book will show you a whole new way to live the Atkins lifestyle that's easier and more effective than any previous book has offered. Welcome back. You'll love the updated Atkins.

Or perhaps you're new to the Atkins programme. Read on and find out why the Atkins lifestyle is the key to not just a slimmer body but also a healthier life. Not only is doing Atkins easier than ever, a growing number of researchers have recently conducted experiments aimed at better understanding how carbohydrate restriction impacts health. In the last few years more than fifty basic and applied studies have been published which, in addition to validating the safety and effectiveness of the Atkins Diet, also provide new insights into ways to optimise the Atkins lifestyle.

We'll tell you how the right foods will help you take charge of your weight, boost your energy and generally make you feel better. You'll learn everything that you need to know now and for a lifetime of weight control. You'll also come to understand that:

- Excess weight and poor health are two sides of the same coin.
- The quality of the food you eat affects your quality of life.
- Atkins is a way of eating for life, not a quickie weight-loss diet.
- Activity is the natural partner of a healthy diet.

Before telling you more about *New Atkins for a New You*, let's establish the logic of a low-carbohydrate lifestyle.

BEAT THE EPIDEMIC OF OBESITY

Here's a pop quiz for you. When eaten in large amounts, which macronutrient raises your blood levels of saturated fats and triglycerides: protein, fat or carbohydrate? You're probably tempted to answer *fat*. But the correct answer is *carbohydrate*. Second question: Which of the three *lowers* your HDL ('good') cholesterol? Again, the answer is carbohydrate.

In the last four decades the percentage of overweight American adults and children has ballooned, and the same is true in the UK. As Albert Einstein once remarked, 'Insanity is doing the same thing over and over, but expecting different results'. In this time frame the medical and nutritional establishment has told Americans and Brits to follow the Food Guide Pyramid, skimp on calories, avoid fat and focus on eating carbohydrate foods. We now consume less saturated fat than they did forty years ago but have replaced those calories – and added another 200 a day – with carbohydrates. Clearly something is seriously wrong with the way we eat.

So has the American and British population become thinner? Quite the contrary! Today, more than 65 per cent of American adults are overweight. Likewise, the prevalence of type-2 diabetes has skyrocketed. And the same trend can be seen in the UK. Are you a part of this statistical nightmare? Or are you at risk of becoming part of it? If so, this book provides the tools to escape that fate. But it's not just enough to read the words, you must also truly take responsibility for your health. Remodeling your eating habits – like making any major life change – takes commitment. But if you're truly ready to exchange your old habits for new ones, your reward will be the emergence of a slimmer, healthier, sexier, more energetic person – the new you!

New Atkins for a New You will make clear that doing Atkins isn't about eating only beef, bacon and butter. Rather, it's about finding how many carbohydrates you can tolerate and making good choices among carbohydrate-, protein- and fat-rich foods. In terms of carbohydrates, that means a wide array of vegetables and other whole foods. And if you chose not to eat meat or fish or any animal protein – whether for personal or other reasons – or to minimise their intake, you can still do Atkins.

CHANGE IS GOOD

In its almost forty-year evolution the Atkins Diet has seen a number of modifications reflecting emerging nutritional science. This book reflects the latest thinking on the diet and nutrition and introduces several significant changes including:

- A daily requirement of a substantial amount of high-fibre 'foundation vegetables'.
- An easy way to reduce or eliminate symptoms that sometimes accompany the initial conversion to a low-carb approach.
- Ways to smooth the transition from one phase to the next, ensuring the gradual and natural adoption of healthy, permanent eating habits.
- Detailed advice on how to maintain weight loss, including a choice of two paths in Phase 4: Lifetime Maintenance.

- The ability to customise the programme to individual needs, including variations for vegetarians and vegans.
- An understanding that we eat many of our meals outside the home with detailed suggestions on how to plan for them and what to eat on the road, in fast-food places or in different kinds of restaurants.

The book is full of other small but significant updates, again based on recent research. For example, we now know that consuming caffeine in moderation actually modestly assists fat burning. So your eight daily cups of fluid can include some coffee and other beverages in addition to water.

Simplicity, versatility and sustainability are essential for any dietary programme to succeed – long term. Atkins meets all three challenges.

1. **Simplicity.** Above all, the goal of this book is to make Atkins simple to do. In a nutshell, here it is: The key to slimming down and enhancing your health is to train your body to burn more fat. And the way to do that, quickly and effectively, is by cutting back on sugars and other refined carbohydrates and allowing fat – including your own body fat – to become your primary source of energy. (Before you know it, you'll understand why fat is your friend.) This book will give you all the tools you'll need to make this metabolic shift.

2. **Versatility.** Atkins now allows you to personalise the programme to your lifestyle and food preferences. If you've tried Atkins before and found it too difficult, too restrictive, you'll be very pleasantly surprised with the updated approach. For example:

   - You determine which phase to start in and when to move to the next phase.
   - You can eat lean cuts of meat and poultry – or none at all, if you prefer.

- You can do Atkins and still honour your own culinary heritage.
- You choose when to begin a fitness programme and what activities to pursue.
- You select one of the two approaches to Lifetime Maintenance that better suits your needs.

3. **Sustainability.** Atkins doesn't just help you shed weight and leave you there. We know – as you do – that the problem with every weight-loss programme is keeping the weight off for the long term. Understanding the power of fat burning is equally essential to lifetime weight maintenance. Importantly, the four-phase programme trains you to gauge your personal tolerance for carbohydrates, so that you can tailor a programme that not only fits you to a T but also enables you to permanently banish excess weight and maintain improved health indicators. And once you find a way of eating that you can live with, yo-yo dieting will be a thing of the past.

HOW TO USE THIS BOOK

Four sections allow you to get started on the programme quickly, complete with lists of acceptable foods and meal plans, plus provide a grounding in nutrition and the scientific foundations of the Atkins approach.

- Part I covers the basics of nutrition, looking at carbohydrates, protein and fats, and explains how and why Atkins works. We'll introduce the four phases that form the continuum of the Atkins Diet:
  - Phase 1: Induction
  - Phase 2: Ongoing Weight Loss (OWL)
  - Phase 3: Pre-Maintenance
  - Phase 4: Lifetime Maintenance

You'll also learn all about 'Net Carbs' and how to count them. (For brevity, we'll often refer to carbohydrates as carbs.) Once you understand these basics and commit yourself to concentrating on whole foods, you'll find it easier than ever to slim down and shape up. You'll also learn how the wrong foods – think of those made with sugar and refined grains – keep you overweight, tired and sluggish and increase your risk for health problems.

- Part II tells you how to do Atkins on a day-to-day basis and transition easily from one phase to the next. We'll guide you through the process of exploring the amounts and types of food that are right for you, with extensive lists of acceptable foods for each phase, as you customise the programme to your needs. You'll find a wide variety of choices in the types of foods you can eat, whether dining in or eating out.

- Part III includes detailed meal plans, recipes for all phases of the diet and guides to eating out.

- Part IV is for those of you who want to learn how Atkins can improve cardiovascular risk factors, reverse metabolic syndrome (pre-diabetes) and manage diabetes. We'll give you the short course and provide lots of reference material in case you happen to love reading scientific journals or want to share these chapters with your physician.

Just as you can tailor Atkins to your needs, you can read this book as you wish. If you're eager to get started immediately, simply start with Part II, but please circle back later to learn how and why Atkins works. At the very least read the review sections at the end of the chapters in Part I. As the 'Success Stories' sprinkled throughout the book make clear, until you understand the nutritional grounding of the Atkins Diet, it's all too easy to regard it merely as a tool for quick weight loss – instead of a healthy and permanent lifestyle.

In Part I you'll also make the acquaintance of the metabolic bully, which threatens your resolve to stay on the weight loss path, and its enemy – and your ally – the Atkins Edge. This powerful tool helps you slim down, without experiencing the hunger or cravings usually associated with weight loss. Other diets may come and go, but Atkins endures because it has always worked. As doctors, nutritionists and researchers, we're committed to making Atkins simpler than ever. After all, the easier it is, the more likely you are to stick with it, and – bottom line – achieve success. We can assure you that Dr Robert C Atkins, who was a pioneer in low-carb nutrition, would approve of the science-based changes introduced in this book, particularly any that make the programme easier for you and enable you to keep excess weight off long term. The growing worldwide epidemics of obesity and diabetes mean that it's not a moment too soon.

Stephen D Phinney, MD, PhD
Jeff S Volek, PhD, RD
Eric C Westman, MD, MHS

WHY IT WORKS:

It's All About Nutrition

Chapter 1

KNOW THYSELF

> Any diet that skimps on natural fats is inherently
> unsatisfying, making it extremely difficult to sustain
> long term and almost certainly doomed to failure.

Did you once delight in eating whatever you wanted without gaining a gram? Were you athletic in secondary school? Was your weight never a problem until after you got your first high-stress job, started your family or approached the menopause? Have you been diagnosed with high cholesterol, or are you at risk for type-2 diabetes? If you're reading this book and the answer to any of these questions is 'yes', it's a safe assumption that your days of carefree eating are long gone.

Or maybe you've spent a good part of your adult life on the diet merry-go-round. You hop on to lose some weight, then dismount as soon as you've lost it. When you regain the weight – as most of us inevitably do – you jump back on and so forth. You might have even done Atkins several years ago and banished that extra padding. But when you reverted to your habitual way of eating, the lost kilograms returned with a vengeance. Maybe you felt under the weather in the first week or two of Atkins, found the programme too restrictive or had some concerns about its healthfulness. Perhaps you simply got bored.

Since you're reading this book, we trust that you're giving Atkins a second chance. Thanks to some significant changes, you'll find that the programme is now far easier to do. And new research makes it clear that Atkins is a healthy way to eat. It's one of the few low-carb diets subjected to extensive independent research. In studies that compared people following a low-calorie programme to those controlling their carbohydrates, the groups that reduced their carbs showed greater weight and fat loss, better compliance, the ability to keep weight off long term and higher satisfaction with food choices. We'll circle back to some of the research later in this chapter.

Another possibility is that you're a veteran of the low-fat approach that left you unsatisfied, hungry, testy and fantasising about forbidden feasts, before ultimately giving it up. Or you've spent the last decade or so sampling every diet craze that came on the shelves only to regain the weight – and perhaps even a little extra weight – for all your efforts.

Whether you're new to Atkins, have returned after wandering in the dietary wilderness or are a confirmed Atkins follower interested in recent modifications, you've come to the right place. Atkins has never been just about weight, so there's also a seat at the table for already slim folks who want to improve their physique, increase their energy, overcome health problems or simply feel better. Whatever your story, it's time to get off the diet merry-go-round and on to a permanent path to lifetime slimness, vitality and good health.

TIME TO TAKE CONTROL

Does this sound familiar? Each time you've tried a new weight-loss approach or renewed your commitment to stick with a programme, you experience euphoria and a sense of empowerment. And you probably enjoyed some initial good results. But then you didn't follow through, and soon you'd find yourself in a downwards spiral. You blamed yourself for your weakness, lack of control and inability to defer the momentary pleasure of a piece of chocolate or a packet of crisps for the long-term goal of a trimmer, more attractive you. And as all too many of you may have already learnt, the challenges of losing weight pale compared to the real work of keeping it permanently at bay. The American humourist Erma Bombeck was on to something when she quipped, 'In two decades I've lost a total of 789 pounds. I should be hanging from a charm bracelet'. But when it comes to your health and your psyche, the cycle of losing, regaining, losing and so forth is no laughing matter. Nor are the guilt, shame and sense of failure that accompany it.

By the end of this chapter, you'll have met the metabolic bully that stands in the way of your losing weight and achieving optimal health. We'll also introduce you to the Atkins Edge, the powerful tool that distinguishes Atkins from other diets and lets you outsmart the bully. The Atkins Edge converts your body to a fat-burning machine. Yes, we're talking about using your spare tyre, beer belly, thunder thighs, heroic hips, jiggling bum or wherever your fat deposits have landed as your primary energy source. Just as important, the process of literally restoring your body to its best shape will not only make you feel good about your body and proud of your resolve, you'll almost surely find that the sense of empowerment and confidence spills over into your personal and professional life. Feeling powerful is an aphrodisiac, so don't be surprised to find that your sex life also revives!

IS ATKINS FOR YOU?

To help you decide whether Atkins can help you slim down – and stay there – and address any health issues, consider the following questions.

ARE YOU HAPPY WITH YOUR WEIGHT? If so, congratulations! But even if you're content with your appearance, you may find it an effort to maintain your weight, or you may have health problems that could be alleviated by changing your diet. Or perhaps you want to reconfigure your body by trading fat for muscle, as Atkins can do, especially if you also embark on a training programme.

Bottom line: Atkins is an effective and sustainable way to shed weight – quickly and safely.

WHAT ARE YOUR WEIGHT-LOSS GOALS? If you have just a few pesky kilograms to lose, you can probably take them off in a month or so. Some people lose up to 7 kilograms (15 pounds) in the first two weeks on Atkins. Countless individuals have lost more than 45 kilograms (7 stones) – and you could, too. You'll meet some of them in this book and can read more of their success stories on www.atkins.com. Naturally, individual results vary considerably, depending upon age, gender, activity level, metabolic resistance and other factors, plus – of course – how carefully you follow our instructions. Bottom line: You can lose a little or a lot on Atkins.

DO YOU HAVE OTHER HEALTH ISSUES YOU WANT TO CORRECT OR HEAD OFF? Individual results vary, but generally, if you go easy on carbs and focus on vegetables and other whole food carbs, you'll almost surely find that your triglycerides diminish, your 'good' cholesterol rises and your markers of inflammation improve. If you have high blood pressure, you should see your numbers drop. Those with elevated blood sugar and insulin levels will also see improvement. Most Atkins followers who once had to take medications and/or insulin for type-2 diabetes to control their blood sugar or diuretics to counteract fluid retention have been able, with their doctor's help, to reduce their dosage and even stop taking the drugs once they've adapted to the Atkins programme. Atkins also addresses other health issues such as insulin resistance and metabolic syndrome.[4] Controlling carbs is also a time-tested and viable treatment for epilepsy.[5] Bottom line: Atkins is a healthy diet and, for those with medical problems, is also a corrective diet that can significantly reduce the risks for disease.

WERE YOU SUCCESSFUL SHORT TERM BUT NOT LONG TERM ON OTHER DIETS? Any diet that's not sustainable is almost certainly doomed to failure. About 95 per cent of people who lose weight regain it – usually within a few years.[6] The point is that once you've slimmed down, raw willpower alone is not enough for you to succeed in the long term. You also need an ally, and this is where the Atkins Edge comes in. Numerous studies show better maintenance of weight loss after one and two years with Atkins compared to low-fat diets.[7] Bottom line: On Atkins, you lose the weight and can then maintain that loss, making it a diet for life.

ARE YOU UNABLE TO LOSE WEIGHT OR MAINTAIN WEIGHT LOSS BY COUNTING CALORIES AND AVOIDING FAT? A diet that skimps on natural fats is inherently unsatisfying, making it extremely difficult to sustain long term, as is a calorie-restricted diet that leaves you perpetually hungry. Atkins, on the other hand, allows you to eat many delicious foods that contain healthy fats. In fact, research shows that when people on Atkins eat as much as they want, most end up naturally eating a suitable number of calories.[8] Bottom line: On Atkins, there's no need to skimp on fats or count calories.

ARE YOU ALWAYS HUNGRY OR PLAGUED BY CRAVINGS ON OTHER DIETS? A low-fat diet is almost always a high-carb diet, which quickly converts to glucose in your bloodstream, especially in the case of low-quality carbs. The result is a roller coaster of blood sugar highs and lows that zap your energy and leave you craving another 'fix' of quickly metabolised carbs a few hours after a meal. Bottom line: Eating the Atkins way (which includes two snacks a day) means you need never go hungry.

ARE YOUR FAVOURITE FOODS DOUGHNUTS, SWEETS, CHIPS, CRISPS AND OTHER HIGH-CARB FOODS? The more of these foods you eat, the more you crave, setting up a vicious cycle of overeating foods that don't sustain your energy and have little nutritional value. A high-carb snack merely repeats the cycle. Bottom line: Eliminating sugars, refined carbs and other high-carb foods from your diet allows you to get off the blood sugar roller coaster.

DO YOU GAIN WEIGHT EASILY EVEN THOUGH YOU DON'T OVEREAT? It's a sad fact that some people put on weight more easily and lose weight more slowly than others.[9] However, if you can't drop excess weight when you're truly not overeating, this may be an indication that your body doesn't tolerate carbs well, which can be a precursor of type-2 diabetes. Controlling your carb intake nips the problem in the bud. Bottom line: Doing Atkins allows your body to bypass problems handling carbohydrates.

WERE YOU INITIALLY SUCCESSFUL ON ATKINS IN THE PAST BUT REGAINED WEIGHT? If you regained weight after losing it, you'll learn how to refine the lessons you learnt about weight loss and apply them to the bigger challenge of slimming down for good. Bottom line: Atkins focuses on weight maintenance from day 1.

DID YOU GET HUNG UP ON INDUCTION AND DIDN'T MOVE THROUGH THE OTHER PHASES? All too many people confuse Induction, the first phase that kickstarts weight loss, for the entire Atkins programme. Remaining in Induction may produce quick weight loss, but it doesn't teach you how to achieve permanent weight control. You may also become bored with the food choices, which could diminish your commitment to stay with Atkins. Bottom line: This time you can be comfortable exploring the range of foods that will enable you to keep losing weight – and ultimately maintain your new weight.

HAVE YOU TRIED ATKINS BEFORE BUT DROPPED OUT BEFORE LOSING MUCH WEIGHT? If you found the programme too restrictive, you'll be pleased to know that it's now far more flexible. For example, you can now enjoy a satisfying variety of vegetables from the beginning. You'll also learn how to dine out easily and safely – on any cuisine. If you felt the food was too expensive, we'll help you avoid overeating protein and provide you with a list of meat cuts that won't break your budget. Bottom line: Anyone can do Atkins anywhere, and that includes vegetarians and vegans.

THIS TIME WILL BE DIFFERENT

If you're a veteran of the weight-loss wars, we can promise you that you're in for a surprise: this time will be different. But first of all you must understand that shedding weight and getting healthy isn't just a matter of willpower. There are biological reasons why you feel hungry – or not. Earlier in this chapter we mentioned the metabolic bully, which undermines your determination and tries to derail your efforts at weight loss. Because the glucose from carbohydrates must always be tapped first as a source of energy, there's rarely any need to access your body fat if you eat a typical carb-heavy diet. So eating lots of carbohydrates acts as a metabolic bully: it blocks your body from burning its own fat, just like a playground bully who keeps other kids from using the swings.

But don't despair. You now have access to a valuable tool that will allow you to burn your own body fat for energy and keep hunger at bay. When you cut back on carbs sufficiently, your body transitions to a primarily fat-burning metabolism, forcing the bully to step aside. The messages your body transmits to your brain will change dramatically. Instead of hearing, 'I'm tired and hungry. Feed me sweet, starchy foods this minute', that nagging voice will be blissfully silent. You'll actually find that you can go for several hours without even thinking about food.

Scientists refer to it as a fat-burning metabolism, but we call this ally the Atkins Edge. It enables you to stop the metabolic bully in its tracks so you lose fat weight without experiencing undue hunger, cravings, energy depletion or any sense of deprivation. When you burn fat for energy all day (and all night), your blood sugar remains on a relatively even keel. Without question, the Atkins Edge makes it easier to stay the course and succeed in meeting your goals. Now that you know that eating too much sugar and other refined carbohydrates stands in the way of losing weight and restoring your energy, we ask again, is Atkins for you? Perhaps the more logical question is: Why wouldn't Atkins be right for you?

NO CARBS, NOT!

The most persistent misconception about Atkins is that it's a no-carb diet. From the first printing of *Dr Atkins' Diet Revolution* in 1972 onwards, the advice has always been to limit – not eliminate – carbs. In fact, this first version of the programme included salads from day 1. Over the years, the number and amount of vegetables permissible in Phase 1 has increased significantly, in large part because of a better understanding of the benign role of fibre in carbs. Atkins is actually about ultimately discovering which whole foods, including vegetables, fruits, nuts, pulses and whole grains – all of which contain carbohydrates – you're able to eat without interfering with weight loss, weight maintenance or metabolic health. Finding out how much fibre-rich carbohydrate you can eat while still maintaining your Atkins Edge is key to your long-term success.

GROUNDED IN RESEARCH

Now that you realise the power of the Atkins Diet, let's take a brief look at some of the recent research that has evaluated its safety and efficacy. This newer research builds upon older information on carbohydrate-restricted diets, including the use of low-carbohydrate diets by a variety of Aboriginal hunting cultures that persisted for thousands of years. In the last decade a multitude of studies on restricted carbohydrate intake has dramatically changed the research landscape. Among these are seven studies lasting from six months to two years, usually comparing the Atkins Diet to other common weight-loss strategies.[10] In terms of total weight loss, in each case individuals on Atkins did at least as well as – and usually better than – than those on other diets, despite the fact that they could consume as many calories as they wanted to as long as they stayed within the carb guidelines.

Moreover, risk factors such as high blood triglycerides, low HDL cholesterol levels and elevated blood pressure consistently showed improvement with carbohydrate restriction. Whether over months or years, the various parameters were as good, and in most cases better, with the Atkins Diet. In no case did Atkins worsen any important parameter. It's worth mentioning that in each of these seven studies, the subjects received varying degrees of ongoing dietary support after the first few weeks or months. And they didn't select the diet that appealed to them; instead they were randomly assigned to one of the various diets, which would tend to limit the degree of success in the group as a whole. Nonetheless groups assigned to Atkins did better on average than those assigned a high-carbohydrate diet.

Another study didn't use the Atkins Diet per se, although it was initially similar to the Induction phase, nor did it compare a low-carb programme to other diets. But this research, done in Kuwait, demonstrated the magnitude of beneficial change that a low-carb diet can provide when subjects receive ongoing support.[11] In this case, sixty-six obese individuals, some with elevated blood sugar and cholesterol, consumed 80 to 100 grams (3 to 4 ounces) per day of protein from meat and fish, 20 grams (0.7 ounces) of carbohydrate from salad vegetables, 5 tablespoons of olive oil for cooking and dressing vegetables and a multivitamin/multimineral supplement. After twelve weeks the carbohydrate intake was raised to 40 grams (1.5 ounces) per day (similar to that in Ongoing Weight Loss), including some berries. The subjects were monitored and supported as outpatients for a year, at which time their average weight loss was more than 27 kilograms (4.3 stones). In addition, a subgroup with elevated blood sugar (some were diabetic) experienced a rapid reduction, bringing them within eight weeks into the normal range, where it remained for the duration of the study. This diet outperformed that of any of the randomised groups in the other seven studies due in part to the fact that the subjects chose their diet, rather than being assigned to it. Additionally, the supportive office staff counselled them, including giving them specific advice on the kind of fat to eat, showing what's possible when a safe and effective low-carb diet is combined with an enabling support staff in a clinical setting.

In the following chapters we'll cover the basics of the diet and talk more about the Atkins Edge and how it enables you to remain in control – and vanquish the metabolic bully that has threatened to take over your life. We'll also offer lots of practical advice on how to deal with the challenges you'll face day in and day out; but first turn the page to meet Traci Marshall, who lost about 45 kilograms (7 stones) on Atkins.

SHEDDING THE 'BABY WEIGHT'

Two pregnancies left Traci Marshall heavier than she had ever been and with a number of serious health problems. Now that she's lost about 41 kilograms (6.4 stones) on Atkins, her health is restored, along with her figure and zest for life.

VITAL STATISTICS

Current phase: Ongoing Weight Loss

Daily Net Carb intake: 40–45 grams (1.5–1.6 ounces)

Age: 42

Height: 167.6 cm (5 ft 6 in)

Before weight: 121.1 kg (19 stones)

Current weight: 78 kg (12.3 stones)

Weight lost: 41.7 kg (6.6 stones)

Goal weight: 68 kg (10.7 stones)

Former waist/hips measurement: 101.6 cm/123.2 cm (40 in/48.5 in)

Current waist/hips measurement: 74.9 cm/97.8 cm (29.5 in/38.5 in)

Former blood pressure: 160/90

Current blood pressure: 118/74

Current triglycerides: 48

Current HDL ('good') cholesterol level: 58 mg/dL

Current LDL ('bad') cholesterol level: 110 mg/dL

Current total cholesterol level: 178 mg/dL

Has your weight always been an issue?

Yes. I'd done Atkins in 1997 and lost about 20 kilograms (3.2 stones) in two and a half months. I kept that off without effort and felt terrific until 2003, when I got pregnant. I had morning sickness the whole time and spent three months in bed. By the time I became pregnant with our second son, I was 41 years old and it was an even more difficult pregnancy.

What health problems did you have?

I'd developed hypertension and had a heart murmur while I was expecting. Afterwards I also suffered from post-natal anxiety.

What got you back on Atkins?

I'd actually gone back to Atkins after my first son's birth and had lost 11.3 of the 22.7 extra kilograms (1.8 of the 3.6 extra stones) I'd gained before realising I was having another baby. I now understand that I could have done the Lifetime Maintenance phase while pregnant. My doctor was totally supportive about my returning to Atkins after my second son's birth. By this time, I'd read several of Dr Atkins's books and knew that I was highly intolerant of carbs and that Atkins was a lifestyle change, not just a weight-loss diet. I remembered how great it felt to live Atkins every day and stay slim. I wanted that back!

What health improvements have you seen?

My blood pressure and lipids are great. My doctor is really happy with my progress. My heart murmur has disappeared. I sleep better. I have way more energy, and exercise is something I look forward to now.

What's your fitness routine?

I walk with the kids three days a week and go by myself on other days. I belong to a gym, where I do some cardio, but have come to realise that staying active is not just going to the gym. Recently, I started doing modified press-ups, leg extensions and other callisthenics. Almost immediately, weight loss picked up. I've learnt to love exercise because it feels awesome!

What was the worst thing about being overweight?
I didn't feel like me. I felt lost in a huge body. I wanted to hide, and I was so embarrassed for my children to have a heavy mum.

How did you handle the challenge of having a lot of weight to lose?
I only thought about 5 kilograms (10 pounds) at a time. Now that I'm closer to my goal, I only think about 2.5 kilograms (5 pounds) at a time.

How would you describe your eating style?
I eat everything that other people eat, I just eat it differently. So today I'm baking a pumpkin pie for my husband, and I'm making low-carb pumpkin cheesecake for myself, baking it in single servings in muffin tins. For breakfast, I might have Brussels sprouts mashed with cream and butter and a pork chop cooked in olive oil with garlic. Lunch is usually a big salad with onion, tomato, avocado, a piece of chicken and my own salad dressing. Snacks are usually berries and nuts. For dinner, we'll have a protein and a vegetable. I'll make rice or sweet potatoes for the rest of the family, and I'll have another low-carb vegetable.

Has doing Atkins affected how you feed your family?
Absolutely. If you teach kids how to eat, they'll eat right. I'm raising them on the Atkins lifestyle. I try not to have white potatoes in the house except at holiday times. I won't buy anything with high-fructose corn syrup. I read the labels of everything to make sure of the ingredients.

What words of wisdom can you offer other people?
Plan ahead. Make more than you need for a single meal so
that you always have something ready. Satisfy sweet cravings
with a cup of coffee with cream and low-carb sweetener.
Motivate yourself by looking at old photos when you were at
a good weight. Keep a food journal. Learn to adapt recipes,
like using aubergine strips in lieu of pasta.

What was the most difficult thing for you?
The hardest part is just making the commitment to start.
Once you get going it just feels so good. For me it gets easier
the longer I stay on Atkins.

Chapter 2

THE ROAD AHEAD

> As long as you consider a short-term diet as a solution,
> you're doomed to an on-again, off-again battle with
> your weight.

One of the main reasons for the failure of most efforts to slim down is that people simply can't sustain the prescribed way of eating. Boredom or dissatisfaction with the permissible foods, concern about the adequacy of the diet or sheer hunger ultimately causes dieters to revert to their old habits. Eating is pleasurable, and any weight control approach that makes food the enemy is doomed to failure. In contrast, Atkins makes food your friend and is all about choice rather than denial. By the time you've completed this chapter, you'll have a better understanding of the several pieces of the puzzle that come together to give you the Atkins Edge. This metabolic advantage will power you with a steady source of energy – and empower you to stay with the programme.

THE D-WORD

Most people are hung up on the secondary meaning of the word 'diet': a limited period of deprivation to lose weight. That short-term thinking is what has got so many 'dieters' into the same bind. They hop on to the diet wagon, lose a little excess baggage, then hop (or fall) off and regain the same old kilograms..

As long as you consider a short-term diet as a solution, you're doomed to an on-again, off-again battle with your weight. Things are different in Atkins land. First of all, losing weight the low-carb way needn't involve deprivation. Secondly, although Atkins has all too often mistakenly been perceived as just a weight-loss diet (and without question, it does help people lose weight swiftly and effectively), it's really a lifestyle that enriches your life in many ways. That's why the programme's formal name is the Atkins Nutritional Approach. You can still call it the Atkins Diet – we do – as long as you remember that it's a much bigger tent. Atkins is a way of eating that will enhance the quality of your life. After three progressively liberal phases, the Atkins programme culminates in Lifetime Maintenance.

LET'S PREVIEW THE PHASES

Part II of this book is devoted to the four phases, but for now we'll briefly introduce them to make it crystal clear that Atkins is truly a recipe for life rather than simply a weight-loss diet.

PHASE 1: INDUCTION, is where most – but not all – people start. It lasts for a minimum of two weeks, but feel free to continue there a bit longer if you have a lot of weight to lose. In Induction you'll train your body to burn fat, which will kick-start weight loss. To do so you'll confine yourself to a daily intake of 20 grams (0.7 ounces) of Net Carbs. (See the sidebar 'What Are Net Carbs?') Of those 20 carb grams, at least 12 to 15 grams (0.4 to 0.5 ounces) should be in the form of what we call 'foundation vegetables', which you'll eat every day, along with protein and healthy, natural fats. Off the menu is anything made with sugar, fruit juices and concentrates, and flour or other grains.

PHASE 2: ONGOING WEIGHT LOSS, or OWL, is when you continue to explore foundation vegetables and begin adding back foods such as berries, nuts and seeds – and perhaps even some pulses. You'll slowly increase your daily carb intake by 5 grams (0.2 ounces) at a time until you find your personal tolerance for consuming carbs while continuing to lose weight, known as your Carbohydrate Level for Losing (CLL). You typically stay in this phase until you're about 4.5 kilograms (10 pounds) from your goal weight.

PHASE 3: PRE-MAINTENANCE, broadens the range of acceptable whole food carbs in the form of other fruits, starchy vegetables and finally whole grains. (However, not everyone can add back all these foods or eat them on a regular basis.) As long as you continue to lose weight, you can slowly increase your daily carb intake in 10-gram (0.4-ounce) increments. When you reach your goal weight, you'll test out the level of carb intake you can handle without regaining kilograms or losing the precious metabolic adaptations you've achieved. This level is known as your Atkins Carbohydrate Equilibrium (ACE). Once your weight has stabilised for a month and your food cravings are under control, you're ready to move on.

PHASE 4: LIFETIME MAINTENANCE, is really not a phase at all but a lifestyle. You'll continue to consume the varied whole foods diet of Pre-Maintenance, adhering to your ACE and regularly monitoring your weight and measurements. Two approaches to Lifetime Maintenance address the needs of people across a range of ACEs. Some people may need to keep their intake of carbohydrates low and avoid certain foods to continue to enjoy the health benefits of carbohydrate restriction; others will have more latitude to consume more and a greater variety of carbohydrate foods.

In the next chapters we'll get into the specifics of what you should be eating from day 1 and what you'll add back as you slim down and your new eating habits become ingrained. We'll also discuss the few foods that you're better off steering clear of. The Atkins approach is not about banning foods lacking in nutrients and full of carbs, but it does make clear the dangers they present to weight control and overall good health. We trust that once you understand how these foods sabotage your good efforts, you'll pretty much ban them yourself for good.

WHAT ARE NET CARBS?

The only carbs that matter when you do Atkins are Net Carbs, aka digestible carbs or impact carbs. Fortunately, you don't have to be a food scientist or maths whizz to figure out how to calculate them. Simply subtract the number of grams of dietary fibre in whole foods from the total number of carbohydrate grams. How come? The answer is that although it's considered a carbohydrate, fibre doesn't impact your blood sugar level. So unlike other carbs, it doesn't act as a metabolic bully. Let's do the maths. About 70 grams (2.5 ounces) of steamed French beans contains 4.9 grams (0.17 ounces) of carbs, of which 2.0 grams (0.07 ounces) are fibre, so subtract 2.0 from 4.9 and you get 2.9 grams (0.1 ounces) of Net Carbs. Here's an even more dramatic example: about 50 grams (1.8 ounces) of cos lettuce contains 1.4 grams (0.05 ounces) of carbs, but more than half the carbs (1.0 gram) are fibre, for a Net Carb count of 0.4 gram (0.01 ounces). No wonder you can eat lots and lots of salad leaves on Atkins!

When it comes to low-carb foods, you subtract grams of sugar alcohols (including glycerine), as well as of fibre, from total grams of carbs to get the Net Carb count.

Tip: For a Carb Counter that provides total carbs, Net Carbs and other nutritional data for hundreds of foods, go to www.atkins.com/Program/FourPhases/CarbCounter.aspx.

WHAT ARE SUGAR ALCOHOLS?

Many low-carb products are sweetened with such ingredients as glycerine, mannitol, sorbitol, xylitol, erythritol, isomalt, lactitol and maltitol. These forms of sugar, called sugar alcohols (or polyols), provide a sweetness and mouthfeel similar to that of sugar without all the calories and unwanted metabolic effects. Because sugar alcohols are not fully absorbed by the gut, they provide roughly half the calories that sugar does, although each one varies slightly. The incomplete and slower absorption results in a minimal impact on blood sugar and insulin response. This means that sugar alcohols don't significantly interfere with fat burning, making them acceptable on Atkins. Other benefits may include promotion of colon health and prevention of cavities. However, a portion of sugar alcohols is not absorbed, which can produce a laxative effect and cause some gastrointestinal problems when they are consumed in excess. Individual tolerances vary, so it is best to test the waters slowly. Most people find that they can handle 20 to 30 grams (0.7 to 1 ounce) a day without undesirable effects.

MEASURING YOUR PROGRESS

Most people lose kilograms quickly and steadily in the first few weeks of Atkins – in fact, some people lose up to 7 kilograms (15 pounds – just over a stone) in the first two weeks on the programme. But numerous factors influence your individual weight-loss pattern. If you have just a few pounds to lose, they may be more resistant to your efforts. Men tend to lose more quickly than women do. Younger people typically have an advantage over the middle-aged or older. Hormonal changes such as the menopause can definitely slow your metabolism and make it more difficult to banish kilograms. Some people naturally have a slower metabolism. Certain prescription medicines can also interfere with weight loss. Your spouse or friend may well lose at a different rate than you do. Just remember that getting slim and trim isn't a contest. Rather, it's a process of discovering how your own body works.

Those of you with a significant amount of weight to lose typically see steady progress week after week, but it's natural to experience some ups and downs, and with time almost everyone sees a slow down in weight loss. Lost centimetres also indicate progress, sometimes even when kilograms won't budge. That's why we encourage you to unroll the tape measure whenever you hop on the scales. As you'll come to understand, your goal is not just a smaller clothing size and a trimmer body, it's also to enjoy good health and well-being. If you start out with type-2 diabetes or hypertension, both of which tend to improve promptly on Atkins, your improved numbers will give you and your doctor evidence that the diet is working. We'll give you more detail on how diabetes and other serious conditions respond to Atkins in Part IV.

WATER WEIGHT AND FAT WEIGHT

As with any weight-loss programme, some of the initial weight loss you'll experience is water weight. After all, one half to two thirds of your body is composed of water. Atkins naturally has a diuretic effect that starts within the first few days, which is why drinking plenty of water is important, as is taking a multivitamin/ multimineral, to ensure that you don't deplete your stores of electrolytes (sodium, potassium, magnesium). (We'll discuss which supplements are important shortly.) So if you lose 4.5 to 6.8 kilograms (10 to 15 pounds) in the first few weeks, you'll be saying goodbye to some unnecessary water weight along with the initial fat weight. But once that excess water is gone, you'll be losing primarily body fat. The Atkins Diet has been shown time and time again to result in significant fat loss, especially from the stomach area. In head-to-head comparisons, Atkins consistently outperforms other diets in terms of fat loss. The majority of studies indicate that when carbohydrate intake is reduced and protein intake is modestly increased, there's a greater percentage of fat loss and better retention of lean body mass. But after that, as long as you follow our food intake guidelines, you can be secure in the knowledge that the vast majority of your ongoing weight loss will come from fat.

WHAT TO EXPECT

Your body makes a number of adjustments as it begins to focus on burning primarily fat, after which you will have gained the metabolic advantage we call the Atkins Edge. However, in those first few weeks, as your body makes this transition, you might encounter a few symptoms. The most common are headaches, dizziness, weakness, fatigue – sometimes referred to as Atkins flu – and constipation. Fortunately, all are quite easy to avoid. We'll touch on them here and then give you more complete instructions on how to manage them in Chapter 7.

As mentioned above, type-2 diabetes and hypertension sometimes improve dramatically when you are on a low-carb programme, so the need for certain medications diminishes. Close co-operation with your doctor is essential so that you don't confuse the effects of too high a dose of a medication with doing Atkins itself. Also, it's not a good idea to begin a new or more intense exercise programme at the same time you start the programme. Give your body the benefit of two to three weeks to adjust before tackling a new exercise regime. On the other hand, if you are already very active or work out regularly and can continue to do so without any loss of energy, feel free to continue.

Consuming carbohydrates makes you retain water, but shifting over to fat burning has a diuretic effect, meaning you'll excrete more salt along with fluid. If you used to feel bloated and no longer do, that's a good thing. Moreover, if you have high blood pressure, the diuretic effect may mean that your numbers will come down nicely in the first few days or weeks. But for many of the rest of us, fluid loss can be too much of a good thing. To manage this problem, simply drink plenty of water and make sure to consume a minimum of half a teaspoon of salt each day. You can do this with salt itself, a couple of cups of salty broth or a measured amount of soya sauce. Follow this regimen from the start, and headaches, dizziness, fatigue or constipation should not be a problem. Adding this modest sodium supplement – no, this does not make Atkins a high-salt diet – is one of many science-based changes in Atkins. We'll give you more details about this practice (and the few exceptions for those who should not follow it) in Chapter 7.

NUTRITION BASICS

You probably have a general idea that foods contain various amounts of protein, fat and carbohydrates, which are commonly considered macronutrients. Does it matter whether you eat more or less of one or another? For that matter, what is a Calorie? And how do calories relate to carbs? Let's start with the easy stuff. Macronutrients are the three nutrient families that provide the body with needed energy – in the form of calories – to carry out all the bodily functions necessary for life. A few foods contain a single macronutrient such as sugar (all carbohydrate) and olive oil (all fat). Most foods, however, contain two or all three macronutrients. For example, 240 millilitres (8 fluid ounces) of whole milk contain 8 grams (0.3 ounces) of protein and about the same amount of fat, as well as more than 11 grams (0.4 ounces) of carbohydrate. About 115 grams (4 ounces) of field mushrooms contain almost 6 grams (0.2 ounces) of carbohydrate – of which nearly 2 grams (0.07 ounces) are fibre – a miniscule amount of fat and almost 3 grams (0.1 ounces) of protein.

A Calorie (aka kilocalorie) is simply a unit of food energy. In this book we use the word 'Calorie' (with a capital C) to designate a kilocalorie, and the word 'calorie' in reference to energy in general. Your body needs the energy in macronutrients, not just for physical activity but also for all its other functions, including breathing, staying warm, processing nutrients and brain activity. A gram of protein or carbohydrate contains 4 Calories, while a gram of fat contains 9 Calories. So gram for gram, fat is a more concentrated source of energy. Some of the raw materials in macronutrients are turned into energy almost immediately; others are broken down into various components that are used for energy later.

ATKINS IS DIFFERENT FROM OTHER DIETS

To succeed on Atkins, you may need to forget what you've learnt on other diets. Here's why:

	LOW-FAT DIET	LOW-CARB DIET	COMMENTS
Methodology	Count calories, restrict all fat	Count carbs, eliminate trans-fats	Satiating foods eaten on Atkins minimise hunger, moderating calorie intake
Eat mostly	Carbs of all sorts	Healthy fats, protein, healthy carbs	Avoid sugar, pasta, bread and other refined-carb foods that raise blood sugar levels
Weigh foods	Yes	No	Who takes scales to a restaurant?
Count calories	Yes	No	Atkins emphasises quality, not low-calorie food
Count carbs	No	Yes	All you need is a Carb Counter to track your intake
Eat prepared foods	Yes (on some programmes)	No	You eat healthful whole foods, not expensive ready meals
Snacks	Yes, but calorie-restricted	Yes, twice a day	Who wouldn't prefer cheese, nuts or guacamole to a celery stick?

HOW FOOD BECOMES ENERGY – AND FAT

Human metabolism is complex, but we'll make it as simple as possible. This chemical process converts food into either energy or the body's building blocks, which then become part of your organs, tissues and cells. Eating the right foods can improve your body's metabolism, particularly how it handles fat. When you eat fewer carbohydrate foods – relying mostly on vegetables rich in fibre – your body switches to burning fat instead of carbs as its primary fuel source. The average normal-weight person carries about 100,000 Calories worth of energy in fat stores – hypothetically, that's enough to run at a steady pace for more than 200 hours – and some of us have much more than that. The Atkins Edge, more than any other diet, gives you the key to unlock that energy for fuel.

The concept of carbs as a metabolic bully should help you understand the implications of the switch from burning carbohydrates to burning fat. Here's how it works. When you eat carbohydrates, they're digested and converted to glucose (sugar), which your bloodstream transports throughout your body. This means that carbohydrate intake is largely responsible for blood sugar fluctuations. It's also important to understand that it's not only the amount of carbohydrates but also their quality that determine the extent of that impact. For example, eating a bowl of brown rice and beans raises your blood sugar level much more slowly and less dramatically than, say, consuming a doughnut, a glass of orange juice or a bowl of sweetened cereal. (Food need not taste sweet to convert rapidly to glucose. Prime examples are mashed potatoes and white bread.)

The amount of sugar circulating in your blood is actually very small – just a few teaspoons – so to keep your blood sugar level normal after a big carbohydrate dose, the absorbed glucose has to be rapidly transported out of your blood and into your cells. This is the job of the hormone insulin, which signals your cells to remove glucose from your bloodstream. Once inside a cell, three things can happen to glucose:

- It can be burnt immediately for energy.
- It can be stored in limited amounts for later use as a starchlike material called glycogen.
- It can be converted to fat.

If a cell chooses this last option, making fat from glucose, it's a one-way street. There's no way that fat can be made back into glucose. It has to be either burnt as fat or stored as fat.

In addition to its function as a traffic officer directing glucose into cells, insulin controls the release of stored fat from your fat cells. The higher your insulin level, the less fat is released back into your system to be used as fuel. So when you eat a high-carb meal, particularly one high in refined starches and sugar, your insulin shoots up to remove the glucose from your blood and tuck it away in cells, and your fat usage simultaneously goes way down. Simply put, your body always gives carbs priority treatment.

Why do carbs always get the kid-glove treatment? It's because your body has only a limited ability to store carbs: at most about half a day's energy supply. (Contrast this to body fat stores: even a thin person tends to carry a two-month reserve supply.) So it makes sense that we burn as much carbohydrate as we can as soon as it's digested and absorbed – otherwise we'd quickly run out of places to store it. Add to that the rapid pace at which sugar and other refined carbs are digested, and the whole process can get pretty dramatic. Now imagine this process taking place three, four or five times a day, each time shutting off fat burning as your insulin level escalates to deal with the rising tide of blood sugar. Your body has no other options once you've eaten a carb-rich meal, because this metabolic bully always has to have its way. Because of this biologic imperative, fat calories are always pushed to the back of the line – where more than likely they are stored, and stored and stored.

This whole process is quite silent for most of us, as long as we're young and healthy, but some people have trouble with these wide swings in blood glucose. If your insulin response is too great or lasts too long, your blood sugar level drops – and bam! Your energy level crashes. You may recognise it as a slump a few hours after lunch. You may have trouble concentrating, feel sleepy and often crave something such as chocolate, crisps or sweets. Then guess what happens a few hours later? Just rerun the tape. Keep up this pattern for years, and you may develop insulin resistance, meaning that more and more insulin is required to transport the same amount of glucose. What has happened is that your body is giving in to the bully and the stage is set for developing metabolic syndrome and even type-2 diabetes. (We'll discuss this in depth in Chapter 12.)

Compared to the span of evolution, our bodies haven't had much time to learn how to deal with all these new refined carbohydrates and sugars that have come to dominate our diet only in the last half century or so. And all along, you were blaming your thunder thighs on salad dressing and scrambled eggs! The ability to carry a bit of energy in the form of fat actually helped our distant ancestors survive during prolonged intervals between meals (hunting doesn't always deliver each meal on time) and in times of famine. However, today, when most people eat three big meals full of refined carbs each day – not to mention sweetened double lattes and mid-afternoon chocolate bars – they seldom get the opportunity to draw on their backup fat stores. As long as we keep making glucose into fat and let the bully blockade it there, we're doomed to being heavy.

Fortunately, finding the Atkins Edge gives you an exit ramp off the blood sugar roller coaster by switching your body over to burning mostly fat for energy. When you eat foods composed primarily of protein, fat and fibre, your body produces far less insulin. (If you eat a large amount of protein, some of it can convert to glucose, but protein doesn't provoke the secretion of nearly as much insulin as carbs do.) And when the carbs you do eat are in the form of high-fibre whole foods, which convert to glucose relatively slowly, you shouldn't experience extremes in your blood sugar levels. Your body needs to produce much less insulin, so your blood sugar level holds steady, along with your energy level.

By changing the balance of fats, carbohydrates and protein in your diet, you convert your body to burning primarily fat instead of constantly making it switch back and forth between carbs and fat. There's nothing strange or risky about this perfectly normal metabolic process. You burn your own body fat for energy, and as a welcome side effect you lose weight. Just in case you missed the point earlier, eating fats doesn't make you fat as long as you give your body permission to burn them. Place the blame where it belongs: overeating and overresponding to carbs. And herein lies the theme of this book – and the premise of the Atkins Diet.

We know that you're raring to begin Atkins, but hold your horses. We've deliberately placed the next three chapters on macronutrients before Part II, where you'll get the nitty-gritty on how to do Atkins. Better to take a little bit of time reading this now than later on having to say, 'Oops, I should have read that before I rushed into this and went astray!' The more you understand the importance of what you put into your mouth, the more you'll be committed to choosing a healthful way to eat for the rest of your life. Most people who failed on Atkins in the past actually were doing some misconception of Atkins. When you understand the correct way to eat (and why) and how slower, steady weight loss leads to lifetime weight control, your likelihood of long-term success increases greatly.

REVIEW POINTS

- Atkins is a lifetime approach to eating, not just a weight-loss diet.
- Atkins is comprised of four progressively liberal phases.
- Curb your carb intake and you convert your body to burning primarily fat for energy.
- When you begin to tap into your body's fat stores, you foil the metabolic bully that normally blocks access to your fat stores.

- This metabolic adaptation, known as the Atkins Edge, provides a steady source of energy, helping control your appetite and eliminating or reducing carb cravings.
- You'll lose water weight first on Atkins, as you do on any weight-loss diet, but fat loss will quickly follow.
- Consuming a modest amount of salt eliminates or moderates symptoms that may accompany the diet's diuretic effect and the metabolic shift to burning fat.
- The amount and quality of the carbohydrate foods you eat impact the amount of insulin in your bloodstream.
- Fat is easily stored in your body, but there is limited storage space for carbohydrate, so any excess converts to fat.

Now let's meet Janet Freedman, who is slim for the first time in her adult life.

SUCCESS AT LONG LAST

From age 7, when she was seriously injured in an accident, the artist and author Janet Freedman had struggled with her weight. After spending months in bed being stuffed with food – including daily milkshakes to heal her bones – she emerged as a chunky little girl who grew into a chunky woman. But that's now history.

VITAL STATISTICS

Current phase: Ongoing Weight Loss

Daily Net Carb intake: 30 grams (1 ounce)

Age: 64

Height: 160 cm (5 ft 3 in)

Before weight: 71.4 kg (11.3 stones)

Current weight: 60 kg (9.5 stones)

Weight lost: 11 kg (1.8 stones)

Current blood pressure: 110/70

Former triglycerides: 181

Current triglycerides: 83

Former HDL ('good') cholesterol: 41 mg/dL

Current HDL ('good') cholesterol: 54 mg/dL

What was your first effort to slim down?

I began the 'old' Weight Watchers when I was nineteen. I lost the excess weight but remember lying in bed at night unable to sleep because my stomach hurt from hunger. Needless to say, I ultimately stopped the programme and regained the weight I'd lost. Over many years I've tried a series of unsuccessful diets. Meanwhile, I gained additional weight during two pregnancies and even more as I aged. In 2004 I entered a study at the local hospital that focused on a low-calorie, low-fat diet (DASH) that included weekly educational meetings. I lost weight slowly but was hungry most of the time.

Did you have related health issues?
Yes. My cholesterol levels required increased medication, my joints ached and I felt old and tired. I also wasn't able to fully participate in the exercise component of the DASH diet due to my 'bad knees and hips', which my doctor attributed to arthritis. Both coronary artery disease and diabetes run in my family, and I thought it was just a matter of time.

What made you turn to Atkins?
At the end of the study, I continued to eat the low-fat, low-calorie way, maintaining my weight through extreme diligence. I still felt deprived, and in the last year I followed that diet, I lost only 1.8 kilograms (4 pounds). Meanwhile, my cholesterol numbers, which were supposed to come down, kept climbing. A friend told me how she lost weight and improved her health on Atkins. Since I still wasn't anywhere near a normal weight and I knew I couldn't continue the low-fat torture any longer, I decided to try it.

How did you do?
I reached my goal weight in five months and then set a goal of another 2.3 kilograms (5 pounds), which I've surpassed. I've been able to reduce my cholesterol medicine dose, and my dry skin has disappeared. My joints no longer ache, so I've been able to increase my exercise. I fully expect to see further improvement as I continue this amazing lifestyle. And I fit into size-10 trousers, which I've never worn in my entire life!

What is your fitness regimen?
I started walking at home on a treadmill for five minutes at 2.4 kilometres (1.5 miles) per hour. As I've lost weight and my knee and hip pain has decreased, I've doubled my speed and added an incline. I now walk for twenty to thirty

minutes three or four times a week. Other days I ride a stationary bike, do a series of core exercises and a short free-weight routine.

What were the worst things about being overweight?
People who are of normal weight have no idea of the agonies that young overweight people endure. I know that it left its mark on my self-esteem and confidence. All those continually unsuccessful diets only added to the pain.

What do you like about Atkins?
I love that it is healthy and sensible and promotes real food. The awful gnawing hunger disappears. Hunger has always made me abandon previous attempts to lose weight. No longer. When I went to my son's wedding, I was surrounded by lots of empty-calorie, high-carb foods, but I wasn't tempted, even by the wedding cake. The excessive hunger and cravings are gone.

What words of wisdom can you offer to other people?
Read everything you can about Atkins. Follow the guide-lines, and give the plan two weeks to see what it can do for you. The Atkins Community will provide you with advice and support.

Anything else you want to add?
I got fat following the government's advice. Now my body is telling me that this is the right way to eat and the advice I'd been getting for years was dead wrong.

Chapter 3

THE RIGHT CARBS IN
THE RIGHT AMOUNTS

White flour is better suited for glue for primary-school art projects than for nutrition. Refined grains and the insidious sweet 'poison' known as sugar fuel the food-processing industry, but such products damage the health and quality of life of people who are struggling with carb overload.

In addition to taking control of your weight and your health, an equally important and related goal is to discover a nutrient-rich pattern of eating that supplies you with a steady stream of energy. It's vital that you understand the basics of nutrition, but you also need to learn to read your own body's signals. Rebalancing your diet is the first step in this personalisation process.

You probably know some lucky individuals who seem to be able to eat everything and never gain a gram. (Don't hate them.) Then there are the rest of us who struggle with a metabolism that can't handle the high carbohydrate load typical of the modern, processed-food diet. Fortunately, your body will behave differently if you feed it differently. All you have to do to stop the struggle is to banish the metabolic bully by activating the fat-burning switch, aka the Atkins Edge. In this chapter we'll focus on how much and which carbohydrates you should be eating to do so. In following chapters we'll explore the roles of protein and fat in weight management.

WHAT ARE CARBS?

First let's clarify some terms. Carbs come in two general 'flavours': sugars and starches (also called simple and complex). The most common simple carbs are glucose, fructose and galactose, each containing a single sugar unit. These simple sugars can be partnered to make sucrose (glucose and fructose) or the milk sugar lactose (glucose and galactose). Sucrose is the main sugar in granulated sugar, honey, maple syrup, brown sugar, cane syrup and molasses. Starches, on the other hand, are composed of long chains of glucose, but when they're digested they break down into their component glucose parts. Starches make up the majority of carbs in breads, pasta, cereals, rice and potatoes. The leafy greens and other vegetables that are key to the Atkins Diet contain relatively small amounts of both sugars and starches, so they're often called 'non-starchy' vegetables.

WHAT DO CARBS DO?

Carbohydrates provide energy, but if you're trying to lose weight, you clearly must reduce your energy intake – in the form of taking in fewer calories. Using that logic, lowering your carbohydrate intake makes sense. But there's another, more important reason to curb carbs. By increasing your insulin levels, dietary carbohydrates control your body's use of fat for fuel. Insulin acts as an immediate roadblock, inhibiting your use of body fat. As we explained in the previous chapter, when you eat lots of carbs, they hobble your body's ability to burn fat. And that's why you can't shed that unwanted fat weight.

WHY EAT CARBOHYDRATES?

If carbs are such metabolic bullies, why eat them? Many foods that contain them also offer a range of beneficial minerals, vitamins, antioxidants and other micronutrients, giving them a place in a healthy diet. The preferable carbohydrates come from foods with a modest number of grams (after fibre grams have been subtracted) per serving and are usually those that are digested and absorbed slowly, so that they don't interfere with your overall steady supply of energy. Unprocessed carbohydrates, such as those found in vegetables, some fruits, nuts, pulses and whole grains, are also good sources of fibre and water. High fibre content is one reason why most complex carbs are absorbed more slowly than sugars and processed carbs.

Most vegetables and other whole food carbohydrates are fine in moderation, but in the typical Western diet, a huge proportion of the foods consumed is not leafy greens, cooked vegetables, berries and other low-sugar fruits and whole grains. Instead, they're foods made of ground-up grains, refined starches and various forms of sugar. Think of pasta and biscuits. Other foods, such as crisps and muffins, bear little resemblance to their origins. Even foods that appear at first glance to be healthful are often packed with sugar. Take low-fat yoghurt, a favourite 'diet' food. Of the 21 grams (0.74 ounces) of carbohydrates in a 115-gram (4-ounce) pot of a popular brand of strawberry yoghurt, 19 grams (0.67 ounces) come from sugar!

Atkins is not just about identifying and avoiding foods full of empty carbohydrates, it's also about finding the right carbs – in the right amounts – to suit your individual metabolism. You'll hold off eating some whole food carbohydrates in the initial weight loss phases of Atkins as you learn how sensitive your body is to carb intake. Instead, you'll focus initially on leafy greens and other non-starchy vegetables. Some people have a metabolism that may eventually tolerate moderate amounts of pulses, whole grains and even some starchy vegetables. All these foods are on the acceptable food lists for later phases of the Atkins Diet, but other individuals find that even these starchy whole food carbohydrates interfere with weight loss and/or maintenance. In that case, they should be avoided or eaten only occasionally. You'll know which group you fall into after several weeks or months on Atkins.

DO YOU SEEK COMFORT IN CARBS?

An inability to stay away from certain foods may not be a true addiction akin to alcoholism or dependence upon opiates, but eating these foods is still playing with fire when it comes to your health.

- Are your favourite foods bread, crisps and other snack foods and/or biscuits, pastry and other sweets?
- Are you unable to just have one (or two) portions? Do you snack on these foods throughout the day?
- When you're bored or depressed, do you turn to these comfort foods?
- Are you hungry again a couple of hours after a meal or snack?
- Do you find yourself eating such foods even when you're not hungry just because they're in front of you?
- Are you often tired, irritable, headachy or unable to deal with stress or to focus in the afternoon or at other times?

All these symptoms are evidence that you're caught in a vicious cycle of craving the very carbohydrate-rich foods that raise and then precipitously drop your blood sugar level. Unlike a true addiction, in this case you do have a choice. If you can stay away from such foods for a week or two, which will give you the Atkins Edge, you'll soon find that you can be much more comfortable without them.

A FRUIT IS NOT A VEGETABLE

Although fruits and vegetables are often considered interchangeable, they're more different than similar, both botanically and metabolically. Nonetheless, the US Department of Agriculture (USDA) Food Guide Pyramid continues to group them together. Not a good idea. Most fruits are significantly higher in sugar and therefore behave very differently in your body than do lettuces, French beans and other non-starchy vegetables. On Atkins, you'll postpone eating almost all fruits until you're past Induction. The exceptions are olives, avocados and tomatoes, which – believe it or not – are all botanically fruits but behave metabolically more like vegetables. The next fruits you'll reintroduce in OWL are berries, which are relatively low in carbs and packed with both antioxidants and fibre. A helpful way to think about fruit is to regard it as a condiment to enhance a meal or snack.

WATCH OUT FOR THE BAD GUYS

In contrast to whole foods that contain carbs, refined-grain products, sugary treats and many other ready-prepared foods – the list is nearly endless – supply calories but are almost devoid of beneficial nutrients. To complicate matters, there's sugar and then there's *sugar*. The sugars in fruits are natural, which is not to say that you can consume them mindlessly even when you're in Lifetime Maintenance. Sugar also occurs naturally in dairy products, vegetables and other carbohydrate foods. But added sugars, which – as the name suggests – boost the level in foods, are a huge problem. Added sugars can be either manufactured or natural, so the honey in honey mustard, for example, is still added sugar. According to the USDA, each person in the United States consumes an average of 70 kilograms (154 pounds) of added sugar per year, up from an average of 56 kilograms (123 pounds) in the early 1970s. This translates into nearly 750 calories a day.[1]

This insidious sweet 'poison' fuels the food-processing industry but damages the health and quality of life of people who are struggling with carb overload. Practically every item in the centre aisles of the supermarket contains added sugar. Learn how to spot it by carefully reading both the Nutrition Facts panel and the list of ingredients on the product label. In addition to the obvious culprits such as fizzy drinks, baked goods, fruit drinks, desserts, sweets and cereals, added sugars lurk in sauces, salad dressings, tomato ketchup, pickled products and even baby food. All manufactured sugars are full of empty carbs and have been implicated in a host of health problems from cavities to insulin resistance. Sounds as though nothing could be worse, right? Wrong!

THE MOST DANGEROUS CHARACTER OF THEM ALL

High-fructose corn syrup (HFCS) deserves a special place in the rogues' gallery of sugars. A manufacturing process that increases the fructose content of corn syrup (which starts out as pure glucose) creates HFCS, making it taste much sweeter. The end product typically contains 55 per cent fructose and 45 per cent glucose. In contrast, table sugar has equal parts fructose and glucose. Ah, you ask, what's a mere 5 per cent difference among friends? As you'll learn below, this extra 5 per cent of 'sugar' as fructose is fated to turn into fat.

HFCS has infiltrated our food supply. Some public health officials link the doubling in the rate of obesity in the last four decades to the growing use of HFCS to sweeten fizzy drinks.[2] In 1970 it was found that, on average, each year Americans consumed about 225 grams (8 ounces) of HFCS. Fast-forward to 1997 and annual consumption per person was a staggering 28 kilograms (62.5 pounds).[3] From 1975 to 2000 annual fizzy drink consumption alone soared from an average of 95 litres (160 pints) to 190 litres (320 pints) per person![4]

Supporters argue that sucrose, which is half fructose and half glucose, occurs naturally in fruits, and humans have eaten it for thousands of years. That's why you'll see HFCS listed on food labels – and hawked in advertisements – as 'all natural', even though factories produce it in massive quantities. Although chemically similar to the fructose in fruits, HFCS in processed foods is problematic because of the sheer quantity involved.

Whole fruits (and vegetables) contain a relatively small amount of fructose, which is packaged with fibre and healthy antioxidants and other micronutrients. The manufactured stuff is just empty calories with none of fruits' benefits.

Though most cells in your body can metabolise glucose quickly, fructose is processed primarily in the liver, where most of it turns to fat. From there it takes a direct route to your love handles. Though our forebears did OK with the small amount of natural fructose present in fruits, today we're taking in massively greater amounts. Frankly, our bodies weren't made to deal with it as a recent study makes crystal clear. Two groups of overweight people were told to eat their usual diet. Individuals in one group had to consume one quarter of their daily calories as a specially made beverage sweetened with glucose. People in the other group had to consume an otherwise identical beverage sweetened with fructose. There were no other dietary requirements or limitations. As expected, everyone gained weight, but only the fructose-consuming subjects gained fat in the tummy – the most dangerous place to carry extra weight. They also showed increases in insulin resistance plus significantly higher levels of triglycerides. None of these indicators was present in the glucose group. Pass up any product that lists HFCS as an ingredient.

THE WILLPOWER MYTH

THE MYTH: Successful weight loss is simply a matter of willpower.

THE REALITY: Like hair colour, you inherit your metabolism, and metabolic characteristics vary greatly among individuals. Some of the best demonstrations that genes control metabolism involve research on identical twins. When many sets of twins were given the same reduced-calorie diet, all of them lost weight. However, the amount of weight loss (and fat loss) varied widely across the whole group. And guess what? The individuals within each pair of identical twins lost very similar amounts of weight. That means that people with the same genes respond to energy restriction in the same way, but people with a different genetic make-up (in this case, the different pairs of twins) have a wide range of responses, some losing easily and others very slowly. The same similarity of response within each pair of twins and wide variation across the sets of twins occurred when they were put on an exercise programme that burnt 1,000 calories a day. So don't be frustrated if someone else is losing weight faster than you. If despite doing everything right, you're experiencing snail-like progress, you can blame some of it on your great-grandparents!

AGAINST THE GRAIN

A little over a century ago, a Swiss invention changed forever the diet of people around the world. The steel roller transformed the milling of grain, making it possible to quickly and cheaply produce white flour and other refined grains. The good news turned out to be the bad news. White bread, once the exclusive preserve of the rich, was now available to anyone. However, by removing the oil-rich germ and fibre-rich bran, flour was stripped of virtually all of its essential nutrients. Only after millions of people worldwide died as a result of malnutrition from eating a diet based on bread made with white flour did the governments act, mandating that flour be fortified with a number of essential vitamins and minerals to replace some of the micronutrients removed in the germ and bran. This new and supposedly improved white flour was dubbed 'enriched'.

With or without fortification, white flour is better suited as glue for primary-school art projects than for nutrition. White flour may still help kill people; it just takes longer, as diabetes and cardiovascular disease take their toll. Nonetheless, like sugar and its kin, refined flour and other refined grains – HFCS is a refined-corn product – have become mainstays of our diet. As a society we are just as hooked on highly processed grains as we are on sugar. Sadly people around the globe are following in our dietary footsteps.

Just as drinking an energy drink, aka sugar water with some taurine, guarana, fruit flavouring or a splash of fruit juice added, is not the same as eating the fruit itself, grains that have been robbed of their essential nutrients are pale imitations of the whole food originals. For many people there's a place for granary bread, steel-cut oatmeal, brown rice, quinoa and the like in the later phases of Atkins. Refined grains are a whole different story. It may be unreasonable to expect you never again to touch foods made with them once you're in Lifetime Maintenance, but don't pretend that they hold much in the way of nutrition. If it turns out that you have insulin resistance that doesn't improve with weight loss – although, fortunately, it usually does – even whole grains may be more than your metabolism can tolerate.

CARBS CAN MAKE YOU FAT

We'll look at the misconception that eating fat makes you fat in detail in Chapter 5. But carbohydrates, and to a lesser extent protein, can also metabolise into body fat. Guess what a farmer feeds a pig or a steer when he wants to fatten it for market? That's right: grain. An increasingly popular theory is that the chief culprit in our expanding waistlines is not fat but sugar, HFCS and white flour – the penultimate metabolic bullies. Consider the all-too-typical Western-style diet: a 'toaster tart' and orange juice for breakfast, an on-the-run lunch of soup in a cup and a packet of crisps and a microwave dinner of breaded chicken and mashed potatoes – topped off with a few cans of fizzy drinks and 'junk food' snacks throughout the day. You could easily be looking at 300 grams (11 ounces) of carbs. Moreover, most of these carbs are coming from refined grains and various forms of sugar. Low-calorie, low-fat diets also rely heavily on carbs, including lots of those less nutritious ones. In contrast, the carbs you eat on Atkins come primarily from whole foods, especially vegetables.

When you do Atkins you *rebalance* your intake of the three macronutrients, removing the roadblock to burning fat for energy. That roadblock is – guess what? – a high blood insulin level resulting from a diet that includes too many carbohydrates. This change in diet, which allows you to burn mostly fat for energy – making it easy to lose weight – is the Atkins Edge.

REVIEW POINTS

- Consuming less carbohydrate relative to fat and protein, and only as many whole food carbs as your metabolism can tolerate, will enable you to lose weight and keep it off.
- Consuming too many carbohydrates, even those in whole foods, blocks burning fat for energy.
- Significantly decreasing carb consumption causes your body to burn its built-up reserves of its preferred fuel, fat, for energy, a perfectly natural process.
- Eating sugar, refined grains and other nutrient-deficient foods results in spikes in blood sugar; avoiding them eliminates both the spikes and slumps.
- Increased consumption of high-fructose corn syrup (HFCS) has been linked to the recent surge in obesity.
- Whole food carbs contain more fibre, which slows the digestive process and minimises hunger.
- Gram for gram, whole food carbs are packed with far more micronutrients than manufactured ones.

After reading the next success story, that of Julian Sneed, who lost more than 45 kilograms (7 stones) on Atkins, move on to Chapter 4 to find out how eating protein plays a major role in weight control.

THE BIG THREE-O

Heavy since he was a teenager, twenty-something Julian Sneed decided it was time to get serious about his weight – and health. He's already shed well over 45 kilograms (7 stones) and is still going strong, proving he can be fitter in his thirties than in his twenties.

VITAL STATISTICS

Current phase: Ongoing Weight Loss

Daily Net Carb intake: 50–75 grams (1.8–2.6 ounces)

Age: 30

Height: 185.4 cm (6 ft 1 in)

Before weight: 138.8 kg (21.9 stones)

Current weight: 90 kg (14.2 stones)

Weight lost: 48.5 kg (7.6 stones)

Goal weight: 84 kg (13.2 stones)

Has your weight always been an issue?
As a kid I played basketball, and I was still slim as a young teen. But when I was seventeen, we moved from New York to North Carolina and I went from going everywhere on foot to driving everywhere. Plus, there were lots of family barbecues and other gatherings with much richer food than I was used to. By the time I was eighteen, I weighed 109 kilograms (17.1 stones). Later my job as a manager in a fast-food restaurant, where I could eat as much as I wanted, also made it difficult to control my weight.

How did you hear of Atkins?
My supervisor at the restaurant had lost about 45 kilograms (7 stones) on Atkins. She gave me *New Diet Revolution* to

read, but for a while it just gathered dust. When I did get around to reading it in April of 2007, I weighed more than 136 kilograms (21 stones) and knew very little about nutrition. It seemed strange, but tell me that I can eat steak and eggs and I'm there!

Did you have any health problems other than your weight?
No, but diabetes, hypertension and heart disease all run in the family. My doctor told me that I needed to do something or it was just a matter of time.

What happened after you started the diet?
I lost an incredible 22.7 kilograms (3.6 stones) in five months. At this point I was happy that I got my weight down to 116 kilograms (18.3 stones). I felt great and kept the weight off for almost two years.

What made you return to Atkins?
I was turning thirty in July of 2009, and I decided to commit myself to getting fitter and healthier. I went back to Induction and lost 7.3 kilograms (1.1 stones) in two weeks, before moving on to OWL. When I turned thirty, I weighed 106.6 kilograms (16.8 stones), but I knew I was just getting started.

When did you add an exercise component to your programme?
I began walking 3.2 kilometres (2 miles) every other day my second time in Induction. After my birthday, I joined a gym and hired a personal trainer. At first, I struggled with her regimen, but now I love it and my body has changed. I regularly jog 6.4 kilometres (4 miles) five days a week without stopping, lift weights every other day and work out on exercise machines.

What do you eat on a typical day?
For breakfast, I might have oatmeal with sucralose and cream and three eggs. Lunch is a big salad with grilled chicken and dressing. For dinner, my favourite vegetable is French beans, which I might have with turkey and sometimes some brown rice. I eat whole grains a few times a week, but never anything white or bleached. I have an apple every other day and sometimes even half a banana. My snacks are usually almonds, but if my energy is low or I'm hungry, I'll have a piece of grilled chicken or some tuna.

You're getting close to your goal weight. What's next?
I want to see how fit I can get. My goal weight is now 84 kilograms (13.2 stones), but my larger objective is to be fit enough to join the police force within a year. You need to be able to run 4.8 kilometres (3 miles) and do 100 press-ups. I'm up to fifty now. I feel like I can do anything and it's not just about weight. The sky's the limit!

What advice do you have for others?
I want anyone else who struggles with his weight to know that you can do it, too. You'll learn so much about yourself. My first experience with Atkins was all about weight loss, but later I got into another place and realised that it's really about good health. I'm sort of a perfectionist so I counted carbs faithfully, which I recommend. I wanted to get slim and fit so badly that I was able to resist certain foods in the beginning. Now you could put me down in front of a table full of unhealthy foods and they wouldn't tempt me in the least. That can happen to you if you do Atkins right.

Chapter 4

THE POWER OF PROTEIN

Its satiating nature means that a diet higher in protein results in better weight loss. When you replace some carbohydrate with protein in your diet, you experience fewer fluctuations in blood sugar.

Protein foods are crucial to your health and your low-carb lifestyle. Protein works hand in glove with dietary fat to allow you to cut down on carbs. We'll look first at the many important roles that protein plays, including its role in preserving lean tissue while promoting fat loss. Then we'll show you how to ensure you're getting adequate protein. Finally, you'll learn why Atkins is *not* a high-protein diet.

PROTEIN WORKS OVERTIME

Protein is a component of every cell and organ in your body. Proteins are made from twenty different amino acids that are linked together like a strand of pearls. When you eat protein foods, the digestive process breaks the links apart so the amino acids can be absorbed into your bloodstream. There, they are transported throughout your body to provide the building blocks necessary to construct and repair cells. Without a continuous supply of amino acids, your existing cells shrink and new cells cannot be produced. When you embark on a weight-loss diet, you want to shrink the cells that store body fat, but not muscle and other critical cells. Eating protein also increases blood levels of amino acids contributing to:

- Increased satiety (a sense of fullness)
- More stable blood sugar levels
- Burning of more calories

A number of studies have shown that consuming protein is more satiating than consuming either carbohydrate or fat. This may be one reason why diets with more than the minimum amount of protein have been shown to result in better weight loss. When you replace some carbohydrate with protein in your diet, you experience fewer fluctuations in blood sugar. Digesting and metabolising protein consumes more than twice the energy (about 25 per cent) as processing either carbohydrate or fat. This means you burn more calories when digesting protein than when digesting the two other macronutrients. Higher-protein diets have been linked to prevention of obesity and muscle loss, as well as a reduced risk of developing metabolic syndrome, type-2 diabetes and heart disease.[3]

A common assumption is that *a calorie is a calorie*. Advocates of this concept suggest that only the total calories consumed count and the proportions of carbohydrate, protein and fat don't impact weight loss and body composition. Needless to say, this is a contentious issue among nutritionists. Why? Because unlike in lab animals or hospital patients, people live in the real world, making these factors hard to assess accurately week after week. Research shows that higher-protein diets are associated with greater retention of lean body mass during weight loss – independent of calorie intake – providing strong evidence that diets lower in carbs and higher in protein have beneficial effects on body composition.[4]

The proteins in your body are constantly being both torn down and built up. In adults protein breakdown and synthesis are usually in balance, so the amount of lean body mass (muscle and organ tissue) remains pretty constant. When slimming down, you want to lose only fat. But with most diets about one quarter of the total lost weight normally come from lean body mass. The key to maintaining lean mass is to keep your protein synthesis greater than or equal to your protein breakdown. Not surprisingly, up to a point eating protein foods boosts protein synthesis, while inadequate protein intake may result in lost lean body mass – not a good thing. This is another reason that we recommend consuming some protein at every meal, including breakfast.

BEEF ON A BUDGET

A careful look at the offerings in the meat section or counter of your supermarket can literally pay off at the till. In addition to making purchases when more expensive items are on sale and freezing them for future use, look for less-expensive cuts to pare your budget. The same cuts are sold under an array of names.

For roasting: Sirloin, topside, top rump or fore rib.

For braising: These leaner cuts are less expensive than those suited to roasting. They are browned to seal the meat before being slowly cooked. Braising steak is ideal for casseroles. Silverside is a good choice for a pot roast. Brisket is another budget-friendly cut that benefits from long, slow cooking.

For grilling griddling and frying: Fillet steak is a tender cut, while rump and sirloin steak are firmer with a more intense flavour.

Beef mince: The leanest mince is made from steak, which is why minced steak is more expensive.

PAIR EXERCISE WITH PROTEIN

The body's efficient use of dietary protein increases with exercise. Consuming enough protein combined with significant weight-bearing (resistance) activity such as walking up and down stairs or lifting weights can help preserve and tone your muscles during weight loss. With significant weight-bearing exercise, it may even be possible to add some lean body mass.

In that case, you're basically trading fat for muscle. The more you can preserve and tone muscle while losing fat, the better you'll feel and look. You'll also be in better shape, more able to heft a couple of bags of groceries up the steps or keep pace with your kids. But that's not all. The added benefit of more muscle is that whether you're working up a sweat or flopped on the sofa, you'll still be burning more calories than someone at the same weight who has a greater percentage of body fat.

Just to be clear, you don't have to actually work out – although physical activity is important – especially for maintaining weight loss on Atkins. Nonetheless, many people discover a new interest in fitness as they shed weight. Individuals with a lot of weight to lose may find that they need to slim down a bit before they can exercise comfortably. The choice is up to you. We'll discuss the role of physical activity in greater depth in Part II.

HOW MUCH PROTEIN?

In the UK the government's recommended dietary allowance (RDA) for protein is 55 grams (2 ounces) for adults between nineteen and fifty years old. The US government recommends 0.36 grams (0.1 ounces) per pound of body weight for adults a day. For a person weighing 68 kilograms (10.7 stones), that's about as much as you'd consume in a large chicken breast and a handful of nuts. It's important to understand that the RDA reflects the *minimum*, not the optimal, amount of protein an average healthy person needs. Many factors increase your minimum protein needs such as your age, gender, body composition (ratio of fat to lean body mass) and whether you're still growing, are pregnant, have inflammation or are dieting. Even the amount of stress you may be under can be a factor. Research indicates that adults benefit from protein intakes above the RDA, particularly when they're losing weight.[5]

HOW MUCH PROTEIN DO *YOU* NEED?

The ranges below for women and men should give you an idea of the flexibility in protein intake allowed across all phases of the Atkins Diet, while the listing for typical protein intake will cover the general protein needs of most people.

RECOMMENDED PROTEIN RANGES AND TYPICAL PROTEIN INTAKES FOR WOMEN AND MEN, BASED UPON HEIGHT

Height	Recommended Protein Range	Typical Protein Food Intake	Recommended Protein Range	Typical Protein Food Intake
	WOMEN		MEN	
(In shoes, 2.5-cm/1-in heels)	Grams (ounces) per day	Grams (ounces) per day	Grams (ounces) per day	Grams (ounces) per day
147.3 cm (4 ft 10 in)	63–125 g (2.2–4.4 oz)	370 g (13 oz)		
149.9 cm (4 ft 11 in)	64–130 g (2.3–4.6 oz)	400 g (14 oz)		
152.4 cm (5 ft 0 in)	65–135 g (2.3–4.8 oz)	400 g (14 oz)		
154.9 cm (5 ft 1 in)	66–138 g (2.3–4.9 oz)	400 g (14 oz)		
157.5 cm (5 ft 2 in)	68–142 g (2.4–5 oz)	425 g (15 oz)	74–154 g (2.6–5.4 oz)	450 g (16 oz)
160 cm (5 ft 3 in)	70–145 g (2.5–5.1 oz)	425 g (15 oz)	75–157 g (2.7–5.5 oz)	480 g (17 oz)
162.6 cm (5 ft 4 in)	71–149 g (2.5–5.3 oz)	450 g (16 oz)	76–159 g (2.7–5.6 oz)	480 g (17 oz)
165.1 cm (5 ft 5 in)	73–152 g (2.6–5.4 oz)	450 g (16 oz)	78–162 g (2.8–5.7 oz)	480 g (17 oz)
167.6 cm (5 ft 6 in)	75–156 g (2.7–5.5 oz)	450 g (16 oz)	79–165 g (2.8–5.8 oz)	480 g (17 oz)
170.2 cm (5 ft 7 in)	76–159 g (2.7–5.6 oz)	480 g (17 oz)	81–168 g (2.9–5.9 oz)	510 g (18 oz)
172.3 cm (5 ft 8 in)	78–162 g (2.8–5.7 oz)	480 g (17 oz)	82–171 g (2.9–6 oz)	510 g (18 oz)
175.3 cm (5 ft 9 in)	80–166 g (2.8–5.9 oz)	510 g (18 oz)	84–175 g (3–6.1 oz)	510 g (18 oz)
177.8 cm (5 ft 10 in)	81–169 g (2.9–6 oz)	510 g (18 oz)	86–178 g (3–6.3 oz)	540 g (19 oz)
180.3 cm (5 ft 11 in)	83–173 g (2.9–6.1 oz)	510 g (18 oz)	87–182 g (3–6.4 oz)	540 g (19 oz)
182.9 cm (6 ft 0 in)	85–176 g (3–6.2 oz)	540 g (19 oz)	89–186 g (3.1–6.6 oz)	565 g (20 oz)
185.4 cm (6 ft 1 in)			91–190 g (3.2–6.7 oz)	565 g (20 oz)
188 cm (6 ft 2 in)			93–194 g (3.3–6.8 oz)	600 g (21 oz)
190.5 cm (6 ft 3 in)			95–199 g (3.4–7 oz)	600 g (21 oz)
193 cm (6 ft 4 in)			98–204 g (3.5–7.2 oz)	625 g (22 oz)

THE RULE OF SEVENS

Now that you know about how many grams (or ounces) of protein you should be aiming for each day, simply follow the Rule of Sevens. About 30 grams (1 ounce) of cooked chicken, meat, tofu, nuts, other protein food or hard cheese, a 240-millitre (8-fluid-ounce) glass of dairy or a large egg is equivalent to about 7 grams (0.2 ounces) of protein. Consume 10 to 25 of these 30-gram (1-ounce) units daily, depending upon your height and choice within the ranges above, and you'll be satisfying your needs. These visual comparisons should help estimate the number of grams (or ounces) in portions:

FOOD	VISUAL
30 grams (1 ounce) meat, poultry, tofu, etc.	Small matchbox/remote car key
85 grams (3 ounces) meat, poultry, tofu, etc.	Deck of cards/mobile phone
225 grams (8 ounces) meat, poultry, tofu, etc.	Slim paperback book
85 grams (3 ounces) fish	Chequebook/iPod
30 grams (1 ounce) hard cheese	Four dice

Spread your protein consumption out over the day, eating at least 115 to 175 grams (4 to 6 ounces) at each meal, including breakfast; tall men may need 225 grams (8 ounces). Unless your initial portions are larger, there's usually no need to reduce your protein consumption as you move through the phases. On the other hand, if you're finding it difficult to lose weight and doing everything else by the book, you may want to decrease your protein portions if you're at the high end of our suggested intake range to see if that may be the hold-up.

One way to judge if you're getting enough protein is simple: take the satiety test. After you've consumed what you consider an adequate amount of protein (which naturally comes with a modest dose of natural fat), ask yourself if you're satisfied. If you are, fine. If not, have a bit more. If you're still hungry, try adding some olive oil, cream or one of our delicious salad dressings or sauces. You need pay closer attention to your protein intake only if you think you might be eating too little or too much.

Don't waste time calculating the amount of protein you should be eating during weight loss as a percentage of your total macronutrient intake. Instead, as shown in the previous table, base your optimal protein intake upon your height and gender. You can choose from the midpoint of the recommended protein range, or you can choose to have more or less within the range. The typical food intake figures will guide you to the size of the portions you should be eating.

THE MORE VARIETY, THE BETTER

When most people think of protein, particularly in the context of the Atkins Diet, they envision beef and other meat, poultry, fish, shellfish, eggs and dairy products. Animal products are all good sources of protein, but they're hardly the only ones. Nor are they the only ones you can eat on Atkins. In much of the world people rely in large part on plant sources such as nuts and seeds, pulses and whole grains for protein. Even vegetables contain small amounts. Animal protein is considered a complete, or whole, protein, meaning it contains all nine essential amino acids (those your body cannot make on its own). Many (but not all) plant sources have reduced levels of one or more of the nine essential amino acids, so they're considered incomplete proteins. It can be challenging to satisfy most or all of your protein needs from plant sources when you're on Atkins, but it's perfectly possible, as we'll discuss in Chapter 6.

We can't stress strongly enough that the best diet for you is one composed of foods you love. When it comes to protein, you may be content to eat beef, chicken, dairy and eggs and ignore most other protein sources. But if variety is the spice of your life, make an effort to have fish and shellfish two or three times a week, as well as sampling pork, lamb and perhaps veal. You may also enjoy venison, turkey, duck or even pheasant; real adventurers might branch out into goat, rabbit or even ostrich.

The more varied your overall diet, the more likely you are to obtain the full range of vitamins, minerals and other micronutrients your body needs for optimal health. And the more varied your sources of protein, the more apt you are to consume a balance of amino acids and the essential fats you'll learn about in the next chapter. The point is you can do whatever works for you in terms of taste and cost, as long as you take foods' carb content into consideration. Protein sources with relatively more fat tend to be more satiating, so, for example, you may feel full sooner after eating duck than a chicken breast. Because they're lower in fat (except for tofu and nut butters), plant proteins also tend to be less satiating, another reason to add healthy fats in cooking and to be keenly aware of the carb content of vegetable protein sources.

Our position has always been that when you control carb consumption, there's no need to avoid fatty cuts of meat or to trim the fat. However, if you prefer, feel free to use leaner cuts. Just be sure to serve them with a crumbling of blue cheese or compound butter or a salad dressing or some olive oil on vegetables in the same meal. Again, it's your choice.

ATKINS IS NOT A HIGH-PROTEIN DIET

Let us set your mind to rest about concerns that Atkins is overly high in protein and can therefore cause certain health problems. With a typical intake of 370 to 625 grams (13 to 22 ounces) of protein foods daily, Atkins can hardly be considered a high-protein diet. Instead, we regard it as an *optimal* protein diet. In any case, most of the concerns about eating too much protein are unfounded in that they're based on limited or flawed research. For example, the misconception that a high-protein intake can damage kidneys probably arose from the fact that individuals who *already have advanced kidney disease* cannot clear away the waste from even a moderate protein intake. There's absolutely no evidence that any healthy person has experienced kidney damage from eating the amount of protein consumed on Atkins. Far more dangerous is failure to drink enough water, as dehydration is a much greater stressor on the kidneys.

A high-protein diet has been shown to increase calcium excretion in the urine, prompting concern about a negative effect on bone health. However, recent research indicates that this loss of calcium is offset by increased absorption of calcium and the net effect is increased bone mass.[6] Concerns about an increased risk of developing osteoporosis in healthy individuals are likewise unfounded.[7]

REVIEW POINTS

- Protein requirements should be based on your height, taking into consideration your activity level and other personal factors.
- Your protein needs will best be met by including protein in each meal.
- Eating a bit more than the RDA for protein helps preserve muscle mass, especially during weight loss.
- The satiating quality of protein helps to keep you from overeating.
- Our recommended protein-intake range has been linked to a reduction in obesity and improvement in many other health problems.
- You'll be eating plenty of protein, but Atkins is not a high-protein diet.

In the next chapter you'll learn about the crucial role that dietary fat plays in weight control and good health. But first, let's visit with Loralyn Hamilton, who dispatched her excess weight fourteen years ago – for good.

DOING WHAT COMES NATURALLY

For fourteen years and counting, Loralyn Hamilton has followed Atkins to keep her weight under control and to boost her energy. As she's come to know how her body works and to trust her instincts, living a low-carb lifestyle has become second nature.

VITAL STATISTICS

Current phase: Lifetime
  Maintenance
Daily Net Carb intake: 80–100
  grams (3–3.5 ounces)
Age: 35

Height: 167.6 cm (5 ft 6 in)
Before weight: 74.8 kg
  (11.8 stones)
Current weight: 60 kg (9.3 stones)
Weight lost: 15.9 kg (2.5 stones)

What motivated you to try Atkins?
The first time I did Atkins was when I was a fresher in college. I needed to be careful about what I ate ever since I was fourteen, but it wasn't until I was nineteen that I put on 13.6 kilograms (2.1 stones). Also, I wasn't feeling well. I was so tired that I couldn't easily walk from one class to another, and mentally it was very difficult. Judging from my mid-morning and mid-afternoon sugar crashes, my doctor said that I was borderline hypoglycaemic. He told me to cut back on the sugar and eat more protein. After reading about the Atkins Diet, I decided to try it. I lost 15.9 kilograms (2.1 stones), had a lot more energy and the sugar crashes stopped.

Did you experience any major hurdles?
Plateaus, of course, and getting those last 2.25 kilograms (5 pounds) off was difficult. As a college student, it was difficult to find food that I could eat. Every time I went somewhere and ordered a cheeseburger without a bun, everyone thought I was crazy. For me, now it is the norm.

Did you incorporate fitness into your lifestyle?
I bought a little treadmill and walked on it for five minutes a day, slowly getting up to fifteen minutes a day, five days a week. Now I stretch and work out for about ten minutes a day on the glider.

Did you fall off the wagon at any point?
No, but I intentionally migrated off a couple of times. Once I tried Slim-Fast, but I was hungry all the time and was not a nice person on it! When I became pregnant, I was in the Lifetime Maintenance phase, and although I thought I could stay there I wasn't really sure about the impact of it, so I took a moderately low-carb approach. I hope to become pregnant again soon, and this time I will stay in the Maintenance Phase.

After fourteen years, is doing Atkins second nature?
My husband eats the same way I do, which makes it easy. In fact, on our first date we discovered we both watched our carbs. I'd never dated anyone else who did. We follow our own version of Atkins simply because we know what works for us and what doesn't. After a while you come to know your system. Occasionally, I'll have a piece of bread or pancakes with sugar-free syrup. If they make me feel extra hungry the next day, I eat plenty of meat and butter and salad dressing to satiate myself.

So basically you find it easy to maintain your weight?
Yes. I weigh myself about three times a week. It's a motivational thing for me. My weight cycles between 59 and 61.2 kilograms (9.3 and 9.6 stones). When I'm at the top end of that, I can take off the extra 1.4 to 2.3 kilograms (3 to 5 pounds) quickly, but my body doesn't want to go below 59 kilograms (9.3 stones). If I realise I'm consuming too many carbs, I'll have eggs for breakfast and chicken or beef and some vegetables for lunch and dinner and the weight comes off in a week or so.

What tips can you offer other people about maintaining their weight long term?
Most people need to realise that they will be able to incorporate the foods they love back into their lifestyle once they know their ACE and therefore how their body processes carbs. Focusing on the good things you can eat and enjoy works better than focusing on those you can't handle. You have to retrain your mind to think of the benefits. Resistance only makes you want something more. If you think of wanting an inappropriate food as something temporary, you can push through the difficult points and stay on track.

Chapter 5

MEET YOUR NEW FRIEND: FAT

The simplistic idea that eating fat makes you fat has no scientific basis, despite the old saying that you are what you eat. More accurately, you are what your body chooses to store from what you eat.

It's time to stop thinking of dietary fat as your enemy. One more time, loud and clear: fat is a key source of energy and essential nutrients, and you cannot live without it. As against the grain as it may be, replacing sugars and refined carbohydrates with natural fats also plays an important role in helping with weight control. In fact, fat can be a high-energy food that gives you a metabolic edge, what we call the Atkins Edge. When you increase your intake of fat in place of carbs, you'll experience a higher and more consistent energy level.

But first, let's explain a few terms and definitions. When scientists refer to fat, they usually use the term 'fatty acids', which are part of a group of substances called lipids. And because they are insoluble in water, dietary fats enable your body to absorb the fat-soluble vitamins A, D, E and K as well as certain other micronutrients in vegetables.

MULTITASKING FATS

Fat-containing cells cushion many parts of your body, including bones and organs, and help to insulate us from cold. Fatty acids are also vital ingredients in membranes, which are basically the wrappers that act as the cells' gatekeepers, controlling what comes in and goes out. Many of our cells, including brain cells, contain specific essential fatty acids that are necessary for healthy brain function, enabling our nerves and hormonal system to send signals to the rest of our body, among other important functions.

All well and good, you are probably saying, but what I really want to know is how can fat make me thin? As you already know, along with protein, fat helps increase satiety. And because fat carries flavour, it makes food more satisfying. So what? Let's say for the sake of argument that 500 Calories of fat give you as much satiety as 1,000 Calories of refined carbs. Which is the better choice if you want to lose weight? Fat in the diet also slows the entry of glucose into the bloodstream, moderating the highs and lows of blood sugar that can lead to renewed hunger soon after eating carbs. Bottom line: Eat fats in place of carbs and you're less apt to overeat. These entwined properties are essential to the processes of both losing weight and then keeping it off.

Despite all these benefits, dietary fat has been demonised over the last half century. For too long the public and even some nutrition scientists have bought into the simplistic idea that eating fat makes you fat. That's remarkable because there's no compelling research that shows that natural fat is bad for you. In fact, it's just the opposite. First, in and of itself, properly selected dietary fat isn't a threat to health. Secondly, there are now hard data to demonstrate that consuming as much as 60 per cent of calories as fat in the early phases of Atkins poses no health hazard. But there is a big *but*! It's the *combination* of fat and a relatively high intake of carbohydrates – particularly refined ones – that can become a deadly recipe for obesity, diabetes, cardiovascular disease and a host of other ills. We've touched on it before, but in this chapter we'll prove to you that dietary fat is fine in the context of a low-carb lifestyle.

CONFUSION OVER CALORIES

The higher calorie content per gram of fat compared to that of protein and carbohydrate has undoubtedly added to the phobia about eating fatty foods. (A gram of fat contains 9 Calories; a gram of protein or carbohydrate contains 4 Calories.) Gram for gram, reducing the amount of fat you eat would appear to be the best way to reduce calories, but the *weight* of food is not what counts. It's all about what foods *do* once they enter your body, and fat can do wonderful things when consumed in combination with the right ratio of carbs. Statistics reveal that fat intake by Americans hasn't changed much from 1971 to 2000.[1] The same cannot be said for carbohydrates. Their intake has increased in tandem with skyrocketing rates of obesity. In actuality, people have replaced some of their dietary fat with an even greater amount of carbohydrates. The real culprit is increased calorie intake in the form of carbs, aided and abetted by a lack of regular activity. Absolute fat intake has stayed about the same or actually decreased slightly. So much for the 'eat fat, get fat' misconception.

Moreover, there's a reason why restricting only calories may not get you the weight-loss results you desire. Much as petrol fuels a car, your body runs on energy provided by the food you eat. Just as you conserve fuel by driving at a lower speed, your body conserves valuable energy when it senses that food is in short supply. This self-regulating process was a life-saver in the days when our ancestors had to endure periods of food scarcity. When fewer calories come in, your metabolism gets stingy with the calories it expends. So calories from healthy fats may be the very thing you need to get your metabolism tuned to the right mix of fuels and sustain your energy level.

WHAT HAPPENS TO DIETARY FAT?

What occurs when you eat fatty foods depends upon what else is on your plate and how your body responds to it. If you're young and active, you may be able to eat lots of fat – and carbs – and stay slim. On the other hand, if you've lost that youthful resilience, live a sedentary lifestyle and continue certain dietary habits, you're likely to accumulate body fat. If you're already overweight and eating lots of carbs – with or without much fat – you'll rarely if ever tap into your excess body fat as an energy source. Instead, it just continues to accumulate year after year. This is why the low-fat/high-carb approach has failed to work for so many of us. But cutting down on carbs releases you from this fat-holding pattern. When your carb intake is low, your body recovers its capacity to burn fat, so your fat intake can be relatively high without any adverse effect on your weight or health.

Some people mistakenly assume that a marriage of Atkins and a low-fat diet is the best of both worlds. Not so! As long as you're restricting carbohydrates, the dietary calories from fat are used directly for energy and are unlikely to be stored. Yummy foods such as nuts, guacamole, whipped cream, olives, pesto, butter and chicken salad made with mayonnaise help to provide satiety so you can keep your appetite under control. They also ensure an adequate calorie intake so your metabolism doesn't turn itself down to 'low', slowing weight loss. Protein can't do the job on its own. The team of fat and protein keeps you from feeling deprived.

So what happens if you try to cut out fats in an effort to coax the weight to come off faster? In short, problems arise, all of which can be managed but require close medical supervision. So, yes, doctors do sometimes put hospital patients on a low-carb and low-fat programme to resolve serious metabolic issues, but such a programme must be closely supervised. Eating sufficient fats is key to making Atkins work safely. So stop worrying and start enjoying.

Fat metabolism is perfectly natural for your body, and the fastest path to getting into the fat-burning mode is the Induction phase, in which you wean your body away from its carb and glucose habit. It can take several weeks to fully convert your metabolism to burning primarily fat, but after the first week of restricting carbs, you'll be most of the way there. However, even one high-carb meal will slow your conversion progress.

Another common misconception is that eating fatty foods initiates the burning of body fat. Not so. It's simply the restriction of carbohydrates that acts as the stimulus.[2] Nor is dietary fat burnt before body fat. Rather, existing body fat stores intermingle with incoming dietary fat, much as the remaining fuel in your petrol tank mixes with new fuel when you start pumping more in. So when you're adapted to fat metabolism, some of the ingredients in the blend burn faster, the rest are recirculated and the blend is remixed on a regular basis. This way your body gets to pick and choose which fats it burns and which it keeps for later. As we will tell you over and over again, you're not what you eat. Rather, you are what your body chooses to store from what you eat. Your job is to give it good choices and let it do its job.

THE CHOLESTEROL MYTH

THE MYTH: Eating fatty foods raises cholesterol to dangerous levels.

THE REALITY: The idea of eating less carbohydrate and more fat inevitably raises the spectre of cholesterol and its relationship to cardiovascular health. But calm down. Like fats, cholesterol is a lipid. And like them, it's essential for life, in this case, normal cellular function, hormone production and infection fighting. Unlike fat, however, cholesterol has no calories, so your body doesn't burn it for energy. Though you do absorb some cholesterol from eating animal products – plants contain none – your own liver makes the vast majority of the cholesterol in your body from scratch, independently of how much cholesterol you eat. So, yes, the amount of cholesterol in your diet influences your cholesterol levels somewhat, but so does your genetic predisposition and, most important, the mix of other nutrients you eat. Give your body the right combination of nutrients and it will figure out how to safely process cholesterol.

THREE 'FLAVOURS' OF FAT

Although most foods contain a mixture of fat – the three main classes are based on chemical structure – they're typically categorised by their predominant fat.

- *Monounsaturated fatty acids* (MUFAs) are found in olive oil, rapeseed oil, groundnut oil and most other nut oils, as well as avocados. MUFAs are usually liquid at room temperature.
- *Polyunsaturated fatty acids* (PUFAs) are always liquid both at room temperature and in the refrigerator. They're found mostly in oils from vegetables, seeds and some nuts. Sunflower oil, safflower oil, flaxseed oil, soya bean oil, corn oil, cottonseed oil, grapeseed oil and sesame oil are all high in PUFAs. So are the oils in fatty fish such as sardines, herring and salmon.
- *Saturated fatty acids* (SFAs) tend to remain solid at room temperature. Butter, lard, suet, palm oil and coconut oil are all relatively rich in saturated fats.

Remember, most fatty foods contain more than one type of fat. For example, rapeseed oil contains twice as much monounsaturated fat as polyunsaturated fat, so it's considered a MUFA. And although most people assume all the fat in a steak is saturated, certain cuts of beef actually contain almost as much MUFA as SFA and even a small amount of PUFA.

THE SATURATED FAT MYTH

THE MYTH: Saturated fat is to blame for a host of health ills.

THE REALITY: Nothing could be further from the truth. Recent research actually points to the benefits of saturated fat as part of a balanced intake of natural fats. Harvard researchers found that the higher their subjects' intake of SFA, the less plaque they had in their arteries.[3] And although some types of SFAs increase cholesterol levels, replacing dietary carbohydrate with either protein or any kind of fat lowers your blood triglyceride level and elevates HDL ('good') cholesterol levels.[4] Moreover, the number of small dense LDL ('bad') particles actually decreases, becoming the fluffy, less risky type.[5] So where did the SFA go? When carb intake is restricted, the body makes less saturated fat and simultaneously burns more of it. And strange but true, research shows that during the weight-loss phases of Atkins if you eat saturated fat, the less carbohydrate you eat, the more you reduce the saturated fat levels in your blood.[6] Even in the weight-maintenance phases of Atkins, the increased intake of saturated fat is associated with decreased blood levels of SFAs.

All three of these classes of fats can be healthy, but getting the right balance in your diet is important to give your body the variety it needs. At present a Western-style diet tends to be high in polyunsaturates, which is fine for people who eat a low-fat diet. However, at higher levels of fat intake, certain PUFAs lower both 'good' and 'bad' cholesterol. Though the latter is desirable, the former is not – it increases the risk for heart disease – so we recommend that you not add much more PUFAs. (This advice does not apply to fatty fish, as discussed below.)

MUFAs, on the other hand, lower LDL ('bad') cholesterol and triglyceride levels without lowering HDL ('good') cholesterol levels. The higher the proportion of these oils you eat, the better, starting with olive oil. Dress salads and vegetables alike with extra virgin olive oil. For cooking, your best bets are virgin olive oil, rapeseed oil and high-oleic safflower oil (which is labelled for high-heat use), all rich in MUFAs and with relatively high smoke points. Safflower imparts no taste to foods. Both rapeseed oil and safflower oil are inexpensive; however, rapeseed oil should be refrigerated to guard against rancidity. Rapeseed oil also can impart an off taste when heated. Feel free to cook with butter and add a knob to vegetables, meat or fish at the table. Coconut oil is also fine in the context of a low-carb diet. Take care not to heat oils to their smoking point or burn them as that causes chemical changes that can turn a good fat bad.

Interestingly, no matter which natural fats you eat, when you have the Atkins Edge your body has its way with them. When body fat from people of all ethnic and geographic groups is analysed, it tends to be primarily MUFA. This means that your body picks and chooses from what you give it to obtain its preferred mix for storage as body fat.

DOUBLE-TALK ABOUT TRANS-FATS

In the last decade researchers have found that an increased intake of trans-fats is associated with an increased heart attack risk.[7] More recently, trans-fats have been shown to increase the body's level of inflammation.[8] (For more on trans-fats and inflammation, see Chapter 11.) Since 2006, the Food and Drug Administration (FDA) in the United States has mandated that the Nutrition Facts panel indicate the amount and percentage of trans-fats in all packaged foods. Though the FDA did not ban trans-fats outright, leaving it to the consumer to be vigilant, the result was that many manufacturers reduced the amount in their products or eliminated them altogether. Among the numerous products that recently were or may still be made with trans-fats are fried foods, baked goods, biscuits, crackers, sweets, snack foods, frostings and vegetable shortenings. Most margarine products have been reformulated, but as long as a product contains less than 0.5 grams (0.02 ounces) of trans-fat per serving, a manufacturer can claim that it's free of trans-fats. To be sure that there are *no* trans-fats in a product, also check the list of ingredients, where trans-fats are listed as 'shortening' or 'hydrogenated vegetable oil' or 'partially hydrogenated vegetable oil'. If you see any of these words in the ingredient list, just say no. Also, avoid deep-fried foods in fast-food and other restaurants.

ESSENTIAL FATS

The essential fatty acids (EFAs) are two families of compounds among dietary fats that your body cannot produce on its own. Both omega-3 and omega-6 EFAs are polyunsaturated fats essential to your health and well-being. The former start their way up the food chain as the leaves of green plants and green algae and end up in the fat of shellfish and cold-water fish. Omega-6 fats are found primarily in seeds and grains as well as in chickens and pigs, which pass along to us much of these essential fats from the feed they ate. Unless you're following a very-low-fat diet, you're likely to get much more than the recommended amount of omega-6s – far in excess of what your ancestors or even your grandparents did. The latest recommendation from the American Heart Association is that 5 to 10 per cent of your daily calories should be made up of omega-6s. That intake is associated with a reduced risk for cardiovascular disease.[9]

Both omega-6 and omega-3 EFAs are needed for human cell membranes to function; however, the two compete with each other to get into membranes, so keeping their intake in balance is important. In the current Western-style diet, which relies heavily on products made from soya, corn and their oils, omega-6s dominate. In addition, the meat of animals fattened on soya and corn is full of omega-6 fats. This is true of the British diet, too, where omega-3 levels have fallen due to the increased consumption of white fish, which is low in omega-3. This has led to a decrease in the consumption of oil-rich fish such as trout, sardines and salmon, which are high in omega-3. As a result, the ideal dietary ratio of 1 to 1 between omega-6 and omega-3 EFAs has been disrupted. For example, soya bean oil has an omega-6 to omega-3 ratio of 10 to 1 and corn oil a ratio of 100 to 1! Perfect balance is difficult to achieve, so 2 to 1 or 3 to 1 omega-6 to omega-3 is a more realistic goal. To achieve a desirable ratio:

- Emphasise olive, rapeseed, high-oleic safflower and other high-MUFA oils for dressing foods and cooking.
- Eat foods or take supplements rich in omega-3s such as cold-water ocean fish or fish oil. (See the sidebar 'Where to Get Your Omega-3s'.)
- Avoid corn oil, soya bean oil, sunflower oil, cottonseed oil and groundnut oil, which are all high in omega-6s.

WHERE TO GET YOUR OMEGA-3S

Salmon and such other cold-water fish such as tuna, sardines, herring and anchovies are superb sources of omega-3s. Why these fish and not their tropical counterparts? The colder the water, the more omega-3 fat fish need to survive. Farmed salmon now has omega-3 levels that come close to those of wild-caught salmon. Even 55 to 85 grams (2 to 3 ounces) of water-packed canned tuna provide one day's requirement of omega-3s. If you don't like the taste of fish or fish oil capsules, an alternative is fish oil with lemon or orange oil to mask the fish taste. Non-fish sources – flaxseed, almonds, walnuts and rapeseed oil – are generally not as concentrated as fish oil and contain a form of omega-3 that your body must process extensively to convert to usable omega-3. A new product that may appeal to vegetarians or others who prefer not to use fish oil is a DHA supplement extracted from microalgae. It's about as close as you can get to what fish low on the food chain eat. The American Heart Association recently increased its dietary recommendation from two to three portions of fatty fish a week, or 1 gram (0.04 ounces) of omega-3s a day.

When your body burns fat for energy, both omega-3 and omega-6 fats are metabolised, along with monounsaturated and saturated fat. In fact, the omega-3 fats are actually burnt off faster than the others.[10] As a result, after significant weight loss, a person tends to have reduced stores of this EFA, making it all the more important to consume omega-3s both during weight loss and for some time afterwards. (See the sidebar 'Where to Get Your Omega-3s'.) On the other hand, one of the benefits of carbohydrate restriction is that it allows your body to make better use of the EFAs it does have in order to construct good membranes. This means that the combination of cutting back on carbs and adding omega-3 fats to your diet is an excellent way to improve your cell membrane function.

If you're confused about the difference between dietary fat and essential fats, a helpful analogy is petrol and motor oil. Both petrol and motor oil are derived from the stuff that gushes from oil wells, but the former goes into your car's petrol tank and the latter into the crankcase. Petrol is burnt for energy, while motor oil lubricates the machinery so that it runs without friction, reducing wear and tear. Dietary fats differ from each other in many ways, but most contain a mixture of non-essential fats, the saturates and monounsaturates, and essential fats, the omega-6s and omega-3s that are in the polyunsaturated group. Think of the non-essential fats as fuel and the essential fats as metabolic lubricators.

THE REBALANCING ACT

You now understand that to effectively reboot your metabolism you'll have to change the ratio of carbohydrate, fat and protein in your diet. If your first reaction is, 'Yuck. I don't want to eat lots of fat', please take a careful look at the Phase 1: Induction meal plans in Part III. You'll see that in a typical day, you'll be eating a cornucopia of vegetables along with ample muscle-building protein. To enhance those foods, you'll add your favourite acceptable salad dressings, sauces and oils. If you're at a loss for ideas, our recipe section, also in Part III, focuses on such sauces, dressings and condiments.

SAVOUR, DON'T SMOTHER

It's essential that you eat enough natural fats to provide satiety, the satisfying sense of fullness, keep your fat metabolism humming along and make foods tasty. But that doesn't mean you should eat so much that you end up with a calorie bomb. For most of us on Atkins, our natural appetite response gives us good guidance as to how much fat to eat. But here are some tips. Use enough oil when sautéing food to keep it from sticking to the pan. Use about a tablespoon of oil (plus lemon juice or vinegar) to dress a small salad. These are general guidelines. Petite women may need less, and tall men may be able to have more. Feel free to swap one fat source for another. For example, if you don't use cream in your coffee, you can have a bit more cheese. If you have two salads a day and need more olive oil for dressing, forgo a knob of butter. You get the picture. A typical day's intake of fat might include the following:

- 2 tablespoons oil for dressing salads and cooking
- 1 tablespoon butter
- 25–30 grams (1 ounce) cream
- 55 grams (2 ounces) cheese
- 2–3 eggs
- 2–3 servings of meat, poultry, fish or shellfish
- 10 olives and/or ½ Haas avocado
- 55 grams (2 ounces) nuts or seeds (after the first two weeks of Induction)

REVIEW POINTS

- Dietary fat is essential to good health and plays a key role in weight control.
- In the context of a low-carb diet, natural fats pose no health risk; rather, it is the combination of fat and a high intake of carbohydrates that is linked to heart disease and other serious conditions.
- As long as you're eating a high-carb diet, you won't burn your own body fat for energy. But reduce carb intake enough, and you will burn both dietary and body fat.
- A low-fat version of Atkins is unnecessary and unadvisable without proper medical supervision.
- Your body uses three kinds of fat for fuel: monounsaturated, polyunsaturated and saturated.
- The standard Western-style diet is tilted towards polyunsaturated fat. To restore the proper balance, use olive and other monounsaturated oils for cooking and dressing vegetables.
- When you control your carb intake, there is no health risk in eating foods high in saturated fats.

- Eating fatty fish several times a week or taking an omega-3 supplement can remedy the imbalance between omega-6 and omega-3 essential fatty acids.
- Your cholesterol levels are primarily a factor of your genetics, not your diet.

Now let's move on to Part II, where you'll learn how to personalise Atkins to meet your needs and food preferences and embark on your healthy new lifestyle. But first, meet Sara Carter, who, after losing about 45 kilograms (7 stones) left her job and started her own business.

SUCCESS STORY 5

NEW BODY, NEW CAREER

After Sara Carter trimmed 45 kilograms (7 stones) from her frame, she became motivated to leave her desk job and start her own business. Eight years later, she's still slim and her business is thriving.

VITAL STATISTICS

Current phase: Lifetime
  Maintenance
Daily Net Carb intake:
  50–60 grams (1.8–2.1 ounces)
Age: 46
Height: 175 cm (5 ft 9 in)
Before weight: 106.8 kilograms
  (16.8 stones)
Current weight: 61.2 kilograms
  (9.6 stones)

Weight lost: 45 kilograms (7 stones)
Former blood sugar: 163 mg/dL
Current blood sugar: 80 mg/dL
Current HDL cholesterol: 50 mg/dL
Current LDL cholesterol: 111 mg/dL
Former total cholesterol: 235 mg/dL
Current total cholesterol: 175 mg/dL
Current triglycerides: 66 mg/dL

Has your weight always been an issue?
I was heavy for years. I carried most of my weight below my waist, and when I was wearing stretch trousers and standing with my legs together I looked like a double scoop on an ice cream cone. My weight would fluctuate, depending upon what diet my mother had me on, but I was always hungry, cranky and sneaking food.

What motivated you to try Atkins?
My mother was diagnosed with diabetes about eight years ago and told to lose weight or else. Her weight just started coming off. Well, I was not about to have my mother be thinner than me! So I started Akins, too, and wow! I lost 3.6 kilograms (8 pounds) the first day and 31.8 kilograms (5 stones) in three months. This was the only diet that felt natural to me. Every other diet was a fight, like 'die' with a 't'. Eating the Atkins way was how I always wanted to eat but was told was wrong.

How long did it take you to lose the 45 kilograms (7 stones)?
I stayed in Induction for two weeks to get rid of my carb cravings, then moved to OWL, where I lost most of the weight. I lost weight every single day. When I got close to my goal weight, I started adding carbs until I got to between 50 and 60 grams (1.8 and 2.1 ounces) a day. All in all, it took me six months to go from a size 26 to a size 8. Later, when I would grocery shop, I would pick up a 25-kilogram (50-pound) bag of dog food and heft it over my shoulder just to see what it felt like; I would be amazed that I'd lugged around the equivalent of two bags for years.

Did you see any health benefits?

After three months, my total cholesterol went from 235 – interestingly, the same number as my start weight in pounds – to 170, all the while I was eating a four-egg omelette with cheese for breakfast every day. My blood sugar went from about 163 to 104. Once I was taking many tablets for depression and pain from fibromyalgia and sometimes had to walk with a walking stick because my knees were starting to buckle. Now that I watch my carb and gluten intake, I only need to take ibuprofen sometimes. My mother is doing well, too. She lost 27.2 kilograms (4.3 stones) and doesn't need any diabetes medications at this time. And my dad is doing Atkins, too.

How did losing weight change other things in your life?

For twenty years I sat in a chair working as a secretary until I decided to start my own business. I clean up foreclosed properties, which means that I'm lifting things, mowing lawns and hauling rubbish all day. I'm not an exercise person, but I'm so active now that I don't need to.

After eight years, do you watch what you eat?

It's still a battle but I keep a tight rein on myself. I can eat pretty much what I want to because I'm so active, but I weigh myself every other day. It's become a habit not to put sugar in my coffee. It shoots through me like a rocket. And eating bread makes me feel tired and sick. It's difficult to stay away from certain foods, but I know how I'll feel if I eat them and ask myself whether the price is worth paying. Usually, it isn't.

What advice can you offer other people?

Always have food handy that can quell cravings. I precook chicken breasts and microwave them when I'm in a hurry. I often have to leave the house without making breakfast, so I keep sliced pepperoni and roast beef in the fridge so I can grab them and go. I'm in the car a lot, so I always keep Atkins bars and a tin of mixed nuts there for snack attacks. And I know where the convenience shops are so that if I get caught without a snack on me, I can buy one quickly.

Part II

WHAT TO EAT:

How to Tailor Atkins to Your Needs and Goals

Chapter 6

ATKINS FOR YOU: MAKE IT PERSONAL

You can customise Atkins to your own metabolism, goals
and time frame – for example, choosing to start in OWL
instead of Induction. Just as important, you can mould
the programme to your culinary preferences and dietary
restrictions.

Now that you understand why and how Atkins works, let's
focus on the nitty-gritty of doing it. After covering the
basics, we'll show you how to tailor it to your needs, including
deciding which path to pursue at several forks in the road. As
long as you understand and adhere to the underlying principles
of the programme, this approach will provide you with lots of
freedom as you give your body permission to burn primarily fat
for energy, which, as you've learnt, is the essence of the Atkins
Edge. But first, let's review the principles underlying Atkins.

Atkins is based upon seven concepts that ensure optimal
health and weight control. We introduced most of these principles in Part I, but let's review them quickly.

- *Focus on Net Carbs.* This means that you count only the grams
  of carbohydrate that impact your blood sugar level, not total
  carbs, since fibre doesn't sabotage your body's use of fat.
- *Eat adequate protein.* In addition to building and fortifying all
  the cells in your body, protein helps you feel full and keeps your
  blood sugar and insulin levels on an even keel. Have a minimum

of 115 to 175 grams (4 to 6 ounces) of protein with each meal. Taller men may need closer to 225 grams (8 ounces).

- *Understand the power of fat.* Fat carries flavour, making food satisfying and filling, working hand in hand with protein. Increase your intake of monounsaturated fats, while holding back on most polyunsaturated fats with the exception of omega-3s. Saturated fats are fine in the context of a low-carb diet.

- *Get adequate fibre in food.* In addition to its role in blood sugar management, fibre is filling, so it helps make you feel full, moderating your hunger.

- *Avoid added sugar and refined carbs.* Eliminating these empty carbs is essential to good health, appetite management and weight control.

- *Supplement your diet with vitamins, minerals and other vital nutrients.* Although Atkins is a whole foods diet, it's hard to achieve optimal levels of some micronutrients such as omega-3 fatty acids and vitamin D on any eating programme.

- *Explore and find enjoyable forms of physical activity* to incorporate into your lifestyle as your weight loss and improved energy level allow.

WHAT YOU'LL EAT

You now know that your objective is to curb your carbs while eating more healthy fat along with adequate protein. You'll be getting your carbs primarily, at least in Induction, from the leafy greens and other non-starchy vegetables known as foundation vegetables. You'll find an extensive list of Acceptable Foods for Induction in the next chapter, along with foods to avoid in this phase. With each of the next two phases we'll provide similar lists of acceptable foods. (Foods for Lifetime Maintenance are the same as those for Pre-Maintenance.) Some people will be able to add back most or all of these foods; others will not. We'll help you to understand what works for you and what doesn't. Unless you're blessed with total recall, photocopy these lists. That way you can have this crucial information – which will be the key to your success – with you at all times. Over time, of course, it will become second nature.

LEARN TO COUNT

Central to doing Atkins is lowering your carbohydrate intake enough to unlock the gate that blocks fat burning. The initial amount that works for just about everyone is 20 grams (0.7 ounces) of Net Carbs a day. So for at least the first two weeks of Phase 1: Induction, your objective is to stay at or very close to that number. Counting grams of Net Carbs allows precision as long as your portions match those listed in the carb gram counter. (For most ready-prepared foods, you'll have to read the Nutrition Facts panel to find the carb count, subtracting fibre from total carbohydrate to calculate Net Carbs.) Our Induction-level meal plans in Part III are designed to ensure that you eat about 20 grams of Net Carbs per day, of which 12 to 15 grams (0.4 to 0.5 ounces) will come from foundation vegetables.

Be sensible, not obsessive, about both carbs and portions. You needn't split hairs about whether a serving contains 0.4 or 0.8 grams of Net Carbs. Round off to 0.5 grams in the first case and 1.0 gram in the second, as we've done in our meal plans. Nor will you hit 20 grams of Net Carbs exactly each day. Your intake may be a couple of grams under 20 one day and a little over the next. Don't count calories, although we do ask you to use common sense. In the past some individuals made the mistake of thinking that they could stuff themselves with protein and fat and still lose weight. If the weight is falling off, forget about calories. But if the scales won't budge or it seems to be taking you forever to lose, you might want to do a reality check regarding your calorie intake. (See page 61.) You could probably guess that too many calories will slow your weight loss, but here's a surprise: too *few* will slow down your metabolism, also threatening your progress.

THOU SHALT EAT REGULARLY . . .

That's right. No starving yourself! Regardless of the phase in which you start, you should be eating three regular-sized meals (with your choice of up to two snacks) every day. You may be surprised by how quickly that old devil hunger diminishes when you eliminate the blood sugar roller coaster. One reason we want you to put something into your stomach at least three times a day is to provide enough protein to prevent lean tissue loss, as well as to avoid cravings that may tempt you to hijack the office vending machine. Also, a low-carb late-afternoon snack, perhaps half an avocado or 55 grams (2 ounces) or so of cheese, will make you less likely to chow down everything in sight at dinner. Are snacks mandatory? Not if your appetite is under control at meals and you're not feeling fatigued. Try cutting out one or both snacks, see what happens and proceed accordingly. Or simply cut back a bit at meals and continue the snacks. Some people do best on four or five small meals. Do what works for you.

. . . AND DRINK REGULARLY

There are numerous health reasons for drinking adequate fluid. When you're not properly hydrated – and many people are borderline dehydrated much of the time – your body releases a hormone that makes your kidneys retain salt and water, but it does this at the expense of wasting your body's stores of potassium. This essential mineral is vital to keeping your muscles and heart happy. The key to maintaining a healthy amount of potassium is to drink plenty of water, eat your foundation vegetables *and* consume a modest amount of salt every day (unless you're on a diuretic medication). We'll discuss how to do this in detail in Chapter 7. Consuming adequate salt, particularly in Induction, keeps your circulation primed and your energy level high. People often misread the body's signal for more fluid as hunger, so staying well hydrated also helps you not overeat.

To determine if you're drinking enough fluids, simply check the colour of your urine, which should be clear or pale yellow. Also make sure that you're passing urine at least every four to six hours. Thirst is clearly a sign as well, but you need to rehydrate long before you actually feel thirsty. Despite the old saying that everyone should drink eight 240-millilitre (8-fluid-ounce) glasses of water a day, individual needs vary. Larger, more active people need more than small, sedentary folks. Vigorous exercise or airplane travel (thanks to the dry air) increases your needs as well.

The bulk of your daily fluids should come from water, clear broth and herbal teas. Drinking coffee and other caffeinated beverages increases urine output, but research indicates that it doesn't contribute to creating water or electrolyte imbalances.[1] Caffeine also gently assists the body in burning fat.[2] That means that you can count coffee and caffeinated tea (in moderation) towards your fluid intake. You won't be drinking fruit juice (with the exception of small amounts of lemon and lime juice) or fizzy drinks sweetened with sugar or high-fructose corn syrup, all of which are full of carbs. The same goes for milk – and that includes skimmed milk, which is naturally rich in milk sugar (lactose). Spread out your fluid intake over the day, although you may want to stop a couple of hours before bedtime to avoid middle-of-the-night trips to the toilet.

SUPPLEMENTARY INSURANCE

Vitamins, minerals, antioxidants and other micronutrients in food are just as vital to your health as protein, fat and carbohydrate. Vitamins and minerals help to convert calories into useful energy and perform a host of other functions that are vital for your body's optimal performance. With lots of vegetables, ample protein and healthy fats, at the very least you'll be getting the daily minimum of micronutrients that you need. You should also take a daily multivitamin with minerals that includes magnesium and calcium but no iron (unless your doctor has diagnosed you as iron-deficient). Also take an omega-3 supplement to ensure a proper balance of essential fatty acids. Finally, consider taking additional vitamin D if you don't spend a lot of time in the sun.

BECOME GOAL-ORIENTED

As with any new endeavour, the first step is to set specific goals. We encourage a realistic long-term weight goal. If you're dealing with health issues, work with your healthcare provider to quantify both long-term and short-term goals. Blood sugar, insulin, triglycerides and blood pressure indicators usually improve quickly on Atkins, but changes in some markers may take up to six months. As with any journey, you need to know your destination or you might get lost or distracted along the road. The more specific your goal, the more likely you'll achieve it. For example:

- I want to lose 13.5 kilograms (2 stones) in six months.
- I want to be able to fit into Mum's size-12 wedding dress for my wedding in June.
- I want to get my blood sugar level down to normal in the next three months.
- I want to maintain my 13.5-kilogram (2-stone) weight loss for a year.

Don't make the mistake of setting yourself up for failure by trying to return to the Twiggy figure you may have had thirty years ago. But don't sell yourself short, either. There's usually no reason why you can't be slim again – or even for the first time. Having that goal weight firmly planted in your mind will help you to confront momentary temptations. Setting short-term goals is equally important, especially if you know you have a long road ahead of you. Stepped goals provide an ongoing sense of accomplishment, so you don't start feeling that you'll never reach your ultimate goal. If you have a long way to go, you might set interim goals in 4.5-kilogram (10-pound) increments or smaller clothes sizes. If your weight loss goals are more modest, 2.3-kilogram (5-pound) increments may be more appropriate.

Once you've established your goal, imagine how achieving each one of your objectives will make you look and feel. These visualisations should be more than just idle daydreams. Close your eyes, clear your mind and create a distinct image of the new you. Visualise the person you are becoming on a daily basis.

LET'S GET PERSONAL

You can customise Atkins to your own metabolism, goals and time frame, for example, by choosing to start in Phase 2: Ongoing Weight Loss (OWL) instead of Phase 1: Induction. Just as important, you can mould the programme to your culinary tastes and any dietary restrictions you may have. If you don't care to eat beef, fine. Concentrate on poultry, pork, fish and lamb. If you're allergic to dairy products, there are plenty of alternative products that you can enjoy. You can even do Atkins while following kosher dietary rules.* One of the reasons that Atkins is so popular worldwide is that it can be adapted to almost any cuisine.

VERSATILE ENOUGH FOR VEGETARIANS

No, that's not a typo! It's perfectly possible to be a vegetarian – or simply minimise your intake of animal protein, add variety to your meals and trim your food budget – and still do Atkins. The typical Western vegetarian often consumes far too many carbohydrates in the form of pasta and other refined grains. As

* See www.groups.yahoo.com/group/Kosher-Low-Carb.

long as you consume at least two varieties of plant protein each day, you can get a balance of essential amino acids. Which leads to the second challenge. Plant proteins are 'packaged' with carbohydrate. Your objective is to consume enough protein without simultaneously getting so much carbohydrate that it interferes with weight loss or weight maintenance. To adapt Atkins to your needs as a vegetarian:

- Make sure to get sufficient protein in eggs, cheese and soya products (see page 51 to gauge your needs).
- Start in Ongoing Weight Loss at 30 grams (1 ounce) of Net Carbs and introduce nuts and seeds before berries.
- Or, if you have no more than 9 kilograms (1.4 stones) to shed and are willing to swap slower weight loss for more food variety, you may start in Phase 3: Pre-Maintenance, at 50 grams (1.8 ounces) of Net Carbs.
- Add extra olive, rapeseed oil, high-oleic safflower oil, walnut oil, flaxseed oil and other oils to salads and vegetables to make up for the smaller amount of fat in most of your protein sources, so as not to interfere with fat metabolism.

You'll find vegetarian meal plans in Part III. We'll go into greater detail on this variation of Atkins in the chapters on OWL and Pre-Maintenance.

ATKINS FOR VEGANS

It's more challenging for vegans, who don't eat eggs and dairy products, to do Atkins, but it's not impossible. The trick is to get sufficient protein from seeds, nuts, soya products, soya and rice cheeses, seitan, pulses and high-protein grains such as quinoa. Weight loss may proceed more slowly because of the higher carb intake than that of those following the standard Atkins programme. Vegans should make the following modifications:

- Start in Ongoing Weight Loss at 50 grams (1.8 ounces) of Net Carbs so that you can have nuts, seeds and their butters plus pulses from the start.
- If you don't have much weight to lose, start in Pre-Maintenance at 60 grams (2.1 ounces) of Net Carbs, in order to include small amounts of whole grains and other plant protein sources from the start.
- Make sure you're getting sufficient protein in plant sources (see 'How Much Protein Do *You* Need?' on page 51 to gauge your needs).
- In order not to interfere with fat metabolism, add extra flaxseed oil, olive oil, rapeseed oil, walnut oil and other oils to salads and vegetables to make up for the smaller amount of fat in most of your protein sources.

You'll find a 50-gram (1.8-ounce) Net Carbs vegan meal plan in Part III and you can modify the vegetarian plans at higher levels. We'll go into greater detail on this variation of Atkins in the chapters on OWL and Pre-Maintenance.

ATKINS WITH A LATIN BEAT

As the number of Latinos in the United States continues to grow, so, unfortunately do their rates of obesity and diabetes, making them one of the most at-risk populations in that nation. All this argues for overweight Hispanics or those with a family history of obesity or diabetes to seriously consider Atkins, which has been shown to reduce risk factors for type-2 diabetes and even reverse its progression. Although traditional Latin diets include lots of corn, rice and beans, most Latinos didn't suffer from metabolic disorders in disproportionate numbers until they migrated to the United States or started eating the typical American diet full of refined grains, sugar and other processed foods. Yet Hispanic-American people – as well as those of Caribbean dissent – can honour their culinary traditions and still do Atkins. (We understand that from Peru to Puerto Rico, and from Mexico to Cuba, each cuisine is different, so our recommendations are general in nature.) The same is true of Europeans and their diverse culinary traditions. Start in Phase 1: Induction, regardless of the amount of weight you need to lose and focus on simply prepared protein dishes flavoured with traditional seasonings minus high-carb sauces. Specific recommendations appear in the chapters on Ongoing Weight Loss and Pre-Maintenance.

RESEARCH REPORT: LOW-CARB DIETS AND EXERCISE

Two common beliefs of nutritionists and athletes are that it's necessary to consume carbohydrates to have the energy to exercise, and therefore high-carb diets optimise exercise capacity. So, the logic goes because Atkins is a low-carb diet, it must play havoc with your ability to be physically active. Right? Wrong! The reality is that your body adapts to a low-carb diet, allowing access to your fat stores and burning more fat for fuel, which are the same desirable outcomes associated with exercise training. In fact, being able to burn fat for energy and thus spare carbohydrate stores while exercising is a major goal of endurance athletes. From a purely metabolic perspective, the Atkins diet and exercise are highly complementary.

One researcher looked at elite cyclists who ate a diet similar to the Atkins Lifetime Maintenance phase.[3] Given their very low carbohydrate intakes, conventional wisdom would have predicted severely impaired performance. Indeed, for the first week or two they struggled to maintain their training schedule. Four weeks later, however, when the amount of time it took for the cyclists to reach the point of exhaustion was tested, the results were virtually identical to their previous performance while on a high-carb diet. There were, however, dramatic changes in fuel selection. After the four-week period, the cyclists used almost exclusively fat during exercise, making very little use of blood sugar (which remained at the normal level) and muscle glycogen (stored glucose).

Atkins and weight training are highly compatible as well. In another study overweight men followed a diet comparable to the Ongoing Weight Loss phase of Atkins while participating in an intense resistance training programme.[4] After twelve weeks, the men showed extraordinary changes in body composition. They lost an average of

7.3 kilograms (1.1 stones) of fat, attributable mainly to their low-carb diet. Meanwhile, their lean body mass actually increased by 900 grams (2 pounds), credited mainly to the resistance training. These and other studies clearly shatter the common misconception that you need a high-carb diet to benefit from exercise.

GET PHYSICAL – OR NOT

Numerous health benefits are associated with regular physical activity, making it a natural partner to a healthy diet. The primary benefit of exercise regarding weight is to promote long-term weight maintenance. Research reveals that physical activity appears to help some people lose weight but not others, meaning that your genes make this determination.[5] But there are numerous other benefits of regular physical activity, including:

- Increasing your energy level.
- Complementing the effects of a low-carb diet to unlock your fat stores.
- Inducing calmness, thanks to the release of endorphins, which could temper stress experienced as a result of changing eating habits.
- Building muscle (in the case of some types of high-resistance exercise), so you look better in and out of clothes.
- Instilling a sense of accomplishment.

But go slowly. If physical activity is already a part of your life, you may need to reduce the duration or intensity in the first few weeks as you adapt to Atkins before building back up again – or not. Listen to your body's signals. Sedentary people should wait until they are at least two weeks into the programme before adding activity. Build your skills and tolerance gradually so that by the time you reach your goal weight, your fitness programme will help you to maintain it. We also understand that some of you need to trim off a little weight before you move on to exercise. Over time, however, there's no reason why most people can't incorporate physical activity into their routine. Begin with walking, which can be done almost anywhere and is also less likely to result in injuries. You can personalise the type and degree of activity to suit your skills, preferences and schedule. Embarking on a vigorous fitness programme at a later date is one of those possibilities that is entirely up to you.

You may find it easier to incorporate walking and swimming into a busy schedule by combining them with family time, socialising and even chores like walking the dog. Because it's more natural than a formal exercise programme, many people are more likely to stay with such physical activities for the long term. Much like your new eating style, being active should become a habit. Just as you're more likely to eat delicious foods, you're more apt to regularly pursue activities you find enjoyable. The UK government recommends a minimum of a half-hour of moderate activity five days per week.

TALK TO YOUR DOCTOR

See your doctor before embarking on any weight-loss or health-improvement programme, both to make sure that there is no health reason that might interfere with your success and to have baseline tests performed. He or she will check your blood pressure and blood sugar level as well as order a lipid panel (total, HDL and LDL cholesterol and triglycerides) if necessary. In three to six months, or after you've reached your weight goal (whichever comes first), these health markers can serve as bases for comparison. If you're taking any medications, discuss whether they might interfere with weight loss, as certain antidepressants, insulin, steroids and beta-blockers can. Perhaps you can reduce the dosage or switch to another medication. If you're taking insulin, controlling your carb intake will likely reduce your blood sugar level, often necessitating a prompt reduction in your dosage. This is a good thing but you need to discuss with your doctor how to manage it safely. People with high blood pressure also often see a quick improvement, so if you are on diuretics or other medication for this condition, take your own readings and keep in touch with your doctor. *Caution: Do not stop taking or reduce the dosage of any drugs without consulting your doctor.*

GET READY, GET SET

As Henry Ford once said, 'Before everything else, getting ready is the secret of success'. Once you've experienced the appetite-controlling benefits of burning your own body fat, you'll find it much easier to deal with the psychological baggage associated with weight loss. The control you'll wield will enable you to accept on a profound level that you're going to succeed. You'll find that you can get past your history and perhaps a poor self-image and form new habits. With the Atkins Edge, you'll enjoy a wonderful sense of mastery as you realise that you're capable of modifying your responses to certain situations and temptations. Before you begin your Atkins journey, address these motivational and practical matters.

- *Finish reading this book.* You'll want to return to various sections as you enter each new phase but it's important to have an overview before beginning.
- *Get a carbohydrate gram counter.* Print it out from www.atkins. com/Program/FourPhases/CarbCounter.aspx or pick up *Dr Atkins' New Carbohydrate Gram Counter*, which fits in your pocket or handbag.
- *Pick the right time.* Don't embark on Atkins when you're under a lot of stress or unusually busy. You want to have as much control as you can over external events in your first weeks on the programme, to ensure getting off to a good start. Likewise, don't begin over a holiday or just before travelling. On the other hand, don't keep coming up with excuses to delay starting the programme.
- *Make maintaining your goal weight a priority* from day 1.

- *Enlist the support of family and friends*. It's a courtesy to tell them what you're up to, but make it clear that you're not requesting approval or permission. Remember, this is all about taking control of your life and it starts with this decision. Even those nearest and dearest to you may have some ambivalence. Their assistance can buoy you up but their doubt, scorn or refusal to accept your decision could torpedo your efforts. Remind them that you need all the help you can get, which includes not sabotaging your efforts.

- *In with the good and out with the bad*. Stock your kitchen with the right foods and snacks (see Acceptable Induction Foods on page 99). Equally important is to remove everything that's off-limits for now. If housemates or family members aren't joining you on Atkins, isolate the foods that you'll be avoiding for now. Also be sure to have the recommended nutritional supplements to hand.

- *Make meal plans*. Advance planning puts you in the driver's seat. Review the Acceptable Food List and the meal plans for the phase in which you're starting. Get into the habit of planning your meals before you go grocery shopping so you have everything to hand. Otherwise, you may find yourself grabbing the first thing you can find in the fridge or cupboard.

- *Dust off your scales and find a tape measure*. These two tools are equally essential to establishing baseline figures for comparison in the weeks and months to come. Weigh yourself and take your measurements at the chest, waist, upper arms, thighs and hips. Although the scales are not a particularly reliable tool on a day-to-day basis, they're still useful to track your progress. (See the sidebar 'The Myth of the Daily Weigh-in'.)

- *Change small but impactful habits*. If your morning ritual has been to stop by a bakery to get a muffin with your morning cup of coffee, find a place where pastries don't beckon when you get your caffeine fix. If necessary, take another route so you don't end up succumbing to the familiar sweet aroma.

- *Duplicate behaviour that's been successful in other areas of your life.* By regarding being overweight or in poor health as a problem with a potential solution rather than a personal failing, you'll be more able to come to grips with these issues.
- *Develop strategies for social situations.* To succeed on any weight-loss programme, you must decide how to respond to situations that threaten your control before you confront them.
- *Find an Atkins buddy* in the flesh or online to share the load, the successes and the inevitable times when you're tempted to eat foods you know will undermine all your good work to date. Many people find that it's perfectly possible to team up with a friend who lives elsewhere, checking in daily by phone or email.
- *Keep a journal* to track your weight loss and health improvements as well your feelings, goals, challenges and victories. First record your current weight and measurements along with your long- and short-term goals, and include a current photo. (Go to http://community.atkins.com/user/ to use our online journal or print out the format.) Make daily entries and review them regularly to see what's working, where you may have gone off track and what foods may be interfering with continued weight loss or causing cravings.
- *Use interactive aides.* The Atkins website offers a whole toolbox of them at www.atkins.com/low-carb-online-tools.aspx. One tracks your daily carb intake and keeps a record as you proceed. Other tools include a way to track your weight and meal plans customised to your preferences for vegetables and protein sources as well as any food allergies you may have.
- *Participate in online support networks and blogs.* The Atkins Community includes numerous chat rooms. There are also other low-carb and unofficial Atkins sites, but only www. atkins.com is monitored daily for accuracy by an Atkins nutritionist and incorporates the latest research and thinking on the diet.

One more thing: Don't obsess about perfection. At this very moment you're probably making promises to yourself about controlling your weight. If you're like most of us, you'll keep many of those promises and other times you'll fall short. As long as such failures of will occur only occasionally, regard them as an opportunity to revise your strategy and take control from that moment on. We all make mistakes but the biggest mistake is confusing a single error with failure. When you do misstep, acknowledge it to yourself and then keep going in the right direction. Managing your weight and enhancing your health are all about taking charge.

THE MYTH OF THE DAILY WEIGH-IN

THE MYTH: The scales don't lie.

THE REALITY: Unless you wisely interpret what your scales say, it will drive you crazy! Even the newest digital scales suffer from an age-old flaw: They can't tell what's in your body with enough accuracy to give you day-to-day guidance on the progress of your diet. Here's why. A typical adult's body contains about 38 litres (66.5 pints) of water, but it can safely range between 37 and 39 litres (64.8 and 68.2 pints). Since each litre (1.75 pints) weighs about 900 grams (2 pounds), your body weight randomly varies across a 1.8-kilogram (4-pound) 'grey zone'. Thirst and kidney function kick in only when you get to the bottom or top of this zone. Cutting your carb intake to less than 50 grams (1.8 ounces) per day clears some extra water, but that just pushes your 1.8-kilogram (4-pound) grey zone that much lower, without narrowing the range. Add to this the 900 grams to 2.3 kilograms (2 to 5 pounds) of water that premenstrual women typically retain, and you'll see why the scales cannot possibly be completely precise in measuring progress when you're losing, say, 1.4 kilograms (3 pounds) of fat per week. And forget about day to day. Instead, consider these options:

- Don't weigh yourself at all, focusing rather on how your clothes fit and how good you feel.
- Weigh yourself once a week to get a sense of your general progress, thus providing yourself fewer opportunities to hate your scales.

- Weigh yourself daily and record the number in your journal. Each day take the last three values, average them – you can even do this on your mobile phone – and write that number down in a second column. This running three-day mean smoothes out much of the random noise. Even better, keep a running average for the whole week.

Whatever method you prefer, don't let stupid scales and some water control your mood or sense of self-worth.

WHERE SHOULD YOU START?

In the next chapters we'll guide you through the four phases. But first decide whether to start in Phase 1: Induction, or a later phase. You'll find many opportunities to customise the Atkins Diet to your needs, starting with this important decision. For many people Induction is a brief jump-start phase to get them off on the right footing before moving on. Others may remain there longer to achieve considerable weight loss before transitioning to the next phase. We advise people with more weight to lose or certain health issues to start in Induction, but otherwise you can start in Phase 2 or beyond if you prefer. The self-test that follows should help you make the choice that's right for you. Obviously, the more grams of carbs you're consuming – progressively more in each phase – the more slowly excess weight will come off.

Do you have less than 7 kilograms (1 stone) to lose?
If so, you could probably start in Phase 2: Ongoing Weight Loss (OWL), especially if you're young and active. On the other hand, if you're a bit older, you might chose to start in Induction as weight loss will likely occur more slowly.

Do you have from 7 to 14 kilograms (1 to 2 stones) to lose?
You'll probably still want to start in Induction. You can also start in Ongoing Weight Loss if you want to add more variety in food options in exchange for slower weight loss.

Do you have more than 14 kilograms (2 stones) to lose?
You'll definitely want to begin in Induction.

Do you lead a sedentary lifestyle?
Start in Induction unless you have less than 7 kilograms (1 stone) to lose, in which case you could start in Ongoing Weight Loss and lose more slowly.

Have you gained and lost and regained weight for years?
You may have become resistant to weight loss. Start in Induction to get off on the right footing.

Are you over age fifty?
Your metabolism usually slows with the passage of years. Start in Induction and move to Ongoing Weight Loss after two weeks or more if the weight comes off easily and you're so inclined.

Do you have type-2 diabetes?
Start in Induction and remain there at least until you get your blood sugar and insulin levels under control.

Does your waist measure more than 101.5 cm (40 in) if you're a man or is it larger than your hips if you're a woman, and do you have high blood pressure, high triglycerides and low HDL?
Chances are that you have metabolic syndrome, or prediabetes (see Chapter 11). Have your doctor check your blood sugar, blood pressure and insulin levels. Start in Induction, and remain there until you get your blood sugar and insulin levels under control.

Do you have high triglycerides?
Starting in Induction will help you to improve your triglyceride level more quickly.

Are you a vegetarian or vegan?
See pages 83–84 for guidance on where to start.

Even if you decide to start in a later phase, be sure to read the following chapter to understand what foods you can eat and what to expect in your first few weeks on Atkins. Then take a few minutes to make the acquaintance of mum-of-five Jennifer Munoz, who gained weight with each successive pregnancy.

SUCCESS STORY 6

KEEPING UP WITH THE FAMILY

With a family and a full-time job, Jennifer Munoz was short on time and low on energy. After struggling with her weight for years and giving birth to five children, she decided to do Atkins. More than halfway to her goal weight, she loves that she now has the energy to keep up with her kids.

VITAL STATISTICS

Current phase: Ongoing Weight
  Loss
Daily Net Carb intake:
  30–40 grams (1–1.4 ounces)
Age: 33
Height: 160 cm (5 ft 3 in)

Before weight: 89.8 kg
  (14.1 stones)
Current weight: 72.1 kg
  (11.4 stones)
Weight lost: 17.7 kg (2.8 stones)

What motivated you to do Atkins?

Because of my weight, I was tired all the time. My cholesterol was high and so was my blood pressure. There is a history of heart attacks in my family, so I knew I needed to get the extra weight off. Five months after the birth of my daughter, it was time. One of my office-mates at the order management for car dealers firm where I work and I decided to do Atkins together because we'd heard that it was the best way to lose weight.

Had you put on excess weight during your pregnancy?

Actually, I didn't gain that much when I was pregnant, but I sure gained it afterwards. I was eating everything in sight, and on the weekends I'd eat fast food. My family is from Mexico and I love Mexican food – rice, beans and enchiladas – so those high-carb foods weren't helping, either. I've moved away from them because I'm still afraid of them, although I have started using low-carb tortillas.

How did the first few months go?

The beginning was a breeze; I started in Induction and lost 11.3 kilograms (1.8 stones) in the first two months. My blood pressure has normalised so I no longer need medication, and I'm full of energy. Recently, my weight loss has slowed down to about 1.4 or 1.8 kilograms (3 or 4 pounds) a month.

How are you dealing with that?

I keep myself motivated. When I started Atkins, I found a website that takes a photo of you and manipulates it to show how you'll look when you've reached your goal weight. When I am tempted by foods I know I shouldn't eat, I look at that photo and it keeps me going. I also religiously write down everything I eat. My work friend and I try to incorporate exercise by taking three ten-minute walks every day, and I walk everywhere I can. I also get on the treadmill to watch a video when I get home from work. Every day I fill up a huge jug with water and make sure to drink it all.

What do you eat in a typical day?
For breakfast, I might have a sausage and cheese slices. For lunch, it's usually a salad topped with chicken or steak. Or I'll have a taco meat salad without the taco shell. Dinner is similar. I'll grill chicken, a steak, hamburgers or turkey burgers and serve it with lots of salad. I'm not big on cooked vegetables. My usual snacks are cheese slices with cucumbers or pork rinds with lemon juice.

What tips do you have for other people?
Keep junk food out of the house, not just for you but for your kids as well. Have a diet buddy to help you out. Keep your eye on the ball.

Chapter 7

WELCOME TO PHASE 1: INDUCTION

Food is necessary for life. And a major component of succeeding on Atkins is enjoying what you eat. If it's blah, boring or nutritionally inadequate, there's no way you're going to stay the course long enough to become slim and healthy.

Induction, as the name implies, is your initiation into the Atkins Diet. In Induction, also called Phase 1, you'll consume 20 grams (0.7 ounces) of Net Carbs each day, which will come primarily from foundation vegetables. It's not essential to start here, but Induction is the fastest way to blast through the barrier that blocks your fat stores, transforming your cells into an army of fat-burning soldiers. Induction will also likely energise and empower you.

At the end of the last chapter, we asked a series of questions to help you ascertain where you should start Atkins. (We'll do the same at the end of the chapter on each of the next two phases to help you decide whether to stay there or move on.) There are no ironclad rules about the timing. Instead, we'll give you the tools so you can make the choice that's right for you. For example, if you have a lot of weight to shed, you're more likely to see significant results sooner if you stay in Induction longer than two weeks. However, if losing more slowly is a trade-off you're willing to make for reintroducing nuts and berries into your diet and upping your carb intake slightly, that's your choice.

If you haven't already decided whether to start in Induction, a glimpse of what you get to eat in Phase 1 should also help you to make up your mind.

ACCEPTABLE INDUCTION FOODS

This is an extensive list but cannot include all foods. When in doubt, leave it out!

MEAT, FISH AND POULTRY

Most fish, poultry and meat that are not breaded contain few or no carbs. We've noted those that do.

All fish, including:

Cod	Sardines
Halibut	Sole
Herring*	Trout
Plaice	Tuna
Salmon	

All shellfish, including:

Clams	Oysters†
Crabmeat†	Prawns
Lobster	Squid
Mussels‡	

All poultry, including:

Chicken§	Pheasant
Duck	Poussin
Goose	Quail
Ostrich	Turkey§

---

* Avoid pickled herring prepared with added sugar and all 'batter-dipped' fish and shellfish.
† Avoid artificial crab (surimi), sold as crab legs, and other processed shellfish products.
‡ Oysters and mussels contain carbs, so limit your consumption of them to about 115 grams (4 ounces) per day.
§ Avoid processed chicken and turkey products such as chicken nuggets and other products with breading or fillers.

All meat, including:

Beef¶	Pork, bacon, gammon, ham¶
Goat	Veal
Lamb	Venison

Eggs any style, including:

Boiled	Omelettes
Devilled	Poached
Fried	Scrambled

Note: One egg contains 0.6 grams (0.02 ounces) Net Carbs.

SOYA AND OTHER VEGETARIAN PRODUCTS

Product	Serving Size	Grams of Net Carbs
Almond milk, unsweetened	240 ml (8 fl oz)	1.0
Quorn burger	1	4.0
Quorn roast	115 g (4 oz)	4.0
Quorn unbreaded cutlet	1	3.0
Seitan	1 piece	2.0
Shirataki soya noodles	90 g (3 oz) cooked	1.0
Soya 'cheese'	1 slice	1.0
Soya 'cheese'	30 g (1 oz)	2.0
Soya milk, plain, unsweetened	240 ml (8 fl oz)	1.2
Tempeh	85 g (3 oz)	3.3
Tofu, firm	115 g (4 oz)	2.5
Tofu, silken, soft	115 g (4 oz)	3.1
Tofu 'bacon'	2 rashers	2.0
Tofu 'back bacon'	3 rashers	1.5
Tofu bulk 'sausage'	55 g (2 oz)	2.0–5.0 (depending on brand)
Tofu link 'sausage'	2 links	4.0

¶ Some processed meat – think pepperoni, salami and the like – bacon and ham are cured with sugar, which adds to their carb count. Also steer clear of sandwich meats and other meats with added nitrates and such breaded meat products as pre-made meatballs.

Product	Serving Size	Grams of Net Carbs
Vegan 'cheese' no casein	1 slice	5.0
Vegan 'cheese,' no casein	30 g (1 oz)	6.0
Veggie burger	1 burger	2.0
Veggie crumbles	¾ cup	2.0
Veggie 'meatballs'	4–5 balls	4.0

Note: Check individual products for exact carb counts. Quorn products contain milk and eggs, making them unsuitable for vegans. Soya cheeses that contain casein, a milk product, are also unsuitable for vegans.

CHEESE

Most cheese contains less than 1 gram of Net Carbs per 30 grams (1 ounce). You may have up to 115 grams (4 ounces) of cheese per day. As a guide, 30 grams (1 ounce) is about the size of an individually wrapped slice of Cheddar cheese or a bit larger than a 2.5-centimetre (1-inch) cube. A tablespoon or two of any grated cheese contains a negligible amount of carbs. Avoid ricotta and cottage cheese during Induction. Also, steer clear of cheese spreads that contain other ingredients – flavoured cream cheese, for example – that may raise the carb count. Also avoid 'diet' cheese, 'cheese products' and whey cheeses, none of which is 100 per cent cheese. Soya or rice 'cheese' is acceptable, but check the carb count.

Other than that you can enjoy most cheeses, including:

Cheese	Serving Size	Grams of Net Carbs
Blue cheese	2 tablespoons	0.4
Brie	30 g (1 oz)	0.1
Cheddar	30 g (1 oz)	0.4
Cream cheese	2 tablespoons	0.8
Feta	30 g (1 oz)	1.2
Goat's cheese, soft	30 g (1 oz)	0.3

Cheese	Serving Size	Grams of Net Carbs
Gouda	30 g (1 oz)	0.6
Mozzarella, whole-milk	30 g (1 oz)	0.6
Parmesan	30 g (1 oz)	0.9
Emmenthal	30 g (1 oz)	1.0

Note: For a more extensive list of cheeses, see www.atkins.com/Files/AtkinsCarbCounter.pdf.

FOUNDATION VEGETABLES

These include both salad vegetables and others that are usually cooked. They'll continue to be the foundation of your carb intake upon which you will build as you move through the phases. The 12 to 15 grams (0.4 to 0.5 ounces) of Net Carbs of foundation vegetables you'll eat each day are equivalent to approximately 175 grams (6 ounces) of salad leaves and 200 to 300 grams (7 to 11 ounces) of cooked vegetables, depending upon the ones you select.

SALAD VEGETABLES

A serving of raw vegetables is usually roughly the size of your fist. Measure the following salad vegetables raw (except for artichoke hearts). Note that tomatoes, onions and peppers are higher in carbs than are other salad vegetables, so use them in small portions. Also included are other fruits generally thought of as vegetables, such as avocados.

Vegetable	Serving Size	Grams of Net Carbs
Alfalfa sprouts	16 g (0.6 oz)	0.2
Artichoke hearts, tinned	4 pieces	2.0
Artichoke hearts, tinned	1 heart	1.0
Avocado, Haas	½ fruit	1.8
Beans, French, snap, string, wax	55 g (2 oz), raw	2.1
Bibb lettuce	40 g (1.4 oz), raw	0.8
Broccoli florets	35 g (1.2 oz)	0.8

Vegetable	Serving Size	Grams of Net Carbs
Cabbage, green, red, Savoy	70 g (2.5 oz)	1.1
Cauliflower florets	50 g (1.8 oz)	1.4
Celery	1 stalk	0.8
Celeriac	80 g (2.8 oz)	3.5
Chicory	25 g (1 oz)	0.4
Chinese cabbage	70 g (2.5 oz)	0.0
Chives	1 tablespoon	0.1
Cos lettuce	50 g (1.8 oz)	0.4
Cucumber	50 g (1.8 oz)	1.0
Daikon radish	60 g (2 oz)	1.0
Endive	15 g (0.5 oz)	0.1
Escarole	15 g (0.5 oz)	0.1
Fennel	45 g (1.6 oz)	1.8
Greens, mixed	55 g (2 oz)	0.4
Iceberg lettuce	70 g (2.5 oz)	0.2
Loose-leaf lettuce	30 g (1 oz)	1.0
Mesclun	30 g (1 oz)	0.5
Mung bean sprouts	50 g (1.8 oz)	2.1
Mushrooms, button, fresh	35 g (1.2 oz)	1.2
Olives, black	5	0.7
Olives, green	5	0.0
Onion	2 tablespoons, chopped	0.5
Pak choi	70 g (2.5 oz), raw	0.4
Parsley (and all fresh herbs)	1 tablespoon	0.1
Peppers, green	50 g (1.8 oz)	2.1
Pepper, red	50 g (1.8 oz)	2.9
Radicchio	25 g (1 oz)	0.7
Radishes	6	0.5
Rocket	30 g (1 oz)	0.4
Spring onion	25 g (1 oz)	1.2
Spinach	30 g (1 oz)	0.2
Tomato	1 small (85–115 g/3–4 oz)	2.5

Vegetable	Serving Size	Grams of Net Carbs
Tomato	1 medium	3.3
Tomato, cherry	5	2.2
Watercress	15 g (0.5 g)	0.0

COOKED VEGETABLES

Because most of the following vegetables are usually served cooked, we've indicated their carb count as such, unless otherwise noted. Some also appear on the salad vegetable list, but cooking compacts them, which explains the differences in carb counts. A number of these vegetables are slightly higher in carbs than the salad vegetables listed above. Unless otherwise noted, be sure to measure them *after* you cook them. Note that some, such as celeriac, kohlrabi, leeks, mushrooms, onions and pumpkin, are higher in carbs than most, so we have usually indicated smaller portions. You can steam, sauté, stir-fry or braise most of these vegetables. Boiling destroys and/or removes nutrients (unless you drink the broth). *Note*: Vegetables *not* on this list should not be consumed in Induction.

Vegetable	Serving Size	Grams of Net Carbs
Artichoke	½ medium	3.5
Asparagus	6 spears	2.4
Aubergine	50 g (1.8 oz)	2.0
Bamboo shoots, tinned, sliced	60 g (2 oz)	1.2
Beans, French, wax, string, snap	60 g (2 oz)	2.9
Beetroot greens	70 g (2.5 oz)	3.7
Pak choi	85 g (3 oz)	0.2
Broccoli	80 g (2.8 oz)	1.7
Broccoli rabe	85 g (3 oz)	2.0
Brussels sprouts	40 g (1.4 oz)	1.8
Cabbage, green	75 g (2.6 oz)	1.6
Cabbage, red	75 g (2.6 oz)	2.0
Cabbage, Savoy	75 g (2.6 oz)	1.9

Vegetable	Serving Size	Grams of Net Carbs
Cauliflower	60 g (2 oz)	0.9
Celery	75 g (2.6 oz)	1.2
Chard	85 g (3 oz)	1.8
Courgette	115 g (4 oz)	1.5
Dandelion greens	55 g (2 oz)	1.8
Escarole	15 g (0.5 oz)	0.1
Fennel	40 g (1.5 oz)	1.5
Hearts of palm	1 heart	0.7
Kale	65 g (2.3 oz)	2.4
Kohlrabi	85 g (3 oz)	2.3
Leeks	50 g (1.8 oz)	3.4
Mangetout/snap peas in the pod	80 g (2.8 oz)	3.4
Mushrooms, button	15 g (0.5 oz)	2.3
Mushrooms, shiitake	20 g (0.8 oz)	4.4
Mustard greens	70 g (2.5 oz)	0.1
Okra	80 g (2.8 oz)	2.4
Onion	20 g (0.8 oz)	4.3
Peppers, green, chopped	45 g (1.6 oz)	1.9
Peppers, red, chopped	45 g (1.6 oz)	1.9
Pumpkin	60 g (2 oz)	2.4
Rhubarb, unsweetened	120 g (4 oz)	1.7
Sauerkraut	70 g (2.5 oz), drained	1.2
Shallots	2 tablespoons	3.1
Spaghetti squash	40 g (1.4 oz)	2.0
Spinach	90 g (3 oz)	2.2
Spring greens	95 g (3.4 oz)	2.0
Spring onions	50 g (1.8 oz)	2.4
Summer squash	115 g (4 oz)	2.6
Tomato	60 g (2 oz)	4.3
Tomatillo	50 g (1. 8 oz)	2.6
Turnips (white), mashed	80 g (2.8 oz)	3.3
Water chestnuts, tinned	30 g (1 oz)	3.5

SALAD DRESSINGS

Any prepared salad dressing with no more than 3 grams (0.1 ounces) of Net Carbs per serving (1–2 tablespoons) is acceptable. A better – and lower-carb option – is to make your own. (See Recipes in Part III.)

Dressing	Serving Size	Grams of Net Carbs
Blue cheese dressing	2 tablespoons	2.3
Caesar salad dressing	2 tablespoons	0.5
Italian dressing	2 tablespoons	3.0
Lemon juice	2 tablespoons	2.5
Lime juice	2 tablespoons	2.9
Oil and vinegar	2 tablespoons	1.0
Ranch dressing	2 tablespoons	1.4

FATS AND OILS

No carbs to worry about here. A serving size is approximately 1 tablespoon. Oils labelled 'cold pressed' or 'expeller pressed' are preferable because they haven't been subjected to nutrient-destroying heat. Use extra virgin olive oil only for dressing salad and vegetables and sautéing and olive oil, rapeseed oil or high-oleic safflower oil for other cooking. Never use speciality oils such as walnut oil or sesame oil for cooking; instead use them to season a dish after removing it from the heat. Avoid products labelled 'light' or 'low fat' and all margarines and shortening products, which still contain small amounts of trans-fats. The term 'no trans-fats' actually means that a product may contain up to 0.5 grams per serving. (See Chapter 5 for more on selection of oils.)

Butter	Olive oil
Coconut oil	Rapeseed oil
Grapeseed oil	Sesame oil

Groundnut oil   Safflower oil, high-oleic
Mayonnaise*   Walnut oil

NON-CALORIC SWEETENERS

Count each packet as 1 gram (0.04 ounces) of Net Carbs and consume no more than three per day.

Splenda (sucralose)
Truvia or SweetLeaf (natural products made from stevia)
Sweet'N Low (saccharin)
Xylitol (available in health food stores and some supermarkets)

LOW-CARB CONVENIENCE FOODS

Some low-carb food products can come in handy when you're unable to find appropriate food, can't take time for a meal or need a quick snack. More and more companies are creating healthy food products that can be eaten during the Induction phase of Atkins. Just remember two things:

- Not all low-carb bars, shakes and other convenience products are the same. Check both the list of ingredients and the Nutrition Facts panel to ascertain the number of grams of Net Carbs. ('Sugar free' does not necessarily mean 'carb free' or 'low carb'.) Products suitable for Induction should contain no more than 3 grams (0.1 ounces) of Net Carbs per serving.
- Such foods can make doing Atkins easier but don't overdo them. Don't substitute them for any of your 12 to 15 grams (0.4 to 0.5 ounces) of Net Carbs from foundation vegetables.

---

* Most commercial mayonnaise is made with soya bean oil. Find a brand made with rapeseed oil or high-oleic safflower oil and without added sugar. Or make your own with our recipe in Part III.

CONDIMENTS, HERBS AND SPICES

Hidden carbs lurk in many condiments. Read labels carefully and look out for added sugar, flour and cornflour and other off-limits thickeners. Most tomato ketchups, marinades and barbecue sauces contain added sugar (often listed as corn syrup, corn syrup solids, cane syrup or something else). Salt, black and cayenne pepper, most spices, basil, fresh coriander, dill, oregano, rosemary, sage, tarragon, thyme and other dried herbs contain practically no carbs. But make sure that any herb or spice mixture contains no added sugar. The following products are suitable. Check the list of ingredients of any products that aren't listed before consuming them.

Condiment, Herb or Spice	Serving Size	Grams of Net Carbs
Ancho chilli pepper	1 pepper	5.1
Anchovy paste	1 tablespoon	0.0
Black bean sauce	1 teaspoon	3.0
Capers	1 tablespoon	0.1
Chipotle en adobe	2 peppers	2.0
Clam juice	240 ml (8 fl oz)	0.0
Coconut milk, unsweetened	½ cup	1.9
Cocoa powder, unsweetened	1 tablespoon	1.2
Enchilada sauce	4 tablespoons	2.0
Garlic	1 large clove	0.9
Gherkin, pickled	½ pickle	1.0
Ginger	1 tablespoon grated root	0.8
Horseradish sauce	1 teaspoon	0.4
Jalapeño chilli pepper	45 g (1.6 oz)	1.4
Miso paste	1 tablespoon	2.6
Mustard, Dijon	1 teaspoon	0.5
Mustard, yellow	1 teaspoon	0.0
Pasilla chilli pepper	1 pepper	1.7
Pesto sauce	1 tablespoon	0.6

Condiment, Herb or Spice	Serving Size	Grams of Net Carbs
Pickapeppa sauce	1 teaspoon	1.0
Pimento/roasted red pepper	30 g (1 oz)	2.0
Salsa, green (no added sugar)	1 tablespoon	0.6
Salsa, red (no added sugar)	1 tablespoon	1.0
Serrano chilli pepper	50 g (1.8 oz)	1.6
Soya sauce	1 tablespoon	0.9
Tabasco or other hot sauce	1 teaspoon	0.0
Taco sauce	1 tablespoon	1.0
Tahini (sesame paste)	2 tablespoons	1.0
Thai fish sauce	1 teaspoon	0.2
Vinegar, balsamic	1 tablespoon	2.3
Vinegar, cider	1 tablespoon	0.9
Vinegar, red wine	1 tablespoon	1.5
Vinegar, rice (unsweetened)	1 tablespoon	0.0
Vinegar, sherry	1 tablespoon	0.9
Vinegar, white wine	1 tablespoon	1.5
Wasabi paste	1 teaspoon	0.0

BEVERAGES

- Clear broth/bouillon (not low sodium and without added sugars, hydrogenated oils or MSG)
- Soda water
- Cream, double or single (30 to 45 grams/1 to 1.5 ounces a day)
- Caffeinated or decaffeinated coffee
- Caffeinated or decaffeinated tea
- Diet fizzy drinks sweetened with non-caloric sweeteners
- Lemon juice or lime juice; limit to 2 to 3 tablespoons a day. Note that 2 tablespoons of lemon juice contain 2.5 grams (0.09 ounces) Net Carbs; the same amount of lime juice contains 2.9 grams (0.1 ounces).
- Plain or essence-flavoured soda water (must say 'no calories')
- Herbal tea (without added barley or fruit sugars)

- Unsweetened, unflavoured soya or almond milk.
  A 240-millilitre (8-fluid-ounce)
- Water (tap, spring, filtered or mineral)

WHAT'S OFF-LIMITS?

For now you need to stay away from certain foods. Clearly, we cannot list every food you should avoid. Follow these guidelines and use your common sense. Avoid the following:

- Fruits and juices (other than fruits listed with vegetables and lemon and lime juice)
- Caloric fizzy drinks
- Foods made with flour or other grain products (exclusive of low-carb products with no more than 3 grams/0.1 ounces of Net Carbs per serving) and/or sugar, including but not limited to bread, pasta, tortillas, muffins, pastries, biscuits, crisps, cakes and sweets
- Any food with added sugar, no matter what kind. Look for terms such as brown syrup, evaporated cane juice, glucose, dextrose, honey and corn syrup
- Alcohol of any sort
- Nuts and seeds, nut and seed butters (in the first two weeks of Induction), except for flaxseeds, which are acceptable
- Grains, even whole grains: rice, oats, barley, quinoa, buckwheat groats and so on
- Kidney beans, chickpeas, lentils and other pulses
- Any vegetables not on the Acceptable Induction Foods list, including starchy vegetables such as parsnips, carrots, potatoes, yams, sweet potatoes, acorn squash and other winter squash
- Dairy products other than hard cheese, cream, soured cream and butter. No cow's or goat's milk of any sort, yoghurt, cottage cheese or ricotta for now
- 'Low-fat' foods, which are usually high in carbs

- 'Diet' products, unless they specifically state 'no carbohydrates' or have no more than 3 grams (0.1 ounces) of Net Carbs per serving. Most such foods are suitable for low-fat diets, not low-carb plans. Don't be fooled by the words 'sugarless', 'sugar free', 'natural' or 'no sugar added'. Go by the carb content, which must be stated on the label
- 'Junk food' in any form
- Products such as chewing gum, breath mints, cough syrups and drops, even liquid vitamins, which may be filled with sugar or other caloric sweeteners. (You can have breath mints and gums sweetened with sorbitol or xylitol and count 1 gram per piece, up to three a day)
- Any foods with manufactured trans-fats (hydrogenated or partially hydrogenated oils)

When in doubt, pass it up.

TURNING LISTS INTO MEALS

Your objective is to build meals around a wide array of protein sources, natural fats and foundation vegetables. If you love salads, eat them to your heart's content. When it comes to cooked vegetables, choose from more than forty selections, from artichoke to water chestnuts. Steam, sauté, roast or stir-fry vegetables, but don't boil them, which destroys their nutrients, unless you drink the broth or add it to soups. Likewise, meats, poultry, fish, shellfish and tofu may be grilled, griddled, roasted, stir-fried, poached or braised – but not deep-fried. Enjoy the odd fruits that pretend to be vegetables – think avocados, olives and tomatoes – in moderation. Refer to the Induction meal plans in Part III, which you can modify according to your needs as long as you comply with the Acceptable Induction Foods list and tally the carbs.

INDUCTION GUIDELINES

Many people see remarkably fast weight-loss results on Induction. Others find it slow going. Whatever your pace, you'll need to follow the rules precisely to achieve success. This applies equally to those of you who are working on improving your blood sugar and insulin levels or your lipids. Otherwise, you could become frustrated before you've had a chance to see what Atkins can really do for you. Read the following rules of Induction and then read them again to ensure that they're engraved on your brain!

- Eat either three regular-sized meals a day or four or five smaller meals. Don't skip meals or go more than six waking hours without eating.

- At each meal eat at least 115 to 175 grams (4 to 6 ounces) of protein foods. Up to 225 grams (8 ounces) is fine if you're a tall man. There's no need to trim the fat from meat or the skin from poultry, but if you prefer to do so, fine. Just add a splash of olive oil or a knob of butter to your vegetables to replace the fat.

- Enjoy butter, mayonnaise (made from olive oil, rapeseed oil or high-oleic safflower oil), olive oil, high-oleic safflower oil, rapeseed oil and seed and nut oils. Aim for 1 tablespoon of oil on a salad or other vegetables, or a knob of butter. Cook foods in enough oil to ensure they don't burn but no more. Or spritz the pan with a mister of olive oil. See guidelines for oils above.

- Eat no more than 20 grams (0.7 ounces) a day of Net Carbs, 12 to 15 grams (0.4 to 0.5 ounces) of them as foundation vegetables. This means you can eat approximately 175 grams (6 ounces) of salad and 200 to 300 grams (7 to 11 ounces) of cooked vegetables. (See Acceptable Induction Foods on page 99.) Carb counts of vegetables vary.

- Eat only the foods on this list. This is not the time to indulge in treats.

- Learn to distinguish hunger from habit and adjust the quantity you eat to suit your appetite as it decreases. When you're hungry, eat until you feel satisfied but not stuffed. If you're not sure if you're full, wait ten minutes, have a glass of water and eat more only if you're still unsatisfied. If you're not hungry at mealtime, eat a small low-carb snack.
- Don't starve yourself and don't restrict fats.
- Don't assume that any food is low in carbs. Read the labels on ready-prepared foods to discover unacceptable ingredients and check their carb counts (subtract grams of fibre from total grams). Also use a carbohydrate gram counter.
- When dining out be on guard for hidden carbs. Gravy is usually made with flour or cornflour, both no-nos. Sugar is found in salad dressing and may even appear in coleslaw and other deli salads. Avoid any deep-fried or breaded food.
- Use sucralose (Splenda), saccharine (Sweet'N Low), stevia (SweetLeaf or Truvia) or xylitol as a sweetener. Have no more than three packets a day and count each one as 1 gram (0.04 ounces) of carbs.
- To be safe, stick with Atkins low-carb products and only those coded for Induction. Limit them to two a day.
- Drink at least eight 240-ml (8-fluid-ounce) portions of approved beverages each day to prevent dehydration and electrolyte imbalances. Include two cups of broth (not low sodium), one in the morning and one in the afternoon, in this count.
- Take a daily iron-free multivitamin/multimineral combo and an omega-3 fatty acid supplement.

WHAT TO EXPECT IN THE FIRST WEEK

If you've been eating lots of poor-quality carbohydrates, this way of eating will be a significant change for you and it may take some time for your body to adjust. You may also be giving up many of your old high-carb comfort foods, which may leave you feeling emotionally bereft. Both reactions are normal. Record any such feelings in your diet journal, along with a list of the foods you've eaten. You can find online support and answers to specific questions on the Atkins Community forums during this transition (as well as at any other time) as well as link up with Atkins 'newbies' and old hands.

Just because your best friend or spouse lost 3 kilograms (7 pounds) on Atkins in his or her first week of Induction, don't assume it will be the same for you. It's better to begin with no set expectations. Most people lose a bit of water weight in the first few days. Your loss may be more dramatic, or not. And don't skimp fluids or eliminate salt to hasten water loss. Remember that lost centimetres are just as significant. So if your clothes seem to feel a bit looser even if your weight is constant, you're on the right track. This is also why we recommend that you weigh yourself once a week at roughly the same time of day (or use weight averaging) and take your measurements. That way you're more likely to see positive results and not get hung up on your body's normal day-to-day variances.

Everyone is different, and it can take some time to fully switch your metabolism over to burning primarily fat. A low-carb diet is naturally diuretic, which flushes sodium and water from your body. Fatigue, light-headedness upon standing up or with exposure to heat (in a hot shower or hot bath or while mowing the lawn on a hot day, for example), weakness, constipation, chronic headaches and leg cramps are all signs you might not be getting enough sodium. Like fat, salt has been unjustly demonised, despite being essential to life and well-being.

The symptoms described above are not the result of the diet – too little carbohydrate, too much protein or whatever. The real problem is the lack of just a daily pinch of sodium. Yes, individuals who are sensitive to salt may experience bloating and high blood pressure if they eat lots of salt. But interestingly, these conditions are most pronounced when people eat high-carb diets. Adapting to the low-carb state fundamentally changes how your system handles nutrients that might cause problems in a high-carb setting.

Our strategy to restore your sodium balance will stop most symptoms before they begin. In our experience normally salting food to taste is not adequate. So don't wait until you experience symptoms; instead have either two cups of broth, ½ teaspoon of salt or 2 tablespoons of regular soya sauce daily from your first day on Atkins. Start this regimen on your first day on Atkins and continue until your carb intake exceeds 50 grams (1.8 ounces) of Net Carbs.

If you opt for the broth, drink one cup in the morning and another in the mid-afternoon. Ideally, make your own chicken, beef or vegetable broth (see recipes in Part III), but otherwise use regular (not low-sodium) tinned or Tetra Pak broth or a bouillon cube dissolved in water. If you're going to be exercising vigorously, drink one portion about an hour beforehand. If you opt for salt instead, measure out the amount in the morning and sprinkle it on food throughout the day, being sure to use all of it. If you use soya sauce, make sure it is not the low-sodium kind and consume it in at least two portions as a condiment or ingredient in meals.

If you're taking a diuretic medication or have been advised to restrict your salt intake, consult your doctor before adding sodium to your diet. Meanwhile, be sure to eat the recommended amount of vegetables and sufficient protein with every meal as well as drink enough fluids and take your supplements. If symptoms do crop up or remain, you may want to temporarily increase your intake to 25 grams (0.9 ounces) of Net Carbs by eating more foundation vegetables. Or have some nuts or seeds or even 125 millilitres (4 fluid ounces) of tomato juice, which you would not normally have until Ongoing Weight Loss. Once you feel better, eliminate these foods for the time being and return to 20 grams (0.7 ounces) of Net Carbs to speed your weight loss. Follow this advice and you're far less likely to experience symptoms than in the past.

YOUR ALLY, THE ATKINS EDGE

Somewhere towards the end of the first or second week most people feel a dramatic increase in their energy level and sense of well-being. This is a clear signal that you've got the Atkins Edge and can begin to hone your low-carb skills.

Developing new habits and learning how to resist temptation are crucial to your success but they're not enough. Another major component of succeeding on Atkins is enjoying what you eat. If it's blah, boring or nutritionally inadequate, there's no way you're going to stay with the programme long enough to become slim and healthy. Having a large repertoire of enjoyable food choices and making sure that the right foods and ingredients are always in your kitchen is integral to forming habits that will result in a permanently slim you. (See the sidebar 'Don't Get Caught Short'.) Food is necessary for life. Once you discover which types and amounts of food are best for your metabolism, you'll set yourself up for success in terms of health and weight management as well as satisfaction and, yes, pleasure. So let's delve deeper into what you can eat during Induction.

DON'T GET CAUGHT SHORT

You've been following Atkins to the letter, but after a gruelling day at work, the kids are clamouring for dinner and there's nothing in the house that's Atkins-compliant. So you end up eating macaroni and cheese with the family. If this sounds familiar, you need to have an emergency store to hand at all times. Stock your freezer, fridge and cupboard with the following foods and you should always be able to put together a tasty, low-carb meal.

REFRIGERATOR: Eggs, tofu, cheese, herring in cream sauce (without added sugar), rotisserie chicken (not honey basted), sliced roast beef or fresh turkey, hard salami and other cold cooked sliced meats with no added sugar; salad fixings.

FREEZER: Hamburger patties, lamb chops, prawns, chicken breasts in individual resealable freezer bags for quick defrosting in a bowl of warm water.

CUPBOARD: Tuna or salmon in tins or vacuum bags, sardines, crabmeat, clams.

THE VEGETABLE CHALLENGE

One of the things we hear most often from people new to Atkins is that they're having trouble getting enough vegetables into their daily carb tally. New science on the importance of fibre, minerals and phytochemicals in vegetables has changed our recommendations about the amount of vegetables you should eat in Induction to 12 to 15 grams (0.4 to 0.5 ounces) of Net Carbs. Have at least one and preferably two salads a day. To make it easier to track your carbs, we've created mini-recipes for basic main course and side dish salads, which you can modify.

- *Side Dish Salad:* Start with 55 grams (2 ounces) of salad leaves (0.8 gram Net Carbs). Add 6 sliced radishes (0.5 grams), ½ medium tomato (1.6 grams) and a tablespoon of olive oil and a little vinegar, and you've spent only about 4 grams (0.14 ounces) of Net Carbs. Hate radishes or tomatoes? Simply replace them with vegetables of comparable carb counts and you're set to go. Or add a couple of slices of avocado for another gram of carbs.

- *Main Course Salad:* Start with 115 grams (4 ounces) of your favourite salad leaves (1.6 grams Net Carbs). Add 25 grams (1 ounce) sliced spring onions (1.2 grams), 35 grams (1.2 ounces) sliced raw mushrooms (1.4 grams) and 50 grams (1.8 ounces) cucumber slices (1.0 gram) for a total of 5.2 grams (0.2 ounces) of Net Carbs. Top with a grilled chicken breast, prawns, roast beef, tuna, tofu, hard-boiled eggs or another protein source and dress with oil and vinegar for roughly another gram, and you're looking at not much more than 6 grams (0.21 ounces) of Net Carbs. Or pile on low- or no-carb garnishes such as crumbled bacon, diced hard-boiled egg or grated cheese.

Making a salad is no big deal, especially if you invest in a salad spinner. To save time, spin a couple of days' worth of salad leaves, then wrap them gently in a tea towel, seal in a resealable food bag and pop the bag into the vegetable bin in your fridge. Likewise, wash, trim and cut up your other favourite salad veggies and keep in the fridge. Or, to cut out the washing and prep work, buy bagged pre-washed salad leaves and ready-prepared sliced vegetables. Easier yet, stop by a salad bar and load up on acceptable vegetables. The point is don't let anything get into the way of eating fresh greens.

WHAT'S FOR BREAKFAST?

Most people find that it's quite easy to eat Atkins style at lunch and dinner, and it is at breakfast, too, if you get 'egg-cited' about the myriad of ways in which eggs can be prepared. But if eggs aren't your thing you'll need to get a bit more creative, as we explain below. Americans have grown up equating the first meal of the day with sugar, in the form of sweetened cereal, doughnuts, juice drinks, cereal bars and other foods of dubious value, and many British people are following this trend. But in most other countries, breakfasts are much more varied. The Japanese often have soup for breakfast, the Scandinavians delight in smoked fish. Time to broaden your own horizons.

Some of our Induction breakfast suggestions are variations of such dishes, and yes, we admit there's an egg here and there, but they're a far cry from two fried eggs. Remember your goal is not just to control carbs but to also get sufficient protein and fat at every meal including the first meal of the day. The following ideas, which all come in under 4 grams (0.14 ounces) of Net Carbs, should add some variety to your morning repertoire. Some are portable, making them good for weekday mornings, and all serve one unless otherwise indicated.

- *On-the-Run Roll-ups:* Wrap slices of cheese and ham around a couple of cucumber spears and a dab of mayonnaise mixed with mustard. Use sliced turkey or roast beef instead and lettuce leaves or another vegetable. Or wrap cream cheese in smoked salmon.
- *Chocolate-Coconut Shake:* Blend 125 millilitres (4 fluid ounces) unsweetened soya or almond milk, 2 tablespoons no-sugar-added coconut milk, 1 scoop unsweetened whey protein powder, 2 teaspoons cocoa powder, ½ teaspoon vanilla essence, 3 ice cubes and 1 packet sucralose (optional) in a blender until well mixed and frothy.
- *Stuffed Peppers:* Stuff half a pepper with a few tablespoons of pork or turkey bulk sausage and microwave for 10–15 minutes on high or in a 180°C/350°F/Gas Mark 4 oven for 45 minutes. Pour off the excess fat and serve with no-added-sugar salsa or, if desired, with a poached egg and/or grated cheese. Make a batch ahead of time and reheat individual portions.
- *Corned Beef Hash.* Instead of the potatoes called for in most recipes, use white turnips or chopped cauliflower. Or replace the corned beef with leftover chicken or turkey.
- *Veggie Hash Browns.* Sauté cauliflower florets and cut-up white turnips and onions in bacon drippings until browned and tender. Add crumbled bacon or sausage and serve with no-added-sugar tomato ketchup.
- *Grilled Stuffed Mushrooms:* Brush a field mushroom cap with oil. Grill for a minute or two on both sides. Top with browned minced beef and some grated cheese and return to the grill for a minute or two.

- *Egg Fu Yung:* Stir-fry a sliced spring onion with 55 grams (2 ounces) bean sprouts in a little oil until soft, then add two beaten eggs and cook, stirring, for a minute or two. Serve with soya sauce or no-added-sugar salsa. Or replace the sprouts with grated courgette, spinach or vegetable leftovers. Or replace the sprouts with ½ packet well-rinsed and drained shirataki noodles.
- *Morning Soup:* Bring 240 millilitres (8 fluid ounces) of water to the boil. Turn down the heat and add 1 bouillon cube, 115 grams (4 ounces) firm tofu cut into small pieces, ½ packet well-rinsed shirataki noodles and 1 thinly sliced spring onion. Simmer for a few minutes. Ladle into a soup bowl. Or replace the tofu with chunks of leftover chicken, beef or pork and/or add watercress or baby spinach leaves.

While we're on the subject of breakfast, there's no reason to avoid caffeinated coffee. Moderate caffeine intake is actually associated with improved long-term health and regulation of body weight.[1] Coffee contains several antioxidants and has the added benefit of mildly enhancing fat burning.[2] Add cream (but not milk) and/or one of the three acceptable sweeteners if you wish. By the way, an overwhelming desire for caffeine is not a true addiction but simply the result of consuming it regularly. You'll probably notice some withdrawal signs such as a mild headache if you miss your daily dose. This reaction is normal and isn't associated with doing Atkins. However, another common morning beverage, orange juice (along with other fruit juices) is off-limits – think of it as liquid sugar and you'll understand why.

THE MYTH ABOUT EGGS

THE MYTH: Eggs raise cholesterol levels and increase health risks.

THE REALITY: Eggs are one of the most nutrient-dense foods you can consume. One large egg provides 6 grams (0.2 ounces) of high-quality, easily digested protein and all the essential amino acids. Eggs are also a significant source of a number of vitamins and minerals. The yolk of a large egg has about 4 to 5 grams (0.14 to 0.18 ounces) of fat, mainly the unsaturated type, and also contains choline, an important substance necessary for fat breakdown and brain function. Eggs also provide high-quality protein at a lower cost than many other animal-protein foods.

A large body of research over five decades has revealed no association between eating eggs and heart disease. Recent research involving 9,500 overweight but otherwise healthy adults showed that eating one or more eggs a day had no impact on cholesterol or triglyceride levels and didn't increase the subjects' risk of heart disease or stroke.[3] There also appears to be an association with decreased blood pressure. Subjects who ate eggs also lost more weight and felt more energetic than subjects who ate a bagel for breakfast. Both groups were on reduced-calorie diets, and the egg and the bagel breakfasts both contained the same number of calories.[4] Previous research indicated that individuals who ate eggs for breakfast felt more satisfied and were likely to consume fewer calories at lunchtime.[5] Compared to the bagel eaters, egg eaters lost 65 per cent more weight and had a 51 per cent greater reduction in BMI (body mass index). Finally, another study that compared the results of following the Atkins Diet both with and without eggs found that eating three eggs a day is associated with a greater increase in HDL ('good') cholesterol.[6] So go ahead and enjoy your breakfast – or lunch or dinner – of eggs in all their wondrous variety without a smidgen of guilt.

SNACK TIME

Snacks are an important part of the Atkins Diet. A mid-morning and mid-afternoon snack should help keep your energy on a level plane and head off fatigue, jitters, inability to concentrate, ravenous cravings for inappropriate food or overeating at your next meal. But not just any snacks will do: Snacks should be made up of fat and protein. Vegetables (and later berries and other fruits) are fine in moderation, but always eat them with some fat and/or protein to minimise the impact on your blood sugar. In addition to a low-carb shake or bar, here are ten guilt-free Induction-appropriate snacks, each with no more than 3 grams (0.1 ounces) of Net Carbs.

- 30 grams (1 ounce) of cheese slices
- Celery stuffed with cream cheese
- Cucumber 'boats' filled with tuna salad
- 5 green or black olives, perhaps stuffed with cheese
- Half a Haas avocado
- Beef or turkey jerky (cured without sugar)
- A devilled egg
- A lettuce leaf wrapped around grated Cheddar cheese
- Sliced ham rolled around a few raw or cooked French beans
- Two slices of tomato topped with chopped fresh basil and grated mozzarella and heated under the grill for a minute
- 30 grams (1 ounce) of nuts or seeds (after the first two weeks)

After the first two weeks, you can also have one ounce of nuts or seeds.

DESSERT ON INDUCTION

On Atkins, desserts are an option, even in Phase 1. Here's a week's worth of ideas, each with no more than 3 grams (0.1 ounces) of Net Carbs – to finish off a low-carb meal. Once you're past the first two weeks and can eat nuts and seeds your options will open up.

- *Chocolate 'Pudding':* Mix together 2 tablespoons double cream, 1 tablespoon unsweetened cocoa and 1 packet of Splenda. Using a fork or a spatula, blend for a couple of minutes until it reaches the consistency of soft ice cream. Add a drop or two of vanilla essence if desired.
- *Mocha 'Pudding':* Add 1 teaspoon instant coffee granules to the above recipe.
- *Chocolate Coconut 'Pudding':* Add 1 tablespoons dried unsweetened coconut and 1 teaspoon of coconut extract if desired to the basic recipe.

- *Raspberry Mousse:* Follow the recipe on the packet of raspberry sugar-free gelatine and partially set in the fridge. Whip 125 millitres (4 fluid ounces) double cream. Gently blend into the gelatine. Return to the fridge until set. Makes four servings.

- *Lime Mousse:* Use sugar-free lime (or any other flavour) gelatine instead.

- *Rhubarb Compote:* Treat this vegetable like a fruit. Cut 1 stalk into 2.5-cm (1-in) pieces and cook in a saucepan over low heat with a tablespoon of water and 1 packet of sucralose until soft. Serve warm or cold, topped with a little double cream. (Makes 2 servings.)

- *Vanilla Freeze:* In a large cereal bowl dissolve 1 scoop low-carb vanilla protein powder in 125 millitres (4 fluid ounces) of unsweetened soya milk. Add a scoopful of cracked ice and stir until the ice turns the mixture to the consistency of soft ice cream. Add a bit more soya milk if it seems too thick. Or make in a blender after crushing the ice. Sweeten with a little acceptable sweetener if desired.

LET'S EAT OUT

Like many people, you may eat many of your meals outside the home. Fast food may be convenient and inexpensive, but the typical offerings are all too often full of empty carbs: in the roll, crust, breading, condiments and, of course, the chips. Fortunately, there are other options if you take the trouble to find them. Some fried chicken chains now offer grilled or roasted chicken that's not battered or breaded. Watch out for some of the sauces, however, which may be full of sugar. In a pinch, you can always peel off the battered skin of a piece of fried chicken and eat only the meat.

Many fast-food chains now offer salads with ham or chicken and even salad dressings that aren't swimming in sugar. If you ask, most will give you a cheeseburger minus the roll, or just ask for a fork and dispose of the roll yourself. The bigger chains provide complete nutritional data for their foods on their websites. Burger King even allows you to add or subtract the roll or/and condiments and immediately see the nutritional impact. For example, once you remove the roll and tomato ketchup, a Whopper goes from 51 to 3 grams (from 1.8 to 0.1 ounces) of Net Carbs. For specific suggestions on what to order and what to avoid at several national chains, see Chapter 11, 'Low-Carb Fast Food and Restaurant Meals'.

What about your favourite cuisines? Again, as long as you follow certain guidelines, you can dine out on Atkins. Select simple grilled or roasted meats and fish. Avoid deep-fried dishes, which are breaded and may contain harmful trans-fats. Likewise, avoid stews, which may have potatoes or other starchy vegetables in them. Gravy is almost always thickened with flour or cornflour, so steer clear of it. In lieu of potatoes or another starch, ask for an additional portion of (hopefully) fresh vegetables or a side salad.

Nearly every cuisine has a staple food such as potato, bread, rice or pasta, corn or beans. Though it may seem almost impossible to eat Italian cuisine, for example, without a plate of pasta, what really gives any cuisine its identity is certain seasonings and cooking methods. Those elements can be applied to a wide variety of protein sources and vegetables. For advice on how to navigate Italian, Mexican, Indian, Chinese, Japanese and other menus, see Chapter 11, 'Low-Carb Fast Food and Restaurant Meals'.

Regardless of cuisine or prices, all restaurants have some things in common.

- *They're in the service business.* And they love repeat customers. Don't hesitate to ask what's in a dish. There's no need to explain why you're interested. Specify any changes you want such as salad dressing and any sauces on the side and ask that the bread basket, or chips and salsa not be placed on the table.

- *Don't believe the menu.* Though many major chains and some restaurants have done their homework, just because a dish is listed in a 'healthy' or 'low-carb' section of the menu doesn't mean that it actually is. If carb counts aren't listed, take any claims with a large grain of salt.

- *Exercise portion control.* If the portions served to you are too large, don't fall into the trap of feeling that you need to clean the plate – don't eat more than you would normally do.

- *Play it safe with a salad.* Just be sure to order dressing that has an oil-and-vinegar base, whether French, Italian or Greek. Mayo is fine on occasion (sometimes you just can't dodge soya bean oil) as is blue cheese dressing, which is either mayo- or, preferably, soured cream–based. Ask for it on the side for portion control, and ditch any croutons.

- *Ask your server about the dressing* and pass on it if you're not satisfied with the explanation. Many ready-prepared dressings are full of sugar, cornflour or corn syrup.

- *Preview the menu.* Some restaurants post their menus online. Decide what you're going to order before you arrive so you won't be tempted to order less suitable dishes.

- *Steer clear of temptation.* If you're concerned that eating in an Indian restaurant, for example, could tempt you with longtime high-carb favourites, go somewhere else.

ON THE ROAD

Many of us live life on the run, commuting to work, driving kids to school and activities, rushing from one commitment to another. When hunger strikes, you're often at the mercy of a vending machine or snack bar that offers only sugary, starchy options. That's why it's essential to have a repertoire of portable low-carb foods that you can take on the road or on a plane. Some of our Induction-approved snack ideas such as cheese slices are suitable as are, of course, low-carb meal replacement bars and Tetra Pak shakes. One item will do as a snack, but if you're putting together a meal, you'll need to include several items. Pack each item in a separate resealable bag in an insulated bag. Here are some suggestions:

- Sliced vegetables with cream cheese
- Cheese slices or cubes
- Hard-boiled eggs
- Cooked sliced meats
- Nuts and pumpkin seeds (after first two weeks on Induction)
- Vacuum-packed tuna
- Strips of cooked chicken breast, wings or drumsticks, or sliced leftover steak

What about when you're travelling for business or pleasure? Follow our advice for eating out above. If you order from room service, specify what you *don't* want as well as what you do and have the server remove any 'offending' items that make their way into your room. A pair of plump hard rolls staring you in the face as you eat dinner in front of the plasma screen is not a good idea. Likewise, as soon as you're done, put the tray outside the door so you don't end up grazing hours later. Resist the impulse to check out the contents of the room's mini-bar. Other than bottled water, which you can get less expensively elsewhere, it's a minefield studded with sugary and starchy snacks. If you think you may give in to temptation, decline the key to the fridge or return it to the reception desk.

HOW ARE YOU DOING?

After a week or so on Induction, you should have the basics under your belt. If you're thinking, 'It's a breeze!' you've obviously already lost an impressive amount of weight and are feeling energised. Do prepare yourself for a bit of a slow down after you've lost that extra water weight you were carrying. For variety (and to avoid boredom), it's a good idea to start sampling new foods, particularly foundation vegetables, and explore new ways of preparing old favourites.

If you've been writing in your journal each day, you'll be able to see whether you've been eating enough vegetables and drinking enough fluids. You'll also begin to recognise such patterns as an afternoon slump if you're skipping your snack. If you feel hungry on a regular basis, review your protein intake; you're almost certainly not eating enough. You may have already discovered the difference between hunger and habit. If so, bravo! Some people go through life without ever learning the distinction. If you feel weak or light-headed, check on when you had your last cup of broth. If it's been more than six or eight hours, have another.

If your first week wasn't a walk in the park or the weight and waistline aren't going down as fast you'd hoped, a few small adjustments may be all you need to get into first gear. If you've had trouble changing some ingrained habits, now's the time to adjust any missteps and lay the groundwork for a whole new set of habits. This is a much harder task than losing a little weight the first week of a new diet. And we know that change doesn't happen overnight. As you move through the first three phases of Atkins, you'll have the opportunity to hone those new habits. The day will come when you can walk through the biscuit, cracker or snack food aisles or ice cream section of the supermarket without a twinge. Then you'll realise that you've banished one of your old habits. At this very moment it may be hard to believe that that day will ever come. But we promise you it will.

Changing habits is essential but you might simply be someone – and you are not alone – who no matter how faithfully she – unfortunately, this is more often a problem for women – follows the programme, will find it slow going. We profile such a person at the end of this chapter. Metabolic resistance simply means that your body is resistant to losing weight. This may be the case if you have lost and then regained weight in the recent past. If after two weeks on Induction you've lost no weight or merely the 900 grams (2 pounds) that typically constitute water weight, you need to confirm that you're actually doing everything right. It's the rare person who doesn't lose weight on Atkins, so the two most important pieces of advice we can give you are: First, be sure you're in full compliance with the programme and second, be patient. Occasionally, those first few kilograms or pounds are maddeningly slow to disappear from your life. Even if you think you're doing everything right, this quick quiz should point you in the right direction.

Were your expectations unrealistic?
If you've already lost more than 900 grams to 1.4 kilograms (2 to 3 pounds) – some of it water weight – you're on your way. From here on you'll be shedding fat. Although some people do experience more dramatic results, a loss of just a kilogram or two is definitely within the normal range. Continue with the programme and those small increments will add up.
Course correction: Readjust your expectations. After the initial few weeks, your average rate of loss could be as low as 450 to 900 grams (1 to 2 pounds) per week.

Are you eating too much protein?
Sometimes people new to Atkins take the freedom to eat ample amounts of protein to extremes. Protein is essential to fortify your body but overindulging can get in the way of fat burning and stall weight loss.
Course correction: Cut back to a maximum of 175 grams (6 ounces) at each meal (unless you're a tall man who might need a bit more) and follow the guidelines for total daily intake in Chapter 4 and you should see results.

Are you not eating enough or holding back on fat?

Strange as it sounds, eating too little or skipping meals can slow down your metabolism. Eat three meals a day, or if you simply aren't hungry, have a small snack that includes fat and protein. Once you're eating sufficient quantities of both, you should start shedding weight. If your calorie intake dips too low, your metabolism slows to preserve your body's organs and muscle mass.

Course correction: Follow the guidelines on fat intake to ensure that you're getting enough energy to maintain your metabolic rate. Don't follow a low-carb, low-fat diet unless supervised by a medical professional!

Are you eating too many calories?

Although you don't have to count calories on Atkins, if you're overdoing the protein and fat you may be taking in too many calories. We know we said that you don't have to count calories on Atkins, and the vast majority of people don't, but you may need a reality check.

Course correction: See 'Savour, Don't Smother' on page 69 and refer to the recommended protein ranges on page 51. Women should aim for a range of 1,500 to 1,800 calories a day, while men should aim for 1,800 to 2,200. Eat less if you're not losing weight. If you're accustomed to counting calories, you'll know what your range is. If not, a spot check at www.fitday.com will tell you whether or not you're in the correct range. (If you're losing weight nicely, don't worry about calories.)

Are you counting grams of Net Carbs?

If you're just estimating, you may well be consuming too many carbs.

Course correction: Note the carb content of each item you eat in your diet journal. If you're right at about 20 grams (0.7 ounces) of Net Carbs and not losing weight, make sure that you're not exceeding the recommended protein portions.

Are you eating 12 to 15 of your carb grams (0.4 to 0.5 ounces) in the form of foundation vegetables?

If you're not, you may be constipated, which will obviously impact the numbers on your scales and tape measure. The fibre and moisture in vegetables also help you to feel full so you eat less.

Course correction: To learn how to incorporate more foundation vegetables into your meals, see 'The Vegetable Challenge' on page 117.

Are you consuming hidden carbs?

Unless you're reading the labels on all sauces, condiments, beverages and ready-prepared products, you might be unaware that you're consuming added sugars and other carbs. And do they add up fast!

Course correction: Eat nothing that you're not 100 per cent sure contains no hidden carbs.

Are you overdoing low-carb shakes and bars?

The limit is two a day in Induction for products with no more than 3 grams (0.1 ounces) of Net Carbs.

Course correction: If you're having three or more shakes and/or bars a day, cut back to two. (This almost certainly means that you're not eating enough vegetables.) If you're eating two, cut back to one.

Are you using more than three packets a day of non-caloric sweeteners?

Sweeteners themselves contain no carbs, but they're made with a powdered agent to prevent clumping, which contains somewhat less than 1 gram (0.04 ounces) of carbohydrate per packet. Those small amounts can add up all too quickly when your total is 20 grams (0.7 ounces) a day.

Course correction: Cut back to three packets. If that doesn't work, cut out any fizzy drinks sweetened with non-caloric sweeteners.

Are you really, truly drinking at least eight 240-millitre (8-fluid-ounce) glasses of water and other fluids?

Fluid helps you feel full, so you're less likely to overeat.

Course correction: Keep track of your fluid intake, and aim for a minimum of 1.9 litres (3.3 pints).

Are you skipping meals and then getting ravenous before the next meal?

One reason we recommend a mid-morning and mid-afternoon snack is to keep you from getting so hungry that you lose the internal gauge that alerts you when you've eaten enough.

Course correction: Eat three meals and two snacks to keep your appetite under control.

Are you taking over-the-counter medicines that could slow your weight loss?

Non-steroidal anti-inflammatory drugs (NSAIDs), including aspirin, ibuprofen, naproxen and ketoprofen cause water retention and may block fat burning. Other over-the-counter medicines can also interfere with weight loss.

Course correction: Cut back on these medicines if possible. If you need further pain relief, use paracetamol, which is not an NSAID. Your doctor may be able to suggest alternative anti-inflammatory remedies.

Are you taking prescription medications that could slow weight loss?

There are many pharmaceuticals that can interfere with weight loss. They include oestrogens in hormone-replacement therapies and birth-control pills, many antidepressants, insulin and insulin-stimulating drugs, anti-arthritis drugs (including steroids), diuretics and beta-blockers.

Course correction: Speak to your doctor about whether or not you can use another prescription drug. Caution: Do not stop or reduce the dosage of any drugs without medical consultation.

Are you under stress?

Stress plays a profound role in weight-loss efforts. When you produce a lot of the stress hormone cortisol, your body releases more insulin to buffer its effects. Insulin, as you now know, is the fat-storing hormone, and it deposits fat around the waist first. Insulin also causes sodium retention, which in turn makes you hold water. If your waist is as large as or larger than your hips, you may be particularly sensitive to cortisol, which is one reason why we recommend you take your measurements before you begin Atkins.

Course correction: Meditation, biofeedback, low-intensity exercise and yoga are all known stress reducers.

OTHER MEASURES OF SUCCESS

What if you're not losing weight – or have lost very little – but have carefully reviewed all the questions and answers above and can honestly say that none apply to you? You may have not had any extra water (bloating) to start with and therefore didn't experience the usual water weight loss. But sometimes there's no explanation for slow weight loss. Your body has its own agenda and timetable. It isn't a duplicate of anyone else's body. In the long run, it nearly always responds to sensible management, but in the short run, it may decide to go its own way for its own inexplicable reasons. Be patient. You can outwait it. After the first few weeks, you'll have adapted to the diet by switching your metabolism to burning fat and will start to lose weight.

Remember, too, that whittling off weight is not the only way to measure success. Look at the other markers. Are you feeling better than you used to? Do you have more energy? If so, good things are happening to your body. Have you tried on those clothes that felt a little too tight just a few weeks ago and found them looser? Hopefully, you've followed our advice about measuring your chest, waist, hips, thighs and upper arms. If you're reducing your circumference, the scales will eventually catch up. It's a mistake to ignore this advice. You may be losing weight but building a little muscle. If so, that's great news. Your clothes will fit better and soon the scales will catch up with the measuring tape.

Increasing your activity may be helpful as you move through the phases. Continue to take it easy in the first two weeks of Induction, but if you stay in this phase longer, you may decide that it's time to get moving. If you've been a bona fide couch potato for years, take it slowly. Perhaps a short walk around the neighbourhood after dinner is all you can manage now, but even small efforts can add up. If exercise has been an asset for you in the past, it's time to switch to the 'on' button for good. If you've always been active, think about ramping up your activity level a bit as your weight comes down. Many of you will find Atkins and exercise naturally complement each other.

READY TO MOVE ON? IT'S UP TO YOU

By the end of your second week on Induction, it's decision time. Even if you got off to a rocky start, by the end of the second week you should have corrected any missteps and your results will show it. You should be reducing your weight and waistline – although perhaps not as fast as you had hoped – and feeling energised. After the first week, low energy is very often a sign that you are not regularly consuming enough salt. Review the paragraphs about how to address sodium depletion in the previous chapter. Getting adequate salt also eliminates or minimises other symptoms that may accompany switching to fat metabolism.

If you're not feeling satisfied with your meals and snacks, you're probably not eating enough protein and/or fat. Again the combination will moderate your appetite and boost your energy level. You may also be missing the filling benefit of fibre if you're not eating the recommended amount of foundation vegetables. Skipping meals or snacks may also increase the likelihood of giving in to cravings for sugary, starchy and other unacceptable foods. As you now know, sugars and refined carbs block fat burning.

You know what to do. So just do it. Let go of the carbs! Instead of saying that Atkins is too restrictive, explore the great foods you can eat and fill yourself up so hunger doesn't overtake your good intentions. If you can stick to the programme for just two weeks, you'll experience the Atkins Edge. Among its other beneficial effects, burning fat for energy moderates hunger and cravings. Without it, it's unlikely that you'll be able to realise your dream of a healthier, slimmer body.

DECISION TIME

Based upon your experience in the last two weeks plus your weight goal, you've come to one of the forks in the road. It's time to decide whether to stay in Induction or move on to Phase 2: Ongoing Weight Loss, or even to Phase 3: Pre-Maintenance. Having a large amount of weight to lose is a common reason to stay longer in Induction, as you'll lose a bit more quickly and consistently in this phase than in subsequent ones. If you're content for now with the Induction food choices, you should consider staying put. But as always, the choice is yours. On the other hand, if you're close to your goal weight, losing very quickly or being tempted to stray because of limited food choices it's time to move to OWL.

Don't make the mistake of staying in Induction too long just because you love how the weight is peeling off. Eventually, it's important to move through the phases to ensure that you have cured yourself of your old habits and can reintroduce foods without halting your weight loss or provoking cravings. Losing weight fast is exhilarating, but it will likely be a temporary fix if you don't find your comfort zone for eating in the 'real world'. Deliberately slowing your rate of weight loss as you approach your goal will make it easier to make the lost weight history – permanently. You needn't worry about any health risks of staying in Induction, but you do need to work on moving up the ladder so you can find your tolerance for carbs, whether it's 30, 50, 60 or more grams a day.

Move to OWL if . . .

- You're already within 7 kilograms (1 stone) of your goal weight. It's important for you to move on to learn a new permanent way of eating.
- You're bored with your current food choices.
- You've been in Induction for several months and are more than halfway to your goal. Again it's important for most people to cycle through the phases.

You may choose to stay in Induction if . . .

- You still have more than 14 kilograms (2 stones) to lose.

You should stay in Induction for now if . . .

- You still have a large amount of weight to lose.
- You're still struggling with carb cravings.
- You have not been fully compliant with Induction.

- If you still have elevated blood sugar or blood pressure levels.
- Your weight loss is slow and you aren't physically active.

Move on to Pre-Maintenance if . . .

- You're within 4.5 kilograms (10 pounds) of your goal weight and still losing at a brisk pace.

BEYOND TWO WEEKS

If you do choose to stay put in Induction, you'll remain at 20 grams (0.7 ounces) of Net Carbs a day, but you can add nuts and seeds to your list of acceptable foods. A couple of tablespoons (30 grams/1 ounce) of walnuts, almonds, pecans, pumpkin seeds or other seeds or nuts makes a great snack. Or sprinkle them on a salad or cooked vegetables.

After two weeks, assuming that you're feeling well, many of you should be considering incorporating physical activity into your programme if you've not already done so. A regular walking programme is a great way to begin. Once you get into the habit, you'll realise the benefits in terms of toning your body and improving your mood. Finally, remember to keep your diet (and fitness) journal up to date, tracking foods as you add them back to spot any problems.

As you say goodbye to Induction, turn the page to learn how to move to Phase 2: Ongoing Weight Loss. Even if you're moving directly to Pre-Maintenance, it's important for you to review the content on OWL. But first, read on the next page about Rebecca Latham's success with Atkins after trying numerous other diets.

SUCCESS STORY 7

HUNGRY NO MORE

After eating at 'starvation level' for decades without being able to lose weight, Rebecca Latham decided to join her husband on the Atkins Diet. Unusually resistant to weight loss, she is finally seeing results and closing in on her goal weight.

VITAL STATISTICS

Current Phase: Pre-Maintenance
Daily Net Carb intake: 25 grams
 (0.9 ounces)
Age: 54
Height: 160 cm (5 ft 3 in)
Before weight: 68 kg (10.7 stones)

Current weight: 63.5 kg (10 stones)
Weight loss: 4.5 kg (10 pounds)
Goal weight: 55 kg (9.3 stones)
Former BMI: 26.6
Current BMI: 24.8
Current blood pressure: 120/80

What made you decide to do Atkins?
When my husband was diagnosed with metabolic syndrome, our doctor recommended the Atkins Diet and I decided to join him. I'd started gaining weight at thirty years old and over the next twenty years slowly put on 18 kilograms (2.9 stones).

Did you have any relevant health issues?
I have oestrogen dominance and an underactive thyroid. Although there's heart disease and diabetes in my family, my lipids and other health markers were always normal.

Have you tried other weight-loss programmes?
You name it, I've tried it! I've suffered through numerous diet programmes. My husband and I were doing 'The Zone'

just before we began Atkins. We'd both just lost about a kilogram (2.2 pounds), but we were starving!

Had you done Atkins before?
Yes, years ago, but now I know that I was doing it incorrectly. I was eating no vegetables, and I kept cutting calories until I was down to 1,000 and then I quit.

So what was different this time?
I read a few Atkins books, as well as *Good Calories, Bad Calories* by Gary Taubes, which was influential in getting me to try Atkins again. I found out at www.atkins.com that severely limiting calories would make me stop losing. I know I would have failed again without the support of the Atkins Community forum. I also now know that even though weight loss may happen slowly, a reduced waistline also indicates success. I've lost almost 12.5 centimetres (5 inches) at my navel alone!

How did you customise Atkins to your needs?
My hormonal imbalance and hypothyroidism made it extremely difficult to lose weight. So Atkins nutritionist Colette Heimowitz gave me a modified version of Induction to follow. I started at 11 grams (0.4 ounces) of Net Carbs, with 8 of them coming from foundation vegetables. Now that I'm in Pre-Maintenance, I'm at 25 grams (0.9 ounces) of Net Carbs, with at least 15 of them coming from vegetables. Occasionally, I also eat nuts, berries, yoghurt, apple sauce and pulses.

What is your fitness regimen?
I started walking and lifting weights about three weeks after starting Atkins. When I started, my muscles were wasted and

I was very weak. My doctor had told me to lose 15.9 kilograms (2.5 stones) of fat and to gain 4.5 kilograms (10 pounds) of muscle. When I reached 63.5 kilograms (10 stones), the 4.5 kilograms (10 pounds) I'd lost actually represented the loss of almost 7.7 kilograms (1.2 stones) of fat and the gain of almost 3.2 kilograms (7 pounds) of muscle!

Chapter 8

MOVING TO PHASE 2: ONGOING WEIGHT LOSS

Initially, the differences between Induction and Ongoing Weight Loss (OWL) are relatively minor, but the gradual additions to your diet mark the beginning of your return to a permanent way of eating. Your objective in OWL is to find how many carbs you can consume while continuing to lose weight, keep your appetite under control and feel energised.

Welcome to Phase 2: Ongoing Weight Loss, or OWL to Atkins insiders. Initially, the differences between phases 1 and 2 are relatively minor, but the gradual additions to your diet mark the beginning of the return to a permanent way of eating. Everything else remains the same as in Induction. You'll count Net Carbs. You'll eat the recommended amounts of protein and plenty of natural fats. You'll continue to drink about eight glasses of water and other acceptable fluids and make sure that you're getting enough salt (assuming that you don't take diuretic medications). And you'll continue with your multivitamin/multimineral and omega-3 supplements.

There is, however, one key distinction between the two phases: the slightly broader array of acceptable foods in Ongoing Weight Loss. Still, despite eating more carbs and gradually introducing a greater variety of them, it's best to regard these two changes as baby steps. Perhaps the biggest mistake you can make when you move from Induction to OWL is to regard the transition as dramatic.

Most people spend the majority of their (weight-loss) time in this phase. Unless you have just a little weight to lose and plan to be on your way quickly to Phase 3: Pre-Maintenance, you'll have plenty of time to get familiar with Ongoing Weight Loss. We recommend that you stay here until you're only 4.5 kilograms (10 pounds) from your goal weight. If you're beginning your Atkins journey in this phase, be sure to read the previous chapters on Induction, which are key to understanding much of OWL and preparing properly before beginning the programme.

In this chapter, in addition to helping you transition to this phase, we'll look at how to:

- Gradually increase your carb intake in 5-gram (0.18-ounce) increments without stopping weight loss and/or prompting the return of old symptoms.
- Reintroduce foods in a certain order.
- Address challenges such as plateaus and carb creep.
- Find your personal tolerance for carb consumption in this phase, known as your Carbohydrate Level for Losing (CLL).
- Integrate physical fitness into your weight control programme.
- Customise OWL to suit your needs.

LEARN THE LINGO

Newcomers to Atkins are sometimes confused by abbreviations tossed around by insiders. Here's how to translate them:

NET CARBS: Generally grams of total carbohydrates minus grams of fibre.

OWL: Ongoing Weight Loss, Phase 2 of Atkins.

CLL: Carbohydrate Level for Losing, the maximum number of grams of Net Carbs you can eat each day and continue to lose weight.

ACE: Atkins Carbohydrate Equilibrium, the maximum number of grams of Net Carbs you can eat each day and maintain your weight.

TRANSITION JITTERS

Before we describe exactly how to do Ongoing Weight Loss, let's address an important issue. With the freedom to choose among more carbohydrate foods comes the risk of getting out of your safety zone. After holding yourself back in Induction, you may be afraid that you'll go too far in OWL. Undoubtedly, this is one reason why some people have a hard time weaning themselves away from Induction. Furthermore, by the time you get to OWL, your initial enthusiasm may be flagging slightly and you may find it harder to focus on the work that remains. You're not alone. We'll hold your hand every step of the way. You can always backtrack a bit if a new food causes a problem. Let's take a moment to put your transition in perspective.

Are you daunted by what still remains ahead?
Of course you are. If you're on the plump side, it took a while to pad your body by eating the wrong foods. If you're struggling with health issues, they didn't occur overnight, either. As the hare in Aesop's fable learnt in his race with the turtle, slow and steady wins the race. Learn to celebrate your small and incremental victories instead of focusing only on the ultimate goal.

Are you using all the tools and help available?
Writing in your journal and reviewing it a few days later can often offer valuable perspectives. That seeming regain of a half a kilogram (a pound) or so suddenly isn't so bad a week later, when you've re-lost it along with another kilogram (or a couple of pounds). Having a friend and/or tapping into the online support network on www.atkins.com can also prove invaluable when you need a shoulder to cry on or a platform to let off steam.

Do you have more energy than before you started Atkins?
If you're eating enough protein, fat, vegetables and salt, you
should be bursting with energy. If not, once again we remind you
not to skip meals or skimp on protein. To maintain your energy
if you're middle-aged or older, you may need to increase your
protein intake within the recommended range for your height by
eating a bit more meat, poultry and fish. Cutting out sugars and
other poor-quality carbohydrates should also have eliminated
that all-too-common affliction, the mid-afternoon slump. If
you've started exercising or increased your physical activity
recently, you've probably also noticed that both your energy
level and endurance have increased.

How about your moods?
Most Atkins followers report a sense of exhilaration along with
increased energy during or shortly after the first few weeks on
Atkins. That's another benefit of the Atkins Edge. Hopefully
you're also experiencing a whole complex of positive emotions
about other changes you can make in your life. Physical activity
is a known mood enhancer as well. That's not to say that you
probably haven't battled temptation and perhaps occasionally
succumbed to it. We're willing to bet that on at least one occasion you've found yourself in a situation where there was nothing
you could eat. At such times when the scales and the measuring
tape just won't budge or seem headed in the wrong direction,
you may have wondered whether this new lifestyle is worth it.
All of this is perfectly normal. The mere fact that you're now
transitioning to OWL is proof of your success to date.

BEGINNING IN OWL
If you've decided to start in OWL, rather than Induction, you
presumably have one or more of these reasons:

- You're 7 kilograms (1 stone) or less from your goal weight.
- Your weight loss goal is modest and you're physically very active.
- No matter what your current weight is, you want more variety in your diet than Induction offers and are willing to lose weight a bit more slowly.
- You're a vegetarian or a vegan.
- Weight isn't an issue, but you want to feel better and have more energy.

HOW TO DO OWL

Initially, you'll increase your daily carb intake by just 5 grams to 25 grams (0.18 to 0.9 ounces) of Net Carbs and then gradually move up in 5-gram (0.18-ounce) increments, slowly building upon your Induction carbohydrate food choices. In addition to the Acceptable Induction Foods (page 99), you can now begin to select foods from the Acceptable Foods for OWL below. (Be sure to also check out the meal plans for Phase 2 in Part III, which incorporate many of them.) Our recommendation is that you add nuts and seeds first, then berries and a few other fruits, then additional dairy choices and only then pulses. Those of you who remained in Induction beyond the first two weeks are probably already enjoying the satisfying crunch of walnuts, almonds, pumpkin seeds, pine kernels and such. But if the sweetness of a few berries (with the emphasis on *few*) matters more to you than a few nuts, rearrange the order to suit your preferences. We call these different food groups the rungs on the carb ladder. (See the sidebar 'The Carb Ladder.') Later, we'll address the needs of those who want to limit their intake of animal protein or omit it altogether or are interested in a Latino culinary heritage.

Add only one new food within a certain group at a time. That way if something reawakens food cravings, causes gastric distress or interferes with your weight-loss journey, you can easily identify it. So, for example, you might start with a small portion of blueberries one week. Assuming that they cause no problems, you could then move on to strawberries in a day or two.

THE CARB LADDER

The carb ladder assists you in two ways. First, it provides a logical progression with which to add carbohydrate foods. Secondly, it prioritises their amount and frequency. On the lower rungs are the foods you should be eating most often. On the top rungs are the foods that – even in Lifetime Maintenance – will put in an appearance only occasionally, rarely or never depending upon your tolerance for carbs.

Rung 1: Foundation vegetables: leafy greens and other low-carb vegetables

Rung 2: Dairy foods high in fat and low in carbs: cream, soured cream and most hard cheeses

Rung 3: Nuts and seeds (but not chestnuts)

Rung 4: Berries, cherries and melon (but not watermelon)

Rung 5: Whole milk yoghurt and fresh cheeses, such as cottage cheese and ricotta

Rung 6: Pulses including chickpeas, lentils and so on

Rung 7: Tomato and vegetable juice 'cocktail' (plus more lemon and lime juice)

Rung 8: Other fruits (but not fruit juices or dried fruits)

Rung 9: Higher-carb vegetables such as winter squash, carrots and peas

Rung 10: Whole grains

REALISTIC EXPECTATIONS

If you shed kilograms quickly on Induction, be aware that this reliable and exhilarating pace won't continue indefinitely. Your average weekly loss will almost certainly slow as you increase your carb intake and your weight drops. This is deliberate as you gradually add more carbohydrates in greater variety and slowly adopt a new, sustainable way of eating. You may find the path ahead much like driving in heavy traffic: you'll crawl along at a snail's pace for a few miles, perhaps picking up speed for a while and then stopping, slowing and so forth. This bumpy progress will try your patience no doubt, but knowing that it's not unusual should help you to cope. We'll revisit how you may be able to influence your progress below.

HOW TO REINTRODUCE CERTAIN FOODS

There are three important points to understand as you begin to reintroduce foods. First, if you've been estimating carb counts, now is the time to start counting them. Second, you're increasing your range of foods but not the *amount* of food that you're eating day to day by very much. As you continue to add small amounts of carbohydrate foods, you don't have to do anything other than make sure you're not overdoing your protein intake. Let your appetite be your guide. Stay hydrated, and the moment you feel you've had enough, stop eating. If you've always been a member of the clean-plate club now is the time to resign. Or dish out less from the start. Finally, not everyone will necessarily be able to reintroduce all the acceptable foods for this phase; some will be able to eat them only rarely.

As you add new foods, you'll substitute some of them for other carb foods you're already eating, but not your 12 to 15 grams (0.4 to 0.5 ounces) of Net Carbs from foundation vegetables. For example, you can now have cottage cheese in lieu of some of the hard cheese you've been eating in Induction. Instead of an afternoon snack of green olives, you might switch to macadamias. You'll still be eating those Induction-friendly foods but you can branch out a bit. As long as you're tracking your carb intake, eating the recommended amount of vegetables and feeling full but not stuffed, you should do fine. Your protein portions at each meal should remain within the roughly 115-to-175-gram (4-to-6-ounce) range.

We can't stress enough that writing in your diet journal is particularly important as you start to add foods back in. This process doesn't always happen smoothly, and you'll want to know which food is causing which response, so if necessary you know which to keep away from. Keep on noting what you're adding, how much and your reactions, if any.

ACCEPTABLE FOODS FOR OWL
NUTS AND SEEDS

Most people start by reintroducing nuts and seeds and butters made from them. Avoid honey-roasted and smoked products. About 30–55 grams (1–2 ounces) of walnuts, pecans or pumpkin seeds makes a perfect snack. (The listing below provides portions equivalent to 30 grams/1 ounce.) Or sprinkle them over salads or cottage cheese. Salted nuts are fine, but understand that they can be notoriously difficult to eat in moderation. Store nuts and seeds in the fridge or freezer to avoid rancidity. Peanuts, cashews and roasted soya beans ('soya nuts') are not true nuts. The latter two are higher in carbs than true nuts, so go easy on them. (Chestnuts are very starchy and high in carbs, making them unsuitable for OWL.) Heart-healthy fibre helps to moderate the carb counts of nuts and seeds, but their healthy fats make them all high in calories, so keep your intake to no more than 55 grams (2 ounces) a day. Almond, macadamia and other nut or seed butters are a great alternative to peanut butter, but avoid products such as Nutella that include sugar or other sweeteners. Nut meals and flours broaden your cooking options.

Tip: When you buy a large packet of nuts or seeds, divide it into 30-gram (1-ounce) servings; place them in small resealable bags and store in the freezer. There's no need to weigh anything; if it's a 450-gram (1-pound) bag, simply divide the contents into sixteen equal portions. When you're ready for a nut snack, consume one – and only one – bag. Or count out the suitable number of a particular kind of nut, following the portion guidelines below, and return the rest of the bag or container to the fridge. Nut portions are approximately 30 grams (1 ounce), but the size of each kind of nut can vary considerably, so adjust accordingly.

Nut or Seed	Serving Size	Grams of Net Carbs
Almonds	24 nuts	2.3
Almond butter	1 tablespoon	2.5
Almonds, ground	4 tablespoons	3.0
Brazil nuts	5 nuts	2.0
Cashews	9 nuts	4.4
Cashew butter	1 tablespoon	4.1
Coconut, shredded unsweetened	¼ cup	1.3
Macadamias	6 nuts	2.0
Macadamia butter	1 tablespoon	2.5
Hazelnuts	12 nuts	0.5
Peanuts	22 nuts	1.5
Peanut butter, natural	1 tablespoon	2.4
Peanut butter, smooth	1 tablespoon	2.2
Pecans	10 halves	1.5
Pine kernels (piñons)	2 tablespoons	1.7
Pistachios	25 nuts	2.5
Pumpkin seeds, hulled	2 tablespoons	2.0
Sesame seeds	2 tablespoons	1.6
Soya 'nuts'	2 tablespoons	2.7
Soya 'nut' butter	1 tablespoon	3.0
Sunflower seeds, hulled	2 tablespoons	1.1

Nut or Seed	Serving Size	Grams of Net Carbs
Sunflower seed butter	1 tablespoon	0.5
Tahini (sesame paste)	1 tablespoon	0.8
Walnuts	7 halves	1.5

BERRIES AND OTHER FRUITS

There's a good reason why the first (sweet) fruits you'll add back are berries. They're relatively high in fibre – the seeds help – which lowers their Net Carb gram count. They're also packed with vitamins and antioxidants. The brighter the colour of a fruit or vegetable, the higher its antioxidant level. And what could be bolder than the blue, black and red of most berries? Melon (but not watermelon) and cherries are slightly higher in carbs than most berries. Eat them in moderation – and only after introducing berries – to ensure that they don't stimulate cravings for more sweet things. All fruits should be regarded as garnishes, not major components of a meal or snack.

Have fresh berries with a little cheese, cream, soured cream or whole-milk yoghurt to mute the impact on your blood sugar. Add some berries to a breakfast smoothie. Toss them into a green salad or blend them into a vinaigrette dressing. You may also have small (1-tablespoon) portions of preserves made without added sugar. Each tablespoon should provide no more than 2 grams (0.7 ounces) of Net Carbs.

Fruit	Serving Size	Grams of Net Carbs
Blackberries, fresh	36 g (1.3 oz)	2.7
Blackberries, frozen	38 g (1.3 oz)	4.1
Blueberries, fresh	37 g (1.3 oz)	4.1
Blueberries, frozen	39 g (1.4 oz)	3.7
Boysenberries, fresh	31 g (1.1 oz)	2.7
Boysenberries, frozen	33 g (1.2 oz)	2.8
Cherries, sour, fresh	39 g (1.4 oz)	2.8

Fruit	Serving Size	Grams of Net Carbs
Cherries, sweet, fresh	35 g (1.2 oz)	4.2
Cranberries, raw	28 g (1 oz)	2.0
Currants, fresh	28 g (1 oz)	2.5
Gooseberries, raw	75 g (2.6 oz)	4.4
Loganberries, raw	36 g (1.3 oz)	2.7
Melon, cantaloupe balls	44 g (1.6 oz)	3.7
Melon, Crenshaw balls	44 g (1.6 oz)	2.3
Melon, honeydew balls	44 g (1.6 oz)	3.6
Raspberries, fresh	31 g (1.1 oz)	1.5
Raspberries, frozen	62 g (2.2 oz)	1.8
Strawberries, fresh, sliced	42 g (1.5 oz)	1.8
Strawberries, frozen	55 g (2 oz)	2.6
Strawberry, fresh	1 large	1.0

CHEESE AND DAIRY PRODUCTS

You can now also reintroduce the remaining fresh cheeses, which are slightly higher in carbs than the ones you could eat in Induction. A 115-gram (4-ounce) portion of either cottage cheese or ricotta with 30–55 grams (1–2 ounces) of nuts provides plenty of protein for one meal. Avoid low-fat and fat-free cottage cheese and ricotta products, which are higher in carbs. Top some salad leaves with either one for a quick lunch or some berries for breakfast. Yoghurt lovers can now savour natural, unsweetened, whole-milk yoghurt. Greek yogurt is even lower in carbs. Do make sure you buy the 'original' whole-milk, unflavoured kind. Sprinkle on some sweetener or stir in a tablespoon of sugar-free fruit syrup or no-added-sugar preserves if you prefer. Berries, either fresh or frozen, and yoghurt are natural partners. But steer clear of processed yoghurt made with fruit or other flavourings or with any added sugar. Likewise, avoid low-fat and non-fat yoghurt products, which invariably deliver a bigger carb hit. Once more with feeling: 'low calorie' doesn't necessarily mean low carb.

Cheese or Dairy Product	Serving Size	Grams of Net Carbs
Cottage cheese, 2% fat	115 g (4 oz)	4.1
Cottage cheese, creamed	115 g (4 oz)	2.8
Milk, whole, evaporated	2 tablespoons	3.0
Ricotta, whole milk	115 g (4 oz)	3.8
Yoghurt, low carb	115 g (4 oz)	3.0
Yoghurt, natural, unsweetened, whole-milk	115 g (4 oz)	5.5
Yoghurt, Greek, natural, unsweetened whole-milk	115 g (4 oz)	3.5

PULSES

Most members of the bean family, including lentils, chickpeas, soya beans, split peas, navy beans, black beans and dozens of others (but not snap beans or mangetout, which are fine in Induction) are known as pulses. Many of them are dried; a few, such as butter beans and edamame, are also available fresh or frozen. Vegans and many vegetarians rely on pulses to help meet their protein needs. Their high fibre and protein content make pulses filling. Despite their fibre, they're significantly higher in carbs than the foundation vegetables you've been eating in Induction. There's also a wide range in their carb counts as you'll see below. If and when you do begin to reintroduce pulses, use small portions and regard them as a garnish. Avoid baked beans, which are full of sugar, and other products such as beans in tomato sauce with sugar or starches and bean dips. Always check carb counts and the ingredients list before purchasing any product.

Tip: Black soya beans are far lower in carbs than black (or turtle) beans [1 gram of Net Carbs per 85 grams (3 ounces) of cooked beans, compared to 12.9 grams for black beans], with no trade-off in taste.

Pulse	Serving Size	Grams of Net Carbs
Black beans	45 g (1.6 oz)	6.5
Black-eyed beans	45 g (1.6 oz)	6.2
Borlotti beans	45 g (1.6 oz)	6.3
Broad beans	45 g (1.6 oz)	6.0
Butter beans	45 g (1.6 oz)	6.5
Cannellini beans	45 g (1.6 oz)	8.5
Chickpeas	45 g (1.6 oz)	6.5
Great Northern beans	45 g (1.6 oz)	6.3
Haricot beans	45 g (1.6 oz)	9.1
Hummus	2 tablespoons	4.6
Kidney beans	45 g (1.6 oz)	5.8
Lentils	50 g (1.8 oz)	6.0
Peas, split	50 g (1.8 oz)	6.3
Pigeon peas (red gram)	45 g (1.6 oz)	7.0
Pinto beans	45 g (1.6 oz)	7.3
Refried beans, tinned	60 g (2 oz)	6.5
Soya beans, black	90 g (3 oz)	1.0
Soya beans, green edamame	40 g (1.4 oz)	3.1

Note: Serving sizes for dried pulses are after cooking. Serving sizes for fresh pulses are for shelled beans.

VEGETABLE AND FRUIT JUICES

Most fruit juices might as well be liquid sugar, making them completely off-limits. The exceptions are lemon and lime juice, a couple of tablespoons of which are acceptable each day in Induction. In OWL you can double that amount to serve over fish or make beverages or low-carb desserts. It's amazing how much flavour you can get from 4 tablespoons of these juices, but that amount does contain more than 5 grams (0.18 ounces) of Net Carbs. You can now also introduce small portions of tomato juice or tomato juice cocktail.

Juices	Serving Size	Grams of Net Carbs
Lemon juice	4 tablespoons	5.2
Lime juice	4 tablespoons	5.6
Tomato juice	125 ml (4 fl oz)	4.2
Tomato juice cocktail	125 ml (4 fl oz)	4.5

LOW-CARB PRODUCTS SUITABLE FOR OWL

Not all low-carb foods are created equal. Manufacturers use a host of different sweeteners and other ingredients, some of which may give you gastric distress, tempt you to overeat or reawaken cravings you thought you'd put to rest. In addition to the bars and shakes you can enjoy in Induction, you may be able to handle some other low-carb products in OWL. In each case we've provided the maximum acceptable carb count for a single serving. Always read the Nutrition Facts panel and list of ingredients before purchasing any product. Any sweet or salty food may stimulate you to overindulge. Deluding yourself that you can eat large quantities of a certain food just because a small portion of it is low in carbs is, well, delusional. Purchase and use these products with care. Low-carb products can be very convenient, but they're no substitute for vegetables and other unprocessed foods. Try products one at a time and limit yourself to two servings a day of such foods. Again, if the carb count of a specific product exceeds the amount listed below, pass it up.

Low-Carb Product	Serving	Maximum Grams of Net Carbs
Low-carb bagels	1	5.0
Low-carb bake mix	¾ cup	5.0
Low-carb bread	1 slice	6.0
Low-carb chocolate/sweets	34 g (1.2 oz)	3.0
Low-carb dairy drink	250 ml (8 fl oz)	4.0
Low-carb pancake mix	2 pancakes	6.0
Low-carb pitta	One 15-cm (6-in)	4.0

Low-Carb Product	Serving	Maximum Grams of Net Carbs
Low-carb bread rolls	1	4.0
Low-carb soya chips	28 g (1 oz)	5.0
Low-carb tortillas	One 18-cm (7-in)	4.0
No-added-sugar ice cream	70 g (2.5 oz)	4.0

TO YOUR HEALTH – IN MODERATION

Say cheers! Now that you're in OWL, you can have alcohol if you wish – if experience shows that you can handle it. There are several things to consider about consuming alcohol while losing weight. Most mixers, including tonic water, are incredibly high in carbs, especially any made with fruit juice. (Sugar-free tonic water is acceptable.) So are flavoured brandy and other liqueurs (although aged brandy and Cognac are low in sugar). Although most spirits contain no carbs, your body will metabolise alcohol before fat (in this respect, alcohol is a macronutrient), so drinking slows down fat burning and may slow your weight loss. And, of course, be sure to count the carbs.

Drink alcohol neat or on the rocks with a lemon twist. A 350-millilitre (12-fluid-ounce) serving of regular beer contains up to 13 grams (0.5 ounces) of carbs, which is clearly too high for OWL. A single light beer or, better yet, low-carb beer should be your brew of choice in this phase, and keep it to one. A glass of wine with dinner can make a basic meal a special occasion, but steer clear of sugary wine coolers and sweet dessert wines. You may find that you're more susceptible to the effects of alcohol while doing Atkins. And because alcohol can make you drop your inhibitions, you may find it more difficult to stay away from crisps and other high-carb snack foods that often accompany alcohol. For all these reasons, the best advice we can give you is to go easy. If you have trouble reining yourself in, you might be better off avoiding alcohol until you're more in control.

Beverage	Serving Size	Grams of Net Carbs
Beer, 'light'	350 ml (12 fl oz)	7.0
Beer, low-carb	350 ml (12 fl oz)	3.0
Bourbon	30 ml (1 fl oz)	0.0
Champagne	125 ml (4 fl oz)	4.0

Beverage	Serving Size	Grams of Net Carbs
Gin	30 ml (1 fl oz)	0.0
Mixers, sugar-free	1 serving	4.0
Rum	30 ml (1 fl oz)	0.0
Scotch	30 ml (1 fl oz)	0.0
Sherry, dry	50 ml (2 fl oz)	2.0
Vodka	30 ml (1 fl oz)	0.0
Wine, dry dessert	100 ml (3.5 fl oz)	4.0
Wine, red	100 ml (3.5 fl oz)	2.0
Wine, white	100 ml (3.5 fl oz)	1.0

TROUBLESHOOTING

Sooner or later almost everyone finds that his/her weight loss temporarily halts. As you become increasingly accustomed to eating the low-carb way, it's all too easy to get sloppy about tracking your carbs. Instead of the 35 grams (1.2 ounces) of Net Carbs you *think* you're consuming, for example, you might actually be closer to 55 (or even 75). Whether as a result of sloppiness, cockiness, overconfidence or testing the limits, 'carb creep' can stop weight loss in its tracks. Worse, you may lose your body's adaptation to burning primarily fat – the Atkins Edge. It's tempting to call this a plateau. But the first thing you should do is to look carefully at your recent behaviour and make corrections if necessary. Ask yourself these questions:

- Have you truly been eating the right foods, or have you been tempting fate with inappropriate ones? Eliminate any questionable foods.
- Are you actually counting carbs? If you've been careless or stopped counting, go back to the carb level at which you were losing weight and remain there until weight loss resumes.
- Have you been too enthusiastic about adding back fruits? If so, eliminate fruits other than berries, and if necessary cut back on your berry portions.

- Are you eating excessive amounts of protein? Cut back to the mid-range for your height but maintain your intake of fat.

HITTING A PLATEAU

The pace of weight loss is always erratic, but the definition of a plateau is when you lose nothing despite doing everything right over a period of at least *four* weeks. If your clothes are fitting better and you've lost centimetres, if not weight, you're not truly on a plateau. Keep on doing what you're doing. A plateau can try the patience of a saint. But patience is exactly what you need plenty of. To get things moving by, in addition to the suggestions above, trying some or all of these modifications:

- Tighten up your journal discipline. Write everything down.
- Decrease your daily intake of Net Carbs by 10 grams (0.35 ounces). You may have exceeded your tolerance for carbs while losing and inadvertently stumbled upon your tolerance for maintaining your new weight. Once weight loss resumes, move up in 5-gram (0.18-ounce) increments again.
- Count all your carbs, including lemon juice, sweeteners and so on.
- Find and eliminate 'hidden' carbs in sauces, drinks and processed foods that may contain sugar or starches.
- Increase your activity level; this works for some but not all people.
- Increase your fluid intake to a minimum of eight 240-ml (8-fluid-ounce) glasses of water (or other non-caloric fluids) daily.
- Cut back on artificial sweeteners, low-carb products and fruits other than berries.
- Do a reality check on your calorie intake. (See page 128 in Chapter 7.)
- If you've been consuming alcohol, cut back or abstain for now.

If none of these modifications makes the scales budge for a month you're truly on a plateau. Frustrating as it is, the only way to outsmart it is to be patient and wait. Continue to eat right and follow the other advice above, and your body (and the scales) will eventually comply.

PUSHING THE LIMITS

Let's look at another all-too-common reason for a slow down or stall. Call it a form of self-delusion. This is a conscious form of behaviour, unlike carb creep. You may have found that you could have an occasional slice of regular bread or even sneak in a bowl of your favourite ice cream and still continue to pare off the weight. 'I have a really high metabolism', you might tell yourself, 'so I can push the limits and still have Atkins work for me'. Sooner or later – probably sooner, however – your weight loss will grind to a halt and you may experience renewed hunger and carb cravings, which then leads to eating more of the very foods you should stay away from.

Both carb creep and knowingly eating inappropriate foods can sabotage weeks or even months of hard work. Whether conscious or unconscious, such actions may conspire to make you think you cannot stick to the programme and to throw in the towel. Don't do it! You now know you can trim down on Atkins. You just need to use the knowledge that you've gained. If certain foods – low-carb bread or fruits, for example – appear to be encouraging cravings or you simply can't stop eating them, eliminate them for a few weeks and then try to reintroduce them. Or not. There's no rule saying that you have to push your Net Carb intake beyond 30 or 40 grams (1 or 1.4 ounces) a day.

But first, don't hate yourself for having fallen off the wagon. Such things happen. Have a talk with yourself about what made you vulnerable. Were you at a social gathering? Did you come back from a cycle ride or the gym and feel entitled? Were you ravenous and the right foods weren't in the fridge? Were you feeling sorry for yourself for some reason and needed a 'treat'? Whatever the reason, note it in your journal along with your plan of how to avoid getting into this fix again. Remember the ability to burn off your own body fat is a valuable gift you've given yourself. Don't abuse it.

If you've had a bad day regarding your carb intake, simply eat properly the next day – and the following days. Your weight loss will likely slow down and you may feel some cravings. If you've been completely out of control for more than a few days, you may need to return to Induction for a week or two until you get your appetite and cravings under control. If you eat a high-carb meal and are particularly sensitive to carbohydrates, it could take up to a week to return to burning primarily fat for energy. That's a high price to pay for the pleasure of a plate of chips.

TRIGGER FOODS

OK, admit it. Like most of us you've probably at one time eaten a whole packet of biscuits, a super-large packet of crisps, or an entire cheesecake. The specifics may differ, but the guilt, self-disgust, physical discomfort and overall sense of having lost control are similar. This behaviour is to not to be confused with having a craving for more carbs several hours after a high-carb meal. With a trigger food, it's a more immediate thing. You can't stop with one. The next thing you know you're back for just another taste and then more, again and again, until it's gone. When the packet is almost empty, you think, 'What the heck, I might as well finish it off', even though the physical desire for it may have passed.

If you live alone or with an understanding partner, you may be able to simply banish your trigger foods from the house. But until you deal with the underlying reason why they provoke an uncontrollable reaction, you're at their mercy when you do come across them. In many cases trigger foods are associated with

pleasurable past experiences. Chocolate-chip biscuits may remind you of coming home after school and finding the house
filled with their sweet aroma. You may associate those biscuits
with the love and the security that you may feel is now missing
in your life. Perhaps pistachio ice cream reminds you of stopping
at a certain restaurant in happier days before your parents got
divorced. Understanding why certain foods hold a power over
you may help you to take control.

THE URGE TO BINGE

The Atkins Edge can also be your ally in controlling such urges.
So here's the test: If you're at or just below your carb threshold,
it's normal to feel comfortably empty at times without having
to feel hungry. But if you're above your carb threshold, feeling
empty *always* triggers hunger. If you feel really hungry before
meals or if you experience binge eating, try reducing your average
daily carb intake until the hunger or urge to binge goes away.
In the simplest terms bingeing can be a symptom of consuming
excess carbs, so that you're no longer able to burn your own fat
reserves and experience the appetite control that comes with
shifting your metabolism.

Here are more practical ways to deter binges:

- Never shop for food when you're hungry.
- Don't wait until you're ravenous to eat.
- Don't buy food you know you'll eat in the car on the way home.
  (Better yet, don't eat while driving!)
- Understand when you're eating for emotional reasons rather
  than for hunger.
- Call your diet friend immediately when in the grip of a trigger
  food.
- Ask your partner or housemate for help when you feel out of
  control.

- Eat mindfully. Don't eat in front of the television or at the cinema, when you may lose track of how much and what you're eating.
- Always have suitable snacks in the house. If chocolate is a problem for you, have a substitute such as a low-carb bar always to hand.

WHAT WILL OWL BE LIKE FOR YOU?

Though everyone's experience is unique, following are two possible scenarios for the first couple of months in OWL. Individuals with less weight to lose typically spend a shorter time in this phase compared to others with many kilograms to lose.

SCENARIO 1

- Week 1: You move to 25 daily grams (0.9 ounces) of Net Carbs, continuing to consume 12 to 15 grams (0.4 to 0.5 ounces) of carbs in the form of foundation vegetables and reintroducing one type of nuts or seeds, then another each day or every few days. You lose another 1.4 kilograms (3 pounds).
- Week 2: You move up to 30 grams (1 ounce) of Net Carbs, branching out into berries, one type at a time, and perhaps some melon. By the end of the week, you've lost 900 grams (2 pounds) but find that you're craving more fruits.
- Week 3: You move to 35 grams (1.2 ounces) of Net Carbs and avoid the berries and melon. Instead, you try some Greek yoghurt one day, ricotta another day and then cottage cheese. Another 900 grams (2 pounds), say goodbye to your body.
- Week 4: You advance to 40 grams (1.4 ounces) of Net Carbs, reintroducing small portions of berries without stimulating cravings this time. You lose another 900 grams (2 pounds).
- Week 5: You move to 45 grams (1.6 ounces) of Net Carbs, treating yourself to a small alcoholic beverage over the weekend to celebrate the loss of another 900 grams (2 pounds).

- Week 6: You advance to 50 grams (1.8 ounces) of Net Carbs but don't add another new food group. You're surprised and pleased to lose another 1.4 kilograms (3 pounds).
- Week 7: You move up to 55 grams (1.9 ounces) of Net Carbs and have a small portion of lentil salad one day, some edamame another day and a cup of split pea soup another day. You lose another kilogram (2.2 pounds).
- Week 8: You increase your intake to 60 grams (2.1 ounces) of Nets Carbs and introduce low-carb bread as a 'shelf' for your egg or tuna salad lunches. Nonetheless, you trim off another 900 grams (2 pounds).

SCENARIO 2

- Week 1: You move to 25 grams (0.9 ounces) of Net Carbs a day, reintroducing nuts and seeds one kind at a time. Your weight loss stalls for the week.
- Week 2: You stay at 25 grams (0.9 ounces) of Net Carbs but lay off the nuts and seeds and replace them with more foundation vegetables. By the end of the week, you've lost 900 grams (2 pounds).
- Week 3: You remain at 25 grams (0.9 ounces) and try the nuts and seeds again. This time you seem to be able to tolerate them, but you lose only 450 grams (1 pound).
- Week 4: Frustrated with your slow progress, you remain at 25 grams (0.9 ounces) of Net Carbs. You lose 900 grams (2 pounds) by week's end.
- Week 5: You increase your carb count to 30 grams (1 ounce) but add no new foods. Another 450 grams (1 pound) vanishes.
- Week 6: Encouraged by your ability to handle the nuts and seeds, you try introducing berries without changing your Net Carb count. You find that the berries provoke cravings, making it hard to be compliant. Although you lose another 450 grams (1 pound), it is a struggle.

- Week 7: You decide to forgo berries for the time being but go up another 5 grams to 35 grams (1.2 ounces) of Net Carbs. You find yourself struggling with hunger again and lose nothing for a week.
- Week 8: You drop back to 30 grams (1 ounce) of Net Carbs, having a small serving of berries every other day. You drop another 450 grams (1 pound) and your cravings retreat.

If your experience resembles Scenario 1, you'll find it relatively easy to introduce new foods and increase your overall intake of carbs. Scenario 2 is clearly a different situation. Your own experience could be anywhere along this spectrum or you might lose at a faster rate, even into the second or third month on Atkins. You might be able to increase your Net Carb intake week by week without a slow down, or you may find you need to move at a snail's pace so as to not interfere with weight loss or reactivate hunger and cravings. Progressing slowly also allows you to identify trigger foods you may find hard to eat in moderation. (Review the discussion of trigger foods on page 158.)

Not everyone will be able to reintroduce all Acceptable Foods for OWL, and some people will be able to tolerate some only occasionally and/or in small amounts. This is particularly true of pulses and low-carb grain products, which many people find that they cannot reintroduce until they're in a later phase, or possibly never. Sometimes a food that initially gives you trouble can be reintroduced later without adverse consequences.

YOUR PERSONAL TOLERANCE FOR CARBS

As the two scenarios demonstrate, your objective in OWL is to determine how many carbs you can consume and continue to lose weight, keep your appetite under control and feel energised. If relevant, you'll also want to see an improvement in various health markers. Phase 2 also enables you to explore and decide which foods you can and cannot handle. All this is part of the process of finding your personal Carbohydrate Level for Losing (CLL).

Think of it as exploring your dietary neighbourhood while avoiding the metabolic bully's turf. People doing Atkins report a broad range of CLLs. Those with a higher tolerance may have a CLL of 60 to 80 grams (2.1 to 2.8 ounces) or even higher. Still others find that they can't move much beyond the 25 grams (0.9 ounces) of Net Carbs that initiate OWL. If you're losing less than a 450 grams (1 pound) a week on average, you're probably close to your CLL and should not increase your carb intake. If your weight loss rate picks up, you may be able to raise your carb intake slightly. Your goal should be to enjoy as broad a range of foods as possible, but not at the risk of losing the benefits of carb restriction, namely continued weight loss, appetite control, the absence of obsessive thoughts about food, high energy and a general sense of well-being.

It's always better to stay slightly below your carb tolerance limit than to overshoot it and then have to go backwards. The delicate balancing act of finding your personal CLL is crucial to truly understanding your metabolism so you can ultimately maintain a healthy weight. That said, it may take a bit more 'backing and forthing' until you identify your CLL. As long as you stay in OWL, you'll remain at or around that number, and both weight and your waistline should continue to disappear.

Your CLL is influenced by your age, gender, level of physical activity, hormonal issues, medications you may be taking and other factors. Again, younger people and men tend to have an advantage. Increasing your activity level or exercise programme may or may not raise it. No matter what your tolerance for carbs, however, it's perfectly normal to lose in fits and starts. And, as you know, the scales aren't a perfect tool to measure the positive changes you're experiencing.

After a month or two in OWL, you should have a pretty good idea of where your CLL will land. This in turn will likely predict the path that you'll follow after this phase. If your experience is like Scenario 1, you'll most likely find you can add back a variety of carbohydrate-containing foods and exceed 50 grams (1.8 ounces) of Net Carbs a day without losing the Atkins Edge. However, if your experience is more like Scenario 2, you may find that you have difficulty introducing carbohydrate foods higher on the carb ladder and have a CLL of somewhere between 25 and 50. In Chapter 10 we'll detail two different approaches that allow you to customise your permanent diet to your individual needs.

PERSONALISE OWL

Once you have the basics of Ongoing Weight Loss under your belt – that same belt that you've probably had to tighten a notch or two – it's time to learn how to customise OWL to suit your needs, culinary heritage or preferences and metabolism. Assuming that you're continuing to slim down steadily, you may be able to change the order established in the carb ladder, as long as you stick to your daily quota of carbs. So if you prefer to add berries before nuts or yoghurt before berries, give it a try. But don't try this with pulses (unless you're a vegetarian or vegan), which are higher in carbs. What is not negotiable is continuing to get at least 12 to 15 grams (0.4 to 0.5 ounces) of Net Carbs from foundation vegetables. Also be sure to:

- Discontinue any new food if cravings result.
- Keep portions small.
- Count – don't estimate – your carbs.
- Record any reactions such as weight gain, change in energy level or cravings in your diet journal and modify your choices accordingly.

OWL FOR VEGETARIANS

See Part III for Ongoing Weight Loss vegetarian meal plans, which start at 30 grams (1 ounce) of Net Carbs, allowing you to eat all unsweetened dairy products except milk (whether whole, skimmed or semi-skimmed) and buttermilk. If you're one of the many people who opt for the occasional meatless meal or even a meatless day or two each week, these guidelines and meal plans will help you as well.

Meat substitutes may be made from textured vegetable protein (TVP), soya protein (tofu and tempeh), wheat gluten (seitan) and even fungi (Quorn), among other ingredients. (See Acceptable Induction Foods: Soya and Vegetarian Products on page 100 for a more comprehensive list.) Some of these products contain added sugars and starches and some are breaded, so read the list of ingredients carefully. In OWL avoid tempeh products that include rice or another grain. Others contain eggs, which place them off-limits for vegetarians who eschew eggs. Many products have suitable carb counts – aim for no more than 6 grams (0.2 ounces) of Net Carbs per serving so you can continue to get most of your carbs from foundation vegetables. Other tips for vegetarians:

- Most non-animal protein sources (except for tofu and nut butters) are low in fat. Continue to get enough healthy fats in other dishes by dressing vegetables and salads with olive oil and other monounsaturated oils and eating high-fat snacks such as half a Haas avocado or some olives.
- Add back nuts and seeds before berries. Nuts and seeds contain fat and protein that will make Atkins easier to do and more effective.
- Tempeh, made with fermented soya beans, is higher in protein than tofu and more flavourful. Sauté tempeh with veggies in a stir-fry, crumble it into chilli, soup or sauces, or marinate and grill it.

- If you don't eat eggs, simply ignore the egg recipes on the meal plans and substitute crumbled tofu for scrambled eggs – a pinch of turmeric provides an appealing yellow hue. For baking, use an egg substitute product. A number of eggless breakfast suggestions appear on page 119.
- Vegetarians may add back pulses before other OWL-acceptable foods, but do so in extreme moderation (2-tablespoon servings), using them as garnishes on soups or salads.

The following suggestions apply to vegans as well as vegetarians. Shakes made with plain unsweetened soya milk (or almond milk), soya (or hemp) protein, berries and a little sweetener can make a tasty breakfast. Use tofu in shakes (try it puréed with peanut or almond butter for added protein) or sautéed with vegetables to substitute for scrambled eggs. Mayonnaise made with soya instead of eggs, mixed with crumbled tofu, chopped celery and onions, and a little curry powder makes a tasty eggless salad. Silken tofu can be used in desserts, as can agar-agar in jellies.

There are numerous soya and rice cheeses, soya burgers and other analogues described above, as well as non-dairy 'soured cream' and 'yoghurt'. Dairy substitutes tend to be lower in carbs than their counterparts, although some cheeses are actually higher. Read the labels as always. As long as these products don't contain added sugar or fillers, they're acceptable in Atkins. Products such as 'bacon', 'sausage', 'burgers' and 'meatballs' usually contain just a few carbs per serving.

Seitan is made with wheat gluten (the protein component of wheat) and is used for many meat analogues. It can be stir-fried but its texture improves when it is simmered, braised or oven-baked. Vegans should avoid Quorn products made from fungi, which include milk solids and egg protein.

OWL FOR VEGANS

It's clearly more challenging for vegans to do Atkins but not impossible. If you're a vegan, you probably rely heavily on beans and other pulses, whole grains and nuts and seeds as protein sources. Because you don't eat any dairy products, eggs, meat or fish, it's not possible to satisfy your protein needs in Induction. By beginning in OWL at a higher carb intake than vegetarians or omnivores, however, it's possible to do a version of Atkins that's free of all animal products.

- Start in OWL at 50 grams (1.8 ounces) of Net Carbs, advancing by 5 grams of Net Carbs each week or every few weeks as long as you continue to shed weight, until you're 4.5 grams (10 pounds) from your goal weight.
- You can eat Induction-acceptable vegetables and OWL-acceptable nuts and seeds and their butters, berries and other OWL-acceptable fruits and pulses from the start.
- Consume enough soya products and other analogues to meet your protein guidelines, being sure to have at least two different types of protein a day so as to get a mix of essential amino acids.
- Be sure to add extra flaxseed oil, olive oil, walnut oil and other natural oils to salads and vegetables to make up for the minimal amount of fat in most of your protein sources.

Follow the initial Ongoing Weight Loss Meal Plan for Vegans in Part III. It may take you longer to get into a primarily fat-burning mode as your initial carb intake is more than twice that of Induction's 20 grams (0.9 ounces) of Net Carbs. You also need to be especially alert to cravings and unreasonable hunger at the higher level of carb intake. After a week at 50 grams (1.8 ounces) of Net Carbs, assuming that you're losing weight and not experiencing cravings, you can move up to 55 grams (1.9 ounces), adapting the vegetarian meal plans to your needs.

OWL WITH A LATIN BEAT

Now that you're in OWL, follow the general guidelines for the phase and continue to focus on eating simply prepared protein dishes. Keep the following in mind.

- Reintroduce pulses only after you've reintroduced nuts and seeds, berries and additional dairy products.
- If you feel you must have pulses earlier try adding one type of bean at a time – and always in moderation – as a garnish (2 tablespoons cooked). Stop eating them if they arouse cravings or slow your weight loss.
- You may try to introduce low-carb tortillas (or make your own, using Atkins All-Purpose Bake Mix), but back off if they cause cravings or you can't stop at two.
- If beans or low-carb tortillas turn out to be trigger foods and you can't stop with a small portion, cease and desist.
- Put off on trying to reintroduce grains (including corn and rice) and starchy vegetables until you reach Phase 3: Pre-Maintenance.
- Remember that pulses, grains and starchy vegetables are among the foods that have got you in trouble in the past, and it's likely that they'll never again become the mainstay of your diet even when you reach Phase 4: Lifetime Maintenance.

WHAT'S FOR BREAKFAST IN OWL?

Once you're again eating nuts, seeds and berries, a whole new array of breakfast options is at your fingertips. In addition to our Induction ideas (see page 119) and numerous egg options here are a week's worth of ideas to tickle your taste buds. With one exception, each contains no more than 6 grams (0.2 ounces) of Net Carbs per serving. Unless indicated, each recipe serves one.

Granola-topped Cheese: Top 115 grams (4 ounces) ricotta or cottage cheese (not low-fat) with a mixture of 1 tablespoon chopped walnuts and 2 tablespoons flaxseed meal. Add a packet of sweetener if desired.

Almost Muesli: This classic Swiss breakfast gets a low-carb update. Mix 2 tablespoons flaxseed meal and 1 tablespoon chopped almonds with 125 millilitres (4 fluid ounces) natural whole-milk Greek or low-carb yoghurt. Add 1 packet of sweetener and cinnamon to taste. Top with berries if desired.

Strawberry Smoothie: In a blender add 2 tablespoons of unsweetened whey protein powder, 150 millilitres (6 fluid ounces) plain unsweetened chilled almond milk, 1 packet of sweetener, 2 tablespoons double cream, 55 grams (2 ounces) frozen strawberries, and ¼ teaspoon pure vanilla essence. Blend until smooth, adding a little water if too thick.

Tropical Green Smoothie: It sounds weird, but it's delicious. In a blender add 2 tablespoons unsweetened whey protein powder, ¼ Haas avocado, 50 millilitres (2 fluid ounces) coconut milk, 2 ice cubes and 125 millilitres (4 fluid ounces) unsweetened chilled almond milk. Blend until smooth, adding a little water if too thick.

Pumpkin Smoothie: This recipe is slightly higher in carbs than the others. In a blender add 4 tablespoons pumpkin purée (not pumpkin pie mix), 2 tablespoons unsweetened whey protein powder, 150 millilitres (6 fluid ounces) plain unsweetened soya milk, 2 tablespoons double cream, 1 packet sweetener, ¼ teaspoon nutmeg or allspice and 2 ice cubes. Blend until smooth, adding water if too thick.

Nutty Blueberry Pancakes: Beat 2 medium eggs with 1 tablespoon double cream and 1 tablespoon rapeseed oil or high-oleic safflower oil. In another bowl mix 55 grams (2 ounces) ground almonds and 55 grams (2 ounces) flaxseed meal with ¼ teaspoon salt and 2 teaspoons cinnamon. Add 60 to 90 millilitres (2 to 3 fluid ounces) seltzer water or soda water. Combine with the egg mixture. Ladle on to a hot frying pan, dot with a few blueberries each and flip when

the underside is pale brown. Serve with sugar-free syrup. Makes six
10-centimetre (4-inch) pancakes. Serves 2.

Avocado Boat: Top half a Haas avocado with 175 grams (6 ounces) of
cottage cheese and garnish with no-added-sugar salsa.

SNACK TIME

You'll continue your mid-morning and mid-afternoon snack habit
in OWL, but in addition to the snacks suitable for Induction, most
people can now branch out a bit more. None of these ten sweet
and savoury snacks contains more than 5 grams of Net Carbs:

- 115 grams (4 ounces) of unsweetened whole-milk yoghurt
  mixed with 2 tablespoons no-added-sugar grated coconut and
  1 packet of sweetener.
- Celery sticks stuffed with peanut or another nut or seed butter.
- Cucumber 'boats' filled with ricotta and sprinkled with
  seasoned salt.
- 2 chunks of melon wrapped in slices of ham or smoked salmon.
- Kebab of 2 strawberries, 2 squares Emmenthal cheese and
  2 cubes white turnip.
- *Nutty Cheese Dip:* Blend 2 tablespoons cream cheese,
  1 tablespoon grated mature Cheddar, a few drops of hot pepper
  sauce, a pinch of paprika and 1 tablespoon chopped pecans.
  Serve with red pepper strips.
- *Blue Cheese Dip:* Blend 2 tablespoons blue cheese into
  3 tablespoons unsweetened natural whole-milk yoghurt. Serve
  with courgette spears or another vegetable.
- A scoop of cottage cheese topped with 2 tablespoons no-sugar-
  added salsa.
- Mix 125 millilitres (4 fluid ounces) tomato juice and
  1 tablespoon soured cream in a bowl and you've got yourself a
  refreshing cold creamed soup. Top with chunks of avocado if
  desired.

- Mash 40 grams (1.5 ounces) blueberries with 2 tablespoons mascarpone cheese and top with flaxseed meal.

WHAT'S FOR DESSERT IN OWL?

Once you're eating nuts and berries, your dessert options increase exponentially, but dessert needn't be an every-night occasion. If you've planned for it during the day by setting aside the roughly 6 grams of Net Carbs or less that these treats include, that's fine. Most of the Induction mini-recipes on page 122 can be garnished with nuts or berries. (Also see the recipes at www.atkins.com/recipes.) Each recipe serves one unless otherwise indicated.

- *Chocolate-Peanut Whip:* Using a spatula, blend together 1 tablespoon cocoa powder, 1 tablespoon smooth peanut butter and 1 packet of sweetener. Whip 2 tablespoons of double cream into soft peaks and gently fold into the peanut butter mix. Also delicious with almond butter.
- *'Blue' Cheese:* Mash 40 grams (1.5 ounces) blueberries with 1 packet of sweetener. Mix with 2 tablespoons cream cheese and 1 tablespoon double cream.
- *Raspberry Parfait:* Beat 125 millilitres (4 fluid ounces) double cream until soft peaks form. Add 115 grams (4 ounces) mascarpone and 2 packets of sweetener. Beat just until smooth. Using 60 grams (2 ounces) raspberries, layer with the dairy mixture in 2 parfait glasses. Serves 2.
- *Nutty Rhubarb Parfait:* Make the Rhubarb Compote on page 123. Cool before layering with the whipped cream–mascarpone mixture above. Top with chopped nuts. Serves 2.
- *Strawberry-Rhubarb Compote:* Follow the recipe for Rhubarb Compote on page 123, but add 85 grams (3 ounces) sliced strawberries and cook briefly with the rhubarb. Serves 2.

- *Cantaloupe-Orange Smoothie:* In a blender mix 1 scoop unsweetened whey protein powder, 125 millilitres (4 fluid ounces) unsweetened soya milk, 1 packet of sweetener, 1 scoopful of cracked ice, 45 grams (1.6 ounces) cantaloupe balls and ¼ teaspoon orange extract. Pulse until the mixture is the consistency of soft ice cream.

- *Lime-Coconut Mousse:* Using an electric mixer, beat together 55 grams (2 ounces) soft cream cheese and 4 packets of sweetener until smooth. Slowly add 4 tablespoons lime juice, beating until creamy. Beat in 1 teaspoon coconut essence and 240 millilitres (8 fluid ounces) double cream until fluffy. Place in four bowls, sprinkle with unsweetened coconut flakes and refrigerate until serving. Serves 4.

PHYSICAL ACTIVITY: YOUR PARTNER IN ACHIEVING HEALTH AND GOOD LOOKS

Now that you're out of Induction, have your energy back and have shed some weight, consider adding physical activity to your shape-up and health-improvement programme. If you're not accustomed to being physically active, build up slowly. There's no need for expensive gym or club memberships, lessons, machines, weights or workout kit. All you really need are a good pair of walking shoes or a yoga mat, some loose clothes and perhaps some large empty milk bottles you can fill with water to use as weights and a resistance band, which might set you back a few pounds. If you have a stationary bike or other machine sitting unused in the cellar or garage, dust it off and climb aboard. If you're embarking on a walking programme, it's worth investing in a pedometer. No, it's not essential, but it sure is empowering to tally your weekly kilometres in your journal.

Not sure how to fit activity into your already busy schedule? Try devoting half an hour of the time you usually spend watching television or surfing the web to physical activity. Or multitask by watching the news while doing leg lifts. Get up half an hour earlier to do yoga or stretches. Walk up and down the stairs for ten minutes before breakfast. Take a walk on your lunch break. If you live near your job, walk or cycle to work rather than take the car or bus. Or walk your kids to school rather than driving them if you live close by. (With childhood obesity on the rise, you could be doing them a favour.) There has to be a half-hour in the day that you can devote to exercise if you put your mind to it. If weekdays are truly impossible, schedule time on the weekends when you can make it a family activity. Once you begin to feel its myriad of good effects, as with your new way of eating, physical activity will likely become a habit.

TIME TO MOVE TO PRE-MAINTENANCE?

Our usual recommendation is that you proceed to Phase 3 when you're about 4.5 kilograms (10 pounds) from your goal weight. To decide when and if it's time for you to move to Phase 3, ask yourself the following questions:

Have you been losing steadily and are now 4.5 kilograms (10 pounds) from your goal weight?
If so, it's time to segue into your new permanent way of eating, which is the purpose of Pre-Maintenance.

Do you have more than 4.5 kilograms (10 pounds) to go but are continuing to lose weight at a CLL of 50-plus without cravings and nagging hunger, but are keen for more food choices?
You can try going directly to Pre-Maintenance but return to OWL quickly if weight loss ceases and any previous symptoms return.

Do you still have more than 4.5 kilograms (10 pounds) to lose and . . .

- Your weight loss is stalled?
- Certain foods still trigger cravings?
- You're eating inappropriate foods on occasion?
- Your blood sugar and insulin levels are not yet normalised?

If so, you're better off staying in OWL for the time being.

Alternatively, does this describe your situation?

- You were able to lose weight in Induction but can't seem to budge in OWL.
- The greater choice of foods is creating problems with cravings and unreasonable hunger.
- You may have even regained some lost weight in OWL.

If so, you may be someone who is particularly sensitive to carbohydrates and has to keep his/her carb intake low indefinitely. If your weight loss has stalled for more than four weeks and you're experiencing symptoms that are making it difficult to stay with OWL, this is usually not the time to consider moving to another phase. You've probably reached your Atkins Carbohydrate Equilibrium (ACE) – or exceeded it – sooner than you expected. Just to be clear, your CLL is the daily carb intake level that lets you keep losing weight, and your ACE is the level that lets you hold your weight stable. For some people these two numbers can be pretty low and close together, 30 and 45 grams (1 and 1.6 ounces), for example. Say you've reached a daily intake of 40 grams (1.4 ounces) of Net Carbs. If you're still losing weight but are experiencing hunger, this level may be destabilising indicators that you'd recently brought under control.

When you bump up against your ACE before reaching your goal, it means that the metabolic bully is back and needs to be dispatched. Here's how. Reduce your carbohydrate intake by

5 grams for one or two weeks. If you feel no better and are still not losing, reduce another 5 grams. A better CLL for you may be 35 or even 30 grams (1.2 or 1 ounce) or less. Look at your foods as well. If, for example, you've recently added berries and suspect that they may be the culprit, eat them a couple of times a week instead of every day. Add no new food groups until you feel better. Once you stabilise, you can continue to try to add new OWL foods as long as both your weight loss and your overall feelings of well-being remain. When you're 4.5 kilograms (10 pounds) from your goal weight, move to Pre-Maintenance.

However, if you're consuming somewhere between 25 and 50 grams (0.9 and 1.8 ounces) of Net Carbs, cannot increase your CLL and you are 4.5 kilograms (10 pounds) from your goal weight, there's no point in trying to introduce foods higher on the carb ladder. Instead, stay in OWL until you reach your goal weight, maintain it for a month and then follow the lower-carb approach to Lifetime Maintenance designed for people who are more sensitive to carbs. You may need to back down on carbs and increase your fat intake. Don't feel bad if you find that your CLL is quite low. Instead, be grateful that Atkins allows you to find the individualised level that will allow your body to correct or stabilise the underlying condition and keep the bully at bay.

We'll conclude this chapter with a brief recap of OWL.

- Begin OWL at 25 grams (0.9 ounces) of Net Carbs per day.
- Increase your intake in increments of 5 grams at the pace that is comfortable for you, listening carefully to your body's signals as well as charting your weight-loss progress.
- Reintroduce carbohydrate foods in the following order: nuts and seeds, berries and a few low-carb fruits, additional dairy products, vegetable juices and pulses, understanding that not everyone can reintroduce all these foods.
- Continue to consume the recommended amounts of protein and plenty of natural fats and to count your carbs.

- Continue to drink about eight glasses of water and other acceptable fluids and maintain your sodium intake with sufficient broth, salt or soya sauce as long as you are consuming 50 grams (1.8 ounces) or less of Net Carbs per day.
- Use certain low-carb products in moderation if you can handle them.
- Continue to take your daily multivitamin/multimineral and omega-3 supplements.
- Continue or begin to be active or exercise if you can do so comfortably.
- Understand that weight loss moves erratically and you may experience plateaus.

Even if you're not moving on to Pre-Maintenance yet or at all, do make a point of reading the next chapter. Meanwhile, read about Jessie Hummel's return to health and vigour, thanks to losing weight on Atkins.

SUCCESS STORY 8

BACK IN SHAPE

When he couldn't squeeze into an old suit, Jessie Hummel realised it was time to do something about his weight. Three years later both his excess weight and his bad habits are history.

VITAL STATISTICS

Current phase: Lifetime
  Maintenance
Daily Net Carb intake:
  60–70 grams (2.1–2.5 ounces)
Age: 65

Height: 183 cm (6 ft)
Before weight: 103 kg (16.3 stones)
Current weight: 88 kg (13.9 stones)
Weight lost: 15 kg (2.4 stones)

Had you always had problems with your weight?
No. Until I reached my sixties, I had never dieted a day in my life. But when I turned sixty, my metabolism changed and I retained weight. The hardest part of being heavy was looking in the mirror, but the defining moment came when I wanted to wear my black suit to funeral services for one of my brothers-in-law and found that I couldn't squeeze into it. At the service some people who hadn't seen me in years commented to my wife, 'Jessie looks the same, except he's fatter'.

What made you decide on Atkins?
When I was younger, I knew about Atkins, but it was my wife who suggested I try it because she knows how much I enjoy my evening cocktail. Even though you can add alcohol in Ongoing Weight Loss, I didn't have a drink until I reached my goal weight. And I haven't had any sugar or bread since I've been on the Atkins Diet.

Did you have any health issues that were factors?
Several years back, carrying around the extra weight, my left knee went chronic on me with pain and discomfort. My doctor said, 'Welcome to arthritis', which I could trace back to my youth. Well, once I had lost the weight, which took about four months, my knees no longer hurt. My doctor was fine with my doing Atkins, but he did want to check my cholesterol every six months and my readings have been fine. Now he tests it just once a year.

What was the most difficult thing for you?
This will sound strange but it was hard for me to eat three times a day. I never used to eat breakfast or even lunch unless I had a business meeting. I just wasn't hungry but I knew it

was important to eat regularly. Even now I usually just have an Atkins bar for lunch.

How about exercise?

After losing weight, I started a daily aerobic fitness programme that works about 80 per cent of my body. Now that I'm retired my passion is swimming, which is excellent exercise. I have to swim every day. Fortunately, we live in Florida and have a heated pool, but getting in and out of it in the winter is still a challenge. I'm in as good shape as when I was in the military years ago.

What inspired you to stick with the programme?

I'm a self-motivator, but while I was losing weight, weighing myself once every week helped. I also changed my habits so that things I did for years like late-night snacking are no longer a part of my life. Now that I'm at my goal weight, wearing trousers with a 91-centimetre (36-inch) waist, down from 107 centimetres (42 inches), is a daily reminder of what I've achieved. Even though my wife is a terrific cook, and from time to time she tempts me with certain dishes, I just say no.

Have you had any trouble maintaining your weight?

No. Based upon my weekly weigh-in, I adjust my carb intake within a 10-gram (0.4-ounce) range so that I never put on more than a kilogram (2.2 pounds), which I then take off immediately.

What advice can you offer other people?

Give away your old clothes that no longer fit. Establish new habits. Find a form of exercise you love to do and do it.

Chapter 9

INTO THE HOME STRETCH: PRE-MAINTENANCE

> The last kilograms and centimetres are often the most
> stubborn to let go, particularly if you try to advance
> your carb intake too quickly. This phase could take as
> long as three months or even more, but that's fine. Now
> is the time to think like a tortoise, not like a hare.

For those of you who began Atkins in Induction or Ongoing Weight Loss (OWL), the end is in sight. (Of course you know that 'the end' is really only the beginning of your new lifestyle.) If your goal was to slim down, it's within your grasp. If you were determined to lower your blood pressure and your blood sugar and insulin levels or improve your cholesterol and triglyceride levels, your indicators should show marked improvement. Just for fun, flip back through some of the entries in your diet journal to remind yourself of how far you've come in the last several months (or weeks if your objectives were small). Your achievements are the result of keeping your eye on the big picture, feeding your body in a way that minimises temptation and not letting minor setbacks derail you.

Let's put one issue to rest. Many people don't understand why Atkins is made up of four phases instead of three. Once you reach your goal, you're done, right? Wrong! Difficult as losing weight is it pales in comparison to the challenge of maintaining your healthy new weight. Almost anyone can stick with any diet for weeks – or even months. But permanently changing your way of eating is much more difficult. That's why Phase 3: Pre-Maintenance and Phase 4: Lifetime Maintenance are distinct. In Phase 3 you'll attain your goal weight and then make sure that you can stay right there for a month. (Some people remain in Ongoing Weight Loss, or OWL, until they reach their goal weight as discussed in the last chapter.) This dress rehearsal prepares you for the real show, the rest of your life in Lifetime Maintenance. Regard Pre-Maintenance as the beginning of your transition to a permanent and sustainable way of eating.

Whether the Carbohydrate Level for Losing (CLL) that you found in OWL is 30 or 80 grams (1 or 2.8 ounces) of Net Carbs, you've obviously hit upon a mix of nutrients that works for you, at least for weight loss. Give yourself a round of applause as you begin to whittle away those last kilograms and centimetres and normalise your health indicators. Check out the Phase 3 meal plans in Part III to get an idea of how you're likely to be eating in Phase 3, in which many of you will have the opportunity to test the waters with the remaining carbohydrate food groups. These include fruits other than berries, starchy vegetables and whole grains. Which is not to say that you have to eat these foods or even that you can eat them.

You'll explore your tolerances for foods higher on the carb ladder as you increase your overall carb intake (generally in 10-gram increments) until you reach and maintain your goal weight for a month. Although this seems like a relatively small goal, particularly if you've already trimmed a substantial amount of extra weight, the last kilograms and centimetres are often the most stubborn to let go, particularly if you try to advance your carb intake too quickly. This phase could take as long as three months or even more, but that's fine. Now is the time to think like a tortoise, not like a hare. But first it's time for a reality check.

Are you impatient to reach your goal?
Of course you are. It's natural to want to cross the final hurdles when the finish line is in sight. But it's important to understand that achieving your goal weight is only one battle in the war that you'll be waging for permanent weight management. In addition to saying goodbye to those final 4.5 kilograms (10 pounds) of excess fat, you want to identify your overall tolerance for carbohydrates as well as which foods you can and cannot handle. In this phase you'll fine-tune those two concepts. Hard as it may be at this crucial time, keep your focus on the process, which will naturally lead to your desired results. If you rush to shed those last pesky bit of weight, you may never learn what you need to know to keep them off for good.

Are you anxious to get back to your old way of eating?
If you're feeling deprived and looking forward to revisiting all your old food friends as soon as possible, you're heading for disaster. Unless you're blessed with superhuman powers of self-control or the metabolism of a superhero – in which case we doubt you'd be reading this book – it's simply unrealistic to think you can drop weight and/or get your blood sugar, blood pressure and lipids under control and then return to your old way of eating without repercussions. In fact, no matter how you lose weight, abandoning your new way of eating once you reach your goal almost inevitably leads to weight regain. If you return to a high-carb diet – usually laden with heavily processed foods – you'll also likely experience the attendant health problems we've already mentioned and will discuss in detail in Part IV. In this chapter we'll help you define a reasonable way to eat on a regular basis. If you plan to celebrate reaching your goal with pasta, chips and doughnuts, why are you wasting your time slimming down on Atkins? You'll simply be hopping back on to the diet seesaw. Those of you who previously achieved

your goal weight on Atkins only to gain back the weight have learnt this lesson the hard way. Again, Pre-Maintenance trains you for a life-long way of eating.

Have you achieved good results to date but only with considerable effort?

You may have lost weight only to gain some of it back. If you've followed the programme to the letter and found that certain foods reawakened cravings, you may have moved beyond your Carbohydrate Level for Losing (CLL). Or you may have progressed too quickly. As you now know, both can reawaken the sleeping metabolic bully. Frustrating as these experiences have surely been, the silver lining is that they've given you valuable information on what you can and cannot eat. Knowledge is power. Even if you don't like everything you've learnt, your hard-earned education about your body's response to carbohydrates will allow you to work within its comfort range – and put you, not that packet of biscuits or the pizza, in control.

Was your experience in OWL an exercise in frustration?

You may have found that reintroducing certain foods stalled your weight loss or actually made you regain some weight. Perhaps you became reacquainted with some of the old familiar demons: cravings, out-of-control appetite and mid-afternoon fatigue. Maybe you felt that you'd jumped back on that blood sugar roller coaster. Like it or not, it may be that your body is particularly sensitive to carbohydrates and you'll have to continue to keep your intake low to avoid regaining weight and experiencing other harmful metabolic effects. You may need to heal your metabolism by continuing at a relatively low carb level for the foreseeable future. As you'll learn in the next chapter, we've tailored Lifetime Maintenance to provide a version that allows you to safely keep your carb intake at no more than 50 grams (1.8 ounces) of Net Carbs.

BEGINNING IN PRE-MAINTENANCE

If you're starting out with 4.5 to 9 kilograms (10 to 20 pounds) to lose or are presently happy with your weight and are changing your diet for health reasons, you may start in this phase at 40 grams (1.4 ounces) of Net Carbs a day, increasing by 10-gram weekly increments until you approach your Atkins Carbohydrate Equilibrium (ACE), discussed below. If weight is not your issue, you'll know that you've exceeded your ACE when you develop cravings or unreasonable hunger, your energy level drops or your health indicators stop improving or revert to previous levels. Read the preceding chapters on Induction and Ongoing Weight Loss (OWL) and follow the guidelines described above. If you have more weight to lose but are unwilling to limit your food choices and willing to trade off with a slower pace of weight loss, you can also start in this phase. Understand, however, that moving through the four phases maximises fat burning, even if you spend relatively little time in the earlier ones. If you see no (or unsatisfactory) results on Pre-Maintenance after two weeks, you should probably start over in OWL at 30 grams (1 ounce) of Net Carbs.

Vegans or vegetarians with modest weight loss goals or those who simply want to feel better and more energetic may also start Atkins in Pre-Maintenance as discussed below.

WHAT TO EXPECT IN PRE-MAINTENANCE

As you increase your carb intake and home in on your goal weight, you may lose an average of as little as 250 grams (a half pound) a week, which is perfectly natural. All the while you'll be learning the eating habits that will guide you for the rest of your life. As in OWL, you'll experiment as you figure out what you can and can't eat. This process of testing your limits or even temporarily backing off – using your weight change as the imperfect indicator you now know it is – is all part of the learning curve.

There's a good likelihood that at some point you'll find yourself on a plateau. If you experienced one or more of the inexplicable cessations of weight loss in OWL, you'll know what to do. If you haven't plateaued before, go back to 'Hitting a Plateau' on page 156 and carefully reread that section. Dealing patiently with and learning from a plateau is essential to your continued success. (If you seem to be getting nowhere despite following these suggestions, it's likely that you've happened upon your ACE prematurely and need to drop back 10 to 20 grams/0.4 or 0.7 ounces of Net Carbs to continue losing.) After all your ultimate success in Lifetime Maintenance is achieving a permanent plateau – aka your goal weight. You may get discouraged and be tempted to revert to OWL (or even Induction) to banish the last pesky bit of weight as soon as possible. Don't do it! Pre-Maintenance is where you learn how to eat in the real world of family dinners, business lunches, family gatherings, holidays and myriad occasions in which food plays a major role.

THE BASICS OF PRE-MAINTENANCE

Now that you're in Phase 3, you'll still follow pretty much the same routine you have until now to stay in a fat-burning mode. You must know it by heart by now: count your carbs and be sure that 12 to 15 grams (0.4 to 0.5 ounces) of your total daily Net Carb intake is made up of foundation vegetables. They'll continue to be the platform upon which you build as you add back new carbohydrate foods. Also, keep eating the recommended amounts of protein and sufficient natural fats to feel satisfied at the end of each meal. Continue to drink plenty of water and other acceptable drinks, consume enough salt, broth or soya sauce (unless you take diuretics) if your Net Carb intake is 50 grams (1.8 ounces) or less, and take your supplements.

So what's different? You'll slowly increase your daily Net Carb intake in 10-gram weekly increments as long as weight loss continues and follow the Pre-Maintenance meal plans in Part III. In effect, you're swapping the pace of your weight loss for a slightly higher CLL. But if this brings your weight loss to a grinding halt or you gain back half a kilogram (1 pound) or so that remains longer than a week, simply drop back 10 grams (0.4 ounces). Stay there for a couple of weeks, and if slight weight loss resumes try increasing your carb intake by 5 grams to see if you get the same reaction you did with a 10-gram increase. You may end up remaining at the same CLL that you were at in OWL, even as you reintroduce some of the acceptable foods for this phase. Once you exceed 50 grams (1.8 ounces) of Net Carbs, you need not continue to consume salty broth, soya sauce or a half teaspoon of salt each day.

ACCEPTABLE FOODS FOR PRE-MAINTENANCE

In addition to the foods you can eat in Induction and OWL, the following foods are acceptable in Pre-Maintenance – if your metabolism can tolerate them. You can also add small portions of whole milk (125 millilitres/4 fluid ounces contain almost 6 grams Net Carbs) or buttermilk, but not semi-skimmed or skimmed types. If you're lactose-intolerant, you can have lactose-free dairy products or buttermilk (also in 125-millilitre/4-fluid-ounce portions). Eat nothing that isn't on these three lists unless you know the carb count and the ingredients (including added sugars). Follow the carb ladder (page 145) starting with pulses, unless you've been able to reintroduce them in OWL – as vegetarians and vegans almost certainly have.

PULSES

Though pulses are relatively high in carbs, they also contain lots of fibre and contribute protein to meals. Introduce them one by one and in small portions. If you love a bowl of lentil soup on a chilly day, a side dish of steamed edamame or a snack of hummus, this step will make you happy. If beans are not your thing, simply skip this group of carbohydrate foods. (For a list of pulses with carb counts, see page 152.)

OTHER FRUITS

Assuming you didn't have trouble reintroducing moderate portions of berries, cherries and melon in OWL, you can now experiment with other fruits. As you'll see below carb counts vary significantly. Remember that all fruits are high in sugar and should be treated as a garnish. Start by introducing small portions of such relatively low-carb fresh fruits as plums, peaches, apples, tangerines and kiwi fruits. One small ripe banana, on the other hand, packs about 21 grams (0.7 ounces) of Net Carbs and its close relative, the plantain, even more. Avoid tinned fruit. Even fruit packed in juice concentrate or 'lite' syrup is swimming in added sugar.

Continue to stay away from fruit juice, other than lemon and lime juice. A 240-millilitre (8-fluid-ounce) glass of unsweetened apple juice, for example, racks up 29 grams (1 ounce) of Net Carbs, and orange juice (even freshly squeezed) is a close runner-up. Without the fibre to slow its absorption, fruit juice hits your metabolism like a sledgehammer. Likewise, dried fruits including apricots, raisins, prunes and apple slices, have concentrated sugars, elevating their carb count. But as you can see in this table, there are lots of fruit choices that come in at less than 10 grams (0.4 ounces) of Net Carbs per portion. The following carb counts are for fresh fruits.

Fruit	Serving Size	Grams of Net Carbs
Apple	½ medium	8.7
Apricot	3 medium	9.2
Banana	1 small	21.2
Cherimoya (Custard apple)	80 g (2.8 oz)	24.3
Figs, fresh	1 small fruit	6.4
Grapes, green	75 g (2.6 oz)	13.7
Grapes, purple	75 g (2.6 oz)	7.4
Grapes, red	75 g (2.6 oz)	13.4
Grapefruit, red	½ fruit	7.9
Grapefruit, white	½ fruit	8.6
Guava	85 g (3 oz)	5.3
Kiwi fruit	1 fruit	8.7
Kumquat	4 fruits	7.5
Loquat	10 fruits	14.2
Lychee	95 g (3.4 oz)	14.5
Mango, sliced	85 g (3 oz)	12.5
Orange	1 medium fruit	12.9
Orange sections	60 g (2 oz)	8.4
Nectarine	1 medium fruit	13.8
Papaya	½ small fruit	6.1
Passion fruit	60 g (2 oz)	7.7
Peach	1 small fruit	7.2
Pear, Bartlett	1 medium fruit	21.1
Pear, Bosc	1 small fruit	17.7
Persimmon	½ fruit	12.6
Pineapple	85 g (3 oz)	8.7
Plantain	75 g (2.6 oz)	21.0
Plum	1 small fruit	3.3
Pomegranate	¼ fruit	6.4
Quince	1 fruit	12.3
Star fruit	65 g (2.3 oz)	2.8
Tangerine	1 fruit	6.2
Watermelon, flesh only	75 g (2.6 oz)	5.1

STARCHY VEGETABLES

Vegetables such as winter squash, sweet potatoes and root vegetables such as carrots, beetroots and parsnips have their virtues. All root vegetables are rich in minerals, and brightly coloured ones are full of antioxidants. But the flip side is that these same vegetables are significantly higher in carbs than foundation vegetables are. You'll want to keep your portions of these new vegetables small unless you have a very high tolerance for carbs. Even within this grouping, carb counts vary greatly. Carrots and beetroots, for example, come in well below corn on the cob and potatoes. And a single serving of cassava exceeds the total carb intake for a day in Induction, with taro a close runner-up.

Vegetable	Serving Size	Grams of Net Carbs
Beetroot	85 g (3 oz)	6.8
Burdock	60 g (2 oz)	12.1
Calabaza (Spanish pumpkin), mashed	120 g (4 oz)	5.9
Carrot	1 medium	5.6
Cassava (yuca), mashed	100 g (3.5 oz)	25.1
Corn	75 g (2.6 oz)	12.6
Corn on the cob	1 ear	17.2
Jerusalem artichoke*	75 g (2.6 oz)	11.9
Parsnips, cooked	80 g (2.8 oz)	10.5
Potato, baked	½ potato	10.5
Squash, acorn, baked	120 g (4 oz)	7.8
Squash, acorn, steamed	120 g (4 oz)	7.6
Squash, butternut, baked	100 g (3.5 oz)	7.9
Swede	120 g (4 oz)	5.9
Sweet potato, baked	½ potato	12.1
Taro	65 g (2.3 oz)	19.5
Xanthosoma (yautia), sliced	65 g (2.3 oz)	29.9
Yam, sliced	75 g (2.6 oz)	16.1

*All vegetables are measured after cooking, except for Jerusalem artichoke.

WHOLE GRAINS

This is usually the last food group to be reintroduced (if at all) and with good reason. Gram for gram, grains are generally the highest in carb content of any whole food. You'll note that we refer to this category as *whole* grains, not simply grains. Oats, buckwheat, brown rice and other whole grains are good sources of fibre, B vitamins, vitamin E and minerals such as zinc and magnesium. But they and products made with them – granary bread, for one – come with a high carb price tag. Even for people with a relatively high ACE, these foods could bait the metabolic bully. Introduce them with care and if tolerated, consume them in moderation.

Whole Grain	Serving Size	Grams of Net Carbs
Barley, hulled	90 g (3 oz)	13.0
Barley, pearled	75 g (2.6 oz)	19.0
Bulgar wheat	90 g (3 oz)	12.8
Couscous, whole wheat	80 g (2.8 oz)	17.1
Cracked wheat	90 g (3 oz)	15.0
Kasha (buckwheat groats)	85 g (3 oz)	14.0
Millet	85 g (3 oz)	19.5
Oat bran*	2 tablespoons	6.0
Oats, rolled*	50 g (1.8 oz)	19.0
Polenta*	2 tablespoons	10.6
Quinoa	45 g (1.6 oz)	27.0
Rice, brown	100 g (3.5 oz)	20.5
Rice, wild	80 g (2.8 oz)	16.0
Wheat berries	90 g (3.2 oz)	14.0

*With these exceptions, all measurements are for cooked grains.

PROCEED WITH CAUTION

Refined grains and processed foods made with them are a very different story. Their high carb count is accompanied by scant nutritional value. As much as possible, continue to stay away from refined grains such as white flour and bread and crackers made from them. Refined grains including white rice have been stripped of their valuable bran and germ (the seed embryo, which is rich in antioxidants, fatty acids and other micronutrients).

You'll note that the list of Acceptable Foods for Pre-Maintenance doesn't list processed foods such as bread, pasta, pitta bread, tortillas, crackers, breakfast cereals and the like, as carb counts vary significantly from one manufacturer to another. While you should continue to check the Nutritional Facts panel on all processed products, foods that incorporate grains particularly qualify as minefields. In addition to avoiding foods with trans-fats and added sugar, watch out for white or 'enriched' flour. Baked goods made with wholemeal or other whole grains – look for 100 per cent whole grain – tend to be higher in fibre and therefore lower in carbs as well as higher in micronutrients. If white flour is the first item on the ingredients list followed by whole grain flour, forget about it.

SMALL CHANGES, BIG IMPACT

Even if you're able to incorporate most or all carb foods into your diet, here are some tips to avoid sparking weight regain and the return of symptoms indicating sensitivity to carbs.

- Instead of rice or pasta as a base for sauces, curries and other dishes, use shredded lettuce or cabbage, mung bean sprouts, grated raw courgette or daikon radish, spaghetti squash or shirataki noodles (made from soya beans and a non-starchy yam).
- Eat carrots raw instead of cooked, which pushes up the carb count.
- Certain fruits are lower in carbs before they're fully ripe. A few slices of a green pear make a tart addition to a tossed salad without adding too many carbs. Grated green papaya makes a great slaw dressed with unsweetened rice vinegar and sesame oil.

- Wrap sandwich fixings in nori, the sheet seaweed used for sushi, instead of wraps or tortillas. Avocado and either salmon or sliced chicken are a natural combo, as are tuna salad and shredded lettuce.

- Regard half a jacket potato as a portion. Slice the potato lengthways before baking, and when it's done mash the pulp with blue cheese, pesto or herb butter.

- Some wholegrain flat breads are high in fibre and relatively low in Net Carbs, making them a good choice for open-faced sandwiches. Scandinavian bran crisps are even lower in carbs.

- Make your own muesli or granola with rolled oats, chopped nuts and seeds and ground flaxseed. Serve a 40-gram (1.4-ounce) portion with natural whole-milk yoghurt, some berries or half a chopped-up apple and some sweetener if you wish.

- Sprinkle small portions of barley, bulgar, buckwheat, wheat berries or wild rice on to salads or soups for a texture treat without much carb impact.

WHAT DOES PRE-MAINTENANCE LOOK LIKE?

As before, you'll add the acceptable new foods gradually, one group at a time as long as you can handle them and one food at time within each group. It's important to continue to record in your journal how you respond to each new food because you're now entering territory full of foods that may have triggered cravings and possibly binges in the past. So let's look at three scenarios of how your first several weeks of Pre-Maintenance might go.

SCENARIO 1

Say that you've left OWL with a CLL of 50.

- Week 1: You move up to 60 grams (2.1 ounces) of Net Carbs a day, sampling a few different kinds of pulses over the week, during which you lose another 450 grams (1 pound).

- Week 2: You move to 70 grams (2.5 ounces) of Net Carbs and reintroduce small portions of new fruits. You lose no weight and struggle with cravings for more fruits.

- Week 3: You drop back down to 60 grams (2.1 ounces) of Net Carbs and continue with small portions of fruits, being sure to have them with cream, yoghurt or cheese. The cravings diminish and you lose 225 grams (half a pound) over the week.
- Week 4: You remain at 60 grams (2.1 ounces) of Net Carbs and reintroduce small portions of carrots, sweet potatoes and peas on alternate days. You lose another 450 grams (1 pound) by week's end.
- Week 5: You move to 70 grams (2.5 ounces) of Net Carbs and cautiously introduce tiny portions of whole grains every other day, shedding 225 grams (half a pound) by week's end.
- Week 6: You move to 80 grams (2.8 ounces) of Net Carbs and continue to carefully try different fruits, pulses, starchy vegetables and occasionally whole grains. By the end of the week, you've lost another 225 grams (half a pound).

SCENARIO 2

Again, assume you had a CLL of 50 upon leaving OWL.

- Week 1: You move up to 60 grams (2.1 ounces) of Net Carbs a day. You couldn't care less if you ever eat another pulse again, but you sample a few different kinds of fruits over the week. Your weight is unchanged at week's end.
- Week 2: You remain at 60 grams (2.1 ounces) of Net Carbs and find yourself craving more fruits, so you make sure to always combine it with cheese, cream or yoghurt and you manage to lose 225 grams (half a pound).
- Week 3: You move to 65 grams (2.3 ounces) of Net Carbs and reintroduce small portions of carrots, sweet potatoes and peas on alternate days. By week's end, you've regained 450 grams (1 pound).
- Week 4: You drop back to 55 grams (1.9 ounces) of Net Carbs and continue to cautiously consume both fruits and some

starchy vegetables. Although you don't regain weight, you don't lose any, either.

- Week 5: You move up to 60 grams (2.1 ounces) of Net Carbs and reduce the starchy vegetables. By the end of the week, you've lost 225 grams (half a pound) and wonder whether you're getting pretty close to your ACE.
- Week 6: You continue at this carb level and avoiding the starchy vegetables, losing 225 grams (half a pound) that week.

SCENARIO 3

Now let's assume that you left OWL with a CLL of 35.

- Week 1: You move to 45 grams (1.6 ounces) of Net Carbs, adding small portions of pulses. Although your weight remains stable, by the end of the week, you've had some ravenous episodes and feel bloated.
- Week 2: You drop back to 35 grams (1.2 ounces) of Net Carbs and reduce the pulses. Your weight loss resumes, and the bloating and cravings disappear.
- Week 3: You're feeling good and slowly losing weight, so you decide not to push your luck and remain at 35 grams (1.2 ounces) of Net Carbs for another week.
- Week 4: You move up to 40 grams (1.4 ounces) of Net Carbs and try reintroducing small pulse portions. You continue to feel good and lose another 225 grams (half a pound).
- Week 5: You move up to 45 grams (1.6 ounces) of Net Carbs and add small amounts of fruits, which produce cravings and stall weight loss.
- Week 6: Understanding that feeling good and in control is more important than trying to push things, you back down to 40 grams (1.4 ounces) of Net Carbs, experimenting with new foods in small portions until you've achieved your goal weight.

As you can see, there is a tremendous variation in how individuals respond to increases in carb intake and to different foods. Your own scenario will undoubtedly differ. Also remember that your weight can vary by a kilogram (or a couple of pounds) or so from day to day, independently of increments in carb intake and different foods. That's why it's important to continue to use the weight-averaging method described on page 93.

YOUR CARB TOLERANCE

Like it or not, you may find that there are some foods you simply cannot handle or must eat very carefully in order to not regain weight and stimulate cravings. Likewise, if elevated blood sugar or metabolic syndrome has been an issue for you, it's likely that you'll need to be very careful about introducing higher-carb foods. (For more on metabolic syndrome, see Chapter 13.) Knowing your limits will enable you to have a realistic approach to meal planning once you're in Lifetime Maintenance. Anxious as you may be to reach your goal weight, achieving it in a way that's close to the way that you'll be eating to sustain that new weight makes it more likely you'll succeed long term.

Once you've achieved your goal weight but before you move to Lifetime Maintenance, you'll have to find your Atkins Carbohydrate Equilibrium (ACE). In contrast to your CLL, which relates to weight loss, your ACE is the number of grams of Net Carbs you can eat each day while *neither losing nor gaining* weight. Many people end up with an ACE of 65 to 100 grams (2.3 to 3.5 ounces) of Net Carbs, but some people have a considerably lower ACE and a very few people an even higher one.

It's important to understand that looking merely at weight loss can oversimplify the issue of carb tolerance. Your energy level, ability to concentrate, tendency to retain fluid and, of course, the old signals of unreasonable hunger and carb cravings must also be considered. For example, even if you're losing weight at a CLL of, say, 50 grams (1.8 ounces) of Net Carbs a day, you might still be reawakening food cravings or blood sugar swings or experiencing lack of energy, which could make maintaining that level of carb intake problematic long term. Why are we bringing this up? Because some people for a variety of reasons find that they do best with 25 to 50 grams (0.9 to 1.8 ounces) of Net Carbs in either the weight-loss or weight-maintenance phase. Your objective is not to push your carb intake to the absolute limit but to advance to the point where you're comfortable and don't stimulate the return of any of the old symptoms that originally got you into trouble. Finding your ACE is not just a matter of getting to the right weight: if you're pushing your ACE too high, it is probably not sustainable.

What's unique about the low-carb way of eating compared to other diets is that adhering first to your CLL and later your ACE results in profound changes in your metabolism, enabling you to better control your intake of calories. The flip side is that if you exceed your ACE, you're forcing your body to burn more glucose while inhibiting fat breakdown and utilisation. This makes it harder to control appetite and feel satiated with the result that you'll almost certainly regain lost pounds. You'll lose the Atkins Edge and the metabolic bully will rear its ugly head again, blocking fat burning.

CUSTOMISING PRE-MAINTENANCE

We generally recommend that you introduce carbohydrate foods in the sequence shown by the carb ladder in both OWL and Pre-Maintenance. But if you're continuing to lose weight at a reasonably regular pace and the foods you've reintroduced recently haven't sparked uncontrollable hunger or other symptoms, you may be able to change the order. If you'd rather have a small serving of brown rice with your chicken curry than sink your teeth into a crisp apple, that's your choice. But be alert to the dangers. The desire for a certain food, particularly one higher in carbs, may be a sign that you'll have trouble handling it in moderation. As always, count carbs to make sure you're not exceeding your revised CLL and watch for those familiar warning signals.

GETTING (THE FAT) UP THERE

From everything we've told you so far, you'd think that it's the carbs in your diet that stop weight loss at your goal. That's partially true because carbs do exert a strong control over your metabolism – the bully thing. But when you move from losing weight to maintaining weight, you need to increase your consumption of healthy, natural fats slightly to meet your maintenance energy needs. No, you don't need to measure or count your intake of fatty foods. With your appetite as your guide, you just need to let it happen. We'll tell you how in the next chapter. All you need to know for now is that as you approach your goal weight, you may become aware of something that hunting peoples have known about for centuries: 'fat hunger'. It's a different and subtler feeling than the crash you may experience after a sugar rush. But if you find yourself staring into the fridge and eyeing the butter, cheese or salad dressing, you've probably been skimping on fat. Learning to recognise and respond appropriately to fat hunger is an important skill for success in Lifetime Maintenance.

THE RIGHT WEIGHT FOR YOU

When you began your journey on Atkins, we advised you to establish your goals, including a target weight. Undoubtedly, you've kept this number and the image of yourself at that size in your mind's eye. You may be zeroing in on that figure (pun definitely intended) at this very moment. But setting a goal weight is more of an art than science. Following the Atkins Diet seems to allow people to find their natural healthy weight, which might be higher or lower than the one you'd originally envisioned.

It's not uncommon at this point for people to find themselves not at their initial goal. So what do you do if you work your way through Pre-Maintenance and reach a point where you're able to stabilise your weight but it's slightly higher than the number you were targeting? If it's merely a matter of a kilogram (or a couple of pounds) or so and you're pleased with how you look and feel, this is the right weight for you. After all, wouldn't you rather be at a weight that you can maintain relatively easily instead of waging an ongoing struggle to be 1 to 2 kilograms (3 to 4 pounds) thinner?

But what if it's more than a kilogram or so (a couple of pounds)? If you haven't already jumped on to the activity wagon, one option is to finally climb aboard. Do keep in mind that not everyone is genetically programmed to lose a lot of weight by exercising. Nonetheless, even if you don't shed some more weight, you may be able to shape your body with weight-bearing exercise. The other option is to be patient, hone your maintenance skills and give your mind and body a break for six months or so. If you find that you're unduly stressing yourself by trying to lose 25 kilograms (3.5 stones) in one fell swoop, sometimes it's better to lose say, 13.5 kilograms (2 stones) and then move to Lifetime Maintenance to stabilise your weight by practising your new habits. After at least six months – your body is likely to resist further weight loss before that rest period – you can return to OWL to lose some or much of the remaining excess weight, before returning to Pre-Maintenance to shed the last 4.5 kilograms (10 pounds).

What about the opposite scenario? You've lost the 10 kilograms (1.8 stones) you set as your goal but now realise that you could probably pare off another 2 kilograms (5 pounds). Just stay at the same level of carb intake you're presently at and the rest of the weight should drop off slowly.

PRE-MAINTENANCE FOR SPECIAL GROUPS

Whole grains usually loom large for vegetarians and vegans, and starchy vegetables are often important components of their meals. However, they're among the very foods that may have got you in trouble in the past. Follow the general guidelines for reintroduction and think of these foods as well as pulses as side dishes rather than the mainstays of a meal. You may find that over time you can tolerate larger portions as long as you avoid refined grains and most processed foods. Both vegetarians and vegans should add back starchy grains followed by whole grains before higher-carb fruits (other than the berries and melon acceptable in OWL).

Likewise, pulses, starchy vegetables, grains and tropical fruits are key components of Hispanic-American and Caribbean cuisines. Again, it is this very combination of foods (often in the context of Western junk-food culture) that's likely led to weight gain and other metabolic danger signals. If you're able to reintroduce all these foods, we recommend the following ways to minimise weight regain and elevated blood sugar and insulin levels.

- Continue to season protein dishes with traditional seasonings but avoid carb-laden sauces.
- Continue to focus on foundation vegetables such as garlic, sweet and chilli peppers, chayote, jicama, nopales, tomatillos, pumpkin, cauliflower and white turnips – along with that delicious fat: avocado.
- Reintroduce such starchy vegetables and tubers as calabaza, cassava (yuca), potatoes, taro, yams (ñame), xanthosama (yautia) and plantains in small amounts and one by one. Have them rarely and be on the alert for signals that you cannot tolerate the carb load. Gram for gram, they're among the highest-carbohydrate foods.
- Use brown rice instead of white rice, and keep serving sizes small. Do the same with corn (maize).

- Use pulses that are relatively low in carbs, such as black soya beans, pinto beans and red kidney beans.
- Treat all fruits, but particularly bananas, plantains, cherimoya (custard apples) and mangos, as garnishes, rather than major components of a meal.
- Continue to eat low-carb or corn (maize) tortillas in moderation. (A conventional 15-centimetre/6-inch corn tortilla contains about 11 grams/0.4 ounces of Net Carbs compared to 3 or 4 grams/0.1 ounces for a low-carb one; a low-carb 15-centimetre/6-inch tortilla is comparable in carb count, in contrast to the roughly 15 grams/0.5 ounces of Net Carbs in a conventional flour tortilla.)

Your long-term objective is to honour your culinary heritage without falling back into the same eating patterns that got you into trouble in the first place. This juggling act will inevitably involve some compromises.

WOULDN'T YOU RATHER?

Paradoxically, the closer you get to your weight goal, sometimes the harder it is to stick to your resolve. This slow down can leave you vulnerable to instant gratification. 'I'm not losing much anyway so why not have that chocolate cupcake?' you say to yourself. For a moment that momentary pleasure seems more important than how you'll look in that new swimming costume or expensive suit. Assuming that you're continuing to eat enough fat, protein and fibre to remain satiated, often the ability to continue the programme is a matter of having a list of reasons to remind yourself why it's worth resisting temptation. These may reside in your head, in your diet journal or even on your PDA. Here are some ideas that should stimulate you to come up with your own list. Say to yourself – I love to . . .:

- Be able to see my feet when I look down.
- Slide easily into my trousers instead of waging a tug-of-war.

- Get admiring looks.
- Have a social life.
- Feel pleasantly full but not stuffed after a meal.
- Feel at ease when nude.
- Feel sexually desirable.
- Wear clothes that show off rather than hide my body.
- No longer have to avoid mirrors.
- Feel full of energy.
- Participate in activities with my family.
- Know my size no longer embarrasses my spouse or children.
- Feel healthy and comfortable with myself.
- Know that I'm in control of my destiny.

READY TO MOVE ON TO LIFETIME MAINTENANCE?

Of all the phases the whether-to-move-on question is easiest in Pre-Maintenance. It's a simple black-and-white issue.

Have you reached your goal weight and maintained it for a month? If so, it's time to move on to the rest of your life in Lifetime Maintenance.

Have you not yet reached your goal weight? Have you not maintained it for a month? Have some newly reintroduced foods triggered cravings that are making it hard for you to stay in control and provoked other symptoms?

If the answer to any of the above questions is 'yes', you're clearly not ready to move on. (The exception is the decision to take a holiday from weight loss and go to Lifetime Maintenance, resuming weight loss after at least six months, as described above.) Review this chapter and proceed slowly. Yo-yo dieting can make you resistant to weight loss. You may need to reduce your ACE to lose and then maintain your goal weight.

**Have you reached your goal weight and your ACE is somewhere
between 25 and 50? Did you have type-2 diabetes or did you
have any signs of metabolic syndrome before you began Atkins?**
If many of the foods considered acceptable for Pre-Maintenance
give you trouble and/or your ACE is close to the number of grams
of Net Carbs (50 or less) that you were consuming in OWL,
you should consider the lower-carb version of the Lifetime
Maintenance programme described in the next chapter. This is
particularly the case if you still have metabolic syndrome (see
Chapter 13) or type-2 diabetes (see Chapter 14).

In the next chapter we'll look at how Lifetime Maintenance –
which you can customise to your individual circumstances – will
enable you to make your new weight permanent as you continue
to retain your health and vitality. But first, read how Jennifer
Kingsley finally adopted Atkins as her lifestyle after using it
twice as a quickie diet.

SUCCESS STORY 9

THE THIRD TIME'S A CHARM

After two experiences with Atkins and the loss of more than
45 kilograms (7 stones), Jennifer Kingsley gained much of
it back during pregnancy. Once she understood that Atkins
is more than a weight-loss diet, she was able to finally say
goodbye to foods that made her heavy, depressed and subject
to ailments.

VITAL STATISTICS

Current phase: Lifetime
  Maintenance
Daily Net Carb intake: 120 grams
  (4.2 ounces)
Age: 39

Height: 162.5 cm (5 ft 4 in)
Before weight: 104 kg (16.4 stones)
Current weight: 53 kg (8.4 stones)
Weight lost: 51 kg (8 stones)

Has your weight always been an issue?

Growing up I was definitely heavier than most of the other girls. In secondary school I was dealing with backaches, knee pain from an injury, nearly debilitating PMS symptoms, depression, etc. At nineteen years old I was told I had high cholesterol. I slowly began to gain weight after my first son was born. Eventually, I just stopped weighing myself. I estimate that I was at least 104 kg (16.4 stones).

What motivated you to try Atkins?

Shopping for clothes was the most painful experience. I finally broke down crying in the middle of a department store after weeks of looking for a dress to wear to a special event. After that, I constantly made excuses not to accept invitations. Then in December of 2002 I learnt that my boyfriend was to be best man in a wedding in February. I knew just the dress in my wardrobe that I wanted to wear. Problem was it was several sizes too small. So I started Atkins – and six weeks later, I wore that dress to the wedding.

Why didn't you stay with Atkins?

At the reception I ate whatever I wanted. That night I felt really sick and I realised that over the last few months on Atkins I hadn't felt the old aches, pains and bloated stomach. And I wasn't depressed. But it was really hard to start Atkins again. I didn't have the wedding to keep me motivated and

I could still fit into my old clothes. At first, that is. When they kept getting tighter and tighter, I realised I didn't want to be back where I was before – crying in the middle of a department store.

What got you back on track?

A coworker was preparing for her wedding and I wanted to get back to a size 14 again, so we started Atkins together in July of 2003. By June of the following year, I reached what I *thought* was my goal. Then I wondered, 'Maybe I could get into a size 12 again'. When I reached a size 10, I went out and bought a new wardrobe. But it turned out that I was on a plateau. Suddenly, I was wearing a size 8 and then a 6, and finally a 4. I weighed 54.4 kilograms (8.6 stones) and happily stayed there until July of 2006.

What happened then?

I realised I was pregnant. My weight gain was mostly normal at first. But I wasn't sure how to maintain my low-carb way of eating while pregnant – or even if I could. My doctor told me to get plenty of whole grains. So I did. Almost immediately I wanted every simple carbohydrate I could get my hands on. My exhaustion returned along with aches and pain. At one point my doctor even tested me for gestational diabetes because of my excessive weight gain. After my son was born, I breastfed him. People told me nursing helps shed weight but I was gaining a half kilogram (1 pound) or so each week until I was back up to 77 kilograms (12 stones). I gained a bit more before I found the Atkins website and backed into Lifetime Maintenance, which got me down to 68.5 kilograms (10.8 stones). Once my son weaned himself in March of 2008, I decided to return to Induction.

What was different this time?

I spent several months reacquainting myself with the diet on the Atkins website and message board. I began to understand there was a lot more to Atkins than dieting. I realised that the only time I truly felt good in my life was while I was on Atkins. There was obviously a nutritional reason for many of those health problems. This time I focused on my nutritional needs – not just my weight loss. By September of that year, I had lost the 'baby weight' and was back into my pre-pregnancy clothes.

What did you learn about yourself in the process?

On Atkins my depression is gone. My chronic fatigue, yearly urinary tract infections, back and knee pain and bloating are all gone, too. And cholesterol? One doctor called my blood work 'stellar'. I also realised that I get ill when I eat gluten. I have two cousins with coeliac disease, and once I researched it I realised that whether or not I actually have coeliac disease myself, gluten is a major problem for me. Now I avoid wheat altogether but I can eat some other whole grains such as oats and teff.

What's your fitness routine?

I do yoga regularly but haven't been able to go to the gym as much as I would like. Having a three-year-old around is actually quite a bit of exercise!

What advice can you offer other people?

Visit the Atkins Community message board. The support I've received has been incredible and I hope to return the favour by supporting others. I know that this is still a journey for me. I continue to learn and grow. There is no finish line.

Chapter 10

KEEPING IT OFF: LIFETIME MAINTENANCE

Long-term success with weight maintenance has both practical and psychological components. Fortunately, you've already learnt and practised many of the skills necessary for this momentous task.

You've done it! You've reached the goal for which you've striven long and hard and proved that you have the persistence to realise your dreams. You're now officially out of the weight-loss phases of Atkins and into Phase 4: Lifetime Maintenance, aka the rest of your life. The very fact that you've found your ACE and reached your goal weight is proof that what you've been doing works for you. Keep it up – with certain modifications – and you should be able to extend that success. If you started Atkins to resolve such health issues as high blood sugar or insulin levels, hypertension or unfavourable lipid levels in addition to losing weight, you'll obviously want to maintain your improvements in these markers as well.

Regardless of your health when you began Atkins, now is the time to revisit your healthcare provider. (If your weight-loss journey has lasted more than six months, you may have already have done so.) You'll almost surely receive good news. Obviously, you don't need your doctor to tell you that you've lost 13.5 kilograms (2 stones) – or whatever – but you'll likely discover that you've also scored some significant improvements in your health indicators. That news should relieve any lingering concerns you may have about the healthfulness of following a low-carb lifestyle.

As you well know, making these changes permanent is at least as challenging as achieving them. Success with weight maintenance has both practical and psychological components and we'll help you deal with both. Fortunately, whether or not you realise it, you've already learnt and practised many of the skills necessary for this momentous task. Think about it:

- You've developed a whole set of new habits.
- You've experienced the empowerment that comes with controlling what you put into your mouth.
- You know how many carbs you can consume without regaining weight.
- You can distinguish between empty carbs and nutrient-dense carbs.
- You understand why eating sufficient fat is key to appetite control and the Atkins Edge.
- You've learnt how to distinguish between hunger and habit and between feeling satisfied and feeling stuffed.
- You recognise the signs that a certain food or pattern of eating triggers cravings.
- You've experienced the exhilaration of feeling good and full of energy.

Before you started your weight-loss journey, we asked you why you would consider *not* doing Atkins when its benefits are so obvious. Now we ask you a similar question. Knowing what you now know and succeeding as you have, why would you ever go back to your old way of eating – letting sugars and other processed carbs bully your metabolism – which is almost sure to result in weight regain and the re-emergence of health problems and self-esteem issues?

PROTECT YOUR WEIGHT LOSS BUT MAINTAIN YOUR WEIGHT

Early in this book we talked about the two definitions of the word 'diet'. Now that you've lost that extra padding, it's time to focus on the word's primary definition: a way of living. Because your weight-loss diet has smoothly morphed into your permanent lifestyle, there shouldn't be any big surprises. The lessons that you've learnt about which foods to eat in which amounts remain valid now that your goal is to hold steady.

You want to arrive at a place where you're mindful of your weight but not obsessed with it. Weigh and measure yourself once a week. As you knows the scales may 'lie', thanks to natural day-to-day weight fluctuations within a 1.8-kilogram (4-pound) range, but the measuring tape tends to be less variable. (For a review of weight averaging, see page 93.) If your measurements consistently increase and your clothes feel and look tight, it's time to act. As long as you've gained no more than 2.3 kilograms (5 pounds), simply drop down 10 to 20 grams (0.35 to 0.7 ounces) of Net Carbs below your ACE and the extra weight should retreat. But it's not just a matter of weight. It's equally important to stay alert for cravings, unreasonable hunger, lack of energy and other familiar indicators that you may be veering away from your fat-burning safety zone and losing the Atkins Edge. All these may signal that you're consuming too many carbs or that you're sensitive to the effects of one or more recently added foods. As you adjust your intake accordingly with every passing week, you'll get a better idea of your limits.

Now that you're no longer trying to trim weight and reduce your waistline, you clearly need more energy from food sources since you're no longer relying on your body fat for some of your fuel. Most people find that their appetite increases slightly as they approach their body's healthy natural weight, even as they stay within their ACE. It's important to understand that the extra fuel to keep your weight stable should come primarily from dietary fat so that you remain in a fat-burning mode. If you find that your weight is dropping below the desired level or experience fat hunger, you'll need to allow a little more fat into your diet.

FAT REMAINS YOUR FRIEND

When you were losing, say, an average of 450 grams (1 pound) a week, each day you were burning about 500 Calories of your body fat for energy. As you transition into Lifetime Maintenance your body doesn't really care where your favourite fuel comes from hour by hour: inside – your stores of body fat – or outside – dietary fat. Say that you're consuming 75 grams (2.6 ounces) of Net Carbs per day (300 Calories) and 425 grams (15 ounces) of protein (roughly 400 Calories); together they add up to just 700 Calories. If you're a 162.5-centimetre (5-foot 4-inch) -tall woman and your body is burning 1,800 Calories a day, the other 1,100 Calories have to come from fat. Why not simply increase your protein intake instead? Because, as you learnt in Chapter 5, the amount of protein you've been eating all along is close to optimal and more isn't better. As for adding more carbs, once you've found your Atkins Carbohydrate Equilibrium (ACE) it's likely to remain your upper limit for the foreseeable future.

If you ignore this advice and continue to add carbs beyond your ACE, you'll soon be revisited by the same old demons of hunger and carb cravings. Overconsuming carbs only invites that metabolic bully back into your life. Your metabolism is already adapted to efficiently moving fat into your cells and using it for energy rather than storing it for later use, providing a sustained and predictable fuel supply. Perhaps you've noticed that once you've adapted to a low-carb diet and are complying with your ACE, you can be an hour or two late for a meal and not feel desperate. How so? The answer is that even when you're at your goal weight you still have a couple of months' worth of energy reserve tucked away as body fat. This means that your muscles, your liver and your heart are getting a continuous uninterrupted flow of energy directly from fat. Even your brain, which requires more than 500 Calories per day, gets much of its energy from fat. If you've banished 13.5 kilograms (2 stones) of body fat since you started Induction, your body has burnt off an awesome 100,000 Calories more than you ate. And there's no reason your metabolism can't continue that same burn rate for fat – keeping the Atkins Edge – as you maintain your new weight.

How can you add fat calories in a palatable way? Follow the meal plans for Pre-Maintenance, adding small portions of salad dressings, sauces and spreads. Many cultures have used sauces, gravies and meat drippings this way for millenia. (For more ideas, see the sidebar 'Delectable Choices' and try the recipes for sauces in Part III.) There's no need to count fat grams or calories. Just let your taste and appetite dictate without letting fat phobia get in your way. It may take a while to learn to trust your instincts. Fat has an inherent ability to satisfy your appetite and to keep you feeling satisfied longer than the same amount of carbohydrate. You'll probably get a giggle out of the fact that you, who once had a weight problem, now have to be careful not to go too far in the opposite direction.

DELECTABLE CHOICES

Add some of the following healthy fats to those you've been eating throughout your weight-loss journey to maintain your goal weight without fat hunger or carb cravings. Each portion provides 100 or so Calories of healthy fat. The difference in energy intake between OWL and Lifetime Maintenance for most people is somewhere between 300 and 500 Calories, so making this dietary transition is as simple as adding three to five of these portions to your existing daily intake. See the recipes in Part III for more delicious choices.

- 1 tablespoon oil for dressing salads
- 1 tablespoon butter or herb butter/oil mix
- 2 tablespoons cream
- 5 g (2 oz) cheese
- 10 large ripe olives with a teaspoon of olive oil
- ½ Haas avocado
- 30 g (1 oz) almonds, walnuts, pecans or macadamias
- 1 tablespoon mayonnaise (from rapeseed oil, high-oleic safflower oil or olive oil)
- 2 tablespoons pesto
- 2 tablespoons nut butter

Here's one more issue *not* to worry about. You may be concerned that you can't digest all this fat. With the possible exception of someone who has had gall bladder surgery, this is not likely to be a problem. Why? Have you ever eaten a pint of ice cream at one time? Honestly now, the last thing on your mind back then was worrying that your digestive system couldn't handle 75 grams (2.6 ounces) of fat in less than an hour, right? Given that experience, why would you worry about whether it can handle 50 to 60 grams (1.8 to 2.1 ounces) of fat as part of a whole foods meal?

CUSTOMISING LIFETIME MAINTENANCE

Throughout this book you've learnt how the versatility of Atkins allows you to tailor the diet to your particular needs and preferences. You've already made many choices as you worked towards your goal weight. Likewise, there's no one-size-fits-all maintenance programme. The single most important decision that you'll confront is this: what do I need to do to keep off the weight I've lost and maintain my health long term? From experience we've learnt that you must do something different than you did in the past because maintenance doesn't just happen.

You already know about the tremendous variation among individual ACEs, which enables some people to consume considerably more carbs each day than others without regaining weight or seeing the return of cravings, low energy and other symptoms. Others find that they just feel better with a lower intake of carbs. Just as we've advised you to increase your overall carb intake – and the variety of carb foods – slowly in the weight-loss phases, we want you to think carefully about your carb intake in Lifetime Maintenance. Rather than push yourself to a level that makes maintenance hard to sustain, you may be happier and more successful at a lower level. In fact, you may even find you'll prefer to back down 5 or 10 grams from the ACE you achieved in Pre-Maintenance. Remember the goal here is to banish the weight you've lost for good, not win some contest for having the highest ACE in your neighbourhood!

HEALTH AND YOUR ACE

If you have a condition such as hypertension, diabetes, a high triglyceride level or low HDL cholesterol level, all of which indicate a risk of developing cardiovascular disease, you may find that they're better controlled if you remain at a lower level of carb intake than the ACE determined by your ability to maintain your weight. Rest assured there's no risk in staying between 25 and 50 grams (0.9 to 1.8 ounces) of Net Carbs. This is particularly worth considering if you previously needed medication to control any of these conditions. Ask yourself two interlocking questions:

- Do I feel safer and better on the medication(s)?
- Or do I feel safer and better on a diet that gives me equal or better control of this condition with less medication or none at all?

For some people, staying at or less than 50 grams (1.8 ounces) per day of Net Carbs gives them a better long-term response to these conditions. If ongoing health issues require medication or you've experienced weight regain despite your best efforts, you may also want to reduce your ACE. In effect, your choice of foods can work like your medicine. (Depending upon how severe the condition, you may still be able to cut back on or eliminate your medication at a somewhat lower level of carb intake.) Your best approach to Lifetime Maintenance is to understand all of your options and keep them open as you move forwards. If you have to work hard to maintain your weight at a higher ACE, you may later decide that it's too stressful to do so. Or you may find that some of your health indicators have worsened. At that point you might choose to reduce your carb intake to improve your life. Alternatively, if you've been able to maintain your weight for some time and/or your blood pressure, blood sugar, blood lipids or other metabolic indicators remain in the low-risk range, you may consider gradually increasing your carb intake. Your ACE is never carved in stone and you can raise or lower it as experience dictates.

TWO SUSTAINABLE PATHS

If you've done well with Atkins so far you'll very likely continue to do so by following one of two Lifetime Maintenance options: one at 50 grams (1.8 ounces) of Net Carbs or less and the other above 50 grams (1.8 ounces). In either case, with the exception of omega-3s (such as fish oil or flaxseed oil), it's best to continue to stay away from high-polyunsaturated-fat vegetable oils such as corn oil, soya bean oil, sunflower oil, cottonseed oil and groundnut oil. Instead, focus on olive oil, rapeseed oil and high-oleic safflower oil. Also feel free to continue to eat saturated fats. Each option meets all of your energy and essential nutrient needs and will be tailored to your individual metabolism. It's likely that you already have a pretty good idea which path is the one for you based upon your metabolism, your ACE and your experiences in OWL and Pre-Maintenance

LIFETIME MAINTENANCE WITH AN ACE OF 50 OR LESS

The simplest description of this approach is Ongoing Weight Loss with a bit more variety and some additional fat. Here's how to do it.

- Remain at the ACE you identified in Pre-Maintenance.
- Continue to eat the same healthy whole foods you've come to rely on:
  - About 115 to 175 grams (4 to 6 ounces) of protein foods at each meal
  - Enough healthy fats to keep you satisfied
  - The right balance of fats
  - At least 12 to 15 grams (0.4 to 0.5 ounces) of Net Carbs from foundation vegetables
- Continue to consume 2 servings of broth (not low sodium), 2 tablespoons of soya sauce or half a teaspoon of salt each day unless you're taking a diuretic medication or your doctor has advised you to restrict salt).
- In addition to Acceptable Induction and OWL foods, continue to eat any Acceptable Pre-Maintenance foods you've been able to reintroduce.
- If you find it hard to eat moderate portions of any food, new or otherwise, or it causes cravings, stay away from it.
- If you still have indicators of metabolic syndrome or type-2 diabetes despite your weight loss, don't keep increasing your carb intake. Instead, if you're not satiated try increasing your fat intake as described above. (For more on how Atkins addresses these health conditions, see Part IV.)
- Follow the meal plans for OWL at the appropriate number of grams of Net Carbs, but add more healthy natural fats as your appetite dictates.
- Continue your multivitamin/multimineral and omega-3 supplements.

LIFETIME MAINTENANCE WITH AN ACE ABOVE 50

This path can be best described as your last month of Pre-Maintenance, again with a bit more fat. The main difference from the lower-carb path described above is that you can select from a broader range of carbohydrate-containing foods. With greater variety, however, comes a greater risk of temptation so you may need to exercise extra vigilance to conform to your ACE. Here's how to do it.

- Remain at the ACE you identified in Pre-Maintenance.
- Continue to eat the same healthy whole foods you've come to rely on:
  - About 115 to 175 grams (4 to 6 ounces) of protein foods at each meal
  - Enough healthy fats to keep you satisfied
  - The right balance of fats
  - At least 12 to 15 grams (0.4 to 0.5 ounces) of Net Carbs from foundation vegetables
- Continue to add new foods as your ACE allows as long as they don't stimulate excessive hunger and cravings. If they do, give them a miss and try to reintroduce them at a later date. Stay away from any foods that provoke old bad habits.
- If you drop below your desired goal weight, increase your fat intake as described above.
- Broth or other ways to introduce salt are no longer necessary but you may continue to consume them if you prefer.
- Follow the Pre-Maintenance meal plans at your ACE but add more healthy natural fats as your appetite dictates.
- Continue your multivitamin/multimineral and omega-3 supplements.

Perhaps the best way to think of the two paths in Lifetime Maintenance is like a pair of non-identical twins. They share many similarities but have some significant differences, as summarised below.

DAILY INTAKE IN TWO LIFETIME MAINTENANCE PATHS

ACE	Above 50 Grams of Net Carbs	Below 50 Grams of Net Carbs
Foundation vegetables	Minimum 12–15 grams	Minimum 12–15 grams
Total daily protein (meals plus snacks)	Women: 350–510 grams (12–18 oz) Men: 450–625 grams (16–22 oz)	Women: 350–510 grams (12–18 oz) Men: 450–625 grams (16–22 oz)
Healthy natural fats	As your appetite dictates	As your appetite dictates
Total grams of Net Carbs	50–100	25–50
Range of carbohydrate foods possible	Foundation vegetables Nuts and seeds Berries and other fruits Pulses Starchy vegetables* Whole grains*	Foundation vegetables Nuts and seeds Berries Other foods possible*
Broth/bouillon/salt	Optional	2 servings (unless you are hypertensive or on diuretic medication)

*If your ACE allows.

NEW TASTES, NEW HABITS

Now that you've slimmed down and shaped up, you may have found that other things are changing in your life as well. Perhaps your social life has improved. The downside, of course, is that social situations can test your resolve. As long as you don't exceed your ACE, you should have the Atkins Edge in your corner, but you also need to learn strategies for coping with situations that crop up at work, when dining out or travelling, and more. To a large extent your carbohydrate threshold, aka your ACE, will influence how you'll address these 'real-world' issues and situations, but don't underestimate the importance of your mindset.

Whether your ACE is 30 or 100, as you develop new habits they'll ultimately become second nature. You'll probably notice that you increasingly gravitate to healthful foods and find it easier to stay away from problematic ones. Again we advise you, as much as possible, to avoid table sugar, high-fructose corn syrup (HFCS), other forms of sugar and foods made with them, including fruit juice, energy drinks and commercial smoothies. Once you get out of the sugar habit, you'll likely find that such foods lose their hold over you and may taste overly sweet. And now that you know that such foods wreak havoc on your body's ability to burn fat, sabotaging your efforts at weight control, you have good reason to avoid them.

The same goes for foods made with white flour or other refined grains. White bread, pasta, potatoes, polenta and other starchy foods may now not taste as wonderful as you remembered them. In fact, much of the flavour and satisfaction you associated with such foods comes from the herbs, spices and fats served with them – not the food itself. You can savour olive oil, butter, cream, soured cream, Parmesan cheese and a myriad of tasty condiments on salads, vegetables, meat, fish and a variety of other foods without the downside of metabolic interference.

Does this mean you can never again enjoy another piece of Granny's apple pie or a bowl of pasta or a stack of pancakes with maple syrup? One should never say 'never'. We know as well as you do that it's quite hard to live on this planet and not be tempted to occasionally eat such foods. If your weight has stabilised and you aren't experiencing cravings, you might allow yourself an occasional exception to your low-carb diet. Just remember that such empty carbs take you out of fat-burning mode. On the other hand, there's a thin line between the 'just one taste' mentality and carb creep. If you're regularly having a forkful of problem foods here and a spoonful there, you could be heading for trouble. It's not that you can't recover from the temporary metabolic shift away from fat burning given a few days of firm resolve, but you should understand what happens when you do. For many people it's the equivalent of playing with fire. You've spent a lot of time and effort building your 'metabolic house' – it would be a shame to burn it down.

GOODBYE TO OLD HABITS

Even as you settle into your new lifestyle, it's all too common to find yourself caught short as you find it hard to break habits you've had for years, perhaps even decades. Whether it's having cake during your coffee break or a jumbo container of popcorn at the cinema or eating comfort foods when you're lonely or depressed, these routines can exert a powerful influence on you. How can you change habits that may seem relatively innocuous in and of themselves but cumulatively can jeopardise all the new habits you've carefully developed over the last several months? Here's a four-step way to come to grips with the situation.

1. Identify the habits that are threatening your commitment to weight maintenance and good health. List them in your diet journal.

2. Check to see if you'd eaten enough of the right foods in the twelve hours before you were tempted to revert to your old behaviour. Habits and cravings can be a way your body says, 'You're not feeding me enough'.

3. Look at both the short- and long-term risks these habits pose. For example, short term might be reawakening cravings that threaten your resolve and long term might be increasing your susceptibility to the type-2 diabetes in your family history.

4. Come up with a replacement habit and record it in your journal. For example, swap the cake for your favourite low-carb bar and make sure to always have a supply at work. Take a small packet of salted nuts and a bottle of water to the cinema with you and don't go near the snack bar. In fact, your new habit doesn't have to relate to food. Any eating that's motivated by anything other than hunger is a prime candidate for radical change. Maybe a short walk after dinner with your spouse can replace dessert. You can practise yoga rather than eat chocolate when you're feeling blue. Develop a plan of action for each new habit. If you spend too much time alone watching television in the evenings, join a book club

or health club, or get involved in community activities. Look at both the long- and short-term benefits these new habits offer. Having a clear vision of how your new habit can help you maintain your healthy lifestyle, feel good about yourself and increase the prospect of a long, healthy life is a strong motivator.

Finally, don't put yourself down if you occasionally fall back into an old habit. It takes a while to break old habits and make new ones.

AVOIDANCE VERSUS EXPERIENCE

We talked about empty carbs above. But you can also all too easily exceed your ACE with carbohydrate foods on the three Acceptable Foods lists. Even with a relatively high ACE, you need to continue to be mindful of what you eat. Your approach may differ from how your best friend or spouse does it. For some people the solution is to 'just say no' to any carbs not on their personal list of suitable foods – basically, a behaviour pattern of avoidance. These individuals have decided that it just isn't worth trying out foods that aren't in their comfort zone. Others adopt this strategy after experimenting with how much and what kinds of carbs they can handle. Through hard-won experience they've identified the line they cannot cross. For some people it's a distinct line, for others it's a buffer zone. The 'distinct liners' behave the way a person who realises that she/he can't handle alcohol does: experience leads to avoidance. People who find that they can be somewhat more flexible around foods with higher carb counts behave much like someone who can handle alcohol in moderation. To a large extent, the thickness of your line is likely to depend on your ACE. If you've found you do best at 40 grams (1.4 ounces) of Net Carbs a day you have a thin line and will probably find it wise to adopt a restrictive mindset about stepping over it. But if your ACE is 90, you may have learnt that your buffer zone can be a bit wider.

If experience tells you that you can handle it, knowing you can have a small portion of dessert at a dinner party or an occasional half bagel without endangering your hard-won goal weight is empowering. It's equally empowering to know that strict avoidance of anything on the other side of the 'line' best protects your sense of control and physical well-being. In either case, you have to explore where you fit into this spectrum by carefully testing your response to different foods and backing away when you find that you've gone too far.

STRATEGISING YOUR SOCIAL LIFE

Advance planning is also key to not exceeding your limits. If you're going to be, say, at a wedding or holiday celebration that could prove to be a minefield of problematic foods, consider these survival tactics:

- Have a substantial snack or even a meal before the event to temper your appetite.
- Look at the various offerings, decide what you're going to have and stick with them. If you do choose to eat a high-carb food, pick your poison. If you going to splurge on pasta salad, pass on the dessert.
- Make only one trip to the buffet table.
- Eat only until you're satisfied but not stuffed.
- Drink alcohol in moderation, both because your body burns it before carbs and fat and so as not to let down your inhibitions and eat inappropriate foods. Pass on any drinks that contain fruit juice or sugar.
- If your host or hostess pressures you to have just one piece of pie or cake, politely say that you're too full. Or take a small taste, say it is delicious and then claim that you're so full you can't eat any more.

What about when you're on holiday or a business trip to a dining mecca? After all, it would be a shame to go to Paris, Rome or New York and not sample some of the local delicacies. Here are some ideas of how to enjoy the cuisine without overdoing it.

- Have eggs or a low-carb shake for breakfast and a salad with protein for lunch. That should leave a bit of a margin to enjoy the local specialty – in moderation, of course. (Also see the sidebar, 'Thumbs Down, Thumbs Up'.)
- Explore the range of local foods. The seafood in Italy is justly famous. Chose a local speciality that's prepared without breading or starchy sauces.
- The moment you get home, return to your ACE if you've not gained weight.
- If you've put on a little weight, drop back 10 to 20 grams (0.35 to 0.7 ounces) of Net Carbs until you restore your goal weight.

THUMBS DOWN, THUMBS UP

Your long-term success in maintaining your healthy new weight will depend in large part on the small choices you make every day. Here are just a few alternatives to foods that can get you into trouble:

Thumbs Down	Thumbs Up
Tortilla chips	Salted nuts or seeds
Crackers	Bran crispbread
Potato crisps	Soya crisps
Glazed/honey-cured ham	Regular ham
Chicken or turkey kiev	Turkey breast
Tuna-mayo sandwich	Tuna salad plate
Beef Wellington	Roast beef
Breaded scampi	Sautéed or grilled prawns
Stuffed clams	Steamed clams

Thumbs Down	Thumbs Up
Crab cakes	Steamed or sautéed crabs
Chicken nuggets	Grilled chicken
Smoothie	Atkins Advantage shake
Fruit juice	Berries or other fruits
Muffin	Atkins Day Break bar
Chocolate bar	Atkins Endulge bar
Brownie	Atkins Advantage bar
Flavoured yoghurt	Full-fat yoghurt with fresh berries
Almost any dessert	Berries and cream

THE MIND GAME

In addition to developing new habits and eating filling foods in the form of protein, fat and fibre, there's a third component that comes into play in order to stay in charge of your intake. We're talking about the relationship between your emotions and food. Find a time when you know you won't be disturbed and record in your journal your feelings about your accomplishments, your new looks and your sense of what's possible. We know we've said it before, but please pay special attention this time. If you're like many people who've recently transformed themselves, you may be on an emotional high with all sorts of plans for the future. Now that you know you can take charge of your eating habits, your health and your physical self, you realise that there are many other changes you can make as well. Consider how this empowering experience may help you to open other doors in your life – if it hasn't already. List them as possible goals. Certainly, several of our 'Success Stories' demonstrate that changing one's appearance or making health improvements often leads to major life shifts. What have you dreamt of doing but put aside because you didn't think you could achieve it? Now is the time to dust off those dreams and go for them.

Also record in your journal any disappointments that you may have experienced in the last few weeks. It's not uncommon to feel a complex mix of emotions upon reaching your goal weight. Among other things, you no longer have the ongoing reduction in your weight and measurements to reinforce your motivation. Also it's all too easy to have blamed all your problems in the past on being overweight and then feel let down when certain issues remain after the weight departs. For example, you may have assumed that once you subtracted all that weight and reduced your waistline, you'd see your career blossom. Or you may have thought that your social life would improve once you slimmed down. Guess what? You still have to work at making changes. If you were always shy about your size, it's unrealistic to assume that you'll promptly become an extrovert as you shrink. After all, you've changed your body, not had a personality transplant! It may take you some time to achieve the confidence that goes with that terrific-looking person you see in the mirror.

Sometimes, however, it isn't just a matter of becoming comfortable with that changed person. All too often formerly heavy people find that they have a hard time letting go of their old self-image. It's not that they don't want to but they are so used to seeing themselves as unattractive, overweight and unworthy that they continue to think of themselves that way. Some of this can be dealt with at the conscious level. For example, simply taping before and after photos of yourself to your mirror can provide a constant reminder of how much you've changed for the better.

PERCEPTION AND REALITY

The part of your brain that enables you to touch your finger to your nose with your eyes closed also tells you for example how much space you occupy. Try this exercise if you've lost more than 13.5 kilograms (2 stones):

- Put two straight-back chairs back-to-back in the middle of the room.
- Stand by one chair and pull it out just far enough that your eye tells you there's enough space to pass between them with your hips barely brushing the chair backs.
- Now step between the chairs to see how good your eye was at judging your width.

We've found that most people who've recently lost a significant amount of weight pull the chair out too far, often by several centimetres. People who've been the same weight for more than two years, however, are usually accurate to within 2.5 centimetres (1 inch). This how-wide-am-I instinct apparently takes between six and twelve months to adjust after major weight loss. And this is only one sense-of-self instinct out of many, all of which take time to realign after you lose weight. In the meantime you need to consciously tell yourself, 'I'm doing great and I'm proud of myself'.

LIFE GOES ON

The real risk here is that if you continue to hang on to your old image of yourself, sooner or later you may revert to that reality because it's familiar territory. The other image, the one expressed by your new physique, is still filled with uncertainty. And life goes on with all its messiness. You may be looking and feeling great but your kids will still get sick, talk back, break things and bicker with their siblings. Your partner will not always be a model of understanding and support. You may lose your job. Your car won't promise to never break down. You get the picture: you've made a major change in a big part of your life, but in case you haven't noticed the world doesn't revolve around you.

It's important to find a way to air such concerns, whether in the Atkins online community or with your friends or family members. Don't let setbacks (whether real or perceived) in your personal and work life drive you back to your old way of eating. In our success stories you've already met nine people like you who confronted their weight and their inner demons. Reread some of their stories and you'll see that they often struggled not just with their new weight but with their sense of self. It may take some time before you feel completely comfortable with the new you, the permanently slim you.

TO EXERCISE OR NOT: THAT IS THE QUESTION

If you've reached Lifetime Maintenance, you've already made great strides in achieving a healthy body. If you haven't already done so, now is the time to consider incorporating some enjoyable forms of physical activity into your lifestyle. More often than not they'll enrich your Atkins experience and offer additional health benefits. Studies indicate that people who are physically active have a better chance of maintaining their weight loss than do compared to sedentary folks. For some of you the role of exercise in controlling your weight may be small – genetics play a major role – but there are other reasons to consider adopting an exercise routine. For example, bone health and minimising the risk of osteoporosis are closely linked to activity, especially resistance, or weight-bearing, exercise. Whether you're in your twenties and want to improve your athletic performance or in your eighties and want to maintain normal daily activities, resistance exercises are also the most efficient way to increase your muscle endurance, strength and power.

Such sustained rhythmic exercises as swimming, cycling and running are great ways to improve your heart and circulatory and respiratory systems. These endurance forms of exercise also complement many of the metabolic adaptations induced by the Atkins Diet such as increased fat burning. Do you have to exercise two hours a day to keep your weight under control and maintain appetite control, lack of food cravings and other benefits? Absolutely not! Remember, if you continue to follow the programme's principles you'll have the Atkins Edge, so you don't need to overdo the exercise to control the metabolic bully. But to optimise mental and physical health and well-being, most of us benefit from regularly finding time to exercise.

THINGS CHANGE

Now that you're getting comfortable with your new lifestyle and feeling that the struggle you've had with your weight is finally history, don't forget this important point. The only constant in life is change. Imagine one or more of these situations:

- You join a swimming team and start competing in meets.
- You leave your desk job for one that involves more physical labour.
- You start bicycling 5 kilometres (3 miles) to and from work instead of taking the bus.
- You move from the country to the city and walking becomes your usual mode of transportation.

It's possible that any of these changes will increase your daily energy use, enabling you to eat a bit more, either as whole food carbohydrates or as healthy, natural fats, to stay at your goal weight.

Now consider these situations:

- You suffer a ski injury and spend several months in a cast.
- You have a new baby in the house and find yourself stressed and sleep-deprived.
- Your doctor prescribes antidepressants to help you to deal with a family crisis.
- A new job requires frequent travel, interfering with your fitness regimen.

Chances are that any of the above will reduce your daily energy use, meaning you'll need to lower your ACE to maintain your weight.

Now let's take a longer view. If you're forty years old, exercise regularly and have no health issues, you may be able to continue to manage your weight by staying at your ACE for years to come. As we've discussed before numerous factors – some in your control and others not (including your genes) – influence your metabolism, which in turn determines your ACE. Ageing tends to slow your metabolism; so can certain drugs and hormonal changes. As long as you're attuned to the implications of such changes, you can stay in charge of your weight by either eating fewer carbs, upping your activity level (which works for some people) or both.

TO ERR IS HUMAN

We know and you know that occasionally there is the chance that you'll slip up. The following three situations should help you to handle smaller and bigger indiscretions.

Small stuff. You find yourself devouring an apple turnover, a raisin bagel or another high-carb food of dubious value. *Recovery tactic:* Once your weight has been stable for several months, it's likely that such an indiscretion won't impact your weight, although it might make you feel sluggish for a day or two. Once you realise what you're doing, stop immediately and get back on track with the healthful way you've been eating.

A week of carb overindulgence: You spend a week in Mexico and succumb to the lure of quesadillas and margaritas. Not only do you gain weight, you're also plagued with carb cravings. *Recovery tactic:* Since most of the weight gain from a brief episode of carb overindulgence is water, the best antidote is to reduce your carb intake. As soon as you get home, drop 20 daily grams

(0.7 ounces) of Net Carbs below your ACE. If the excess weight won't budge and you're still experiencing cravings, return to OWL for a week or two until things are back under control.

Falling off the wagon: An event such as a breakup with a partner, a lost job or another major disappointment sends you back to your old, unhealthy eating habits. Even a positive event such as beginning a relationship with someone who doesn't follow the Atkins lifestyle can trigger a lapse from your new eating habits. After several weeks and gained weight you're feeling disgusted with yourself. Your pre-Atkins symptoms have returned with a vengeance and you can't fit into your new clothes. *Recovery tactic:* First of all, don't berate yourself. Get off the guilt trip, which will just lead to more destructive eating. Instead go back to OWL until your cravings are under control. Then move to Pre-Maintenance to restore your goal weight and maintain it for a month.

These three examples illustrate several points. First, the longer you wait to take action, the more aggressive your response needs to be. A minor slip-up may require no action other than to examine why it happened and plan future defences. A binge or period during which you depart from your low-carb way of eating demands more proactive measures. Regard any such departure as a learning experience of how thin is the line between your carb threshold and overdoing it. It also clearly demonstrates how a cascading series of events can threaten your long-term weight control programme. More important, however, you'll realise that you can reverse the tide. It's as simple as this: You were in control. You fell out of control. Now you know what you have to do to take control again.

At this moment while you're still new to Lifetime Maintenance you may honestly believe you'll never go backwards. Maybe you're one of those remarkably strong people who never do, but if you're like many of us, you will occasionally slip up.

Just remember that you have all the skills you need to execute a fast reverse and then move forwards with the rest of your life full of health and vitality.

TWO OUTCOMES

Undoubtedly, the question running through your head is: 'Will I really be able to stay slim and control my eating habits for the rest of my life?' Without claiming to be fortune-tellers, we can predict whether or not you'll succeed in making your goal weight your permanent weight. That's right. We don't even have to meet you. Ask yourself these questions:

1. Are you someone who couldn't wait to reach your goal weight so you could eat all those foods you've been missing?
2. Do you believe that now that you've slimmed down, you'll be able to keep the excess weight off by eating almost anything in moderation and practising self-control?
3. Do you want to push your carb intake as high as you possibly can?
4. Do you understand that only by permanently changing your way of eating will you avoid repeating the past?
5. Do you understand the role that certain foods play in controlling your appetite?
6. Do you realise that it's better to not push your carb threshold to the maximum but to settle at a level that you can sustain without cravings?

If you answered 'yes' to any of the first three questions, we predict that your weight will creep (or maybe even lurch) back along with the attendant health problems. Before you know it, you'll be starting Induction again or trying a new diet. But if you can honestly answer 'yes' to questions 4, 5 and 6 – and abide by them – we predict that you'll achieve long-term success. If you're in the second group, you should be able to get on with your life without worrying constantly about your weight and health.

ADVICE FOR LIFE

If you didn't pass the test above with flying colours, memorise the correct answers to all six questions. For sustained success, also remind yourself frequently of all the things that you've learnt in your weight-loss journey. Continue to consume at least 12 to 15 grams (0.4 to 0.5 ounces) of your Net Carbs in the form of foundation vegetables and abide by these twenty tips and you'll make your goal weight your lifetime weight:

1. *Rely on satisfying foods.* Protein foods keep you feeling pleasantly full and are fundamentally self-limiting. Almost everyone has eaten a couple of dozen biscuits in an evening at some time in his or her life, but how many people have eaten as many hard-boiled eggs at one sitting? Other than a contestant at a country fete, probably no one!

2. *Don't skimp on natural fats.* Even though you're now at your goal weight, you're still burning mostly fat for energy along with a relatively small portion of carbohydrates. Since you're no longer losing weight, it's your dietary fat that's keeping your body warm and your muscles working. Never forget that getting enough fat in your diet keeps your appetite and cravings under control.

3. *Remember the magic number.* Never, ever let yourself gain more than 2.3 kilograms (5 pounds) without taking action to restore your goal weight.

4. *Go easy on the fruits.* Eating too many fruits pushes up your insulin level and makes you store fat. Even with a relatively high ACE, you should probably confine yourself to no more than two daily servings. With a low ACE, you're better off with at most one serving of berries. Regardless of your carb

tolerance, concentrate on those with lower carb counts and more fibre such as berries, cherries, melon and that vegetable that pretends it's a fruit: rhubarb.

5. *Keep sipping.* Drink plenty of fluids and take your supplements.

6. *Always read labels.* Be alert to added sugar and other ingredients best avoided in ready-prepared foods.

7. *Steer clear of trigger foods.* You know what they are. Keep them out of the house if at all possible.

8. *Make compromises with excess carbs an increasingly less common behaviour.* It's unlikely that the occasional pizza or ice cream cone will never pass your lips. But if you're going to succeed long term, you'll figure out how to recover, return to your ACE and minimise such lapses in the future.

9. *Keep moving.* Staying active will increase the likelihood that you'll keep your weight under control. Increasing your activity may also help in the event that your weight starts to trend upwards. Weight-bearing and resistance exercise will increase your strength while toning your muscles so you look even better.

10. *Track your numbers.* Weigh and measure yourself weekly or use weight averaging so you can nip in the bud any gains that result from 'carb creep'.

11. *Eat before you go.* Having a protein-plus-fat snack or even a meal before you go to a 'food-centric' event will take the edge off your hunger and make you more able to resist inappropriate items on the buffet table.

12. *Take it with you.* When at work, on the road or even at the cinema, pack snacks such as nuts or cheese so you won't be tempted by the usual sky-high-carb offerings.

13. *Use low-carb specialty foods carefully.* Bars, shakes and other specialty foods can replace their high-carb analogues, eliminating any sense of deprivation.

14. *Compromise when necessary* (and learn from the experience). When there are no good options, make the best choice available.

15. *Stay in touch.* Continue to share with another Atkins 'graduate' and check in with others on the Atkins Community website. The challenges don't cease, although they should get easier over time and you may be able to help others reach their goals.

16. *Get rid of your 'fat' wardrobe.* If you have nothing to wear that hides extra weight, you'll have an early alert system if you start to regain weight and an economic incentive to take immediate action.

17. *Prepare, prepare, prepare.* If you're eating out, check the menu online beforehand, if available. If you're going grocery shopping, make a list and stick to it. Anticipating situations in which temptation might well rear its ugly head is a powerful strategy.

18. *Act quickly.* If you detour from Atkins for a day or more, get back on track as as possible. The longer you're off, the harder it may be to resume.

19. *Remind yourself.* Review your diet journal occasionally and take a peek at your 'before' photo.

20. *Savour your power.* Remind yourself regularly of the tremendous accomplishment you have made and how it impacts not just you but your family and friends. You've made yourself healthier and more attractive and inspired others to do the same.

THE WAY WE WERE DESIGNED TO EAT

To conclude this portion of the book, we remind you once again that by controlling your carbohydrate intake you make your body burn primarily body fat and dietary fat for energy. This in turn allows you to lose weight and later maintain that new weight, while also improving a host of health indicators. Known as the Atkins Edge, this metabolic adaptation also allows you to enjoy a steady source of energy, making excessive hunger and cravings for carbohydrate foods a thing of the past. With that tool at your disposal, permanent weight control is within your grasp.

After reading Part III, 'Eating Out, Eating In: Atkins in the Real World', move on to Part IV, where we discuss the compelling research that confirms that consuming a high-fat, moderate-protein diet, which describes Atkins, improves a broad range of health indicators that impact heart health, metabolic syndrome and diabetes.

EATING OUT, EATING IN:

Atkins in the Real World

Chapter 11

LOW-CARB FAST FOOD AND RESTAURANT MEALS

From fast food to fine cuisine, we've got you covered. Check our restaurant guides, and then in Chapter 12 move on to our delicious low-carb recipes and meal plans for every phase.

EATING ON THE RUN

When you're on the road, grabbing lunch between appointments or taking the family out without breaking the bank, chances are that you'll be visiting some of the big chain fast-food eateries. Here are some lower-carb options that won't blow your diet. This is not to say that these foods should be your daily fare or that some of them aren't high in calories, have a few grams of added sugar or contain trans-fats.

BURGER KING/WWW.BK.CO.UK

Thumbs up: Minus the bun: All burgers and Whoppers and grilled chicken sandwiched; flame-grilled garden salad (remove the carrots if you're in earlier phases); Breakfast in Bread (minus the bun and cheese); Veggie Burger OK for phases 3 and 4 (minus the bun).
Thumbs down: Garden Salad.

KFC/WWW.KFC.CO.UK

Thumbs up: Roasted chicken Caesar or Caesar side salad, both without croutons; roasted chicken salad; most chicken wing dishes.

Thumbs down: All fried, breaded or crispy dishes and salads; most sides.

MCDONALD'S/WWW. MCDONALDS.CO.UK

Thumbs up: Minus the bun: Burgers or cheeseburgers; grilled chicken salad or grilled chicken and bacon salad; scrambled eggs and sausage patty minus the bun; Caesar Dressing.

Thumbs down: Burgers with buns; Chicken McNuggets; all breaded chicken and side dishes; wraps; all other salad dressings.

SUBWAY/WWW.SUBWAY.CO.UK

Thumbs up: Any sub can be ordered as a salad (toss any croutons), including Subway Club, tuna, ham, turkey breast and beef.

Thumbs down: Any sub.

DINING OUT

Whether your tastes run to shish kebab or sashimi, Chicken Piccata or Tandoori Chicken, fajitas or fatoushe, you can eat out with ease in almost any cuisine while complying with your low-carb lifestyle. Here's a peek at what's good to order and what's off the menu so you can navigate menus in ten different languages.

ITALIAN RESTAURANTS

Order dishes that feature chicken, veal, seafood or pork with the flavourings that mark the cuisine, but without the sides of pasta, rice or polenta.

Thumbs up: Prosciutto with melon (OWL) or asparagus; Parmigiano Reggiano; antipasto (assorted meat, cheese and marinated vegetables); caponata (aubergine and caper salad) and most other salads;

meat, fish and poultry entrées such as Veal Saltimbocca, Chicken
Piccata or Veal Scaloppini (if not breaded, floured or battered).
Thumbs down: Any pasta or risotto dish; pizza; deep-fried calamari
or mozzarella; garlic bread; baked clams; Fettuccine Alfredo;
Aubergine (or veal or chicken) Parmesan.

Tip: For starters, ask for a bowl of olives instead of the bread basket. To end the
meal, order caffè breve, made with cream instead of cappuccino made with milk.

GREEK RESTAURANTS

Olives, olive oil, lemons, aubergines, courgettes, spinach, fennel, vine leaves, yoghurt, garlic, mint, dill, rosemary and tahini
(ground sesame seeds) play starring roles in this healthful cuisine.

Thumbs up: Tzatziki (cucumber, yoghurt and garlic dip); Tarama-
salata (creamy fish-roe spread); Avgolemono soup; feta and other
sheep's and goat's cheeses; roasted, skewered (souvlaki) or grilled or
braised lamb, beef, pork and chicken; gyro platter; grilled prawns,
octopus or fish.
Thumbs down: Pitta bread; rice-stuffed vine leaves; Skordalia
(garlic-potato spread); Spanakopita or Tyropita tarts; Moussaka,
Pastitsio (lamb with pasta), pilafs, fried calamari and baklava.

Tip: A Greek restaurant is almost always a good low-carb bet for a Greek salad full
of feta cheese, olives, olive oil, lettuce, tomatoes and fresh basil. Ask for more feta
instead of the stuffed vine leaves that are a typical garnish.

MIDDLE EASTERN RESTAURANTS

Many popular dishes are built around rice, chickpeas and lentils. Instead, concentrate on lamb and other meat dishes. Aubergine also gets star treatment.

> *Thumbs up:* Babaganoosh (roasted aubergine mixed with garlic and tahini); Loubieh (French beans cooked with tomatoes) and other vegetable dishes; grilled skewered dishes: lamb shish kebab, kofta (lamb mince and onion balls) and Shish Taouk (chicken pieces). In later phases: Hummus, labnee (thickened yoghurt with mint), tabbouleh, fatoushe and kibbeh.
>
> *Thumbs down:* Falafel and other chickpea dishes, pitta and baklava.

Tip: Instead of using pitta bread to dip, ask for celery sticks, green pepper chunks or cucumber spears.

MEXICAN RESTAURANTS

There's much more to this cuisine than the tortillas, beans and rice in Mexican restaurants, whether following the traditional Mexican style or one of the American styles such as Tex-Mex style, New Mexico-style and Cal-Mex style. The primary seasonings of garlic, chillies, fresh coriander and cumin can be found in any number of carb-smart dishes.

> *Thumbs up:* Salsa (with no added sugar) or guacamole (with jicama strips for dipping); jicama salad; grilled chicken wings; Sopa de Albondigas (meatball and vegetable soup); 'naked fajitas' (minus tortillas and beans); grilled chicken (Pollo Asado) or fish (pescado); Camarones al Ajili (prawns in garlic sauce); chicken or turkey mole.

Thumbs down: Tortilla chips or nachos; any taco, tamale, burrito or tortilla, or enchilada platter or dish; stuffed jalepeño peppers or Chiles Rellenos; quesadillas, chimichangas or flautas; prawn enchiladas.

Tip: Ask for dishes such as Enchiladas Verdes without the tortilla and with the sauce atop the chicken. Or order a tostada/taco salad with beef or chicken minus the rice and beans and leave the tostada itself, just as you would a plate.

FRENCH RESTAURANTS

French food is actually a collection of regional specialties and includes everything from bistro fare to haute cuisine. Many French sauces such as Hollandaise are based on butter or olive oil and thickened with egg yolks rather than flour.

Thumbs up: French onion soup (without bread topping); curly endive salad; Coquilles St Jacques (scallops in cream sauce); Steak au Poivre, Entrecôte or Tournedos Bordelaise; Veal Marengo, Coq au Vin (minus potatoes and carrots); Boeuf Bourguignon; mussels in white wine sauce or Bouillabaisse (skip the bread for dipping); Duck à l'Orange; cheese plate for dessert.

Thumbs down: Alsatian tart, Vichyssoise, Croque Monsieur, pommes frites and any other potato dish, Crêpes Suzette.

INDIAN RESTAURANTS

India has several distinct cuisines, many based on rice, wheat or pulses. But there's still plenty of protein and low-carb vegetables on the typical menu, which also offers many options for vegetarians and vegans.

Thumbs up: Tandooris (meats, fish and vegetables baked in a clay oven); meat and fish curries; grilled prawns, meat or chicken kebabs; raita (yoghurt and cucumbers – after Induction); korma, saag and paneer (cheese curd) dishes; chicken Shorba soup.

Thumbs down: Naan and other breads; dhals, including mulligatawny soup (in Pre-Maintenance and Lifetime Maintenance); biryani dishes; chutneys made with added sugar; samosas and fritters.

CHINESE RESTAURANTS

The regional cuisines include Szechuan, Hunan, Cantonese and Shandong, but rice is a staple of all of them. Order a small portion of brown rice if you can handle whole grains.

Thumbs up: Egg-drop soup (made without cornflour) or hot-and-sour soup; sizzling prawn platter, steamed or stir-fried tofu with vegetables; steamed beef with Chinese mushrooms; stir-fried chicken with garlic; Peking Duck and Moo Shu Pork (minus pancakes and plum sauce).

Thumbs down: Any sweet-and-sour dishes; fried wontons, egg rolls, spring rolls; white or fried rice; any breaded or battered or noodle-based dish.

> *Tip:* Most Chinese dishes rely on a sauce thickened with cornflour, as do many soups. Request the sauce on the side; better yet, ask for it prepared without sugar or cornflour.

JAPANESE RESTAURANTS

Again, rice is a staple as are noodles. As an island nation Japan, has many seafood dishes, but a number of other protein sources have found their way into the cuisine.

Thumbs up: Miso soup; sashimi; Shabu-Shabu; grilled fish or squid; Negamaki (spring onions/asparagus tips wrapped in sliced beef); steamed and grilled vegetables; pickled vegetables (oshinko), including daikon radish, Japanese aubergine and seaweed; Sunomono salad (cucumbers, seaweed, crab); edamame (in the later phases).
Thumbs down: Prawn and vegetable tempura; sushi; gyoza (fried dumplings); seafood noodle dishes; sukiyaki and beef teriyaki (there is sugar in the sauces).

THAI RESTAURANTS

A blend of Chinese and Indian culinary traditions, Thai food has its own unique combination of seasonings: coconut milk, lemongrass, tamarind, fresh coriander, turmeric, cumin, chilli paste, dried prawns, fish sauce, lime juice and basil. In general, stick to sautéed dishes and avoid noodle-based ones and dipping sauces.

Thumbs up: Tom Yum Goong (prawn soup) or Gai Tom Kha (chicken and coconut milk soup); Nuuryungnamtok or Yum Plamuk (main-dish salads with sliced steak or squid, respectively); sautéed prawns, spring onion, pork, beef or vegetable dishes; curries (without potatoes); steamed fish (sauce on the side); green papaya salad.
Thumbs down: Dumplings and spring rolls: fried and white rice; Pad Thai and any other noodle dish; deep-fried fish.

KOREAN RESTAURANTS

Korean cuisine is a blend of Mongolian, Japanese and Chinese elements with many dishes ideal for carb-conscious diners.

Thumbs up: Grilled or stewed fish and shellfish; marinated grilled pork, beef and chicken dishes (omit rice or noodles); ditto for Kalbi Tang (beef-rib stew); any bulgogi (barbecue – minus the sugary sauce); Shinsollo (hot pots); tofu; kimchi (fermented vegetables with chillies); pickles.
Thumbs down: Noodle-based soups; dumplings; any rice dish; Pa Jon (spring onion pancake).

Chapter 12

RECIPES AND MEAL PLANS

Numerous low-carb cookery books and hundreds of recipes at www.atkins.com and other low-carb websites make it easy to produce Atkins-friendly meals. For that reason, and because we simply don't have space to include too many recipes in this book, we've taken a different approach: with the exception of the broths, these dishes aren't designed to be eaten alone. Instead, use these delectable sauces, marinades, salad dressings and flavoured butters to complement or enhance meat, poultry, fish or tofu, as well as salad leaves and other vegetables, while complying with your weight-management programme. Even your family members who aren't on Atkins will enjoy these tasty recipes. In addition to a protein source and vegetables, just make some brown rice, sweet potatoes or another nutrient-rich starch for them.

Master several of these simple recipes and you'll be able to:

1. Add flavour and variety to basic meals so you'll never get bored eating low-carb.
2. Find delicious ways to consume all the healthy natural fats you need to do Atkins properly.
3. Make low-carb alternatives to condiments such as barbecue sauce and cocktail sauce that are usually full of added sugars.

Different non-caloric sweeteners have varying degrees of sweetness. We've left the choice of sucralose, saccharin, xylitol or stevia up to you in most cases where a recipe for a sauce, salad dressing or marinade calls for a sweetening agent, unless the recipe calls for 2 or more tablespoons, in which case we've specified xylitol, which is not as sweet as the other three alternatives.

For each recipe we've provided appropriate phases, nutritional data, the number and size of servings and the total amount of time it takes to make as well as the active time. For example, a sauce may need to simmer for an hour to blend flavours but take only ten minutes to assemble. In the case of specialist ingredients, we've provided sources or alternatives.

So let's get cooking!

RECIPE INDEX

MARINADES AND RUBS

BROTHS

SAUCES

There are countless sauces and many ways to make them. Sauces that get their rich texture from cream, butter, oil or puréed ingredients are a boon for people who are watching their carb intake. Mayonnaise, Hollandaise and basil pesto, for example, rely on eggs, cream or oil to do the thickening. Even sauces that aren't usually low carb such as barbecue sauce are easy to adapt, as our recipes demonstrate. Similarly adaptable are pan sauces, which are usually made by thickening the drippings of roast beef, turkey or another main dish with a roux (a flour and fat mixture). Condiments such as tartar sauce, salsa, aioli and other zesty complements to meals are another type of sauce.

In most recipes we've relied on oils such as olive oil and rapeseed oil that are primarily monounsaturated. Occasionally, small amounts of the polyunsaturated sesame oil or groundnut oil are specified to remain faithful to a sauce inspired by an Asian cuisine.

Also check these sauces on www.atkins.com: Chimichurri Sauce, Béarnaise Sauce, Classic Mint Sauce, Creamy Herb Sauce, Pico de Gallo (tomato salsa), Guacamole and Simplest Turkey Gravy.

Velouté Sauce

Don't be intimidated by the French name. This tasty sauce is easy to make. The classic version relies on flour as thickener, but our version makes it a perfect low-carb accompaniment. The specific broth depends on whether you'll be using the sauce with poultry, meat or fish.

Phases: 1, 2, 3, 4
Makes: 4 (125-ml/4-fl-oz) servings
Active Time: 5 minutes
Total Time: 15 minutes

475 ml (16 fl oz) Chicken Broth or Beef Broth (page 285 or 287), or tinned or Tetra Pak chicken, beef or fish broth
½ teaspoon salt
⅛ teaspoon pepper
1 tablespoon ThickenThin not/Starch thickener
2 tablespoons unsalted butter

Combine broth, salt and pepper in a small saucepan over medium-high heat; bring to the boil. Whisk in thickener; simmer, stirring occasionally, until sauce thickens, about 3 minutes. Remove from heat; swirl in butter until melted. Serve warm or refrigerate in an airtight container for up to 5 days.

PER SERVING: Net Carbs: 1 gram; Total Carbs: 3 grams; Fibre: 2 grams; Protein: 3 grams; Fat: 6 grams; Calories: 70

Tip: ThickenThin not/Starch thickener thickens sauces the way cornflour or flour does, but without the carbs. All its carbs are fibre, so it has no grams of Net Carbs per serving. You can order it online from low-carb food websites. Alternatively, you can use xanthan gum or psyllium husks, two other low-carb thickeners available from low-carb food websites and in health food shops – follow the product's advice on the amount to use.

Béchamel Sauce

Béchamel is a mild sauce that can be used in soufflés or simmered with finely chopped vegetables or meats. Traditionally thickened with a mixture of flour and fat, our version uses double cream and a low-carb thickener instead.

Phases: 1, 2, 3, 4
Makes: 6 (60-ml/2-fl-oz)
   servings
Active Time: 10 minutes
Total Time: 30 minutes

240 ml (8 fl oz) double cream
240 ml (8 fl oz) water
½ small onion, roughly chopped
1 teaspoon salt
¼ teaspoon pepper
Pinch ground nutmeg
1 tablespoon ThickenThin not/Starch thickener
1 tablespoon butter

Combine cream, water, onion, salt, pepper, and nutmeg in a small saucepan over medium heat; bring to a simmer. Remove from heat; let stand 15 minutes.

Strain cream mixture; return to saucepan over medium heat. Whisk in thickener; cook until sauce thickens, about 3 minutes. Remove from heat; swirl in butter until melted. Use straight away.

PER SERVING: Net Carbs: 2 grams; Total Carbs: 3 grams; Fibre: 1 gram; Protein: 1 gram; Fat: 17 grams; Calories: 160

Mushroom Gravy

This low-carb gravy gets its rich flavour from sautéed mushrooms rather than from pan drippings. For a vegetarian version, replace the chicken broth with vegetable broth.

Phases: 1, 2, 3, 4
Makes: 10 (60-ml/2-fl-oz) servings
Active Time: 25 minutes
Total Time: 35 minutes

50 grams (2 ounces) butter, divided
1 small onion, finely chopped
¼ teaspoon salt
⅛ teaspoon pepper
275 g (10 oz) sliced mixed mushrooms
2 garlic cloves, minced
2 teaspoons soya sauce
2 teaspoons red wine vinegar
475 ml (16 fl oz) chicken broth or Chicken Broth (page 285)
1½ teaspoons ThickenThin not/Starch thickener
2 teaspoons fresh chopped thyme

Melt 15 g (½ oz) of the butter in a non-stick frying pan over medium-high heat. Add onion, salt and pepper and sauté until soft, about 3 minutes. Add mushrooms and sauté until golden brown, about 8 minutes. Add garlic and sauté until fragrant, about 30 seconds. Add soya sauce and vinegar; simmer until evaporated, about 30 seconds. Add broth and boil until mixture is reduced by one third, about 10 minutes. Stir in thickener and thyme; simmer until sauce thickens, about 2 minutes. Remove from heat; swirl in remaining 15 g (½ oz) butter until melted. Serve warm.

PER SERVING: Net Carbs: 2 grams; Total Carbs: 3 grams; Fibre: 1 gram; Protein: 2 grams; Fat: 5 grams; Calories: 60

Mayonnaise

Ready-prepared mayonnaise may be convenient, but it's usually made with soya bean oil and often with added sugar. Home-made mayonnaise is delicious, especially spooned over steamed vegetables. Use it to make tuna, prawn or egg salad or as a base for dips or sauces such as Tartar Sauce (page 252) and Rémoulade (page 253).

Phases: 1, 2, 3, 4
Makes: 8 (2-tablespoon) servings
Active Time: 10 minutes
Total Time: 10 minutes

1 large egg yolk (see note on page 250)
2 teaspoons fresh lemon juice
1 teaspoon Dijon mustard
½ teaspoon salt
⅛ teaspoon pepper
120 ml (4 fl oz) olive oil or rapeseed oil

Combine egg yolk, lemon juice, mustard, salt and pepper in a medium bowl; add oil in a slow and steady stream, whisking constantly until sauce is very thick. Serve straight away or refrigerate in an airtight container for up to 4 days. If mayonnaise is too thick, stir in 1 to 2 teaspoons water to thin.

PER SERVING: Net Carbs: 0 grams; Total Carbs: 0 grams; Fibre: 0 grams; Protein: 0 grams; Fat: 29 grams; Calories: 260

VARIATIONS
Blender Mayonnaise

Assemble ingredients for Mayonnaise, substituting a whole egg for the egg yolk. Combine egg, lemon juice, mustard, salt and pepper in a blender and pulse to combine. With blender running on low speed, pour in the oil in a thin, steady stream. If the mixture becomes too thick and the oil is no longer incorporating, pulse the blender.

Herb Mayonnaise

Prepare Mayonnaise according to directions, adding 3 tablespoons chopped fresh herbs, such as parsley, fresh coriander, thyme or basil.

Lime Mayonnaise

Prepare Mayonnaise according to directions, substituting lime juice for the lemon juice and adding 2 teaspoons grated lime zest.

Chilli-Coriander Mayonnaise

Prepare Mayonnaise according to directions, substituting lime juice for the lemon juice and adding 3 tablespoons chopped fresh coriander and 2 teaspoons chilli powder.

Note: The very young and very old, those with compromised immune systems and pregnant women should avoid consuming raw eggs.

Aïoli

Delicious atop poached chicken or fish, this garlicky mayonnaise also can be used as a dip for fresh vegetables, making it a perfect low-carb snack food.

Phases: 1, 2, 3, 4	2 garlic cloves, peeled
Makes: 8 (2-tablespoon)	½ teaspoon salt
servings	2 large egg yolks (see note, above)

Active Time: 10 minutes
Total Time: 10 minutes

1 teaspoon Dijon mustard
120 ml (4 fl oz) olive oil
120 ml (4 fl oz) rapeseed oil

Mince garlic on a chopping board and sprinkle with salt. With the blade of a heavy knife, mash the garlic and salt into a paste. Transfer to a medium bowl. Add egg yolks and mustard; mix well. Combine olive oil and rapeseed oil in a small jug. Slowly whisk in oil a few drops at a time until the mixture begins to thicken. Add oil slightly faster, pouring in a slow, steady stream, whisking constantly, until very thick.

PER SERVING: Net Carbs: 0 grams; Total Carbs: 0 grams; Fibre: 0 grams; Protein: 1 gram; Fat: 29 grams; Calories: 270

VARIATION
Rouille
Prepare Aïoli according to directions, adding ½ small roasted red pepper that has been mashed into a purée and ⅛ teaspoon cayenne pepper with the egg yolks.

Dill Sauce
Dill sauce is the classic accompaniment to cold fish (particularly poached salmon), meat and poultry dishes. Also try it with eggs and vegetables.

Phases: 1, 2, 3, 4
Makes: 12 (2-tablespoon) servings
Active Time: 10 minutes
Total Time: 40 minutes

120 ml (4 fl oz) Mayonnaise (page 249)
115 g (4 oz) soured cream
7 g (¼ oz) chopped dill
1½ tablespoons Dijon mustard
2 tablespoons double cream
1 tablespoon lemon juice
Salt and pepper to taste

In a small bowl, whisk together mayonnaise, soured cream, dill, mustard, cream and lemon juice. Stir in salt and pepper. Cover and refrigerate for at least 30 minutes to allow flavours to blend.

PER SERVING: Net Carbs: 1 gram; Total Carbs: 1 gram; Fibre: 0 grams; Protein: 1 gram; Fat: 10 grams; Calories: 100

VARIATION
Caper-Dill Sauce

Prepare Dill Sauce according to directions, substituting a pinch of cayenne pepper for the black pepper and stirring in 2 tablespoons drained, chopped capers.

Tartar Sauce

Tartar sauce is a breeze to make, and making it yourself ensures that it will have no added sugar. This classic is particularly good with crab cakes and other fried seafood, but try it over vegetables, too.

Phases: 1, 2, 3, 4	120 ml (4 fl oz) Mayonnaise (page 249)
Makes: 8 (generous	4 tablespoons finely chopped dill pickle gherkin
2-tablespoon) servings	2 tablespoons finely chopped onion
Active Time: 10 minutes	1 tablespoon drained, chopped capers
Total Time: 10 minutes	2 teaspoons Dijon mustard
	½ teaspoon granular non-caloric sweetener

Combine mayonnaise, gherkin, onion, capers, mustard and sugar substitute in a small bowl. Serve straight away or refrigerate in an airtight container for up to 5 days.

PER SERVING: Net Carbs: 1 gram; Total Carbs: 1 gram; Fibre: 0 grams; Protein: 0 grams; Fat: 22 grams; Calories: 205

VARIATION

Rémoulade

Prepare Tartar Sauce according to directions, omitting the onion and adding 1 finely chopped hard-boiled egg, 1 tablespoon minced parsley and 1 teaspoon minced tarragon. If possible, replace the gherkin with 1 tablespoon finely chopped sour gherkin.

Mustard-Cream Sauce

Serve this savoury sauce over chicken, pork or veal cutlets or poached salmon or chicken breasts.

Phases: 1, 2, 3, 4	120 ml (4 fl oz) double cream
Makes: 4 (generous	1 spring onion, chopped
2-tablespoon) servings	1½ tablespoons coarse-grain mustard
Active Time: 5 minutes	¼ teaspoon pepper
Total Time: 5 minutes	¼ teaspoon salt

Pour cream into a small frying pan and bring to the boil over high heat. Stir in spring onion and cook, stirring frequently, until cream thickens slightly, about 4 minutes. Remove from heat and stir in mustard, pepper and salt.

PER SERVING: Net Carbs: 1 gram; Total Carbs: 1 gram; Fibre: 0 grams; Protein: 5 grams; Fat: 11 grams; Calories: 110

Cocktail Sauce

Unlike most commercial cocktail sauces, this easy-to-make recipe contains no added sugars. Use this tangy sauce on prawn cocktail or raw oysters or your favourite baked or (non-breaded) fried seafood.

Phases: 1, 2, 3, 4	240 g (8½ oz) no-sugar-added tomato ketchup
Makes: 8 (generous	3 tablespoons prepared horseradish, drained
2-tablespoon) servings	½ teaspoon grated lemon zest (optional)
Active Time: 5 minutes	1 tablespoon fresh lemon juice
Total Time: 1 hour, 5 minutes	Hot pepper sauce

Combine tomato ketchup, horseradish, lemon zest and lemon juice in a small bowl; stir in hot sauce to taste. Cover and refrigerate for at least 1 hour to allow flavours to blend.

PER SERVING: Net Carbs: 3 grams; Total Carbs: 5 grams; Fibre: 2 grams; Protein: 0 grams; Fat: 0 grams; Calories: 25

Barbecue Sauce

Most commercial barbecue sauces are full of sugar or high-fructose corn syrup. Feel free to customise the sauce to your preferences or to the recipe you'll use this sauce with – more or less cayenne pepper, more or less vinegar and other spice combinations.

Phases: 2, 3, 4
Makes: 10 (scant 2-tablespoon) servings
Active Time: 25 minutes
Total Time: 25 minutes

1 tablespoon olive oil
1 small onion, finely chopped
2 tablespoons tomato purée
1 teaspoon chilli powder
1 teaspoon ground cumin
¾ teaspoon garlic powder
¾ teaspoon powdered mustard
¼ teaspoon ground mixed spice
⅛ teaspoon cayenne pepper
350 g (12 oz) no-sugar-added tomato ketchup
1 tablespoon cider vinegar
2 teaspoons Worcestershire sauce
2 teaspoons xylitol
¼ teaspoon instant coffee granules

Heat oil in a medium saucepan over medium-high heat. Add onion and sauté until soft, about 3 minutes. Add tomato purée, chilli powder, cumin, garlic powder, mustard, mixed spice and cayenne pepper; cook until fragrant, about 1 minute. Stir in tomato ketchup, vinegar, Worcestershire sauce, sugar substitute and coffee; simmer, stirring occasionally, until very thick, about

8 minutes. Serve warm or at room temperature or refrigerate in an airtight container for up to 3 days.

PER SERVING: Net Carbs: 4 grams; Total Carbs: 7 grams; Fibre: 3 grams; Protein: 0 grams; Fat: 1.5 grams; Calories: 45

Peanut Sauce

Peanut sauce is a standard in the cuisines of Southeast Asia, particularly Thailand and Indonesia. Use it as a dip for chicken, lamb, beef or tofu kebabs or with any grilled meat or poultry. Also try it on raw or steamed vegetables. Be sure to use natural peanut butter without hydrogenated oils and sweeteners. If you don't have fish sauce, substitute soya sauce.

Phases: 3, 4
Makes: 8 (generous 2-tablespoon) servings
Active Time: 10 minutes
Total Time: 10 minutes

1 tablespoon groundnut oil
1 tablespoon minced fresh ginger
2 garlic cloves, minced
¼ teaspoon red pepper flakes
130 g (4½ oz) chunky natural peanut butter
60 ml (2 fl oz) water
1 tablespoon unseasoned rice wine vinegar
1 tablespoon Thai fish sauce (*nam pla*)
1 tablespoon non-caloric sweetener
175 ml (6 fl oz) unsweetened coconut milk

Heat oil in a small saucepan over medium-high heat. Add ginger, garlic and pepper flakes and sauté until ginger and garlic start to brown, about 1 minute. Add peanut butter, water, vinegar, fish sauce and sugar substitute; cook, stirring, until smooth, about 1 minute.

Remove from heat and stir in coconut milk. Serve straight away or refrigerate in an airtight container for up to 5 days. If sauce is too thick, stir in 1 to 2 tablespoons water.

PER SERVING: Net Carbs: 5 grams; Total Carbs: 6 grams; Fibre: 1 gram; Protein: 4 grams; Fat: 15 grams; Calories: 170

Raita

Cooling raita is a staple in Indian and Middle Eastern cuisines. It cools hot curries but it's also great with mild dishes and spiced grilled meats and even as a dip.

Phases: 2, 3, 4
Makes: 8 (60-ml/2-fl-oz)
  servings
Active Time: 15 minutes
Total Time: 1 hour,
  15 minutes

1 medium cucumber, peeled, deseeded, grated and squeezed
  dry
375 g (13 oz) natural full-fat yoghurt
2 tablespoons chopped fresh mint
2 tablespoons chopped fresh coriander
½ teaspoon salt
⅛ teaspoon curry powder

Combine cucumber, yoghurt, mint, coriander, salt and curry powder in a medium bowl. Cover and refrigerate for 1 hour to allow flavours to blend.

PER SERVING: Net Carbs: 3 grams; Total Carbs: 3 grams; Fibre: 0 grams; Protein: 2 grams; Fat: 1.5 grams; Calories: 35

VARIATION
Tzatziki

Prepare Raita according to directions, omitting the mint, fresh coriander and curry powder and adding 2 tablespoons extra virgin olive oil, 1 minced garlic clove and 2 teaspoons fresh lemon juice. For a more authentic dish, use Greek yoghurt, which is thicker and richer – and lower carb – than the standard supermarket variety.

Romesco Sauce

This traditional Spanish sauce gets body and flavour from puréed peppers and almonds – a terrific low-carb combination. Use it on grilled meats, vegetables, poultry and eggs.

Phases: 2, 3, 4

Makes: 12 (generous
   3-tablespoon) servings

Active Time: 25 minutes

Total Time: 45 minutes

3 medium red peppers, halved lengthways, seeds removed

120 ml (4 fl oz) extra virgin olive oil

75 g (3 oz) blanched sliced almonds

2 garlic cloves, crushed

1 small tomato, deseeded

2 teaspoons sherry vinegar

2 teaspoons paprika

Salt to taste

Cayenne pepper to taste

Place peppers, skin side up, on a grill pan in a preheated grill (or on a skewer over a gas hob set on high heat); cook, turning occasionally, until skin is charred, about 8 minutes. Transfer to a large bowl and cover with cling film. Allow to steam for 20 minutes; peel and deseed.

Meanwhile, heat oil in a medium frying pan over medium heat. Add almonds and garlic and sauté until golden, about 3 minutes. Combine peppers, almonds, tomato, garlic, vinegar and paprika in a food processor or blender and purée. Season with salt and cayenne pepper to taste. Serve straight away or refrigerate in an airtight container for up to 3 days.

PER SERVING: Net Carbs: 2 grams; Total Carbs: 3 grams; Fibre: 1 gram; Protein: 1 gram; Fat: 11 grams; Calories: 120

Alfredo Sauce

One of the simplest and best of all pasta sauces, Alfredo sauce is versatile enough to dress up steamed vegetables as well. For the best flavour, buy blocks of Parmesan and Pecorino Romano and grate them yourself.

Phases: 1, 2, 3, 4	25 g (1 oz) unsalted butter
Makes: 6 (60-ml/2-fl-oz) servings	350 ml (12 fl oz) double cream
Active Time: 10 minutes	50 g (2 oz) Parmesan, grated
Total Time: 20 minutes	50 g (2 oz) Pecorino Romano, grated
	⅛ teaspoon pepper
	Pinch ground nutmeg

Melt butter in a medium saucepan over medium heat. Add cream and simmer until reduced to 240 ml (8 fl oz), about 10 minutes. Remove from heat; stir in Parmesan, Pecorino Romano, pepper and nutmeg until the cheeses have melted and sauce is smooth. Serve straight away.

PER SERVING: Net Carbs: 2 grams; Total Carbs: 2 grams; Fibre: 0 grams; Protein: 4 grams; Fat: 28 grams; Calories: 280

VARIATION
Vodka Sauce
Prepare Alfredo Sauce according to directions, adding 3 tablespoons tomato purée and 2 tablespoons vodka to the double cream before reducing.

Basic Tomato Sauce
This versatile sauce is great not just with meatballs or on low-carb or shirataki pasta, but also on sautéed courgettes, onions or peppers.

Phases: 2, 3, 4	60 ml (2 fl oz) extra virgin olive oil
Makes: 6 (120-ml/4-fl-oz) servings	1 medium onion, finely chopped
Active Time: 15 minutes	½ medium celery stick, finely chopped
Total Time: 40 minutes	2 garlic cloves, chopped
	1 teaspoon dried basil
	800 g (28 oz) tinned crushed tomatoes
	Salt and pepper to taste

Heat oil in a medium saucepan over medium heat. Add onion,
celery and garlic and sauté until the vegetables are very soft, about
6 minutes. Add basil and cook, stirring, 30 seconds.

Stir in tomatoes. Bring to the boil; reduce heat to medium-low
and simmer, partially covered, until thickened, about 30 minutes.
Season with salt and pepper and serve hot.

PER SERVING: Net Carbs: 9 grams; Total Carbs: 12 grams; Fibre: 3 grams; Protein: 2 grams; Fat: 10
grams; Calories: 140

Carbonara Sauce

This rich sauce is best for long strands of shirataki (or low carb
pasta such as spaghetti or fettuccine in later phases). It can also
be served over sauteed aubergine, onions or peppers. Time the
cooking so that the pasta or vegetable base is still very hot when
you pour the sauce on. This allows the eggs to continue to cook
and thicken.

Phases: 1, 2, 3, 4
Makes: 6 (60-ml/2-fl-oz)
  servings
Active Time: 20 minutes
Total Time: 20 minutes

6 rashers bacon, cut into 5-mm (¼-in) pieces
2 garlic cloves, minced
175 ml (6 fl oz) double cream
50 g (2 oz) Parmesan, grated
⅛ teaspoon pepper
2 large eggs

Cook bacon in a medium frying pan over medium heat until crisp,
about 6 minutes. Transfer bacon to a plate lined with kitchen
paper; set aside. Spoon off all but 2 tablespoons fat; return frying
pan to heat. Add garlic and sauté until fragrant, about 30 seconds.
Add cream, Parmesan and pepper; simmer until cheese has
melted, about 1 minute.

Meanwhile, lightly beat eggs in a medium bowl; slowly whisk
hot cream mixture into eggs until completely combined. Return
mixture to frying pan over low heat; simmer, stirring constantly,

until it begins to thicken, about 3 minutes. Remove from heat; stir in reserved bacon. Serve straight away.

PER SERVING: Net Carbs: 2 grams; Total Carbs: 2 grams; Fibre: 0 grams; Protein: 8 grams; Fat: 17 grams; Calories: 190

Basil Pesto

Despite its low carb content, this recipe is not coded for Induction because it contains nuts, but it is certainly appropriate after the first two weeks. Toasting the nuts enhances the flavour. Add more garlic if you prefer. Mix pesto with mayonnaise or soft cream cheese for a quick dip or thick sauce to spoon over fish, chicken, beef or steamed vegetables. It's also great on top of slices of tomato and mozzarella.

Phases: 2, 3, 4
Makes: 4 (50-g/2-oz) servings
Active Time: 10 minutes
Total Time: 10 minutes

75 g (3 oz) fresh basil leaves
50 g (2 oz) pine kernels
40 g (1½ oz) Parmesan, grated
1 garlic clove, peeled
½ teaspoon salt
75 ml (2½ fl oz) extra virgin olive oil

Combine basil, pine kernels, Parmesan, garlic and salt in a food processor or blender; pulse until finely chopped. Add oil in a slow and steady stream with machine running; process until fairly smooth but not puréed. Serve straight away or refrigerate in an airtight container for up to 3 days or freeze for up to one month.

PER SERVING: Net Carbs: 1 gram; Total Carbs: 3 grams; Fibre: 2 grams; Protein: 5 grams; Fat: 29 grams; Calories: 280

VARIATION
Rocket-Walnut Pesto
Prepare Basil Pesto according to directions, substituting rocket for the basil and walnuts for the pine kernels.

Sun-dried Tomato Pesto
A tasty twist on the classic Basil Pesto (page 260), this sauce can be mixed with soured cream or cream cheese for a tasty dip. Found near the produce section of the supermarket, dry-packed sun-dried tomatoes are much less expensive and fresher tasting than oil-packed ones.

Phases: 2, 3, 4
Makes: 8 (3-tablespoon)
  servings
Active Time: 10 minutes
Total Time: 15 minutes

40 g (1½ oz) sun-dried tomatoes (not packed in oil)
475 ml (16 fl oz) boiling water
60 ml (2 fl oz) water
175 ml (6 fl oz) extra virgin olive oil
15 g (1/2 oz) basil leaves
40 g (1½ oz) pine kernels, toasted
3 tablespoons grated Pecorino Romano
1 garlic clove

Combine sun-dried tomatoes and boiling water in a bowl; leave until tomatoes are pliable, about 10 minutes. Drain; squeeze out excess liquid.

Combine tomatoes, water, oil, basil, pine kernels, Pecorino Romano and garlic in a blender; pulse until fairly smooth. Serve straight away or refrigerate in an airtight container for up to 2 days or freeze for up to 1 week.

PER SERVING: Net Carbs: 3 grams; Total Carbs: 4 grams; Fibre: 1 gram; Protein: 2 grams; Fat: 24 grams; Calories: 240

Salsa Cruda

This uncooked tomato sauce is delicious over vegetables and makes a summery dish when tossed with grilled shrimp or chicken. If your tomatoes are on the acidic side, add ½ teaspoon granulated sucralose.

Phases: 1, 2, 3, 4	4 medium tomatoes, deseeded and chopped
Makes: 10 (50-g/2-oz) servings	60 ml (2 fl oz) extra virgin olive oil
Active Time: 15 minutes	3 tablespoons chopped fresh basil
Total Time: 45 minutes	1 tablespoon red wine vinegar
	1 garlic clove, minced
	½ teaspoon salt
	¼ teaspoon pepper

Combine tomatoes, oil, basil, vinegar, garlic, salt and pepper in a medium bowl. Leave for 30 minutes before serving.

PER SERVING: Net Carbs: 1.5 grams; Total Carbs: 2 grams; Fibre: 0.5 grams; Protein: 0 grams; Fat: 5.5 grams; Calories: 60

Tip: It's a good idea to wear rubber gloves to prevent skin irritation when chopping jalapeños. Also, be careful not to rub your eyes after touching the peppers.

Tomatillo Salsa (Salsa Verde)

Break out of your red salsa rut! This green salsa is tangy and slightly spicy and has a bit of crunch, too. If you haven't experimented with tomatillo, a member of the tomato family that's particularly low in carbs, this is a good first recipe to try.

Phases: 2, 3, 4
Makes: 12 (50-g/2-oz) servings
Active Time: 15 minutes
Total Time: 15 minutes

450 g (1 lb) tomatillos, husked and chopped

½ small red onion, finely chopped

5 tablespoons chopped fresh coriander

2 tablespoons fresh lime juice

2 tablespoons extra virgin olive oil

1 jalapeño, finely chopped (see note on page 262)

½ teaspoon salt

⅛ teaspoon pepper

Mix tomatillos, onion, coriander, lime juice, oil, jalapeño, salt and pepper in a medium bowl. Leave for 30 minutes to allow flavours to blend. Serve chilled or at room temperature. Refrigerate leftovers in an airtight container for up to 3 days.

PER SERVING: Net Carbs: 4 grams; Total Carbs: 6 grams; Fibre: 2 grams; Protein: 1 gram; Fat: 5 grams; Calories: 70

Hollandaise Sauce

This is the classic sauce for asparagus, broccoli and Eggs Benedict, but don't overlook it for fish and shellfish. This recipe calls for clarified butter – meaning the milk solids are removed, which makes the sauce more stable. If you prefer, simply melt the butter and add it in step 2 without straining it.

Phases: 1, 2, 3, 4
Makes: 16 (2-tablespoon) servings
Active Time: 15 minutes
Total Time: 25 minutes

350 g (12 oz) unsalted butter

3 large egg yolks

3 tablespoons water

1 tablespoon fresh lemon juice

½ teaspoon salt

⅛ teaspoon pepper

Line a sieve with a damp kitchen paper and set over a bowl. Bring butter to the boil in a small saucepan over medium heat; cook until foam on top falls to the bottom and the butter begins to clear, about 8 minutes. Pour butter though sieve; set aside.

Combine egg yolks and water in the top of a double boiler set over (not in) simmering water set over medium-low heat; simmer until mixture has tripled in volume, about 3 minutes. Add butter in a slow and steady stream, whisking constantly until sauce thickens. Whisk in lemon juice, salt and pepper; serve right away.

PER SERVING: Net Carbs: 0 grams; Total Carbs: 0 grams; Fibre: 0 grams; Protein: 1 gram; Fat: 18 grams; Calories: 160

Brown Butter Sauce

Butter cooked just until it browns has a lovely nutty flavour and aroma. This simple French classic pairs well with any white fish or scallops, eggs and vegetables.

Phases: 1, 2, 3, 4	115 g (4 oz) unsalted butter
Makes: 4 (2-tablespoon)	1 tablespoon lemon juice
servings	½ teaspoon salt
Active Time: 10 minutes	⅛ teaspoon pepper
Total Time: 10 minutes	

Melt butter in a small saucepan over medium heat; cook until butter begins to brown and smell nutty, about 5 minutes. Remove from heat; stir in lemon juice, salt and pepper. Serve straight away.

PER SERVING: Net Carbs: 0 grams; Total Carbs: 0 grams; Fibre: 0 grams; Protein: 0 grams; Fat: 23 grams; Calories: 200

COMPOUND BUTTERS AND OILS

Butter-Oil Blend

This mix is high in monounsaturated fats and includes some omega-3 fatty acids. It also has a nice mouthfeel and spreads the way soft margarine does. Serve on vegetables, fish or meat.

Phases: 1, 2, 3, 4
Makes: 32 (1-tablespoon) servings
Active Time: 5 minutes
Total Time: 5 minutes

225 g (8 oz) salted butter
120 ml (4 fl oz) light olive oil
120 ml (4 fl oz) rapeseed oil

Blend butter and both oils in a food processor until smooth. Scrape into a container with a snap top. Keeps in the refrigerator for up to one month.

PER SERVING: Net Carbs: 0 grams; Total Carbs: 0 grams; Fibre: 0 grams; Protein: 0 grams; Fat: 16 grams; Calories: 110

Herb-Butter Blend

This savory version of the Butter-Oil Blend is delicious on vegetables, fish and meats.

Phases 1, 2, 3, 4
Makes: 32 (1-tablespoon) servings
Active Time: 7 minutes
Total Time: 7 minutes

½ teaspoon salt
1 teaspoon finely ground black pepper
120 ml (4 fl oz) light olive oil
2 cloves garlic, peeled
3 sprigs fresh oregano leaves, leaves only
5–10 fresh basil leaves
225 g (8 oz) salted butter
120 ml (4 fl oz) rapeseed oil

Place salt, pepper, olive oil, garlic, oregano and basil in a food processor. Pulse until herbs are finely ground and there are no visible specks of pepper (30–60 seconds total). Add butter and rapeseed oil, blending until smooth. Scrape into a container with a snap top and refrigerate up to 1 month.

PER SERVING: Net Carbs: 0 grams; Total Carbs: 0 grams; Fibre: 0 grams; Protein: 0 grams; Fat: 12.5 grams; Calories: 110

Parsley Butter

Top vegetables or grilled meats and poultry with this seasoned butter or use it to cook eggs. Substitute a minced clove of garlic and a little onion if shallots aren't available. Feel free to substitute chopped fresh coriander for the parsley, lime juice for the lemon juice and a pinch of cayenne pepper for the pepper.

Phases 1, 2, 3, 4	75 g (3 oz) salted butter, at room temperature
Makes: 4 (2-tablespoon)	1 small shallot (or garlic), minced
servings	2 tablespoons minced parsley
Active Time: 10 minutes	2 teaspoons fresh lemon juice
Total Time: 2 hours, 10 minutes	¼ teaspoon salt
	⅛ teaspoon pepper

Combine butter, shallot, parsley, lemon juice, salt and pepper in a medium bowl; blend well to distribute ingredients thoroughly. Spoon seasoned butter on to greaseproof paper; roll paper around butter to form a log. Twist ends to secure butter; roll gently across work surface to form an even cylinder. Refrigerate until chilled, at least 2 hours and up to 1 week. Slice into small pats and use as desired.

PER SERVING: Net Carbs: 1 gram; Total Carbs: 1 gram; Fibre: 0 grams; Protein: 0 grams; Fat: 17 grams; Calories: 150

Herb-flavoured Oil

Use herb oils to garnish vegetables, soups and meats or in salad dressings.

Phases 1, 2, 3, 4	1 bunch fresh leafy herbs, such as basil, parsley or coriander
Makes: 16 (1-tablespoon) servings	240 ml (8 fl oz) extra virgin olive oil or rapeseed oil
Active Time: 10 minutes	
Total Time: 8 hours	

Bring a large pot of salted water to the boil. Have a bowl of cold water ready. Add the herbs (stems and all) to the boiling water and leave until just softened and bright green, about 30 seconds. Drain and plunge into cold water to stop cooking. Drain again and pat dry with kitchen paper.

Combine herbs and oil in a blender. Blend until smooth. Transfer to a glass jar, cover and refrigerate 8 hours or overnight.

Strain oil through a fine-mesh sieve. Refrigerate oil in an airtight container for up to 1 week.

PER SERVING: Net Carbs: 0 grams; Total Carbs: 0 grams; Fibre: 0 grams; Protein: 0 grams; Fat: 14 grams; Calories: 130

SALAD DRESSINGS

To get the most monounsaturated fats and minimise your consumption of polyunsaturates, of which we already get plenty, make salad dressings with olive oil – use the extra virgin type – and rapeseed oil. A few of our dressings call for another oil to lend a certain flavour. In recipes that call for rice vinegar, be sure to use the unseasoned kind with no added sugar. For additional salad dressings such as Lemon Vinaigrette, Green Goddess Dressing and Garlic Ranch Dressing, go to www.atkins.com.

Caesar Salad Dressing

This is the classic dressing for a Caesar salad made with cos lettuce, but it enlivens any salad leaves. For a real treat make this
dressing with home-made Mayonnaise (page 249).

Phases: 1, 2, 3, 4
Makes: 4 (2-tablespoon)
  servings
Active Time: 5 minutes
Total Time: 5 minutes

55 g (2 oz) mayonnaise
3 tablespoons grated Parmesan
1 tablespoon anchovy paste
1 tablespoon fresh lemon juice
2 garlic cloves, finely chopped
2 teaspoons extra virgin olive oil
1 teaspoon Worcestershire sauce
1 teaspoon Dijon mustard
½ teaspoon pepper
Hot pepper sauce

Combine mayonnaise, Parmesan, anchovy paste, lemon juice,
garlic, oil, Worcestershire sauce, mustard, pepper and hot sauce
in a small bowl. Use straight away or refrigerate in an airtight
container for up to 2 days.

PER SERVING: Net Carbs: 1.5 grams; Total Carbs: 1.5 grams; Fibre: 0 grams; Protein: 2 grams; Fat: 15
grams; Calories: 150

Greek Vinaigrette

Serve this tangy lemon-garlic dressing on iceberg lettuce with
some black olives, red onions, tomatoes, cucumbers and feta
cheese for a Greek salad. Add grilled prawns to turn it into a
hearty supper salad.

Phases: 1, 2, 3, 4

Makes: 4 (2-tablespoon)
    servings

Active Time: 7 minutes

Total Time: 7 minutes

90 ml (3 fl oz) extra virgin olive oil

1 garlic clove, finely minced

½ teaspoon dried oregano, crumbled

½ teaspoon salt

¼ teaspoon pepper

2 tablespoons fresh lemon juice

1 teaspoon red wine vinegar

Whisk together oil, garlic, oregano, salt and pepper in a small bowl; whisk in lemon juice and vinegar. Use straight away or refrigerate in an airtight container for up to 2 days.

PER SERVING: Net Carbs: 1 gram; Total Carbs: 1 gram; Fibre: 0 grams; Protein: 0 grams; Fat: 20 grams; Calories: 185

Hot Bacon Vinaigrette

Perfect for a winter meal, this hot dressing wilts the salad leaves. Serve it over spinach, iceberg, tender chicory or cos. Add a few hard-boiled eggs, and/or a little leftover roast chicken to make a filling lunch or a light dinner.

Phases 1, 2, 3, 4

Makes: 6 (2-tablespoon)
    servings

Active Time: 12 minutes

Total Time: 12 minutes

6 rashers thick-cut bacon, cut into 5-mm (¼-in) strips

60 ml (2 fl oz) sherry vinegar

60 ml (2 fl oz) extra virgin olive oil

Salt and pepper

Brown bacon in a frying pan over medium heat, stirring occasionally, until crisp, about 10 minutes. Using a slotted spoon, transfer to a kitchen paper–lined plate to drain; keep bacon fat in frying pan. Add vinegar and oil; whisk, scraping up browned bits from bottom of pan. Season to taste with salt and pepper. Pour over salad leaves while still hot.

PER SERVING: Net Carbs: 0 grams; Total Carbs: 0 grams; Fibre: 0 grams; Protein: 3 grams; Fat: 12.5 grams; Calories: 125

Tip: Instead of whisking salad dressing ingredients, you can use a blender or place them in a jar with a tight-fitting lid and shake it vigorously.

Sherry Vinaigrette

Serve this creamy dressing over spinach, watercress, rocket or other dark leafy greens.

Phases: 1, 2, 3, 4
Makes: 6 (2-tablespoon) servings
Active Time: 3 minutes
Total Time: 3 minutes

2 tablespoons sherry vinegar
1 small shallot, minced
1 teaspoon Dijon mustard
½ teaspoon salt
¼ teaspoon pepper
90 ml (3 fl oz) extra-virgin olive oil

Combine vinegar, shallot, mustard, salt and pepper in a small bowl. Add oil in a slow, steady stream, whisking until dressing thickens. Use straight away or refrigerate in an airtight container for up to 2 days.

PER SERVING: Net Carbs: 0.5 grams; Total Carbs: 0.5 grams; Fibre: 0 grams; Protein: 0 grams; Fat: 13.5 grams; Calories: 125

Creamy Coleslaw Dressing

This makes enough dressing for 225 g (8 oz) green cabbage, shredded.

Phases: 1, 2, 3, 4
Makes: 12 (2-tablespoon) servings
Active Time: 15 minutes
Total Time: 15 minutes

175 g (6 oz) mayonnaise
55 g (2 oz) soured cream
2 tablespoons cider vinegar
1 garlic clove, chopped
1 teaspoon caraway seeds
½ teaspoon salt
¼ teaspoon pepper

Combine mayonnaise, soured cream, vinegar, garlic, caraway seeds, salt and pepper in a small bowl. After adding dressing to cabbage, cover and refrigerate for at least 30 minutes before serving.

PER SERVING: Net Carbs: 0.5 grams; Total Carbs: 0.5 grams; Fibre: 0 grams; Protein: 0 grams; Fat: 12 grams; Calories: 110

Fresh Raspberry Vinaigrette

If your berries are tart, you may want to add the sugar substitute, but in-season berries are likely to be fine without it.

Phases: 2, 3, 4
Makes: 8 (2-tablespoon)
  servings
Active Time: 10 minutes
Total Time: 10 minutes

65 g (2½ oz) fresh raspberries
2 tablespoons water
3 tablespoons red wine vinegar
1 teaspoon granular non-caloric sweetener (optional)
1 shallot, minced
¾ teaspoon salt
½ teaspoon pepper
½ teaspoon pepper
120 ml (4 fl oz) extra virgin olive oil

Purée raspberries and water in a blender; strain into a bowl. Stir in vinegar, sugar substitute, shallot, salt and pepper. Add oil in a slow stream, whisking until dressing thickens. Use straight away or refrigerate in an airtight container for up to 2 days.

PER SERVING: Net Carbs: 1 gram; Total Carbs: 0 grams; Fibre: 1 gram; Protein: 0 grams; Fat: 14 grams; Calories: 130

Blue Cheese Dressing

Drizzle this thick and creamy dressing over iceberg lettuce or other salad leaves or serve as a dip for fresh vegetables or chicken wings or on top of cold roast beef. If you can, make the dressing

a day ahead to let the flavours develop. Home-made Mayonnaise
(page 249) produces scrumptious results.

Phases 1, 2, 3, 4	115 g (4 oz) blue cheese, crumbled
Makes: 14 (2-tablespoon) servings	115 g (4 oz) mayonnaise
	115 g (4 oz) soured cream
Active Time: 10 minutes	75 ml (2½ oz) double cream
Total Time: 10 minutes	1 tablespoon fresh lemon juice
	½ teaspoon Dijon mustard
	½ teaspoon pepper

Combine blue cheese, mayonnaise, soured cream, double cream,
lemon juice, mustard and pepper in a medium bowl, mashing with
a fork to break up the cheese. Use straight away or refrigerate in an
airtight container for up to 3 days.

PER SERVING: Net Carbs: 1 gram; Total Carbs: 1 gram; Fibre: 0 grams; Protein: 2 grams; Fat: 12 grams;
Calories: 120

Italian Dressing

This traditional favourite achieves the perfect ratio of oil to vinegar. If you don't have a garlic press, crush the cloves with the flat
side of a knife and then mince them very finely.

Phases: 1, 2, 3, 4	175 ml (6 fl oz) extra virgin olive oil
Makes: 8 (2-tablespoon) servings	60 ml (2 fl oz) red wine vinegar
	2 tablespoons fresh lemon juice
Active Time: 10 minutes	2 garlic cloves, pressed
Total Time: 10 minutes	3 tablespoons minced fresh parsley
	1 tablespoon minced fresh basil
	2 teaspoons dried oregano
	½ teaspoon red pepper flakes
	¼ teaspoon salt
	¼ teaspoon pepper
	½ teaspoon granular non-caloric sweetener

Combine oil, vinegar, lemon juice, garlic, parsley, basil, oregano, red pepper flakes, salt, pepper and sugar substitute in a jar with a tight-fitting lid; shake vigorously. (This can also be done in a blender.) Use straight away or refrigerate in an airtight container for up to 3 days.

PER SERVING: Net Carbs: 1 gram; Total Carbs: 1 gram; Fibre: 0 grams; Protein: 0 grams; Fat: 21 grams; Calories: 200

Roasted Garlic-Basil Dressing

Roasted garlic emulsifies this creamy dressing, keeping it from separating into oil and vinegar. Roasting tames the garlic's pungency, resulting in a paste that's actually sweet. If you have a ceramic garlic roaster, use it instead of kitchen foil.

Phases: 1, 2, 3, 4
Makes: 15 (2-tablespoon) servings
Active Time: 10 minutes
Total Time: 90 minutes

1 large garlic bulb
265 ml (8½ fl oz) extra virgin olive oil
75 ml (½ fl oz) unseasoned rice wine vinegar
10 fresh basil leaves
30 g (1 oz) grated Parmesan (optional)
½ teaspoon salt
1 teaspoon pepper
2 tablespoons xylitol

Preheat the oven to 200°C/400°F/Gas Mark 6. Trim the top 5 mm (¼ in) off the garlic bulb to expose the cloves. Place on a large square of kitchen foil, drizzle the top with a tablespoon of olive oil and close tightly to form a packet. Bake until garlic is very soft, about 45 minutes. Remove from oven and leave to cool at room temperature for about 25 minutes.

Place vinegar, basil and grated Parmesan in food processor and pulse until very finely ground. Separate garlic into cloves. Squeeze roasted garlic out of skins into food processor and add olive oil, salt and pepper. Process until smooth, 2 or 3 minutes.

Refrigerate in a squeeze bottle or closed container for up to a week.

PER SERVING: Net Carbs: 1 gram; Total Carbs: 1 gram; Fibre: 0 grams; Protein: 0 grams; Fat: 20 grams; Calories: 180

Ranch Dressing

An all-American favourite, this home-made version of the creamy garlic-and-herb dressing is smooth and satisfying.

Phases: 1, 2, 3, 4
Makes: 8 (2½-tablespoon) servings
Active Time: 10 minutes
Total Time: 10 minutes

175 g (6 oz) mayonnaise
120 ml (4 fl oz) double cream
2 tablespoons chopped fresh parsley
2 tablespoons chopped chives
2 teaspoons fresh lemon juice
2 teaspoons Dijon mustard
1 garlic clove, minced
1 teaspoon chopped fresh dill
½ teaspoon salt
¼ teaspoon pepper

Whisk mayonnaise, cream, parsley, chives, lemon juice, mustard, garlic, dill, salt and pepper in a small bowl. Use straight away or refrigerate in an airtight container for up to 3 days.

PER SERVING: Net Carbs: 1 gram; Total Carbs: 1 gram; Fibre: 0 grams; Protein: 0 grams; Fat: 22 grams; Calories: 200

Sweet Mustard Dressing

Use this sweet-and-sour dressing to bring out the best in any salad containing meat or cheese, or to dress up steamed green vegetables.

Phases: 1, 2, 3, 4
Makes: 10 (2-tablespoon)
  servings
Active Time: 10 minutes
Total Time: 10 minutes

80 g (3 oz) coarse-grain mustard
75 ml (2½ fl oz) cider vinegar
60 ml (2 fl oz) sugar-free maple syrup
½ teaspoon salt
¼ teaspoon pepper
150 ml (¼ pint) rapeseed oil

Combine mustard, vinegar, syrup, salt and pepper in a small bowl. Add oil in a slow, steady stream, whisking until dressing thickens. Use straight away or refrigerate in an airtight container for up to 2 days.

PER SERVING: Net Carbs: 1 gram; Total Carbs: 1 gram; Fibre: 0 grams; Protein: 1 gram; Fat: 15 grams; Calories: 140

Carrot-Ginger Dressing

This colourful dressing adds exotic flavour to iceberg lettuce, steamed French beans or chicken, salmon or low-carb or shirataki noodle salads.

Phases: 3, 4
Makes: 12 (3-tablespoon)
  servings
Active Time: 15 minutes
Total Time: 15 minutes

3 medium carrots, grated
3 tablespoons minced fresh ginger
40 g (1½ oz) white onion, chopped
60 ml (2 fl oz) unseasoned rice vinegar
60 ml (2 fl oz) water
1 tablespoon soya sauce
1 tablespoon dark sesame oil
1 teaspoon salt
½ teaspoon granular non-caloric sweetener
120 ml (4 fl oz) rapeseed oil

Purée carrots, ginger, onion, vinegar, water, soya sauce, sesame oil, salt and sugar substitute in a blender. With motor running, add oil in a slow, steady stream until dressing thickens. Use straight away or refrigerate in an airtight container for up to 1 day.

PER SERVING: Net Carbs: 1 gram; Total Carbs: 2 grams; Fibre: 1 gram; Protein: 0 grams; Fat: 10 grams; Calories: 100

Creamy Italian Dressing

This creamy dressing, bold with aged cheese, herbs and spices, might become your favourite. If you don't have Italian seasoning to hand use a combination of basil, oregano and parsley instead.

Phases: 1, 2, 3, 4
Makes: 10 (2-tablespoon)
  servings
Active Time: 10 minutes
Total Time: 15 minutes

50 g (2 oz) mayonnaise
75 ml (2½ fl oz) white wine vinegar
2 tablespoons sugar substitute
30 g (1 oz) Parmesan, grated
1 garlic clove, minced
2 teaspoons dried Italian seasoning
¼ teaspoon red pepper flakes
¼ teaspoon salt
¼ teaspoon pepper
2 tablespoons chopped fresh parsley

Whisk mayonnaise, vinegar and sugar substitute in a medium bowl. Stir in Parmesan, garlic, Italian seasoning, pepper flakes, salt, pepper and parsley until well blended. Leave for 5 minutes. Use straight away or refrigerate in an airtight container for up to 3 days; stir before using.

PER SERVING: Net Carbs: 2 grams; Total Carbs: 2 grams; Fibre: 0 grams; Protein: 1 gram; Fat: 10 grams; Calories: 100

Parmesan-Peppercorn Dressing

This simple dressing is especially good with shaved fennel or strongly flavoured greens and vegetables. To crack whole peppercorns, place them under a heavy-based pan and press down on them, or use a pestle and mortar.

Phases: 1, 2, 3, 4
Makes: 8 (2-tablespoon)
  servings
Active Time: 10 minutes
Total Time: 10 minutes

3 tablespoons fresh lemon juice
3 tablespoons grated Parmesan
1 garlic clove, chopped
1 teaspoon red wine vinegar
1 teaspoon granular non-caloric sweetener

1 teaspoon cracked black peppercorns
½ teaspoon salt
120 ml (4 fl oz) extra virgin olive oil

Combine lemon juice, Parmesan, garlic, vinegar, sugar substitute, peppercorns and salt in a small bowl. Add oil in a slow, steady stream, whisking until dressing thickens. Use straight away or refrigerate in an airtight container for up to 3 days.

PER SERVING: Net Carbs: 1 gram; Total Carbs: 1 gram; Fibre: 0 grams; Protein: 1 gram; Fat: 15 grams; Calories: 140

VARIATION
Lemon-Dill Vinaigrette
Prepare Parmesan Peppercorn Dressing according to directions, replacing the Parmesan with 1 tablespoon drained capers and 1 tablespoon chopped fresh dill.

French Dressing
Try this classic sweet-tart American salad dressing with crisp pieces of iceberg lettuce and wedges of sweet ripe tomatoes. If you don't have garlic powder, crush one garlic clove with the flat side of a chef's knife and add it to the dressing; remove and discard the garlic before serving or storing.

Phases: 1, 2, 3, 4
Makes: 10 (2-tablespoon) servings
Active Time: 10 minutes
Total Time: 10 minutes

120 g (4 oz) low-carb tomato ketchup
125 ml (4 fl oz) rapeseed oil
60 ml (2 fl oz) cider vinegar
1 tablespoon xylitol
½ teaspoon salt
¼ teaspoon garlic powder
Pinch cayenne pepper

Whisk tomato ketchup, oil, vinegar, sugar substitute, salt, garlic powder and cayenne pepper in a medium bowl. Use straight away or refrigerate in an airtight container for up to 3 days.

PER SERVING: Net Carbs: 1 gram; Total Carbs: 2 grams; Fibre: 1 gram; Protein: 0 grams; Fat: 11 grams; Calories: 110

Russian Dressing

Despite its name, this is an American recipe. It's said that at one time it called for caviar as an ingredient, hence the name. You can also spoon it over cold sliced chicken or hard-boiled eggs.

Phases: 1, 2, 3, 4
Makes: 8 (2-tablespoon) servings
Active Time: 10 minutes
Total Time: 10 minutes

175 g (6 g) mayonnaise
60 g (2½ oz) low-carb tomato ketchup
1 tablespoon finely chopped onion
1 tablespoon chopped fresh parsley
2 teaspoons prepared horseradish
1 teaspoon Worcestershire sauce

Combine mayonnaise, tomato ketchup, onion, parsley, horseradish and Worcestershire sauce in a bowl, mixing well. Use straight away or refrigerate in an airtight container for up to 3 days.

PER SERVING: Net Carbs: 0 grams; Total Carbs: 1 gram; Fibre: 1 gram; Protein: 0 grams; Fat: 17 grams; Calories: 160

Tip: Heinz and other manufacturers make tomato ketchup with no added sugar. If your supermarket doesn't carry it, ask the manager to order it or purchase it online.

MARINADES AND RUBS

Unlike sauces and condiments, marinades and rubs work their magic before cooking.

Marinades are liquids that usually contain an acidic ingredient – wine, vinegar, lemon or lime juice or yoghurt – and flavourings. Meat, chicken, fish and even vegetables are soaked in marinades to heighten their flavours, and enzymes in the acids work to break down fibres. Tough cuts of meat may take several hours (or even days) to become tender when marinated, but delicate fish should be marinated briefly – no more than 20 or 30 minutes – or it may actually 'cook' in the acid, giving your finished dish an unpleasant texture. Whether you're cooking fish, tofu, vegetables, poultry or meat, heed the instructions given in the recipe; if no times are given, err on the side of caution – figure 15 to 20 minutes for fish and tofu, 2 hours for chicken parts or thin steaks, 6 to 8 hours for roasts.

Rubs are dry mixtures of spices and sometimes herbs. As the name suggests, they're rubbed on to cuts of meat and allowed to permeate the meat before cooking. Ideally, you'll have the time to leave the rubbed meat overnight, but even a half-hour will add flavour.

Latin Marinade

Garlic and lime, suggesting a Cuban accent, flavour this marinade. It's particularly good with all cuts of pork and chicken (marinate at least 2 hours and up to 24) and fish and shellfish (marinate no longer than 20 minutes).

Phases: 1, 2, 3, 4
Makes: 8 (2-tablespoon)
    servings (enough for 675 to
    900 g/1½ to 2 lb meat, fish or
    vegetables)
Active Time: 5 minutes
Total Time: 5 minutes

5 garlic cloves, peeled
60 ml (2 fl oz) fresh lemon juice
2 tablespoons fresh lime juice
2 tablespoons chopped coriander leaves
½ small onion, chopped
1½ teaspoons grated orange zest
¾ teaspoon dried oregano
1½ teaspoons salt
175 ml (6 fl oz) rapeseed oil

Combine garlic, lemon juice, lime juice, coriander, onion, orange zest, oregano and salt in a blender; blend until smooth. Add the oil and pulse to combine.

PER SERVING: Net Carbs: 2.5 grams; Total Carbs: 3 grams; Fibre: 0.5 gram; Protein: 0.5 gram; Fat: 21 grams; Calories: 190

Tip: Many of the ingredients in marinades and rubs contain carbohydrates, but since you usually discard the marinade, you'll actually consume only negligible amounts.

Asian Marinade

Try this simple marinade with chicken kebabs, salmon or tuna steaks, pork chops or beef fillet. Marinate chicken and meat for up to 24 hours, fish for up to 2 hours.

Phases: 1, 2, 3, 4
Makes: 6 (2-tablespoon) servings (enough for 450 to 900 g/1 to 1½ lb meat, fish or vegetables)
Active Time: 5 minutes
Total Time: 5 minutes

120 ml (4 fl oz) soya sauce
2 tablespoons unseasoned rice wine vinegar
2 tablespoons xylitol
1 tablespoon grated peeled ginger
2 garlic cloves, minced
2 teaspoons dark sesame oil
2 tablespoons canola oil

Combine soya sauce, vinegar, sugar substitute, ginger, garlic and sesame oil in a bowl. Slowly whisk in vegetable oil until combined.

PER SERVING: Net Carbs: 5 grams; Total Carbs: 5 grams; Fibre: 0 grams; Protein: 1.5 grams; Fat: 4 grams; Calories: 60

Tip: Discard marinades after soaking food. Even if you've refrigerated it, the marinade may harbour potentially harmful bacteria. If you want to use the marinade as a basting sauce or to pass it at the table, it's much safer to reserve some before adding the food, or to make a fresh batch.

Chipotle Marinade

Chipotles en adobo are part of the Mexican cuisine and may be available in cans in the specialist food sections of your supermarket, or try ordering it online. This pastelike marinade is terrific on bone-in chicken, short ribs, all pork cuts and boneless, skinless turkey cutlets.

Phases: 1, 2, 3, 4
Makes: 4 (2-tablespoon)
  servings (enough for about
  450 g/1 lb meat, fish or
  vegetables)
Active Time: 5 minutes
Total Time: 5 minutes

6 garlic cloves, minced
4 chipotles en adobo, finely chopped
2 teaspoons granular non-caloric sweetener
2 tablespoons fresh lime juice
2 tablespoons extra-virgin olive oil
2 teaspoons ground cumin
1 teaspoon salt

Combine garlic, chipotles, sugar substitute, lime juice, oil, cumin and salt in a bowl; mix well.

PER SERVING: Net Carbs: 2 grams; Total Carbs: 3 grams; Fibre: 1 gram; Protein: 1 gram; Fat: 8 grams; Calories: 80

Mediterranean Marinade

Rosemary, garlic and lemon are the base of this versatile marinade. It's great on just about anything you grill, sauté or roast, but particularly chicken, veal chops, aubergine slices, mild-flavoured whole fish such as snapper or bass and sea scallops.

Because it's low in acid, even fish and shellfish can be marinated in it for up to 24 hours.

Phases: 1, 2, 3, 4
Makes: 4 (2-tablespoon)
  servings (enough for about
  450 g/1 lb meat, fish or
  vegetables)
Active Time: 5 minutes
Total Time: 5 minutes
	2 tablespoons Dijon mustard
	2 tablespoons fresh chopped rosemary leaves
	3 garlic cloves, peeled
	1 teaspoon grated lemon zest
	½ teaspoon ground fennel
	½ teaspoon pepper
	1 teaspoon salt
	120 ml (4 fl oz) extra virgin olive oil

Combine mustard, rosemary, garlic, lemon zest, fennel, pepper and salt in a blender. With the motor running, slowly drizzle in the oil until incorporated.

PER SERVING: Net Carbs: 1 gram; Total Carbs: 2 grams; Fibre: 1 gram; Protein: 1 gram; Fat: 29 grams; Calories: 270

Hearty Red Wine Marinade

Steaks, venison, bison or other game, thick onion slices and summer squash are among the foods that stand up well to this full-flavoured marinade. Substitute a small onion for the shallot if you wish.

Phases: 1, 2, 3, 4
Makes: 8 (2-tablespoon)
  servings (enough for 675 to
  900 g/1½ to 2 lb meat, fish or
  vegetables)
Active Time: 5 minutes
Total Time: 5 minutes
	120 ml (4 fl oz) dry red wine
	60 ml (2 fl oz) extra virgin olive oil
	2 tablespoons red wine vinegar
	1 medium shallot, chopped
	1 garlic clove, minced
	2 teaspoons granular non-caloric sweetener
	10 juniper berries (optional)
	2 teaspoons chopped fresh rosemary leaves
	¼ teaspoon coarsely ground black pepper
	¾ teaspoon salt

Combine wine, oil, vinegar, shallot, garlic, sugar substitute, juniper berries, rosemary, pepper and salt in a bowl; mix well.

PER SERVING: Net Carbs: 1 gram; Total Carbs: 1 gram; Fibre: 0 grams; Protein: 0 grams; Fat: 7 grams; Calories: 80

Tip: If you grind whole spices – a clean coffee grinder is ideal for this – to clean it, tear up a slice of bread and whirl it in the machine to form crumbs. The bread will absorb the coffee grinds and oils. Repeat after you've ground the spices to absorb their oils.

BBQ Rub

Use this simple rub to spice up meats before grilling and for roasting as well. Its flavour pairs beautifully with Barbecue Sauce (page 254). Rub this on ribs before cooking and then baste the ribs with the sauce during the last 10 to 20 minutes of grilling or cooking.

Phases: 1, 2, 3, 4
Makes: 12 (1-tablespoon)
  servings (enough for 1.6 to
  1.8 kg/3½ to 4 lb meat or
  fish)
Active Time: 5 minutes
Total Time: 5 minutes

2 tablespoons ground cumin
2 tablespoons garlic powder
2 tablespoons onion powder
2 tablespoons xylitol
1½ tablespoons chilli powder
1½ tablespoons pepper
1 tablespoon salt
1 teaspoon powdered mustard
1 teaspoon ground mixed spice

Combine cumin, garlic powder, onion powder, sugar substitute, chilli powder, pepper, salt, mustard and mixed spice in a bowl; mix well.

PER SERVING: Net Carbs: 3 grams; Total Carbs: 4 grams; Fibre: 1 gram; Protein: 1 gram; Fat: 0.5 gram; Calories: 20

Tip: You can store extra spice rub mixtures in an airtight container in a cool place for up to 2 months.

Moroccan Rub

This is exotic mix is a great flavour booster for lamb, prawns and chicken.

Phases: 1, 2, 3, 4
Makes: 6 (1-tablespoon)
  servings (enough for about
  900 g/2 lb meat or fish)
Active Time: 5 minutes
Total Time: 5 minutes

2 tablespoons plus 2 teaspoons ground cumin
4 teaspoons ground coriander
4 teaspoons salt
2 teaspoons pepper
2 teaspoons ground ginger
2 teaspoons dried oregano
1½ teaspoons granular non-caloric sweetener
1 teaspoon ground cinnamon

Combine cumin, coriander, salt, pepper, ginger, oregano, sugar substitute and cinnamon in a bowl; mix well.

PER SERVING: Net Carbs: 1 gram; Total Carbs: 3 grams; Fibre: 2 grams; Protein: 1 gram; Fat: 1 gram; Calories: 25

Tip: After food has marinated in a dry rub, remove as much as possible along with any juices released before cooking to ensure browning.

Cajun Rub

This is a classic 'blackening' rub for fish steaks such as tuna or swordfish or fillets such as catfish and snapper, but it also works well for poultry or pork chops.

Phases: 1, 2, 3, 4
Makes: 8 (1-tablespoon)
   servings (enough for about 1.3
   kg/3 lb meat or fish)
Active Time: 5 minutes
Total Time: 5 minutes
	2 tablespoons plus 2 teaspoons paprika
	2 tablespoons dried oregano
	1 tablespoon garlic powder
	1 tablespoon salt
	1 teaspoon dried thyme
	1 teaspoon cayenne pepper

Combine paprika, oregano, garlic powder, salt, thyme and cayenne pepper in a bowl; mix well.

PER SERVING: Net Carbs: 1 gram; Total Carbs: 3 grams; Fibre: 2 grams; Protein: 1 gram; Fat: 0 grams; Calories: 15

BROTHS

Drinking two 240-millilitre (8-fluid-ounce) cups of broth helps to eliminate or minimise side effects such as weakness that may result from the diuretic effects of following a very-low-carb (50 daily grams or 1.8 ounces of Net Carbs or less) diet. Along with fluids you can lose sodium (salt) and other minerals. These three broths will keep your electrolytes balanced. Plus, they're far more flavourful and nutritious than tinned or other packaged versions.

Chicken Broth

Each cup of this satisfying broth contains 7 grams (0.2 ounces) of protein, providing about an ounce of protein – far more than any ready-prepared product. The broth is also rich in potassium and magnesium.

Phase 1, 2, 3, 4
Makes: 16 (240-ml/8-fl-oz)
 servings
Active Time: 30 minutes
Total Time: 4 hours, 30 minutes

1 x 1.8-kg (4-lb) chicken
2 small onions
2 centre celery sticks with leaves
2 garlic cloves
2 tablespoons salt
4 litres (7 pints) water
5 parsley sprigs (optional)
5 thyme sprigs (optional)
2 bay leaves (optional)
10 black peppercorns

Combine chicken, onions, celery, garlic, salt, water, optional seasonings and peppercorns in a large pot over medium heat. Bring just to the boil. Reduce heat to low and simmer, covered, for 2 hours. Stir to break up large pieces of chicken. Add enough water to return to original level and simmer 2 to 4 hours longer. Restore water level again; bring to the boil and remove from heat. After stock has cooled slightly, strain and discard all solids (including chicken).

Chill in the refrigerator until fat congeals. Skim off and discard. Transfer broth to small containers; refrigerate for up to 3 days or freeze for up to 3 months.

PER SERVING: Total Carbs: 1 gram; Fiber: 0 grams; Net Carbs: 1 gram; Protein: 7 grams; Fat: 0 grams; Calories: 28

Tip: To ensure a clear broth and optimal flavour, rinse the chicken and the neck, but discard all organs, including the kidney, which is a reddish brown clump against the backbone just inside the cavity.

VARIATION
Beef Broth
Prepare Chicken Stock according to directions above, replacing chicken with 1.8 kg (4 lb) chuck cut of beef.

Vegetable Broth

Canned broths and packaged bouillon cubes can never match the flavour of a home-made stock. In addition, this broth is a good source of potassium, an important mineral during dieting. Use it in place of water or chicken broth in most soup or sauce recipes.

Phase 1, 2, 3, 4
Makes: 16 (1-cup) servings
Active Time: 20 minutes
Total Time: 1 hour, 20 minutes

4 medium leeks, white and light green parts only
2 tablespoons olive oil
2 medium carrots, roughly chopped
2 celery sticks, roughly chopped
115 g (4 oz) mushrooms, sliced
4 garlic cloves, crushed
4 litres (7 pints) water
5 parsley sprigs
5 thyme sprigs
2 bay leaves
5 teaspoons table salt
2 teaspoons lite table salt (a mix of regular salt and
     potassium chloride)
10 peppercorns

Cut leeks in half lengthways and wash in cold water to remove any dirt. Chop roughly.

Heat oil in a large saucepan over medium heat. Add leeks, carrots, celery, mushrooms and garlic; sauté until vegetables are soft but not browned, about 10 minutes. Add water, parsley, thyme, bay leaves, salt and pepper. Bring just to the boil. Cover and reduce heat to low and simmer 1 hour, stirring periodically.

Remove from heat and strain, pressing on vegetables with a spatula or wooden spoon to release liquid. Discard solids and transfer broth to small containers; refrigerate for up to 3 days or freeze for up to 3 months.

PER SERVING: Net Carbs: 2 grams; Total Carbs: 2 grams; Fiber: 0 grams; Protein: 0 grams; Fat: 2 grams; Calories: 26

HOW TO USE THE MEAL PLANS

On the following pages, you'll find a wide array of meal plans that should allow you to move at your own pace through the four phases of Atkins. (See Index of Meal Plans on page 292.) They include a week of plans for Phase 1: Induction. Simply repeat this week, with your own variations, as long as you stay in Induction. (Remember, you can add nuts and seeds after two weeks in Induction if you decide to stay there longer.) We include six weeks at progressively higher levels for Phase 2: Ongoing Weight Loss. The five weeks of plans for Phase 3: Pre-Maintenance, are also suitable for Phase 4: Lifetime Maintenance.

Because vegetarians should start Atkins in Ongoing Weight Loss (OWL), our vegetarian plans start at 30 grams (1 ounce) of Net Carbs in OWL. We recommend that vegans begin Atkins in OWL at 50 grams (1.8 ounces) of Net Carbs. Once vegans begin to lose weight at this level, they can move to higher carb intakes by following the vegetarian meal plans, but substituting plant-based foods for dairy products and eggs.

TWO TIERS

Most of the plans have two tiers. In OWL, you move up in 5-gram increments, so the first week, you'll stay at the lower level. After a week or more at that level, you can move to the next tier. In Pre-Maintenance, you move up in 10-gram increments, so we've provided similarly incremental versions in the first two meal plans for this phase. (See below for more detail on how to read the incremental plans.)

FOCUS ON CARBS

While you're welcome to follow these plans to the letter, they're designed to show how to gradually increase your carb intake and, following the carb ladder (see page 145), to add new foods. Feel free to substitute foods with similar carb counts, swapping asparagus for French beans or cottage cheese for Greek yoghurt, for example.

The meal plans focus on carbs; however, we have not indicated carbs from sugar substitutes, cream, drinks with acceptable sweeteners, most condiments or acceptable desserts. If you add these foods, be sure to make adjustments to remain in the right carb range, so long as you consume at least 12 to 15 grams (0.4 to 0.5 ounces) of Net Carbs as foundation vegetables.

PROTEIN AND FAT

Intake varies from one person to another, so protein and fat portions aren't usually indicated, although both will make up the majority of your calorie intake. Most people eat roughly 113 to 170 grams (4 to 6 ounces) of protein with each meal. Eat enough fat to feel satisfied. We have, however, indicated portions for the few protein foods that also contain carbs, such as bacon and vegetarian and vegan protein sources. Likewise, we've included serving sizes and carb content for salad dressings and a few sauces. Feel free to add other fats such as butter, olive oil and soured cream.

You'll follow the same meal plans for Pre-Maintenance and Lifetime Maintenance, but once you've achieved your goal weight, you'll need to consume more fatty foods to offset the body fat that you were burning during weight loss. Check out our recipes for delicious salad dressings and other condiments.

JUST TO BE CLEAR

We've packed a lot of information into the plans. Here's how to read them:

- Recipes that appear in this book are in bold. See the recipe index on pages 244–245 for page numbers.
- Meals and snacks show the carb content of each item and a subtotal.
- When a meal or snack includes an incremental food for the higher level of Net Carbs, it appears in bold italics.
- When a meal or snack includes an incremental food, the higher level of carb content in the subtotal follows the lower level and is in parentheses.
- The day's total appears at the bottom of each day. In the case of two-tiered plans, the higher level of carb intake appears in parentheses.
- Foundation vegetables are also listed in the day's tally.

Finally, a daily variance at any carb level is natural and fine as long as you don't consistently overshoot your carb tolerance level, as you'll see in the daily totals.

INDEX OF MEAL PLANS

Phase 1: Induction

Each day shows the food item followed by its Grams of Net Carbs.

BREAKFAST

Day 1	Day 2	Day 3	Day 4	Day 5	Day 6	Day 7
2 scrambled eggs — 1 Sausages — 0 30 g steamed spinach — 2	Ground beef sautéed with — 0 25 g spring onions and — 0.5 50 g red peppers, topped with — 2 30 g shredded mozzarella cheese — 0.5	30 g shredded mozzarella cheese melted on 1 medium tomato — 3.5 Low-carb shake — 1	2 slices Swiss cheese — 0.5 Roast turkey slices wrapped around — 0 4 asparagus spears — 2	2 fried eggs — 1 2 Tbsp. no-sugar-added red salsa — 0.5 ½ Haas avocado — 2	Smoked salmon wrapped around — 1 2 Tbsp. cream cheese and — 0.5 50 g sliced cucumber — 2	Bacon strips — 0 1 slice Swiss cheese — 1 1 hard-boiled egg — 0.5 3 asparagus spears — 1.5
Subtotal 3	**Subtotal 3**	**Subtotal 4.5**	**Subtotal 2.5**	**Subtotal 3.5**	**Subtotal 3.5**	**Subtotal 3**

SNACK

Day 1	Day 2	Day 3	Day 4	Day 5	Day 6	Day 7
1 stick string cheese — 0.5 ½ Haas avocado — 2	1 hard-boiled egg — 0.5 1 celery stalk — 1	6 radishes — 0.5 2 slices Muenster cheese — 1	Low-carb bar — 0.5 ½ medium cucumber — 0.5	50 g sliced cucumber — 2 2 slices Cheddar cheese — 1	2 celery stalks — 1 2 Tbsp. Blue Cheese Dressing — 1	10 green olives stuffed with — 1.5 2 Tbsp. cream cheese — 1
Subtotal 2.5	**Subtotal 1.5**	**Subtotal 1.5**	**Subtotal 1**	**Subtotal 3**	**Subtotal 2**	**Subtotal 2.5**

LUNCH

Day 1	Day 2	Day 3	Day 4	Day 5	Day 6	Day 7
Roast beef on 220 g mixed salad greens — 0 50 g mung bean sprouts — 1.5 5 black olives — 2 2 Tbsp. chopped onions — 0.5 2 Tbsp. Lemon-Dill Vinaigrette — 1.5	Grilled chicken on 220 g mixed salad greens with — 0 5 cherry tomatoes — 1.5 2 Tbsp. chopped onion — 2 2 Tbsp. grated Parmesan — 0.5 2 Tbsp. Caesar Dressing — 1.5	Cobb salad: 200 g Cos lettuce — 0 Grilled chicken — 1.5 1 hard-boiled egg — 2 30 g shredded Cheddar cheese — 1.5 35 g raw mushrooms — 0.5 2 Tbsp. Sweet Mustard Dressing — 1.5	220 g mixed salad greens with tinned sardines — 1.5 30 g feta cheese — 0.5 5 black olives — 0.5 5 cherry tomatoes — 1 2 Tbsp. Greek Vinaigrette — 1	1 tin tuna fish on 110 g mixed salad greens — 1.5 80 g cooked broccoli — 1 25 g spring onions — 0.5 4 pieces marinated artichoke hearts — 1 2 Tbsp. Lemon-Dill Vinaigrette — 2	Grilled chicken on 220 g mixed salad greens with — 0 ½ Haas avocado — 1.5 10 black olives — 2 16 g alfalfa sprouts — 1 2 Tbsp. Italian Dressing — 2	Sliced roast beef on 220 g mixed salad greens — 0 30 g shredded mozzarella — 1.5 6 radishes — 0.5 50 g sliced cucumbers — 0.5 1 Tbsp. Parmesan-Peppercorn Dressing — 1
Subtotal 6.5	**Subtotal 6.5**	**Subtotal 7**	**Subtotal 4.5**	**Subtotal 6**	**Subtotal 6.5**	**Subtotal 4.5**

Phase 1: Induction

Day 1

SNACK

Item	Grams of Net Carbs
10 green olives	0
1 slice Cheddar cheese	0.5
Subtotal	**0.5**

DINNER

Item	Grams of Net Carbs
Baked salmon steak topped with	0
2 Tbsp. **Aïoli**	0
6 steamed asparagus spears	2.5
Salad of 60 g rocket	1
5 cherry tomatoes	2
50 g sliced cucumbers	1
2 Tbsp. **Italian Dressing**	1
Subtotal	**7.5**

Total	20
Foundation vegetables	16

Day 2

SNACK

Item	Grams of Net Carbs
½ Haas avocado	2
2 slices Muenster cheese	0.5
Subtotal	**2.5**

DINNER

Item	Grams of Net Carbs
Grilled pork chops	0
60 g mashed cauliflower with	0
30 g shredded Cheddar cheese	2.5
110 g mixed salad greens with	1
6 radishes	2
55 g raw French beans	1
2 Tbsp. **Italian Dressing**	1
Subtotal	**7.5**

Total	21.5
Foundation vegetables	16.5

Day 3

SNACK

Item	Grams of Net Carbs
2 Tbsp. cream cheese on	1
2 celery stalks	1.5
Subtotal	**2.5**

DINNER

Item	Grams of Net Carbs
Grilled tuna steak	0
2 Tbsp. **Herb-Butter Blend**	0
115 g sautéed courgette	1
110 g mixed salad greens	1.5
½ Haas avocado	1
2 Tbsp. blue cheese	0.5
2 Tbsp. **Parmesan-Peppercorn Dressing**	2
Subtotal	**6**

Total	20
Foundation vegetables	12.5

Day 4

SNACK

Item	Grams of Net Carbs
30 g Gouda cheese	0.5
5 green olives	0
Subtotal	**0.5**

DINNER

Item	Grams of Net Carbs
Grilled beef tenderloin	0
115 g steamed courgette	1.5
110 g mixed salad greens with	1
45 g roasted red peppers	3.5
2 Tbsp. chopped onions	1.5
2 Tbsp. **Parmesan-Peppercorn Dressing**	1
Subtotal	**8.5**

Total	20
Foundation vegetables	14.5

Day 5

SNACK

Item	Grams of Net Carbs
Roast turkey slices and	0.5
2 Tbsp. **Aïoli**	0
Subtotal	**0.5**

DINNER

Item	Grams of Net Carbs
Hamburger patty topped with	0
2 Tbsp. sautéed onions and	1.5
15 g sautéed mushrooms and	1
2 slices Cheddar cheese	1
110 g mixed salad greens	1.5
2 Tbsp. **Sweet Mustard Dressing**	1
Subtotal	**6**

Total	20.5
Foundation vegetables	14.5

Day 6

SNACK

Item	Grams of Net Carbs
Low-carb bar	2
1 slice Cheddar cheese	0.5
Subtotal	**2.5**

DINNER

Item	Grams of Net Carbs
Chef salad:	0
200 g Cos lettuce	2
Turkey and ham	0
1 small tomato	2.5
2 Tbsp. chopped onions	1.5
Cheddar cheese	1
2 Tbsp. **French Dressing**	1
Subtotal	**8**

Total	20
Foundation vegetables	15

Day 7

SNACK

Item	Grams of Net Carbs
Low-carb bar	2
1 medium tomato	3.5
Subtotal	**5.5**

DINNER

Item	Grams of Net Carbs
Grilled chicken	0
2 Tbsp. **Brown Butter Sauce**	1.5
90 g steamed spinach	0
110 g mixed salad greens	2.5
30 g endive	1
½ Haas avocado	1
2 Tbsp. **Italian Dressing**	1
Subtotal	**7**

Total	21
Foundation vegetables	14

Phase 2: Ongoing Weight Loss, at 25 and 30 Grams of Net Carbs (30-gram additions in bold italics)

Meal	Day 1	Grams of Net Carbs	Day 2	Grams of Net Carbs	Day 3	Grams of Net Carbs	Day 4	Grams of Net Carbs	Day 5	Grams of Net Carbs	Day 6	Grams of Net Carbs	Day 7	Grams of Net Carbs
BREAKFAST	3 rashers bacon 120 g mashed cauliflower with 30 g shredded Cheddar cheese ***37 g blueberries*** Subtotal	1 2 0.5 ***4*** 3.5 (7.5)	2-egg omelette with 20 g sautéed onion and 60 g shredded Cheddar cheese ***5 large strawberries*** Subtotal	1 1 4.5 ***5*** 6.5 (11.5)	Sliced boiled ham 2 slices Swiss cheese ½ Haas avocado ***37 g blueberries*** Subtotal	0 2 2 ***4*** 4 (8)	Low-carb shake 14 g pecans ***93 g raspberries*** Subtotal	1 1.5 ***5*** 2.5 (7.5)	Turkey sausage sautéed with 25 g spring onions and 140 g shredded green cabbage ***37 g blueberries*** Subtotal	1 0 2 ***4*** 3 (7)	2 fried eggs 90 g steamed spinach 3 bacon strips ***4 large strawberries*** Subtotal	1 0 2 ***4*** 3 (7)	Low-carb bar 1 devilled egg ***36 g blackberries*** Subtotal	2 0.5 ***2.5*** 2.5 (5)
SNACK	2 celery stalks 1 Tbsp. natural peanut butter Subtotal	1.5 2 3.5	30 g almonds 10 green olives Subtotal	2.5 1 3.5	100 g sliced cucumber 60 g walnuts Subtotal	2 0.5 2.5	½ Haas avocado 60 g Cheddar cheese Subtotal	2 3 5	2 slices Provolone cheese around 4 asparagus spears Subtotal	2 1 3	2 celery stalks 2 Tbsp. natural peanut butter Subtotal	1.5 5 6.5	5 Brazil nuts 5 cherry tomatoes Subtotal	1.5 5 6.5
LUNCH	Tinned sardines on 60 g spinach and 100 g Cos lettuce 45 g roasted red peppers 35 g raw broccoli 2 Tbsp. Lemon-Dill Vinaigrette Subtotal	0 0.5 1 3.5 1 1 7	London broil (left over from day 1) over 220 g mixed salad greens and 1 stalk diced celery 1 small tomato ½ Haas avocado 2 Tbsp. Ranch Dressing Subtotal	0 1 0.5 1.5 2 2 7	Tinned salmon mixed with 1 stalk diced celery 2 Tbsp. chopped onions and 2 Tbsp. Blender Mayonnaise over 200 g Cos lettuce 5 black olives Subtotal	0 0.5 1.5 0.5 2.5 2.5 7.5	Grilled chicken (left over from day 3) over 30 g watercress and 90 g leaf lettuce 1 small tomato 55 g raw French beans 2 Tbsp. Blue Cheese Dressing Subtotal	0 0.5 1.5 1.5 1.5 2 7	Grilled prawns over 220 g mixed salad greens 5 black olives 1 small tomato 60 g goat's cheese 2 Tbsp. Lemon-Dill Vinaigrette Subtotal	0 1 1.5 1.5 1 2 7	Hamburger ½ Haas avocado 1 slice Cheddar cheese 1 small tomato 30 g loose-leaf lettuce 2 Tbsp. onions Subtotal	0 2 1.5 1 0.5 1 6	Grilled chicken (left over from day 6) over 120 g baby spinach salad with 30 g feta cheese 30 g walnuts ½ Haas avocado 5 black olives 2 Tbsp. Fresh Raspberry Vinaigrette Subtotal	0 1 1.5 1.5 2 0.5 1 7.5

Phase 2: Ongoing Weight Loss, at 25 and 30 Grams of Net Carbs (30-gram additions in bold italics)

Day 1	Grams of Net Carbs	Day 2	Grams of Net Carbs	Day 3	Grams of Net Carbs	Day 4	Grams of Net Carbs	Day 5	Grams of Net Carbs	Day 6	Grams of Net Carbs	Day 7	Grams of Net Carbs
SNACK													
5 Brazil nuts	2	30 g pecans	1.5	1 slice Cheddar cheese	1.5	30 g walnuts	1.5	30 g pecans	1.5	Low-carb bar	2	80 g steamed broccoli	1.5
1 hard-boiled egg	0.5	Low-carb shake	1	5 cherry tomatoes	1	4 pieces marinated artichoke hearts	2	Low-carb shake	1	1 slice Swiss cheese	1	2 slices Cheddar cheese	1
Subtotal	2.5	Subtotal	2.5	Subtotal	2.5	Subtotal	3.5	Subtotal	2.5	Subtotal	3	Subtotal	2.5
DINNER													
London broil topped with	0	Baked cod	0	Grilled chicken	0	Lamb kebabs cooked with	0	Pork tenderloin	0	Grilled chicken with	0	Rainbow trout	0
20 g sautéed shiitake mushrooms	4.5	***2 Tbsp. Herb-Butter Blend***	0	1 Tbsp. ***Barbecue Sauce***	2	100 g cubed aubergine and	2	***2 Tbsp. Mustard-Cream Sauce***	1	50 g ***Basil Pesto***	1	***2 Tbsp. Butter-Dill Blend***	0
110 g mixed salad greens with	1	160 g steamed broccoli	4.5	90 g steamed spinach	3	40 g cubed onions and	2	60 g cooked French beans topped with	3	120 g mashed cauliflower with	3	1 steamed medium artichoke	7
30 g pine nuts	1.5	110 g mixed salad greens with	1	60 g rocket topped with	1	50 g cubed red peppers	1	30 g slivered almonds	3	30 g shredded Cheddar cheese	0.5	110 g mixed salad greens with	1
30 g crumbled blue cheese	0.5	16 g alfalfa sprouts	1.5	4 pieces marinated artichoke hearts	0	110 g mixed salad greens	2	110 g mixed salad greens with	2.5	120 g rocket	1.5	50 g sliced cucumber	1
2 Tbsp. Fresh Raspberry Vinaigrette	1	***2 Tbsp. Lemon-Dill Vinaigrette***	1	25 g spring onions	2	***2 Tbsp. Greek Vinaigrette***	1	45 g roasted red peppers	1	***2 Tbsp. Fresh Raspberry Vinaigrette***		***2 Tbsp. Italian Dressing***	1
				2 Tbsp. Blue Cheese Dressing	1			***2 Tbsp. Lemon-Dill Vinaigrette***	1				
Subtotal	8.5	Subtotal	8.5	Subtotal	5	Subtotal	9	Subtotal	9	Subtotal	6	Subtotal	10
Total	25 (29)	Total	24 (29)	Total	24.5 (28.5)	Total	25 (30)	Total	26.5 (30.5)	Total	26 (30)	Total	26 (28.5)
Total Foundation vegetables	15	Total Foundation vegetables	15	Total Foundation vegetables	16	Total Foundation vegetables	16	Total Foundation vegetables	17	Total Foundation vegetables	14	Total Foundation vegetables	16

NEW ATKINS FOR A NEW YOU

Phase 2: Ongoing Weight Loss, at 35 and 40 Grams of Net Carbs (40-gram additions in bold italics)

Day 1	Grams of Net Carbs	Day 2	Grams of Net Carbs	Day 3	Grams of Net Carbs	Day 4	Grams of Net Carbs	Day 5	Grams of Net Carbs	Day 6	Grams of Net Carbs	Day 7	Grams of Net Carbs
BREAKFAST													
3 rashers bacon	1	2-egg omelette with	1	Boiled ham slices	0	Low-carb shake	0	Turkey sausage sautéed with	1	2 fried eggs	1	115 g cottage cheese	4
120 g mashed cauliflower with	2	20 g sautéed onion and	4.5	2 slices Swiss cheese	2	30 g almonds	2.5	40 g chopped onions and	4	90 g steamed spinach	2	44 g cantaloupe melon balls	3.5
30 g shredded Cheddar cheese	0.5	20 g sautéed shiitake mushrooms	4.5	½ Haas avocado	2	37 g blueberries	4	50 g red peppers	3	3 strips bacon	0	***44 g melon balls***	3.5
35 g sweet cherries	4	30 g shredded Cheddar cheese	0.5	84 g sliced strawberries	3.5	***88 g cantaloupe melon balls***	3	36 g blackberries	2.5	***35 g sweet cherries***	4	30 g hazelnuts	0.5
Subtotal	3.5 (7.5)	Subtotal	10.5	Subtotal	7.5	Subtotal	7.5 (14.5)	Subtotal	8.5	Subtotal	7 (11)	Subtotal	8 (11.5)
SNACK													
2 celery stalks	1.5	115 g ricotta cheese	4	100 g sliced cucumber	2	½ Haas avocado	2	2 slices Provolone cheese around	2	2 celery stalks	1.5	120 g raw broccoli	1
2 Tbsp. natural peanut butter	5	31 g raspberries	1.5	2 Tbsp. Blue Cheese Dressing	1	2 slices Cheddar cheese	1	4 asparagus spears	1	2 Tbsp. natural peanut butter	5	2 Tbsp. Aioli	0
Subtotal	6.5	Subtotal	5.5	Subtotal	3	Subtotal	3	Subtotal	3	Subtotal	6.5	Subtotal	1
LUNCH													
Tinned sardines on	0	London broil (left over from day 1) over	0	Tinned salmon mixed with	0	Grilled chicken (left over from day 3) over	0	Grilled prawns over	0	Hamburger patty	0	Grilled chicken (left over from day 6) over	0
60 g baby spinach and	0.5	220 g mixed salad greens and	0.5	1 stalk diced celery	1	30 g watercress and	0	220 g mixed salad greens	0	½ Haas avocado	2	120 g baby spinach with	1
100 g Cos lettuce	1	1 stalk diced celery	1	2 Tbsp. chopped onions and	1.5	90 g leaf lettuce	1.5	5 black olives	1.5	1 slice Cheddar cheese	0.5	60 g feta cheese	2.5
45 g roasted red peppers	3.5	1 small tomato	3.5	2 Tbsp. Blender Mayonnaise over	0	1 medium tomato	3.5	1 small tomato	3.5	1 small tomato	2.5	30 g walnuts	1.5
4 pieces marinated artichoke hearts	2	16 g alfalfa sprouts	0	200 g Cos lettuce	1.5	5 black olives	0.5	2 Tbsp. Lemon-Dill Vinaigrette	0.5	30 g leaf lettuce	1	6 radishes	0.5
35 g raw broccoli	1	2 Tbsp. Greek Vinaigrette	2	5 black olives	0.5	2 Tbsp. Blue Cheese Dressing	1	***5 large strawberries***	5	2 Tbsp. onions	1.5	5 black olives	0.5
2 Tbsp. Lemon-Dill Vinaigrette	1			***120 g tomato juice***	4					2 Tbsp. Aioli	0	***2 Tbsp. Fresh Raspberry Vinaigrette***	1
Subtotal	9	Subtotal	7	Subtotal	4.5 (8.5)	Subtotal	6.5	Subtotal	5.5 (10.5)	Subtotal	7.5	Subtotal	7

Phase 2: Ongoing Weight Loss, at 35 and 40 Grams of Net Carbs (40-gram additions in bold italics)

	Day 1	Grams of Net Carbs	Day 2	Grams of Net Carbs	Day 3	Grams of Net Carbs	Day 4	Grams of Net Carbs	Day 5	Grams of Net Carbs	Day 6	Grams of Net Carbs	Day 7	Grams of Net Carbs
SNACK	120 g low-carb yoghurt	3	60 g pistachios	5	60 g pecans	5	30 g almonds	3	60 g pine nuts	3.5	Low-carb bar	3.5	120 g tomato juice	4
	37 g blueberries	4	60 g jicama sticks	2.5	115 g cottage cheese	2.5	120 g low-carb yoghurt	3	115 g cottage cheese	3	115 g ricotta cheese	3	120 g plain whole milk Greek yoghurt	3.5
	Subtotal	7	Subtotal	7.5	Subtotal	7.5	Subtotal	6	Subtotal	6.5	Subtotal	6.5	Subtotal	7.5
DINNER	London broil topped with		Baked cod		Grilled chicken with		Lamb kebabs broiled with		Pork tenderloin		Grilled chicken with		Rainbow trout	0
	60 ml **Mushroom Gravy**	0	2 Tbsp. **Herb-Butter Blend**	0	2 Tbsp. **Barbecue Sauce**	0	100 g cubed aubergine and	4	2 Tbsp. **Mustard-Cream Sauce**	0	50 g **Basil Pesto**	0	2 Tbsp. **Butter-Oil Blend**	0
	½ steamed medium artichoke	3.5	160 g steamed broccoli	3.5	80 g steamed Brussels sprouts	3.5	40 g cubed onions and	1	60 g cooked French beans	2	120 g mashed cauliflower with	3	1 steamed medium artichoke	7
	110 g mixed salad greens with	1	110 g mixed salad greens	1	Salad of 60 g rocket and	1	50 g cubed red peppers	3	110 g mixed salad greens with	3	30 g shredded Cheddar cheese	0.5	110 g mixed salad greens with	1
	50 g sliced cucumber and	0.5	50 g sliced cucumber with	0.5	4 pieces marinated artichoke hearts	1	110 g mixed salad greens	3	45 g roasted red peppers and	6	120 g rocket	1.5	50 g sliced cucumber	1
	2 Tbsp. Lemon-Dill Vinaigrette	1	2 Tbsp. Lemon-Dill Vinaigrette	1	1 small tomato and	1	5 black olives	2.5	50 g sliced cucumber	0.5	1 small tomato	2.5	½ Haas avocado	2
	25 g spring onions	1	***35 g sweet cherries***	4	2 Tbsp. Ranch Dressing	4	2 Tbsp. Greek Vinaigrette	0.5	2 Tbsp. Lemon-Dill Vinaigrette	1	***2 Tbsp. Fresh Raspberry Vinaigrette***	1	2 Tbsp. Italian Dressing	1
	2 Tbsp. Fresh Raspberry Vinaigrette	1							***2 Tbsp. Fresh Raspberry Vinaigrette***	1				
	Subtotal	9	Subtotal	6.5 (10.5)	Subtotal	14	Subtotal	14	Subtotal	12.5	Subtotal	8.5	Subtotal	12
	Total	35 (39)	Total	35 (39)	Total	35 (39)	Total	34.5 (41.5)	Total	34 (39)	Total	35.5 (39.5)	Total	35.5 (39)
	Total Foundation vegetables	17	Total Foundation vegetables	22	Total Foundation vegetables	17.5	Total Foundation vegetables	20	Total Foundation vegetables	21	Total Foundation vegetables	16.5	Total Foundation vegetables	14

Phase 2: Ongoing Weight Loss, at 45 and 50 Grams of Net Carbs (50-gram additions in bold italics)

BREAKFAST

Day 1	Grams of Net Carbs	Day 2	Grams of Net Carbs	Day 3	Grams of Net Carbs	Day 4	Grams of Net Carbs	Day 5	Grams of Net Carbs	Day 6	Grams of Net Carbs	Day 7	Grams of Net Carbs
3 rashers bacon	1	2-egg omelette with	1	Sliced boiled ham	0	115 g creamed cottage cheese	3	Turkey sausage sautéed with	0	2 fried eggs	1	2 Atkins Waffles*	6
120 g mashed cauliflower with	2	20 g sautéed onion and	4.5	2 slices Swiss cheese	2	30 g almonds	2.5	40 g chopped onion	3	70 g steamed beetroot greens	3.5	115 g cottage cheese	4
30 g shredded Cheddar cheese	0.5	20 g sautéed shiitake mushrooms	4.5	½ Haas avocado	2	74 g blueberries	8	140 g shredded green cabbage	2	3 bacon strips	0	88 g cantaloupe melon balls	7.5
88 g honeydew melon balls	7	31 g fresh raspberries	1.5	*120 g tomato juice*	4			30 g shredded Cheddar cheese	0.5	120 g tomato juice	4		
Subtotal	10.5	**Subtotal**	11.5	**Subtotal**	4 (8)	**Subtotal**	7.5 (14.5)	**Subtotal**	5.5	**Subtotal**	8.5	**Subtotal**	17.5

SNACK

Day 1	Grams of Net Carbs	Day 2	Grams of Net Carbs	Day 3	Grams of Net Carbs	Day 4	Grams of Net Carbs	Day 5	Grams of Net Carbs	Day 6	Grams of Net Carbs	Day 7	Grams of Net Carbs
2 celery stalks	1.5	60 g almonds	5	100 g sliced cucumbers	2	½ Haas avocado	2	2 slices Provolone cheese	2	1 celery stalk	1	2 Tbsp. hummus	4.5
2 Tbsp. natural peanut butter	5	115 g ricotta cheese	4	2 Tbsp. hummus	4.5	2 slices Cheddar cheese	1	88 g honeydew melon	1	2 Tbsp. natural peanut butter	7	60 g jicama sticks	2.5
Subtotal	6.5	**Subtotal**	9	**Subtotal**	6.5	**Subtotal**	3	**Subtotal**	3	**Subtotal**	8	**Subtotal**	7

LUNCH

Day 1	Grams of Net Carbs	Day 2	Grams of Net Carbs	Day 3	Grams of Net Carbs	Day 4	Grams of Net Carbs	Day 5	Grams of Net Carbs	Day 6	Grams of Net Carbs	Day 7	Grams of Net Carbs
Tinned sardines on	0	London broil (left over from day 1) over	0	Tinned salmon mixed with	0	Grilled chicken (left over from day 3) over	0	Lamb kebabs (left over from day 4) over	0	Hamburger(s)	0	Grilled chicken (left over from day 6)	0
60 g baby spinach and	0.5	220 g mixed salad greens and	0.5	1 stalk diced celery	0.5	30 g watercress and	0.5	220 g mixed salad greens	0.5	½ Haas avocado	2	Salad of 120 g baby spinach with	1
100 g Cos lettuce	1	2 stalks diced celery	1	2 Tbsp. chopped onions and	1.5	90 g loose-leaf lettuce	1.5	5 black olives	1.5	1 slice Cheddar cheese	0.5	30 g feta cheese	1
45 g roasted red peppers	3.5	1 small tomato	3.5	2 Tbsp. Blender Mayonnaise	2.5	1 medium tomato	2.5	1 small tomato	2.5	1 small tomato	2.5	4 pieces marinated artichoke hearts	2
45 g cooked chickpeas	6.5	45 g cooked kidney beans	6	200 g Cos lettuce	1	45 g cooked black-eyed peas	6	45 g butter beans	7	30 g loose-leaf lettuce	1	1 small tomato	2.5
2 Tbsp. Lemon-Dill Vinaigrette	1	2 Tbsp. Ranch Dressing	1	1 medium tomato	2	2 Tbsp. Lemon-Dill Vinaigrette	0.5	2 Tbsp. Lemon-Dill Vinaigrette	1	2 Tbsp. chopped onions	1.5	2 Tbsp. Greek Vinaigrette	0
1 low-carb pitta	4	*1 low-carb pitta*	4	2 Tbsp. Blue Cheese Dressing	0.5			*1 low-carb bagel*	5	*low-carb hamburger bun*	4	*1 low-carb pitta*	4
Subtotal	12.5 (16)	**Subtotal**	12 (16)	**Subtotal**	8	**Subtotal**	11	**Subtotal**	12.5 (17.5)	**Subtotal**	7.5 (11.5)	**Subtotal**	6.5 (10.5)

Phase 2: Ongoing Weight Loss, at 45 and 50 Grams of Net Carbs (50-gram additions in bold italics)

Day 1	Grams of Net Carbs	Day 2	Grams of Net Carbs	Day 3	Grams of Net Carbs	Day 4	Grams of Net Carbs	Day 5	Grams of Net Carbs	Day 6	Grams of Net Carbs	Day 7	Grams of Net Carbs
SNACK													
5 cherry tomatoes	2	2 slices Cheddar cheese	1	60 g roasted pumpkin seeds	4	30 g walnuts	2	84 g sliced strawberries	1.5	120 g plain whole milk yoghurt	5.5	Low-carb bar	2
120 g low-carb yoghurt	3	60 g jicama sticks	2.5	74 g blueberries	4.5	5 large strawberries	6.5	115 g creamed cottage cheese	5	37 g blueberries	4	60 g walnuts	3
Subtotal	5	Subtotal	3.5	Subtotal	8.5	Subtotal	8.5	Subtotal	6.5	Subtotal	9.5	Subtotal	5
DINNER													
London broil topped with	0	Baked cod topped with	0	Grilled chicken	0	Lamb kebabs cooked with	0	Pork tenderloin	0	Grilled chicken with	0	Rainbow trout	0
60 ml **Mushroom Gravy**	0	2 Tbsp. **Herb-Butter Blend**	0	2 Tbsp. **Barbecue Sauce**	0	100 g cubed aubergine and	4	2 Tbsp. **Mustard-Cream Sauce**	1	50 g **Basil Pesto**	1	2 Tbsp. **Butter-Oil Blend**	0
120 g steamed French beans	2	120 g steamed broccoli	2	160 g steamed Brussels sprouts	3.5	40 g cubed onion and	3	120 g cooked French beans topped with	2	120 g mashed cauliflower with	2	1 steamed medium artichoke	7
110 g mixed salad greens with	6	120 g steamed French beans	3.5	Salad of 60 g rocket topped with	1	50 g cubed red peppers	3	30 g slivered almonds	3	30 g shredded Cheddar cheese	0.5	110 g mixed salad greens with	0.5
50 g mung bean sprouts	1	110 g mixed salad greens with	6	4 pieces marinated artichoke hearts	2	110 g mixed salad greens	1	110 g mixed salad greens with	1	120 g rocket	1.5	5 black olives	2.5
2 Tbsp. crumbled blue cheese	2	50 g mung bean sprouts	1	25 g spring onions	1	*50 g cooked lentils*	6	45 g roasted red peppers and	6	1 small tomato	1	50 g sliced cucumber	1
1 low-carb bread roll	4	4 pieces marinated artichoke hearts	2	2 Tbsp. Lemon-Dill Vinaigrette	2	2 Tbsp. Greek Vinaigrette	0	2 Tbsp. Greek Vinaigrette	0	50 g cooked lentils	6	2 Tbsp. Fresh Raspberry Vinaigrette	1
1 Tbsp. Fresh Raspberry Vinaigrette	0.5	2 Tbsp. Lemon-Dill Vinaigrette	2							2 Tbsp. Italian Dressing	3.5		
Subtotal	10 (14)	Subtotal	16	Subtotal	9.5	Subtotal	10.5 (16.5)	Subtotal	14	Subtotal	14.5	Subtotal	10.5
Total	44.5 (48.5)	**Total**	45.5 (49.5)	**Total**	47 (51)	**Total**	32 (39)	**Total**	46.5 (51.5)	**Total**	46 (50)	**Total**	46.5 (50.5)
Foundation vegetables	17.5	**Foundation vegetables**	17.5	**Foundation vegetables**	22	**Foundation vegetables**	20	**Foundation vegetables**	20	**Foundation vegetables**	17.5	**Foundation vegetables**	17.5

*www.atkins.com/Recipes/ShowRecipe884/Atkins-Cuisine-Waffles.aspx.

Phase 3: Pre-Maintenance and Phase 4: Lifetime Maintenance, at 55 and 65 Grams of Net Carbs (65-gram additions in bold italics)

BREAKFAST

Day 1	Grams of Net Carbs	Day 2	Grams of Net Carbs	Day 3	Grams of Net Carbs	Day 4	Grams of Net Carbs	Day 5	Grams of Net Carbs	Day 6	Grams of Net Carbs	Day 7	Grams of Net Carbs
2-egg omelette	1	1 Atkins Waffle*	6	Smoothie: 120 ml plain unsweetened almond milk	0.5	120 g plain whole milk yoghurt	5.5	120 g plain whole milk Greek yoghurt	5.5	2 scrambled eggs	1	2 Atkins Pancakes**	6
20 g sautéed shiitake mushrooms	4.5	60 g ricotta cheese	2	120 g plain whole milk yoghurt	5.5	Low-carb bar	2	37 g blueberries	2	20 g sautéed onions	4.5	120 g ricotta cheese	4
60 g shredded Cheddar cheese	1	37 g blueberries	8	62 g raspberries	3	85 g mango	12.5	60 g almonds	12.5	60 g shredded Cheddar cheese	1	74 g blueberries	4
		30 g slivered almonds	2.5	30 g almonds	2.5					120 g tomato juice	4		
Subtotal	**6.5**	**Subtotal**	**18.5**	**Subtotal**	**11.5**	**Subtotal**	**20**	**Subtotal**	**20**	**Subtotal**	**10.5**	**Subtotal**	**14**

SNACK

Day 1	Grams of Net Carbs	Day 2	Grams of Net Carbs	Day 3	Grams of Net Carbs	Day 4	Grams of Net Carbs	Day 5	Grams of Net Carbs	Day 6	Grams of Net Carbs	Day 7	Grams of Net Carbs
60 g pine nuts	3.5	2 slices of Swiss cheese	3.5	2 slices Swiss cheese	2	2 slices Swiss cheese around	2	½ Haas avocado	2	Low-carb bar	2	½ Haas avocado	2
72 g blackberries	5.5	4 asparagus spears	5.5	80 g edamame	2	4 spears asparagus	6	85 g mango	12.5	36 g blackberries	2.5	*1 medium carrot stick*	5.5
		1 tsp. Dijon mustard			0.5								
Subtotal	**9**	**Subtotal**	**9**	**Subtotal**	**4.5**	**Subtotal**	**8**	**Subtotal**	**14.5**	**Subtotal**	**4.5**	**Subtotal**	**2 (7.5)**

LUNCH

Day 1	Grams of Net Carbs	Day 2	Grams of Net Carbs	Day 3	Grams of Net Carbs	Day 4	Grams of Net Carbs	Day 5	Grams of Net Carbs	Day 6	Grams of Net Carbs	Day 7	Grams of Net Carbs
Grilled chicken with 2 Tbsp. **Peanut Sauce**	5	Lamb kebabs (left over from day 1)	0	Sliced turkey (left over from day 2) on	0	2 devilled eggs made with	0	Prawns (left over from day 4) topped with	1	Grilled chicken over 220 g mixed salad greens	0	Ham (left over from day 5) and	0
220 g mixed salad greens	1.5	2 Tbsp. hummus	4.5	220 g mixed salad greens and	4.5	2 Tbsp. **Blender Mayonnaise**	1.5	2 Tbsp. **Blender Mayonnaise** and	0	80 g pickled okra	1.5	2 slices Swiss cheese on	1.5
50 g green peppers	2	110 g mixed salad greens	1.5	45 g roasted red peppers	1.5	1 low-carb pitta with	4	1 dill pickle gherkin, chopped	4	45 g roasted red peppers	2	Low-carb bagel with	2.5
60 g chopped jicama	2.5	1 medium tomato	2	2 Tbsp. hummus	3.5	2 Tbsp. hummus	3.5	1 low-carb bagel	4.5	55 g snap peas	5	1 tsp. Dijon mustard	3.5
1 small tomato	2.5	½ Haas avocado	2.5	½ Haas avocado	2	110 g mixed salad greens	2	200 g Cos lettuce	1	2 Tbsp. **Parmesan-Peppercorn Dressing**	6	15 g loose-leaf lettuce	3.5
2 Tbsp. **Creamy Italian Dressing**	2	2 Tbsp. **Greek Vinaigrette**	2	1 small tomato	2.5	1 small tomato	2.5	50 g cooked lentils	2.5			1 small tomato	
				2 Tbsp. **Italian Dressing**	1	2 Tbsp. **Parmesan-Peppercorn Dressing**	1	2 Tbsp. **Italian Dressing**	1			2 Tbsp. hummus	1
Subtotal	**15.5**	**Subtotal**	**12.5**	**Subtotal**	**12.5**	**Subtotal**	**10.5**	**Subtotal**	**14**	**Subtotal**	**16**	**Subtotal**	**12**

Phase 3: Pre-Maintenance and Phase 4: Lifetime Maintenance, at 55 and 65 Grams of Net Carbs (65-gram additions in bold italics)

Day 1	Grams of Net Carbs	Day 2	Grams of Net Carbs	Day 3	Grams of Net Carbs	Day 4	Grams of Net Carbs	Day 5	Grams of Net Carbs	Day 6	Grams of Net Carbs	Day 7	Grams of Net Carbs
SNACK													
120 g plain whole yoghurt	5.5	30 g almonds	2.5	30 g almonds	2.5	35 g sweet cherries	4	120 g tomato juice	4	85 g pineapple	8.5	60 g almonds	4.5
½ medium apple	8.5	½ white grapefruit	8.5	85 g pineapple	8.5	60 g almonds	4.5	60 g goat's cheese	0.5	30 g macadamias	2	½ medium apple	8.5
Subtotal	**14**	**Subtotal**	**11**	**Subtotal**	**11**	**Subtotal**	**8.5**	**Subtotal**	**4.5**	**Subtotal**	**10.5**	**Subtotal**	**13**
DINNER													
Lamb kebabs	0	Roast turkey	0	Fajitas: broiled sliced skirt steak with	0	Sautéed prawns on	0	Baked ham	0	Flank steak	0	Salmon steak over	0
½ sweet jacket potato	12	125 ml **Velouté Sauce**	1			50 g steamed leeks	3.5	60 ml **Mushroom Gravy**	2	45 g cooked butter beans	7	80 g roasted fennel and	3
110 g grilled aubergine	1	*½ jacket potato*	12.5	20 g sautéed onions and	4.5	60 ml **Alfredo Sauce**	2	*100 g mashed butternut squash*	7	*75 g sweet-corn*	7	20 g roasted onions	4.5
110 g mixed salad greens		100 g grilled aubergine	4	90 g sautéed green peppers	8	60 g baby spinach salad	0.5	Salad of 90 g chopped raw fennel and	1	110 g mixed salad greens	1	60 ml **Raita**	3
45 g cooked chickpeas	6.5	110 g mixed salad greens	1	50 g **Salsa Cruda**	1.5	1 small tomato	2.5	60 g chopped jicama	3.5	50 g chopped cucumber	1	Salad of 60 g rocket	0.5
5 black olives	0.5	6 radishes	0.5	*½ corn on the cob*	8.5	*85 g pickled beetroots*	7	2 Tbsp. **Blue Cheese Dressing**	1	1 small tomato	2.5	4 pieces marinated artichoke hearts	2
30 g blue cheese	0.5	2 Tbsp. **Greek Vinaigrette**	0.5	110 g mixed salad greens	1	2 Tbsp. **Creamy Italian Dressing**	1			2 Tbsp. **Creamy Italian Dressing**	1	2 Tbsp. **Fresh Raspberry Vinaigrette**	1
2 Tbsp. **Greek Vinaigrette**	1			2 Tbsp. **Parmesan-Peppercorn Dressing**	1								
Subtotal	**9.5 (21.5)**	**Subtotal**	**7.5 (20)**	**Subtotal**	**14 (22.5)**	**Subtotal**	**10.5 (17.5)**	**Subtotal**	**9 (16)**	**Subtotal**	**13.5 (26)**	**Subtotal**	**14**
Total	**54.5 (66.5)**	**Total**	**54 (66.5)**	**Total**	**55 (63.5)**	**Total**	**57 (64)**	**Total**	**56 (63)**	**Total**	**54 (66.5)**	**Total**	**58 (63.5)**
Foundation vegetables	14.5	Foundation vegetables	14.5	Foundation vegetables	24.5	Foundation vegetables	12	Foundation vegetables	12	Foundation vegetables	20	Foundation vegetables	15

*www.atkins.com/Recipes/ShowRecipe884/Atkins-Cuisine-Waffles.aspx, **www.atkins.com/Recipes/ShowRecipe883/Atkins-Cuisine-Pancakes.aspx.

Phases 3: Pre-Maintenance and 4: Lifetime Maintenance, at 75 and 85 Grams of Net Carbs (85-gram additions in bold italics)

Day 1	Grams of Net Carbs	Day 2	Grams of Net Carbs	Day 3	Grams of Net Carbs	Day 4	Grams of Net Carbs	Day 5	Grams of Net Carbs	Day 6	Grams of Net Carbs	Day 7	Grams of Net Carbs
BREAKFAST													
2-egg omelette	1	1 Atkins Waffle*	1	Smoothie: 120 ml plain unsweetened almond milk with	0.5	2 devilled eggs made with	1	120 g plain whole milk yoghurt	5.5	2 scrambled eggs	1	2 Atkins Pancakes**	6
20 g sautéed shiitake mushrooms	4.5	115 g ricotta cheese	4	120 g plain whole milk yoghurt and	5.5	1 Tbsp. Blender Mayonnaise	0	1 medium orange	13	60 g refried beans	6.5	120 g ricotta	4
60 g shredded Cheddar cheese	1	85 g pineapple	8.5	85 g pineapple and	8.5	1 low-carb pitta with	4	30 g cashews	4.5	60 g shredded Cheddar cheese	1	88 g honeydew melon balls	7
120 g tomato juice	4	30 g slivered almonds	2.5	30 g almonds	2.5	3 Tbsp. Sun-dried Tomato Pesto	3			120 g tomato juice	4		
Subtotal	10.5	Subtotal	17	Subtotal	17	Subtotal	8	Subtotal	23	Subtotal	12.5	Subtotal	17
SNACK													
60 g almonds	5	2 slices Swiss cheese	2	30 g macadamias	2	½ medium apple	8.5	½ Haas avocado	2	Low-carb bar	2	½ Haas avocado	2
88 g cantaloupe melon balls	7.5	1 medium carrot	5.5	120 g tomato juice	5.5	60 g pecans	3	120 g tomato juice	4	72 g blackberries	5.5	1 small tomato	2.5
Subtotal	12.5	Subtotal	7.5	Subtotal	7.5	Subtotal	11.5	Subtotal	6	Subtotal	7.5	Subtotal	4.5
LUNCH													
Grilled chicken with 2 Tbsp. Peanut Sauce	5	Lamb kebabs (left over from day 1)	0	Sliced turkey (left over from day 2) on	0	Beef burger and	0	Prawns (left over from day 4) with	0	Grilled chicken over	0	Ham (left over from day 5) and	0
110 g mixed salad greens	1	110 g mixed salad greens	1	220 g mixed salad greens	1.5	2 slices Swiss cheese and	2	2 Tbsp. Cocktail Sauce	2	220 g mixed salad greens	1.5	2 slices Swiss cheese on	2
50 g green peppers	2	50 g cooked lentils	6	45 g roasted red peppers	3.5	1 small tomato and	2.5	200 g Cos lettuce	2.5	80 g pickled okra	2.5	Low-carb bagel with	5
60 g chopped jicama	2.5	1 medium tomato	3.5	½ Haas avocado	2	60 g hummus wrapped in	9	85 g pickled beetroots	8	90 g roasted red peppers	7	1 tsp. Dijon mustard	0.5
2 medium carrots, grated	11	½ Haas avocado	2	2 small tomatoes	5	15 g loose-leaf lettuce	0.5	***40 g cooked wild rice***	***8***	***75 g sweetcorn***	***12.5***	15 g loose-leaf lettuce	0.5
75 g sweetcorn	***12.5***	2 Tbsp. Creamy Italian Dressing	2.5	***75 g sweetcorn***	***12.5***	Coleslaw: 140 g shredded cabbage and	2	2 Tbsp. Italian Dressing	0.5	55 g snap peas	3.5	50 g sliced cucumber	1
2 Tbsp. Italian Dressing	1	1 low-carb pitta	4	2½ Tbsp. Ranch Dressing	1	1 medium carrot, grated and	5.5			2 Tbsp. Parmesan-Peppercorn Dressing	1	60 g hummus	9
						2 Tbsp. Creamy Coleslaw Dressing	1						
Subtotal	22.5 (35)	Subtotal	19	Subtotal	13 (25.5)	Subtotal	22.5	Subtotal	13 (21)	Subtotal	12.5 (25)	Subtotal	18

Phases 3: Pre-Maintenance and 4: Lifetime Maintenance, at 75 and 85 Grams of Net Carbs (85-gram additions in bold italics)

Meal	Day 1	Grams of Net Carbs	Day 2	Grams of Net Carbs	Day 3	Grams of Net Carbs	Day 4	Grams of Net Carbs	Day 5	Grams of Net Carbs	Day 6	Grams of Net Carbs	Day 7	Grams of Net Carbs
SNACK	1 medium apricot	3	30 g cashews	3	60 g goat's cheese	4.5	70 g sweet cherries	8	88 g honeydew melon balls	7	½ medium apple	8.5	60 g almonds	4.5
	120 g plain whole milk yoghurt	5.5	½ medium apple	4.5	74 g blueberries	8.5	115 g cottage cheese	4	60 g goat's cheese	0.5	60 g macadamias	4	1 medium orange	13
	Subtotal	8.5	Subtotal	8.5	Subtotal	13	Subtotal	12	Subtotal	7.5	Subtotal	12.5	Subtotal	17.5
DINNER	Lamb kebabs	0	Grilled turkey breast	0	Fajitas: broiled sliced skirt steak with	0	Sautéed prawns	0	Baked ham with	0	Flank steak	0	Salmon steak over	0
	90 g cooked chickpeas	13	2 Tbsp. Barbecue Sauce	1	40 g sautéed onions and	4	***100 g cooked brown rice***	10	60 ml Mushroom Gravy	2	½ jacket potato	10.5	80 g roasted fennel and	3
	110 g mixed salad greens	1	***90 g cooked bulgur wheat***	13	90 g sautéed green peppers	3.5	100 g steamed leeks with	9	120 g baked acorn squash	7	220 g mixed salad greens	2	***50 g cooked brown rice***	10.5
	4 pieces marinated artichoke hearts	2	110 g mixed salad greens	2	***120 g refried beans***	13	60 ml Alfredo Sauce	2	Salad of 180 g chopped raw fennel and	0.5	90 g cooked chickpeas	13	40 g roasted onions	9
	30 g blue cheese	0.5	45 g chopped fennel	0.5	50 g Salsa Cruda	2	60 g baby spinach salad with	0.5	60 g chopped jicama	7	2 Tbsp. Fresh Raspberry Vinaigrette	1	60 ml Raita	3
	5 black olives	0.5	1 medium tomato	0.5	110 g mixed salad greens	3.5	1 small tomato	2.5	1 small tomato	2.5			Salad of 60 g rocket	0.5
	1 small tomato	2.5	60 g feta cheese	2.5	2 Tbsp. Parmesan-Peppercorn Dressing	1	85 g pickled beetroots	7	2 Tbsp. Blue Cheese Dressing	2			2 Tbsp. Creamy Italian Dressing	2
	2 Tbsp. Greek Vinaigrette	1	2 Tbsp. Greek Vinaigrette	1			2 Tbsp. Creamy Italian Dressing	1						
	Subtotal	20.5	Subtotal	7.5 (20.5)	Subtotal	13.5 (26.5)	Subtotal	21 (31)	Subtotal	25.5	Subtotal	26	Subtotal	17.5 (28)
	Total	74.5 (87)	Total	74 (87)	Total	73.5 (86)	Total	75 (85)	Total	75 (83)	Total	71 (83.5)	Total	74.5 (85)
	Foundation vegetables	16	Foundation vegetables	13.5	Foundation vegetables	25.5	Foundation vegetables	15	Foundation vegetables	16	Foundation vegetables	16.5	Foundation vegetables	18.5

*www.atkins.com/Recipes/ShowRecipe884/Atkins-Cuisine-Waffles.aspx, **www.atkins.com/Recipes/ShowRecipe883/Atkins-Cuisine-Pancakes.aspx.

Phases 3: Pre-Maintenance and 4: Lifetime Maintenance, at 95 Grams of Net Carbs

Meal	Day 1	g Net Carbs	Day 2	g Net Carbs	Day 3	g Net Carbs	Day 4	g Net Carbs	Day 5	g Net Carbs	Day 6	g Net Carbs	Day 7	g Net Carbs
BREAKFAST	2-egg omelette 60 g shredded Cheddar cheese 1 medium orange **Subtotal**	1 1 13 **15**	1 Atkins Waffle* 115 g ricotta cheese 42 g sliced strawberries 30 g slivered almonds **Subtotal**	6 4 1 2.5 **14.5**	75 g cooked rolled oats 60 g whole milk 37 g blueberries 30 g almonds **Subtotal**	6 4 2 2.5 **14.5**	115 g cottage cheese 85 g mango 60 g almonds **Subtotal**	4 19 3 **28.5**	120 g plain whole milk yoghurt 45 g cooked wheat berries 37 g blueberries 60 g cashews **Subtotal**	5.5 7 4 9 **25.5**	2 scrambled eggs 20 g sautéed onions 30 g shredded Cheddar cheese ½ white grapefruit **Subtotal**	1 4.5 0.5 8.5 **14.5**	2 Atkins Pancakes*** 120 g ricotta ½ red grapefruit **Subtotal**	6 4 8 **18**
SNACK	60 g pine nuts 120 g tomato juice **Subtotal**	3.5 4 **7.5**	2 slices Swiss cheese around 4 asparagus spears 1 tsp. Dijon mustard **Subtotal**	3.5 4 0.5 **7.5**	30 g walnuts 120 g tomato juice **Subtotal**	2 2 **4.5**	2 slices of Swiss cheese 1 medium carrot **Subtotal**	1.5 4 **5.5**	½ Haas avocado 120 g tomato juice **Subtotal**	2 5.5 **7.5**	Low-carb bar 36 g blackberries **Subtotal**	2 4 **6**	½ Haas avocado 1 small tomato **Subtotal**	2 2.5 **4.5**
LUNCH	Grilled chicken with 2 Tbsp. Peanut Sauce 110 g mixed salad greens 50 g green peppers 45 g roasted red peppers 45 g chickpeas 2 Tbsp. Creamy Italian Dressing **Subtotal**	5 1 2 3.5 6.5 2 **20**	Lamb kebabs (left over from day 1) on 2 Tbsp. hummus on 2 pieces fibre crisp bread 110 g salad greens and 2 small tomatoes 2 Tbsp. Greek Vinaigrette **Subtotal**	0 12 2 3.5 6.5 **24**	Sliced turkey (left over from day 2) on 1 slice 100% whole grain bread 220 g mixed salad greens and 45 g roasted red peppers 50 g cooked lentils 2 Tbsp. Fresh Raspberry Vinaigrette **Subtotal**	0 4.5 11 1.5 5 2 **24**	2 devilled eggs topped with 1 Tbsp. Blender Mayonnaise 110 g mixed salad greens topped with 90 g cooked wheat berries and 50 g red peppers 2 Tbsp. Parmesan Peppercorn Dressing **Subtotal**	1 0 1.5 14 3 1 **20**	Tuna fish salad made with 2 Tbsp. Blender Mayonnaise and 1 stalk chopped celery and 2 Tbsp. chopped onion on 1 slice 100% whole wheat bread 200 g Cos lettuce 1 medium carrot, grated 2 Tbsp. Italian Dressing **Subtotal**	1 0 1 14 3 2.5 1 **22.5**	Grilled chicken over 110 g mixed salad greens 2 slices Swiss cheese on 75 g sweetcorn 100 g red peppers 90 g black beans 2 Tbsp. Parmesan Peppercorn Dressing **Subtotal**	0 1 12.5 6 13 1.5 **33.5**	Ham (left over from day 5) and 2 slices Swiss cheese on 1 slice 100% whole wheat bread with 1 tsp. Dijon mustard 15 g loose-leaf lettuce 1 medium tomato 60 g hummus **Subtotal**	0 2 12 0.5 0.5 3.5 9 **27.5**

Phase 3: Pre-Maintenance and Phase 4: Lifetime Maintenance, at 95 Grams of Net Carbs

Day 1	Grams of Net Carbs	Day 2	Grams of Net Carbs	Day 3	Grams of Net Carbs	Day 4	Grams of Net Carbs	Day 5	Grams of Net Carbs	Day 6	Grams of Net Carbs	Day 7	Grams of Net Carbs
SNACK													
88 g cantaloupe melon balls	7.5	30 g cashews	4.5	2 slices Swiss cheese	2	2 Tbsp. hummus	4.5	75 g red grapes	13.5	1 medium carrot	5.5	60 g almonds	4.5
115 g cottage cheese	4	¼ pomegranate	6.5	½ medium apple	8.5	6 spears asparagus	2.5	60 g goat's cheese	0.5	60 g walnuts	3	84 g sliced strawberries	3.5
Subtotal	11.5	Subtotal	11	Subtotal	10.5	Subtotal	7	Subtotal	14	Subtotal	8.5	Subtotal	8
DINNER													
Lamb kebabs with	0	Roast turkey	0	Fajitas: broiled sliced skirt steak with	0	Sautéed prawns	0	Baked ham	0	Flank steak	0	Salmon steak over	0
60 ml **Raita**	3	125 ml **Velouté Sauce**	1	20 g sautéed onions and	4.5	100 g sautéed leeks with	3.5	60 ml **Mushroom Gravy**	2	60 ml **Mushroom Gravy**	2	180 g sautéed spinach topped with	4.5
140 g cooked low-carb penne pasta**	19	100 g cooked brown rice	20.5	45 g sautéed green peppers	2	60 ml **Alfredo Sauce**	2	120 g steamed acorn squash	15	125 g mashed potato	16.5	60 ml **Raita**	3
120 g Brussels sprouts	9.5	1 steamed medium artichoke	7	60 g refried beans	6.5	80 g cooked wild rice	16	Salad of 90 g chopped raw fennel and	3.5	110 g mixed salad greens	1	140 g cooked low-carb penne pasta**	19
110 g mixed salad greens		110 g mixed salad greens topped with	2	50 g **Salsa Cruda**	1.5	60 g baby spinach salad with	0.5	60 g chopped jicama	2.5	30 g goat's cheese	0.5	Salad of 60 g	1
1 medium carrot, grated	5.5	45 g roasted red peppers	5.5	110 g mixed salad greens	3.5	½ Haas avocado	2	1 small tomato	2.5	55 g snap peas	3.5	rocket	0.5
30 g shredded jicama	3.5	1 medium carrot, grated	1.5	½ Haas avocado	2	75 g sweetcorn	12.5	2 Tbsp. Blue Cheese Dressing	2	85 g pickled beetroots	7	4 pieces marinated artichoke hearts	2
2 Tbsp. Greek Vinaigrette	1	2 Tbsp. Greek Vinaigrette	1	2 Tbsp. Parmesan Peppercorn Dressing	1	2 Tbsp. Creamy Italian Dressing	2			2 Tbsp. Fresh Raspberry Vinaigrette	1	1 medium carrot, grated	5.5
												2 Tbsp. Creamy Italian Dressing	2
Subtotal	40.5	Subtotal	39.5	Subtotal	18.5	Subtotal	38.5	Subtotal	26.5	Subtotal	31.5	Subtotal	36.5
Total	94.5	Total	93.5	Total	93.5	Total	94	Total	94.5	Total	95.5	Total	94.5
Foundation vegetables	18.5	Foundation vegetables	20	Foundation vegetables	20	Foundation vegetables	12.5	Foundation vegetables	14	Foundation vegetables	16	Foundation vegetables	15.5

*www.atkins.com/Recipes/ShowRecipe884/Atkins-Cuisine-Waffles.aspx, **www.atkins.com/Products/productdetail.aspx?productID=36, ***www.atkins.com/Recipes/ShowRecipe883/Atkins-Cuisine-Pancakes.aspx.

Phase 2: Ongoing Weight Loss, Vegetarian, at 30 and 35 Grams of Net Carbs (35-gram additions in bold italics)

	Day 1	Grams of Net Carbs	Day 2	Grams of Net Carbs	Day 3	Grams of Net Carbs	Day 4	Grams of Net Carbs	Day 5	Grams of Net Carbs	Day 6	Grams of Net Carbs	Day 7	Grams of Net Carbs
BREAKFAST	2-egg omelette 80 g Swiss chard sautéed with 40 g chopped onion 30 g shredded Cheddar cheese and **_37 g blueberries_**	1 1.5 3 0.5 **_4_**	3 slices tofu 'bacon' 60 g mashed cauliflower with 30 g shredded Cheddar cheese and 2 Tbsp. sautéed onion **_37 g blueberries_**	1 1.5 0.5 2.5 **_4_**	1 veggie burger 2 slices Swiss cheese ½ Haas avocado **_5 large strawberries_**	1.5 1 1 **_5_**	Low-carb shake 60 g pecans **_36 g blackberries_**	2 2 **_5_**	Smoothie: 240 ml plain unsweetened almond milk and 90 g silken soft tofu and 2 Tbsp. low-carb strawberry syrup and 30 g almonds	1 3 0 2.5	2 fried eggs 80 g sautéed okra 2 tofu 'bacon' strips	1 2.5 2	120 g tofu 'sausage' patties 2 slices Cheddar cheese ½ Haas avocado	8 1 2
Subtotal		6 (10)		5.5 (9.5)		6 (11)		4 (9)		6.5		5.5		11
SNACK	1 celery stalk 1 Tbsp. natural peanut butter	1 2.5	30 g almonds Low-carb shake	1 2.5	2 celery stalks 2 Tbsp. Aïoli	2.5 1	½ Haas avocado 2 slices Cheddar cheese	1.5 0	8 asparagus spears 2 Tbsp. Aïoli	2 1	1 small tomato 30 g roasted pumpkin seeds	3 0	60 g walnuts **_44 g cantaloupe melon balls_**	3 **_3.5_**
Subtotal		3.5		3.5		3.5		1.5		3		3		3 (6.5)
LUNCH	120 g firm tofu sautéed with 60 g spinach 1 Tbsp. soya sauce 100 g Cos lettuce 16 g alfalfa sprouts 10 black olives 2 Tbsp. Fresh Raspberry Vinaigrette	1 2.5 1 1 0 1 1	2 devilled eggs on 220 g mixed salad greens 80 g pickled okra 6 radishes 5 black olives 2 Tbsp. Russian Dressing	1 2.5 1 1 1.5 0.5	120 g sautéed seitan on 200 g Cos lettuce with 10 black olives 60 g sliced daikon 2 Tbsp. Caesar Dressing 2 Tbsp. grated Parmesan	1 2.5 0.5 0.5 1 0.5	2-egg omelette 90 g sautéed spinach 220 g mixed salad greens 16 g alfalfa sprouts 2 Tbsp. Blue Cheese Dressing	1 3.5 1.5 1.5 2	4 slices 'turkey'-style 2 slices Provolone cheese 1 tsp. Dijon mustard 220 g mixed salad greens 10 black olives 2 Tbsp. Italian Dressing	1 1.5 0 1 0 1	2 veggie burgers ½ Haas avocado 2 slices Cheddar cheese 30 g loose-leaf lettuce 2 Tbsp. chopped onions 2 Tbsp. Aïoli	4 1 1 0.5 1.5 0.5	2-egg salad made with 1 stalk diced celery and 1 Tbsp. Blender Mayonnaise Salad of 120 g baby spinach with 1 small tomato 2 Tbsp. Sweet Mustard Dressing	1 0.5 0 2.5 1 1
Subtotal		7.5		7.5		6		9.5		4.5		8.5		6

Phase 2: Ongoing Weight Loss, Vegetarian, at 30 and 35 Grams of Net Carbs (35-gram additions in bold italics)

	Day 1	Grams of Net Carbs	Day 2	Grams of Net Carbs	Day 3	Grams of Net Carbs	Day 4	Grams of Net Carbs	Day 5	Grams of Net Carbs	Day 6	Grams of Net Carbs	Day 7	Grams of Net Carbs
SNACK	30 g pecans	1.5	2 sticks string cheese	1	1 dill gherkin pickle	2	30 g goat's cheese	0.5	30 g hazelnuts	0.5	30 g walnuts	1.5	60 g sliced daikon	1
	60 g goat's cheese	1	30 g walnuts	1.5	30 g peanuts	1.5	10 green olives	0	*37 g blueberries*	4	2 Tbsp. blue cheese	0.5	2 Tbsp. Aioli	0
	Subtotal	2.5	Subtotal	2.5	Subtotal	3.5	Subtotal	0.5	Subtotal	0.5 (4.5)	Subtotal	2	Subtotal	1
DINNER	5 veggie 'meatballs' sautéed with	4	120 g Quorn roast with	4	120 g firm tofu baked with	2.5	⅔ cup veggie crumbles sautéed with	4	85 g tempeh sautéed with	3.5	120 g baked firm tofu and	2.5	2 tofu 'hot dogs'	4
	90 g shirataki soya noodles topped with	1	60 ml Mushroom Gravy	2	2 Tbsp. Barbecue Sauce	2	140 g raw shredded green cabbage topped with	2	50 g green peppers served over	2	3 Tbsp. Sun-dried Tomato Pesto over	3	140 g sauerkraut	2
	3 Tbsp. Romesco Sauce	2	60 g steamed French beans	3	40 g steamed Brussels sprouts	2	2 Tbsp. Peanut Sauce	5	140 g raw shredded green cabbage topped with	2	80 g cooked spaghetti squash	4	60 g mashed cauliflower and	1
	110 g mixed salad greens with	2	110 g mixed salad greens	2	Salad of 60 g rocket and	1	110 g mixed salad greens	1	3 Tbsp. Romesco Sauce and	2	Salad of 60 g mesclun and	2	30 g shredded Cheddar cheese	0.5
	1 small tomato	2.5	4 pieces marinated artichoke hearts	2.5	30 g walnuts	1.5	8 asparagus spears	3	30 g grated Parmesan	3	16 g alfalfa sprouts	1	Salad of 110 g mixed salad greens	1
	2 Tbsp. Sweet Mustard Dressing	1	2 Tbsp. Blue Cheese Dressing	1	2 Tbsp. Italian Dressing	1	100 g sliced cucumber	1	½ Haas avocado	1	*62 g raspberries*	3	50 g sliced cucumber	1
							2 Tbsp. Sweet Mustard Dressing	1			2 Tbsp. Fresh Raspberry Vinaigrette	1	2 Tbsp. Italian Dressing	1
	Subtotal	11.5	Subtotal	13	Subtotal	10	Subtotal	18	Subtotal	12.5	Subtotal	11.5 (14.5)	Subtotal	10.5
	Total	31 (35)	Total	30.5 (34.5)	Total	30.5 (35)	Total	30 (35)	Total	30 (34)	Total	33 (36)	Total	31.5 (35)
	Foundation vegetables	12	Foundation vegetables	14.5	Foundation vegetables	12.5	Foundation vegetables	12.5	Foundation vegetables	12	Foundation vegetables	14.5	Foundation vegetables	12

Phase 2: Ongoing Weight Loss, Vegetarian, at 40 and 45 Grams of Net Carbs (45-gram additions in bold italics)

Meal	Day 1	NC	Day 2	NC	Day 3	NC	Day 4	NC	Day 5	NC	Day 6	NC	Day 7	NC
BREAKFAST	2-egg omelette with	1	3 slices tofu 'bacon'	1	1 veggie burger	1.5	Low-carb shake	2	Smoothie: 240 ml plain unsweetened almond milk with	1	2 fried eggs	1	120 g tofu 'sausage' patties	8
	80 g Swiss chard sautéed with	1.5	120 g mashed cauliflower with	1.5	2 slices Cheddar cheese	1	30 g pecans	1	90 g silken soft tofu and	3	2 tofu 'bacon' strips	2	2 tofu 'bacon' strips	2
	40 g chopped onion	3	60 g shredded Cheddar cheese and	3	½ Haas avocado	2	62 g raspberries	3	110 g frozen strawberries and	5	½ Haas avocado	2	½ cup baked chayote squash	2
	30 g shredded Cheddar cheese	0.5	20 g sautéed onion	0.5	37 g blueberries	4			30 g walnuts	1.5	50 g **Tomatillo Salsa**	4	2 slices Cheddar cheese	1
													½ Haas avocado	2
	Subtotal	**6**	**Subtotal**	**6**	**Subtotal**	**9**	**Subtotal**	**6**	**Subtotal**	**10.5**	**Subtotal**	**9**	**Subtotal**	**13**
SNACK	74 g blueberries	8	30 g almonds	2.5	2 celery sticks	2.5	½ Haas avocado	2	***115 g cottage cheese***	4	30 g almonds	2.5	60 g hazelnuts	1
	30 g goat's cheese	0.5	42 g sliced strawberries	0.5	60 g walnuts	2	***115 g cottage cheese***	4	Low-carb bar	2	36 g blackberries	3	***120 g plain whole milk Greek yoghurt***	3.5
	Subtotal	**8.5**	**Subtotal**	**3**	**Subtotal**	**4.5**	**Subtotal**	**2 (6)**	**Subtotal**	**2 (6)**	**Subtotal**	**5.5**	**Subtotal**	**1 (4.5)**
LUNCH	120 g firm tofu sautéed with	1	2 devilled eggs on	1	120 g sautéed seitan on	1	2-egg omelette with	1	4 slices 'turkey'-style	1	2 veggie burgers	4	2-egg salad made with	1
	60 g spinach and	0.5	220 g mixed salad greens	2.5	Salad of 200 g Cos lettuce	1.5	15 g chopped watercress and	3.5	2 slices Provolone cheese	0	1 small tomato	2.5	1 stalk diced celery and	1
	1 Tbsp. soya sauce	1	80 g pickled okra and	1	5 black olives	2.5	60 g Cheddar cheese	1.5	1 tsp. Dijon mustard	1	2 Tbsp. hummus	4.5	2 Tbsp. **Blender Mayonnaise** over	0
	Salad of 100 g Cos lettuce and	2.5	120 g steamed French beans	2.5	60 g sliced daikon and	1.5	220 g mixed salad greens	0.5	220 g mixed salad greens	1.5	2 slices Cheddar cheese	1	120 g baby spinach with	1
	1 small tomato	1	10 black olives	1.5	2 Tbsp. **Caesar Dressing**	6	1 small tomato	1	10 black olives	2.5	30 g loose-leaf lettuce with	1	30 g cooked chickpeas	6.5
	1 stalk chopped celery	0.5	2 Tbsp. **Russian Dressing**	0.5	2 Tbsp. grated Parmesan	0	2 Tbsp. **Blue Cheese Dressing**	1	2 Tbsp. **Italian Dressing**	1	2 Tbsp. **Aïoli**	0	2 Tbsp. **Sweet Mustard Dressing**	1
	2 Tbsp. **Fresh Raspberry Vinaigrette**	1												
	Subtotal	**9**	**Subtotal**	**9**	**Subtotal**	**12.5**	**Subtotal**	**8.5**	**Subtotal**	**7**	**Subtotal**	**13**	**Subtotal**	**10.5**

Phase 2: Ongoing Weight Loss, Vegetarian, at 40 and 45 Grams of Net Carbs (45-gram additions in bold italics)

SNACK

Day	Item	Grams of Net Carbs
Day 1	60 g almonds	5
	115 g cottage cheese	4
	Subtotal	5 (9)
Day 2	30 g almonds	2.5
	120 g plain whole milk yoghurt	5.5
	Subtotal	2.5 (8)
Day 3	1 dill gherkin pickle	2
	120 g plain whole milk Greek yoghurt	3.5
	Subtotal	2 (5.5)
Day 4	30 g walnuts	1.5
	45 g roasted red peppers	3.5
	Subtotal	5
Day 5	30 g walnuts	1.5
	55 g raw French beans	2
	Subtotal	3.5
Day 6	30 g walnuts	1.5
	115 g ricotta cheese	4
	Subtotal	1.5 (5.5)
Day 7	37 g blueberries	4
	2 sticks string cheese	1
	Subtotal	5

DINNER

Day	Item	Grams of Net Carbs
Day 1	5 veggie 'meatballs' sautéed with	4
	90 g shirataki soya noodles topped with	
	3 Tbsp. **Romesco Sauce**	3.5
	110 g mixed salad greens	2
	50 g sliced cucumber	1
	5 asparagus spears	2.5
	2 Tbsp. **Sweet Mustard Dressing**	1
	Subtotal	11.5
	Total	40 (44)
	Foundation vegetables	12.5
Day 2	120 g Quorn roast with	4
	60 ml **Mushroom Gravy**	4
	45 g sautéed red peppers	1
	110 g mixed salad greens	2
	50 g sliced cucumber	1
	2 Tbsp. **Blue Cheese Dressing**	2.5
	2 Tbsp. **Sweet Mustard Dressing**	1
	Subtotal	11.5
	Total	41 (46.5)
	Foundation vegetables	23.5
Day 3	120 g firm tofu grilled and topped with	4
	2 Tbsp. **Barbecue Sauce**	2
	130 g sautéed kale	3.5
	Salad of 60 g rocket	1
	1 small tomato	1
	2 Tbsp. **Italian Dressing**	1
	Subtotal	12.5
	Total	40 (43.5)
	Foundation vegetables	17
Day 4	¾ cup veggie crumbles sautéed with	4
	180 g shirataki soya noodles topped with	4
	2 Tbsp. **Peanut Sauce**	5
	160 g steamed Brussels sprouts	7
	110 g mixed salad greens	2.5
	2 Tbsp. **Sweet Mustard Dressing**	1
	Subtotal	16
	Total	39.5 (43.5)
	Foundation vegetables	17.5
Day 5	85 g tempeh sautéed with	4
	100 g green peppers over	2
	140 g raw shredded green cabbage topped with	5
	3 Tbsp. **Romesco Sauce and**	2
	30 g grated Parmesan	1
	½ Haas avocado	1
	Subtotal	15
	Total	39.5 (43.5)
	Foundation vegetables	13.5
Day 6	120 g baked firm tofu and	2.5
	3 Tbsp. **Sun-dried Tomato Pesto over**	3
	80 g cooked spaghetti squash	4
	Salad of 60 g rocket	2
	50 g sliced cucumber	2
	2 Tbsp. **Fresh Raspberry Vinaigrette**	1
	Subtotal	12
	Total	41 (45)
	Foundation vegetables	15
Day 7	2 tofu 'hot dogs'	2.5
	70 g sauerkraut	1
	120 g mashed cauliflower and	2
	30 g Cheddar cheese	0.5
	110 g mixed salad greens	
	4 pieces marinated artichoke hearts	2
	2 Tbsp. **Italian Dressing**	1
	Subtotal	11.5
	Total	41 (44.5)
	Foundation vegetables	12

Phase 2: Ongoing Weight Loss, Vegetarian, at 50 and 55 Grams of Net Carbs (55-gram additions in bold italics)

BREAKFAST

Day	Food	Grams of Net Carbs
Day 1	2-egg omelette	1
	170 g sautéed Swiss chard and	3.5
	30 g shredded Cheddar cheese and	
	2 Tbsp. sautéed onion and	2.5
	30 g shredded Cheddar cheese	1
	44 g cantaloupe melon balls	3.5
	Subtotal	**11.5**
Day 2	3 slices tofu 'bacon'	1
	60 g refried beans	6.5
	30 g shredded Cheddar cheese	3.5
	120 g tomato juice	
	Subtotal	**11.5**
Day 3	1 veggie burger	1.5
	1 slice Cheddar cheese	6.5
	½ Haas avocado	0.5
	74 g blueberries	4
	Subtotal	**8.5 (12.5)**
Day 4	Low-carb shake	2
	60 g pecans	3
	88 g cantaloupe melon balls	7.5
	Subtotal	**12.5**
Day 5	Smoothie: 240 ml plain unsweetened almond milk and	1
	90 g silken soft tofu and	3
	165 g frozen strawberries and	7
	30 g almonds	2.5
	Subtotal	**13.5**
Day 6	2 fried eggs	1
	80 g sautéed okra	2.5
	2 tofu 'bacon' strips	2
	50 g **Tomatillo Salsa**	
	Subtotal	**9.5**
Day 7	120 g tofu 'sausage' patties	8
	½ cup baked chayote squash	2
	2 slices Cheddar cheese	1
	½ Haas avocado	2
	Subtotal	**13**

SNACK

Day	Food	Grams of Net Carbs
Day 1	*120 g tomato juice*	
	115 g cottage cheese	4
	Subtotal	**4 (8)**
Day 2	5 large strawberries	4
	120 g low-carb yoghurt	4
	Subtotal	**8**
Day 3	115 g cottage cheese	5
	1 small tomato	3
	Subtotal	**8**
Day 4	½ Haas avocado	4
	40 g edamame	2.5
	Subtotal	**6.5**
Day 5	115 g cottage cheese	2
	8 asparagus spears	3
	Subtotal	**2 (5)**
Day 6	120 g plain whole milk Greek yoghurt	3.5
	1 small tomato	2.5
	Subtotal	**6**
Day 7	60 g hazelnuts	1
	36 g blackberries	3
	Subtotal	**4**

LUNCH

Day	Food	Grams of Net Carbs
Day 1	120 g firm tofu sautéed with	1
	100 g green peppers and	4.5
	40 g spring onions	2.5
	1 Tbsp. soya sauce	1
	100 g Cos lettuce	1
	2 Tbsp. Fresh Raspberry Vinaigrette	1
	Subtotal	**12.5**
Day 2	2 devilled eggs on	2.5
	220 g mixed salad greens	4.5
	80 g pickled okra and	2.5
	1 small tomato	1
	4 pieces marinated artichoke hearts	1
	100 g Cos lettuce	1
	2 Tbsp. Russian Dressing	
	Subtotal	**12.5**
Day 3	120 g sautéed seitan on	1
	200 g Cos lettuce	1.5
	10 black olives	2.5
	60 g sliced daikon	2.5
	2 Tbsp. Caesar Dressing	2
	2 Tbsp. grated Parmesan	0
	Subtotal	**9.5**
Day 4	2-egg omelette with	1
	90 g sautéed red peppers and	3.5
	60 g feta cheese	1.5
	110 g mixed salad greens	1
	1 small tomato	2.5
	2 Tbsp. **Sweet Mustard Dressing**	1
	Subtotal	**9.5**
Day 5	4 slices 'turkey'-style	3
	2 slices Swiss cheese	2
	1 tsp. Dijon mustard	0.5
	120 g mesclun greens	2.5
	1 small tomato	1
	10 black olives	2.5
	2 Tbsp. Italian Dressing	
	Subtotal	**11.5**
Day 6	2 veggie burgers	3
	½ Haas avocado	2
	3 Tbsp. hummus	7
	60 g shredded Cheddar cheese	2
	30 g loose-leaf lettuce	1.5
	1 Tbsp. chopped onions	1
	1 Tbsp. Caesar Dressing	0.5
	Subtotal	**10 (17)**
Day 7	2-egg salad made with	1
	1 stalk diced celery and	2
	2 Tbsp. Blender Mayonnaise over	0
	120 g baby spinach with	1
	1 small tomato	2.5
	45 g cooked chickpeas	6.5
	2 Tbsp. Sweet Mustard Dressing	1
	Subtotal	**12.5**

Phase 2: Ongoing Weight Loss, Vegetarian, at 50 and 55 Grams of Net Carbs (55-gram additions in bold italics)

Day 1	Grams of Net Carbs	Day 2	Grams of Net Carbs	Day 3	Grams of Net Carbs	Day 4	Grams of Net Carbs	Day 5	Grams of Net Carbs	Day 6	Grams of Net Carbs	Day 7	Grams of Net Carbs
SNACK													
40 g edamame	3	1 stick string cheese	0.5	***120 g tomato juice***	4	50 g red peppers	4	30 g macadamias	2	60 g pecans	3	***120 g tomato juice***	4
60 g cashews	9	60 g macadamias	4	60 g walnuts	3	2 Tbsp. hummus	3	44 g Crenshaw melon balls	2.5	88 g cantaloupe melon balls	7.5	115 g cottage cheese	4
Subtotal	12	Subtotal	4.5	Subtotal	3 (7)	Subtotal	7	Subtotal	4.5	Subtotal	10.5	Subtotal	4 (8)
DINNER													
5 veggie 'meatballs' sautéed with	4	120 g Quorn roast with	4	120 g firm tofu baked with	4	120 g veggie crumbles sautéed with	4	85 g tempeh sautéed with	4	120 g baked firm tofu and	1.5	2 tofu 'hot dogs'	4
180 g shirataki soya noodles topped with		60 ml **Mushroom Gravy**	2	2 Tbsp. **Barbecue Sauce**	2	180 g shirataki soya noodles topped with		100 g green peppers topped with	2	50 g cooked lentils topped with	6	70 g sauerkraut	1
3 Tbsp. **Romesco Sauce**	2	180 g sautéed green pepper	7.5	110 g mixed salad greens	3	2 Tbsp. **Peanut Sauce**	5	3 Tbsp. **Romesco Sauce** and	3	3 Tbsp. **Sun-dried Tomato Pesto**	3	160 g mashed turnip and	6.5
110 g mixed salad greens	3	20 g sautéed onion	4.5	60 g steamed French beans	1.5	120 g steamed Brussels sprouts	5.5	30 g grated Parmesan	1	110 g salad greens	1	60 g shredded Cheddar cheese	1
50 g sliced cucumber	1	110 g mixed salad greens	1	45 g cooked chickpeas	6.5	110 g mixed salad greens	3	30 g watercress salad	1	6 radishes	0.5	110 g salad greens	1
2 Tbsp. **Sweet Mustard Dressing**	1	2 Tbsp. **Blue Cheese Dressing**	1	2 Tbsp. **Italian Dressing**	1	2 Tbsp. **Blue Cheese Dressing**	1	***45 g black beans***	6.5	2 Tbsp. **Fresh Raspberry Vinaigrette**	2	4 pieces marinated artichoke hearts	2
								2 Tbsp. **Sweet Mustard Dressing**	1			2 Tbsp. **Italian Dressing**	1
Subtotal	11	Subtotal	20	Subtotal	18	Subtotal	18.5	Subtotal	12 (18.5)	Subtotal	14	Subtotal	16.5
Total	51 (55)	Total	50.5 (54.5)	Total	49.5 (53.5)	Total	51 (54)	Total	49.5 (56)	Total	50 (57)	Total	50 (54)
Foundation vegetables	16	Foundation vegetables	21.5	Foundation vegetables	12.5	Foundation vegetables	18.5	Foundation vegetables	13.5	Foundation vegetables	15	Foundation vegetables	18.5

Phase 2: Ongoing Weight Loss, Vegan, at 50 Grams of Net Carbs

Each day column shows the food item followed by its Grams of Net Carbs.

BREAKFAST

	Day 1	Day 2	Day 3	Day 4	Day 5	Day 6	Day 7
Items (Grams of Net Carbs)	120 g tofu 'scrambled eggs' — 2 80 g Swiss chard sautéed with — 1.5 40 g chopped onion — 3 2 Tbsp. grated vegan 'Parmesan cheese' — 1	3 slices tofu 'bacon' — 1.5 60 g refried beans — 6.5 30 g vegan 'Cheddar cheese' — 1.5	1 vegan burger — 2 1 slice vegan 'cheese' — 6 ½ Haas avocado — 2 37 g blueberries — 4	3 tofu 'link sausages' — 6 ½ cup baked chayote squash — 6 240 ml unsweetened almond milk — 2	120 g tofu 'scrambled eggs' — 6 1 small tomato — 2 ½ Haas avocado — 2 1 Tbsp. grated vegan 'Parmesan cheese' — 1	2 tofu 'bacon' strips — 2 80 g sautéed okra — 2.5 1 slice vegan 'cheese' — 6	Smoothie: 240 ml plain unsweetened almond milk and — 2.5 90 g silken soft tofu and — 1 55 g frozen strawberries — 3
Subtotal	7.5		14	14	9	10.5	6.5

SNACK

	Day 1	Day 2	Day 3	Day 4	Day 5	Day 6	Day 7
Items (Grams of Net Carbs)	40 g edamame — 3 2 slices vegan 'cheese' — 12	2 Tbsp. vegan 'cream cheese' — 2 50 g cucumber sliced — 1	240 ml unsweetened almond milk — 2 60 g pecans — 1	31 g boysenberries — 3 60 g hazelnuts — 1	10 green olives, stuffed with — 3 2 Tbsp. vegan 'cream cheese' — 1	1 small tomato — 2.5 10 black olives — 1.5	2 celery stalks — 1.5 50 g guacamole — 1.5
Subtotal	15	3	3	4	4	4	3

LUNCH

	Day 1	Day 2	Day 3	Day 4	Day 5	Day 6	Day 7
Items (Grams of Net Carbs)	120 g firm tofu sautéed with — 2.5 50 g green peppers and — 2 50 g spring onions and — 2.5 1 Tbsp. soya sauce — 1 100 g Cos lettuce — 1 2 Tbsp. Fresh Raspberry Vinaigrette — 1	⅔ cup veggie crumbles sautéed and topped with — 2.5 50 g Salsa Cruda — 2 220 g mixed salad greens with — 2.5 80 g pickled okra and — 1 4 pieces marinated artichoke hearts — 2.5 5 black olives — 0.5 2 Tbsp. Russian Dressing — 0	85 g tempeh sautéed with — 3.5 40 g chopped onion and — 3 1 stalk chopped celery — 0.5 110 g mixed salad greens — 3 50 g cooked lentils and — 2.5 6 radishes — 0.5 2 Tbsp. Sweet Mustard Dressing — 1	2 slices vegan deli 'ham' over — 6 220 g mixed salad greens and — 3 50 g red peppers — 0.5 45 g cooked black beans — 6.5 1 small tomato — 2.5 2 Tbsp. Sweet Mustard Dressing — 1	2 slices vegan deli 'turkey' and — 6 1 slice vegan 'Swiss cheese' with — 1.5 50 g Basil Pesto on — 2.5 1 low-carb pitta — 6.5 110 g mixed salad greens — 2.5 5 black olives — 0.5 2 Tbsp. Italian Dressing — 1	2 vegan burgers — 4 ½ Haas avocado — 2 2 Tbsp. hummus — 4.5 30 g loose-leaf lettuce — 1 2 tomato, chopped onions — 1.5 1 Tbsp. Italian Dressing — 0.5	2 tofu 'hot dogs' with — 4 20 g sautéed onions — 2 110 g mixed salad greens — 4.5 1 small tomato — 1 45 g cooked chickpeas — 6.5 2 Tbsp. Sweet Mustard Dressing — 1
Subtotal	10	12	15.5	20.5	20.5	13.5	20

Phase 2: Ongoing Weight Loss, Vegan, at 50 Grams of Net Carbs

Day 1	Grams of Net Carbs	Day 2	Grams of Net Carbs	Day 3	Grams of Net Carbs	Day 4	Grams of Net Carbs	Day 5	Grams of Net Carbs	Day 6	Grams of Net Carbs	Day 7	Grams of Net Carbs
SNACK													
10 green olives	0	60 g walnuts	3	10 green olives	3	60 g jicama sticks	0	60 g hazelnuts	1	30 g almonds	2.5	60 g walnuts	3
60 g almonds	4.5	44 g Crenshaw melon balls	2.5	1 slice vegan 'cheese'	2.5	2 Tbsp. hummus	5	6 radishes	0.5	31 g raspberries	1.5	1 slice vegan 'Cheddar cheese'	5
Subtotal	**4.5**	**Subtotal**	**5.5**	**Subtotal**	**5.5**	**Subtotal**	**5**	**Subtotal**	**1.5**	**Subtotal**	**4**	**Subtotal**	**8**
DINNER													
5 veggie 'meatballs' sautéed with	4	120 g firm tofu baked with	4	120 g baked tofu and	2.5	85 g tempeh sautéed with	3.5	4 pieces sautéed seitan	8	⅔ cup veggie crumbles sautéed with	8	4 veggie 'meatballs' and	4
180 g shirataki soya noodles topped with	2	1 Tbsp. **Barbecue Sauce**	2	180 g shirataki soya noodles topped with	2	80 g okra and	2	60 g steamed French beans	3	140 g pak choi	3	3 Tbsp. **Romesco Sauce** over	3
3 Tbsp. **Romesco Sauce**	2	60 g steamed French beans	3	50 g **Basil Pesto**	2	15 g button mushrooms and	1	120 g mashed pumpkin	5	50 g red peppers	5	40 g spaghetti squash	2
110 g mixed salad greens and	1	110 g mixed salad greens and	1	80 g braised fennel	3	2 Tbsp. chopped onions	1.5	110 g mixed salad greens	1.5	45 g cooked chickpeas	1	80 g steamed broccoli	1.5
50 g sliced cucumber	1	45 g cooked chickpeas	2.5	110 g mixed salad greens and	3	110 g mixed salad greens and	1.5	6 radishes	0.5	Salad of 140 g shredded green cabbage with	0.5	110 g mixed salad greens	1.5
1 small tomato	2.5	2 Tbsp. **Italian Dressing**	1	1 small tomato	2.5	½ Haas avocado	2.5	40 g edamame	2.5	30 g chopped peanuts and	1	10 black olives	1.5
2 Tbsp. **Sweet Mustard Dressing**	1			2 Tbsp. **Sweet Mustard Dressing**	1	2 Tbsp. **Russian Dressing**	1	2 Tbsp. **Russian Dressing**	0	2 Tbsp. **Coleslaw Dressing**	0.5	2 Tbsp. **Russian Dressing**	0.5
Subtotal	**13.5**	**Subtotal**	**13.5**	**Subtotal**	**16**	**Subtotal**	**13**	**Subtotal**	**20.5**	**Subtotal**	**19**	**Subtotal**	**14**
Total	**50.5**	**Total**	**50.5**	**Total**	**50.5**	**Total**	**52**	**Total**	**50**	**Total**	**50.5**	**Total**	**51.5**
Foundation vegetables	**14.5**	**Foundation vegetables**	**13**	**Foundation vegetables**	**13**	**Foundation vegetables**	**19.5**	**Foundation vegetables**	**16**	**Foundation vegetables**	**17**	**Foundation vegetables**	**19.5**

Phase 3: Pre-Maintenance and Phase 4: Lifetime Maintenance, Vegetarian, at 60 and 70 Grams of Net Carbs (70-gram additions in bold italics)

Meal	Day 1	Grams of Net Carbs	Day 2	Grams of Net Carbs	Day 3	Grams of Net Carbs	Day 4	Grams of Net Carbs	Day 5	Grams of Net Carbs	Day 6	Grams of Net Carbs	Day 7	Grams of Net Carbs
BREAKFAST	115 g cottage cheese	4	2 Atkins Pancakes*	6	Smoothie: 120 ml plain unsweetened almond milk	0.5	2-egg omelette	1	1 Atkins Waffle**	6	120 g plain whole milk Greek yoghurt	3.5	2 scrambled eggs	1
	30 g almonds	2.5	115 g ricotta cheese	4	120 g low-carb yoghurt	3	50 g sautéed leeks	3.5	60 g ricotta cheese	2	88 g honeydew melon balls	7	80 g sautéed okra	2.5
	74 g blueberries	8	31 g raspberries	3	38 g frozen blackberries	4	30 g feta cheese	1	42 g sliced strawberries	2	60 g pecans	3	50 g *Salsa Cruda*	1.5
					1 Tbsp. almond butter	2.5	88 g cantaloupe melon balls	7	30 g slivered almonds	2.5			30 g shredded Cheddar cheese	0.5
	Subtotal	14.5	**Subtotal**	13	**Subtotal**	10	**Subtotal**	12.5	**Subtotal**	12.5	**Subtotal**	13.5	**Subtotal**	5.5
SNACK	2 Tbsp. natural peanut butter	5	60 g walnuts	3	2 slices of Swiss cheese around	2	50 g red peppers	3	1 celery stalk	1	75 g marinated Jerusalem artichoke	12	60 g macadamias	4
	2 celery stalks	1.5	1 medium carrot	5.5	4 asparagus spears	2	60 g almonds	4.5	1 Tbsp. natural peanut butter	2.5	2 slices Cheddar cheese	2	6 large strawberries	6
					1 tsp. Dijon mustard	0.5								
	Subtotal	6.5	**Subtotal**	8.5	**Subtotal**	4.5	**Subtotal**	7.5	**Subtotal**	3.5	**Subtotal**	14	**Subtotal**	10
LUNCH	120 g seitan, sautéed, over	1	2 hard-boiled eggs and	1	1 veggie burgers on	1	120 g firm tofu simmered with	4	2-egg, egg salad made with	2.5	½ cup veggie crumbles sautéed and topped with	2.5	3 slices tofu 'bacon'	1.5
	60 g mesclun greens	0.5	2 tofu 'bacon' strips	2	1 low-carb hamburger bun	4	2 Tbsp. *Barbecue Sauce*	4	2 Tbsp. *Blender Mayonnaise* and	1	30 g shredded mozzarella cheese	0.5	2 slices Swiss cheese on	2
	30 g feta cheese	1	½ Haas avocado	2.5	½ Haas avocado	2	220 g mixed salad greens with	2.5	2 Tbsp. chopped onions and	1.5	60 g refried beans	6.5	1 low-carb bagel	5
	45 g roasted red peppers	3.5	1 small tomato	1	1 small tomato	2.5	40 g edamame	1	1 stalk diced celery on	0.5	55 g shredded mixed greens	0.5	1 tsp. Dijon mustard	0.5
	10 black olives	1.5	25 g spring onions on	3.5	110 g mixed salad greens	1	85 g pickled beetroots	3	1 low-carb pitta	7	50 g *Salsa Cruda*	1.5	15 g loose-leaf lettuce	0.5
	45 g cooked lentils	6	220 g mixed salad greens	1.5	4 pieces marinated artichoke hearts	1.5	60 g goat's cheese	7	110 g mixed salad greens	1	1 low-carb tortilla	4	100 g sliced cucumber	2
	2 Tbsp. *Italian Dressing*	1	2 Tbsp. *Blue Cheese Dressing*	6	5 black olives	1	2 Tbsp. *Greek Vinaigrette*	0.5	2 Tbsp. *Parmesan-Peppercorn Dressing*	1	½ Haas avocado	2	2 Tbsp. hummus	9
					2 Tbsp. *Italian Dressing*	1								
	Subtotal	17	**Subtotal**	11	**Subtotal**	11	**Subtotal**	17	**Subtotal**	15	**Subtotal**	17	**Subtotal**	20.5

Phase 3: Pre-Maintenance and Phase 4: Lifetime Maintenance. Vegetarian, at 60 and 70 Grams of Net Carbs (70-gram additions in bold italics)

Meal	Day 1	Grams of Net Carbs	Day 2	Grams of Net Carbs	Day 3	Grams of Net Carbs	Day 4	Grams of Net Carbs	Day 5	Grams of Net Carbs	Day 6	Grams of Net Carbs	Day 7	Grams of Net Carbs
SNACK	60 g goat's cheese 74 g blueberries **Subtotal**	0.5 8 **8.5**	2 slices Swiss cheese 80 g edamame **Subtotal**	0.5 8 **8.5**	Low-carb bar 44 g honeydew melon balls **Subtotal**	2 6 **8**	35 g sweet cherries 115 g cottage cheese **Subtotal**	2 3.5 **5.5**	120 g plain whole milk Greek yoghurt 37 g blueberries **Subtotal**	3.5 4 **7.5**	60 g jicama sticks 2 Tbsp. Parmesan-Peppercorn Dressing **Subtotal**	2.5 1 **3.5**	50 g red pepper 1 slice Swiss cheese **Subtotal**	3 1 **4**
DINNER	Stuffed pepper: 170 g sautéed tempeh in 2 red pepper halves drizzled with 1 Tbsp. soya sauce and topped with 30 g shredded Cheddar cheese and baked 110 g mixed salad greens ***1 medium carrot, grated*** 1 medium tomato 2 Tbsp. Italian Dressing **Subtotal**	3.5 4.5 1 0.5 1 ***5.5*** 3.5 1 **15 (20.5)**	150 g tofu 'sausage' sautéed with 40 g onions and 50 g green peppers over 100 g steamed butternut squash 110 g mixed salad greens ***40 g cooked wild rice*** 2 Tbsp. Parmesan-peppercorn Dressing **Subtotal**	5 3 2 7 1 ***8*** 1 **19 (27)**	120 g sautéed seitan on 120 g baked acorn squash 220 g mixed salad greens 45 g cooked chickpeas 60 g jicama ***50 g cooked brown rice*** 2 Tbsp. Russian Dressing **Subtotal**	5 10.5 2 4.5 2.5 ***10.5*** 0 **24.5 (35)**	2/3 cup veggie crumbles sautéed with 140 g raw shredded cabbage and 40 g onions ***45 g cooked bulgur wheat*** 1/2 Haas avocado and 1 small tomato 1 Tbsp. Russian Dressing **Subtotal**	3.5 4 1.5 ***6.5*** 2 2.5 0 **13.5 (20)**	120 g firm tofu sautéed with 40 g onions 80 g parsnips 110 g mixed salad greens 2 small tomatoes ***40 g cooked millet*** 2 Tbsp. Parmesan-Peppercorn Dressing **Subtotal**	5 2 8.5 1 5 ***10*** 0 **21.5 (31.5)**	2 tofu 'hot dogs' 60 g mashed pumpkin 110 g mixed salad greens 110 g watercress 5 black olives 2 Tbsp. Sweet Mustard Dressing ***40 g cooked wild rice*** **Subtotal**	2.5 5 1 0.5 0.5 3.5 ***8*** **13 (21)**	2 Quorn unbreaded cutlets 2 Tbsp. Barbecue Sauce 6 asparagus spears ***100 g cooked brown rice*** Salad of 140 g shredded cabbage and 1 medium carrot, shredded 2 Tbsp. Creamy Coleslaw Dressing **Subtotal**	6 4 2.5 ***10.5*** 2 5.5 **20 (30.5)**
Total		61.5 (67)		59.5 (67.5)		61.5 (72)		61 (67.5)		60 (70)		61 (69)		60.5 (71)
Total Foundation vegetables		16		13		14		17.5		13.5		13.5		14

*www.atkins.com/Recipes/ShowRecipe883/Atkins-Cuisine-Pancakes.aspx. **www.atkins.com/Recipes/ShowRecipe884/Atkins-Cuisine-Waffles.aspx

Phase 3: Pre-Maintenance and Phase 4: Lifetime Maintenance, Vegetarian, at 80 and 90 Grams of Net Carbs (90-gram additions in bold italics)

BREAKFAST

Day 1	Net Carbs	Day 2	Net Carbs	Day 3	Net Carbs	Day 4	Net Carbs	Day 5	Net Carbs	Day 6	Net Carbs	Day 7	Net Carbs
115 g cottage cheese	4	2 **Atkins Pancakes***	4	Smoothie: 120 ml plain unsweetened almond milk	0.5	2-egg omelette		1 **Atkins Waffle****	6	Atkins muesli: 3 Tbsp. oat bran and	9	2 scrambled eggs	1
74 g blueberries	8	15 g ricotta cheese	8	240 g plain whole milk yoghurt	5.5	90 g cooked spinach	7	60 g ricotta cheese	2	60 g pecans and	3	80 g sautéed okra	2.5
1 slice low-carb bread	6	168 g sliced strawberries	2.5	38 g frozen blackberries	4	30 g feta cheese		37 g blueberries	4	2 Tbsp. dried unsweetened coconut	2	50 g **Salsa Cruda**	1
1 Tbsp. almond butter	2.5			30 g almonds	2.5	88 g cantaloupe melon balls	7	30 g slivered almonds	2.5	31 g raspberries	1.5	60 g shredded Cheddar cheese	1
										120 g plain whole milk yoghurt	5.5	1 low-carb tortilla	4
Subtotal	20.5	**Subtotal**	14.5	**Subtotal**	12.5	**Subtotal**	12.5	**Subtotal**	11	**Subtotal**	21	**Subtotal**	9.5

SNACK

Day 1	Net Carbs	Day 2	Net Carbs	Day 3	Net Carbs	Day 4	Net Carbs	Day 5	Net Carbs	Day 6	Net Carbs	Day 7	Net Carbs
30 g pistachios	2.5	60 g walnuts	2.5	2 slices Swiss cheese	3	35 g sweet cherries	4	1 celery stalk	1	½ Haas avocado	2	60 g macadamias	2
1 medium carrot	5.5	44 g Crenshaw melon balls	5.5	1 medium carrot	4.5	115 g cottage cheese	4	1 Tbsp. natural peanut butter	2.5	44 g Crenshaw melon balls	4.5	6 large strawberries	4.5
				1 tsp. Dijon mustard									
Subtotal	8	**Subtotal**	8	**Subtotal**	7.5	**Subtotal**	8	**Subtotal**	3.5	**Subtotal**	6.5	**Subtotal**	6.5

LUNCH

Day 1	Net Carbs	Day 2	Net Carbs	Day 3	Net Carbs	Day 4	Net Carbs	Day 5	Net Carbs	Day 6	Net Carbs	Day 7	Net Carbs
120 g seitan, sautéed, over	4	Cobb salad: 2 hard-boiled eggs and	1	2 veggie burgers on	4	120 g firm tofu simmered with	4	2 devilled eggs	2	⅓ cup veggie crumbles sautéed and topped with	1	3 slices tofu 'bacon'	1.5
30 g mesclun greens	0.5	2 tofu 'bacon' strips on	2	1 low-carb hamburger bun	4	2 Tbsp. **Barbecue Sauce** over	2.5	2 Tbsp. chopped onion and	2.5	30 g shredded mozzarella cheese	0.5	2 slices Swiss cheese on	2
4 Tbsp. hummus	9	220 g mixed greens with	2	110 g mixed salad greens	1.5	50 g brown rice	10.5	1 stalk diced celery in	0.5	60 g refried beans	6.5	1 slice 100% whole grain bread	12
30 g feta cheese	0.5	½ Haas avocado	1.5	4 pieces marinated artichoke hearts	2	220 g mixed salad greens with	1.5	1 low-carb pitta	4	55 g shredded mixed greens	0.5	1 Tbsp. Dijon mustard	0.5
50 g red peppers	3	1 small tomato	2.5	60 g jicama	2.5	45 g cooked chickpeas	6.5	110 g mixed salad greens	1.5	75 g sweetcorn	12.5	15 g loose-leaf lettuce	0.5
5 black olives	0.5	25 g spring onions	1	½ Haas avocado	1.5	85 g pickled beetroots	7	45 g cooked lentils	6.5	50 g **Salsa Cruda**	1	2 small tomatoes	5
1 medium tomato	3.5	75 g sweetcorn	12.5	1 medium tomato	3.5	60 g goat's cheese	0.5	40 g cooked wild rice	8	1 low-carb tortilla	4	***4 Tbsp. hummus***	9
2 Tbsp. **Greek Vinaigrette**	1	2 Tbsp. **Blue Cheese Dressing**	1	2 Tbsp. **Italian Dressing**	1	2 Tbsp. **Greek Vinaigrette**	1	2 Tbsp. **Parmesan-Peppercorn Dressing**	0.5				
Subtotal	22	**Subtotal**	23.5	**Subtotal**	20	**Subtotal**	26.5 (33.5)	**Subtotal**	21 (29)	**Subtotal**	27	**Subtotal**	21.5 (30.5)

Phase 3: Pre-Maintenance and Phase 4: Lifetime Maintenance, Vegetarian, at 80 and 90 Grams of Net Carbs (90-gram additions in bold italics)

Day 1	Grams of Net Carbs	Day 2	Grams of Net Carbs	Day 3	Grams of Net Carbs	Day 4	Grams of Net Carbs	Day 5	Grams of Net Carbs	Day 6	Grams of Net Carbs	Day 7	Grams of Net Carbs
SNACK													
60 g goat's cheese	0.5	2 slices Swiss cheese	2	Low-carb bar	2	45 g roasted red peppers	3.5	120 g plain whole milk yoghurt	5.5	120 g jicama sticks	5	50 g red peppers	3
70 g sweet cherries	8.5	80 g edamame	6	1 small fig	6	60 g walnuts	3	44 g Crenshaw melon balls	4.5	2 slices Cheddar cheese	1	2 slices Cheddar cheese	1
Subtotal	9	Subtotal	8	Subtotal	8	Subtotal	6.5	Subtotal	10	Subtotal	6	Subtotal	4
DINNER													
Stuffed pepper: 170 g sautéed tempeh and 50 g cooked brown rice with 1 Tbsp. soya sauce baked in	14	50 g tofu 'sausage' sautéed with	5	120 g sautéed seitan on	5	⅔ cup veggie crumbles sautéed with	4	120 g firm tofu sautéed with	2.5	2 tofu 'hot dogs'	5	2 Quorn unbreaded cutlets	6
2 green pepper halves topped with 30 g shredded Cheddar cheese	0.5	40 g onions and 50 g green peppers over	3.5	120 g baked acorn squash	3	40 g onions and	3	80 g onions and 100 g aubergine	6	140 g sauerkraut	2.5	**_2 Tbsp. Barbecue Sauce_**	4
100 g baked butternut squash	7	100 g steamed butternut squash	10	220 g mixed salad greens	2	140 g raw shredded cabbage	10.5	**_½ sweet jacket potato_**	12	**_½ jacket potato_**	10.5	6 asparagus spears	2.5
110 g mixed salad greens	3.5	110 g mixed salad greens	1	60 g cooked French beans	7	100 g cooked brown rice	1.5	110 g mixed salad greens	0.5	110 g mixed salad greens	1	**_½ sweet jacket potato_**	12
6 radishes	1	1 medium carrot, grated	3.5	45 g cooked chickpeas	1	Chopped salad of ½ Haas avocado	3	1 small tomato	2.5	60 g watercress	0.5	Salad of 140 g shredded cabbage and	2
2 Tbsp. Italian Dressing	1	**_40 g cooked wild rice_**	7	1 medium carrot, grated	5.5	1 small tomato	13	1 medium carrot, grated	5.5	5 black olives	1.5	1 medium carrot, grated	5.5
		2 Tbsp. Parmesan-Peppercorn Dressing	1	**_45 g cooked wheat berries_**	8	**_40 g sweetcorn_**	7	2 Tbsp. Carrot-Ginger Dressing	1	40 g cooked wild rice	2.5	2 Tbsp. Creamy Coleslaw Dressing	0.5
				2 Tbsp. Russian Dressing	1	2 Tbsp. Parmesan-Peppercorn Dressing	0			1 medium carrot, grated	8		
										2 Tbsp. Sweet Mustard Dressing	1		
Subtotal	21 (28)	Subtotal	24.5 (32.5)	Subtotal	31.5 (38.5)	Subtotal	31	Subtotal	33	Subtotal	18.5 (29)	Subtotal	32.5
Total	80 (87.5)	Total	80.5 (88.5)	Total	80.5 (87.5)	Total	83 (90)	Total	82 (90)	Total	79 (89.5)	Total	77.5 (86.5)
Foundation vegetables	12.5	Foundation vegetables	13	Foundation vegetables	13	Foundation vegetables	16.5	Foundation vegetables	15	Foundation vegetables	13	Foundation vegetables	16.5

*www.atkins.com/Recipes/ShowRecipe883/Atkins-Cuisine-Pancakes.aspx, **www.atkins.com/Recipes/ShowRecipe884/Atkins-Cuisine-Waffles.aspx

Phase 3: Pre-Maintenance and Phase 4: Lifetime Maintenance, Vegetarian, at 100 Grams of Net Carbs

Day 1	Grams of Net Carbs	Day 2	Grams of Net Carbs	Day 3	Grams of Net Carbs	Day 4	Grams of Net Carbs	Day 5	Grams of Net Carbs	Day 6	Grams of Net Carbs	Day 7	Grams of Net Carbs
BREAKFAST													
115 g cottage cheese	4	2 Atkins Pancakes*	6	Smoothie: 120 ml plain unsweetened almond milk	1	2-egg omelette	1	1 Atkins Waffle**	6	Atkins muesli: 3 Tbsp. oat bran and	6	2 scrambled eggs	1
74 g blueberries	8	115 g ricotta cheese	4	120 g plain whole milk yoghurt	7	90 g cooked spinach	2	60 g ricotta cheese	2	60 g pecans and	2	80 g sautéed okra and	2.5
1 slice low-carb bread	6	168 g sliced strawberries	8	38 g frozen blackberries	5.5	30 g feta cheese	1	1 orange	13	2 Tbsp. dried unsweetened coconut	2	50 g Salsa Cruda	1.5
2 Tbsp. almond butter	5			30 g almonds	4	1 medium nectarine	14	30 g slivered almonds	2.5	62 g raspberries	3	60 g shredded Cheddar cheese	0.5
										120 g plain whole milk yoghurt	5.5	1 low-carb tortilla	4
Subtotal	23	**Subtotal**	18	**Subtotal**	17	**Subtotal**	18	**Subtotal**	23.5	**Subtotal**	22.5	**Subtotal**	9.5
SNACK													
30 g pistachios	2.5	60 g walnuts	3	2 slices Swiss cheese	2	35 g sweet cherries	4	1 celery stalk	1	½ Haas avocado	2	60 g macadamias	4
1 medium carrot	5.5	44 g Crenshaw melon balls	4.5	1 medium carrot	5.5	115 g cottage cheese	4	1 Tbsp. natural peanut butter	1.5	2 small figs	13	1 medium nectarine	14
				1 tsp. Dijon mustard	0.5								
Subtotal	8	**Subtotal**	7.5	**Subtotal**	8	**Subtotal**	8	**Subtotal**	2.5	**Subtotal**	15	**Subtotal**	18
LUNCH													
120 g seitan, sautéed, over	3.5	Cobb salad: 2 hard-boiled eggs and	1	2 veggie burgers on	4	120 g firm tofu simmered with	4	2-egg salad made with Blender Mayonnaise and	1	⅓ cup veggie crumbles sautéed and topped with	1	3 slices tofu 'bacon'	1.5
30 g mesclun greens	0.5	2 tofu 'bacon' strips on	2	1 low-carb hamburger bun	4	2 Tbsp. Barbecue Sauce over	4	2 Tbsp. chopped onions and	1.5	30 g shredded mozzarella cheese	1.5	2 slices Swiss cheese or	2
4 Tbsp. hummus	9	220 g mixed greens with	2	½ Haas avocado	2	50 g brown rice	10.5	1 stalk diced celery on	1.5	60 g refried beans	6.5	1 slice 100% whole grain bread	12
30 g feta cheese	1	½ Haas avocado	2	1 medium tomato	3.5	220 g mixed salad greens with	1.5	1 low-carb pitta	1.5	55 g shredded mixed greens	0.5	1 tsp. Dijon mustard	0.5
50 g red peppers	3	1 small tomato	1.5	110 g mixed salad greens	1	45 g cooked chickpeas	5.5	110 g mixed salad greens	0.5	75 g sweetcorn	12.5	15 g loose-leaf lettuce	0.5
5 black olives	0.5	5 black olives	0.5	4 pieces marinated artichoke hearts	2	85 g pickled beetroots	6.5	90 g cooked lentils	14	50 g Salsa Cruda	1.5	2 small tomatoes	5
1 medium tomato	3.5	25 g spring onions	1	5 black olives	0.5	60 g goat's cheese	0.5	40 g cooked wild rice	8	1 low-carb tortilla	4	4 Tbsp. hummus	9
2 Tbsp. Greek Vinaigrette	1	75 g sweetcorn	12.5	2 Tbsp. Italian Dressing	1	2 Tbsp. Greek Vinaigrette	1	2 Tbsp. Parmesan Peppercorn Dressing	1				
		2 Tbsp. Blue Cheese Dressing	1										
Subtotal	22	**Subtotal**	23.5	**Subtotal**	18	**Subtotal**	33.5	**Subtotal**	29	**Subtotal**	27.5	**Subtotal**	30.5

Phase 3: Pre-Maintenance and Phase 4: Lifetime Maintenance, Vegetarian, at 100 Grams of Net Carbs

Day 1

SNACK

Item	Grams of Net Carbs
60 g goat's cheese	0.5
½ medium apple	8.5
Subtotal	**9**

DINNER

Item	Grams of Net Carbs
Stuffed pepper: 170 g sautéed tempeh and 100 g cooked brown rice baked with 1 Tbsp. soya sauce in 2 green pepper halves topped with 30 g shredded Cheddar cheese	20
100 g baked butternut squash	3.5
110 g mixed salad greens	0.5
6 radishes	7
2 Tbsp. Italian Dressing	1
	0.5
Subtotal	**38**
Total	**100**
Foundation vegetables	**12.5**

Day 2

SNACK

Item	Grams of Net Carbs
2 slices Swiss cheese	2
75 g red grapes	13.5
Subtotal	**15.5**

DINNER

Item	Grams of Net Carbs
5 oz. tofu 'sausage' sautéed with	
40 g onions and	5
50 g green peppers over	3
130 g steamed butternut squash	10.5
110 g mixed salad greens	3.5
1 medium carrot, grated	0.5
40 g cooked wild rice	7
2 Tbsp. Parmesan-Peppercorn Dressing	1
Subtotal	**37**
Total	**100.5**
Foundation vegetables	**14**

Day 3

SNACK

Item	Grams of Net Carbs
Low-carb bar	2
1 small Bosc pear	17.5
Subtotal	**19.5**

DINNER

Item	Grams of Net Carbs
120 g sautéed seitan on	
120 g baked acorn squash	5
220 g mixed salad greens	3
60 g cooked French beans	10.5
90 g cooked cannellini beans	3
60 g jicama	5.5
90 g cooked wheat berries	8
2 Tbsp. Russian Dressing	1
Subtotal	**41.5**
Total	**99.5**
Foundation vegetables	**16**

Day 4

SNACK

Item	Grams of Net Carbs
45 g roasted red peppers	3.5
60 g walnuts	3
Subtotal	**6.5**

DINNER

Item	Grams of Net Carbs
⅔ cup veggie crumbles sautéed with	
40 g chopped onions and	4
140 g raw shredded cabbage	3
100 g cooked brown rice	2
Chopped salad of ½ Haas avocado	10.5
2 small tomatoes	3
40 g sweetcorn	17
2 Tbsp. Parmesan-Peppercorn Dressing	2.5
Subtotal	**41.5**
Total	**99.5**
Foundation vegetables	**19**

Day 5

SNACK

Item	Grams of Net Carbs
120 g plain whole milk yoghurt	5.5
44 g Crenshaw melon balls	4.5
Subtotal	**10**

DINNER

Item	Grams of Net Carbs
120 g firm tofu sautéed with	
80 g onions and	3
100 g aubergine	2
½ sweet jacket potato	12
110 g mixed salad greens	10.5
1 small tomato	1.5
1 medium carrot, grated	2.5
40 g cooked wild rice	5.5
2 Tbsp. Carrot-Ginger Dressing	6
Subtotal	**33.5**
Total	**99**
Foundation vegetables	**16**

Day 6

SNACK

Item	Grams of Net Carbs
120 g jicama sticks	5
2 slices Cheddar cheese	1
Subtotal	**6**

DINNER

Item	Grams of Net Carbs
2 tofu 'hot dogs'	5
140 g sauerkraut	2.5
½ jacket potato	6
110 g mixed salad greens	2
60 g watercress	0.5
5 black olives	0.5
40 g cooked wild rice	8
1 medium carrot, grated	1
2 Tbsp. Sweet Mustard Dressing	
Subtotal	**29**
Total	**100**
Foundation vegetables	**13.5**

Day 7

SNACK

Item	Grams of Net Carbs
100 g red peppers	6
2 slices Cheddar cheese	1
Subtotal	**7**

DINNER

Item	Grams of Net Carbs
2 Quorn unbreaded cutlets	6
2 Tbsp. Barbecue Sauce	4
6 asparagus spears	2.5
½ sweet jacket potato	12
Salad of 140 g shredded cabbage and	0.5
1 medium carrot, grated	5.5
2 Tbsp. Creamy Coleslaw Dressing	0.5
Subtotal	**32.5**
Total	**97.5**
Foundation vegetables	**19**

*www.atkins.com/Recipes/ShowRecipe883/Atkins-Cuisine-Pancakes.aspx, **www.atkins.com/Recipes/ShowRecipe884/Atkins-Cuisine-Waffles.aspx

Part IV

A DIET FOR LIFE:

The Science of Good Health

Chapter 13

METABOLIC SYNDROME AND CARDIOVASCULAR HEALTH

The words *healthy* and *low fat* seem inextricably linked,
but the rationale for a low-fat diet is based on two overly
simplistic ideas that we now understand to be incorrect.

In this and the following chapter we'll highlight how
carbohydrate-restricted approaches can address cardiovascular
disease (and metabolic syndrome) and diabetes and look at the
impressive body of research in both these areas. (You may want
to share these chapters with your healthcare professional.)

One in four deaths in the United States stems from heart
disease, making it the leading cause of death for both women and
men. Research indicates that there are about 2.3 million people
living in the UK with the condition. Heart disease develops
over decades, and a poor diet can aggravate and accelerate its
progression. Whether you have a strong family history of heart
disease or you're blessed with cardio-protective genes, you can
improve your quality of life by adopting a healthy diet that
targets some of the known modifiable risk factors.

Although the majority of the medical establishment has
focused on LDL cholesterol, an increased understanding of
the progression of heart disease has directed attention and
appreciation towards other risk factors. For example, did you
know that LDL cholesterol is actually a family of particles
of various sizes and that the smallest particles are the most

dangerous ones? The Atkins Diet eradicates small LDL particles like a strategic missile defence system. You'll soon understand the significance of this fact for both cardiovascular disease and metabolic syndrome.

Before we go any further, two brief definitions are in order. In simple terms, metabolic syndrome is a collection of markers that amplify your risk for heart disease, including high blood triglyceride level, low HDL cholesterol level and elevated glucose and insulin levels. Likewise, in simple terms, inflammation is a catch-all word that encompasses the processes by which your body protects you from unfamiliar and potentially damaging substances. As part of your body's natural defence system, a certain amount of inflammation is healthy, especially when it responds to infection, irritation or injury. But once the battle has been fought, inflammation should return to normal levels. Unchecked inflammation, which can be detected during the early phases of heart disease by elevated levels of C-reactive protein (CRP), is now understood to be one of the best predictors of future heart problems. Levels of triglycerides, HDL cholesterol, glucose and insulin are also important markers that provide a complete picture of your overall risk status. We'll explore both conditions in detail below.

This chapter will explore the ascendancy of scientific studies supporting the effectiveness of diets low in carbohydrate as a way to achieve cardiovascular heath. This is true even though you'll be eating plenty of fat. If you've read the rest of this book, we can assume that you've put aside any fear of fat. In case you still have any lingering anxiety, however, the following pages will convince you otherwise. First, let's consider the rationale for a low-fat diet and issue a report.

ARE LOW-FAT DIETS A MAJOR SUCCESS OR A SERIOUS DISTRACTION?

Most of you know that for the last few decades the government agencies concerned with healthcare have beamed forth a strong and unwavering message: reduce your total fat, saturated fat and cholesterol intake to achieve a healthy weight and decrease heart disease. The message has been so unrelenting that the terms 'healthy' and 'low fat' seem inextricably linked, but the rationale for a low-fat diet is based on two overly simplistic ideas that we now understand to be incorrect.

First, fat contains 9 Calories per gram, more than twice the 4 Calories per gram of both protein and carbohydrate. Since fat is more calorically dense, reducing intake of it should be the easiest way to promote weight loss, while still allowing you to eat a greater total volume of food and thus feel satisfied. This logic is expressed in the axiom, 'You are what you eat'. In other words, if you eat fat, you must get fat. The corollary is that if you eat less fat then you'll easily lose body fat. Many Americans and British people have embraced this seemingly intuitive strategy only to find themselves drowning in disappointment.

Our consumption of total fat and saturated fat intake has remained relatively steady and even trended slightly downwards over the last two decades. So why are we experiencing frightening twin epidemics of obesity and diabetes? And why has the metabolic syndrome become a significant health threat to tens of millions of people? Not because we failed to pay attention to dietary recommendations focused on lowering fat. Rather, we replaced fat calories with an abundance of carbohydrate calories, without understanding that many people have a metabolism that cannot process the additional carbohydrate. Basically, the low-fat approach has backfired.

A second reason for the major emphasis on reducing dietary fat, saturated fat and cholesterol is based on the belief that consumption of fatty foods will lead to increased blood cholesterol levels, which in turn will increase the incidence of heart disease. This belief system, often called the 'diet-heart hypothesis', has shaped nutrition policy in this country for the last forty years. Despite decades of research and billions of taxpayer pounds earmarked to prove this hypothesis, there's little evidence to support its basic premise.

The largest and most expensive study in the US on the role of fat in the diet was the Women's Health Initiative, a randomised, controlled trial in which almost 50,000 post-menopausal women aged fifty to seventy-nine were tracked for an average of eight years. Researchers assigned participants either to a low-fat diet that reduced total fat intake and increased the intake of vegetables, fruits and grains, or to a control group who could eat whatever they wanted. Multiple research papers reported on the results of this colossal experiment, which can be summarised as nothing short of a major public health disappointment. A low-fat eating pattern revealed no significant effect on weight loss or the incidence of heart disease, diabetes or cancer.[1] You can see why the low-fat dietary approach to weight control gets a failing score.

METABOLIC SYNDROME

As waistlines expand, so does the epidemic of metabolic syndrome. It's estimated that nearly one of every four American adults has this condition,[2] which puts them on the fast track to developing type-2 diabetes and triples their risk for developing heart disease. The identification of metabolic syndrome two decades ago[3] is now recognised as a turning point in our understanding of metabolism as it plays out in the clinical states of obesity, diabetes and cardiovascular disease. As a theory, metabolic syndrome represents an alternative and conflicting paradigm to the diet-heart hypothesis because elevated LDL cholesterol is typically not a problem in metabolic syndrome. More importantly, the most effective treatment for metabolic syndrome is restriction of carbohydrate, not fat. Restricting dietary fat and replacing it with carbohydrate actually exacerbates many of the problems of metabolic syndrome. The metabolic syndrome paradigm has therefore caused a great deal of distress – and setback – among those advocating low-fat diets.

Metabolic syndrome involves a cluster of markers that predispose people to diabetes and heart disease. Because metabolic syndrome includes the presence of more than one of several potential markers the public health community has struggled with the decision of how best to define, diagnose and treat it. Obesity is a common characteristic, particularly excessive fat in the waist and stomach area, which makes a person look 'apple-shaped'. Problems with fat metabolism manifest as high plasma levels of triglycerides, and although a patient's LDL cholesterol is usually within the normal range, the size of the LDL particles tends to be the small, more dangerous type. High blood pressure is another common marker as is elevated blood glucose. Additional markers include chronically elevated inflammation and abnormal blood vessel function (see the sidebar, 'Do You Have Metabolic Syndrome?').

DO YOU HAVE METABOLIC SYNDROME?

A person is defined as having metabolic syndrome if he or she has three or more of the following markers:[4]

	Men	Women
Waist circumference	≥ 101.5 cm (40 in)	≥ 89 cm (35 in)
Triglycerides	≥ 150 mg/dL*	≥ 150 mg/dL
HDL cholesterol	≤ 40 mg/dL	≤ 50 mg/dL
Blood pressure	≥ 130/85 mm Hg or use of medication for hypertension	≥ 130/85 mm Hg or use of medication for hypertension
Fasting glucose	≥ 100 mg/dL or use of medication for high blood glucose	≥ 100 mg/dL or use of medication for high blood glucose

*Milligrams per decilitre.

Why do the diverse problems that characterise metabolic syndrome tend to show up? The prevailing opinion is that all of them are signs of insulin resistance, which is defined as the diminished ability of a given concentration of insulin to exert its normal biological effect. When insulin resistance develops, it has broad effects on a variety of metabolic pathways that can lead to the specific markers for the metabolic syndrome. But not everyone responds to insulin resistance in the same way: moreover, the time frame in which certain signs develop varies. This variability makes defining – and treating – metabolic syndrome difficult.

Treatment of metabolic syndrome is controversial, with nutritional approaches generally downplayed in favour of multiple medications that target the individual components. Conventional recommendations tend to emphasise caloric restriction and reduced fat intake, even though the metabolic syndrome can best be described as carbohydrate intolerance. Think of it as the first signs of the metabolic bully leaving marks. Low-carbohydrate diets therefore make intuitive sense as a first-line treatment. Let's take a closer look at how they impact the various features of both metabolic syndrome and heart disease.[5]

GLUCOSE AND INSULIN

Increased glucose levels are a signal that the body may be having trouble processing dietary carbohydrate. High insulin levels usually go hand in hand with elevated fasting glucose levels. (See 'Understanding Blood Sugar Readings' on page 347.) Dietary carbohydrate contributes directly to blood glucose levels and is well accepted as the major stimulator of insulin secretion. Lowering carbohydrate intake is the most direct method to achieve better control of both glucose and insulin levels. Could it really be that simple? Yes, it is. The insulin resistance of metabolic syndrome is characterised by intolerance to carbohydrate. If you have lactose intolerance, you avoid lactose. If you have gluten intolerance, you avoid gluten. You get the idea.

Not surprisingly, many studies of low-carbohydrate diets have shown that glucose levels improve significantly in subjects following them.[6] Insulin levels also decrease regardless of glucose tolerance status and even in the absence of weight loss.[7] The reduction in insulin levels throughout the day, even after meals, is crucial to promoting a metabolic environment that allows fat burning. In this way, controlling carbohydrate intake has an important effect on the way the body handles fat along with profound effects on lipid and cholesterol levels. But before we discuss the research on lipids, a quick tutorial on insulin is in order.

HOW INSULIN WORKS

The pancreas makes and releases the hormone insulin in response to increases in blood glucose. Its most recognised function is to restore glucose levels to normal by facilitating the transport of blood glucose into (mainly) muscle and fat cells. However, insulin has a multitude of other effects and is generally described as the 'storage hormone' because it promotes the storage of protein, fat and carbohydrate. For example, insulin facilitates the conversion of amino acids into protein and also promotes the conversion of dietary carbohydrate into either glycogen (the storage form of carbohydrate in the body) or fat. While insulin promotes the storage of nutrients, it simultaneously blocks the breakdown of protein, fat and carbohydrate in the body. Put another way, when insulin is increased, it puts the brakes on burning fat for fuel and at the same time encourages storage of incoming food, mostly as fat. But when you limit your carbohydrate consumption, you stimulate increased fat burning and decreased fat synthesis.

In fact, fat breakdown and fat burning are exquisitely sensitive to changes in the amount of insulin released in response to dietary carbohydrate.[8] Small decreases in insulin can almost immediately increase fat burning several-fold. Insulin also increases glucose uptake and activates key enzymes that transform glucose into fat. Because low-carbohydrate diets significantly blunt insulin levels throughout the day, the Atkins Diet is associated with significant changes in fat metabolism that favour decreased storage and increased breakdown. Translation: You burn more body fat and store less. This is an important adaptation that contributes to a decreased risk for heart disease with better lipid profiles and improvement in all the features of metabolic syndrome. This is why dietary fat is your friend and consuming carbohydrate above your tolerance level acts as a metabolic bully.

CONTROL CARBS TO BURN FAT

Controlling carbohydrate intake and the subsequent decline in insulin levels permits most of the body's cells to use fat almost exclusively for energy, even while an individual is exercising. During Induction and OWL, body fat provides a large share of that energy. During Pre-Maintenance and Lifetime Maintenance, the diet provides most of the needed fuel. Either way, the final effect of the core principle of the Atkins Diet, keeping carb intake at or just below one's individual carb threshold, is the creation of a metabolic state characterised by enhanced mobilisation and utilisation of both dietary and body fat. Many of the beneficial effects of the Atkins Diet on risk factors for metabolic syndrome and heart disease are extensions of this powerful transformation.

THE SATURATED FAT PARADOX

Now that you know that you shouldn't avoid dietary fat on a low-carbohydrate diet, you might still have some scepticism about eating saturated fat. After all, just about every health expert would advise you to limit it, and one of the major criticisms of the Atkins Diet is that it contains more saturated fat than is currently recommended. Let us put your mind at rest.

When one nutrient in the diet decreases, usually one or more other nutrients replace it. In fact, researchers have explored the question of what happens when you reduce saturated fat in the diet and replace it with carbohydrate. A recent meta-study made up of eleven American and European cohort studies that followed more than 340,000 subjects for up to ten years came to the conclusion that replacing saturated fat with carbohydrate increases the risk of coronary events.[10] Yes, according to the best scientific evidence, the very recommendation made by most health experts to reduce saturated fat actually *increases* your chances of having heart disease. Yet this is the same dietary pattern adopted by many Americans.[11] The failure of low-fat dietary approaches is partially explained by the lack of understanding that many people consume more carbohydrates when they lower their saturated fat intake. The culprit is not saturated fat per se. If your carbohydrate intake is low, there's little reason to worry about saturated fat in your diet.

However, if your carbohydrate intake is high, increasing the levels of saturated fat in your diet may become problematic. Higher levels of saturated fatty acids in the blood have been shown to occur in individuals with heart disease.[12] As you now know, the Atkins Diet is all about controlling your carbohydrate intake to ensure that fat remains your body's primary fuel. This explains why on Atkins saturated fat intake is not associated with harmful effects. Two of the authors of this book explored what happens to saturated fat levels in subjects who were placed on the Atkins Diet.[13] In this experiment, the Atkins subjects consumed three times the levels of saturated fat as did subjects consuming a low-fat diet. Both diets contained the same number of calories, meaning that all the subjects were losing weight. After twelve weeks, the Atkins group subjects showed consistently greater reductions in the relative proportion of saturated fat in their blood.

This inverse association between dietary intake and blood concentrations of saturated fat prompted further experiments to validate the effect under controlled conditions. The additional study involved weight-stable men who habitually consumed a typical American diet. They followed a low-carbohydrate diet akin to the Lifetime Maintenance Phase, which contained more saturated fat, than did their regular diet. All foods were prepared and provided to the subjects during each feeding period. Enough food was provided to maintain their weight. After six weeks on the diet, despite consuming more saturated fat the men showed a significant reduction in their blood levels of saturated fat. They also improved their triglyceride and HDL cholesterol levels, LDL particle size and insulin level. This study further supports the conclusion that low dietary carbohydrate is a key stimulus positively impacting the metabolic processing of ingested saturated fat.[14]

These studies clearly show that low-carbohydrate diets high in saturated fat show effects that are very different from results in studies of individuals following a moderate- to high-carbohydrate diet. The likely cause is a combination of less storage and greater burning of saturated fat. This research supports the conclusion that dietary fat, even saturated fat, isn't harmful in the context of a low-carbohydrate diet.[15]

A LONG HISTORY OF SAFE USE

An equally valid indication of the long-term safety of low-carbohydrate diets can be found in the documented experience of Europeans as they explored the North American continent and its established cultures. Very often the most successful explorers were those who adopted the diet of the indigenous cultures, which in many regions consisted mostly of meat and fat with little carbohydrate. Examples of explorers who documented such experiences include Lewis and Clarke, John Rae,[16] Frederick Schwatka[17] and even Daniel Boone.

The explorer whose experience living as a hunter was the most carefully documented was the controversial anthropologist Vilhjalmur Stefansson. After spending a decade in the Arctic among the Inuit in the early 1900s, he wrote extensively about their diet around the same time that scientists discovered the existence of vitamins. Challenged to prove that he could remain healthy on a diet of meat and fat, he ate an Inuit diet under close medical observation for a year. The result, published in a prestigious scientific journal,[18] demonstrated that Stefansson remained well and physically capable while consuming a diet of more than 80 per cent animal fat and about 15 per cent protein.

In addition to recounting some remarkable stories of physical stamina and courage, the reports of these explorers provide valuable insight into the dietary practices of aboriginal hunting societies that lived for millennia on little or no dietary carbohydrate. Of particular importance was the practice of valuing fat over protein, so that the preferred mix of dietary energy was high in fat and moderate in protein. Also of note: Rae, Boone and Stefansson all lived into their eighties despite eating mostly meat and fat for years.

Though these historical lessons don't, in and of themselves, prove the long-term safety of low-carbohydrate diets, they constitute strong supporting evidence. When this accumulated history of safe use is combined with our recent research into the effects of carbohydrate restriction on blood lipids and indicators of inflammation, the inescapable conclusion is that a properly formulated low-carbohydrate diet can be safely utilised for months or even years.

RESEARCH ON SEIZURE CONTROL

In the early 1920s physicians observed that people subject to epileptic seizures experienced relief when they were placed on a total fast for two weeks. However, the benefits of this treatment didn't continue when eating resumed, and a complete fast causes muscle wasting, so this was obviously not a sustainable treatment. But in a series of reports an American physician, Mynie Peterman, demonstrated that a very-low-carb diet produced a similar effect in children, reducing or stopping their seizures, and that this diet could be effectively followed for years.[19]

In 1927 Dr Henry Helmholz reported on more than a hundred cases of childhood seizures treated with Dr Peterman's ketogenic diet.[20] His results indicated that about one third of the children were cured of seizures, one third improved and one third didn't respond to the treatment. A ketogenic diet remained the 'standard of care' for seizure disorders until effective anti-seizure drugs were developed in the 1950s. Between 1922 and 1944, doctors at the Mayo Clinic in Minnesota in the United States prescribed the ketogenic diet to 729 seizure patients, with success rates similar to those originally reported by Dr Peterman.[21] Most of these patients stayed on the diet for a year or two, but some continued it for more than three decades.

The development of anti-seizure drugs with similar efficacy rates superseded the ketogenic diet between 1960 and 1980. Although the diet is equally effective, it's far easier for a doctor to write a prescription for a medicine than it is to educate and motivate an individual or family to make a major dietary change. In the 1990s Dr John Freeman at Johns Hopkins University in Maryland in the United States revived the ketogenic diet and reported that many children whose seizures didn't respond to drugs did respond to the low-carb diet. With Dr Eric Kossoff, Dr Freeman also noted that children experienced fewer side effects from the low-carbohydrate diet than they did from the anti-seizure drugs. For example, not surprisingly their school performance was better when they were off the drugs. These observations have led to a resurgence of interest in low-carbohydrate diets to treat both children and adults suffering from seizures.[22] Today, more than seventy clinics in the United States report the use of this dietary treatment for seizures.

INDICATORS OF IMPROVEMENT

Now let's take a closer look at some of the most common markers improved by low-carbohydrate diets.

TRIGLYCERIDES

Much of the fat circulating in your blood and much of that available to be burnt as fuel is in the form of triglycerides. Increased blood levels of triglycerides are a key feature of metabolic syndrome and have been shown to be an independent risk factor for heart disease. One of the most dramatic and consistent effects of lowering carbohydrate consumption is a reduction in triglyceride levels. In fact, the decline rivals that produced by any current medicines. Most studies focus on fasting levels of triglycerides, but after a meal fat is packaged into triglycerides within the gastrointestinal tract that are dumped into your blood. The liver can also pump out triglycerides after a meal, especially one high in carbohydrate. People who have an exaggerated and prolonged elevation of blood triglycerides, whether from a high-fat or high-carbohydrate meal, have been shown to be at increased risk for heart disease. The good news is that low-carbohydrate diets consistently decrease triglycerides both in the fasting state and in response to meals.[23] Interestingly, this beneficial effect occurs even when weight loss is minimal.[24]

HDL CHOLESTEROL

The clinical significance of increased HDL levels is well established as an important target for good health.[25] Higher levels are desirable because this lipoprotein offers protection against heart disease. Typical lifestyle changes such as exercise and weight loss are often recommended to increase HDL, but their effects are small compared to those achieved by following a low-carbohydrate diet, which consistently outperform low-fat diets in raising HDL levels.[26] The effects are prominent in men and even more so in women.[27] Dietary saturated fat and cholesterol are actually important nutrients that contribute to an increase in HDL cholesterol levels. Replacing carbohydrate with fat has also been shown to increase HDL.

KETONES: WHAT ARE THEY AND WHAT DO THEY DO?

Anti-seizure diets are often referred to as ketogenic diets because restricting carbohydrates requires that the body use an alternative to glucose (blood sugar) as the brain's primary fuel. In place of glucose, the liver uses fat molecules to make acetoacetate and hydroxybutyrate, two compounds known as ketones. The body adopts this same fuel strategy during a total fast of more than a few days. Ketones have got a bad name because they can rise to very high levels in individuals with uncontrolled type-1 diabetes, a state known as diabetic ketoacidosis. However, there is more than a tenfold difference between the ketone levels seen in ketoacidosis and those achieved with a carbohydrate-restricted diet, which we call nutritional ketosis. Equating the two is comparable to confusing a major flood with a gentle shower. Far from overwhelming the body's acid-based defences, nutritional ketosis is a completely natural adaptation that is elegantly integrated into the body's energy strategy whenever carbs are restricted and fat becomes its primary fuel.

LDL CHOLESTEROL

The main target of low-fat diets and many drugs such as statins is to lower concentrations of LDL cholesterol. On average, low-fat diets are more effective at lowering LDL cholesterol levels than are low-carbohydrate diets. But before you attribute this marker to low fat, consider that simply lowering LDL cholesterol by restricting dietary fat doesn't reduce your risk of developing heart disease.[28] Why? An obvious reason is that low-fat diets exacerbate other risk factors; they increase triglycerides and reduce HDL cholesterol. But there's another explanation that relates to the LDL particles themselves. Not all forms of LDL particles share the same potential for increasing heart disease.

Within the category labelled LDL, there is a continuum of sizes, and research shows that smaller LDL particles contribute more to plaque formation in arteries (atherosclerosis) and are associated with a higher risk for heart disease. Although low-fat diets may decrease total LDL concentration, they tend to *increase* the proportion of small particles,[29] making them more dangerous. However, going in the other direction, numerous studies indicate that replacing carbohydrate with fat or protein leads to increases in LDL size.[30] Therefore, it's clear that carbohydrate intake is strongly and directly related to promoting the forms of LDL that contribute to arterial plaque formation,[31] whereas replacing carbohydrates in the diet with fat, even saturated fat, seems to promote the forms of LDL that are harmless.

INFLAMMATION

As discussed above, when inflammation stays elevated because of a repeated insult, such as a poor diet, it is bad news. Researchers now appreciate the importance of this ongoing low-grade condition in contributing to many chronic health problems including diabetes, heart disease and even cancer. We typically think of inflammation in respect to fighting off bacteria and viruses. However other substances including excess carbohydrates and trans-fats can contribute to inflammation. A single high-carbohydrate meal can lead to increased inflammation.[32] Over time eating a high-carbohydrate diet can lead to increased markers of inflammation.[33]

What about low-carbohydrate diets? Levels of CRP, a cytokine marker for inflammation, have been shown to decrease by approximately one third on the Atkins Diet.[34] In subjects with higher levels of inflammation, CRP levels decreased more in response to a low-carbohydrate diet than to a fat-restricted diet.[35] A recently published study compared subjects with metabolic syndrome on a low-fat diet to those who were consuming a very-low-carbohydrate diet. The low-carb group showed a greater decrease in eight different circulating inflammatory markers compared to the low-fat group.[36] These data implicate dietary carbohydrate rather than fat as a more significant nutritional factor contributing to inflammation, although the combination of both increased fat and a high carbohydrate intake may be particularly harmful.

The anti-inflammatory effects of the omega-3 fats EPA and DHA have been shown in cell culture and animal studies as well as in trials using humans.[37] These effects partially explain why these fats appear to have widespread health-promoting effects, especially in reducing the risk of heart disease and diabetes. Several hundred studies have demonstrated the cardio-protective effects of fish oil, and numerous review studies have summarised this body of work.[38] That's why we recommend regular consumption of fatty fish or use of a supplement containing EPA and DHA.

VASCULAR FUNCTION

An early event in heart disease, vascular dysfunction is now considered part of metabolic syndrome because of its likely origins in insulin resistance in cells that line the interior artery walls.[39] An ultrasound technique that measures the ability of an artery in the arm (the brachial artery) to dilate detects the proper functioning of blood vessels.[40] In previous studies a high-fat meal has been shown to temporarily impair dilation of the brachial artery.[41] The adverse effects of single meals high in fat, especially saturated fat, on lipid levels after a meal[42] and on vascular and inflammatory functions have been used as evidence to discourage low-carbohydrate diets. The test subject's prior diet history, however, has a fundamentally important effect on the metabolic response to meals. For example, research has repeatedly shown that adaptation to a very-low-carbohydrate diet results in a substantial reduction in the triglyceride response to a high-fat meal.[43] This means that studies that show short-term harmful effects of a high-fat meal on vascular function may show very different results after subjects are adapted to a low-carbohydrate diet.

When the effects of a high-fat meal on vascular function are assessed in subjects with metabolic syndrome who consumed a high-fat, very-low-carb diet,[44] there is a marked decrease in the triglyceride response to the high-fat meal. In contrast, control subjects consuming a low-fat diet showed little change. After twelve weeks on a very-low-carbohydrate diet, subjects showed improved vascular function after a high-fat meal compared to a control group of subjects who consumed a low-fat diet.

THE ATKINS DIET IS GOOD MEDICINE

A series of low-carbohydrate-diet studies show that improvement in metabolic syndrome is intimately connected with controlling carbohydrate consumption.[45] Although metabolic syndrome can manifest in various ways, the nutritional benefits of a low-carbohydrate diet hold the promise of improving *all* the syndrome's features. Most doctors would treat each symptom individually, with the result that an individual might be taking multiple medications increasing both the expense and the chance of developing side effects. Because having metabolic syndrome means you're on the fast track to diabetes and heart disease, getting all of its components under control is a unique benefit of the Atkins Diet. In the next chapter you'll learn that these same dietary modifications can also reduce the likelihood of developing type-2 diabetes or even reverse its course, as evidenced by our final success story.

WHEN PROFESSIONAL AND PERSONAL WORLDS COLLIDE

His self-diagnosis of diabetes launched the Canadian doctor Jay Wortman on a personal odyssey of discovery and recovery. It also spurred a professional quest to push the boundaries of diabetes management at a time when the disease is becoming a global health crisis.

VITAL STATISTICS

Current phase: Lifetime Maintenance

Daily Net Carb intake: 20–30 grams (0.7–1 ounce)

Age: 59

Height: 175 cm (5 ft 9 in)

Before weight: 94 kg (13.2 stones)

Current weight: 76.6 kg (11.4 stones)

Weight loss: 11.3 kg (1.8 stones)

Current blood sugar: Under 6 mmol/Ll (108 mg/dL)

Current HbA1c: 5.5%

Former blood pressure: 150/95

Current blood pressure: 130/80

Current HDL cholesterol: 91 mg/dL

Current LDL cholesterol: 161 mg/dL

Current triglycerides: 52.4 mg/dL

Current total cholesterol: 272 mg/dL

Current C-reactive protein: 0.3 mg/dL

What is your background?

As a doctor who has focused on Aboriginal health, I was acutely aware of the high rates of diabetes as well as obesity and metabolic syndrome in this population. These epidemics were devastating Aboriginal communities and incurring huge costs for health care services. When I travelled to the affected communities, there was almost a feeling that the situation was hopeless. Even in communities with extra resources and research programmes, we weren't able to reverse the terrible trend.

Did you have a family history of diabetes?

I grew up in a small village in northern Alberta, Canada. Some of my ancestors were settlers in the Hudson Bay area and had intermarried with Aboriginal peoples. Both my maternal grandparents developed type-2 diabetes as did my mother and other close relatives. The Aboriginal genetic tendency towards this disease had slowly snaked its way up through my family tree to bite me.

How did you react to this realisation?

I was stunned. As a doctor, you somehow believe that you're going to be immune to the diseases that you diagnose and treat in others. This, coupled with the fact that I had a very young son, made my self-diagnosis doubly shocking. Of all the concerns about serious health problems and a shortened life expectancy, however, the prospect of not seeing my two-year-old son grow into maturity was the thing that disturbed me most.

I had taken extra training in diabetes in my last year of family medicine residency and knew about the diabetic diet and how lifestyle change was supposed to be the cornerstone of diabetes management. I also knew that for the most part newly diagnosed type-2 diabetics went on drug therapy immediately because of the ineffectiveness of lifestyle interventions and that even then most tended to struggle and fail in their attempts to maintain normal blood glucose values. Further complicating my situation was the fact that I abhorred the use of medication.

Did the diabetes occur out of the blue?

Clearly, I'd been in denial. I'd put on some weight and was fatigued all the time. I struggled through bouts of afternoon drowsiness. I got up at night to urinate, was constantly thirsty and needed to squint to see the television news. My blood pressure was also rising into the zone that would require treatment. I rationalised all these developing problems as the natural and inevitable effects of ageing until it suddenly dawned on me that I had the typical symptoms of diabetes. I tested myself and confirmed that my blood sugar was way too high. In order to buy time while I looked at the recent science and formulated a management plan, I decided not to eat anything that would exacerbate my soaring blood sugar. I immediately stopped eating sugar and starchy foods, but at the time I didn't have a clue about low-carb diets.

What was the result of your dietary shift?
Almost immediately, my blood sugar normalised, followed by a dramatic and steady loss of weight – about 45 grams (1 pound) a day. My other symptoms swiftly vanished, too. I started seeing clearly, the excessive urination and thirst disappeared, my energy level went up and I began to feel immensely better. I bought an exercise bike and started riding it for thirty minutes every day as I continued to avoid starches and sugars. It was my wife who pointed out that I was on the Atkins Diet. She had struggled to lose weight after the birth of our son and had tried various diets. I recall that when she brought home an Atkins book, I was dismissive, suggesting that it was just another of the fad diets and that it probably wouldn't work over the long haul. As I read the book, I realised that I wasn't actually following Dr Atkins' phased approach to carb restriction, I was simply avoiding all carbs.

How did your personal situation impact your practice?
As I began to realise that my simple dietary intervention was rapidly and effectively resolving my own diabetes, I naturally started to look at the broader Aboriginal diabetes epidemic

through this lens. In my travels to First Nations communities I started to question people, especially the elders, about their traditional ways of eating. It was common especially in coastal communities to consume traditional foods such as salmon, halibut and shellfish. Inland, one would eat moose, deer and elk. It was also common to eat modern foods such as potato and pasta salads with the salmon and moose, cakes and biscuits for dessert, all chased with juices and fizzy drinks.

I began to understand that the traditional diet didn't have a significant source of starch or sugar. People ate berries but the vast majority of calories came in the form of protein and fat. A number of seasonal wild plants akin to modern greens were all low in starch and sugar. The traditional diet was looking very much like a modern-day, low-carb diet in terms of its macronutrient content.

How did you test your theory?
Around this time a medical journal published a study in which a group of overweight men were put on the Atkins Diet and followed it for six months. The men lost significant weight and experienced an improvement in their cholesterol levels. I suggested to my two community medicine specialists that we design a similar study for a cohort of First Nations subjects.

I had started speaking to First Nation audiences about my ideas of a link between their changing diet and the epidemics of obesity and diabetes. Ultimately, the Canadian government agreed to fund a trial study to look at the effects of a traditional low-carb diet on obesity and diabetes. I was also able to spend two years on research leave at the University of British Columbia Department of Health Care.

How is your health today?

For about seven years I've adhered to the diet and continue to maintain normal blood sugar and blood pressure and a weight loss of about 11.3 kilograms (1.8 stones). After the first six months, I had my cholesterol checked. I'd become accustomed to eating lots of fatty foods, including my own wickedly delicious low-carb chocolate ice cream recipe. I have to admit I was afraid. I'd been taught that a diet high in saturated fat would lead to an unhealthy lipid profile. Much to my surprise and relief, I had excellent cholesterol. I was clearly on the right track.

My most recent blood tests continue to demonstrate excellent results. Although my total cholesterol and LDL cholesterol are above normal limits, I know from reading the scientific literature that this is not a concern given that the important markers for cardiovascular risk, HDL and triglycerides, are well within normal limits and my C-reactive protein is exceptionally low. With a pattern like this, although I have not tested for small dense LDL, I can assume that my LDL is of the healthy variety. I am convinced that my health is better than it has ever been. I have learnt an enormous amount in an area of science that doctors unfortunately tend to ignore: nutrition.

Has your research been published yet?

At this point, we're collecting data. After statistical analysis, we'll write the paper and submit it for publication in a scientific journal. Meanwhile, the study and how it affected the people of the Namgis First Nation and other residents of Alert Bay is the subject of the documentary *My Big Fat Diet*. (For more information, see www.cbc.ca/thelens/bigfatdiet.)

Chapter 14

MANAGING DIABETES,
AKA THE BULLY DISEASE

Diabetes now affects more than 18 million people in the US and over 2 million people in the UK, but because the early stages can be completely silent, many more are unaware that they have the disease.

The Atkins Diet is more than just a healthy lifestyle. As you've learnt in the previous chapter, this way of eating can significantly reduce your chances of developing heart disease and the metabolic syndrome. Now you'll learn that the Atkins Diet is also an extremely effective tool to manage diabetes. We've previously pointed out that dietary carbohydrates act like a metabolic bully, demanding that they be burnt first and pushing fats to the back of the line, which promotes the buildup of excess fat stores. Just as an individual who has been bullied for years may stop fighting back, some people's bodies eventually give in to the ongoing stress of too much sugar and other refined carbohydrates. The result is type-2 diabetes, which occurs when the body loses its ability to keep blood sugar within a safe range. When this happens, the swings in blood sugar – sometimes too low but mostly too high – start to do their damage.

ONE NAME, TWO DISEASES
Though most people know that diabetes has something to do with insulin, they're generally confused about exactly

what that means. That's not surprising considering that two different conditions (type-1 diabetes and type-2 diabetes) share the name. Both types involve insulin, the hormone that facilitates the movement of glucose into cells to be burnt or stored. Simply put, type-1 diabetes reflects a problem in insulin production that results in low insulin levels. Type-2, on the other hand, reflects a problem in insulin action (insulin resistance), which results in high insulin levels. Type-2 occurs mainly in adults and is the much more common form, representing 85 to 90 per cent of all cases worldwide. Type-1 is more common in children, but thanks to the rapid increase in obesity among younger people, tragically this age group is also now developing type-2 diabetes.

If you've already been diagnosed with type-2 diabetes and have been testing your blood sugar after meals – or you live with someone who does – you've probably noticed that foods rich in carbohydrates drive blood sugar higher than those composed mostly of proteins and fats. If so, this chapter will confirm your suspicions that a healthful diet should limit carbohydrates to an amount that doesn't elevate blood sugar to the level that can inflict damage. And for the rest of us who don't (yet) have diabetes, it will soon become apparent that the best way to prevent this illness is by reducing dietary carbs to the point where they not longer function as a metabolic bully.

A 'SILENT' DISEASE ... BUT AN ENORMOUS EPIDEMIC

About one third of people with type-2 diabetes in the US are unaware that they have this disease, and the same is true for about half a million people in the UK. Fortunately, diagnosing diabetes is as simple as checking a small amount of your blood for its blood sugar (glucose) level or your blood level of haemoglobin A1c (HbA1c), which indicates your blood glucose level over the last several months. Your healthcare provider can perform either of these tests during a check-up (see the sidebar, 'Understanding Blood Sugar Readings' for more on testing). Because diabetes is so common and checking for it is so easy, if you don't know if you have diabetes there's no reason not to find out as soon as possible.

Understanding the role of carbohydrate restriction in the prevention and treatment of diabetes is especially important because of the enormous scope of the diabetes epidemic. Despite the best efforts of the traditional medical approach, which is based upon aggressive use of drugs, the tide of this disease continues to rise. According to the American Diabetes Association the disease now affects 18.2 million people in the United States, but because the early stages of diabetes can be completely silent, 8 million of them are unaware that they have the disease. According to the NHS, over 2 million people in Britain have diabetes, but there's another half a million people with diabetes who but don't know they have it. Nor are the numbers likely to improve soon. As other nations adopt a diet high in sugar and processed carbohydrates, the epidemic has escalated to involve 246 million people worldwide, with projections of 380 million by 2025.

UNDERSTANDING BLOOD SUGAR READINGS

The amount of glucose (sugar) in your blood changes throughout the day and night. Your levels vary depending upon when, what and how much you have eaten and whether or not you've exercised. The American Diabetes Association (ADA) categories for normal blood sugar levels follow based on how your glucose levels are tested.

Fasting blood glucose. This test is performed after you have consumed no food or liquids (other than water) for at least eight hours. A normal fasting blood glucose level is between 60 and 110 mg/dL (milligrams per decilitre). A reading of 126 mg/dL or higher indicates a diagnosis of diabetes. (In 1997 the ADA changed it from 140 mg/dL or higher.) A blood glucose reading of 100 indicates that you have 100 mg/dL.

'Random' blood glucose. This test may be taken at any time with a normal blood glucose range in the low to mid-hundreds. A diagnosis of diabetes is made if your blood glucose reading is 200 mg/dL or higher and you have symptoms of the disease such as fatigue, excessive urination, excessive thirst or unplanned weight loss.

Oral glucose tolerance. After fasting overnight, you'll be asked to drink a sugar-water solution. Your blood glucose levels will then be tested over several hours. In a person without diabetes glucose levels rise and then fall quickly after drinking the solution. If a person has diabetes blood glucose levels rise higher than normal and don't fall as quickly. A normal blood glucose reading two hours after drinking the solution is less than 140 mg/dL, and all readings in the first two hours must be less than 200 mg/dL for the test to be considered normal. Blood glucose levels of 200 mg/dL or higher at any time indicate a diagnosis of diabetes.

Haemoglobin A1c (HbA1c). This is a substance that goes up as a result of high blood glucose levels, and once elevated it stays up for a couple of months. Because blood glucose levels bounce around a lot depending on diet and exercise the HbA1c test offers the advantage of smoothing out a lot of this variability. A level below 5.5 is considered good; a level above 6.5 indicates a diagnosis of diabetes.

As of this writing, the American Diabetes Association is intending to adopt the HbA1c test as a diagnosis for diabetes.

DIABETES AND INFLAMMATION: A CHICKEN-AND-EGG SITUATION?

The underlying cause of type-2 diabetes is a controversial topic. In general, diabetes is a disorder of carbohydrate metabolism caused by a combination of hereditary and environmental factors. The latter includes the composition of the diet, obesity and inactivity. However, many people eat a poor diet and are sedentary but never develop obesity or diabetes. Similarly some obese sedentary people have normal blood sugar levels. Nonetheless, overall obesity and inactivity increase an individual's risk of developing diabetes, but some individuals seem more protected than others. This indicates that genetics play an important role in the development of the disorder. Another important factor is age: Your body may tolerate bad behaviour at age thirty but not necessarily at sixty.

Your body uses the hormone insulin to trigger the movement of blood sugar into the cells, but as you learnt in the previous chapter, at high levels insulin also promotes the metabolic syndrome including excess fat storage, inflammation and the formation of plaque in your arteries. Inflammation has increasingly become a topic of interest because people with type-2 diabetes typically have increased blood levels of inflammation biomarkers such as C-reactive protein (CRP), and this biomarker in turn accurately predicts who will later develop such complications of type-2 diabetes as heart disease, stroke and kidney failure.[1]

More important, however, when large populations of adults without diabetes are screened for CRP levels and then followed for five to ten years the quarter of the population with the highest levels has two to four times the likelihood of subsequently developing diabetes.[2] What this means is that inflammation comes before the overt signs of diabetes develop. In other words, inflammation looks less like an effect of diabetes and more like an (if not *the*) underlying cause. Coming back to our analogy of carbohydrate as a bully, it's simple but appealing to think that dietary carbohydrates repeatedly 'bruise' the body. Further, it would seem that some people respond to this bruising by becoming inflamed, and this inflammation eventually results in damage that causes cells to become insulin-resistant and organs to eventually fail.

So how does this simple analogy help us to understand something as complex as the underlying cause of type-2 diabetes? Well, take away the bully and the bruising stops. Right? In the previous chapter we gave you strong evidence that carbohydrate restriction in people with metabolic syndrome (aka pre-diabetes) results in a sharp reduction in the biomarkers of inflammation. Now we'll show you that type-2 diabetics consuming a low-carb diet experience improvements in blood sugar, blood lipids and body weight – sometimes dramatically so.

A LOOK AT THE RESEARCH

There are several different types of studies used to understand the effect of eating different foods on human health. In previous decades scientists tended to rely on observational studies of what people ate and how that affected their long-term health (nutritional epidemiology), but prospective clinical trials are considered more accurate. Studies on individuals in an 'inpatient' clinical research ward provide tight control over what people eat, but they tend to be limited to a week or two, during which research subjects remain hospitalised with a few notable exceptions.

In other studies researchers give subjects food to take home to eat. However, there's no assurance that people won't eat other food in addition to the supplied meals. Finally, another type of research involves instructing people to buy and eat certain foods and return for instruction and support – often over a period of several years. These 'outpatient' or 'free-living' studies tell us a lot about whether a certain diet is sustainable in the 'real-world' setting. But the interpretation of such studies is limited because people don't necessarily follow the dietary instructions. Here are some examples of studies that have shown that the Atkins Diet is a safe and effective treatment for type-2 diabetes.

INPATIENT STUDIES

In a pioneering study done thirty years ago, seven obese type-2 diabetics were placed on a very-low-calorie ketogenic diet, first as inpatients and later as outpatients.[3] Initially, these subjects had fair-to-poor blood glucose control despite the fact that they were already taking 30 to 100 units of insulin per day. Within twenty days of starting the low-carbohydrate diet, all the subjects were able to discontinue their insulin injections. Nonetheless, their blood glucose control improved as did their blood lipid profiles. The authors noted that blood glucose control improved much more rapidly than did the rate at which they lost weight, indicating that carbohydrate intake was the primary determinant of glucose control and insulin requirement rather than obesity itself.

In a 2005 inpatient study ten obese people with type-2 diabetes were fed their usual diet for seven days, followed by a low-carbohydrate diet (the Induction phase of Atkins) of 20 grams (0.7 ounces) of carbs a day for fourteen days.[4] In both cases, subjects were allowed to choose how much they ate so the only change after the first week was eliminating most carbohydrate foods. Because this study took place in a research ward, the researchers were able to document the subjects' total food intake. They found that when subjects followed the low-carb diet, they continued to eat about the same amount of protein and fat as before, even after two weeks of carb restriction and although they could have eaten more protein and/or fat to make up for the missing carbohydrate calories if they desired. This means that they naturally ate fewer calories when carbs were restricted. In addition to losing weight, the subjects also showed improvements in their blood glucose and insulin levels. Many were able to eliminate their medications, and their insulin sensitivity improved by 75 per cent on average, similar to the observations of the 1976 study cited above. More important, this recent study showed that instructing people to limit their grams of carbohydrate (without restricting calories or portion size) resulted in their eating less food and rapidly improving their insulin sensitivity.

OUTPATIENT STUDIES

A recent outpatient study compared a low-carbohydrate diet to a portion-controlled, low-fat diet in 79 patients over a three-month period.[5] After three months, subjects in the low-carb group were reportedly consuming 110 grams (4 ounces) of carbohydrate per day (the upper range of the Atkins Lifetime Maintenance phase). Compared to the low-fat group, the low-carb group had improvements in glucose control, weight, cholesterol, triglycerides and blood pressure. In addition, more people in the low-carb group were able to reduce medications than those in the low-fat group.

Another very recent outpatient study compared the Induction phase of Atkins (20 grams of carbohydrate daily) to a reduced-calorie diet (500 calories a day below their previous intake level, low in fat and sugar but high in complex carbs) over a six-month period.[6] They found greater improvements in blood sugar levels and greater weight loss in the Atkins Induction group. What was especially exciting, however, was that individuals who were taking insulin often found the beneficial effects of the low-carb diet quite powerful. Subjects taking from 40 to 90 units of insulin before participating in the study were able to eliminate insulin altogether, while also improving glycaemic control. These results were similar to the inpatient studies described above.

And finally, the Kuwaiti low-carb study cited in Chapter 1 included thirty-five subjects whose blood glucose was elevated at the start of the study. The average value for this group returned into the normal range within eight weeks of following the low-carb diet, and at fifty-six weeks this group's average fasting blood glucose had been reduced by 44 per cent.

In summary, these five studies in a variety of settings all showed dramatic improvements in blood glucose control and blood lipids in type-2 diabetics consuming a low-carb diet. When these studies included a low-fat, high-carb comparison group, the low-carb diet consistently showed superior effects on blood glucose control, medication reduction, blood lipids and weight loss. Weight loss is particularly important because treatment goals for patients with type-2 diabetes always emphasise weight loss if the individual is overweight, yet the drugs used to treat diabetics almost all cause weight gain. So let's look at this briefly as the ability to deliver improved blood sugar control and weight loss distinguishes a low-carb approach from all other non-surgical treatments for type-2 diabetes.

WEIGHING THE OPTIONS: COMMON SIDE EFFECTS OF MEDICATION

On its surface, the management of type-2 diabetes seems pretty easy: just get your blood glucose back down into the normal range. But insulin resistance characterises this form of diabetes; put simply the glucose level 'doesn't want to go down'. This means that the body is less responsive to the most powerful drug used to treat it: insulin. So the dose of insulin that most type-2 diabetics are prescribed is very high. Moreover, because insulin not only drives glucose into muscle cells but also accelerates fat synthesis and storage, weight gain is usually one side effect of aggressive insulin therapy.[7] Other tablets and injected medications have been developed to reduce this effect, but on average the harder one tries to control blood glucose, the greater the tendency to weight gain.[8] The other major side effect of attempting to gain tight control of blood sugar is driving it too low causing hypoglycaemia, which causes weakness, shakiness, confusion and even coma. If these symptoms appear, the advice is to immediately eat a lot of sugar to stop the symptoms, which jump-starts the blood sugar roller coaster all over again. Interestingly, once type-2 diabetics complete the first few weeks of the Atkins programme, they rarely experience hypoglycaemia. That's because of the body's adaptation to burning fat for most of its fuel during carb restriction, in concert with the ability to reduce or stop most diabetic medications (including insulin) within a few days or weeks of starting the Atkins Diet.

So why isn't it good enough just to cut back on one's calories without cutting back on carbs? It's true that going on a diet and losing weight typically improve diabetes control. First of all, dieting won't necessarily result in weight loss and any weight loss may not be sustained. Second, even weight loss is usually not enough to significantly reduce medication dosage. Finally, since diabetic drugs still produce side effects and appetite stimulation, losing weight on a standard diet is a difficult tightrope for a diabetic to walk.

Once you understand this tightrope of weight loss during drug treatment – some would call it a Catch-22 – it's easier to appreciate the advantage of using the Atkins Diet to manage type-2 diabetes. When you remove added sugar, significantly reduce carb intake overall and confine your consumption primarily to the 'foundation vegetables' allowed on Induction, your insulin resistance rapidly improves and blood glucose control improves – usually dramatically. Additionally, most people find that they can stop or substantially reduce their diabetes medications. As a result, the path to meaningful weight loss changes from a tightrope to wide road. As long as you stay within your carb tolerance range, you should be able to navigate your way to health.

IF AND WHEN TO EXERCISE

You might be familiar with many of the potential health benefits of exercise, but you probably don't know that exercise has insulin-like effects. This is relevant for type-2 diabetics with insulin resistance because performing just a single bout of exercise improves insulin resistance for several hours. A number of studies have shown that regular exercise improves blood sugar control, even if it doesn't significantly improve weight loss.[9] Because weight loss is so difficult for people with type-2 diabetes and because doctors have little else to offer (other than medicines) in the way of effective remedies, exercise is always near the top of the list of official guidelines.

Given this information simple logic dictates that we should tell everyone with diabetes to get out and exercise. But not so fast. First, exercise holds an exalted position in diabetic treatment because the usual diets almost always fail. We need to consider what role exercise should play if the tables are turned and you have access to a diet like Atkins that almost always 'works' and that simultaneously causes insulin resistance and blood sugar control to improve significantly. Unfortunately, we don't yet have the perfect answer. Yes, we've proved that once people adapt to the Atkins Diet they're capable of lots of exercise. But no one has done a study of diabetics on Atkins where some of them exercise and some of them don't, to prove that adding exercise to an already successful diet improves blood sugar control or increases weight loss enough to justify the added effort.

Second, if you're diabetic, you're at increased risk for heart attack, and most people with type-2 diabetes are overweight (at least before they start Atkins). So if you were offered the choice of either starting the programme and exercising at the same time, or alternatively starting Atkins first, getting your blood sugar under control, reducing or stopping medications you might be taking for diabetes, and getting some weight off your ankles, knees, hips and lower back, which would you choose?

Clearly, the key question is not really *if* but *when*. The Atkins Diet opens the door for you to exercise, and exercise has a lot of benefits other than weight loss (and may even improve your blood sugar control). As we've said previously, if you're already physically active, keep it up, taking care not to overdo it while you're adapting to fat burning in the first few weeks. But if it's been a while since you did much of anything vigorous, consider giving yourself a few weeks or months to unburden your heart and joints before taking on a 10-kilometre (6-mile) run or trying to burn out the treadmill or pump iron at the gym.

THE CURRENT OFFICIAL GUIDELINES

Okay, we've explained how Atkins offers unique benefits to someone with type-2 diabetes. So why isn't everyone with the disorder doing it? The answer is that the low-fat-diet fad of the last thirty years backed by the food industry and government-sanctioned committees has taken a long time to run its course. Only with the recent research we've cited in the last few chapters has the mainstream medical community begun to be receptive to the value of low-carbohydrate diets. Standard treatment guidelines are beginning to reflect this change. This is where we stand today.

The goal of medical nutrition therapy for type-2 diabetes is to attain and maintain optimal metabolic outcomes, including:

- Blood glucose levels in the normal range or as close to normal as is safely possible to prevent or reduce the risk for complications of diabetes.
- Lipid and lipoprotein profiles that reduce the risk for blood vessel disease (i.e., blockage of blood flow to your heart, brain, kidneys and legs).
- Blood pressure levels that reduce the risk of developing vascular disease.

The American Diabetes Association (ADA) has acknowledged the use of a low-carbohydrate diet in achieving these goals in its 2008 guidelines which include:[10]

- Modest weight loss has been shown to improve insulin resistance in overweight and obese insulin-resistant individuals.

- Weight loss is recommended for all overweight individuals who have or are at risk for the disease.
- Either low-carbohydrate or low-fat calorie-restricted diets may be effective for weight loss in the short term (up to one year).
- Patients on low-carbohydrate diets should have their lipid profiles, kidney function and protein intake (for those with kidney damage) monitored regularly.
- To avoid hypoglycaemia, patients following a low-carb diet who are taking blood sugar-lowering medications need to have them monitored and adjusted as needed.

PRACTICAL POINTERS

How can those of you who are diabetic translate all of this information into action to transform your health? Here are three practical considerations:

1. The focus of this chapter has been on type-2 diabetes because it's usually associated with being overweight, and also because most type-2 diabetics probably won't need insulin injections if they can find and comply with their threshold for carbohydrate tolerance (CLL or ACE). Type-1 diabetics will always need some insulin, making its management much more technical on a carb-restricted diet. Though some doctors are now using the Atkins Diet for selected type-1 diabetics, instructions on how to do this safely are beyond the scope of this book. If you've been diagnosed with type-1 diabetes or if you've ever been diagnosed with diabetic ketoacidosis, you should not try the Atkins Diet on your own. And if you do try it under medical supervision, be sure that you're being instructed and closely monitored by a doctor familiar with Atkins.

2. Second, if you're taking medications to control blood sugar (diabetic drugs) or drugs for high blood pressure, be sure to work closely with your doctor, particularly in the first weeks and

months of the diet. It's during this time that diabetes and blood pressure improve rapidly, which usually requires reducing or stopping the medications used to treat these problems. This should always be done with your doctor's knowledge and consent.

3. Be consistent about sticking with the programme. While we advise this for everyone following a low-carb diet – whether your problem is weight, diabetes, high blood lipids or high blood pressure – consistency is of the greatest importance if you start out with diabetes. This is because type-2 diabetes represents the highest level of insulin resistance, so if you break the diet, your body's return to carbohydrate intolerance will be rapid and the swings in blood sugar wide. If you've got off most of your diabetes or high-blood-pressure drugs in the first two weeks of the diet and celebrate this victory by three days of eating everything in sight, the metabolic bully will come back and you'll return home with these problems once again out of control. Yes, as you lose weight your underlying tendency to be insulin-resistant often improves. But most diabetics still remain somewhat insulin-resistant even after substantial weight loss, so staying at or under your carbohydrate threshold has greater importance for you in order to avoid the long-term medical problems caused by poorly controlled diabetes.

A CHALLENGE THAT'S WORTH THE EFFORT

Using the Atkins Diet to manage type-2 diabetes is probably the most potent use of this powerful tool but it's also the most demanding. Make sure that you (and your doctor) are ready to apply the time and energy necessary to be successful – both in the short term and for years to come. To that end, we have provided a combination of scientific and practical information in this chapter so that both you and your doctor can be assured that this use of the Atkins Diet can be safe and effective.

Acknowledgements

> We are like dwarfs on the shoulders of giants, so that we
> can see more than they, and things at a greater distance,
> not by virtue of any sharpness of sight on our part, or any
> physical distinction, but because we are carried high and
> raised up by their giant size.
>
> —*Bernard of Chartres, 1159*

For a quarter century, as an academic physician doing research on low-carbohydrate metabolism, my life ran parallel to that of Robert C Atkins. Sadly, our paths never crossed. About a decade ago, however, two leaders of a new generation of medical scientists contacted me. Building a bridge between the heretofore separate realms of academic research and the clinical brilliance of Dr Atkins, Dr Eric Westman and Dr Jeff Volek have forged the scientific foundation of the New Atkins. As a result of their efforts and the support of the Atkins Foundation, there has been a resurgence of scientific interest in the Atkins Diet. It has been my very great pleasure to collaborate with them, first on current research studies and now on the creation of this book.

I also wish to thank Drs Ethan Sims, Edward Horton, Bruce Bistrian and George Blackburn for teaching me to subject standard dietary practices to scientific scrutiny. Their guidance helped to shape my life and my career. I also owe a debt of gratitude to my many patients and research subjects for opening my eyes to unanticipated results. And most important, thanks to my lovely family – Huong, Lauren and Eric – for their unquestioning support and their tolerance of my cooking.

—*Stephen D Phinney*

I must first thank those people who have shaped my scientific thinking and specifically contributed to a line of research on carbohydrate restriction. Dr William J Kraemer initially sparked my interest in science and has offered unwavering support for almost twenty years as we have continued to collaborate on research and become best friends. I'm not sure if he qualifies for MENSA, but my coauthor Dr Stephen Phinney is a bona fide nutritional genius. In 1994 I first read his enlightening papers on experiments he conducted in the early 1980s on metabolic adaptations to very-low-carbohydrate diets. A decade later I'm fortunate to consider him a close friend and colleague. Several other colleagues have significantly influenced my views of nutrition and positively impacted my research. Drs Maria Luz Fernandez, Richard Feinman and Richard Bruno are all brilliant collaborators on past and current research projects whose relationships I treasure. I have also been privileged to work with several tireless and talented graduate students over the years, all of whom dedicated countless hours to conducting more than a dozen experiments aimed at better understanding how low-carbohydrate diets improve health.

It's been a pleasure working with Eric Westman and Stephen Phinney. It is also necessary to acknowledge Dr Robert C Atkins, who had a remarkable and permanent impact on my life. His recognition of the importance of science to validate his dietary approach and his generous philanthropy has been a major reason I was able to conduct cutting-edge research on low-carbohydrate diets over the last decade.

I am forever grateful to my selfless mother, Nina, and my father, Jerry, for their unconditional love and support, and all the sacrifices they have made in order to make my life better. My two cherished boys, high-spirited Preston, who recently turned two, and Reese, who was born during the writing of this book, give me a deep sense of purpose and perspective. Coming home to them is the perfect antidote to a stressful day of work. Most important thanks to my beloved wife, Ana, who keeps me balanced and makes life infinitely more fun.

—*Jeff S Volek*

I acknowledge first the enthusiastic love and support of my wife, Gretchen, and our children Laura, Megan and Clay. I learnt to tilt at windmills from my parents, Jack C and Nancy K Westman, and brothers, John C Westman and D Paul Westman. Innumerable friends, colleagues and data-driven academic environments enabled this book – and the science behind it – to materialise.

Thanks to Dr Robert C Atkins and Jackie Eberstein for having the openness to invite me to visit their clinical practice. Thanks to Veronica Atkins and Dr Abby Bloch of the Robert C Atkins Foundation for continuing his legacy. Thanks also to the doctors and researchers who allowed me to visit their practices or collaborate on research studies with them: Mary C Vernon, Richard K Bernstein, Joseph T Hickey, Ron Rosedale, members of the American Society of Bariatric Physicians, William S Yancy Jr, James A Wortman, Jeff

S Volek, Richard D Feinman, Donald Layman, Manny Noakes and Stephen D Phinney.

—*Eric C Westman*

As a team, we wish to acknowledge the Herculean effort expended in bringing together all the components of this book by project editor Olivia Bell Buehl and Atkins nutritionist Colette Heimowitz. Dietician Brittanie Volk developed the meal plans. Thanks also to Monty Sharma and Chip Bellamy of Atkins Nutritionals, Inc, for their insight on the importance of publishing this book and their patience as it took on a life of its own.

Glossary

ACE: See *Atkins Carbohydrate Equilibrium*.

Aerobic exercise: Sustained rhythmic exercise that increases your heart rate; also referred to as cardio.

Amino acids: The building blocks of protein.

Antioxidants: Substances that neutralise harmful free radicals in the body.

Atherosclerosis: Clogging, narrowing and hardening of blood vessels by plaque deposits.

Atkins Carbohydrate Equilibrium (ACE): The number of grams of Net Carbs that a person can consume daily without gaining or losing weight.

Atkins Edge: A beneficial state of fat-burning metabolism caused by carbohydrate restriction that makes it possible to lose weight and maintain weight loss without extreme hunger or cravings; a metabolic edge.

Beta cells: Specialised cells in the pancreas that produce insulin.

Blood lipids: The factors of total cholesterol, triglycerides and HDL and LDL cholesterol in your blood.

Blood pressure: The pressure your blood exerts against the walls of your arteries during a heartbeat.

Blood sugar: The amount of glucose in your bloodstream; also called blood glucose.

BMI: See *Body mass index*.

Body mass index (BMI): An estimate of body fatness that takes into account body weight and height.

Carbohydrate: A macronutrient from plants and some other foods broken down by digestion into simple sugars such as glucose to provide a source of energy.

Cholesterol: A lipid; a waxy substance essential for many of the body's functions, including manufacturing hormones and making cell membranes.

C-reactive protein (CRP): A chemical in blood that serves as a marker for inflammation.

Diabetes: See *Type-1 diabetes* and *Type-2 diabetes*.

Diuretic: Anything that removes fluid from the body by increasing urination.

Essential fatty acids (EFAs): Two classes of essential dietary fats that your body cannot make on its own and that must be obtained from food or supplements.

Fat: One of the three macronutrients; an organic compound that dissolves in other oils but not in water. A source of energy and building blocks of cells.

Fatty acids: The scientific term for fats, which are part of a group of substances called lipids.

Fibre: Parts of plant foods that are indigestible or very slowly digested, with little effect on blood glucose and insulin levels; sometimes called roughage.

Foundation vegetables: Leafy greens and other low-carbohydrate, non-starchy vegetables suitable for Phase 1 and Induction, and the basis upon which later carb intake builds.

Free radicals: Harmful molecules in the environment and naturally produced by our bodies. Excess free radicals can damage cells and cause oxidation.

Glucose: A simple sugar. Also see *Blood sugar.*

Glycogen: The storage form of carbohydrate in the body.

HDL cholesterol: High-density lipoprotein; the 'good' type of cholesterol

Hydrogenated oils: Vegetable oils processed to make them solid and improve their shelf life. See *Trans-fats.*

Hypertension: High blood pressure.

Inflammation: Part of the body's delicately balanced natural defence system against potentially damaging substances. Excessive inflammation is associated with increased risk of heart attack, stroke, diabetes and some forms of cancer.

Insulin: A hormone produced by the pancreas that signals cells to remove glucose and amino acids from the bloodstream and stop the release of fat from fat cells.

Ketoacidosis: The uncontrolled overproduction of ketones characteristic of untreated type-1 diabetes, typically five to ten times higher than nutritional ketosis.

Ketones: Substances produced by the liver from fat during accelerated fat breakdown that serve as a valuable energy source for cells throughout the body.

Ketosis: A moderate and controlled level of ketones in the bloodstream that allows the body to function well with little dietary carbohydrate; also called nutritional ketosis.

LDL cholesterol: Low-density lipoprotein. Formerly known as the 'bad' type of cholesterol, but not all LDL cholesterol is 'bad'.

Lean body mass: Body mass minus fat tissue; includes muscle, bone, organs and connective tissue.

Lipids: Fats, including triglycerides and cholesterol in the body.

Macronutrients: Fat, protein and carbohydrate, the dietary sources of calories and nutrients.

Metabolic syndrome: A group of conditions including hypertension, high triglycerides, low HDL cholesterol, higher-than-normal blood sugar and insulin levels and weight carried in the middle of the body. Also known as syndrome X or insulin resistance syndrome, it predisposes you to heart disease and type-2 diabetes.

Metabolism: The complex chemical processes that convert food into energy or the body's building blocks, which in turn become part of organs, tissues and cells.

Monounsaturated fat: Dietary fat typically found in foods such as olive oil, rapeseed oil, nuts and avocados.

Net Carbs: The carbohydrates in a food that impact your blood sugar, calculated by subtracting fibre grams in the food from total grams. In a low-carb product, sugar alcohols, including glycerine, are also subtracted.

Omega-3 fatty acids: A group of essential polyunsaturated fats found in green algae, cold-water fish, fish oil, flaxseed oil and some other nut and vegetable oils.

Omega-6 fatty acids: A group of essential polyunsaturated fats found in many vegetable oils and also in meats from animals fed corn, soya beans and certain other vegetable products.

Partially hydrogenated oils: See *Trans-fats*.

Plaque: A build-up in the arteries of cholesterol, fat, calcium and other substances that can block blood flow and result in a heart attack or stroke.

Polyunsaturated fats: Fats with a chemical structure that keeps them liquid in the cold; oils from corn, soya bean, sunflower, safflower, cottonseed, grapeseed, flaxseed, sesame seed, some nuts and fatty fish are typically high in polyunsaturated fat.

Pre-diabetes: Blood sugar levels that are higher than normal but fall short of full-blown diabetes.

Protein: One of the three macronutrients found in food, used for energy and building blocks of cells; chains of amino acids.

Pulses: Most members of the bean and pea families, including lentils, chickpeas, soya beans, peas and numerous others.

Resistance exercise: Any exercise that builds muscle strength; also called weight-bearing or anaerobic exercise.

Satiety: A pleasurable sense of fullness.

Saturated fats: Fats that are solid at room temperature; the majority of fat in butter, lard, suet, palm oil and coconut oil.

Statin drugs: Pharmaceuticals used to lower total and LDL cholesterol.

Sucrose: Table sugar composed of glucose and fructose.

Sugar alcohols: Sweeteners such as glycerine, mannitol, erythritol, sorbitol and xylitol that have little or no impact on most people's blood sugar and are therefore used in some low-carb products.

Trans-fats: Fats found in partially hydrogenated or hydrogenated vegetable oil; typically used in fried foods, baked goods and other products. A high intake of trans-fats is associated with increased heart attack risk.

Triglycerides: The major form of fat that circulates in the bloodstream and is stored as body fat.

Type-1 diabetes: A condition in which the pancreas makes so little insulin that the body can't use blood glucose as energy, producing chronically high blood sugar levels and overproduction of ketones.

Type-2 diabetes: The more common form of diabetes; high blood sugar levels caused by insulin resistance, an inability to use insulin properly.

Unsaturated fat: Monounsaturated and polyunsaturated fats.

Notes

Chapter 1: Know Thyself

1. C. D. Gardner, A. Kiazand, S. Alhassan, S. Kim, R. S. Stafford, R. R. Balise, et al., 'Comparison of the Atkins, Zone, Ornish, and LEARN Diets for Change in Weight and Related Risk Factors among Overweight Premenopausal Women: The A TO Z Weight Loss Study: A Randomized Trial,' *The Journal of the American Medical Association* 297 (2007), 969–977; I. Shai, D. Schwarzfuchs, Y. Henkin, D. R. Shahar, S. Witkow, I. Greenberg, et al., 'Weight Loss with a Low-Carbohydrate, Mediterranean, or Low-Fat Diet,' *The New England Journal of Medicine* 359 (2008), 229–241; J. S. Volek, M. L. Fernandez, R. D. Feinman, and S. D. Phinney, 'Dietary Carbohydrate Restriction Induces a Unique Metabolic State Positively Affecting Atherogenic Dyslipidemia, Fatty Acid Partitioning, and Metabolic Syndrome,' *Progress in Lipid Research* 47 (2008), 307–318.

2. Shai et al., 'Weight Loss with a Low-Carbohydrate, Mediterranean, or Low-Fat Diet'; A. J. Nordmann, A. Nordmann, M. Briel, U. Keller, W. S. Yancy, Jr., B. J. Brehm, et al., 'Effects of Low-Carbohydrate vs Low-Fat Diets on Weight Loss and Cardiovascular Risk Factors: A Meta-analysis of Randomized Controlled Trials,' *Archives of Internal Medicine* 166 (2006), 285–293.

3. C. D. Gardner et al., 'Comparison of the Atkins, Zone, Ornish, and LEARN Diets for Change in Weight and Related Risk Factors among Overweight Premenopausal Women.'

4. G. Boden, K. Sargrad, C. Homko, M. Mozzoli, and T. P. Stein, 'Effect of a Low-Carbohydrate Diet on Appetite, Blood Glucose Levels, and Insulin Resistance in Obese Patients with type 2 Diabetes,' *Annals of Internal Medicine* 142 (2005), 403–411; E. C. Westman, W. S. Yancy, Jr., J. C. Mavropoulos, M. Marquart, and J. R. McDuffie, 'The Effect of a Low-Carbohydrate, Ketogenic Diet Versus a Low-Glycemic Index Diet on Glycemic Control in type 2 Diabetes Mellitus,' *Nutrition & Metabolism* (London) 5 (2008), 36.

5. E. H. Kossoff, and J. M. Rho, 'Ketogenic Diets: Evidence for Short- and Long-Term Efficacy,' *Neurotherapeutics* 6 (2009), 406–414; J. M. Freeman, J. B. Freeman, and M. T. Kelly, *The Ketogenic Diet: A Treatment for Epilepsy*, 3rd ed. (New York: Demos Health, 2000).

6. T. A. Wadden, J. A. Sternberg, K. A. Letizia, A. J. Stunkard, and G. D. Foster, 'Treatment of Obesity by Very Low Calorie Diet, Behavior Therapy, and Their Combination: A Five-Year Perspective,' *International Journal of Obesity* 13 suppl. 2 (1989), 39–46.

7. Gardner et al., 'Comparison of the Atkins, Zone, Ornish, and LEARN Diets for Change in Weight and Related Risk Factors among Overweight Premenopausal Women: The A TO Z Weight Loss Study: A

Randomized Trial'; I. Shai et al., 'Weight Loss with a Low-Carbohydrate, Mediterranean, or Low-Fat Diet.'

8. G. Boden et al., 'Effect of a Low-Carbohydrate Diet on Appetite, Blood Glucose Levels, and Insulin Resistance in Obese Patients with type 2 Diabetes'; J. S. Volek, M. J. Sharman, A. L. Gomez, D. A. Judelson, M. R. Rubin, G. Watson, et al., 'Comparison of Energy-Restricted Very Low-Carbohydrate and Low-Fat Diets on Weight Loss and Body Composition in Overweight Men and Women,' *Nutrition & Metabolism* (London) 1 (2004), 13.

9. E. A. Sims, E. Danforth, Jr., E. S. Horton, G. A. Bray, J. A. Glennon, and L. B. Salans, 'Endocrine and Metabolic Effects of Experimental Obesity in Man,' *Recent Progress in Hormonal Research* 29 (1973), 457–496; C. Bouchard, A. Tremblay, J. P. Despres, G. Theriault, A. Nadeau, P. J. Lupien, et al., 'The Response to Exercise with Constant Energy Intake in Identical Twins,' *Obesity Research* 2 (1994), 400–410.

10. Gardner et al., 'Comparison of the Atkins, Zone, Ornish, and LEARN Diets for Change in Weight and Related Risk Factors among Overweight Premenopausal Women: The A TO Z Weight Loss Study: A Randomized Trial'; I. Shai et al., 'Weight Loss with a Low-Carbohydrate, Mediterranean, or Low-Fat Diet'; B. J. Brehm, R. J. Seeley, S. R. Daniels, and D. A. D'Alessio, 'A Randomized Trial Comparing a Very Low Carbohydrate Diet and a Calorie-Restricted Low Fat Diet on Body Weight and Cardiovascular Risk Factors in Healthy Women,' *Journal of Clinical Endocrinology & Metabolism* 88 (2003), 1617–1623; M. L. Dansinger, J. A. Gleason, J. L. Griffith, H. P. Selker, and E. J. Schaefer, 'Comparison of the Atkins, Ornish, Weight Watchers, and Zone Diets for Weight Loss and Heart Disease Risk Reduction: A Randomized Trial,' *The Journal of the American Medical Association* 293 (2005), 43–53; G. D. Foster, H. R. Wyatt, J. O. Hill, B. G. McGuckin, C. Brill, B. S. Mohammed, et al., 'A Randomized Trial of a Low-Carbohydrate Diet for Obesity,' *The New England Journal of Medicine* 348 (2003), 2082–2090; L. Stern, N. Iqbal, P. Seshadri, K. L. Chicano, D. A. Daily, J. McGrory, et al., 'The Effects of Low-Carbohydrate Versus Conventional Weight Loss Diets in Severely Obese Adults: One-Year Follow-up of a Randomized Trial,' *Annals of Internal Medicine* 140 (2004), 778–785; W. S. Yancy, Jr., M. K. Olsen, J. R. Guyton, R. P. Bakst, and E. C. Westman, 'A Low-Carbohydrate, Ketogenic Diet versus a Low-Fat Diet to Treat Obesity and Hyperlipidemia: A Randomized, Controlled Trial,' *Annals of Internal Medicine* 140 (2004), 769–777.

11. H. M. Dashti, N. S. Al-Zaid, T. C. Mathew, M. Al-Mousawi, H. Talib, S. K. Asfar, et al., 'Long Term Effects of Ketogenic Diet in Obese Subjects with High Cholesterol Level,' *Molecular and Cellular Biochemistry* 286 (2006), 1–9.

Chapter 2: The Road Ahead

1. J. S. Volek, M. J. Sharman, A. L. Gomez, D. A. Judelson, M. R. Rubin, G. Watson, et al., 'Comparison of Energy-Restricted Very Low-Carbohydrate and Low-Fat Diets on Weight Loss and Body Composition

in Overweight Men and Women,' *Nutrition & Metabolism* (London) 1 (2004), 13; J. S. Volek, S. D. Phinney, C. E. Forsythe, E. E. Quann, R. J. Wood, M. J. Puglisi, et al., 'Carbohydrate Restriction Has a More Favorable Impact on the Metabolic Syndrome than a Low Fat Diet,' *Lipids* 44 (2008), 297–309.

2. C. D. Gardner, A. Kiazand, S. Alhassan, S. Kim, R. S. Stafford, R. R. Balise, et al., 'Comparison of the Atkins, Zone, Ornish, and LEARN Diets for Change in Weight and Related Risk Factors among Overweight Premenopausal Women: The A TO Z Weight Loss Study: A Randomized Trial,' *The Journal of the American Medical Association* 297 (2007), 969–977; I. Shai, D. Schwarzfuchs, Y. Henkin, D. R. Shahar, S. Witkow, I. Greenberg, et al., 'Weight Loss with a Low-Carbohydrate, Mediterranean, or Low-Fat Diet,' *The New England Journal of Medicine* 359 (2008), 229–241; J. S. Volek et al., 'Carbohydrate Restriction Has a More Favorable Impact on the Metabolic Syndrome than a Low-Fat Diet.'

Chapter 3: The Right Carbs in the Right Amounts

1. See www.ers.usda.gov/publications/sb965/sb965h.pdf for more information.

2. S. S. Elliott, N. L. Keim, J. S. Stern, K. Teff, and P. J. Havel. 'Fructose, Weight Gain, and the Insulin Resistance Syndrome,' *American Journal of Clinical Nutrition* 76 (2002), 911–922; G. A. Bray, S. J. Nielsen, and B. M. Popkin, 'Consumption of High-Fructose Corn Syrup in Beverages May Play a Role in the Epidemic of Obesity,' *American Journal of Clinical Nutrition* 79 (2004), 537–543.

3. Bray, Nielsen, and B. M. Popkin, 'Consumption of High-Fructose Corn Syrup in Beverages May Play a Role in the Epidemic of Obesity.'

4. www.cspinet.org/new/pdf/final_soda_petition.pdf.

5. K. L. Teff, J. Grudziak, R. R. Townsend, T. N. Dunn, R. W. Grant, S. H. Adams, et al., 'Endocrine and Metabolic Effects of Consuming Fructose- and Glucose-Sweetened Beverages with Meals in Obese Men and Women: Influence of Insulin Resistance on Plasma Triglyceride Responses,' *Journal of Clinical Endocrinology & Metabolism* 94 (2009), 1562–1569.

6. C. Bouchard, A. Tremblay, J. P. Despres, A. Nadeau, P. J. Lupien, G. Theriault, et al., 'The Response to Long-Term Overfeeding in Identical Twins,' *The New England Journal of Medicine* 322 (1990), 1477–1482.

7. C. Bouchard, A. Tremblay, J. P. Despres, G. Theriault, A. Nadeau, P. J. Lupien, et al., 'The Response to Exercise with Constant Energy Intake in Identical Twins,' *Obesity Research* 2 (1994), 400–410.

Chapter 4: The Power of Protein

1. G. H. Anderson, and S. E. Moore, 'Dietary Proteins in the Regulation of Food Intake and Body Weight in Humans,' *The Journal of Nutrition* 134 (2004), 974S–979S.

2. E. Jequier, 'Pathways to Obesity,' *International Journal of Obesity and Related Metabolic Disorders* 26 suppl. 2 (2002), S12–S17.

3. F. Q. Nuttall, K. Schweim, H. Hoover, and M. C. Gannon, 'Metabolic Effect of a LoBAG30 Diet in Men with type 2 Diabetes,' *American Journal of Physiology—Endocrinology and Metabolism* 291 (2006), E786–E791; D. K. Layman, P. Clifton, M. C. Gannon, R. M. Krauss, and F. Q. Nuttall, 'Protein in Optimal Health: Heart Disease and type 2 Diabetes,' *American Journal of Clinical Nutrition* 87 (2008), 1571S–1575S.

4. J. W. Krieger, H. S. Sitren, M. J. Daniels, and B. Langkamp-Henken, 'Effects of Variation in Protein and Carbohydrate Intake on Body Mass and Composition during Energy Restriction: A Meta-regression,' *American Journal of Clinical Nutrition* 83 (2006), 260–274.

5. L. J. Hoffer, B. R. Bistrian, V. R. Young, G. L. Blackburn, and D. E. Matthews, 'Metabolic Effects of Very Low Calorie Weight Reduction Diets,' *The Journal of Clinical Investigation* 73 (1984), 750–758; P. G. Davis, and S. D. Phinney, 'Differential Effects of Two Very Low Calorie Diets on Aerobic and Anaerobic Performance,' *International Journal of Obesity* 14 (1990), 779–787.

6. R. P. Heaney and D. K. Layman, 'Amount and Type of Protein Influences Bone Health,' *American Journal of Clinical Nutrition* 87 (2008), 1567S–1570S.

7. Ibid.

Chapter 5: Meet Your New Friend: Fat

1. 'Trends in Intake of Energy and Macronutrients—United States, 1971–2000,' *Morbidity and Mortality Weekly Report (MMWR)* 53 (2004), 80–82.

2. S. Klein, and R. R. Wolfe, 'Carbohydrate Restriction Regulates the Adaptive Response to Fasting,' *American Journal of Physiology* 262 (1992), E631–E636.

3. D. Mozaffarian, E. B. Rimm, and D. M. Herrington,'Dietary Fats, Carbohydrate, and Progression of Coronary Atherosclerosis in Postmenopausal Women,' *American Journal of Clinical Nutrition* 80 (2004), 1175–1184.

4. J. S. Volek, M. J. Sharman, and C. E. Forsythe, 'Modification of Lipoproteins by Very Low-Carbohydrate Diets,' *The Journal of Nutrition* 135 (2005), 1339–1342.

5. Ibid.; R. M. Krauss, 'Dietary and Genetic Probes of Atherogenic Dyslipidemia,' *Arteriosclerosis, Thrombosis, and Vascular Biology* 25 (2005), 2265–2272; R. M. Krauss, P. J. Blanche, R. S. Rawlings, H. S. Fernstrom, and P. T. Williams, 'Separate Effects of Reduced Carbohydrate Intake and Weight Loss on Atherogenic Dyslipidemia,' *American Journal of Clinical Nutrition* 83 (2006), 1025–1031.

6. C. E. Forsythe, S. D. Phinney, M. L. Fernandez, E. E. Quann, R. J. Wood, D. M. Bibus, et al., 'Comparison of Low Fat and Low Carbohydrate Diets on Circulating Fatty Acid Composition and Markers of Inflammation,' *Lipids* 43 (2008), 65–77.

7. R. Micha and D. Mozaffarian, 'Trans Fatty Acids: Effects on Cardiometabolic Health and Implications for Policy,' *Prostaglandins, Leukotrienes and Essential Fatty Acids* 79 (2008), 147–152.

8. D. Mozaffarian, A. Aro, and W. C. Willett, 'Health Effects of Trans-Fatty Acids: Experimental and Observational Evidence,' *European Journal of Clinical Nutrition* 63 suppl. 2 (2009), S5–S21.

9. W. S. Harris, D. Mozaffarian, E. Rimm, P. Kris-Etherton, L. L. Rudel, L. J. Appel, et al., 'Omega-6 Fatty Acids and Risk for Cardiovascular Disease: A Science Advisory from the American Heart Association Nutrition Subcommittee of the Council on Nutrition, Physical Activity, and Metabolism; Council on Cardiovascular Nursing; and Council on Epidemiology and Prevention,' *Circulation* 119 (2009), 902–907.

10. S. D. Phinney, A. B. Tang, S. B. Johnson, and R. T. Holman, 'Reduced Adipose 18:3 Omega-3 with Weight Loss by Very Low Calorie Dieting,' *Lipids* 25 (1990), 798–806.

11. C. E. Forsythe, S. D. Phinney, M. L. Fernandez, E. E. Quann, R. J. Wood, D. M. Bibus, et al., 'Comparison of Low Fat and Low Carbohydrate Diets on Circulating Fatty Acid Composition and Markers of Inflammation,' *Lipids* 43 (2008), 65–77.

Chapter 6: Atkins for You: Make It Personal

1. L. E. Armstrong, D. J. Casa, C. M. Maresh, and M. S. Ganio, 'Caffeine, Fluid-Electrolyte Balance, Temperature Regulation, and Exercise-Heat Tolerance,' *Exercise and Sport Sciences Reviews* 35 (2007), 135–140.

2. D. L. Costill, G. P. Dalsky, and W. J. Fink, 'Effects of Caffeine Ingestion on Metabolism and Exercise Performance,' *Medicine & Science in Sports & Exercise* 10 (1978), 155–158.

3. S. D. Phinney, B. R. Bistrian, W. J. Evans, E. Gervino, and G. L. Blackburn, 'The Human Metabolic Response to Chronic Ketosis without Caloric Restriction: Preservation of Submaximal Exercise Capability with Reduced Carbohydrate Oxidation,' *Metabolism* 32 (1983), 769–776; S. D. Phinney, B. R. Bistrian, R. R. Wolfe, and G. L. Blackburn, 'The Human Metabolic Response to Chronic Ketosis without Caloric Restriction: Physical and Biochemical Adaptation,' *Metabolism* 32 (1983), 757–768.

4. E. E. Quann, T. P. Scheett, K. D. Ballard, M. J. Puglusi, C. E. Forsythe, B. M. Volk et al., 'Carbohydrate Restriction and Resistance Training Have Additive Effects on Body Composition during Weight Loss in Men,' *Journal of the American Dietetic Association* (abstract), 107(8) (April 2007), A14.

5. C. Bouchard, A. Tremblay, J. P. Despres, G. Theriault, A. Nadeau, P. J. Lupien, et al., 'The Response to Exercise with Constant Energy Intake in Identical Twins,' *Obesity Research* 2 (1994), 400–410.

Chapter 7: Welcome to Phase 1: Induction

1. E. Lopez-Garcia, R. M. van Dam, S. Rajpathak, W. C. Willett, J. E. Manson, and F. B. Hu, 'Changes in Caffeine Intake and Long-Term Weight Change in Men and Women,' *American Journal of Clinical Nutrition* 83(2006):674–80.

2. A. G. Dulloo, C. A. Geissler, T. Horton, A. Collins, and D. S. Miller. 'Normal Caffeine Consumption: Influence on Thermogenesis and Daily Energy Expenditure in Lean and Postobese Human Volunteers,'

American Journal of Clinical Nutrition 49 (1989):44–50; K. J. Acheson, B. Zahorska-Markiewicz, P. Pittet, K. Anantharaman, and E. Jéquier, 'Caffeine and Coffee: Their Influence on Metabolic Rate and Substrate Utilization in Normal Weight and Obese Individuals,' *American Journal of Clinical Nutrition* 33 (1980):989–997; K. J. Acheson, G. Gremaud, L. Meirim, F. Montigon, Y. Krebs, L. B. Fay, L. J. Gay, P. Schneiter, C. Schindler, and L. Tappy. 'Metabolic Effects of Caffeine in Humans: Lipid Oxidation or Futile Cycling?' *American Journal of Clinical Nutrition* 79 (2004):40–46.

3. A. I. Qureshi, F. K. Suri, S. Ahmed, A. Nasar, A. A. Divani, and J. F. Kirmani, 'Regular Egg Consumption Does Not Increase the Risk of Stroke and Cardiovascular Diseases,' *Medical Science Monitor* 13 (2007), CR1–CR8.

4. J. S. Vander Wal, A. Gupta, P. Khosla, and N. V. Dhurandhar, 'Egg Breakfast Enhances Weight Loss,' *International Journal of Obesity* (London) 32 (2008), 1545–1551.

5. J. S. Vander Wal, J. M. Marth, P. Khosla, K. L. Jen, and N. V. Dhurandhar, 'Short-Term Effect of Eggs on Satiety in Overweight and Obese Subjects,' *Journal of the American College of Nutrition* 24 (2005), 510–515.

6. G. Mutungi, J. Ratliff, M. Puglisi, M. Torres-Gonzalez, U. Vaishnav, J. O. Leite, et al., 'Dietary Cholesterol from Eggs Increases Plasma HDL Cholesterol in Overweight Men Consuming a Carbohydrate-Restricted Diet,' *The Journal of Nutrition* 138 (2008), 272–276.

Chapter 10: Keeping It Off: Lifetime Maintenance

1. J. O. Hill, and H. R. Wyatt, 'Role of Physical Activity in Preventing and Treating Obesity,' *Journal of Applied Physiology* 99 (2005), 765–770.

Chapter 13: Metabolic Syndrome and Cardiovascular Health

1. B. V. Howard, J. E. Manson, M. L. Stefanick, S. A. Beresford, G. Frank, B. Jones, et al., 'Low-Fat Dietary Pattern and Weight Change over 7 Years: The Women's Health Initiative Dietary Modification Trial,' *The Journal of the American Medical Association* 295 (2006), 39–49; L. F. Tinker, D. E. Bonds, K. L. Margolis, J. E. Manson, B. V. Howard, J. Larson, et al., 'Low-Fat Dietary Pattern and Risk of Treated Diabetes Mellitus in Postmenopausal Women: The Women's Health Initiative Randomized Controlled Dietary Modification Trial,' *Archives of Internal Medicine* 168 (2008), 1500–1511; S. A. Beresford, K. C. Johnson, C. Ritenbaugh, N. L. Lasser, L. G. Snetselaar, H. R. Black, et al., 'Low-Fat Dietary Pattern and Risk of Colorectal Cancer: The Women's Health Initiative Randomized Controlled Dietary Modification Trial,' *The Journal of the American Medical Association* 295 (2006), 643–654; R. L. Prentice, C. A. Thomson, B. Caan, F. A. Hubbell, G. L. Anderson, S. A. Beresford, et al., 'Low-Fat Dietary Pattern and Cancer Incidence in the Women's Health Initiative Dietary Modification Randomized Controlled Trial,' *Journal of the National Cancer Institute* 99 (2007), 1534–1543.

2. E. S. Ford, W. H. Giles, and W. H. Dietz, 'Prevalence of the Metabolic Syndrome among US Adults: Findings from the Third National Health

and Nutrition Examination Survey,' *The Journal of the American Medical Association* 287 (2002), 356–359.

3. G. M. Reaven, 'Banting Lecture 1988: Role of Insulin Resistance in Human Disease,' *Diabetes* 37 (1988), 1595–1607.

4. S. M. Grundy, H. B. Brewer, Jr., J. I. Cleeman, S. C. Smith, Jr., and C. Lenfant, 'Definition of Metabolic Syndrome: Report of the National Heart, Lung, and Blood Institute/American Heart Association Conference on Scientific Issues Related to Definition,' *Circulation* 109 (2004), 433–438.

5. J. S. Volek, M. J. Sharman, and C. E. Forsythe, 'Modification of Lipoproteins by Very Low-Carbohydrate Diets,' *The Journal of Nutrition* 135 (2005), 1339–1342; J. S. Volek and R. D. Feinman, 'Carbohydrate Restriction Improves the Features of Metabolic Syndrome. Metabolic Syndrome May Be Defined by the Response to Carbohydrate Restriction,' *Nutrition & Metabolism* (London) 2 (2005), 31.

6. G. Boden, K. Sargrad, C. Homko, M. Mozzoli, and T. P. Stein, 'Effect of a Low-Carbohydrate Diet on Appetite, Blood Glucose Levels, and Insulin Resistance in Obese Patients with type 2 Diabetes,' *Annals of Internal Medicine* 142 (2005), 403–411.

7. J. S. Volek, M. J. Sharman, D. M. Love, N. G. Avery, A. L. Gomez, T. P. Scheett, et al., 'Body Composition and Hormonal Responses to a Carbohydrate-Restricted Diet,' *Metabolism* 51 (2002), 864–870.

8. M. D. Jensen, M. Caruso, V. Heiling, and J. M. Miles, 'Insulin Regulation of Lipolysis in Nondiabetic and IDDM Subjects,' *Diabetes* 38 (1989), 1595–1601.

9. S. D. Phinney, B. R. Bistrian, R. R. Wolfe, and G. L. Blackburn, 'The Human Metabolic Response to Chronic Ketosis without Caloric Restriction: Physical and Biochemical Adaptation,' *Metabolism* 32 (1983), 757–768.

10. M. U. Jakobsen, E. J. O'Reilly, B. L. Heitmann, M. A. Pereira, K. Balter, G. E. Fraser, et al., 'Major Types of Dietary Fat and Risk of Coronary Heart Disease: A Pooled Analysis of 11 Cohort Studies,' *American Journal of Clinical Nutrition* 89 (2009), 1425–1432.

11. 'Trends in Intake of Energy and Macronutrients—United States, 1971–2000,' *Morbidity and Mortality Weekly Report (MMWR)* 53 (2004), 80–82.

12. L. Wang, A. R. Folsom, Z. J. Zheng, J. S. Pankow, and J. H. Eckfeldt, 'Plasma Fatty Acid Composition and Incidence of Diabetes in Middle-Aged Adults: The Atherosclerosis Risk in Communities (ARIC) Study,' *American Journal of Clinical Nutrition* 78 (2003), 91–98; E. Warensjo, U. Riserus, and B. Vessby, 'Fatty Acid Composition of Serum Lipids Predicts the Development of the Metabolic Syndrome in Men,' *Diabetologia* 48 (2005), 1999–2005.

13. C. E. Forsythe, S. D. Phinney, M. L. Fernandez, E. E. Quann, R. J. Wood, D. M. Bibus, et al., 'Comparison of Low Fat and Low Carbohydrate Diets on Circulating Fatty Acid Composition and Markers of Inflammation,' *Lipids* 43 (2008), 65–77.

14. J. S. Volek, M. L. Fernandez, R. D. Feinman, and S. D. Phinney, 'Dietary Carbohydrate Restriction Induces a Unique Metabolic State Positively Affecting Atherogenic Dyslipidemia, Fatty Acid Partitioning, and Metabolic Syndrome,' *Progress in Lipid Research* 47 (2008), 307–318.

15. S. K. Raatz, D. Bibus, W. Thomas, and P. Kris-Etherton, 'Total Fat Intake Modifies Plasma Fatty Acid Composition in Humans,' *The Journal of Nutrition* 131 (2001), 231–234; I. B. King, R. N. Lemaitre, and M. Kestin, 'Effect of a Low-Fat Diet on Fatty Acid Composition in Red Cells, Plasma Phospholipids, and Cholesterol Esters: Investigation of a Biomarker of Total Fat Intake,' *American Journal of Clinical Nutrition* 83 (2006), 227–236.

16. John Rae, *John Rae's Correspondence with Hudson's Bay Company on the Arctic Exploration, 1844–1855* (London: Hudson's Bay Record Society, 1953).

17. E. A. Stackpole, *The Long Arctic Search: The Narrative of Lt. Frederick Schwatka* (Mystic, Connecticut: Marine Historical Association, 1965).

18. E. F. Dubois and W. S. McClellan, 'Clinical Calorimetry. XLV: Prolonged Meat Diets with a Study of Kidney Function and Ketosis,' *The Journal of Biological Chemistry* 87 (1930), 651–668; V. R. Rupp, M. C. McClellan, and V. Toscani, 'Clinical Calorimetry. XLVI: Prolonged Meat Diets with a Study of the Metabolism of Nitrogen, Calcium, and Phosphorus,' *The Journal of Biological Chemistry* 87 (1930), 669–680.

19. M. G. Peterman, 'The Ketogenic Diet in Epilepsy,' *The Journal of the American Medical Association* 84 (1925), 1979–1983.

20. H. F. Helmholz, 'The Treatment of Epilepsy in Childhood: Five Years' Experience with the Ketogenic Diet,' *The Journal of the American Medical Association* 88 (1927), 2028–2032.

21. H. M. Keith, *Convulsive Disorders in Children* (Boston: Little, Brown, 1963), 167–172.

22. E. H. Kossoff, and J. M. Rho, 'Ketogenic Diets: Evidence for Short- and Long-Term Efficacy,' *Neurotherapeutics* 6 (2009), 406–414.

23. M. J. Sharman, A. L. Gomez, W. J. Kraemer, and J. S. Volek, 'Very Low-Carbohydrate and Low-Fat Diets Affect Fasting Lipids and Postprandial Lipemia Differently in Overweight Men,' *The Journal of Nutrition* 134 (2004), 880–885.

24. M. J. Sharman, W. J. Kraemer, D. M. Love, N. G. Avery, A. L. Gomez, T. P. Scheett, et al., 'A Ketogenic Diet Favorably Affects Serum Biomarkers for Cardiovascular Disease in Normal-Weight Men,' *The Journal of Nutrition* 132 (2002), 1879–1885; J. S. Volek, M. J. Sharman, A. L. Gomez, T. P. Scheett, and W. J. Kraemer, 'An Isoenergetic Very Low Carbohydrate Diet Improves Serum HDL Cholesterol and Triacylglycerol Concentrations, the Total Cholesterol to HDL Cholesterol Ratio and Postprandial Pipemic Responses Compared with a Low Fat Diet in Normal Weight, Normolipidemic Women,' *The Journal of Nutrition* 133 (2003), 2756–2761.

25. P. P. Toth, 'High-Density Lipoprotein as a Therapeutic Target: Clinical Evidence and Treatment Strategies,' *American Journal of Cardiology* 96 (2005), 50K–58K; discussion at 34K–35K.

26. J. S. Volek, M. J. Sharman, and C. E. Forsythe, 'Modification of Lipo-proteins by Very Low-Carbohydrate Diets,' *The Journal of Nutrition* 135 (2005), 1339–1342.

27. J. S. Volek et al., 'An Isoenergetic Very Low Carbohydrate Diet Improves Serum HDL Cholesterol and Triacylglycerol Concentrations, the Total Cholesterol to HDL Cholesterol Ratio and Postprandial Pipemic Responses Compared with a Low Fat Diet in Normal Weight, Normolipidemic Women.'

28. B. V. Howard, L. Van Horn, J. Hsia, J. E. Manson, M. L. Stefanick, S. Wassertheil-Smoller, et al., 'Low-Fat Dietary Pattern and Risk of Cardiovascular Disease: The Women's Health Initiative Randomized Controlled Dietary Modification Trial,' *The Journal of the American Medical Association* 295 (2006), 655–666.

29. D. M. Dreon, H. A. Fernstrom, B. Miller, and R. M. Krauss, 'Low-Density Lipoprotein Subclass Patterns and Lipoprotein Response to a Reduced-Fat Diet in Men,' *The FASEB Journal* 8 (1994), 121–126; D. M. Dreon, H. A. Fernstrom, P. T. Williams, and R. M. Krauss, 'A Very Low-Fat Diet Is Not Associated with Improved Lipoprotein Profiles in Men with a Predominance of Large, Low-Density Lipoproteins,' *American Journal of Clinical Nutrition* 69 (1999), 411–418.

30. Volek, Sharman, and Forsythe, 'Modification of Lipoproteins by Very Low-Carbohydrate Diets'; R. M. Krauss, 'Dietary and Genetic Probes of Atherogenic Dyslipidemia,' *Arteriosclerosis, Thrombosis, and Vascular Biology* 25 (2005), 2265–2272.

31. Krauss, 'Dietary and Genetic Probes of Atherogenic Dyslipidemia.'

32. A. Aljada, J. Friedman, H. Ghanim, P. Mohanty, D. Hofmeyer, A. Chaudhuri, et al., 'Glucose Ingestion Induces an Increase in Intranuclear Nuclear Factor κb, a Fall in Cellular Inhibitor κb, and an Increase in Tumor Necrosis Factor Alpha Messenger RNA by Mononuclear Cells in Healthy Human Subjects,' *Metabolism* 55 (2006), 1177–1185; P. Mohanty, W. Hamouda, R. Garg, A. Aljada, H. Ghanim, and P. Dandona, 'Glucose Challenge Stimulates Reactive Oxygen Species (ROS) Generation by Leucocytes,' *Journal of Clinical Endocrinology & Metabolism* 85 (2000), 2970–2973.

33. S. E. Kasim-Karakas, A. Tsodikov, U. Singh, and I. Jialal., 'Responses of Inflammatory Markers to a Low-Fat, High-Carbohydrate Diet: Effects of Energy Intake,' *American Journal of Clinical Nutrition* 83 (2006), 774–779; S. Liu, J. E. Manson, J. E. Buring, M. J. Stampfer, W. C. Willett, and P. M. Ridker, 'Relation between a Diet with a High Glycemic Load and Plasma Concentrations of High-Sensitivity C-reactive Protein in Middle-Aged Women,' *American Journal of Clinical Nutrition* 75 (2002), 492–498.

34. M. L. Dansinger, J. A. Gleason, J. L. Griffith, H. P. Selker, and E. J. Schae-fer, 'Comparison of the Atkins, Ornish, Weight Watchers, and Zone Diets for Weight Loss and Heart Disease Risk Reduction: A Randomized Trial,' *The Journal of the American Medical Association* 293 (2005), 43–53; K. A. McAuley, C. M. Hopkins, K. J. Smith, R. T. McLay, S. M. Williams, R. W. Taylor, et al., 'Comparison of High-Fat and High-Protein Diets with a

High-Carbohydrate Diet in Insulin-Resistant Obese Women,' *Diabetologia* 48 (2005), 8–16.

35. P. Seshadri, N. Iqbal, L. Stern, M. Williams, K. L. Chicano, D. A. Daily, et al., 'A Randomized Study Comparing the Effects of a Low-Carbohydrate Diet and a Conventional Diet on Lipoprotein Subfractions and C-reactive Protein Levels in Patients with Severe Obesity,' *The American Journal of Medicine* 117 (2004), 398–405.

36. C. E. Forsythe, S. D. Phinney, M. L. Fernandez, E. E. Quann, R. J. Wood, D. M. Bibus, et al., 'Comparison of Low Fat and Low Carbohydrate Diets on Circulating Fatty Acid Composition and Markers of Inflammation,' *Lipids* 43 (2008), 65–77.

37. P. C. Calder, 'Polyunsaturated Fatty Acids and Inflammation,' *Prostaglandins, Leukotrienes and Essential Fatty Acids* 75 (2006), 197–202.

38. T. A. Jacobson, 'Secondary Prevention of Coronary Artery Disease with Omega-3 Fatty Acids,' *American Journal of Cardiology* 98 (2006), 61i–70i.

39. H. O. Steinberg, H. Chaker, R. Leaming, A. Johnson, G. Brechtel, and A. D. Baron, 'Obesity/Insulin Resistance Is Associated with Endothelial Dysfunction. Implications for the Syndrome of Insulin Resistance,' *The Journal of Clinical Investigation* 97 (1996), 2601–2610.

40. M. C. Corretti, T. J. Anderson, E. J. Benjamin, D. Celermajer, F. Charbonneau, M. A. Creager, et al., 'Guidelines for the Ultrasound Assessment of Endothelial-Dependent Flow-Mediated Vasodilation of the Brachial Artery: A Report of the International Brachial Artery Reactivity Task Force,' *Journal of the American College of Cardiology* 39 (2002), 257–265.

41. A. Ceriello, C. Taboga, L. Tonutti, L. Quagliaro, L. Piconi, B. Bais, et al., 'Evidence for an Independent and Cumulative Effect of Postprandial Hypertriglyceridemia and Hyperglycemia on Endothelial Dysfunction and Oxidative Stress Generation: Effects of Short- and Long-Term Simvastatin Treatment,' *Circulation* 106 (2002), 1211–1218; M. J. Williams, W. H. Sutherland, M. P. McCormick, S. A. De Jong, R. J. Walker, and G. T. Wilkins, 'Impaired Endothelial Function Following a Meal Rich in Used Cooking Fat,' *Journal of the American College of Cardiology* 33 (1999), 1050–1055; M. C. Blendea, M. Bard, J. R. Sowers, and N. Winer, 'High-Fat Meal Impairs Vascular Compliance in a Subgroup of Young Healthy Subjects,' *Metabolism* 54 (2005), 1337–1344.

42. Ibid.

43. M. J. Sharman, A. L. Gomez, W. J. Kraemer, and J. S. Volek, 'Very Low-Carbohydrate and Low-Fat Diets Affect Fasting Lipids and Postprandial Lipemia Differently in Overweight Men,' *The Journal of Nutrition* 134 (2004), 880–885; J. S. Volek, M. J. Sharman, A. L. Gomez, T. P. Scheett, and W. J. Kraemer, 'An Isoenergetic Very Low Carbohydrate Diet Improves Serum HDL Cholesterol and Triacylglycerol Concentrations, the Total Cholesterol to HDL Cholesterol Ratio and Postprandial Pipemic Responses Compared with a Low Fat Diet in Normal Weight, Normolipidemic Women,' *The Journal of Nutrition* 133 (2003), 2756–2761.

44. J. S. Volek, K. D. Ballard, R. Silvestre, D. A. Judelson, E. E. Quann, C. E. Forsythe, et al., 'Effects of Dietary Carbohydrate Restriction versus Low-Fat Diet on Flow-Mediated Dilation,' *Metabolism* 58 (2009), 1769–1777.

45. J. S. Volek and R. D. Feinman, 'Carbohydrate Restriction Improves the Features of Metabolic Syndrome. Metabolic Syndrome May Be Defined by the Response to Carbohydrate Restriction,' *Nutrition & Metabolism* (London) 2 (2005), 31; J. S. Volek, M. L. Fernandez, R. D. Feinman, and S. D. Phinney, 'Dietary Carbohydrate Restriction Induces a Unique Metabolic State Positively Affecting Atherogenic Dyslipidemia, Fatty Acid Partitioning, and Metabolic Syndrome,' *Progress in Lipid Research* 47 (2008), 307–318.

Chapter 14: Managing Diabetes, aka the Bully Disease

1. S. D. De Ferranti, and N. Rifai, 'C-reactive Protein: A Nontraditional Serum Marker of Cardiovascular Risk,' *Cardiovascular Pathology* 16 (2007), 14–21; P. M. Ridker, 'Inflammatory Biomarkers and Risks of Myocardial Infarction, Stroke, Diabetes, and Total Mortality: Implications for Longevity,' *Nutrition Reviews* 65 (2007), S253–S259.

2. A. D. Pradhan, J. E. Manson, N. Rifai, J. E. Buring, and P. M. Ridker, 'C-reactive Protein, Interleukin 6, and Risk of Developing type 2 Diabetes Mellitus,' *The Journal of the American Medical Association* 286 (2001), 327–334; J. I. Barzilay, L. Abraham, S. R. Heckbert, M. Cushman, L. H. Kuller, H. E. Resnick, et al., 'The Relation of Markers of Inflammation to the Development of Glucose Disorders in the Elderly: The Cardiovascular Health Study,' *Diabetes* 50 (2001), 2384–2389; G. Hu, P. Jousilahti, J. Tuomilehto, R. Antikainen, J. Sundvall, and V. Salomaa, 'Association of Serum C-Reactive Protein Level with Sex-Specific type 2 Diabetes Risk: A Prospective Finnish Study,' *Journal of Clinical Endocrinology & Metabolism* 94 (2009), 2099–2105.

3. B. R. Bistrian, G. L. Blackburn, J. P. Flatt, J. Sizer, N. S. Scrimshaw, and M. Sherman, 'Nitrogen Metabolism and Insulin Requirements in Obese Diabetic Adults on a Protein-Sparing Modified Fast,' *Diabetes* 25 (1976), 494–504.

4. G. Boden, K. Sargrad, C. Homko, M. Mozzoli, and T. P. Stein, 'Effect of a Low-Carbohydrate Diet on Appetite, Blood Glucose Levels, and Insulin Resistance in Obese Patients with type 2 Diabetes,' *Annals of Internal Medicine* 142 (2005), 403–411.

5. M. E. Daly, R. Paisey, R. Paisey, B. A. Millward, C. Eccles, K. Williams, et al., 'Short-Term Effects of Severe Dietary Carbohydrate-Restriction Advice in type 2 Diabetes—A Randomized Controlled Trial,' *Diabetic Medicine* 23 (2006), 15–20.

6. E. C. Westman, W. S. Yancy, Jr., J. C. Mavropoulos, M. Marquart, and J. R. McDuffie, 'The Effect of a Low-Carbohydrate, Ketogenic Diet Versus a Low-Glycemic Index Diet on Glycemic Control in type 2 Diabetes Mellitus,' *Nutrition & Metabolism* (London) 5 (2008), 36.

7. A. Daly, 'Use of Insulin and Weight Gain: Optimizing Diabetes Nutrition Therapy,' *Journal of the American Dietetic Association* 107 (2007), 1386–1393.

8. H. C. Gerstein, M. E. Miller, R. P. Byington, D. C. Goff, Jr., J. T. Bigger, J. B. Buse, et al., 'Effects of Intensive Glucose Lowering in type 2 Diabetes,' *The New England Journal of Medicine* 358 (2008), 2545–2559.

9. N. G. Boule, E. Haddad, G. P. Kenny, G. A. Wells, and R. J. Sigal., 'Effects of Exercise on Glycemic Control and Body Mass in type 2 Diabetes Mellitus: A Meta-analysis of Controlled Clinical Trials,' *The Journal of the American Medical Association* 286 (2001), 1218–1227.

10. J. P. Bantle, J. Wylie-Rosett, A. L. Albright, C. M. Apovian, N. G. Clark, M. J. Franz, et al., 'Nutrition Recommendations and Interventions for Diabetes: A Position Statement of the American Diabetes Association,' *Diabetes Care* 31 suppl. 1 (2008), S61–S78.

Index

About the Authors

DR STEPHEN D PHINNEY has spent 30 years studying diet, exercise, essential fatty acids and inflammation. He has held positions in the United States at the University of Vermont, the University of Minnesota and the University of California at Davis. Following early retirement from U.C. Davis as professor of medicine, he has worked at the leadership level and later as a consultant in nutrition biotechnology. Dr Phinney has published more than 70 papers in the peer-reviewed literature and has several patents. His medical degree is from Stanford University and his PhD in nutritional biochemistry is from MIT. He also did postgraduate training at the University of Vermont and Harvard University.

DR JEFF S VOLEK is currently an associate professor and exercise and nutrition researcher in the Department of Kinesiology at the University of Connecticut in the United States. In the last decade he has published more than 200 peer-reviewed studies, including seminal work on low-carbohydrate diets that points to the Atkins Diet as a powerful tool to lose weight and improve metabolic health. He has provided some of the most convincing evidence that dietary fat, even saturated fat, can be healthy when consumed in the context of a lower-carbohydrate diet.

DR ERIC C WESTMAN is an associate professor of medicine at the Duke University Health System and director of the Duke Lifestyle Medicine Clinic. He combines clinical research and clinical care in lifestyle treatments for obesity, diabetes, and tobacco dependence. He is an internationally known researcher for his work on low-carbohydrate nutrition. He is currently the vice president of the American Society of Bariatric Physicians and a fellow of the Obesity Society and the Society of General Internal Medicine.

YOU'VE READ THE BOOK. NOW EAT IT.

The best way to lose those extra pounds and keep the weight down is to live the Atkins sweet low sugar lifestyle. And the Atkins range of snacks complement the Atkins diet perfectly, providing the ideal snack at each stage of the diet.

The Day Break Bar – *optimal blend of protein and fibre, available in 4 delicious flavours.*

Advantage Bars – *plenty of protein, fibre and a few net carbs, available in 5 flavours.*

Advantage Ready to Drink Shakes – *ideal for a quick start to the day, straight from the fridge.*

Advantage Shake Mix Powder – *just add water, Vanilla and Chocolate flavours.*

Endulge Bars – *just like your favourite chocolate bars, but with less than 2g of sugar – guilt free!*

Also try **Wheat and Rye Crackers**, **Whole Grain Bread Mix** and **Day Break Crunchy Cereal**.

Atkins snacks are available at selected Boots, Tesco, Sainsbury's, and the NutriCentre, and online at Amazon, Avidlite & Lowcarb Megastore.

Sweet • Sexy • Science

Log on to www.atkins.com for downloadable tools such as our carb counter, meal planners, learn about the products, where to buy and how to register for community membership.

ROYAL BOROUGH OF GREENWICH

KT-493-712

Please return by the last date shown

CH PARK	Mandela	
Len clifton	-- AUG 2022	
Lansdowne		
Tudor	-- OCT 2022	
Colleston	Beacon	
Blosson	-- NOV 2022	
Hawes	BILL WALDEN	
	-- MAR 2024	
-- MAR 2022		
Len clifton		
AUG 2022		

How long had it been since she'd touched someone like this?

All that hard flesh Eve had seen on the beach—felt on the bike—pressed back against her fingers as they splayed out across his chest. Across the shadowy eagle that she knew lived there beneath the saturated cotton shirt. Across Marshall's strongly beating heart.

Marshall was right. They weren't going to see each other again. This might be the only chance she had to know what it felt like to have the heat of him pressed against her. To know him. To taste him.

All she had to do was move one finger. Any finger.

She'd never meant to enter some kind of self-imposed physical exile when she'd set off on this odyssey. It had just happened. And before she knew it she'd gone without touching a single person in any way at all for…

She sucked in a tiny breath. All of it. *Eight months.*

Only one way to find out.

Eve trailed her butterfly fingers lightly up to his collarbone. Beyond to the rigid definition of his larynx, which lurched out of touch and then back in again like the scandalous tease it was.

Strong fingers lifted to frame her face—to lift it—and he brought her eyes to his. They simmered, as bottomless as the ocean around them, as he lowered his mouth towards hers.

Dear Reader,

How far would you go to find someone you love? Would you sell your house? Quit your job? Hit the road in a clapped-out bus and pledge to visit every single town in your country until you find them?

A few years ago a close friend of my sister was reported missing, and through my sister's efforts to spread the word about him I fell into the online world of 'The Missing'. Life is completely excruciating for those who love a missing person. There is no closure, limited information, even more limited progress. Everyone's story has unique facets, but the one thing they all have in common is frustration and heartbreak at being so incredibly powerless.

Her Knight in the Outback began with those feelings. With one woman's decision to make finding her missing brother her absolute priority. It should be no surprise to learn that Eve is in a pretty poor psychological state herself when she first meets biker Marshall Sullivan. She's been on the road for months, hunting for her brother, and she's tired, emotionally devastated, but determined to go on.

The last thing she wants or needs is for one gorgeous man to distract her from her mission to find another.

Her Knight in the Outback is a story about a love that saves someone right at the moment they most need rescuing. I hope that you enjoy the very special romance that forms between a broken woman and her knight in shining…leather.

May love always find you.

Nikki Logan xx

HER KNIGHT
IN THE OUTBACK

BY
NIKKI LOGAN

First published in Great Britain 2015
by Mills & Boon, an imprint of Harlequin (UK) Limited,
Eton House, 18-24 Paradise Road, Richmond, Surrey, TW9 1SR

© 2015 Nikki Logan

ISBN: 978-0-263-25761-8

Harlequin (UK) Limited's policy is to use papers that are natural,
renewable and recyclable products and made from wood grown in
sustain   nform
to the l

Printed
by CP

Nikki Logan lives on the edge of a string of wetlands in Western Australia, with her partner and a menagerie of animals. She writes captivating nature-based stories full of romance in descriptive natural environments. She believes the danger and richness of wild places perfectly mirror the passion and risk of falling in love.

Nikki loves to hear from readers
via nikkilogan.com.au or through social media.
Find her on Twitter: @ReadNikkiLogan
and Facebook: NikkiLoganAuthor

Books by Nikki Logan

Mills & Boon® Romance

Their Miracle Twins
Awakened by His Touch

The Larkville Legacy

Slow Dance with the Sheriff

Mills & Boon® Modern Tempted™

How to Get Over Your Ex
My Boyfriend and Other Enemies
His Until Midnight
The Morning After the Night Before

**Visit the author profile page at
millsandboon.co.uk for more titles**

For Mat

Acknowledgements

With enormous gratitude to Dr Richard O'Regan for his help with the pharmaceutical aspects of this story, which were integral to its resolution. And with deepest respect and compassion for the families of 'The Missing'.

CHAPTER ONE

IT WAS MOMENTS like this that Evelyn Read hated. Life-defining moments. Moments when her fears and prejudices reared up before her eyes and confronted her—just like a King Brown snake, surprised while basking on the hot Australian highway.

She squinted at the distant biker limping carefully towards her out of the shimmering heat mirage and curled her fingers more tightly around the steering wheel.

A moment like this one might have taken her brother. Maybe Trav stopped for the wrong stranger; maybe that was where he went when he disappeared all those months ago. Her instincts screamed that she should press down on her accelerator until the man—the danger—was an hour behind her. But a moment like this might have *saved* her brother, too. If a stranger had only been kind enough or brave enough to stop for him. Then maybe Travis would be back with them right now. Safe. Loved.

Instead of alone, scared…or worse.

The fear of never knowing what happened to him tightened her gut the way it always did when she thought too long about this crazy thing she was doing.

The biker limped closer.

Should she listen to her basest instincts and flee, or respond to twenty-four years of social conditioning and help a fellow human being in trouble? There was probably some kind of outback code to be observed, too, but she'd heard too many stories from too many grieving people to be particularly bothered by niceties.

Eve's eyes flicked to the distant motorbike listing on the side of the long, empty road. And then, closer, to the scruffy man now nearing the restored 1956 Bedford bus that was getting her around Australia.

She glanced at her door's lock to make sure it was secure.

The man limped to a halt next to the bus's bifold doors and looked at her expectantly over his full beard. A dagger tattoo poked out from under his dark T-shirt and impenetrable sunglasses hid his eyes—and his intent—from her.

No. This was her home. She'd never open her front door to a total stranger. Especially not hours from the nearest other people.

She signalled him around to the driver's window instead.

He didn't look too impressed, but he limped his way around to her side and she slid the antique window open and forced her voice to be light.

Sociopaths make a decision on whether you're predator or prey in the first few seconds, she remembered from one of the endless missing-person fact sheets she'd read. She was not about to have 'prey' stamped on her forehead.

'Morning,' she breezed, as if this wasn't potentially a very big deal indeed. 'Looks like you're having a bad day.'

'Emu,' he grunted and she got a glimpse of straight teeth and healthy gums.

Stupidly, that reassured her. As if evil wouldn't floss. She twisted around for evidence of a big damaged bird flailing in the scrub after hitting his motorbike. To validate his claim. 'Was it okay?'

'Yeah, I'm fine, thanks.'

That brought her eyes back to his glasses. 'I can see that. But emus don't always come off the best after a road impact.'

As if she'd know…

'Going that fast, it practically went over the top of me as it ran with its flock. It's probably twenty miles from here now, trying to work out how and when it got black paint on its claws.'

He held up his scratched helmet, which had clearly taken an impact. More evidence. She just nodded, not wanting to give an inch more than necessary. He'd probably already summed her up as a bleeding heart over the emu.

One for the prey column.

'Where are you headed?' he asked.

Her radar flashed again at his interest. 'West.'

Duh, since the Bedford was pointing straight at the sun heading for the horizon and there was nothing else out this way *but* west.

'Can I catch a lift to the closest town?'

Was that tetchiness in his voice because she kept foiling him or because hers was the first vehicle to come along in hours and she was stonewalling him on a ride?

She glanced at his crippled bike.

'That'll have to stay until I can get back here with a truck,' he said, following her glance.

There was something in the sag of his shoulders and the way he spared his injured leg that reassured her even as the beard and tattoo and leather did not. He'd clearly come off his bike hard. Maybe he was more injured than she could see?

But the stark reality was that her converted bus only had the one seat up front—hers. 'That's my home back there,' she started.

'So…?'

'So, I don't know you.'

Yep. That was absolutely the insult his hardened lips said it was. But she was not letting a stranger back there. Into her world.

'It's only an hour to the border.' He sighed. 'I'll stand on your steps until Eucla.'

Right next to her. Where he could do anything and she couldn't do a thing to avoid it.

'An hour by motorbike, maybe. We take things a little more easy in this old girl. It'll take at least twice that.'

'Fine. I'll stand for two hours, then.'

Or she could just leave him here and send help back. But the image of Trav, lost and in need of help while someone drove off and left him injured and alone, flitted through her mind.

If someone had just been brave...

'I don't know you,' she wavered.

'Look, I get it. A woman travelling alone, big scary biker. You're smart to be cautious but the reality is help might not be able to get to me today so if you leave me here I could be here all night. Freezing my ass off.'

She fumbled for her phone.

His shaggy head shook slightly. 'If we had signal don't you think I'd have used it?'

Sure enough, her phone had diminished to *SOS only.* And as bad as that motorbike looked, it wasn't exactly an emergency.

'Just until we get signal, then?' he pressed, clearly annoyed at having to beg. 'Come on, please?'

How far could that be? They were mostly through the desert now, coming out on the western side of Australia. Where towns and people and telecommunications surely had to exist.

'Have you got some ID?'

He blinked at her and then reached back into his jeans for his wallet.

'No. Not a licence. That could be fake. Got any photos of you?'

He moved slowly, burdened by his incredulity, but pulled his phone out and flicked through a few screens. Then he pressed it up against Eve's window glass.

A serious face looked back at her. Well groomed and in a business shirt. Pretty respectable, really. Almost cute.

Pffff. 'That's not you.'

'Yeah, it is.'

She peered at him again. 'No, it's not.'

It might have been a stock photo off the Internet for all

she knew. The sort of search result she used to get when she googled 'corporate guy' for some design job.

'Oh, for pity's sake…'

He flicked through a few more and found another one, this time more bearded. But nothing like the hairy beast in front of her. Her hesitation obviously spoke volumes so he pushed his sunglasses up onto his head, simultaneously revealing grey eyes and slightly taming his rusty blond hair.

Huh. Okay, maybe it was him.

'Licence?'

A breathed bad word clearly tangled in the long hairs of his moustache but he complied—eventually—and slapped that against the window, too.

Marshall Sullivan.

She held up her phone and took a photo of him through the glass, with his licence in the shot.

'What's that for?'

'Insurance.'

'I just need a lift. That's it. I have no interest in you beyond that.'

'Easy for you to say.'

Her thumbs got busy texting it to both her closest friend and her father in Melbourne. Just to cover bases. Hard to know if the photo would make them more or less confident in this dusty odyssey she was on, but she had to send it to someone.

The grey eyes she could now see rolled. 'We have no signal.'

'The moment we do it will go.'

She hit Send and let the phone slip back down into its little spot on her dash console.

'You have some pretty serious trust issues, lady, you know that?'

'And this is potentially the oldest con in the book. Broken-down vehicle on remote outback road.' She glanced at his helmet and the marks that could be emu claws. 'I'll admit your story has some pretty convincing details—'

'Because it's the truth.'

'—but I'm travelling alone and I'm not going to take any chances. And I'm not letting you in here with me, sorry.' The cab was just too small and risky. 'You'll have to ride in the back.'

'What about all the biker germs I'm going to get all over your stuff?' he grumbled.

'You want a lift or not?'

Those steady eyes glared out at her. 'Yeah. I do.'

And then, as though he couldn't help himself, he grudgingly rattled off a thankyou.

Okay, so it had to be safer to let him loose in the back than have him squished here in the front with her. Her mind whizzed through all the things he might get up to back there but none of them struck her as bad as what he could do up front if he wasn't really who he said he was.

Or even if he was.

Biker boy and his helmet limped back towards the belongings piled on the side of the road next to his disabled bike. Leather jacket, pair of satchels, a box of mystery equipment.

She ground the gears starting the Bedford back up, but rolled up behind him and, as soon as his arms were otherwise occupied with his own stuff, she unlocked the bus and mouthed through the glass of her window. 'Back doors.'

Sullivan limped to the back of the Bedford, lurched it as he climbed in and then slammed himself in there with all her worldly possessions.

Two hours…

'Come on, old chook,' she murmured to the decades-old bus. 'Let's push it a bit, eh?'

Marshall groped around for a light switch but only found a thick fabric curtain. He pulled it back with a swish and light flooded into the darkened interior of the bus. Something extraordinary unfolded in front of him.

He'd seen converted buses before but they were usually pretty daggy. Kind of worn and soulless and vinyl. But this…

This was rich, warm and natural; nothing at all like the hostile lady up front.

It was like a little cottage in some forest. All timber and plush rugs in dark colours. Small, but fully appointed with kitchenette and living space, flat-screen TV, fridge and a sofa. Even potted palms. Compact and long but all there, like one of those twenty-square-metre, fold-down and pull-out apartments they sold in flat packs. At the far end—the driving end—a closed door that must lead to the only absent feature of the vehicle, the bed.

And suddenly he got a sense of Little Miss Hostile's reluctance to let him back here. It was like inviting a total stranger right into your bedroom. Smack bang in the middle of absolutely nowhere.

The bus lurched as she tortured it back up to speed and Marshall stumbled down onto the sofa built into the left side of the vehicle. Not as comfortable as his big eight-seater in the home theatre of his city apartment, but infinitely better than the hard gravel he'd been polishing with his butt for the couple of hours since the bird strike.

Stupid freaking emu. It could have killed them both.

It wasn't as if a KTM 1190 was a stealth unit but maybe, at the speed the emu had been going, the air rushing past its ears was just as noisy as an approaching motorbike. And then their fates had collided. Literally.

He sagged down against the sofa back and resisted the inclination to examine his left foot. Sometimes boots were the only things that kept fractured bones together after bike accidents so he wasn't keen to take it off unless he was bleeding to death. In fact, particularly if he was bleeding to death because something told him the hostess-with-the-leastest would not be pleased if he bled out all over her timber floor. But he could at least elevate it. That was generally good for what ailed you. He dragged one of his satchels up onto the sofa, turned and stacked a couple of the bouncy, full pillows down the opposite end and then swung his abused limb up onto it, lying out the full length of the sofa.

'Oh, yeah…' Half words, half groan. All good.

He loved his bike. He loved the speed. He loved that direct relationship with the country you had when there was no car between you and it. And he loved the freedom from everything he'd found touring that country.

But he really didn't love how fragile he'd turned out to be when something went wrong at high speed.

As stacks went, it had been pretty controlled. Especially considering the fishtail he'd gone into as the mob of emu shot past and around him. But even a controlled slide hurt—him and the bike—and once the adrenaline wore off and the birds disappeared over the dusty horizon, all he'd been left with was the desert silence and the pain.

And no phone signal.

Normally that wouldn't bother him. There really couldn't be enough alone time in this massive country, as far as he was concerned. If you travelled at the right time of year—and that would be the *wrong* time of year for tourists—you could pretty much have most outback roads to yourself. He was free to do whatever he wanted, wear whatever he wanted, be as hairy as he wanted, shower whenever he wanted. Or not. He'd given up caring what people thought of him right about the time he'd stopped caring about people.

Ancient history.

And life was just simpler that way.

The stoic old Bedford finally shifted into top gear and the rattle of its reconditioned engine evened out to a steady hum, vibrating under his skin as steadily as his bike did. He took the rare opportunity to do what he could never do when at the controls: he closed his eyes and let the hum take him.

Two hours, she'd said. He could be up on his feet with her little home fully restored before she even made it from the front of the bus back to the rear doors. As if no one had ever been there.

Two hours to rest. Recover. And enjoy the roads he loved from a more horizontal perspective.

'Who's been sleeping in my bed?' Eve muttered as she stood looking at the bear of a man fast asleep on her little sofa.

What was this—some kind of reverse Goldilocks thing?

She cleared her throat. Nothing. He didn't even shift in his sleep.

'Mr Sullivan?'

Nada.

For the first time, it occurred to her that maybe this wasn't sleep; maybe this was coma. Maybe he'd been injured more than either of them had realised. She hauled herself up into the back of the bus and crossed straight to his side, all thoughts of dangerous tattooed men cast aside. Her fingertips brushed below the hairy tangle of his jaw.

Steady and strong. And warm.

Phew.

'Mr Sullivan,' she said, louder. Those dark blond brows twitched just slightly and something moved briefly behind his eyelids, so she pressed her advantage. 'We're here.'

Her gaze went to his elevated foot and then back up to where his hands lay, folded, across the T-shirt over his midsection. Rather nice hands. Soft and manicured despite the patches of bike grease from his on-road repairs.

The sort of hands you'd see in a magazine.

Which was ridiculous. How many members of motorcycle clubs sidelined in a bit of casual hand modelling?

She forced her focus back up to his face and opened her lips to call his name a little louder, but, where before there was only the barest movement behind his lids, now they were wide open and staring straight at her. This close, with the light streaming in from the open curtains, she saw they weren't grey at all—or not *just* grey, at least. The pewter irises were flecked with rust that neatly matched the tarnished blond of his hair and beard, particularly concentrated around his pupils.

She'd never seen eyes like them. She immediately thought of the burnt umber coastal rocks of the far north, where they slid down to pale, clean ocean. And where she'd started her journey eight months ago.

'We're here,' she said, irritated at her own breathlessness. And at being caught checking him out.

He didn't move, but maybe that was because she was leaning so awkwardly over him from all the pulse-taking.

'Where's here?' he croaked.

She pushed back onto her heels and dragged her hands back from the heat of his body. 'The border. You'll have to get up while they inspect the bus.'

They took border security seriously here on the invisible line between South Australia and Western Australia. Less about gun-running and drug-trafficking and more about fruit flies and honey. Quarantine was king when agriculture was your primary industry.

Sullivan twisted gingerly into an upright position, then carefully pulled himself to his feet and did his best to put the cushions back where they'd started. Not right, but he got points for the effort.

So he hadn't been raised by leather-clad wolves, then.

He bundled up his belongings, tossed them to the ground outside the bus and lowered himself carefully down.

'How is your leg?' Eve asked.

'I'll live.'

Okay. Man of few words. Clearly, he'd spent too much time in his own company.

The inspection team made quick work of hunting over every inch of her converted bus and Sullivan's saddlebags. She'd become proficient at dumping or eating anything that was likely to get picked up at the border and so, this time, the team only found one item to protest—a couple of walnuts not yet consumed.

Into the bin they went.

She lifted her eyes towards Sullivan, deep in discussion with one of the border staff who had him in one ear and their phone on the other. Arranging assistance for his crippled bike, presumably. As soon as they were done, he limped back towards her and hiked his bags up over his shoulder.

'Thanks for the ride,' he said as though the effort half choked him.

'You don't need to go into Eucla?' Just as she'd grown used to him.

'They're sending someone out to grab me and retrieve my bike.'

'Oh. Great that they can do it straight away.'

'Country courtesy.'

As opposed to her lack of...? 'Well, good luck with your—'

It was then she realised she had absolutely no idea what he was doing out here, other than hitting random emus. In all her angsting out on the deserted highway, she really hadn't stopped to wonder, let alone ask.

'—with your travels.'

His nod was brisk and businesslike. 'Cheers.'

And then he was gone, back towards the border security office and the little café that catered for people delayed while crossing. Marshall Sullivan didn't seem half so scary here in a bustling border stop, though his beard was no less bushy and the ink dagger under his skin no less menacing. All the what-ifs she'd felt two hours ago on that long empty road hobbled away from her as he did.

And she wondered how she'd possibly missed the first time how well his riding leathers fitted him.

CHAPTER TWO

IT WAS THE raised voices that first got Marshall's attention. Female, anxious and angry, almost swallowed up by drunk, male and belligerent.

'Stop!'

The fact a gaggle of passers-by had formed a wide, unconscious circle around the spectacle in the middle of town was the only reason he sauntered closer instead of running on his nearly healed leg. If something bad was happening, he had to assume someone in the handful of people assembled would have intervened. Or at least cried out. Him busting in to an unknown situation, half-cocked, was no way to defuse what was clearly an escalating situation.

Instead, he insinuated himself neatly into the heart of the onlookers and nudged his way through to the front until he could get his eyeballs on things. A flutter of paper pieces rained down around them as the biggest of the men tore something up.

'You put another one up, I'm just going to rip it down,' he sneered.

The next thing he saw was the back of a woman's head. Dark, travel-messy ponytail. Dwarfed by the men she was facing but not backing down.

And all too familiar.

Little Miss Hostile. Winning friends and influencing people —as usual.

'This is a public noticeboard,' she asserted up at the human mountain, foolishly undeterred by his size.

'For Norseman residents,' he spat. 'Not for blow-ins from the east.'

'Public,' she challenged. 'Do I need to spell it out for you?'

Wow. Someone really needed to give her some basic training in conflict resolution. The guy was clearly a xenophobe and drunk. Calling him stupid in front of a crowd full of locals wasn't the fastest way out of her predicament.

She shoved past him and used a staple gun to pin up another flier.

He'd seen the same poster peppering posts and walls in Madura, Cocklebiddy and Balladonia. Every point along the remote desert highway that could conceivably hold a person. And a sign. Crisp and new against all the bleached, frayed ones from years past.

'Stop!'

Yeah, that guy wasn't going to stop. And now the McTanked Twins were also getting in on the act.

Goddammit.

Marshall pushed out into the centre of the circle. He raised his voice the way he used to in office meetings when they became unruly. Calm but intractable. 'Okay, show's over, people.'

The crowd turned their attention to him, like a bunch of cattle. So did the three drunks. But they weren't so intoxicated they didn't pause at the sight of his beard and tattoos. Just for a moment.

The moment he needed.

'Howzabout we find somewhere else for those?' he suggested straight to Little Miss Hostile, neatly relieving her of the pile of posters with one hand and the staple gun with his other. 'There are probably better locations in town.'

She spun around and glared at him in the heartbeat before she recognised him. 'Give me those.'

He ignored her and spoke to the crowd. 'All done, people. Let's get moving.'

They parted for him as he pushed back through, his hands full of her property. She had little choice but to pursue him.

'Those are mine!'

'Let's have this conversation around the corner,' he gritted back and down towards her.

But just as they'd cleared the crowd, the big guy couldn't help himself.

'Maybe he's gone missing to get away from you!' he called.

A shocked gasp covered the sound of small female feet pivoting on the pavement and she marched straight back towards the jeering threesome.

Marshall shoved the papers under his arm and sprinted after her, catching her just before she re-entered the eye of the storm. All three men had lined up in it, ready. Eager. He curled his arms around her and dragged her back, off her feet, and barked just one word in her ear.

'Don't!'

She twisted and lurched and swore the whole way but he didn't loosen his hold until the crowd and the jeering laughter of the drunks were well behind them.

'Put me down,' she struggled. 'Ass!'

'The only ass around here is the one I just saved.'

'I've dealt with rednecks before.'

'Yeah, you were doing a bang-up job.'

'I have every right to put my posters up.'

'No argument. But you could have just walked away and then come back and done it in ten minutes when the drunks were gone.'

'But there were thirty people there.'

'None of whom were making much of an effort to help you.' In case she hadn't noticed.

'I didn't want their help,' she spat, spinning back to face him. 'I wanted their attention.'

What was this—some kind of performance art thing? 'Come again?'

'Thirty people would have read my poster, remembered it.

The same people that probably would have passed it by without noticing, otherwise.'

'Are you serious?'

She snatched the papers and staple gun back from him and clutched them to her heaving chest. 'Perfectly. You think I'm new to this?'

'I really don't know what to think. You treated me like a pariah because of a bit of leather and ink, but you were quite happy to face off against the Beer Gut Brothers, back there.'

'It got *attention*.'

'So does armed robbery. Are you telling me the bank is on your to-do list in town?'

She glared at him. 'You don't understand.'

And then he was looking at the back of her head again as she turned and marched away from him without so much as a goodbye. Let alone a thankyou.

He cursed under his breath.

'Enlighten me,' he said, catching up with her and ignoring the protest of his aching leg.

'Why should I?'

'Because I just risked my neck entering that fray to help you and that means you owe me one.'

'I rescued you out on the highway. I'd say that makes us even.'

Infuriating woman. He slammed on the brakes. 'Fine. Whatever.'

Her momentum carried her a few metres further but then she spun back. 'Did you look at the poster?'

'I've been looking at them since the border.'

'And?'

'And what?'

'What's on it?'

His brows forked. What the hell *was* on it? 'Guy's face. Bunch of words.' And a particularly big one in red. MISSING. 'It's a missing-person poster.'

'Bingo. And you've been looking at them since the border

but can't tell me what he looked like or what his name was or what it was about.' She took two steps closer. 'That's why getting their attention was so valuable.'

Realisation washed through him and he felt like a schmuck for parachuting in and rescuing her like some damsel in distress. 'Because they'll remember it. You.'

'Him!' But her anger didn't last long. It seemed to desert her like the adrenaline in both their bodies, leaving her flat and exhausted. 'Maybe.'

'What do you do—start a fight in every town you go to?'

'Whatever it takes.'

Cars went by with stereos thumping.

'Listen…' Suddenly, Little Miss Hostile had all new layers. And most of them were laden with sadness. 'I'm sorry if you had that under control. Where I come from you don't walk past a woman crying out in the street.'

Actually, that wasn't strictly true because he came from a pretty rough area and sometimes the best thing to do was keep walking. But while his mother might have raised her kids like that, his grandparents certainly hadn't. And he, at least, had learned from their example even if his brother, Rick, hadn't.

Dark eyes studied him. 'That must get you into a lot of trouble,' she eventually said.

True enough.

'Let me buy you a drink. Give those guys some time to clear out and then I'll help you put the posters up.'

'I don't need your help. Or your protection.'

'Okay, but I'd like to take a proper look at that poster.'

He regarded her steadily as uncertainty flooded her expression. The same that he'd seen out on the highway. 'Or is the leather still bothering you?'

Indecision flooded her face and her eyes flicked from his beard to his eyes, then down to his lips and back again.

'No. You haven't robbed or murdered me yet. I think a few minutes together in a public place will be fine.'

She turned and glanced down the street where a slight *doof-*

doof issued from an architecturally classic Aussie hotel. Then her voice filled with warning. 'Just one.'

It was hard not to smile. Her stern little face was like a daisy facing up to a cyclone.

'If I was going to hurt you I've had plenty of opportunity. I don't really need to get you liquored up.'

'Encouraging start to the conversation.'

'You know my name,' he said, moving his feet in a pubward direction. 'I don't know yours.'

She regarded him steadily. Then stuck out the hand with the staple gun clutched in it. 'Evelyn Read. Eve.'

He shook half her hand and half the tool. 'What do you like to drink, Eve?'

'I don't. Not in public. But you go ahead.'

A teetotaller in an outback pub.

Well, this should be fun.

Eve trusted Marshall Sullivan with her posters while she used the facilities. When she came back, he'd smoothed out all the crinkles in the top one and was studying it.

'Brother?' he said as she slid into her seat.

'What makes you say that?'

He tapped the surname on the poster where it had *Travis James Read* in big letters.

'He could be my husband.' She shrugged.

His eyes narrowed. 'Same dark hair. Same shape eyes. He looks like you.'

Yeah, he did. Everyone thought so. 'Trav is my little brother.'

'And he's missing?'

God, she hated this bit. The pity. The automatic assumption that something bad had happened. Hard enough not letting herself think it every single day without having the thought planted back in her mind by strangers at every turn.

Virtual strangers.

Though, at least this one did her the courtesy of not referring to Travis in the past tense. Points for that.

'Missing a year next week, actually.'

'Tough anniversary. Is that why you're out here? Is this where he was last seen?'

She lifted her gaze back to his. 'No. In Melbourne.'

'So what brings you out west?'

'I ran out of towns on the east coast.'

Blond brows lowered. 'You've lost me.'

'I'm visiting every town in the country. Looking for him. Putting up notices. Doing the legwork.'

'I assumed you were just on holidays or something.'

'No. This is my job.'

Now. Before that she'd been a pretty decent graphic designer for a pretty decent marketing firm. Until she'd handed in her notice.

'Putting up posters is your job?'

'Finding my brother.' The old defensiveness washed through her. 'Is anything more important?'

His confusion wasn't new. He wasn't the first person not to understand what she was doing. By far. Her own father didn't even get it; he just wanted to grieve Travis's absence as though he were dead. To accept he was gone.

She was light-years and half a country away from being ready to accept such a thing. She and Trav had been so close. If he was dead, wouldn't she feel it?

'So…what, you just drive every highway in the country pinning up notices?'

'Pretty much. Trying to trigger a memory in someone's mind.'

'And it's taken you a year to do the east coast?'

'About eight months. Though I started up north.' And that was where she'd finish.

'What happened before that?'

Guilt hammered low in her gut for those missing couple of months before she'd realised how things really were. How she'd played nice and sat on her hands while the police seemed to achieve less and less. Maybe if she'd started sooner—

'I trusted the system.'

'But the authorities didn't find him?'

'There are tens of thousands of missing people every year. I just figured that the only people who could make Trav priority number one were his family.'

'That many? Really?'

'Teens. Kids. Women. Most are located pretty quickly.'

But ten per cent weren't.

His eyes tracked down to the birthdate on the poster. 'Healthy eighteen-year-old males don't really make it high up the priority list?'

A small fist formed in her throat. 'Not when there's no immediate evidence of foul play.'

And even if they maybe weren't entirely healthy, psychologically. But Travis's depression was hardly unique amongst *The Missing* and his anxiety attacks were longstanding enough that the authorities dismissed them as irrelevant. As if a bathroom cabinet awash with mental health medicines wasn't relevant.

A young woman with bright pink hair badly in need of a recolour brought Marshall's beer and Eve's lime and bitters and sloshed them on the table.

'That explains the bus,' he said. 'It's very…homey.'

'It is my home. Mine went to pay for the trip.'

'You sold your house?'

Her chin kicked up. 'And resigned from my job. I can't afford to be distracted by having to earn an income while I cover the country.'

She waited for the inevitable judgment.

'That's quite a commitment. But it makes sense.'

Such unconditional acceptance threw her. Everyone else she'd told thought she was foolish. Or plain crazy. Implication: like her brother. No one just…nodded.

'That's it? No opinion? No words of wisdom?'

His eyes lifted to hers. 'You're a grown woman. You did what you needed to do. And I assume it was your asset to dispose of.'

She scrutinised him again. The healthy, unmarked skin under the shaggy beard. The bright eyes. The even teeth.

'What's your story?' she asked.

'No story. I'm travelling.'

'You're not a bikie.' Statement, not question.

'Not everyone with a motorbike belongs in an outlaw club,' he pointed out.

'You look like a bikie.'

'I wear leather because it's safest when you get too intimate with asphalt. I have a beard because one of the greatest joys in life is not having to shave, and so I indulge that when I'm travelling alone.'

She glanced down to where the dagger protruded from his T-shirt sleeve. 'And the tattoo?'

His eyes immediately darkened. 'We were all young and impetuous once.'

'Who's Christine?'

'Christine's not relevant to this discussion.'

Bang. Total shutdown. 'Come on, Marshall. I aired my skeleton.'

'Something tells me you air it regularly. To anyone who'll listen.'

Okay, this time the criticism was unmistakable. She pushed more upright in her chair. 'You were asking the questions, if you recall.'

'Don't get all huffy. We barely know each other. Why would I spill my guts to a stranger?'

'I don't know. Why would you rescue a stranger on the street?'

'Not wanting to see you beaten to a pulp and not wanting to share my dirty laundry are very different things.'

'Oh, Christine's dirty laundry?'

His lips thinned even further and he pushed away from the table. 'Thanks for the drink. Good luck with your brother.'

She shot to her feet, too. 'Wait. Marshall?'

He stopped and turned back slowly.

'I'm sorry. I guess I'm out of practice with people,' she said.

'You're not kidding.'

'Where are you staying?'

'In town.'

Nice and non-specific. 'I'm a bit… I get a bit tired of eating in the bus. On my own. Can I interest you in something to eat, later?'

'I don't think so.'

Walk away, Eve. That would be the smart thing to do.

'I'll change the subject. Not my brother. Not your…' *Not your Christine?* 'We can talk about places we've been. Favourite sights.' Her voice petered out.

His eyebrows folded down over his eyes briefly and disguised them from her view. But he finally relented. 'There's a café across the street from my motel. End of this road.'

'Sounds good.'

She didn't usually eat out, to save money, but then she didn't usually have the slightest hint of company either. One dinner wouldn't kill her. Alone with a stranger. Across the road from his motel room.

'It's not a date, though,' she hastened to add.

'No.' The moustache twisted up on the left. 'It's not.'

And as he and his leather pants sauntered back out of the bar, she felt like an idiot. An adolescent idiot. *Of course* this was not a date and *of course* he wouldn't have considered it such. Hairy, lone-wolf types who travelled the country on motorbikes probably didn't stand much on ceremony when it came to women. Or bother with dates.

She'd only mentioned a meal at all because she felt bad that she'd pressed an obvious sore point with him after he'd shown her nothing but interest and acceptance about Travis.

facepalm

Her brother's favourite saying flittered through her memory and never seemed more appropriate. Hopefully, a few hours and a good shower from now she could be a little more socially appropriate and a lot less hormonal.

Inexplicably so.

Unwashed biker types were definitely not her thing, no matter how nice their smiles. Normally, the *eau de sweaty man* that littered towns in the Australian bush flared her nostrils. But as Marshall Sullivan had hoisted her up against his body out in the street she'd definitely responded to the powerful circle of his hold, the hard heat of his chest and the warmth of his hissed words against her ear.

Even though it came with the tickle of his substantial beard against her skin.

She was *so* not a beard woman.

A man who travelled the country alone was almost certainly doing it for a reason. Running from something or someone. Dropping out of society. Hiding from the authorities. Any number of mysterious and dangerous things.

Or maybe Marshall Sullivan was just as socially challenged as she was.

Maybe that was why she had a sudden and unfathomable desire to sit across a table from the man again.

'See you at seven-thirty, then,' she called after him.

Eve's annoyance at herself for being late—and at caring about that—turned into annoyance at Marshall Sullivan for being even later. What, had he got lost crossing the street?

Her gaze scanned the little café diner as she entered—over the elderly couple with a stumpy candle, past the just-showered Nigel No Friends reading a book and the two men arguing over the sports pages. But as her eyes grazed back around to the service counter, they stumbled over the hands wrapped around *Nigel*'s battered novel. Beautiful hands.

She stepped closer. 'Marshall?'

Rust-flecked eyes glanced up to her. And then he pushed to his feet. To say he was a changed man without the beard would have been an understatement. He was transformed. His hair hadn't been cut but it was slicked back either with product or he truly had just showered. But his face…

Free of the overgrown blondish beard and moustache, his eyes totally stole focus, followed only by his smooth broad forehead. She'd always liked an unsullied forehead. Reliable somehow.

He slid a serviette into the book to mark his place and closed it.

She glanced at the cover. *'Gulliver's Travels?'*

Though what she really wanted to say was…*You shaved?*

'I carry a few favourites around with me in my pack.'

She slid in opposite him, completely unable to take her eyes off his new face. At a loss to reconcile it as the under layer of all that sweat, dust and helmet hair she'd encountered out on the road just a few days ago. 'What makes it a favourite?'

He thought about that for a bit. 'The journeying. It's very human. And Gulliver is a constant reminder that perspective is everything in life.'

Huh. She'd just enjoyed it for all the little people.

They fell to silence.

'You shaved,' she finally blurted.

'I did.'

'For dinner?' Dinner that wasn't a date.

His neatly groomed head shook gently. 'I do that periodically. Take it off and start again. Even symbols of liberty need maintenance.'

'That's what it means to you? Freedom?'

'Isn't that what the Bedford means to you?'

Freedom? No. Sanity, yes. 'The bus is just transport and accommodation conveniently bundled.'

'You forget I've seen inside it. That's not convenience. That's sanctuary.'

Yeah…it was, really. But she didn't know him well enough to open up to that degree.

'I bought the Bedford off this old carpenter after his wife died. He couldn't face travelling any more without her.'

'I wonder if he knows what he's missing.'

'Didn't you just say perspective was everything?'

'True enough.'

A middle-aged waitress came bustling over, puffing, as though six people at once was the most she'd seen in a week. She took their orders from the limited menu and bustled off again.

One blond brow lifted. 'You carb-loading for a marathon?'

'You've seen the stove in the Bedford. I can only cook the basics in her. Every now and again I like to take advantage of a commercial kitchen's deep-fryer.'

Plus, boiling oil would kill anything that might otherwise not get past the health code. There was nothing worse than being stuck in a small town, throwing your guts up. Unless it was being stuck on the side of the road between small towns and kneeling in the roadside gravel.

'So, you know how I'm funding my way around the country,' she said. 'How are you doing it?'

He stared at her steadily. 'Guns and drugs.'

'Ha-ha.'

'That's what you thought when you saw me. Right?'

'I saw a big guy on a lonely road trying really hard to get into my vehicle. What would you have done?'

Those intriguing eyes narrowed just slightly but then flicked away. 'I'm out here working. Like you. Going from district to district.'

'Working for who?'

'Federal Government.'

'Ooh, the Feds. That sounds much more exciting than it probably is. What department?'

He took a long swig of his beer before answering. 'Meteorology.'

She stared. 'You're a *weatherman*?'

'Right. I stand in front of a green screen every night and read maximums and minimums.'

Her smile broadened. 'You're a weatherman.'

He sagged back in his chair and spoke as if he'd heard this one time too many. 'Meteorology is a science.'

'You don't look like a scientist.' Definitely not before and, even clean shaven, Marshall was still too muscular and tat-tooed.

'Would it help if I was in a lab coat and glasses?'

'Yes.' Because the way he packed out his black T-shirt was the least nerdy thing she'd ever seen. 'So why are my taxes funding your trip around the country, exactly?'

'You're not earning. You don't pay taxes.'

The man had a point. 'Why are you out here, then?'

'I'm auditing the weather stations. I check them, report on their condition.'

Well, that explained the hands. 'I thought you were this free spirit on two wheels. You're an auditor.'

His lips tightened. 'Something tells me that's a step down from weatherman in your eyes.'

She got stuck into her complimentary bread roll, buttering and biting into it. 'How many stations are there?'

'Eight hundred and ninety-two.'

'And they send one man?' Surely they had locals that could check to make sure possums hadn't moved into their million-dollar infrastructure.

'I volunteered to do the whole run. Needed the break.'

From...? But she'd promised not to ask. They were sup-posed to be talking about travel highlights. 'Where was the most remote station?'

'Giles. Seven hundred and fifty clicks west of Alice. Up in the Gibson Desert.'

Alice Springs. Right smack bang in the middle of their mas-sive island continent. 'Where did you start?'

'Start and finish in Perth.'

A day and a half straight drive from here. 'Is Perth home?'

'Sydney.'

She visualised the route he must have taken clockwise around the country from the west. 'So you're nearly done, then?'

His laugh drew the eyes of the other diners. 'Yeah. If two-thirds of the weather stations weren't in the bottom third of the state.'

'Do you get to look around? Or is it all work?'

He shrugged. 'Some places I skip right through. Others I linger. I have some flexibility.'

Eve knew exactly what that was like. Some towns whispered to you like a lover. Others yelled at you to go. She tended to move on quickly from those.

'Favourites so far?'

And he was off… Talking about the places that had captivated him most. The prehistoric, ferny depths of the Claustral Canyon, cave-diving in the crystal-clear ponds on South Australia's limestone coast, the soul-restoring solidity of Katherine Gorge in Australia's north.

'And the run over here goes without saying.'

'The Nullabor?' Pretty striking with its epic treeless stretches of desert but not the most memorable place she could recall.

'The Great Australian Bight,' he clarified.

She just blinked at him.

'You got off the highway on the way over, right? Turned for the coast?'

'My focus is town to town.'

He practically gaped. 'One of the most spectacular natural wonders in the world was just a half-hour drive away.'

'And half an hour back. That was an hour sooner I could have made it to the next town.'

His brows dipped over grey eyes. 'You've got to get out more.'

'I'm on the job.'

'Yeah, me, too, but you have to live as well. What about weekends?'

The criticism rankled. 'Not all of us are on the cushy public servant schedule. An hour—a day—could mean the difference between running across someone who knew Travis and not.'

Or even running into Trav himself.

'What if they came through an hour after you left, and pausing to look at something pretty could have meant your paths crossed?'

Did he think she hadn't tortured herself with those thoughts late at night? The endless what-ifs?

'An hour afterwards and they'll see a poster. An hour before and they'd have no idea their shift buddy is a missing person.' At least that was what she told herself. Sternly.

Marshall blinked at her.

'You don't understand.' How could he?

'Wouldn't it be faster to just email the posters around the country? Ask the post offices to put them up for you.'

'It's not just about the posters. It's about talking to people. Hunting down leads. Making an impression.'

Hoping to God the impression would stick.

'The kind you nearly made this afternoon?'

'Whatever it takes.'

Their meals arrived and the next minute was filled with making space on the table and receiving their drinks.

'Anyway, weren't we supposed to be talking about something else?' Eve said brightly, crunching into a chip. 'Where are you headed next?'

'Up to Kalgoorlie, then Southern Cross.'

North. Complete opposite to her.

'You?' His gaze was neutral enough.

'Esperance. Ravensthorpe. With a side trip out to Israelite Bay.' Jeez—why didn't she just draw him her route on a serviette? 'I'm getting low on posters after the Nullabor run. Need an MP's office.'

His newly groomed head tipped.

'MP's offices are obliged by law to print missing-person posters on request,' she explained. 'And there's one in Esperance.'

'Convenient.'

She glared at her chicken. 'It's the least they could do.'

And pretty much all they did. Though they were usually carefully sympathetic.

'It must be hard,' he murmured between mouthfuls. 'Hitting brick walls everywhere you go.'

'I'd rather hit them out here than stuck back in Melbourne. At least I can be productive here.'

Sitting at home and relying on others to do something to find her brother had nearly killed her.

'Did you leave a big family behind?'

Instantly her mind flashed to her father's grief-stricken face as the only person he had left in the world drove off towards the horizon. 'Just my dad.'

'No mum?'

She sat up straighter in her seat. If Christine-of-the-dagger was off the table for discussion, her drunk mother certainly was. Clearly, the lines in her face were as good as a barometric map. Because Marshall let the subject well and truly drop.

'Well, guess this is our first and last dinner, then,' he said cheerfully, toasting her with a forkful of mashed potato and peas. There was nothing more in that than pure observation. Nothing enough that she felt confident in answering without worrying it would sound like an invitation.

'You never know, we might bump into each other again.'

But, really, how likely was that once they headed off towards opposite points on the compass? The only reason they'd met up this once was because there was only one road in and out of the south half of this vast state and he'd crashed into an emu right in the middle of it.

Thoughtful eyes studied her face, then turned back to his meal.

'So you're not from Sydney, originally?'

Marshall pushed his empty plate away and groaned inwardly. Who knew talking about nothing could be so tiring? This had to be the greatest number of words he'd spoken to anyone in weeks. But it was his fault as much as hers. No dag-

ger tattoo and no missing brother. That was what he'd stipu-
lated. She'd held up her end of the bargain, even though she
was clearly itching to know more.

Precisely why he didn't do dinners with women.

Conversation.

He'd much rather get straight to the sex part. Although that
was clearly off the table with Eve. So it really made a man wonder why the heck he'd said yes to Eve's 'not a date' invitation.
Maybe even *he* got lonely.

And maybe they were now wearing long coats in Hades.

'Brisbane.'

'How old were you when you moved?' she chatted on, oblivious to the rapid congealing of his thoughts. Oblivious to the
dangerous territory she'd accidentally stumbled into. Thoughts
of his brother, their mother and how tough he'd found Sydney
as an adolescent.

'Twelve.'

The word squeezed past his suddenly tight throat. The logical part of him knew it was just polite conversation, but the
part of him that was suddenly as taut as a crossbow loaded a
whole lot more onto her innocent chatter. Twelve was a crap
age to be yanked away from your friends and the school where
you were finding your feet and thrust into one of the poorest
suburbs of one of the biggest cities in the country. But—for
the woman who'd only pumped out a second son for the public benefits—moving states to chase a more generous single-
parent allowance was a no-brainer. No matter who it disrupted.

Not that any of that money had ever found its way to him
and Rick. They were just a means to an end.

'What was that like?'

Being your mother's meal ticket or watching your older
brother forge himself a career as the local drug-mover?

'It was okay.'

Uh-oh…here it came. Verbal shutdown. Probably just as
well, given the direction his mind was going.

She watched him steadily, those dark eyes knowing something was up even if she didn't know exactly what. 'Uh-huh…'

Which was code for *Your turn next, Oscar Wilde*. But he couldn't think of a single thing to say, witty or otherwise. So he folded his serviette and gave his chair the slightest of backward pushes.

'Well…'

'What just happened?' Eve asked, watching him with curiosity but not judgment. And not moving an inch.

'It's getting late.'

'It's eight-thirty.'

Seriously? Only an hour? It felt like eternity.

'I'm heading out at sunrise. So I can get to Lake Lefroy before it gets too hot.'

And back to blissful isolation, where he didn't need to explain himself to anyone.

She tipped her head and it caused her dark hair to swing to the right a little. A soft fragrance wafted forwards and teased his receptors. His words stumbled as surely as he did, getting up. 'Thanks for the company.'

She followed suit. 'You're welcome.'

They split the bill in uncomfortable silence, then stepped out into the dark street. Deserted by eight-thirty.

Eve looked to her right, then back at him.

'Listen, I know you're just across the road but could you… would you mind walking me back to the bus?'

Maybe they were both remembering those three jerks from earlier.

'Where do you park at night?' He suddenly realised he had no idea where she'd pulled up. And that his ability to form sentences seemed to have returned with the fresh air.

'I usually find a good spot…'

Oh, jeez. She wasn't even sorted for the night.

They walked on in silence and then words just came tumbling out of him.

'My motel booking comes with parking. You could use that if you want. I'll tuck the bike forward.'

'Really?' Gratitude flooded her pretty face. 'That would be great, thank you.'

'Come on.'

He followed her to the right, and walked back through Norseman's quiet main streets. Neither of them spoke. When they reached her bus, she unlocked the side window and reached in to activate the folding front door. He waited while she crossed back around and then stepped up behind her into the cab.

Forbidden territory previously.

But she didn't so much as twitch this time. Which was irrationally pleasing. Clearly he'd passed some kind of test. Maybe it was when the beard came off.

The Bedford rumbled to life and Eve circled the block before heading back to his motel. He directed her into his bay and then jumped out to nudge the KTM forward a little. The back of her bus stuck out of the bay but he was pretty sure there was only one other person in the entire motel and they were already parked up for the night.

'Thanks again for this,' she said, pausing at the back of the bus with one of the two big rear doors open.

Courtesy of the garish motel lights that streamed in her half-closed curtains, he could see the comfortable space he'd fallen asleep in bathed in a yellow glow. And beyond it, behind the door that now stood open at the other end of the bus, Eve's bedroom. The opening was dominated by the foot of a large mattress draped in a burgundy quilt and weighed down with two big cushions.

Nothing like the sterile motel room and single country bed he'd be returning to.

'Caravan parks can be a little isolated this time of year,' she said, a bit tighter, as she caught the direction of his gaze. 'I feel better being close to…people.'

He eased his shoulder against the closed half of the door

and studied her. Had she changed her mind? Was that open door some kind of unconscious overture? And was he really considering taking her up on it if it was? Pretty, uptight girls on crusades didn't really meet his definition of uncomplicated. Yet something deep inside hinted strongly that she might be worth a bit of complication.

He peered down on her in the shadows. 'No problem.'

She shuffled from left foot to right. 'Well…'night, then. See you in the morning. Thanks again.'

A reluctant smile crossed his face at the firm finality of that door slamming shut. And at the zipping across of curtains as he sauntered to the rear of the motel.

Now they were one-for-one in the inappropriate social re-action stakes. He'd gone all strong and silent on her and she'd gone all blushing virgin on him.

Equally awkward.

Equally regrettable.

He dug into his pocket for the worn old key and let himself into his ground floor room. Exactly as soulless and bland as her little bus wasn't.

But exactly as soulless and bland as he preferred.

CHAPTER THREE

'THIS BUS NEVER stops being versatile, does it?'

Eve's breath caught deep in her throat at the slight twang and comfortable gravel in the voice that came from her left. The few days that had passed since she'd heard his bike rumble out of the motel car park at dawn as she'd rolled the covers more tightly around her and fell back to sleep gave him exactly the right amount of stubble as he let the beard grow back in.

'Marshall?' Her hand clamped down on the pile of fliers that lifted off the table in the brisk Esperance waterfront breeze. 'I thought you'd headed north?'

'I did. But a road train had jack-knifed across the highway just out of Kal and the spill clean-up was going to take twenty-four hours so I adjusted my route. I'll do the south-west anti-clockwise. Like you.'

Was there just the slightest pause before 'like you'? And did that mean anything? Apparently, she took too long wondering because he started up again.

'I assumed I'd have missed you, actually.'

Or hoped? Impossible to know with his eyes hidden behind seriously dark sunglasses. Still, if he'd truly wanted to avoid her he could have just kept walking just now. She was so busy promoting *The Missing* to locals she never would have noticed him.

Eve pushed her shoulders back to improve her posture,

which had slumped as the morning wore on. Convenient co-incidence that it also made the best of her limited assets.

'I had to do Salmon Gums and Gibson on the way,' she said. 'I only arrived last night.'

He took in the two-dozen posters affixed to the tilted up doors of the bus's luggage compartment. It made a great road-side noticeboard to set her fold-out table up in front of.

He strolled up and back, studying every face closely.

'Who are all these people?'

'They're all long-termers.' *The ten per cent.*

'Do you know them all?'

'No,' she murmured. 'But I know most of their families. Online, at least.'

'All missing.' He frowned. 'Doesn't it pull focus from your brother? To do this?'

Yeah. It definitely did.

'I wouldn't be much of a human being if I travelled the entire country only looking after myself. Besides, we kind of have a reciprocal arrangement going. If someone's doing something special—like media or some kind of promotion—they try to include as many others as they can. This is something I can do in the big centres while taking a break from the road.'

Though Esperance was hardly a metropolis and talking to strangers all day wasn't much of a break.

He stopped just in front of her, picked up one of Travis's posters. 'Who's "we"?'

'The network.'

The sunglasses tipped more towards her.

'The missing-persons network,' she explained. 'The fami-lies. There are a lot of us.'

'You have a formal network?'

'We have an informal one. We share information. Tips. Successes.'

Failures. Quite a lot of failures.

'Good to have the support, I guess.'

He had no idea. Some days her commitment to a bunch of

people she'd never met face to face was the only thing that got her out of bed.

'When I first started up, I kept my focus on Trav. But these people—' she tipped her head back towards all the faces on her poster display '—are like extended family to me because they're the family of people I'm now close to. How could I not include them amongst *The Missing*?'

A woman stopped to pick up one of her fliers and Eve quickly delivered her spiel, smiling and making a lot of eye contact. Pumping it with energy. Whatever it took…

Marshall waited until the woman had finished perusing the whole display. *'The Missing?'*

She looked behind her. 'Them.'

And her brother had the biggest and most central poster on it.

He nodded to a gap on the top right of the display. 'Looks like one's fallen off.'

'I just took someone down.'

His eyebrows lifted. 'They were found? That's great.'

No, not great. But at least found. That was how it was for the families of long-timers. The Simmons family had the rest of their lives to deal with the mental torture that came with feeling *relief* when their son's remains were found in a gully at the bottom of a popular hiking mountain. Closure. That became the goal somewhere around the ten-month mark.

Emotional euthanasia.

Maybe one day that would be her—loathing herself for being grateful that the question mark that stalked her twenty-four-seven was now gone because her brother was. But there was no way she could explain any of that to someone outside the network. Regular people just didn't get it. It was just so much easier to smile and nod.

'Yes. Great.'

Silence clunked somewhat awkwardly on the table between them.

'Did you get out to Israelite Bay yet?' he finally asked.

'I'll probably do that tomorrow or Wednesday.'

His clear eyes narrowed. 'Listen. I have an idea. You need to travel out to the bay and I need to head out to Cape Arid and Middle Island to survey them for a possible new weather station. Why don't we team up, head out together? Two birds, one stone.'

More together time in which to struggle with conversation and obsess about his tattoos. Was that wise?

'I'll only slow you down. I need to do poster drops at all roadhouses, caravan parks and campsites between here and there.'

'That's okay. As far as the office is concerned, I have a couple of days while the truck mess is cleared up. We can take our time.'

Why did he seem so very reluctant? Almost as if he was speaking against his will. She scrunched her nose as a prelude to an *I don't think so*.

But he beat her to it. 'Middle Island is off-limits to the public. You can't go there without a permit.'

'And you have a permit?'

'I do.'

'Have you forgotten that this isn't a tourist trip for me?'

'You'll get your work done on the way, and then you'll just keep me company for mine.'

'I can get my work done by myself and be back in Esperance by nightfall.'

'Or you can give yourself a few hours off and see a bit of this country that you're totally missing.'

'And why should I be excited by Middle Island?'

'A restricted island could be a great place for someone to hide out if they don't want to be discovered.'

The moment the words left his mouth, colour peaked high on his jaw.

'Sorry—' he winced as she sucked in a breath '—that was… God, I'm sorry. I just thought you might enjoy a bit of downtime. That it might be good for you.'

But his words had had their effect. If you needed a permit and Marshall had one, then she'd be crazy not to tag along. What if she let her natural reticence stop her and Trav was there, camping and lying low?

'I'll let you ride on my bike,' he said, as though that made it better. As if it was some kind of prize.

Instantly her gut curled into a fist. 'Motorbikes kill people.'

'People kill people,' he dismissed. 'Have you ever ridden on one?'

If riding tandem with a woman in the midst of a mid-life crisis counted. 'My mother had a 250cc.'

'Really? Cool.'

Yeah, that was what she and Travis had thought, right up until the day it killed their mother and nearly him.

'But you haven't really *ridden* until you've been on a 1200.'

'No, thanks.'

'Come on… Wouldn't you like to know what it's like to have all that power between your legs?'

'If this is a line, it's spectacularly cheesy.'

He ignored that. 'Or the freedom of tearing along at one hundred clicks with nothing between you and the road?'

'You call that freedom, I call that terror.'

'How will you know until you try it?'

'I'm not interested in trying it.'

He totally failed at masking his disappointment. 'Then you can tail me in the bus. We'll convoy. It'll still be fun.'

Famous last words. Something told her the fun would run out, for him, round about the time she pulled into her third rest stop for the day, to pin up posters.

'There's also a good caravan park out there, according to the travel guides. You can watch a west coast sunset.'

'I've seen plenty of sunsets.'

'Not with me,' he said on a sexy grin.

Something about his intensity really wiggled down under her skin. Tantalising and zingy. 'Why are you so eager for me to do this?'

Grey eyes grew earnest. 'Because you're missing everything. The entire country. The moments of joy that give life its colour.'

'You should really moonlight in greeting-card messages.'

'Come on, Eve. You have to go there, anyway, it's just a few hours of detour.'

'And what if Trav comes through in those few hours?' It sounded ridiculous but it was the fear she lived with every moment of every day.

'Then he'll see one of dozens of posters and know you're looking for him.'

The simple truth of that ached. Every decision she made ached. Each one could bring her closer to her brother or push her further away. It made decision-making pure agony. But this one came with a whole bundle of extra considerations. Marshall-shaped considerations. And the thought of sitting and watching a sunset with him even managed to alleviate some of that ache.

A surprising amount.

She sighed. 'What time?'

'How long are you set up here for?'

'I have permission to be on the waterfront until noon.'

'Five past noon, then?'

So eager. Did he truly think she was that parched for some life experience? It galled her to give him all the points. 'Ten past.'

His smile transformed his face, the way it always did.

'Done.'

'And we're sleeping separately. You know…just for the record.'

'Hey, I'm just buying you a sunset, lady.' His shrug was adorable. And totally disarming.

'Now go, Weatherman—you're scaring off my leads with all that leather.'

Her lips said 'go' but her heart said *stay*. Whispered it, really. But she'd become proficient in drowning out the fancies of her heart. And its fears. Neither were particularly productive in keeping her on track in finding Travis. A nice neutral... nothing...was the best way to proceed.

Emotionally blank, psychologically focused.

Which wasn't to say that Marshall Sullivan couldn't be a useful distraction from all the voices in her head and heart.

And a pleasant one.

And a short one.

They drove the two hundred kilometres east in a weird kind of convoy. Eve chugging along in her ancient bus and him, unable to stand the slow pace, roaring off ahead and pulling over at the turn-off to every conceivable human touch point until she caught up, whacked up a poster and headed out again. Rest stops, roadhouses, campgrounds, lookouts. Whizzing by at one hundred kilometres an hour and only stopping longer for places that had people and rubbish bins and queued-up vehicles.

It was a horrible way to see such a beautiful country.

Eventually, they made it to the campground nestled in the shoulder crook of a pristine bay on the far side of Cape Arid National Park, its land arms reaching left and right in a big, hug-like semicircle. A haven for travellers, fishermen and a whole lot of wildlife.

But not today. Today they had the whole place to themselves.

'So many blues...' Eve commented, stepping down out of the bus and staring at the expansive bay.

And she wasn't wrong. Closer to shore, the water was the pale, almost ice-blue of gentle surf. Then the kind of blue you saw on postcards, until, out near the horizon it graduated to a deep, gorgeous blue before slamming into the endless rich blue of the Australian sky. And, down to their left, a cluster of weathered boulders were freckled by a bunch of sea lions sunning themselves.

God...so good for the soul.

'This is nothing,' he said. Compared to what she'd missed

all along the south coast of Australia. Compared to what she'd driven straight past. 'If you'd just chuck your indicator on from time to time…'

She glanced at him but didn't say anything, busying stringing out her solar blanket to catch the afternoon light. When she opened the back doors of the bus to fill it with fresh sea air, she paused, looking further out to sea. Out to an island.

'Is that where we're going?'

Marshall hauled himself up next to her to follow her gaze. 'Nope. That's one of the closer, smaller islands in the archipelago. Middle Island is further out. One of those big shadows looming on the horizon.'

He leaned half across her to point further out and she followed the line of his arm and finger. It brought them as close together as they'd been since he'd dragged her kicking and cursing away from the thugs back in Norseman. And then he knew how much he'd missed her scent.

It eddied around his nostrils now, in defiance of the strong breeze.

Taunting him.

'How many are there?'

What were they talking about? Right…islands. 'More than a hundred.'

Eve stood, staring, her gaze flicking over every feature in view. Marshall kept his hand hooked around the bus's ceiling, keeping her company up there. Keeping close.

'Trav could be on any of them.'

Not if he also wanted to eat. Or drink. Only two had fresh water.

'Listen, Eve…'

She turned her eyes back up to his and it put their faces much closer than either of them might have intended.

'I really am truly sorry I said that about your brother. It was a cheap shot.' And one that he still didn't fully understand making. He wasn't Eve's keeper. 'The chances of him being out there are—'

'Tiny. I know. But it's in my head now and I'm not going to be able to sleep if I don't chase every possibility.'

'Still, I don't want to cause you pain.'

'That's not hurting, Marshall. That's helping. It's what I'm out here for.'

She said the words extra firmly, as if she was reminding both of them. Didn't make the slightest difference to the tingling in his toes. The tingling said she was here for him.

What did toes ever know?

He held her gaze much longer than was probably polite, their dark depths giving the ocean around them a run for its money.

'Doesn't seem a particularly convenient place to put a weather station,' she said finally, turning back out to the islands.

Subtle subject change. *Not.* But he played along. 'We want remote. To give us better data on southern coastal weather conditions.'

She glanced around them at the whole lot of nothing as far as the eye could see. 'You got it.'

Silent sound cushioned them in layers. The occasional bird cry, far away. The whump of the distant waves hitting the granite face of the south coast. The thrum of the coastal breeze around them. The awkward clearing of her throat as it finally dawned on her that she was shacked up miles from anywhere—and anyone—with a man she barely knew.

'What time are we meeting the boat? And where?'

'First thing in the morning. They'll pull into the bay, then ferry us around. Any closer to Middle Island and we couldn't get in without an off-road vehicle.'

'Right.'

Gravity helped his boots find the dirt and he looked back up at Eve, giving her the space she seemed to need. 'I'm going to go hit the water before the sun gets too low.'

Her eyes said that a swim was exactly what she wanted. But the tightness in her lips said that she wasn't about to go wandering through the sand dunes somewhere this remote with a virtual stranger. Fair enough, they'd only known each other hours. Despite having a couple of life-threatening moments between them. Maybe if she saw him walking away from her, unoffended and unconcerned, she'd feel more comfortable around him. Maybe if he offered no pressure for the two of them to spend time together, she'd relax a bit.

And maybe if he grew a pair he wouldn't care.

'See you later on, then.'

Marshall jogged down to the beach without looking back. When he hit the shore he laid his boots, jeans and T-shirt out on the nearest rock to get nice and toasty for his return and waded into the ice-cold water in his shorts. Normally he'd have gone without, public or not, but that wasn't going to win him any points in the *Is it safe to be here with you?* stakes. The sand beneath his feet had been beaten so fine by the relentless Southern Ocean it was more like squidging into saturated talcum powder than abrasive granules of sand. Soft and welcoming, the kind of thing you could imagine just swallowing you up.

And you wouldn't mind a bit.

His skin instantly thrilled at the kiss of the ice-cold water after the better part of a day smothered in leather and road dust, and he waded the stretch of shallows, then dived through the handful of waves that built up momentum as the rapid rise of land forced them into graceful, white-topped arcs.

This was his first swim since Cactus Beach, a whole state away. The Great Australian Bight was rugged and amazing to look at right the way across the guts of the country but when the rocks down to the sea were fifty metres high and the ocean down there bottomless and deadly, swimming had to take a short sabbatical. But swimming was also one of the things that kept him sane and being barred from it got him all twitchy.

Which made it pretty notable that the first thing he *didn't do* when he pulled up to the beautiful, tranquil and swimmable shores of Esperance earlier today was hit the water.

He went hunting for a dark-haired little obsessive instead.

Oh, he told himself a dozen lies to justify it—that he'd rather swim the private beaches of the capes; that he'd rather swim at sunset; that he'd rather get the Middle Island review out of the way first so he could take a few days to relax—but that was all starting to feel like complete rubbish. Apparently, he was parched for something more than just salt water.

Company.

Pfff. Right. That was one word for it.

It had been months since he'd been interested enough in a woman to do something about it, and by 'interested' he meant hungry. Hungry enough to head out and find a woman willing to sleep with a man who had nothing to offer but a hard, one-off lay before blowing town the next day. There seemed to be no shortage of women across the country who were out to salve a broken heart, or pay back a cheating spouse, or numb something broken deep inside them. They were the ones he looked for when he got needy enough because they didn't ask questions and they didn't have expectations.

It took one to know one.

Those encounters scratched the itch when it grew too demanding…and they reminded him how empty and soulless relationships were. All relationships, not just the random strangers in truck stops and bars across the country. Women. Mothers.

Brothers.

At least the women in the bars knew where they stood. No one was getting used. And there was no one to disappoint except himself.

He powered his body harder, arm over arm, and concentrated on how his muscles felt, cutting his limbs through the surf. Burning from within, icy from without. The familiar, heavy ache of lactic acid building up. And when he'd done all the examination it was possible to do on his muscles, he focused on the water: how the last land it had touched was Antarctica, how it was life support for whales and elephant seals and dugongs and colossal squid and mysterious deep-trench blobs eight kilometres below the surface and thousands of odd-

shaped sea creatures in between. How humans were a bunch
of nimble-fingered, big-brained primates that really only used
the millimetre around the edge of the mapped oceans and had
absolutely no idea how much of their planet they knew nothing about.

Instant Gulliver.

It reminded him how insignificant he was in the scheme of
things. Him and all his human, social problems.

The sun was low on the horizon when he next paid attention,
and the south coast of Australia was littered with sharks who
liked to feed at dusk and dawn. And while there had certainly
been a day he would have happily taken the risk and forgotten the consequences, he'd managed to find a happy place in
the *Groundhog Day* blur that was the past six months on the
road, and could honestly say—hand on heart—that he'd rather
not be shark food now.

He did a final lazy lap parallel with the wide beach back
towards his discarded clothes, then stood as soon as the sea
floor rose to meet him. His hands squeezed up over his lowered lids and back through his hair, wringing the salt water out
of it, then he stood, eyes closed, with his face tipped towards
the warmth of the afternoon sun.

Eventually, he opened them and started, just a little, at Eve
standing there, her arms full of towel, her mouth hanging open
as if he'd interrupted her mid-sentence.

Eve knew she was gaping horribly but she was no more able to
close her trap than rip her eyes from Marshall's chest and belly.

His *tattooed* chest and belly.

Air sucked into her lungs in choppy little gasps.

He had some kind of massive bird of prey, wings spread and
aloft, across his chest. The lower curve of its majestic wings
sat neatly along the ridge of his pectorals and its wing tips
followed the line of muscle there up onto his tanned, rounded
shoulders. Big enough to accentuate the musculature of his
chest, low enough to be invisible when he was wearing a

T-shirt. It should have been trashy but it wasn't; it looked like he'd been born with it.

His arms were still up, squeezing the sea water from his hair, and that gave her a glimpse of a bunch of inked characters—Japanese, maybe Chinese?—on the underside of one full biceps.

Add that to the dagger on the other arm and he had a lot of ink for a weatherman.

'Hey.'

His voice startled her gaze back to his and her tongue into action.

'Wow,' she croaked, then realised that wasn't the most dignified of beginnings. 'You were gone so long...'

Great. Not even capable of a complete sentence.

'I've been missing the ocean. Sorry if I worried you.'

She grasped around in the memories she'd just spent a couple of hours accumulating, studying the map to make sure they hadn't missed a caravan park or town. And she improvised some slightly more intelligent conversation.

'Whoever first explored this area really didn't have the best time doing it.'

Marshall dripped. And frowned. As he lowered his arms to take the towel from her nerveless fingers, the bird of prey's feathers shifted with him, just enough to catch her eye. She struggled to look somewhere other than at him, but it wasn't easy when he filled her field of view so thoroughly. She wanted to step back but then didn't want to give him the satisfaction of knowing she was affected.

'Cape Arid, Mount Ragged, Poison Creek...' she listed with an encouraging lack of wobble in her voice, her clarity restored the moment he pressed the towel to his face and disguised most of that unexpectedly firm and decorated torso.

He stepped over to the rock and hooked up his T-shirt, then swept it on in a smooth, manly shrug. Even with its overstretched neckline, the bird of prey was entirely hidden. The idea of him hanging out in his meteorological workplace in a government-appropriate suit with all of that ink hidden away under it was as secretly pleasing as when she used to wear her best lingerie to section meetings.

Back when stupid things like that had mattered.

'I guess it's not so bad when you have supplies and transport,' he said, totally oblivious to her illicit train of thought, 'but it must have been a pretty treacherous environment for early explorers. Especially if they were thirsty.'

She just blinked at him. What was he saying? What had she asked?

He didn't bother with the rest of his clothes; he just slung the jeans over his shoulder and followed her back up to camp with his boots swinging in his left hand.

'Nice swim?' Yeah. Much easier to think with all that skin and ink covered up.

'I've missed it. The water's so clean down here.'

'Isn't ocean always clean?'

'Not at all. It's so easy to imagine the Southern Ocean being melt straight from Antarctica. Beautiful.'

'Maybe I'll take a dip tomorrow.' When Marshall was otherwise engaged.

They fell to silence as they approached the bus. Suddenly the awkwardness of the situation amplified. One bus. Two people. One of them half-naked and the other fresh from a bout of uncontrollable ogling. As though her-on-the-bed and him-on-the-sofa was the only social nicety to be observed. There was a bathroom and TV space and…air to consider. She was used to having the bus entirely to herself, now she had to share it with a man for twenty-four hours. And not just any man.

A hot man.

A really hot man.

'Um. You take the bus to change, I'll just—' she looked around for inspiration and saw the quirky little public outhouse in the distance '—check out the facilities.'

Oh, good Lord…

'Thanks. I'll only be a few minutes.'

Her, too. Most definitely. There was a reason she'd held out until she found a live-in transport with a toilet built into it. Public toilets in remote Australia were not for the faint of heart.

As it turned out, this one was a cut above average. Well maintained and stocked. Some kind of eco-composting number. It was only when she caught herself checking out how the pipework operated that she knew just how badly she was stalling. As if toilets were anywhere near that fascinating.

Come on, Read, man up.

Returning revealed Marshall to have been as good as his word. He was changed, loosely groomed and waiting outside the bus already. *Outside.* Almost as though he was trying to minimise his impact on her space.

He held his new bike helmet out to her.

'Come on.' He smiled. 'I promised you a ride. While we still have light.'

It took approximately twenty-five seconds for Eve to get over her concern that Marshall only had one motorbike helmet and he was holding it out to her. After that, she was all about survival of the fittest.

'I don't remember agreeing to this—'

'You'll love it, Eve. I promise.'

She glared up at him. 'Just because you do?'

'Because it's brilliant. And fun.'

No. Not always fun. She'd lost one and nearly two people she loved to a not-so-fun motorbike. Though that could just as easily have been a car, her logical side whispered. Or a bus. Or a 747. Tragedies happened every single day.

Just that day it happened to them.

'Think of it like a theme park ride,' he cajoled. 'A roller coaster.'

'That's not really helping.'

'Come on, Eve. What else are we going to do until it's dark?'

Apart from sit in the bus in awkward silence obsessing on

who was going to sleep where…? She glanced sideways at the big orange bike.

'I'll keep you safe, I promise. We'll only go as fast as you're comfortable with.'

His siren voice chipped away at her resistance. And his vow—*I'll keep you safe*. For so long she'd been all about looking after her father and brother. When was the last time someone offered to look after *her*?

'Just slow?'

Of course there was small print, but it came delightfully packaged in a grin full of promise. 'Until you're ready for more.'

He seemed so incredibly confident that was going to happen. Her bottom lip wiggled its way between her teeth. She *had* always wondered what it would be like to ride something with a bit more power. If by *always* she meant after two hours of watching a leather-clad Marshall dominate the machine under him. And if by *ride* she meant pressing her thighs into his and her front to that broad, strong back, both of them hepped up on adrenaline. It was a seductive picture. The kind of picture that was best reserved for her and a quiet, deluded night in the bus. She hadn't imagined it would ever go from fantasy to opportunity.

He held the helmet out again.

'You'll slow the moment I ask?' she breathed.

'Cross my heart.'

Yeah, not really selling it. Everyone knew what came after that line…

But it was only when she was about to lower her hand away from the helmet that she realised she'd even raised it. What was she going to do, live in fear of motorbikes for the rest of her life? No one was even sure what had caused her mother's accident—even Trav, after he'd come out of the coma, couldn't shed much light. Tragic accident. Could have happened to anyone. That was the final verdict.

'You'll drive safely?'

Come on, Read, suck it up.

Sincerity blazed in his solemn grey gaze. 'I'll be a model of conservatism.'

How long had it been since she'd done something outside of the box? Or taken any kind of risk? She used to be edgy, back before life got so very serious and she took responsibility for Travis. And her risks had almost always paid off. That was part of the thrill.

Hadn't she once been known for that?

Here was a gorgeous man offering to wrap her around him for a little bit. And the price—a bit of reckless speed.

It had been years since she'd done something reckless. Maybe it would be good for her.

She took a deep breath and curled her fingers around the helmet's chin strap.

The KTM hit a breath-stealing speed in about the same time it took her to brave opening her eyes. The road whizzed below them in such a blur it was like riding on liquid mercury.

At least that was how it felt.

She immediately remembered the excitement of riding behind her mother, but her mother's bike had never purred like this one. And it had never glued itself to the road like the tyres on this one.

Maybe if it had, all their lives would have been very different now.

She pressed herself more fully into Marshall's hard back and practically punched her fingertips through his leather jacket from clenching it so hard.

'Is this top speed?' she yelled forward to him.

His hair whipped around above her face as he shook his head and shouted back. 'We're only doing seventy kilometres.'

'Don't go any faster,' she called.

She hated the vulnerable note in her voice, but she hated more the thought of hitting the dirt at this kind of speed. In

Travis's case it had been trees but she felt fairly certain that you didn't need trees to be pretty badly injured on a bike.

Marshall turned his face half back to her and smiled beneath his protective sunglasses, nodding once. She'd just have to trust those teeth.

The roads of the national park were long and straight and the bike sat atop them beautifully so, after a few tense minutes, Eve let her death grip on his jacket ease slightly and crept them back to rest on Marshall's hips instead. Still firm, but the blood was able to leach back into her knuckles.

For a death machine he handled it pretty well.

Ahead, the road bent around a monolithic chunk of rock and he eased off the gas to pass it carefully. The bike's lean felt extreme to her and her grasp on his leather jacket completely insufficient, so her fingers found their way under it and hooked onto the eyelets of his jeans.

A few paltry sweatshop stitches were the only thing between her and certain doom.

While the engine was eased, Marshall took the opportunity to call back to her, half turning, 'Doing okay?'

Eyes front, mister!

'Stop staring down,' he shouted. 'Look around you.'

She let her eyes flutter upwards as he turned his attention back to the oncoming road. The entire park was bathed in the golden glow of afternoon light, the many different textures changing the way the light reflected and creating the golden equivalent of the ocean. So many different shades.

And—bonus—the speed didn't seem anywhere near as scary as staring down at the asphalt.

It was almost like being in the Bedford. Sans life-saving steel exoskeleton.

She didn't want to look like a complete wuss, and so Eve did her best to ease herself back from where her body had practically fused with his. The problem with that was as soon as he changed up gears, she brushed, breasts first, against his back. And then again.

And again, as he shifted up into fourth.

Okay, now he was just messing with her. She was having a difficult enough reaction to all that leather without adding to the crisis by torturing her own flesh. Leaning into him might be more intimate, but it felt far less gratuitous and so she snuggled forward again, widening her legs to fit more snugly around his. Probably not how a passenger was supposed to ride—the fact her bottom had left the pillion seat in favour of sharing his leathery saddle proved that—but that was how it was going to be for her first ever big boy's motorcycle experience.

And if he didn't like it he could pull over.

Minutes whizzed by and she grew captivated by the long stretches of tufted grass to her left, the parched, salt-crusted trees and coastal heath to her right and the limestone outcrops that practically glowed in the late-afternoon light. So much so that, when Marshall finally pulled them to a halt at a lookout point, she realised she'd forgotten all about the speed. Her pulse was up, her exposed skin was flushed pink and her breath was pleasantly choppy.

But she hadn't died.

And she wasn't ready for it to be over.

'I can see why she—why *you* like this,' she puffed, lifting the visor on her helmet and leaning around him. 'It's a great way to see the country.'

'Are you comfortable?'

His innocuous words immediately reminded her of how close she was pressed against him—wrapped around him, really—and she immediately went to correct that.

'Stay put,' he cautioned. 'We're about to head back.'

She leaned with him as he turned the bike in a big arc on an old salt flat and then bumped back onto the tarmac. As if she'd been doing this forever. And, as he roared back up to speed, she realised how very much in the *now* she'd been. Just her, Marshall, the road, the wind and the national park.

No past. No future. No accidents. No inquests. No Travis.

And how nice that moment of psychological respite was.

The light was totally different heading back. Less golden. More orange. And fading fast. He accessed a fifth gear that he'd spared her on the first leg and even still, when he pulled back in near the bus, the sun was almost gone. She straightened cold-stiffened limbs and pulled off his helmet.

'How was that?' he asked, way more interest in his eyes than a courtesy question. He kicked the stand into position and leaned the bike into the solid embrace of the earth.

'Amazing.'

The word formed a tiny breath cloud in the cool evening air and it was only then she realised how cold she was. The sun's warmth sure departed fast in this part of the country.

He followed her back towards the bus. 'You took a bit to loosen up.'

'Considering how terrified I was, I don't think I did too badly.'

'Not badly at all. I felt the moment when the fear left your body.'

The thought that she'd been pressed closely enough to him to be telegraphing any kind of emotion caused a rush of heat that she was very glad it was too dim for him to see. But he stepped ahead of her and opened the back of the Bedford and caught the last vestiges of her flush.

'How are you feeling now about motorcycles?'

His body blocked the step up into the bus and so she had no choice but to brush past him as she pulled herself up.

'It's still a death trap,' she said, looking back down at him. 'But not entirely without redeeming qualities.'

Not unlike its owner, really.

CHAPTER FOUR

'I WAS THINKING of steak and salad for dinner,' Eve said, returning from her little bedroom newly clad in a sweater to take the edge off the cool coastal night.

Lord, how domestic. And utterly foreign.

'You don't need to cook for me, Eve. I ate up big at lunchtime in anticipation.'

'I was there, remember? And while it certainly was big you probably burned it all off with that epic swim earlier.'

And Lord knew, between the lusting and the fearing for her life, she'd just burnt all hers off, too.

Preparing food felt natural; she'd been doing it for Travis for so many years. Moreover, it gave her something constructive and normal to do for thirty minutes, but Marshall wasn't so lucky. He hovered, hopelessly. After the comparative intimacy of the bike ride, it seemed ludicrous to be uncomfortable about sharing a simple meal. But he was, a little.

And so was she. A lot.

'Here.' She slid him a bottle opener across the raw timber counter of the Bedford's compact little kitchen. 'Make yourself useful.'

She nodded to a small cabinet above the built-in television and, when he opened it, his eyebrows lifted at the contents. 'I thought you didn't drink?'

That rattled a chuckle from her tight chest.

'Not in bars—' with men she didn't know, and given her

familial history '—but I like to sample the local wines as I move around.'

She brought her solitary wineglass out from under the bench, then added a coffee mug next to it. The best she could do.

'You take the glass,' she offered.

He took both, in fact, poured two generous servings of red and slid the wineglass back her way. 'I guess you don't entertain much?'

'Not really out here for the social life,' she said. But then she relented. 'I did have a second glass once but I have no idea where it's gone. So it's the coffee mug or it's my toothbrush glass.'

And didn't that sound pathetic.

'You're going to need another storage cupboard,' he murmured, bringing the mug back from his lips and licking the final drops off, much to her sudden fascination. 'We're headed for serious wine country.'

'Maybe I just need to drink faster.'

He chuckled and saluted her with the mug. 'Amen to that.'

What was it about a communal glass of vino that instantly broke down the awkwardness barrier? He'd only had one sip and she'd had none, yet, so it wasn't the effects of the alcohol. Just something about popping a cork and swilling a good red around in your glass—or coffee mug—the great equaliser.

Maybe that was how her mother had begun. Social and pleasant. Until one day she woke up and it wasn't social any more. Or pleasant.

'So tell me,' Eve started, continuing with her food prep, 'did you have much competition for half a year in the bush checking on weather stations?'

He smiled and leaned across to relieve her of the chopping knife and vegetables from the fridge. 'I did not.'

It was too easy to respond to that gentle smile. To let her curiosity have wings. To tease. 'Can't imagine why not. Why did you accept it?'

'Travel the country, fully paid. What's not to love?'

'Being away from your friends and family?'

Being away from your girlfriend. She concentrated hard to keep her eyes from dropping to the bottom of the biceps dagger that peeked out from under his sleeve.

'Not all families benefit from being in each other's faces,' he said, a little tightly.

She stopped and regarded him. 'Speaking from experience?'

Grey eyes flicked to hers.

'Maybe. Don't tell me,' he nudged. 'You have the perfect parents.'

Oh...so far from the truth it was almost laughable. The steaks chuckled for her as she flipped them. 'Parent singular. Dad.'

He regarded her closely. 'You lost your mum?'

'Final year of school.'

'I'm sorry. New subject?'

'No. It's a long time ago now. It's okay.'

'Want to talk about it?'

Sometimes, desperately. Sometimes when she sat all alone in this little bus that felt so big she just wished she had someone sitting there with her that she could spill it all to. Someone to help her make sense of everything that had happened. Because she still barely understood it.

'Not much to talk about. She was in an accident. Travis was lucky to survive it.'

His fathomless gaze grew deeper. Full of sympathy. 'Car crash?'

Here it came...

'Motorbike, actually.'

His eyes flared and he spun more fully towards her. 'Why didn't you say, Eve?'

'I'm saying now.'

'Before I press-ganged you into taking a ride with me,' he gritted, leaning over the counter.

'I could have said no. At any time. I'm not made of jelly.'

Except when Marshall smiled at her a certain way. Then anyone would be forgiven for thinking so.

'I never would have—'

'It wasn't the bike's fault. It's good for me to remember that.'

He took a long, slow breath and Eve distracted herself poking the steaks.

'A 250cc, you said. Not your usual family wagon.'

'Oh, we had one of those, too. But she got her motorcycle licence not long after having Travis.' Like some kind of statement. 'She rode it whenever she didn't have us with her.'

Which was often in those last five years.

'I think it was her way of fighting suburbia,' she murmured. Or reality, maybe.

'But she had your brother with her that day?' Then, 'Are you okay to talk about this?'

Surprisingly, she was. Maybe because Marshall was a fellow motorbike fanatic. It somehow felt okay for him to know.

'Yeah—' she sighed '—she did. Trav loved her bike. He couldn't wait to get his bike permit. I think she was going to give him the Kawasaki. He'd started to learn.'

'How old was he when it happened?'

'Fourteen.'

'Five years between you. That's a biggish gap.'

'Thank God for it. Not sure I could have handled any of it if I'd been younger.'

It was hard enough as it was.

It was only when Marshall's voice murmured, soft and low, over her shoulder and he reached past her to turn off the gas to the steaks that she realised how long she'd been standing there mute. Her skin tingled at his closeness.

'New subject?'

'No. I'm happy to talk about my family. I just forget sometimes…'

'Forget what?'

Sorrow washed through her. 'That my family's different now. That it's just me and Dad.'

'You say that like...'

Her eyes lifted. 'That's the reality. If Trav is missing by force, then he's not coming back. And if he's missing by choice...'

Then he's not coming back.

Either way, her already truncated family had shrunk by one more.

'You really believe he could be out here somewhere, just... lying low?'

'I have to believe that. That he's hurting. Confused. Off his meds. Maybe he doesn't think he'd be welcome back after leaving like he did. I want him to know we want him back no matter what.'

Marshall's head bobbed slowly. 'No case to answer? For the distress he's caused?'

Her hand fell still on the spatula. For the longest time, the only sound came from the low-burn frying pan. But, eventually, her thoughts collected into something coherent.

'I ask myself is there anything he could do that would make me not want to have him back with us and the answer is no. So giving him grief for what he did, or why he did it, or the manner in which he did it... It has no purpose. I just want him to walk back in that door and scuff the wall with his school bag and start demanding food. The *what*, *why* and *how* is just not relevant.'

Intelligent eyes glanced from her still fingers to her face. 'It's relevant to you.'

'But it's not important. In the scheme of things.'

Besides, she already had a fairly good idea of the *why*. Travis's escalating anxiety and depression seemed blazingly obvious in hindsight, even if she hadn't seen it at the time. Because she hadn't been paying attention. She'd been far too busy shrugging off her substitute mother apron.

Thinking about herself.

She poked at the steak again and delicious juices ran from it and added to the noise in the pan. She lifted her wineglass with her free hand and emptied a bit into the pan. Then she took a generous swig and changed the subject.

'So, who is Christine?'

No-man's-land the last time they spoke, but they weren't spending the night under the same roof then. They barely knew each other then.

We barely know each other now! a tiny voice reminded her.

But they did. Maybe not a heap of details, but they knew each other's names and interests and purpose. She'd seen him half naked striding out of the surf, and she'd pressed up against him a grand total of two times now and had a different kind of glimpse at the kind of man he was under all the leather and facial hair. He struck her as…safe.

And sometimes safe was enough.

But right now *safe* didn't look entirely happy at her words. Though he still answered.

'Was,' he clarified. 'Christine was my girlfriend.'

Clang. The pan hit the stovetop at his use of the past tense. There was the answer to a question she didn't know she'd been dying to ask. Unexpected butterflies took flight deep in her gut and she busied herself with a second go at moving the frying pan off the heat.

'Recent?'

His strong lips pursed briefly as he considered answering. Or not answering. 'Long time ago.'

Yeah, the ink didn't look new, come to think of it. Unlike the one she'd seen under his biceps.

Which meant he could still be someone else's hairy biker type. That she was having a quiet steak with. Under a gem-filled sky. Miles from anywhere. After a blood-thrilling and skin-tingling motorbike ride…

She shook the thoughts free. 'Childhood sweetheart?'

Tension pumped off him. 'Something like that.'

And suddenly she disliked Christine intensely. 'I'm sorry.'

He shrugged. 'Not your doing.'

She studied the tight lines at the corner of his mouth. The

mouth she'd not been able to stop looking at since he'd shaved and revealed it. Tonight was no different. 'So…there's no Christine now? I mean someone like Christine?'

His eyes found hers. 'You asking if I'm single?'

'Just making conversation. I figured not, since you were on a pilgrimage around the country.'

'It's my job, Eve. Not everyone out here is on some kind of odyssey.'

That stung as much as the sea salt she'd accidentally rubbed in her eye earlier. Because of the judgment those words contained. And the truth. And because they came from him.

But he looked contrite the moment they fell off his lips.

'You don't like talking about her, I take it?' she murmured.

He shook his head but it was no denial.

'Fair enough.' Then she nodded at his arm. 'You might want to get that altered though.'

The tension left his face and a couple of tiny smile lines peeked out the corners of his eyes. 'I couldn't have picked someone with a shorter name, huh? Like Ann. Or Lucy.'

Yep. Christine sure was a long word to tattoo over.

'It's pretty florid, too. A dagger?'

The smile turned into a laugh. 'We were seventeen and in love. And I fancied myself for a bit of a tough guy. What can I say?'

Eve threw some dressing on the salad and gave it a quick toss.

'She got a matching one I hope?'

'Hers just said *Amore*. Multi-purpose.'

'*Pfff.* Non-committal. That should have been your first warning.'

She added a steak to each of their plates.

'With good reason, it turns out.'

'Christine sucked?'

That earned her a chuckle. She loved the rich, warm sound because it came from so deep in his chest. 'No, she didn't. Or I wouldn't have fallen for her.'

'That's very charitable.'

He waved his coffee mug. 'I'm a generous guy.'

'So…I'm confused,' she started. 'You don't want to talk about her, but you don't hold it against her?'

'It's not really about Christine,' he hedged.

'What isn't?' And then, when he didn't respond, 'The awkward silence?'

'How many people end up with their first love, really?'

She wouldn't know. She hadn't had time for love while she was busy raising her family. Or since. More's the pity.

'So where did she end up?'

The look he gave her was enigmatic. But also appraising. And kind of stirring. 'Not important.'

'You're very complicated, Marshall Sullivan.'

His smile crept back. 'Thank you.'

Eve leaned across the counter and lifted the hem of his sleeve with two fingers to have a good look at the design. Her fingertips brushed the smooth strength of his warm biceps and tingled where they travelled.

She cleared her throat. 'Maybe you could change it to *pristine*, like the ocean? That way, you only have to rework the first two letters.'

Three creases formed across his brow as he looked down. 'That could actually work…'

'Or *Sistine*, like the chapel.'

'Or *intestine*, like the pain I get from smelling that steak and not eating it.'

They loaded their plates up with fresh salad and both tucked in.

'This is really good.'

'That surprises you?'

'I didn't pick you as a cook.'

She shrugged. 'I had a rapid apprenticeship after Mum died.'

She munched her way through half her plate before speaking again.

'Can I ask you something personal?'

'Didn't you already do that?'

'About travelling.'

His head tilted. 'Go ahead.'

'Do you…' Lord, how to start this question? 'You travel alone. Do you ever feel like you've forgotten how to be with somebody else? How to behave?'

'What do you mean?'

'I just…I used to be so social. Busy schedule, urban life-style, dinners out most evenings. Meeting new people and chatting to them.' Up until the accident, anyway. 'I feel like I've lost some of my social skills.'

'Honestly?'

She nodded.

'Yeah, you're missing a few of the niceties. But once you get past that, you're all right. We're conversing happily now, aren't we?'

Give or take a few tense undercurrents.

'Maybe you just got good at small talk,' he went on. 'And small talk doesn't take you far in places like this. Situations like this. It's no good at all in silence. It just screams. But we're doing okay, on the whole.'

She rushed to correct him. 'I didn't mean you, specifi-cally—'

'Yeah, you did.'

'What makes you say that?'

'Eve, this feels awkward because it *is* awkward. We don't know each other and yet I was forced into your world unnatu-rally. And now a virtual stranger is sitting ten feet from your bed, drinking your wine and getting personal. Of course it's uncomfortable.'

'I'm not…it's not uncomfortable, exactly. I just feel really rusty. And you don't deserve that. You've been very nice.'

The word *nice* hit him visibly. He actually winced.

'When was the last time you had someone in your bus?' he deviated.

Eve racked her brain… Months. Lots of months. 'Long

enough for that second wineglass to end up right at the back of some cupboard.'

'There you go, then. You're out of shape, socially, that's all.'

She stared at him.

'Let's make a pledge. I promise to be my clunky self when you're around if you'll do the same.' He drew a big circle around the two of them and some tiny part of her quite liked being in that circle with him. 'This is a clunk-approved zone.'

'Clunk-approved?'

'Weird moments acknowledged, accepted and forgiven.'

Why was it so easy to smile, with him? 'You're giving me permission to be socially clumsy?'

'I'm saying I'll understand.'

It was so much easier to breathe all of a sudden. 'All right. Sounds good.'

And on that warm and toasty kindred-spirit moment…

'Are you done?' she checked.

He scooped the last of his steak into his mouth and nodded.

'Hop up, I'd like to show you something.'

As soon as he stood up and back, she pinched the tall stool out from under him and clambered onto it. That allowed her to pop the latch on what looked to anyone else like a sunroof. It folded back onto the bus with a thump. She boosted herself up and into the void, wriggling back until her bottom was thoroughly seated and her legs dangled down into the bus.

'Pass the wine up,' she asked.

He did, but not before adding a generous splash to both their vessels. Then he hoisted himself up opposite her—disgustingly effortlessly—and followed her gaze, left, up out into the endless, dark sky over the Southern Ocean.

'Nice view.'

Essentially the same view as when they'd stood up on the Bedford's back step, just a little higher, but somehow it was made all the more spectacular by the location, the wine and the darkness.

And the company.

'I like to do this when the weather's fine.' Though usually alone.

'I can see why.'

The sky was blanketed with light from a gazillion other solar systems. The full you'll-never-see-it-in-the-city cliché. Eve tipped her head back, stared up and sighed.

'Sometimes I feel like I might as well be looking for Trav out there.' She tossed her chin to the trillions of unseen worlds orbiting those million stars. 'It feels just as unachievable.'

He brought his eyes back down from the heavens. Back to hers.

'It was such a simple plan when I set off. Visit every town in Australia and put posters up. Check for myself. But all it's done is reinforce for me how vast this country is and how many ways there are for someone to disappear. Living or dead.'

'It's a good plan, Eve. Don't doubt yourself.'

She shrugged.

'Did you do it because you truly thought you'd find him? Or did you do it because you had to do something?'

Tears suddenly sprang up and she fought them. It took a moment to get the choke out of her words.

'He's so young. Still a kid, even if the law says otherwise. I was going crazy at home. Waiting. Hoping each day would be the day that the police freed up enough time to look into Trav's case a bit. Made some progress. My heart leaping every time the phone rang in case it was news.'

Fighting endlessly with her father, who wanted her to give up. To accept the truth.

His truth.

'So here you are,' he summarised, simply. 'Doing something constructive. Does it feel better?'

'Yeah. When it's not feeling totally futile.'

It was too dark for the colour of his eyes to penetrate, but his focus fairly blazed out from the shadows under his sockets. 'It's only futile when it stops achieving anything. Right now it's keeping you sane.'

How did this total stranger know her better than anyone else—better than she knew herself?

Maybe because it took one to know one.

She saluted him with her wine. 'Well, aren't we a pack of dysfunctional sad sacks.'

'I'm not sad,' Marshall said, pretty proudly.

What was his story? Curiosity burnt, bright and blazing. The intense desire to *know* him.

'Nothing to say about being dysfunctional?'

'Nope. Totally guilty on that charge.'

The wind had changed direction the moment the sun set, and its heat no longer affected the vast pockets of air blanketing the southern hemisphere. They were tickled by its kiss but no longer buffeted, and it brought with it a deep and comfortable silence.

'So,' Marshall started, 'if I want to use the bus's bathroom during the night I'm basically in your bedroom, right? How's that going to work?'

She just about gave herself whiplash glancing up at him.

'Uh...'

The bus's little en suite bathroom was on the other side of the door that separated it from the rest of the bus. And from Marshall.

Groan. Just another practicality she hadn't thought through thoroughly.

That's because you just about fell over yourself to travel with him for a bit.

'Or I can use the campsite toilet,' he suggested.

Yes! Thank the Lord for public services.

'It's not too bad, actually.' If you didn't mind rocks on your bare feet at three in the morning and spiders in the dark. 'What time do we need to be up?'

As soon as the words tumbled over her lips she regretted

them. Why was she ending the moment of connection so soon after it had begun?

'The boat's coming at eight.'

And dawn was at six. That was two hours of daylight for the two of them to enjoy sharing the clunk-approved zone together. 'Okay. I'll be ready.'

He passed her his mug, then swung himself down and in and took it and hers and placed them together on the bench below. Eve wiggled to the edge of the hatch and readied her arms to take her weight.

'You all right?'

'Yeah, I do it all the time.' Though she just half tumbled, half swung, usually. Gravity fed. Completely inelegant. 'I don't normally have an audience for this bit.'

His deep voice rumbled, 'Here, let me help…'

Suddenly two strong hands were around her waist, pressed sure and hot against her midriff, and she had no choice but to go with them through the roof and back inside the bus. Marshall eased her down in a far less dramatic manner than she was used to, but not without bunching her sweater up under her breasts and leaving her stomach totally exposed as she slid the length of his body. Fortunately, there were no bare hands on bare skin moments, but it was uncomfortable enough to feel the press of his cold jeans stud against her suddenly scorched tummy.

'Thanks,' she breathed.

He released her and stood back, his lashes lowered. 'No problem.'

Instantly, she wondered what the Japanese symbol for 'awkward' was and whether she'd find that tattooed anywhere on his body.

And instantly she was thinking about hidden parts of his body.

She shook the thought free. 'Well…I guess I'll see you in the morning. I'll try and be quiet if you're not up.'

'I'll be up,' he pledged.

Because he was an early riser or because he wasn't about to let her see him all tousled and vulnerable?

Or because all the touching and sliding was going to keep him awake all night, too.

CHAPTER FIVE

IT HAD BEEN a long time since Marshall had woken to the sounds of someone tiptoeing around a kitchen. In this particular case, it was extra soft because the kitchen was only two metres from his makeshift bed.

He'd heard Eve wake up, start moving around beyond that door that separated them all night, but then he'd fallen back into a light morning doze to the entirely feminine soundtrack. You had to live with someone to enjoy those moments. And you had to love them to live with them. And trust them to love them.

Unfortunately, trust and he were uneasy companions.

He'd been in one relationship post-Christine—a nice girl with lots of dreams—and that hadn't ended well. Him, of course. Just another reminder why going solo was easier on everyone concerned. Family included.

Thoughts of his brother robbed him of any further shut-eye. He pulled himself upright and forked fingers through his bed hair.

'Morning,' Eve murmured behind him. 'I hope I didn't wake you?'

'No. I was half awake, anyway. What time is it?'

'Just after six.'

Wow. Went to show what fresh air, hours of swimming and a good drop of red could do for a man's insomnia. He sure couldn't attribute it to the comfort of his bed. Every muscle creaked as he sat up, including the ones in his voice box.

'Not comfortable?'

'Better than my swag on the hard outback dirt.' Even though it really wasn't. There was something strangely comfortable about bedding down on the earth. It was very…honest. 'I'll be back in a tick.'

The morning sun was gentle but massively bright and he stumbled most of the way towards the campsite toilet. Even with her not in her room, the thought of wedging all of himself into that compact little en suite bathroom… It was just too personal.

And he didn't do personal.

'I have eggs or I have sausages,' she announced when he walked back in a little later. 'They won't keep much longer so I'm cooking them all up.'

'Nah. I'll be all right.'

'You have to eat something; we're going to be on the water all day.'

'That's exactly why I don't want something.'

She stopped and stared. 'Do you get seasick?'

'Doesn't really fit with the he-man image you have of me, does it?' He slid back onto his stool from the night before and she passed him a coffee. 'Not horribly. But bad enough.'

'How about some toast and jam, then?'

She was determined to play host. 'Yeah, that I could do.'

That wouldn't be too disgusting coming back up in front of an audience.

She added two pieces of frozen bread to the toaster and kept on with her fry-up. If nothing else, the seagulls would love the sausages.

'Is that okay?' she said when she finally slid the buttered toast towards him.

'Just trying to think when was the last time I had toast and jam.' Toast had been about all his mother stretched to when he was a kid. But there was seldom jam.

'Not a breakfast person?'

'In the city I'd grab something from a fast food place near work.'

'I'm sure your blood vessels were grateful.'

Yeah… Not.

'Mostly it was just coffee.' The liquid breakfast of champions.

'What about out here?'

'Depends. Some motels throw a cooked breakfast in with the room. That's not always a nice surprise.'

'Well, this is a full service b & b, so eat up.'

Eating with a woman at six o'clock in the morning should have felt wrong but it didn't. In fact, clunk-approved zone moments aside, he felt pretty relaxed around Eve most of the time. Maybe because she was uptight enough for the both of them.

'Marshall?'

'Sorry. What did you say?'

'I wondered how the boat would know where to come and get us?'

'They'll just putter along the coast until they see us waving.'

'You're kidding.'

'Well, me waving, really. They're not expecting two.'

'That's very casual,' she said. 'What if they don't come?'

'Then I'll call them and they'll come tomorrow.'

Dark eyebrows shot up. 'You're assuming I'd be happy to stay an extra night.'

'If not, we could just head back to Esperance and pick up the boat there,' he admitted. 'That's where it's moored.'

Her jaw gaped. 'Are you serious? Then why are we here?'

'Come on, Eve. Tell me you didn't enjoy the past twenty-four hours. Taking a break. Enjoying the scenery.'

Her pretty eyes narrowed. 'I feel like I've been conned.'

'You have—' he grinned around the crunch of toast smeared with strawberry jam '—by the best.'

She didn't want to laugh—her face struggled with it—but there was no mistaking the twisted smile she tried to hide by turning and plating up her eggs. Twisted and kind of gorgeous. But all she said was…

'So, talk to me about the island.'

The boat came. The *Vista II*'s two-man crew easily spotted the two of them standing on the rocks at the most obvious point of the whole beach. One of them manoeuvred a small inflatable dinghy down onto the stillest part of the early-morning beach to collect them.

The captain reached down for Eve's hands and pulled her up onto the fishing vessel and Marshall gave her a boost from below. Quite a personal boost—both of his hands starting on her waist but sliding onto her bum to do the actual shoving. Then he scrambled up without assistance and so did the old guy who had collected them in the dinghy that he hastily re-tethered to the boat.

'Thanks for that,' she murmured sideways to Marshall before smiling broadly at the captain and thanking him for real.

'Would you have preferred fish-scaly sea-dog hands on your butt?' Marshall murmured back.

Yeah. Maybe. Because she wouldn't have had to endure his heat still soaking into her. She already had enough of a fascination with his hands…

The next ten minutes were all business. Life vests secured, safety lecture given, seating allocated. Hers was an old square cray pot. Marshall perched on a box of safety gear.

'How long is the trip to Middle Island?' she asked the captain as soon as they were underway.

'Twenty minutes. We have to go around the long way to avoid the wrecks.'

'There are shipwrecks out here?' But as she turned and looked back along the one-hundred-strong shadowy islands of the Recherche Archipelago stretching out to the west, the question suddenly felt really foolish.

Of course there were. It was like a visible minefield of islands.

'Two right off Middle Island.'

As long as they didn't add the *Vista II* to that list, she'd be happy. 'So almost no one comes out here?'

'Not onto the islands, but there's plenty of fishing and small boating traffic.'

'And no one's living on Middle Island?'

Marshall's eyes glanced her way.

'Not since the eighteen-thirties, when Black Jack Anderson based himself and his pirating outfit there,' the captain volunteered.

Huh. So it *could* be lived on. Technically.

Eve turned her gaze towards the distant shadow that was becoming more and more defined as the boat ate up the miles and the captain chatted on about the island's resident pirate. Maybe Marshall's theory wasn't so far-fetched. Maybe Trav could be there. Or have been there in the past. Or—

And as she had the thought, she realised.

Travis.

She'd been awake two whole hours and not given her brother the slightest thought. Normally he was on her mind when her eyes fluttered open each day and the last thing she thought about at night. It kept her focused and on mission. It kept him alive in her heart.

But last night all she'd been able to think about was the man settling in just metres and a bit of flimsy timber away from her. How complicated he was. How easy he was to be around. How good he smelled.

She'd been pulled off mission by the first handsome, broad-shouldered distraction to come along. Nice. As if she wasn't already excelling at the Bad Sister of the Year award.

Well… No more.

Time to get back in the game.

'Eve?' Marshall's voice drifted to her over the sound of the outboard. 'Are you okay?'

She kept her eyes carefully averted, as though she was focusing on the approaching island, and lied.

'Just thinking about what it would be like to live there...'

They travelled in silence, but Eve could just about feel the moments when Marshall would let his eyes rest on her briefly. Assessing. Wondering. The captain chatted on with his semi-tour talk. About the islands. About the wildlife. About the wallabies and frogs and some special lizard that all lived in harmony on the predator-free island. About the southern rock lobster and abalone that he and his mate fished out of these perilous waters. About how many sharks there were lurking in the depths around them.

The promise of sharks made her pay extra attention as she slid back down the side of the *Vista II* into the inflatable and, before long, her feet were back on dry land. Dry, deserted land.

One glance around them at the remote, untouched, unin-habitable terrain told her Trav wasn't hiding out here.

As if there'd really been a chance.

'Watch where you step. The barking gecko is protected on this island.'

'Of course it is,' she muttered.

Marshall just glanced at her sideways. The fishermen left and promised to return for them in a couple of hours. A ner-vous anxiety filled her belly. If they didn't return, what would she do? How would she survive here with just a day's supply of water and snacks and no shelter? Just because Black Jack Whatsit got by for a decade didn't mean she'd last more than a day.

'So,' Marshall said after helping to push the inflatable back offshore, 'you want to explore on your own or come with me?'

Explore on my own—that was the right answer. But, at the same time, she didn't know anything about this strange little island and she was just as likely to break her ankle on the far-thest corner from Marshall and his little first-aid kit.

'Is it safe?' she asked, screening her eyes with her hands and scanning the horizon.

'If you don't count the death adders, yeah.'

She snapped her focus straight back to him. 'Are you kidding?'

'Nope. But if you're watching out for the geckos you'll almost certainly see the snakes before you tread on them.'

Almost certainly.

'I'm coming with you.'

'Good choice. Feel like a climb?' She turned and followed his gaze up to the highest point on the island. 'Flinders Peak is where the weather station would go.'

He assured her it was only one hundred and eighty-five metres above sea level but it felt like Everest when you were also watching every footfall for certain death—yours or a protected gecko's.

Marshall pointed out the highlights to the west, chatted about the nearest islands and their original names. Then he halted his climb and just looked at her.

'What?' she asked, puffing.

'I'm waiting for you to turn around.'

They'd ascended the easiest face of the peak but it had obscured most of the rest of the island from their view. She turned around now.

'Oh, my gosh!'

Pink. A crazy, wrong, enormous bubblegum-pink lake lay out on the eastern corner of the island. Somehow everyone had failed to mention a bright pink lake! 'What is it?'

'Lake Hillier.'

'It's so beautiful.' But so unnatural. It just went to show how little she knew about the natural world. 'Why is it pink?'

'Bacteria? The type of salt? Maybe something new to science. Does it matter?'

'I guess not.' It was just curiously beautiful. 'Can we go there?'

'We just got up here.'

'I know, but now I want to go there.'

So much! A bit like riding on his bike, little moments of

pleasure managed to cut through her miserable thoughts about Travis.

He smiled, but it was twisted with curiosity. And something else.

'What?' she queried.

'This is the first time I've seen you get really passionate about anything since I met you.'

'Some things are just worth getting your pulse up about.' And, speaking of which...

He stepped a little closer and her heartbeat responded immediately.

'Lakes and lizards do it for you?'

'*Pink* lakes and geckos that *bark*,' she stressed for the slow of comprehension. Right on cue, a crack of vocalisation issued from a tuft of scrubby foliage to their left. She laughed in delight. But then she caught his expression.

'Seriously, Marshall... *What?*' His focus had grown way too intense. And way too pointed. She struggled against the desire to match it.

'Passion suits you. You should go hiking more often.'

Her chest had grown so tight with the climb, his words worsened her breathlessness. She pushed off again for the final peak. And for the pure distraction of physical distress.

'I get how the birds get here,' she puffed, changing the subject, 'and the crustaceans. But how did the mammals arrive here? And the lizards?'

For a moment, she thought he wasn't going to let it go but he did, gracefully.

'They didn't arrive, they endured. Back from when the whole archipelago were peaks connected to the mainland. There used to be a lot more until explorers came along and virtually wiped them out.'

Eve looked up at a circling sea eagle. 'You can't tell me that the geckos didn't get picked off by hungry birds, before.'

'Yeah, but in balance. They live in *refugia* here, isolation from the world and its threats. Until the first cat overboard, anyway.'

Isolation from the world and its threats. She kind of liked the sound of that. Maybe that was what Trav was chasing when he walked out into the darkness a year ago. Emotional *refugia.*

She stumbled on a rock as she realised. Not a year ago…a year ago *tomorrow.* Not only had she failed to think about Travis for entire hours this morning but she'd almost forgotten tomorrow's depressing anniversary.

Her joy at their spectacular view drained away as surely as the water far below them dragged back across the shell-speckled beach where they'd come ashore.

Marshall extended his warm hand and took her suddenly cold one for the final haul up the granite top of Flinders Peak, and the entire south coast of Western Australia—complete with all hundred-plus islands—stretched out before them. The same sense of despair she'd felt when staring up at the stars the night before washed over Eve.

Australia was so incredibly vast and so incredibly empty.

So much freaking country to look in.

She stood, immobile, as he did what they'd come to do. Photographing. Measuring. Recording compass settings and GPS results. Taking copious notes and even some soil and vegetation samples. He threw a concerned glance at her a couple of times, until he finally closed up his pack again.

'Eve…'

'Are you done?'

'Come on, Eve—'

'I'm going to head down to the lake.' But there was no interest in her step, and no breathlessness in her words. Even she could hear the death in her voice.

'Stop.'

She did, and she turned.

'What just happened? What did I do?'

Truth sat like a stone in her gut. 'It wasn't you, Marshall. It was me.'

'What did *you* do?'

More what she didn't do.

'Eve?'

'I shouldn't be here.'

'We have a permit.'

'No, I mean I shouldn't be wasting time like this.'

'You're angry because you let yourself off the hook for a few hours?'

'I'm angry because I only have one thing to do out here. Prioritising Travis. And I didn't do that today.'

Or yesterday, if she was honest. She might have pinned up a bunch of posters, but her memories of yesterday were dominated by Marshall.

'Your life can't only be about your brother, Eve. It's not healthy.'

Health. A bit late now to be paying attention to anyone's health. Her own. Her brother's. Maybe if she'd been more alert a couple of years back…

She took a deep breath. 'Are you done up here?'

A dozen expressions ranged across his face before he answered. But, when he did, his face was carefully neutral. 'We have a couple of hours before the boat gets back. Might as well have a look around with me.'

Fine. He could make her stay…

But he couldn't make her enjoy it.

It took the best part of the remaining ninety minutes on the island but Marshall managed to work the worst of the stiffness from Eve's shoulders. He did it with easy, undemanding conversation and by tapping her natural curiosity, pointing out endless points of interest and intriguing her with imaginary tales of the pirate Anderson and his hidden treasure that had never been recovered.

'Maybe his crew took it when they killed him.' She shrugged, still half-numb.

Cynical, but after the sad silence of the first half-hour he'd take it. 'Seems a reasonable enough motive to kill someone. You know, if you were a bloodthirsty pirate.'

'Or maybe there never was any treasure,' she posed. 'Maybe Anderson only managed to steal and trade enough to keep him and his crew alive, not to accrue a fortune. Maybe they weren't very good pirates!'

'You've seen the island now. Where would you bury it if it did exist?'

She glanced around. 'I wouldn't. It's too open here. Hard to dig up without being seen by the crew.' Her eyes tracked outward and he followed them to the guano-blanketed, rocky outcrop just beyond the shores of Middle Island. 'Maybe over there? Some random little cave or hollow?'

'Want to go look?'

She turned wide eyes on him. 'I'm not about to swim fully clothed across a shark-infested channel to an outcrop covered in bird poo filled with God knows what bacteria to hunt for non-existent treasure.'

'You have no soul, Evelyn Read,' he scoffed.

'I do have one and I'd prefer to keep it firmly tethered to my body, thanks very much.'

He chuckled. 'Fair enough. Come on, let's see if the lake looks as impressive up close.'

It didn't. Of course it didn't. Wasn't there something about rose-coloured glasses? But it wasn't a total disappointment. Still officially pink, even once Eve filled her empty water bottle with it.

'You're not planning on drinking that?' he warned.

'Nope.' She emptied it all back into the lake and tucked the empty bottle into her backpack for later recycling. 'Just trying to catch it out being trickily clear.'

They strolled around the lake the long way, then headed back down to the only decent beach on the island. A tiny but sandy cove formed between two outcrops of rocky reef. The place the boat had left them. Marshall immediately tugged his shoes and socks off and tied them to his own pack, which he stashed on a nearby rock, then made his way out a half-dozen metres from where Eve stood discovering that the sand was actually comprised of teeny-tiny white shells.

'Water's fine…' he hinted. 'Not deep enough for predators.'

She crossed her arms grumpily from the shore. 'What about a stingray?'

He splashed a little forward in the waves that washed in from the current surging between the islands. 'Surfing stingrays?'

'Where lakes are pink and lizards bark? Why not?'

'Come on, Eve. Kick your shoes off.'

She glared at him, but eventually she sank onto one hip and toed her opposite runner and sock off, then she did the same on the other foot. Though she took her sweet time putting both carefully in her pack and placing the lot next to his backpack on the hot sand.

'Welcome to heaven,' he murmured as she joined him in the shallows. Her groan echoed his as her hot and parched feet drank up the cold water, too. They stood there like that, together, for minutes. Their hearts slowing to synchronise with the waves washing up and into their little minibay.

Just…being.

'Okay,' Eve breathed, her face turned to the sky. 'This was a good idea.'

He waded a little further from her. 'My ideas are always good.'

She didn't even bother looking at him. 'Is that right?'

'Sure is.'

He reached down and brushed his fingers through the crystal-clear water then flicked two of them in her general direction.

She stiffened—in body and in lip—as the droplets hit her. She turned her head back his way and let her eyes creak open. 'Thanks for that.'

'You had to know that was going to happen.'

'I should have. You with a mental age of twelve and all.'

He grinned. 'One of my many charms.'

She flipped her cap off her head, bent down and filled it with fresh, clean water and then replaced the lot on her head, drenching herself in salty water.

'Well, that killed my fun,' he murmured.

But not his view. The capful of water had the added benefit of making parts of her T-shirt and cargos cling to the curves of her body even more than they already were. And that killed any chance of him cooling down unless he took more serious measures. He lowered himself onto his butt in the shallows and lay back, fully, in the drink.

Pants, shirt and all.

'You know how uncomfortable you're going to be going back?' Her silhouette laughed from high above him, sea water still trickling off her jaw and chin.

He starfished in the two feet of water. 'Small price to pay for being so very comfortable now.'

Even with her eyes mostly shaded by the peak of her cap, he could tell when her glance drifted his way. She was trying not to look—hard—but essentially failing. He experimented by pushing his torso up out of the water and leaning back casually on his hands.

'Easy to say…'

But her words didn't sound easy at all. In fact, they were as tight as her body language all of a sudden.

Well, wasn't *that* interesting.

He pushed to his feet and moved towards her, grinning. Primarily so that he could see her eyes again. Her hands came up, fast, in front of her.

'Don't you dare…'

But he didn't stop until he stood just a centimetre from her upturned hands. And he grinned. 'Don't dare do this, you mean?'

'Come on, Marshall, I don't want to get wet.'

'I'm not the one with a soggy cap dripping down my face.'

'No, you're just soaked entirely through.'

And, with those words, her eyes finally fell where she'd been trying so hard not to look. At his chest, just a finger flex away from her upturned hands.

'I'm beginning to see what Anderson might have liked about this island,' he murmured.

She huffed out a slow breath. 'You imagine he and his crew took the time to roll around in the shallows like seals?'

The thought of rolling around anything with Eve hadn't occurred to him today, but now it was all he could do to squeeze some less charged words past the evocative image. 'Flattering analogy.'

The *pfff* she shot out would have been perfectly at home on a surfacing seal. Her speech was still tinged with a tight breathlessness.

'You know you look good. That was the point of the whole submerge thing, wasn't it? To see how I'd react?'

Actually, getting cool had been the point. Once. But suddenly that original point seemed like a very long time ago. He dropped his voice with his glance. Straight to her lips. 'And how will you react, Eve?'

Her feminine little voice box lurched a few times in her exposed throat. 'I won't. Why would I give you the satisfaction?'

'Of what?'

'Of touching you—'

If she could have bitten her tongue off she would have just then, he was sure. 'Is that what you want to do? I'll step forward. All you have to do is ask.'

Step forward into those still-raised hands that were trembling ever so slightly now.

But she was a tough one. Or stubborn. Or both.

'And why would I do that?'

'Because you really want to. Because we're all alone on a deserted island with time to kill. And because we'll both be going our separate ways after Esperance.'

Though the idea seemed laughable now.

She swallowed, mutely.

He nudged the peak of her cap upwards with his knuckle to better read her expression and murmured, 'And because this might be the only chance we'll have to answer the question.'

Her eyes left his lips and fluttered up to his. 'What question?'

He stared at her. 'No. You have to ask it.'

She didn't, though he'd have bet any body part she wanted to.

'Tell you what, Eve, I'll make it easier for you. You don't have to ask me to do it, you just have to ask me *not* to do it.'

'Not do what?' she croaked.

He looked down at her trembling fingers. So very, very close. 'Not to step forward.'

Beneath the crystal-clear water, his left foot crept forward. Then his right matched it. The whole time he kept his glance down at the place that her palms almost pressed on his wet chest.

'Just one word, Eve. Just tell me to stop.'

But though her lips fell open, nothing but a soft breath came out of them.

'No?' His body sang with elation. 'All righty, then.'

And with the slightest muscle tweak at the backs of his legs, he tipped his torso the tiny distance it needed to make contact with Eve's waiting fingers.

CHAPTER SIX

DEAR LORD...

How long had it been since she'd touched someone like this? More than just a casual brushing glance? All that hard flesh Eve had seen on the beach—*felt* on the bike—pressed back against her fingers as they splayed out across his chest. Across the shadowy eagle that she knew lived there beneath the saturated cotton shirt. Across Marshall's strongly beating heart.

Across the slight rumble of the half-caught groan in his chest.

One he'd not meant to make public, she was sure. Something that told her he wanted this as much as she secretly did.

Or, as her fingers trembled, not so secretly, now.

Marshall was right. They weren't going to see each other again. And this might be the only chance she had to know what it felt like to have the heat of him pressed against her. To know him. To taste him.

All she had to do was move one finger. Any finger.

She'd never meant to enter some kind of self-imposed physical exile when she'd set off on this odyssey. It had just happened. And, before she knew it, she'd gone without touching a single person in any way at all for...

She sucked in a tiny breath. All of it. Eight months.

Puppies and kittens got touch deprivation, but did grown women? Was that what was making her so ridiculously fluttery now? Her father's goodbye hug was the last time she'd had anyone's arms around her and his arms—no matter how strong they'd once been back when she was little—had never felt as sure and rooted in earth as Marshall's had as he'd lowered her from the bus's roof last night. And that had been fairly innocuous.

What kind of damage could they do if they had something other than *help* in mind?

How good—how *bad*—might they feel? Just once. Before he rode off into the sunset and she never got an answer.

Only one way to find out.

Eve inched her thumb down under the ridge of one well-defined pectoral muscle. Nervously jerky. Half expecting to feel the softness of the ink feathers that she could see shadowed through the saturated T-shirt. But there was no softness, only the silken sleeve of white cotton that contained all that hard, hot muscle.

God, he so didn't feel like a weatherman.

Marshall's blazing gaze roasted down on the top of her wet head, but he didn't move. Didn't interrupt. He certainly didn't step back.

Eve trailed her butterfly fingers lightly up along the line of the feathers, up to his collarbone. Beyond it to the rigid definition of his larynx, which lurched out of touch and then back in again like the scandalous tease it was.

Strong fingers lifted to frame her face—to lift it—and he brought her eyes to his. They simmered, as bottomless as the ocean around them as he lowered his mouth towards hers.

'Ahoy!'

Tortured lungs sucked in painfully further as both their gazes snapped out to sea, towards the voice that carried to them on the onshore breeze. Eve stumbled back from all the touching into the buffeting arms of the surf.

'Bugger all decent catch to be had,' the gruff captain shouted as he motored the *Vista II* more fully around the rocks, somehow oblivious to the charged moment he'd just interrupted. 'So we headed back early.'

Irritation mingled with regret in Marshall's storm-grey depths but he masked it quickly and well. It really wasn't the captain's fault that the two of them had chosen the end of a long, warm afternoon to finally decide to do something about the chemistry zinging between them.

'Hold that thought,' he murmured low and earnest as he turned to salute the approaching boat.

Not hard to do while her body screamed in frustration at the interruption, but give her fifteen minutes… Give her the slightest opportunity to think through what she was doing with half her senses and…

Marshall was right to look anxious.

But, despite what she expected, by the time the *Vista II*'s inflatable dinghy transferred them and their gear safely on deck, Eve's awareness hadn't diminished at all. And that was easily fifteen minutes. During the half-hour sea journey back to the campsite beach that followed—past seals sunning themselves and beneath ospreys bobbing on the high currents and over a swarm of small stingrays that passed underneath—still the finely tuned attention her body was paying to Marshall didn't ebb in the slightest.

She forced conversation with the two-man crew, she faked interest in their paltry fishy catch, she smiled and was delightful and totally over-compensated the whole way back.

She did whatever she needed to shake free of the relentless grey eyes that tracked her every move.

After an emotional aeon, her feet were back on mainland sand and the captain lightly tossed their last backpack out of the inflatable and farewelled her before exchanging a few business-related words with Marshall. Moments later, her hand was in the air in a farewell, her smile firmly plastered on and she readied herself for the inevitable.

Marshall turned and locked eyes with her.

'Don't know about you,' he said, 'but I'm famished. Something about boats…'

Really? He was thinking about his stomach while hers was twisted up in sensual knots?

'Have we got any of those sausages from breakfast still in the fridge?'

Um...

Not that he was waiting for her answer. Marshall lugged his backpack up over his shoulder and hoisted hers into his free hand and set off towards the track winding from the beach to the campsite. Eve blinked after him. Had she fantasised the entire moment in the cove? Or was he just exceptional at separating moments?

That was then, this was now. Island rules, mainland rules? What gave?

Warm beach sand collapsed under her tread as she followed him up the track, her glare giving his broody stare all the way back from Middle Island a decent run for its money.

They polished off the leftover sausages as soon as they got back to the bus. At least, Marshall ate most of them while she showered and then she nibbled restlessly on the last one while he did, trying very hard not to think about how much naked man was going on just feet from where she was sitting.

Soapy, wet, naked man.

Had the bus always been quite this warm?

'I think I would have been better off washing in the ocean,' he announced when he walked back in not long after, damp and clean and freshly clothed. Well, freshly clothed in the least used of three pairs of clothes he seemed to travel with. 'Lucky I didn't drop the soap because I wouldn't have been able to retrieve it.'

'I think the previous owners were hobbits,' Eve said, determined to match his lightness.

He slumped down next to her on the sofa. 'The hot water was fantastic while it lasted.'

Yeah. The water reservoir was pretty small. Even smaller as it ran through the onboard gas heater. 'Sorry about that. I guess Mr and Mrs Hobbit must have showered at different ends of the day.'

Not usually a problem for a woman travelling alone. The hot water was hers to use or abuse. And that had worked pretty well for her so far.

'So what's the plan for tonight?' Marshall said, glancing at her sideways.

Lord, if she wasn't fighting off visuals of him in the shower, she was hearing smut in every utterance. *Tonight.* It wasn't a very loaded word but somehow, in this tiny space with this über-present man, it took on piles of new meaning.

'Movie and bed—' She practically choked the word off.

But Marshall's full stomach and warm, fresh clothes had clearly put the damper on any lusty intentions. He didn't even blink. 'Sounds good. What have you got?'

Apparently an enormous case of the hormones, if her prickling flesh and fluttery tummy were any indication. But she nodded towards one of the drawers on the opposite side of the bus and left him to pick his way through the DVD choices. The mere act of him increasing the physical distance helped dilute the awareness that swirled around them.

He squatted and rifled through the box, revealing a stretch of brown, even skin at his lower back to taunt her. 'Got a preference?'

'No.'

Yeah. She'd have preferred never to have said yes to this excruciating co-habitation arrangement, to be honest. But done was done. She filled her one wineglass high for Marshall and then poured filtered water into her own mug where he couldn't tell what she was drinking. Maybe if he was sedated, that powerful, pulsing thrum coming off him would ease off a bit.

And maybe if she kept her wits about her she'd have the strength to resist it.

He held up a favourite. 'Speaking of hobbits…'

Yes! Something actiony and not at all romantic. He popped the disc at her enthusiastic nod, then settled back and jumped through the opening credits to get straight into the movie. Maybe he was as eager as she was to avoid conversation.

It took about ten minutes for her to remember that Middle Earth was definitely *not* without romance and then the whole movie became about the awkwardness of the longing-filled screen kiss that was swiftly approaching. Which only reminded her of how robbed she'd felt out in that cove to have the press of Marshall's lips snatched away by the approach of the *Vista II.*

Which was a ridiculous thing to be thinking when she should be watching the movie.

Hobbits quested. Wraiths hunted. Dramatic elven horse chase. Into the forests of Rivendell and then—

'Are we in the clunk zone, Eve?' Marshall suddenly queried. She flicked her eyes to her left and encountered his, all rust-flecked and serious and steady.

'What?'

Which was Eve-ish for *Yes...yes, we are.*

'Did I stuff things up this afternoon by kissing you?'

'You didn't kiss me,' she managed to squeeze out through her suddenly dry mouth.

But that gaze didn't waver. 'Not for want of trying.'

A waft of air managed to suck down into her lungs. 'Well, the moment has passed now so I think we're cool.'

'Passed?' he asked without smiling. 'Really?'

Yeah… She was a liar.

'That was hours ago,' she croaked.

'I wouldn't know,' he murmured. 'Time does weird things when you're around.'

Her brain wanted to laugh aloud, but the fluttering creatures inside her twittered girlishly with excitement. And they had the numbers.

'I think you're being adversely affected by the movie,' she said, to be safe.

'I'm definitely affected by something.'

'The wine?'

His smile was as gorgeous as it was slow. 'It is pretty good.'

'The company?'

'Yeah. 'Cos that's been terrific.'

She let her breath out in a long, apologetic hiss. 'I'm being weird.'

'You're weird so often it's starting to feel normal.'

'It's not awkward for you?'

His large hand slid up to brush a strand of hair from across her lips. 'What I'm feeling is not awkwardness.'

There went the whole dry mouth thing again. 'What are you feeling?'

'Anticipation.'

The fantastical world on-screen might as well have been an infomercial for all the attraction it suddenly held. Their already confined surroundings shrank even further.

'Maybe the moment's gone,' she said bravely.

He didn't move. He didn't have to. His body heat reached out and brushed her skin for him. 'Maybe you're in denial.'

'You think I'm that susceptible to low lighting and a romantic movie?'

Sure enough, there was a whole lot of elven-human longing going on on-screen. Longing and whispering against an intimate, beautiful soundtrack. Seriously, why hadn't she insisted on something with guns?

'I think the movie was an admirable attempt.'

'At what?' she whispered.

'At not doing this…'

Marshall twisted himself upright, his fingers finding a safe haven for his nearly empty wineglass. His other hand simultaneously relieved her of her mug and reached past her to place it on the sideboard. It legitimised the sudden, closer press of his body into hers.

'Now,' he breathed, 'what were you about to say?'

Heat and dizziness swilled around her and washed all sense out to sea. 'When?'

'Back in the cove. Was it no?' Grey promise rained down on her. 'Or was it yes?'

Truly? She had to find the courage to do this again? It had been hard enough the first time. Though, somehow, having already confessed her feelings made it easier now to admit the truth. She took the deepest of breaths, just in case it was also her last.

'It wasn't no.'

Those beautiful lips twisted in a confident, utterly masculine smile. 'Good.'

And then they found hers. Hot and hard and yet exquisitely soft. Pressing into her, bonding them together, challenging her to respond. She didn't at first because the sensation of being kissed after so very long with no touch at all threw her mind into a state of befuddlement. And she was drowning pleasantly in the sensation of hard male body pressed against hers. And sinking into the clean, delicious taste of him.

But she'd always been a sure adaptor and it only took moments for her feet to touch bottom and push off again for the bright, glittery surface. Her hands crept up around Marshall's shoulder and nape, fusing them closer. Her chin tilted to better fit the angle of his lips. The humid scorch of his breath teased and tormented and roused her, shamefully.

Revived her.

God, she'd missed hot breath mingling with hers. Someone else's saliva in her mouth, the chemical rush that came with that. Tangling tongues. Sliding teeth. And not just any tongue, breath and teeth but ones that belonged with all that hard flesh and ink and leather.

Marshall's.

'You taste of wine, Weatherman,' she breathed.

His eyes fixated on her tongue as she savoured the extra flavour on her lips. 'Maybe it's your own?'

'I had water.'

He lifted back slightly and squinted at her. 'Trying to get me drunk?'

'Trying to fight the inevitable.'

His chuckle rumbled against her chest. 'How's that working out for you?'

Gentle and easy and undemanding and just fine with something as casual as she needed. Wanted. All that she could offer.

And so she gave him access—tempting him with the touch of her tongue—and the very act was a kind of psychological capitulation. Her decision made. Even before she knew she was making it.

She trusted Marshall, even if she didn't know him all that well. He'd been careful and understanding and honest, and her body was *thrumming* its interest in having more access to his. With very little effort she could have his bare, hot skin against hers and her fingertips buried in the sexy curve of all that muscle.

He was gorgeous. He was intriguing. He was male and he was right here in front of her in living, breathing flesh and blood. And he was offering her what she suspected would be a really, really good time.

Did the rest really matter?

One large, hot hand slid up under her T-shirt and curled around her ribcage below her breast as they kissed, monitoring the heart rate that communicated in living braille onto his palm. Letting her get used to him being there. Doing to her exactly what she longed to do to him. Letting her stop him if she wanted. But no matter how many ways he twisted against her, the two of them couldn't get comfortable on the narrow little sofa. No wonder he'd struggled to sleep on it last night. And all the while she had an expansive bed littered with cloud-like pillows just metres away.

Eve levered herself off the sofa, not breaking contact with Marshall's lips or talented hands as he also rose, and she stretched as he straightened to his full height.

'Bed,' she murmured against his teeth.

His escalating kisses seemed to concur. One large foot bumped into hers and nudged it backwards, then another and the first one again. Like some kind of clunky slow dance, they worked their way back through the little kitchen, then through the en suite bathroom and toward unchartered territory. Her darkened bedroom. All the time, Marshall bonded them together either with his lips or his eyes or the hands speared into her hair and curled around her bottom.

There was something delightfully complicit about the way he used his body to steer her backwards into the bedroom while she practically tugged him after her. It said they were equals in this. That they were both accountable and that they both wanted it to happen.

Below her socked feet, the harder external floor of the en suite bathroom gave way to the plush carpet of the bedroom. Marshall's hands slid up to frame her face, holding it steady for the worship of his mouth. His tongue explored the welcome, warm place beyond her teeth just as much as she wanted him to explore this unchartered place beyond the doorway threshold.

A gentle fibrillation set up in the muscles of her legs, begging her to sink backwards onto her bed. The idea of him following her down onto it only weakened them further.

'Eve…' he murmured, but she ignored him, pulling back just slightly to keep the bedward momentum up. It took a moment for the cooler air of the gap she created to register.

Her eyes drifted open. They dropped to his feet, which had stopped, toes on the line between carpet and timber boards.

Hard on the line.

Confusion brought her gaze back up to his.

'I don't expect this,' he whispered, easing the words with a soft brush of his lips. And, when she just blinked at him, his eyes drifted briefly to the bed in case she was too passion-dazzled to comprehend him.

She pulled again.

But those feet didn't shift from the line and so all she achieved was more space between them. Such disappointing, chilly space. At least the hot grasp of his hand still linked them.

'Marshall…?'

'I just wanted to kiss you.'

Ditto! 'We can kiss in here. More comfortably.'

But the distance was official now and tugging any more reeked of desperation so she grudgingly let his hand drop.

'If I get on that bed with you we won't just be kissing,' he explained, visibly moderating his breathing.

'And that's a problem because…?'

'This isn't some roadhouse.'

Confusion swelled up around her numb brain. 'What?'

'You don't strike me as the sex-on-the-first-date type.'

Really? There was a type for these things? 'I don't believe in types. Only circumstances.'

'Are you saying you're just up for it because it's convenient?'

Up for it. Well, that sucked a little of the romance out of things. Then again, romance was not why she'd put her tongue in his mouth just minutes ago. What she wanted from Marshall was what he'd been unconsciously promising her from the moment they'd met.

No strings.

No rules.

No consequences.

'I'm tired of being alone, Marshall. I'm tired of not feeling anything but sadness. I need to feel something good.' A guarded wariness stole over his flushed face and she realised she needed to give him more than that. 'I have no illusions that it's going to go anywhere; in fact, I need it to be short. I don't want the distraction.'

He still didn't look convinced.

'I haven't so much as touched another human being in months, Marshall.'

'Any port in a storm, then?'

God knew it would be stormy between them. As wild and tempestuous as any sea squall. And just as brief.

'We've covered a lot of ground in our few days together and I trust you. I'm attracted to you. I need *you*, Marshall.'

All kinds of shapes seemed to flicker across the back of his intense gaze.

'But I'm not about to beg. Either you want me or you don't. I'll sleep comfortably tonight either way.' *Such lies!* 'Can you say the same?'

Of course he wanted her. It was written in the heave of his chest and the tightness of his muscles and the very careful way he wasn't making a single unplanned move. He wanted what she was offering, too, but there was something about it that he didn't want. Just…something.

And something was enough.

Eve went to push past him, back to the movie, making the disappointing decision for both of them.

But, as she did, his body blocked her path and his left foot crossed onto carpet. Then his right, backing her towards the bed. And then he closed the door on the sword fights of Middle Earth and plunged them into darkness, leaving only the smells and sounds and tastes of passion between them.

CHAPTER SEVEN

EVERY MUSCLE IN Eve's body twinged when she tried to move. Not that she could move particularly far with the heavy heat of Marshall's arm weighing her down. But in case she somehow managed to forget how the two of them had passed the long night, her body was there to remind her. In graphic detail.

Languid smugness glugged through her whole system.

She gave up trying to softly wiggle out of captivity and just accepted her fate. After all, there were much worse ways to go. And to wake up. Right now, her brain was still offering spontaneous flashbacks to specific moments of greatness between them last night, and every memory came with a sensation echo.

Beside her, Marshall slept on in all his insensible glory. Buried face first in her pillows, relaxed, untroubled. It was very tempting just to lie here until lunchtime committing Sleeping Beauty to memory.

Although there was her bladder…

Ugh.

She took more decisive action and slid Marshall's arm off her chest, which roused him sufficiently to croak as she sprang to her feet. 'Morning.'

When was the last time she'd *sprung* anywhere? Usually she just hauled herself out of bed and gritted her teeth as she got on with the business of living.

'Morning yourself. Just give me a sec.'

Easing her bladder just a couple of metres and a very thin

en suite bathroom wall away from Marshall was an unexpectedly awkward moment. It seemed ridiculous after everything
they'd shared in the past twelve hours to have to concentrate
her way through a sudden case of bashful bladder. As soon as
she was done and washed, she scampered back into the toasty
warm and semi-occupied bed.

'You're better than an electric blanket,' she sighed, letting
the heat soak into her cold feet.

'Feel free to snuggle in.'

Don't mind if I do. She was going to milk this one-night
stand for every moment she could.

Marshall hauled her closer with the same strong arm that
had held her captive earlier, her back to his chest in a pretty
respectable spoon.

His voice rumbled down her spine. 'How are you feeling?'

Wow. Not an easy question to answer, and not one she'd expected him to ask. That was a very *not* one-night stand kind of
question. Thank goodness she wasn't facing him.

'I'm...' What was she? Elated? Reborn? She couldn't say
that aloud. 'I have no regrets. Last night was absolutely what
I expected and needed. And more. It was amazing, Marshall.'

It was only then that she realised how taut the body behind
her had become. Awkwardness saturated his words when they
eventually came.

'Actually, I meant because of today.'

She blinked. 'What's today?'

'One year?'

A bucket of icy Southern Ocean couldn't have been more
effective. The frigid wash chased all the warmth of Marshall's
hold away and left her aching and numb. And barely breathing.

Travis. Her poor, lost brother. Twelve months without a boy
she'd loved her whole life and she'd let herself be distracted by
a man she'd known mere moments by comparison.

She struggled for liberty and Marshall let her tumble out
of bed to her feet.

'I'm fine,' she said tightly. 'Just another day.'

He pushed onto his side, giving her a ringside seat for the giant raptor on his chest. She'd so badly wanted to see it last night but the room was too dark. And now she was too gutted to enjoy it.

'Okay...'

Mortification soaked in. What was wrong with her? How much worse to know that, for those first precious moments of consciousness, she hadn't even remembered she *had* a brother. She'd been all about Marshall.

What kind of a sister was she, anyway?

You wanted to forget, that little voice inside reminded her cruelly. *Just for one night. Wasn't that the point?*

Yes. But not like this. Not entirely.

She hadn't meant to *erase* Travis.

'It's a number,' she lied, rummaging in a drawer before dragging on panties and then leggings.

'A significant one,' Marshall corrected quietly.

She pulled a comfortable sweater on over the leggings. 'It's not like it took me by surprise. I've been anticipating it.'

Marshall sat up against the bed head and tucked the covers up around his waist ultra-carefully. 'I know.'

'So why are you making it into an issue?'

Ugh... Listen to herself...

Storm-grey eyes regarded her steadily. 'I just wanted to see how you were feeling this morning. Forget I mentioned it. You seem...great.'

The lie was as ridiculous as it was obvious.

'Okay.'

What was wrong with her? It wasn't Marshall's fault that she'd sought to use him for a bit of escapism. He'd fulfilled his purpose well.

Maybe too well.

'So, should we get going right after breakfast?' she asked brightly from the en suite bathroom as she brushed her hair. Hard to know whether all that heat in her cheeks was residual passion from last night, anger at herself for forgetting today or embarrassment at behaving like a neurotic teen.

Or all of the above.

A long pause from the bed followed and she slowed the drag of the bristles through her hair until it stilled in her hand.

'I've got to get back on the road,' she added, for something to fill the silence.

She should never have left it, really. She replaced the brush and then turned to stand in the bathroom doorway. Trying to be grown up about this. 'We both have jobs to do.'

What was going on behind that careful masculine expression? It was impossible to know. He even seemed to blink in slow motion. But his head eventually inclined—just.

'I'll convoy as far as the South Coast Highway,' he started. 'Then I'll head back to Kal. The road should be open by now.'

Right.

Was that disappointment washing through her midsection? Did she imagine that last night would have changed anything? She *wanted* them to go their separate ways. She'd practically shouted at him that this was a one-off thing. Yet bitterness still managed to fight its way through all her self-pity about Travis.

'Yeah. Okay.'

That was probably for the best. Definitely.

'Do you want me to take some posters for the Norseman to Kalgoorlie stretch? That'll save you doubling back down the track.'

It physically hurt that he could still be considerate when she was being a jerk. A twinge bit deep in her chest and she had to push words through it. Her shoulder met the doorframe.

'You're a nice man, Marshall Sullivan.'

His blankness didn't alter. And neither did he move. 'So I've been told.'

Then nothing. For ages. They just stared at each other warily.

Eventually he went to fling back the covers and Eve spun on the spot before having to face the visual temptation of everything she'd explored with her fingers and lips last night, and made the first excuse she could think of.

'I'll get some toast happening.'

Nice.

Just what every man wanted to hear from a woman he'd spent the night with. Not 'fantastic' or 'unforgettable'. Not 'awe-inspiring' or 'magnificent'.

Nice.

He'd heard that before, from the Sydney kids who had clambered over him in their quest to get closer to Rick and his chemical smorgasbord. From friends and girls and the occasional tragic teacher.

He'd always been the *nicer* brother.

But not the one everyone wanted access to.

Sticks and stones…

Problem was, Eve's lips might have been issuing polite compliments but the rest of her was screaming eviction orders and, though he'd only known her a couple of days, it was long enough for him to recognise the difference. He'd had enough one-off encounters with women to know *get out of my room* when he saw it. Despite all the brave talk last night, she was *not* comfortable with the aftermath of their exhausting night together.

And he was all too familiar with eyes that said something different from words. He'd had them all his life.

He'd been right in assuming Eve wasn't a woman who did this a lot; she was most definitely under-rehearsed in the fine art of the morning-after kiss-off. If he'd realised there'd be no lingering kisses this morning he would have taken greater care to kiss her again last night just before they fell into an exhausted slumber twisted up in each other.

Because Eve had just made it very clear that there would be no more kissing between them.

Ever.

He'd worked his butt off last night giving her the kind of

night she clearly needed from him. Making sure it was memorable. And, if he was honest, giving Eve something to think about. To regret. Maybe that was why it stung even more to see her giving it exactly zero thought this chilly morning.

Wham-bam, thank you, Marshall.

Somewhere, the universe chuckled to itself as the cosmic balance evened up. That was what he got for usually hotfooting it out the next morning the way Eve just had.

Only generally to fire up his motorcycle, not the toaster.

What did he expect? Days wrapped up in each other's arms here in this ridiculous little bus while his remaining weeks on the project ticked ever closer to an end and her bank balance slowly drained away? Neither of them had the luxury of indefinite leisure. He wasn't stupid.

Or maybe he was…because Evelyn Read was definitely not a one-off kind of woman and some deep part of him had definitely hoped for more than the single night they'd both agreed on between kisses. Which meant it was probably just as well that was all he was getting. Eve had no room for another man in her single-track life.

And he was done being a means to an end.

He pulled yesterday's T-shirt back on and rather enjoyed the rumples and creases. They were like little trophies. A reminder of how the shirt had been thoroughly trampled underfoot in their haste to get each other naked. A souvenir of the disturbingly good time he'd had with her beyond her bedroom door.

'Don't burn it,' he murmured, passing into the tiny kitchenette intentionally close to her, just to get one more feel of her soft skin. His body brushed the back of hers.

Her feet just about left the floor, she jumped that fast and high. Then a sweet heat coloured along her jawline and her lips parted and he had to curl his fingers to stop himself from taking her by the hand and dragging her back to that big, warm bed and reminding her what lips were made for.

It felt good to torture Eve, just a little bit. It sure felt good to surprise her into showing her hand like that. To shake the ambivalence loose. To watch the unsteadiness of her step. She might call a halt to this thing just getting going between them but he wasn't going to go easily.

He kept on moving past her, ignoring the sweet little catch in her breath, and he stopped at the back doors, flung them open and then stretched his hands high to hook them on the top of the bus, stretching out the kinks of the night, knowing how his back muscles would be flexing. Knowing how the ink there would flash from beneath his T-shirt. Knowing how that ink fascinated her.

If she was going to drive off into the horizon this morning, she sure wasn't going to do it with a steady brake foot.

Yup. He was a jerk.

He leapt down from the bus and turned to his KTM, and murmured to the bitter cold morning.

'*Nice*, my ass.'

The bus's brake lights lit up on the approach to the junction between the Coolgardie and South Coast Highways and Marshall realised he hadn't really thought this through. It was a big intersection but not built for pulling over and undertaking lingering farewells. It was built for turning off in any of the four points of the compass. His road went north, Eve's went further west.

But the uncertain blink of her brake lights meant she, too, was hesitating on the pedal.

She didn't know what to do either.

Marshall gave the KTM some juice and pulled up in the turn lane beside her instead, reassuring himself in the mirror that there was no one on the remote highway behind them. Eve dropped her window as he flipped his helmet visor.

'Good luck with the rest of your trip,' he called over the top of his thrumming engine and her rattling one.

'Thank you.' It was more mouthed than spoken.

God, this was a horrible way of doing this. 'I hope you get some news of your brother soon.'

Eve just nodded.

Then there was nothing much more to say. What could he say? So he just gave her a small salute and went to lower his visor. But, at the last moment, he found inspiration. 'Thank you for coming with me yesterday. I know you would have rather been back on the road.'

Which was code for *Thanks for last night, Eve.* If only he were the slightest bit emotionally mature.

She nodded again. 'I'm glad I did it.'

Middle Island, he told himself. Yesterday. That was all.

And then a car appeared on the highway in his mirror, way back in the distance, and he knew they were done.

He saluted again, slid his tinted visor with the obligatory squished bugs down between them and gave the bike some juice. It took only seconds to open up two hundred metres of highway between them and he kept Eve in his mirrors until the Bedford crossed the highway intersection and was gone from view, heading west.

Not the worst morning-after he'd ever participated in, but definitely not the best.

He was easily the flattest he could remember being.

He hadn't left his number. Or asked for hers. Neither of them had volunteered it and that was telling. And, without a contact, they'd never find each other again, even if they wanted to.

Eve Read would just have to be one of those memories he filed away deep inside. He added *The Crusader* to his list of badly handled flings.

Except she didn't feel like a fling. She felt like forever. Or what he imagined forever must feel like. Crazy. He'd known her all of five minutes. So the lingering sense that things weren't done between them was...

Ridiculous.

The shimmering haze of her exhaust as she couldn't speed away from him fast enough told a very different story.

Trees and wire fences and road signs whizzed by the KTM

in a one-hundred-and-ten-kilometre-per-hour blur. Plus a sheep or two.

Would he have stayed if she'd asked? If she'd crawled back into bed this morning and snuggled in instead of running an emotional mile? If he hadn't—like a freaking genius—brought up her most painful memory when she was half-asleep and vulnerable to his words?

Yeah. He would have stayed.

But it was the *why* that had him by the throat.

Eve was pretty but not beautiful, bright but not spectacular, prickly as a cactus and more than a little bit neurotic. She should have just been a charming puzzle. So what was with the whole curl-up-in-bed urge? He really wasn't the curl up type.

She's your damsel, man.

The words came burbling up from deep inside him, in his brother's voice. The kind of conversations they used to have way back when. Before they went down opposite off ramps of the values highway. Before Rick's thriving entrepreneurial phase. Certainly before Christine switched teams—and brothers. Back when Rick gave him stick for being a soft touch for girls in need of a knight on a white charger.

Orange charger, in his case.

Relief surfed his veins.

Yeah, this was about Eve's brother. That was all it was, this vague sense that leaving her was wrong. There was nothing more meaningful or complicated going on than that. He hated the helplessness he saw behind Eve's eyes and the flat nothing she carried around with her. It made him feel powerless—his least favourite emotion.

She's not yours to fix, Inner Rick nudged.

No, but was there really nothing more he could offer her than platitudes and some help with the posters and one night of sweaty distraction? He was a resourceful guy. He had connections.

And then it hit him…

Exactly why he'd chosen to place a woman he'd just met

and a man he hadn't seen in ten years next to each other at the dinner table of his subconscious.

His brain ticked over as fast as his tyres ate up the highway. If a person was going to go off grid, they might ditch their bank accounts in favour of cash, stop filing tax returns and opt out of claiming against Medicare. But what was Eve the most cut up about—? That Travis was struggling with his panic disorder, alone. And what did people who were being treated for disorders do? They took drugs. And who knew everything there was to know about drugs?

Rick did.

Enough to have driven his kid brother away years before. Enough to have made a thriving business out of supplying half of Sydney with their chemical needs. Enough to have a world of dodgy contacts inside the pharmaceutical industry—legal and otherwise.

Marshall eased off the throttle.

That meant he was just one uncomfortable phone call away from the kind of information that the cops would never think to access. Or be able to. Not ethical, probably not even legal, but since when did Rick let something as insignificant as the law stand between him and his goals?

Of course it would mean speaking to his brother, but maybe a decade was long enough with the silent treatment. Lord knew, Rick owed him.

Marshall down-geared and, as he did, his rapid pulse started to slow along with his bike. The pulse that had kicked up the moment parting from Eve was upon him. Back at the intersection. A kind of anxiety that he hadn't felt in a long, long time—since before he'd stopped letting himself care for people.

The descending thrum of his blood and the guttural throb of his bike colluded to soak him in a kind of certainty about this plan. As if it was somehow cosmically meant to be. As if maybe this was why he'd met Eve in the first place.

Because he could help her.

Because he could save her.

That was all this was. This…unsettling obsession. It was his Galahad tendency. Evelyn Read needed *help*, not *him*. And he was much more comfortable with the helping part.

He hit his indicator and looked for a safe place to pull over. He fished around in the depths of his wallet for a scrap of paper he'd almost forgotten he still carried. Ratty and brown edged, the writing half-faded. Rick's phone number. He punched the number into his phone but stopped short of pressing Dial.

This was Rick. The brother who'd made his teenage years a living hell. Who'd lured his girlfriend away from him just because he could. The brother who'd been the real reason that most of his friends craved his company and half the teachers gave him special treatment. They'd all wanted an in with *The Pharmacist*.

Rick was the reason he couldn't bring himself to trust a single soul, even now. Rick had taken the lessons they'd both learned from their mother about love and loyalty—or absences thereof—and turned the hurt into a thriving new industry where a lack of compassion for others was a corporate asset.

He'd made it work for him, while his little brother struggled in his shadow.

It had taken him years to fortify himself against those early lessons. His mother's. His brother's. And here he was, straddling his bike and contemplating leaping off the edge of his personal fortress of solitude to help someone he barely knew. He'd kicked the door of communication closed between every part of his old life and here he was, poised to take to that door with a crowbar and crack it open again.For a virtual stranger.

No…*for Eve*.

And Eve mattered.

He thumbed the dial button and listened as the number chirped its ominous melody. Took three deep breaths as it rang and rang. Took one more as a gruff voice picked up.

Marshall didn't waste time with niceties.

'You said to call if I ever needed you,' he reminded his brother. 'Did you mean it…?'

* * *

Rick had been at first surprised, then wary, when he recognised Marshall's serious tone after so very long. But—typical of the brother he remembered—Rick took the call at face value and accepted the subtext without comment. He listened to the request, grizzled about the dubiousness of what he'd been asked to do, but committed to help. And, despite anything else he'd done in his life, Rick Sullivan was the personification of tenacity. If he said he'd get this done, then, one way or another, some time Marshall's phone would be ringing again.

End of day, that was all that really mattered. Eve needed results more than he needed to maintain the moral high ground.

Rick even managed to go the entire phone call without getting personal.

The leathers of Marshall's jacket creaked as he exhaled. 'Thank you for your help, Rick. I swear it's not for anything too dodgy.'

'This whole thing is dodgy,' his brother muttered. 'But I'll do it because it's you. And because dodgy is where I do my best work. It might take a while, though.'

'No problem.'

Eve had been waiting twelve months. What was one more?

'I might find nothing.'

'Understood.'

'And one day maybe you can tell me what we're doing. And who for.'

He tensed up, mostly at the suggestion that there'd be a 'one day'. As if the door couldn't be closed once jemmied open.

'What makes you think there's a "who"?'

'Because you don't get invested in things, brother. Ever. You're Mr Arm's Length. But I can hear it in your voice. This matters.'

'Just let me know how you go,' he muttered. Eve was not someone he would trust his brother with, even mentally. He wasn't about to share any details.

'So…you want to know whether she's okay?' Rick asked, just before they ended the call.

'Christine?' Speaking of not trusting Rick… A few years ago, he would have felt the residual hurt deep in his gut. But now it just fluttered to earth like a burnt ember. Maybe the history really was history now.

'No, not Christine. I have no idea where she ended up.'

That bit. That Rick hadn't even kept his prize after working so very hard to take it from him.

'I meant Mum,' Rick clarified. 'Remember her?'

Everything locked up tight inside Marshall. He'd closed the door on Laura Sullivan the same day he'd locked Rick out of his life. The two of them were a package deal. The moment she'd realised her enterprising oldest son was going to be a far better provider than the Government, she'd made her allegiance—and her preference—totally clear.

That wasn't something you forgot in a hurry… Your own mother telling you to go.

'No. I'm good.'

There didn't seem much else to say after that.

It took just a moment to wind the call up and slip his phone back into his pocket. He'd get a new number just as soon as Rick gave him the info he needed. But he didn't hit the road again straight away. Instead, he sat there on the highway, bestride his KTM, breathing out the tension.

You don't get invested in things.

Well, that pretty much summed him up. Work. Life. He had a good ethic but he never let himself care. Because caring was a sure way of being disappointed. Or hurt. Life in his brother's shadow had taught him that. And as life lessons went, that one had served him well.

Until now.

As Rick had readily pointed out, he was invested now. With Eve—a woman he barely knew. He was more intrigued and conflicted and turned inside out for a woman he'd known just days than the people he'd grown up with. Maybe because she didn't want anything from him that she wasn't prepared to own. She had no agenda. And no ulterior motive.

Eve just…was.

And maybe he'd found a way to help her. Or maybe not. But he sure wasn't going to be able to do it from here.

He'd just sent her off down the highway with absolutely no way of locating her again. No email. No number. No forwarding address. How many Reads might there be in Melbourne? He couldn't shake the screaming thought that this was the only moment he had left. Right now, Eve was rattling down a long, straight road that only went to one place. After that, she could head off in any of five different routes into tourist country and his chances of finding her would evaporate. Tension coiled inside him like a spring…

And that was when he knew.

This wasn't just about helping Eve. If it was, he could just take whatever information his brother dug up straight to the authorities. Let them do the rest. This wasn't just about some cosmic interference to help her find her brother. That unfamiliar, breath-stealing tightness in his chest was panic. And he didn't do panic because that implied caring.

He'd no sooner let himself care for someone than void a ten-year stalemate with his criminal brother to get something that might ease Eve's pain. Eve—a complex, brittle, single-minded angel. The most intriguing woman he'd met in…more than years. The woman who'd barrelled through his defences and wedged herself there between his ribs. Just below his heart.

Oh, crap…

From where he sat, he could see the endless stretch of highway ahead—north to Kalgoorlie, where he could pick up his work trail where he'd left it a few days ago. But, in his mirror, he could see the long straight run behind him, back to the four-way turn-off. Back to a one hundred per cent chance of catching up with the bus before it turned off the western highway.

Back to the possibility he'd been too cowardly to explore.

Back to Eve.

He started his engine, dropped his visor and let his eyes lift to the northern horizon. Towards work and the conclusion of this trip and his safe, comfortable life.

But then they dropped again to the mirror, and the road he'd just travelled.

Sure, she might tell him to get lost. And if she did, he would.

But what if she didn't…?

In the end, his hands made the decision before his head did, and a leathered thumb hit his indicator before pulling the KTM's handlebars right, out across the empty highway and then back onto the opposite shoulder.

Before he could second-guess himself, he gunned the accelerator and roared off towards the south.

Towards the unknown.

CHAPTER EIGHT

IT COULD BE ANYONE—that speck in the distance behind her.

Car. Bike. Truck. It was too small for one of the massive road trains that liked to thunder past at breakneck speed, but a smaller truck, maybe.

Eve forced her eyes forward and ignored the impulse to check again. Plenty of people drove this road into Western Australia's tourist region. People who had far more legitimate reasons to be heading this way than *he* did.

Marshall was heading north. Back to his weather stations. Back to reality.

Which was exactly what she should be doing. Middle Island had been a nice couple of days of escapism—for both of them—but they both had jobs to be doing.

And Travis was her job.

He always had been.

If the past couple of days had taught her anything, it was that she couldn't take her eyes off the prize—or the map—for a moment. Look how fast she'd been swayed from her purpose. Besides, Marshall couldn't get out of there fast enough this morning. Not once he saw her in full neurotic mode. He was probably congratulating himself right now on a bullet well dodged.

The speck in her rear-vision mirror grew larger. But not large enough to be a truck. A car, then.

Or smaller, her subconscious more than whispered.

No.

Why would Marshall return? He hadn't left anything behind in her bus—she'd checked twice. And their parting had been as unequivocal as it was awkward. And definitely for the best. She was on a mission and didn't need the distraction. No matter how compelling.

And boy, was he ever. He'd been an intriguing curiosity while tattooed and hairy. Clean shorn and well educated, he was entrancing. Naked, he was positively hypnotic. All the better for being a long, long way from her.

She glanced helplessly back at the mirror and her pulse made itself known against the fragile skin of her throat.

Not a car.

Her gaze split its time between looking ahead and looking back, then the forward-looking part became a glance and then a mere flick to keep the bus on a straight and safe line.

Plenty of motorbikes in the sea. Impossible to even know what colour this one was yet.

Her gaze remained locked on her mirror.

If it was orange—if it was *him*—that didn't have to mean anything. Their one night together had probably been so good because it was a one-off. No past, no future. Just the very heated and very comfortable present. Even if Marshall was coming back for a second go at last night, there was nothing that said she had to oblige—no matter what her pulse recommended.

No matter how enticing the promise of a few more hours of mental *weightlessness* he brought.

A dull mass settled between her shoulder blades. She couldn't afford to be weightless. Not until her journey was complete and Travis was home.

Her own thought tripped her up. She'd never thought about this journey being over. What she would do. Would work have her back? She'd resigned with notice, so there were no burnt bridges there, but could she go back to meetings and minutes and deadlines? Would she have the patience? What would she be like after it was all over? Could she be *normal* now that she knew how secretly cruel the world really was?

As for weightless… Would she ever feel that way again?

Or was that just another disloyalty to Travis? To be worrying about any of it?

She'd put herself first once before and look how that had ended. Travis had melted down completely the moment she took her eyes off him.

She glanced up again, just in time to see a flash of black and orange changing into the inside lane and then roaring up beside her.

All the breath squeezed up tight in her suddenly constricted chest.

He was back.

Marshall whizzed by on her right, then changed lanes into the vanguard position and weaved in the lane in a kind of high-speed wave. She took several long, steadying breaths to bring the mad thump of her heart back into regular rhythm.

Should she stop? Hear what he had to say?

No. If he wanted her to pull over he'd be braking, slowing her. But he was pacing her, not slowing her. Guiding her onward. Besides, not far now until the turn-off to the Ravensthorpe poster drop. If he had something to say he could say it there.

And she'd listen politely and when it came to the time to part again she'd try and be a bit more erudite than her poor effort this morning.

Two vehicles whizzed by in the opposite direction, marking their entry into tourist country. *Tourism.* That was what she and Marshall were doing, right? Exploring the unchartered country that was each other. Enjoying the novelty. But how many tourists sold up and moved to the places they visited? How many stayed forever? No matter how idyllic.

Right. Because the real world eventually intruded.

And her reality was Travis.

Marshall wiggled his motorbike again and seemed to be

waiting for something. Did he seriously worry that she hadn't recognised him? She gave her headlights a quick flash of acknowledgement and his weaving ceased.

He placed himself squarely in the centre of their lane and let his bike eat up the highway.

And Eve did her best not to fixate on the strong breadth of his back and breathless imaginings about what it would be like to peel all that leather right off him.

The Bedford's front doors were as reluctant to open as Eve was to pass through them. But Marshall had made fast work of slinging the KTM onto its stand and pulling off his helmet. As he sauntered towards her on his thick-soled riding boots, he forked fingers through his thick helmet hair to ruffle it up.

Her first thought—on the clench of her stomach—was that finger-forking his hair was her job.

Her second thought—on the clench of her heart at the sound and smell of his creaking leathers as he stopped in front of her—was that she was completely screwed.

'Forget something?' she managed to squeeze out from the top of the Bedford's steps. More for something to say, really, because if he'd actually come back for his favourite socks she was going to be really crushed. She kept her body language as relaxed as was possible in a body ready to flee.

'Yeah,' he murmured, stepping up onto the bottom step, 'this.'

One gloved hand came up and lifted her chin as if he was holding a crystal flute and his lips brushed against hers. Then the brush got harder, closer. So...*so* much better. He turned his head and deepened the kiss, stroking his tongue into her mouth and against her own. Just when she'd thought no one would ever kiss her like that again.

She wavered there on the top step, the closest thing to a swoon she'd ever experienced.

'I didn't say goodbye properly,' he finally breathed against her astonished mouth. 'Now I don't want to say it at all.'

'You left,' she said between the head spins.

'But I'm back.'

'What about work?'

'What about it? There are plenty of weather stations still on my list. I'll just flex my route.'

What about my *work?* was what she really needed to be asking. Because how much of it was she going to get done with him around? If the past couple of days was any indication.

'You just assume I want to carry on where we left off?'

Just because she *did*… He wasn't to know that.

'I'm not assuming anything. If you send me away I've wasted…what…an hour of my time and a couple of bucks in fuel. Those are reasonable stakes.'

She pulled free. 'Charming.'

His grin managed to warm her right through, even as her heart screamed at her not to fall for it.

'Do you want me to go?'

She stared at him. Remembered how it felt to be with him. To be *with* him. And the thought of watching him drive off again was almost unbearable.

'I should,' she breathed.

'That's not a no.'

'No.' She stared at him. 'It's not.'

His puppy-dog grin graduated into a full, brilliant, blazing smile. 'Come on, then. Let's get some posters up. Time's a-wasting.'

He stepped down off the bus and held a hand out to help her. His eyes were screened by sunglasses but she could clearly see the trepidation still in the stiffness of his body. What she did next mattered to him. And that made her feel a whole lot better. She glanced at his outstretched hand. The unexpected chivalry excited and troubled her at the same time. She'd been jumping down off the Bedford's steps all by herself for eight months.

But just because she *could* didn't mean it wasn't a rare treat not to have to.

How would it feel to share this burden, just for a bit?

Would Travis understand?

After an age, she slid her bare fingers into his leathery ones and accepted his help.

But they both knew that taking his hand was saying yes to a whole lot more.

Marshall followed Eve as she chugged the Bedford into the biggest town in the Great Southern region behind the two-dozen cars that constituted peak hour in these parts. When she pulled up in a big open car park, Marshall stood the KTM and then jogged off to find something for them to eat. When he got back with it, she was set up and ready to go. Table and chair in place, bus sides up and covered in posters.

'I need to find the MP's office,' she announced. 'I'm getting low on posters.'

'Didn't you do that before?'

'Nope. Somebody distracted me.'

Yeah. He was probably supposed to feel bad about that. 'Too bad.' He winced.

'You don't look very sympathetic,' she admonished.

He just couldn't stop smiling. What was that about? 'MP's office was a few doors down from where I got lunch. I'll show you.'

Then it was her turn to smile. 'Thank you.'

She weighted down anything on her display that might blow away, grabbed a flash drive from her wallet and hurried alongside him. The door to the MP's office set off an audible alert as they entered.

'Hi there,' a friendly young woman said from behind the reception desk, addressing him. He looked straight at Eve, who slid the flash drive over the counter. 'Welcome to Albany.'

'Can you run off a hundred of these, please?'

The woman frowned and didn't touch the flash drive. 'What is it?'

'A missing-person poster,' Eve elucidated, but it didn't bring any hint of recognition. 'MP's offices are supposed to run off copies for free.'

A little explanation wasn't exactly an Open Sesame.

'Let me just check,' the woman said, stalling.

Eve looked as if she wanted to say more but his hand on her wrist forestalled it. A few moments later the woman came back, smiling, and chirped, 'Won't be long!'

Eve turned to the window and the port view beyond it and curled her arms around her torso.

Every day must have moments like these for her. When simple things like a bit of public bureaucracy suddenly reared up in front of her like a hurdle in her efforts to find her brother. No wonder she was so tired.

That kind of emotional ambush would be exhausting.

'Good morning,' a male voice said and Eve turned from her view.

An overly large, overly suited man with a politician's smile approached, hand outstretched. 'Gerald Harvey, MP.'

'Evelyn Read,' she murmured, sliding her fingers into his.

He followed suit. 'Marshall Sullivan.'

'You have a missing person?' the man asked and barrelled onwards before she could answer. 'I'm very sorry for your loss.'

'My loss?'

The statement seemed to stop Eve cold, and only the new colour in her face gave Gerald Harvey a hint that he might have put his finely shod foot in it. 'Your…uh…circumstances.'

Marshall stepped in closer behind her and placed his hand on Eve's lower back, stroking gently.

'Thank you,' she said to the man, more evenly than he would have expected based on her expression.

Harvey took the first poster that his assistant printed and read it aloud, rolling the name over his tongue like wine. 'Travis James Read.'

Just in case Eve didn't know who she'd been looking for the past year.

'Can't say I've seen him but someone might have. Are you circulating these in town?'

'All over the country.'

The man laughed. 'Not all over it, surely.'

Eve didn't waver. 'All over it. Every town. Every tourist stop.'

He stared as the poster in his hand fell limply over his substantial fist, and Marshall watched the interplay of disbelief and pity play over his ruddy face. Then it coalesced into kind condescension.

'That's a lot of posters.'

Brilliant. Of all the things he could have noted about Eve's extraordinary endeavour...

'Yes.'

'And fuel.'

Okay, enough was enough.

'Eve,' he interjected, 'how about we go back to the bus and I'll come back for the posters in fifteen minutes? You should get started. Don't want to miss anyone.'

Ironic, given her life was all about missing someone.

He thanked the MP and then bustled her out into the street, instantly feeling the absence of the tax payer–funded office heating. She didn't speak. Didn't confront him or rant. She'd turned inwards somewhere in that brief encounter and wasn't coming out any time soon.

He could endure the silence no longer than five minutes.

'Did I ever look at you like that?' he eventually asked as they walked back towards the main street. The mixture of pity and polite concern. As if she might not be all that mentally well herself.

His direct question dragged her focus back to him. Brown eyes reached into his soul like a fist and twisted. 'A little bit.'

Great. No wonder she'd taken a while to warm up to him. Maybe she still was.

'It's not crazy,' he insisted suddenly, stopping and turning her towards him. 'It's not common, sure, but what you're doing is…logical. Under the circumstances. I get it.'

'You do?'

He waved his hand towards her poster display of all *The Missing* as they approached. 'I imagine every one of their families would like to have the courage and commitment to do what you've done. To get out here and look, personally. To do something proactive. To know you've done as much as you possibly can.'

She tossed her head back in the direction of the MP's office. 'That reaction is pretty common.'

'People don't know what to say, I guess.'

She stared up at him. 'You didn't have that problem.'

Something bloomed deep inside on learning that she had forgiven him for whatever first impression he'd left her with. Enough to shrug and joke, 'I'm exceptional.'

The sadness cracked and her mouth tipped up. 'So you say.'

'Go,' he nudged. 'Get started. I'll go back and manage Mr Charm, and then I'll go find us a camping site after I've dropped your new posters to you.'

She seemed to do a full-body sigh. 'Thank you.'

'No problem. Back in a few.'

He turned back for the MP's office but only got a few steps before turning again. He was back beside her in moments.

'Wha—?'

It took no effort at all to pull her into his arms and tuck her safe and warm beneath his chin. To wrap his arms firmly around her so that nothing and no one could get between them.

How had it not occurred to him before now to hug Eve?

This was a woman who needed repeat and regular hugging. On prescription. And he was happy to be her spoonful of sugar. Her slim arms crept around his waist and hooked behind his back, and the rest of her pressed into his chest as she sagged into him. Stroking her hair seemed obvious.

Around them, the sounds of a busy coastal town clattered on.

But inside their bubble there was only the two of them.

'That guy was a dick,' he announced against her ear.

'I know,' she muffled into his chest.

'I'm sorry that happened.'

She wriggled in closer. 'You get used to it.'

'You shouldn't have to.'

'Thank you.'

He curled her in closer, resting his chin on her head.

'Um…Marshall?' she eventually mumbled.

'Yeah?'

'Aren't you going to get us a site?'

'Yep. Leaving now.'

Around them traffic did its thing and somewhere a set of traffic lights rattled off their audible alert.

'Marshall?'

His fingers stroked her hair absently. 'Hmm?'

'We're making a scene.'

He opened one eye and, sure enough, a couple of locals walked by, glancing at them with amused smiles on their faces.

He closed the eye again and tucked her in even closer.

'Screw 'em.'

'Gotta say, you have a strange idea of what constitutes a "camping site".'

'I'm funded to stay in motels.' Marshall shrugged. 'You might as well benefit.'

'Are all your *motels* quite this flash?' She leaned on the word purposefully because the waterside complex was more of a resort than anything.

'Well, no. But you put me up the last two nights so I have some budget savings. And there's hardly anyone else here out of season so you can take as much car park room as you need for the bus.'

Because she'd be sleeping in the car park while he spread out in the suite's big bed all alone?

She glanced at him. Maybe she'd misunderstood what his return meant. But she wasn't brave enough to ask aloud. Or maybe that was actually a really good idea. A tempestuous one-night stand was one thing but a second night—that needed some managing.

'Come on. At least check it out since you're here.'

She followed him up to the second storey, where the suite's balcony looked out over a parkland walkway below to the turquoise, pine tree–lined swimming bay that curled left and right of them. The rest of the suite was pretty much made of either sofa or bed. Both enormous. A large flat-screen TV adorned the walls between local art and something tantalising and white peeked out at her, reflected, through the bathroom door.

Her breath sucked in. Was that a…?

'Spa?'

'Yeah, I think so,' he said a little sheepishly. Had it suddenly dawned on him that this was all starting to look a little *boom-chick-a-wah-wah*? 'It came with the room.'

How long had it been since she'd soaked her weary body? And having a spa, or lounging on the sofa, or sitting on the balcony with a glass of wine didn't have to mean she was staying the night here. Her own bed was pretty comfy, thanks very much.

She glanced at the crack in the bathroom door again and wondered how she could ask him for access without it sounding like a come-on. Or an invitation.

As usual, Marshall came to her rescue with the lift of one eloquent eyebrow and the careful and chivalrous choice of words.

'You want first crack?'

It took her about a nanosecond to answer in the positive and about two minutes to sprint back to the bus and get some clean clothes. It was only as she took the stairs back up two by two that she realised what the bundle of comfortable leggings and track top in her arms meant.

They weren't going back out again tonight.

So, that meant room service for dinner. Nice and cosy, just the two of them.

Wow. Her subconscious was really going to make this tough

for her. But the siren song of the bubbles was so strong she didn't care.

Bubbles. Heaven.

'It's a fast filler,' Marshall announced as she burst back into the room, more eager than she'd felt in a long time.

Oh, right…filling. Nature's brakes. Eve stood, a bit at a loss, shifting from foot to foot in the room's entryway.

'It has a shower, too,' he volunteered, bright light glinting in the grey of his eyes. 'You could get straight in and then just shower until the water level is high enough.'

She loved her bus, but its shower pressure was as weak as it was brief. The chance for a proper shower was overwhelming. 'Oh, my gosh, really?'

'Your face is priceless.' He grinned. 'You like a spa, I take it.'

'I used to have a jet bath,' Eve admitted to him. And then to herself, 'I miss it.'

Not that she'd given her big four-person bath much thought when she put her house on the market. Because brothers before bubbles, right? But—oh—how she missed the great soak at the end of a long, hard week. And out here where every week was long and hard…

'Go on,' he nudged. 'Get in there.'

Her thanks were practically a squeak as she slipped into the bathroom and closed the door behind her. She waited a moment too long to flip the lock—worrying how Marshall might read the click after such a long, silent pause—but decided to leave it. If he had something nefarious in mind, he'd had plenty of more isolated opportunities to perpetrate his crime. Not to mention the fact they'd already slept together.

Besides, sneaking into a woman's bathroom was beneath a man like Marshall.

He's a good man.

It took no time at all to get naked and under the thundering commercial shower as the water slowly rose up over her calves. Hot, hot water pounded down on her shoulders and back, then over her hair as she plunged fully under it.

Warm and reassuring and…home. The water brought with it a full-body rush of tingles.

Unexpected tears rushed to her support.

She'd been doing this so long. Being on the road. Was it okay to admit she was tired? That didn't have to mean she loved Travis any less, did it? The water thundered on and she lifted her face to let the fresh water wash away her guilty tears. Eventually, though, the spa reached a generous level of fullness and she killed the overhead stream and slid down into the piping-hot pool. Her groan was inevitable and the long sigh that followed the perfect punctuation.

When was the last time she'd felt so…buoyant? When was the last time she'd just closed her eyes and floated? The water's heat did its job and immediately soaked into muscles she'd forgotten didn't always feel this way, including a few that had only been aching since the marathon of last night.

Was it only twenty-four hours ago that she and Marshall had twisted up in each other's arms? And legs. And tongues. Like some kind of fantasy. Had it even really happened? If it had really happened, wouldn't he be in here with her? Not respectfully waiting on the other side of a closed—but not locked—door.

She lifted one hand to better position it and the cascading tinkle echoed in the silent bathroom.

'Marshall…'

'Yeah?'

Water splashed slightly as she started in the bath at the speed and closeness with which he answered. The door was right next to her head but he sounded close enough to be in here with her. Her eyes went to the mirror reflection of the door instinctively, but she knew before they got there what they'd find.

Marshall wasn't really the Peeping Tom type. If he wanted to look, he'd just knock and enter and stare at her until she was as much a hot puddle as the spa water around her.

Because he's a good man, and he knows what he wants.

So what was he doing? Just lurking there? Or did the suite have some kind of weird acoustic thing going on?

She cleared her throat gently. 'Are you busy?'

'Nope. Just unwinding.' Pause. 'Why?'

'I just thought…maybe we could talk.'

'Didn't you want to relax?'

'It's a bit…quiet.'

'I thought you'd be used to that after eight months on the road.'

Yeah. He had a point. Astonishing what two days of company did for a girl.

'Normally I'd have music in my bathroom.' Classical. Mellow.

That deep voice was rich with humour. 'You want me to sing something?'

The very idea added to her hot-water tingles. 'Talking will be fine.'

'Okay.' Another pause. 'What do you want to talk about?'

'I don't know. Where you grew up? Your family? Anything, really.'

The door gave a muffled rattle and Eve wondered if he'd leaned on it. She took the complimentary sponge from its packet and filled it with warm water, then squeezed it down her arms.

Rinse. Repeat.

The slow splashes filled the long silence and the steam started working on her pores. And her soul.

'I'm not sure my history will be particularly conducive to relaxation.'

The tightness in his voice paused her sponge mid-swab. 'Really, why?'

'My family's about as functional as yours.'

Dead, drunken mother and AWOL brother was going to be tough to top. But her curiosity was piqued. 'Where are they now?'

'They're still in Sydney.'

'That doesn't sound so very dramatic.'

'Growing up had...its challenges.'

Her sponging resumed. Eve closed her eyes and let herself tune in to the low rumble of his voice. 'Like what?'

Was that a resigned sigh through the door?

'My family weren't all that well off, but we didn't starve. We were okay.'

Uh-huh...?

'But it was the nineties. The decade of excess and success, and all that.'

Eve lay her head against the back of the bath and just listened.

'I have a brother, too, Eve,' Marshall went on. 'And poverty wasn't really his thing. So he took matters into his own hands and got quite...creative. Before long, the whole neighbourhood knew he was the go-to for whatever soft-core drug they needed.'

She opened her eyes and stared at the bathroom ceiling. After a moment she murmured, 'Your brother was a dealer?'

'An entrepreneur, according to him.'

Right. 'How long did that last?'

'Until very recently I couldn't have answered that at all. But let's just say business is as good as ever for Rick. I don't really see him any more.'

No wonder Marshall could empathise about Travis. He knew exactly what it was like to lose a brother.

'Whose decision was that?'

The only sound in the long, long silence that followed was the dripping of the shower into the spa.

'It's complicated,' he finally said.

Yeah, wasn't it always?

'I struggled growing up with Rick for a brother.'

'Because he was a criminal?'

'Because he was a hero.' He snorted. 'This was the back suburbs, remember. Pretty rough area to grow up. People loved him, they loved what he sold and they scrambled to be part of his inner circle. And sometimes that meant scrambling over me.'

There was something so…suppressed in his voice.

Eve lifted her head. 'Are you talking about girls?'

'Girls. Friends. Even a teacher or two with insalubrious habits.'

Oh, poor teenage Marshall. 'You resented him.'

'No, I loved him.'

'But you hated that,' she guessed.

'It meant I was no different to them. The sycophants. I just wanted to despise him and be done with it.'

So, there were many ways to lose a brother, then.

'Do you miss him?' she whispered.

'I did. For a long while. It felt like he was all I had, growing up. But I just focused my attention on my work and suddenly a decade had passed and I hadn't really thought about him at all. Or my mother. Or Christine. Or what they were all doing together.'

She pushed herself up a little more. 'Christine is with your brother?'

'She was.'

The door rattled slightly again, but not the knob. Down lower. And that was when Eve realised how very close they were sitting to each other. Him sunk down onto the floor of the suite, leaning on the door. Her lying back in warm luxury.

And only a single thin wall between them.

No wonder Marshall was wary of people. And no wonder the tight pain in his voice. 'I'm sorry. I should have asked you about something else.'

'It's okay. I got myself out. It's history now.'

'How do you go from a bad neighbourhood to working for the Federal Government?'

He laughed and she realised how attached she'd become to that sexy little chuckle.

'It will shock you to learn that meteorology is not the sexiest of the sciences.'

Not sexy? Had any of them *seen* Marshall Sullivan?

'But that meant there were scholarships going wasting, and one of them came to me. And it came with on-campus residency.'

'The scholarship was your ticket out?'

'At first, but soon I came to love meteorology. It's predictive. Stats and signs and forecasting. You always know what's coming with weather.'

'No surprises?' she murmured.

'I guess I was just looking for a life where you could spot the truth of something before it found you.'

Yeah. Given he'd been used by his earlier friends, cast off by his mother and then betrayed by his brother, maybe that wasn't surprising.

'It suits you.'

'Being a weatherman?'

'Busting the stereotype.' And how. 'I'm sorry I called you Weatherman.'

'I don't mind it as a nickname. As long as it's coming from you.'

'Why?' She laughed. 'What makes me so special?'

His answer, when it came, was immediate. 'How long have you got?'

The same kind of warmth that was soaking into her from without started to spread out from within. But she wrestled it back down. She couldn't afford to be feeling warm and fuzzy about anyone right now.

She made much of sitting up straighter in the spa bath. The bathroom equivalent of shuffling papers. 'Speaking of specials…what's on the menu tonight?'

Subtle, Read, real subtle.

But he let it go after a breath-stealing moment of indecision. 'Give me a second, I'll check.'

Good man, knows what he wants and compassionate.

Marshall Sullivan was just getting harder and harder to not like.

CHAPTER NINE

THIS WASN'T GOING to end well for him…

It had dawned on Marshall, somewhere between sitting at the bathroom door with his head tipped back against the timber and watching Eve tuck so enthusiastically into a bowl of Italian soup, that not everyone was rewarded for goodness. Any more than they were rewarded for doing the right thing.

Hadn't he got that by now?

But done was done. He'd made his choice and he was here. Only time would tell whether it was a crazily fatalistic or brilliantly optimistic decision. But since he was here and since she hadn't driven him off the road, he could use the time practically. He could try and get to know Eve a bit more. Understand her.

Maybe that way he could get a sense of her truth before it hit him like a cyclone.

'Can I ask you what happened with Travis?' he asked, passing his empty plate into the long fingers she reached out and starting at the most obvious point. 'When he disappeared.'

Her bright, just-fed eyes dulled just a little.

'One day he was there—' she shrugged '—the next he was gone.'

'That simple?'

'It wasn't simple.'

'Losing someone never is.'

He fell to silence and waited her out. It had certainly worked well enough on him while she was in the bath. He'd offered up much more than he'd ever shared with anyone else.

'She was drunk,' Eve finally murmured and he didn't need to ask who. 'She'd passed the few hours of Travis's Under-Fifteens hockey at the nearest pub. As far as anyone could tell, she thought she was okay to drive.'

Oh. Crap. Drunk and in charge of the safety of a fourteen-year-old boy.

'Was she an alcoholic?' That certainly explained Eve's moderate approach to liquor.

Her dark head slowly nodded. 'And the whole neighbourhood got to hear about it.'

He let his hands fall between his splayed thighs. Stared at them. 'That's a lot for a girl to handle.'

'It was a lot for all of us to handle,' she defended. 'Travis watched Mum die, Dad endured her reputation being trashed and I...'

'What did you do?'

'I coped. I got on with things. Took over caring for them both.'

'A lot of pressure.'

'Actually, it was okay then.' *Then...* 'It gave me something to focus on. Purpose.

'Dad pulled Trav out of school for the last few months of the year and that might have been a mistake. It took him from his friends, his sport, his structure. He lost his way a bit. He got back into it the next year and got okay grades but he was never cheeky and joyous again. I think we all just got used to the new, flat Travis.' She took a big swallow of water. 'Maybe we got used to a new *us*, too.'

Yeah. Numbness crept up on a person...

'It wasn't easy, those first couple of years. At first it was all about getting him out of the hospital, but then life had to... We had to just get on with it, you know?'

Yep. He certainly did know all about just getting on... Story of his life. But not everyone could do it. There were times *he* really wanted to just opt out. In some ways maybe he had.

'What changed? To make him leave?'

Her beautiful face pinched up slightly. 'Um…'

Whatever it was, it was hurting her.

'There was an inquest the year he went, and there was all this media interest in the accident again.'

'Years later?'

'A legal queue, I guess.' Her slight shoulders shrugged and he'd never wanted to hold someone more in his life. But she looked so fragile he worried she'd shatter. 'So much pressure on all of us again.'

He shifted closer. Leaned into her. 'He couldn't take it?'

Her head came up but she didn't quite meet his eyes. 'I couldn't. I desperately wanted to understand what happened but I couldn't go through it all again. Supporting Dad, mothering Travis. Just as things were getting normal. I just couldn't do it while we relived the accident over and over again.'

Suddenly her blazing need to find her brother began to make more sense.

'What did you do?'

'I went back to my own place. Replaced the dead pot plants with new ones, cleaned the gutters, threw out years of junk mail, started easing back into my own life.'

'And what did Travis do?'

'I didn't abandon them,' she defended hotly. 'I still visited, did sisterly things. But they were both men. They needed to step up, too. They agreed.'

He said nothing, knowing the question was almost certainly in his eyes. *But…?*

'Trav was finding it harder than any of us realised. The inquest brought it all back just as he might have started to become stronger. He turned eighteen, and drifted further and further from us emotionally.' She shook her head. 'And then he just left. Right in the middle of the inquest. We thought he'd just taken off for a few days to avoid the pressure but then it was a week, and then two. We finally reported him missing when we hadn't heard anything for a month.'

'You blame yourself.'

Her slim shoulders lifted and then sagged again. 'I wasn't there for him.'

'Yeah, you were. For years.'

'But I withdrew.'

'You *survived*. Big difference.'

Her tortured eyes lifted. 'Why wouldn't he talk to me? If he was struggling.'

Yeah—she'd been carrying that around a while; he recognised the signs of soul baggage.

'Eighteen-year-old boys don't talk to anyone about their feelings, Eve. I've been that kid.'

Old agony changed her face. He pulled her into his arms. 'You aren't responsible for Travis being missing.'

'That's what people say, isn't it,' she said against his chest. 'In this kind of situation. But what if I am?'

Okay, so she'd heard this before and still not believed it. A rough kind of urgency came over him.

'What if it had nothing to do with you and everything to do with a young boy who watched his mother die? On top of the day-to-day trauma of having an alcoholic for a mother. My own mother was no prize,' he admitted, 'but she was at least present.'

He'd almost forgotten that she was Eve's mother, too. She seemed so disconnected from her past. 'What if you had turned up on his doorstep every single day and he had still done this?'

Tortured eyes glistened over. 'He's my brother.'

'He's a grown man, Eve.'

'Only just. Eighteen is still a kid. And with the anxiety disorder, and depression…'

'Which he was being treated for, right? He was on it.'

'Then why did he leave?'

It was always going to come back to that question, wasn't

it? And Eve was never going to be free of the big, looming question mark. 'Only Travis knows.'

She fell to an anguished kind of silence, picking at the fabric on the sofa beneath her. Marshall stacked up the rest of the dishes and put the lot outside his door on the tray left there by the staff and quietly turned back. He crossed to her and held out a hand.

'Come on.'

She peered up at him with wide, hurt eyes. 'Where are we going?'

'I'm walking you home. I think you need to be in your own place right now, surrounded by familiar things.'

She didn't argue for once. Instead, she slipped her fingers into his and let him pull her up and towards the suite's door.

'It's not really my place,' she murmured as they stepped out into the hall. 'And most of them aren't my things.'

How weird that such sorrowful words could bring him such a lurch of hope. If Eve wasn't all that attached to the Bedford or its contents maybe there was hope for him yet. Maybe he could wedge himself a place in her distracted, driven world.

He kicked off one of his shoes and left it wedged in the doorway so that he didn't lock himself out.

Down in the almost empty car park he opened the bus for her and followed her through to her bedroom. She didn't so much as glance at that presumption, and she didn't look the slightest bit anxious that he might stay. She just accepted it as though they'd been doing it for years.

He pressed his key-card into her hand. 'Breakfast on the balcony at eight?'

'Okay.'

He flipped back her bed covers and waited for her to crawl in, then he folded them back over her and tucked her so firmly in that she resembled something that had just tumbled out of a sarcophagus.

'It's not your fault, Eve.'

He was going to tell her that every day of their lives if he had to.

She nodded, but he wasn't foolish enough to think that she actually believed it. Maybe she just accepted that he didn't think so. Bending brought him dangerously close to her lips, but he veered up at the last moment and pressed his to her hot forehead instead.

'Breakfast. Eight o'clock.'

She didn't agree. She didn't even nod. But her eyes were filled with silent promise and so he killed the lights and backed out of the room and then the bus, giving the big back door a security rattle before leaving her snug and safe inside.

It went against everything in him to leave her in the car park, but Eve had been doing this a long time and she was a grown, competent woman. Just because she'd opened up a little and shown him some of her childhood vulnerability didn't mean he could treat her like the child she'd almost been when her mother killed herself and nearly her brother.

As hard as that was.

He limped along on one shoe and returned to the big, lonely suite.

A gentle kind of rocking roused Marshall out of a deep, comfortable sleep. The suite was as dark as an outback road but he knew, instantly, what was going on.

Except it wasn't eight o'clock. And this wasn't morning.

A warm, soft body slid in next to him, breathing carefully. He shunted over a bit to make room, but she only followed him, keeping their bodies close.

'Eve…?'

As if there was any question.

She snuggled up hard into his side. 'Shh. It's late.'

Or early, he suspected. But he wasn't about to argue with whatever God had sent her back to him, and he wasn't about to ruin a good thing by reading something into this. Instead, he took it—and Eve—at face value and just gathered her into him so that his sleepy heat could soak into her cold limbs.

But he wasn't so strong that he could resist pressing his lips to her hair and leaving them there.

And she wasn't of a mind to move away, apparently.

'I have no expectations,' he murmured against her scalp. 'If you tell me that going our separate ways yesterday felt okay to you then that's cool, I know where I stand. But it felt anything but okay to me and I came back so that we could just—'

'Finish things up more civilly?'

'—*not* finish things up,' he said into the dark. 'Maybe just explore this a little more. See where it goes.'

Her breathing filled his ears. His heart.

'I slept with you because you were riding off into the horizon the next day,' she whispered.

He turned a little more towards her, trying to make her out in the dark. 'And I slept with you knowing that. But then I discovered something about horizons.'

'What?' she mumbled.

'They're an awfully long way away.'

She pushed up onto one elbow, robbing him of her warmth. 'So…you're just going to ride shotgun for the next…what—days? Weeks?'

'Until we know.'

Her voice sounded tantalisingly close to his ear. 'Know what?'

'Whether we have potential.'

'You're in the middle of an epic road trip. It's a terrible time to be looking for potential.'

She was right. He should be aiming for fast, casual and uncomplicated. Like she had.

'That's the thing, Eve. I wasn't looking. It seems to have found me.'

She had nothing to say to that, but her steady breathing told him she was still awake.

Listening.

Thinking.

He bundled her back in close and fell with her—lips to hairline—into a deep slumberous heaven.

CHAPTER TEN

WAKING THE NEXT morning was like an action replay of the morning before—but without all the action. This time, he didn't catch Eve creeping out of bed. This time, she was not freaking out and sucking all the warmth out of the room. This time, she was not back-pedalling madly from what they'd shared the night before.

Even though what they'd shared overnight was more intimate and meaningful than anything they'd done with each other back at the campsite.

Two bodies, pressed together in sleep. Wrapped around each other. Talking.

No sex.

But infinitely more loaded.

'Morning,' she murmured before her eyes even opened.

'How long have you been awake?'

'Long enough to feel you staring.'

'It's the novelty.' He chuckled.

Come on. Open them...

But she just smiled and squirrelled in closer, as if she was getting ready to go back to sleep.

'It's eight o'clock,' he pointed out.

And then her eyes opened—drugged, languorous, and he'd never seen anything quite so beautiful.

'No, it's not.'

'Yeah, it really is.'

And this was a workday for both of them. Technically.

Her eyes fluttered shut and she wiggled deeper into the covers. Okay, so he was going to have to be the brave one.

'So, look at you in my bed...' he hinted.

One eye half opened and he waited for the quip to follow. Something sharp and brilliant and completely protective. But he didn't get one. Her second eye opened and locked on him, clear and steady.

'I just woke up in the middle of the night,' she murmured, 'and knew this is where I wanted to be.'

Right. What could he say to that? This was what he'd come back for, wasn't it? To see what might grow between them. Wasn't that what he'd been murmuring at midnight about? Yet, now that he was faced with it, it suddenly seemed overwhelmingly real.

He cleared his throat. 'Breakfast?'

'In town, maybe? After I get set up.'

Right. Work.

'I have to do my thing today, too.' For the people paying him.

'Where's the weather station?'

He told her and she asked a question or two. More than enough to muddle his mind. He was in bed with a living, breathing, *radiating* woman and they were talking about the weather again. Literally. But somehow it didn't feel like small talk. It felt big.

And then it hit him why.

They were having a *couple* conversation. Comfortable. Easy. And they were having it in bed. Where all conversations should happen. And that was enough to scare him upright.

'I'm going to grab a shower, then I'll get us some food while you set up.'

She pushed up onto her elbows, blinking. 'Sorry if I made things weird.'

He forced a relaxed smile onto his face.

'Not weird. Just—' *dangerously appealing* '—new.'

He padded into the bathroom and put himself under the shower Eve had enjoyed so much the night before. Images filled his head—of Eve standing with the water streaming over her slight body, head tipped back, issuing those sounds he'd heard while he leaned on the doorframe out in the hall. How badly he'd wanted to step inside and join her. Shower with her until the end of time. And now, here he was freaking out that his dreams might be coming true.

In his world, dreams didn't come true.

They shattered.

It was so hard to trust the good feelings.

He nudged the taps and cut out half of the hot water feed and then made sure to keep his shave brief.

When he emerged, Eve was gone.

For half a heartbeat the old doubts lurched to the surface but then he remembered she had no clothes up here, only what she'd crept up the stairs in, and he opened the suite door a crack and peered down through the hallway window. Like a seasoned stalker. Long enough to see Eve heading back across the car park.

Come on, man. Pull it together. This is what you wanted.

He'd just learned the hard way not to want. It only led to disappointment.

So Eve had opted for more comfortable accommodation overnight. No biggie. That was hardly a declaration of passion. She'd snuggled in and enjoyed the heat coming off him, and today she was all about Travis again.

Eve was always about Travis.

It was part of what intrigued him about her. That fathomless compassion.

But it was part of what scared him, too. Because how could there be room for him with all that emotion already going on?

He quickly shrugged something decent on and ran a quick comb through his hair so that when she swiped the suite's door he was clothed and everything that needed brushing was brushed.

He threw her a neutral smile. 'Good to go?'

The pause before she answered was full of silent query. 'Yep. Meet you in front of the Town Hall?'

Wherever that was. 'Yup.'

The question mark shifted from her eyes to her soft smile but she simply turned and let him follow her back down to where his bike was parked. She headed for the bus.

'Egg and bacon burger?' he called.

'Sounds great.'

Great.

Okay, so it was officially his turn to be off. Most guys would be stoked to wake up to a warm, willing body but, instead of converting the opportunity to a goal, he'd let it get under his skin. Weird him out. Not the best start, true, but Eve didn't look too tragic about it. Her mind was back on her brother already.

As was always the way.

The bumbling MP yesterday was pretty normal, in Eve's experience. In fact, he'd been more tactful than many of the people she'd tried to explain herself to in the past.

Herself… Her choices.

But the only people who'd understood her odyssey the way Marshall had were the other family members in her missing-persons network. Which did, in fact, make him pretty darned exceptional.

Eve smiled and passed a poster to an older lady who stopped to peruse her display. The stranger took her time and looked at every single face before wandering off, which Eve particularly appreciated. Nothing worse than the glancers. Glancing was worse than not looking at all, in some ways. Eve knew it was a big ask to hope that people might remember one face, let alone dozens, but there was no chance of people remembering them from the wall displays in post offices that were half obscured by piles of post packs or pull-down passport photo screens most of the time.

Something inside her had shifted last night when Marshall

told her about his brother. As if he went from adversary to equal in her mind. He'd effectively lost a brother, too—to circumstance—so he knew what it was like to give up on a family member.

Except, in Marshall's case, he was the one who'd walked away.

And didn't that tear her up. Half of her wanted to hug him for the personal strength it must have taken to leave an intolerable family situation so young. The other half wanted to shake him and remind him he had a brother. A living, breathing brother.

And those weren't to be sneezed at.

She never would have picked him for the product of a rough neighbourhood, even with all the tattoos. He was just too *normal*. Beneath the 'keep your distance' leather smokescreen. But to find out that someone so close to him was neck-deep in criminal activity… That just made what he'd done with his life even more remarkable. Finished school, tackled university and then got himself the straightest and smartest of straight, smart jobs.

Meteorology.

A tiny smile crept, unbidden, to her lips. Who knew that she'd ever get quite so hot and bothered by a weatherman?

Yet here she was, very much bothered. And decidedly hot under the covers.

At least she had been last night.

Crawling in with him hadn't been quite the spontaneous exercise she'd confessed. The sprint across the car park had been as sobering as it was chilly and she had plenty of opportunity to think better of it. But she hadn't—because a big part of her had wanted him to roll over, see her and just keep on rolling. Up and over onto her. To make love to her like he had the first time—all breathless and uninhibited.

Another taste of lightness.

Her days were consumed by her brother—couldn't someone

else have her nights? When she'd normally be asleep? Wouldn't it be okay to let go just for those few short hours? To forget?

But Marshall hadn't taken advantage. He'd just tugged her close, murmured hot, lovely words in her ear and pulled her into unconsciousness behind him. And it was only as she'd fallen asleep that she'd realised how badly she wanted *not to* do the obvious thing. The easy thing.

Sleeping with Marshall was easy.

Falling for him would be treacherous.

But morning would always come. And it dragged reality with it.

Eve's reality was that she still had a monumental task ahead of her. Marshall had chased her up the highway to see what might form between them if they gave it a chance, but how could there be any kind of something between them while she had this dismal marathon to complete?

Good sex was one thing. A *happy families* future was quite another.

She had no room for anything beyond right now.

And both of them knew that *happy families* was just a myth. They knew it firsthand.

'Thank you,' she murmured belatedly to the man who took a poster as though from an unattended pile. She'd been so lost in thought, that might as well have been true.

Nope, she hadn't promised Marshall anything more than *right now* and he hadn't asked for it.

Two people could go a long way on *right now*.

The south-western corner of Western Australia was packed with small, wine-rich country towns, each with unique personality and spaced close enough for tourists to hop from one to another on their weekend trails.

Papering the two hundred square kilometres ahead with posters was going to be a much bigger job than the two thousand before it.

But they did a good job together, she and Marshall. When

he wasn't working, or they weren't curled up together in her bus or a motel room, he'd be with her, plastering Trav's face all over the towns they visited. Handing her the pins or the tape or the staple gun. Nothing she couldn't have done for herself but—boy—was it good not to have to.

Somehow, having someone to share all of this with made it more bearable. And she hadn't realised how unbearable it had become. How utterly soul-destroying. Until she felt her soul starting to scab over.

She glanced sideways at Marshall's handsome face. How fast she'd adapted to having him here by her side during her displays of *The Missing*. How willing she'd been to bring him into her journey.

A problem shared…

A man approached from the far end of the street, folded paper in his hands. He looked grim and twitchy.

'Movie tonight?'

Marshall's voice pulled her focus back to him. The two of them hadn't braved a movie since *that* night in her bus. As if the entire art form was now too loaded. The last time they'd settled in to watch a movie together they'd ended up sharing so much more.

'Maybe,' she said breathlessly. A girl couldn't live on spooning alone. And she was fairly sure neither could a man. They were well overdue for a rematch. The way Marshall's eyes locked on hers said maybe he thought so, too.

The stranger still hovered and it was only as he turned away, stuffing the paper in his pocket, that Eve's brain finally comprehended that he wanted to say something.

'I'm sorry,' she called, stretching taller in her seat. 'Can I help you?'

The man slowed. Turned.

'Do you know him?' he said, holding up the crumpled paper as he approached. It was one of her posters.

A tingle tickled between her shoulders and grew outwards

until gooseflesh puckered under her shirt. 'He's my brother. Why? Do you recognise him?'

The man stepped one pace closer. 'Not sure. He looks familiar.'

Eve shot to her feet. 'What do you mean?'

'Just that I feel like I've seen him before. But I don't want to get your hopes up if I'm wrong…'

'I don't need certainty,' she was quick to reassure, 'just leads.'

She felt Marshall's heat as he stood behind her and her heart began to hammer. God, she'd been so wrapped up in the promise in his eyes she'd nearly let this guy walk off. A guy who might know something.

'Where do you think you know him from?' Marshall asked.

The guy switched focus. 'I really can't say. Just…somewhere. And recently.'

'How recent? Two months? Six?' Eve could hear the urgency in her own voice but was incapable of easing it. A big hand fell on her shoulder as if to physically suppress her.

'Where do you live?' Marshall asked, much more casually.

The guy responded to his even tone. 'Here. In Augusta. But I don't think I know him from here.'

God, the idea of that. That Travis might be right here in this little seaside town…

'Somewhere else?'

'I run trucks. Maybe I saw him on one of those. In another—'

'What other town?' Eve pressed, and Marshall squeezed harder.

Are you freaking kidding me? The first reasonable lead she'd had in nearly nine months and Marshall wanted her to relax? Every nerve in her body was firing in a soup of adrenaline.

'Where do you do your runs?' Marshall asked calmly.

'Anywhere in the South West,' the man said, visibly uncomfortable at having started the conversation at all. He immediately started retreating from his earlier thoughts. 'Look, I'm probably wrong—'

Deep panic fisted in her gut.

'*No!* Please don't start second-guessing yourself,' Eve rushed on, critically aware that her urgency was pushing him further away. She fought to breathe more evenly. God, how close she'd come to just not calling out to him.

What was happening to her?

'The subconscious is a powerful thing,' she urged. 'It probably knows something your conscious mind can't quite grasp.'

The man's eyes filled with pity and, in that moment, she saw herself as others must. As Marshall must.

Obsessed. Desperate. Pathetic.

And she didn't like his view of her one little bit.

Lines appeared on the man's time-weathered brow. 'I'm just not sure…'

'How about just jotting down the routes you usually take?' Marshall grabbed another poster, flipped it over to the blank side and handed it and a pen to the man. 'We can take it from there.'

More lines formed in his weathered skin. 'I have two-dozen routes. That'll take time…'

They were losing him. And the best lead she'd had in an age…

Eve dashed to the front of the bus and rummaged in the glove box with clammy hands for the maps she carried detailing every region she was in. One was marked up with her own routes—to make sure she never missed a town or junction—but her spare was blank, a clean slate. She thrust the spare into the man's hands.

'On this then, just highlight the routes you take. I can do the rest.'

Possibility flickered over his face. 'Can I take this with me?'

The fist squeezed harder. Not because she risked losing a four-dollar map. But she risked losing a tangible link with Travis. 'Can't you do it here…?'

'Take it,' Marshall interrupted. 'Anything you can give us will be great.'

The stranger's eyes flicked between the two of them 'Hopefully, I can be clearer somewhere…away from here.'

Eve took two steps towards the man as he retreated with the map in his hand. She spun to Marshall. 'I should go with him.'

His strong hand clamped around her wrist. 'No. You should let him go somewhere quiet and do what he has to do. He's not going to be able to concentrate with you hovering over him.'

Hovering…! As if they were talking about her chaperoning a teenage date and not possibly finding her brother. 'I just want to—'

'I know exactly what you want, Eve, and how you're feeling right now. But stalking the guy won't get you what you need. Just leave him be. He'll come back.'

'But he's the first person that's seen Travis.'

'*Possibly* seen Travis, and if you push any harder he's going to decide he never actually saw a thing. Leave him to his process, Eve.'

She glanced up the street, hunting for the man's distinctive walk. Two blocks away she spotted him, turning into the local pub. She swung baleful eyes onto Marshall.

'Leave him to his process,' he articulated.

Deep inside she knew he was right, but everything in her screamed for action. Something. Anything.

'Easy for you to say!'

He took a long breath. 'There's nothing easy about watching you suffer, Eve.'

'Try feeling it some time,' she muttered.

She turned away roughly but he caught her. 'I do feel it. In you. Every day—'

'No, I mean try *feeling* it, Marshall. From this side of the fence.'

'It's not about sides—'

'Spoken like someone who's more used to cutting people out of their life than being cut out.'

For a moment she thought he was going to let that go, but he was a man, not a saint. Words blew warmly behind her ear as Marshall murmured in this public place, 'And what's that supposed to mean, exactly?'

'What you imagine it means, I'm sure,' she gritted.

'Eve, I know this is frustrating—'

She spun on him. 'Do you, Marshall? You've been travelling with me all of ten days. Multiply that by twenty-five and then tell me how you think I should be feeling as my only lead walks away from me and into a bar.'

His lips tightened but he took several controlled breaths. 'You need an outlet and I'm convenient.'

Spare me the psychoanalysis!

'How did this become about you?' she hissed. 'This is about me and Travis.'

She glanced at the pub again and twisted her hands together.

Warm fingers brought her chin around until her eyes met his. '*Everything* is about Travis with you, Eve. Everything.'

That truly seemed to pain him.

The judgment in his gaze certainly hurt her. 'Forgive me for trying to stay focused on my entire purpose out here.'

The words sounded awful coming off her lips, doubly so because, deep down, she knew he didn't deserve her cruelty. But did he truly not get the importance of this moment? How rare it was. How it felt to go nearly nine months without a single lead and then to finally get one?

A lead she'd almost missed because she was so off mission.

She dropped back into her seat.

All week she'd been going through the motions. Putting up posters, staffing her unhappy little table, answering questions about the faces in her display. But she hadn't actively promoted. She hadn't forced posters on anyone. She hadn't made a single real impression.

All she'd done was sit here looking at Marshall. Or thinking about him when he was gone. Letting herself buy into his hopeless fantasy.

She'd failed Travis. Again.

And she'd nearly missed her only lead.

Marshall sat back and considered her in silence. And when he spoke it was careful but firm.

'I think it might be time to stop, Eve.'

She did stop. All movement, all breath. And just stared.

'Maybe it's time to go home,' he continued. 'This isn't good for you.'

When she finally spoke it was with icy precision.

'How good for me do you imagine it is sitting around the house, wondering whether Travis is alive or dead and whether anyone will give him more than the occasional cursory check twice a year?'

'It's been a year—'

'I know. I've been living it every single day. But I'm nearly done.'

'You're not nearly done. You still have one third of the country to go.'

'But only ten per cent of the population,' she gritted.

'That's assuming that you haven't missed him already.' *And assuming he is still alive.* The words practically trembled on those perfect lips.

She glared. 'What happened to "What you're doing is logical"?'

'I meant that. I completely understand why you're doing it.'

'And so…?'

'I don't like what *it's doing to you*, Eve. This search is hurting you. I hate watching it.'

'Then leave. No one's forcing you to stay.'

'It's not that easy—'

But whatever logical, persuasive thing he was about to say choked as she ran over the top of him. 'Maybe you're just unhappy that I'm putting him ahead of you. Maybe your male ego can't handle taking second place.'

She'd never seen someone's eyes bruise before, but Marshall's did. And it dulled them irreparably.

'Actually, that's the one thing I'm more than used to.'

The fist inside tightened further. How could she do this? How could she choose between two men she cared so much about? Marshall was, at least, stable and healthy and capable of looking after himself. Travis was...

Well, who knew what Travis was? Or where.

But his need was unquestionably greater.

She ripped the emotional plaster off and pushed to her feet. 'I think it's time for us to go our separate ways.'

The bruising intensified. 'Do you?'

'It's been lovely—'

'But you're done now?'

'Come on, Marshall, how long would we have been able to keep this up, anyway? Your circuit's coming to an end.' And her funds were running out.

Her casual dismissal turned the vacuum behind his lids to permafrost. 'Is that right?'

'I don't have room for you, Marshall.'

'No, you really don't, do you.'

'I need to stay focused on Travis.'

'Why?'

'Because he needs me. Who else is going to look for him?' Or look *out* for him. Like she should have all along.

'Face facts, Eve,' he said, face gentle but words brutal. 'He's either gone or he's *choosing* to stay away. You said it yourself.'

Her breaths seemed to have no impact on the oxygen levels in her body. Dark spots began to populate the edges of her vision. 'I can't believe that.'

'People walk away all the time. For all kinds of reasons.'

'Maybe *you* do.'

His voice grew as cold as her fingers. 'Excuse me?'

She started to shake all over. 'I should have thought to seek your perspective before. I have an expert on cutting loose right here with me. You tell me why a perfectly healthy young man would just walk away from his family.'

Marshall's face almost contorted with the control he was trying to exert. 'You think I didn't struggle, leaving them?'

'As far as I can see, you crossed a line through them and walked away and you seem no worse for wear. That's quite a talent.'

'Are you truly that self-absorbed,' he whispered, 'that you can't appreciate what that was like for me?'

'Yet you chose it.'

Where were these words coming from? Just pouring like toxic lava over her lips. Uncontrollable. Unstoppable.

Awful.

'Sometimes, Eve, all your choices are equally bad and you just have to make one.'

'Just go and don't look back?' she gritted. 'Who does that?'

Something flared in his eyes. Realisation. 'You're angry at Travis. For leaving.'

I'm furious *at Travis for leaving*, she screamed inside. But outwardly she simply said, 'My brother left against his will.'

How many police counsellors had she had that argument with? Or fights with her father.

'What if he didn't?' Marshall urged. 'What if he left because he couldn't imagine staying?'

Pfff... 'Someone's been reading up on the missing-persons websites.'

'Don't mock me, Eve. I wanted to understand you better—'

'Those people were desperate or scared or sick. The Travis I know wouldn't do that.'

'Maybe he wasn't your Travis, have you thought about that? Maybe he's not the kid brother you raised any more.'

The trembles were full-body shudders now.

Marshall stepped closer. Lowered his voice. 'Do you see how much of your life he's consumed, Eve? This obsessive search. It's ruining you.'

'If I don't do it, who will?' she croaked.

'But at what cost?'

'My time. My money. All mine to spend.'

He took her hand. 'And how much of life are you missing while you're out here spending it? I'm right here, Eve. Living. Breathing. But any part of you that might enjoy that is completely occupied by someone who's—'

His teeth cracked shut.

Nausea practically washed over her. 'Go on. Say it.'

'Eve—'

'Say it! You think he's dead.'

'I fear he's a memory, one way or another. And I think that memory is stopping you from living your life just as much as when your mother died.'

'Says the man who hides out behind a face full of hair and leather armour to avoid facing his demons.'

Marshall took a long silent breath.

'This has become an unhealthy obsession for you, Eve. A great idea, practically, but devastating personally. You stripped yourself away from all your support structures. Your colleagues. Your friends. Your family. The people who could have kept you healthy and sane.'

'So we're back to me being crazy?'

'Eve, you're not—'

'You need to go, Marshall,' she urged. 'I can't do what I have to do with you here. That guy nearly walked off because I was off my game. I was busy mooning after you.'

'This is my fault?'

She wrapped her arms around her torso. 'I nearly let my only lead in a year walk off because I was distracted with you.'

'I guess I should at least be happy I'm a distraction.'

Misery soaked through her. 'You are much more than a distraction, but don't you get it? I don't have room for you—for us—in my life. In my heart.'

'You don't have room for happiness? Doesn't that tell you anything?'

'I don't get to be happy, Marshall,' she yelled, heedless of the passers-by. 'Not until Travis is back home where he belongs.'

Those dreadful words echoed out into the seaside air.

'Do you hear yourself, Eve? You're punishing yourself for failing Travis.'

The muscles around her ribs began to squeeze. Hard. 'Thank you for your concern but I'm not your responsibility.'

'So, I just walk away from you, knowing that you're slowly self-destructing?'

'I will be fine.'

'You won't be fine. You'll search the rest of the country and what will you do when you get back to your start point and you've found no sign of him? Start again from the top?'

The thought of walking away from this search without her brother was unimaginable.

'I will always look for him,' she vowed.

And that wasn't fair on someone as vibrant as Marshall. Hadn't he been sidelined enough in his life? She shook her head slowly.

'Find someone else, Marshall. Please.'

Someone who could offer him what he needed. Someone who wouldn't hurt him. Someone who could prioritise him.

'I don't want someone else, Eve,' he breathed. 'I want you.'

Those three simple words stole the oxygen from her cells. The words and the incredibly earnest glitter of Marshall's flecked grey eyes that watched her warily now.

Of all the times. Of all the places. Of all the men.

The seductive rush of just letting all of this go, curling herself into Marshall's arms and letting him look after her. Letting him carry half of all this weight. Of parking the bus for good somewhere and building a new life for herself with whatever she had left. With him. Of little grey-eyed kids running amuck in the sand dunes. Learning to fish. Hanging out with their dad.

But the kids of her imagination morphed, as she watched, into Travis when he was little. Scrabbling along the riverbank at the back of their house. Getting muddy. Just being a kid. A kid she loved so completely.

Eve took several long breaths. 'If you care for me as much

as you say you do, then what I need should matter to you. And what I need is my brother. Home. Safe. That's all I've got room for.'

'And then what?'

She lifted her eyes to his.

'After that, Eve. What's the plan then? You going to move in with him to make sure he stays safe? Takes his medication? Stays healthy? How far does this responsibility you feel go?'

The truth…? Just as there was nothing but black after not finding Travis, there was nothing but an opaque, uncertain mist after bringing him home. She'd just never let herself think about either outcome in real terms. She'd just focused on the ten kilometres in front of her at all times.

And the ten kilometres in front of her now needed to be solo.

She twisted her fingers into his. 'You're a fantastic guy, Marshall. Find someone to be happy with.'

'I thought I was working on that.'

It was time for some hard truths. 'You're asking me to choose between a man I've loved my whole life and a man I've—'

She caught herself before the word fell across her lips, but only just.

—*known ten days.*

No matter how long it felt.

Or how like love.

'Would I like to be important to you?' he urged. 'Yes. Would I like, two years from now, to live together in a timber cottage and get to make love to you twice a day in a forest pool beside our timber cabin? Yes. I'm not going to lie. But this is the real world. And in the real world I'm not asking you to choose *me*, Eve. I'm begging you to choose *life*. You cannot keep doing this to yourself.'

She stepped a foot closer to him, close enough to feel his warmth. She slid her unsteady hand up the side of his face and curled her fingers gently around his jaw.

'It's a beautiful image, Marshall,' she said past the ball of hurt in her chest. 'But if I'm going to indulge fantasies, it has to be the one where that guy with the map comes back and it leads me to finding Travis.'

The life drained right out of his face and his eyes dropped, but when they came back up they were filled with something worse than hurt.

Resignation.

This was a man who was used to coming last.

'You deserve to be someone's priority, Marshall,' she whispered. 'I'm so sorry.'

His eyes glittered dangerously with unshed truth and he struggled visibly to master his breathing, and then his larynx.

Finally he spoke.

'I'm scared what will happen to you if I can't be there with you to hold you—to help you—when you find him, or when you don't,' he enunciated. 'Promise me you'll go home to your father and start your life over and pick up where you left off.'

'Marshall—'

'Promise me, Eve. And I'll go. I'll leave you in peace.'

Peace. The very idea of that was almost laughable. Not knowing the true nature of the world, as she did now. Blissfully ignorant Eve was long gone.

And so she looked Marshall in the eye.

And she lied.

CHAPTER ELEVEN

Dɪᴅ Eᴠᴇ ʜᴀᴠᴇ any idea how bad she was at deceit?

Or maybe she just saved her best lies for the ones she told herself. There was no way on earth that this driven, strong woman was going to go back to suburbia after this was all over.

She was too far gone.

And, try as he might, she was not letting him into her life long enough for him to have any kind of influence on what happened from here. His job was to walk away. To respect her decision.

To do what his brain said was right and not what his heart screamed was so very wrong.

I'm choosing Travis.

His gut twisted in hard on itself. Wasn't that the story of his life? Had he really expected the very fabric of the universe to have changed overnight? Eve needed to finish this, even if she had no true idea of what that might mean.

He needed her to be whole.

He just hadn't understood he was part of the rending apart.

He rested his hand over Eve's on his cheek, squeezed gently and then tugged hers down and over.

'I hope you find him,' he murmured against the soft skin of her palm.

What a ridiculously lame thing to say.

But it was definitely better than begging her to change her mind. Or condemning her to search, half-crazed, forever.

He stepped back. And then back again. And the cold air between them made it easier to take a very necessary third step. Within a few more, he was turning and crossing the road without a backward glance.

Which was how he generally did things.

You crossed a line through them and walked away.

Did she truly believe that he could cauterise entire sections of his life without any ill effect? That he was that cold? His issues arose from caring too much, not too little. But maybe she was also right about it being a life skill, because experience was sure going to help him now.

This was every bit as hard as walking away from his mother and brother.

Eve was not going to be okay. He could feel it in his bones. She had no idea how much she needed him. Someone. Anyone. And if he could feel that protective of her after just a few short weeks, how much must she burn with the need to find and protect the baby brother she'd loved all his life?

He kept walking up the main street through town but then turned down a side street as soon as he was out of her view and doubled back to slide in the side door of a café fronting onto the same road he'd just walked down. From his table he could see Eve, behind her display table, rocking back and forth in the cold air.

If that guy didn't come back soon, he was going to go and drag him out of that pub and frogmarch him back up the street. If Eve wasn't going to walk away from this whole crusade, and she wasn't going to have him by her side, then he was going to do everything he could to make sure that it all came out okay.

So that *she* came out okay.

The waitress delivered his coffee and he cupped his frigid hands around it and watched the woman who'd taken up residence in the heart he'd assumed was empty. The organ he thought had long since atrophied from lack of use.

She sat, hunched, surrounded by *The Missing*, curled forwards and eyes downcast. Crying in body if not in tears. Looking for all the world as bereft and miserable as he felt.

She wasn't trying to hurt him. She hadn't turned into a monster overnight. She was just overwhelmed with the pressure of this unachievable task she'd set herself.

She just had priorities. And he couldn't be one of them. It was that simple.

At least she'd been honest.

And if he was going to be, she'd never pretended it was otherwise. She'd never promised him more than right now. No matter what he'd hoped for.

So maybe he was making progress in life after all. At this rate he might be ready for a proper relationship by the time he was in his sixties.

Out on the street, Eve's body language changed. She pushed to her feet, as alert and rigid as the kangaroos they drove past regularly, her face turned towards the sea. A moment later, the guy from the pub shuffled back into view, handed her the folded map and spoke to her briefly, pointing a couple of times to places on the map.

Marshall's eyes ignored him, staying fixed on the small face he'd come to care so much about. Eve nodded, glanced at the map and said something brief before farewelling him. Then she sank back down onto her chair and pulled the map up against her chest, hard.

And then the tears flowed.

Every cell in his body wanted to dump his coffee and jog back across the road. To be there for her. To hold her. Impossible to know whether the guy had been unable to help, after all, and the tears were heartbreak. Or maybe they were joy at finally having a lead. Or maybe they were despair at a map criss-crossed with dozens of routes which really left her no further ahead than she'd started.

He'd never know.

And the not ever knowing might just kill him.

His fingers stilled with the coffee cup halfway to his mouth.

At last, he had some small hint of what hell every day was for Eve. Of why she couldn't just walk away from this, no matter how bad it was becoming for her. Of why she had no room for anything—or anyone—else in her heart. Adding to the emotional weight she carried around every day was not going to change the situation. Loving her, no matter how much, was not going to transform her. There was only one thing that would.

Someone needed to dig that brother of hers out from under whatever rock he'd found for himself. For better or worse.

A sudden buzzing in his pocket startled him enough to make him spill hot coffee over the edge of his mug and he scrambled to wipe the spillage with a napkin with one hand while fishing his phone out with the other.

He glanced at the screen and then swiped with suddenly nerveless fingers.

'Rick?'

'Hey,' his brother said. 'I've got something for you.'

Thank God for Rick's shady connections. And for health regulators. And maybe for Big Brother.

And thank God, for Eve's sake, that Travis Read was, apparently, still alive.

Rick had hammered home that the kid's name wouldn't have appeared anywhere on official records, if not for a quietly implemented piece of legislation at the start of the year. Even this was an *unofficial* record.

Accessing it certainly was—his brother had called in a number of very questionable favours getting something useful.

'The trouble with the Y-Gen is that they soon work out how to fly under the digital radar,' Rick had said over the phone. 'But he came undone by refilling his Alprazolam in his real name, even though he did it off the health scheme to stay hidden.

'As of February,' he'd continued, 'it became notifiable in order to reduce the amount of doc-shopping being done by addicts. Your guy wouldn't have known that because the GPs aren't required to advise their patients of its existence; in fact it's actively discouraged. And people call *me* dodgy...'

Marshall had ignored Rick's anti-government mutterings and scribbled the details down on the first thing at hand. The name of the drug. The town it was filled in. Ironic that prioritising his mental health had led to Travis's exposure. An obscure little register inside the Department of Health was pretty much the only official record in the entire country that had recent activity for Travis Read. Lucky for him, his brother knew someone who knew someone who knew some*thing* big about a guy in the Health Department's IT section. Something that guy was happy to have buried in return for a little casual database scrutiny.

Marshall's muttered thanks were beyond awkward. How did you thank someone for breaking innumerable laws on your behalf? Even if they did it every day.

'Whoever you're doing this for, Marsh...' Rick had said before hanging up '...I hope they know what this cost you. I sure do.'

That was the closest he'd come to acknowledging everything that went down between them in the past. He'd added just one more thing before disconnecting.

'Don't leave it so long next time.'

And then his brother was gone. After ten years. And Marshall had a few scribbled words on half a coffee-stained napkin. The pharmacy and town where Travis Read had shown his face a few months earlier.

Northam. A district centre five hours from where he was sitting.

Marshall pulled up his map app and stared at it. If Eve's intelligence was hereditary, then chances were her brother wouldn't be dumb enough to get his medical care in the town in which he was hiding out. So, he desktopped a wobbly fifty-kilometre radius around Northam and ruled out anything in the direction of the capital city. Way too public. It was also ninety-five per cent of the state's population and so that left him with only two-dozen country towns inside his circle.

If it was *him* trying to go underground, he'd find a town that was small enough to be under-resourced with government types, uninteresting enough to be off the tourist trail, but not so small that his arrival and settling in would draw attention. That meant tiny communities were out and so were any of the popular, pretty towns.

Agricultural towns were in because they'd be perfect for a man trying to find cash work off the books.

All of that filtering left him just a couple of strong candidates inside his circle. One was the state's earthquake capital and drew occasional media attention to itself that would be way too uncontrollable for a kid intent on hiding out.

That left only some towns on the southern boundary of his circle.

One was on a main route south—too much passing traffic and risk of exposure. Another too tiny.

The third was Beverley, the unofficial weekend headquarters for a biker gang and must regularly receive police attention.

He was about to cross that one through when he reconsidered. What better place to hide out than in a town filled with people with many more secrets to keep than Travis? People and activity that kept the tourists away and the authorities well and truly occupied. And where better for a newcomer to assimilate seamlessly than a town with a transient male population?

Beverley made it onto his top three. And he made a mental note to wear as much leather as he owned.

One day's drive away and he could spend a day each hunting in all three.

Then at least he would know.

It could be him.

Hard to say under the scrappy attempt at facial hair. The best of all the options he'd seen in the past couple of days, anyway. Marshall settled in at the bar and ordered something that he couldn't remember just five seconds later. Then he pulled out his phone and pretended to check his messages while covertly grabbing an image of the man that might be Eve's brother.

Evidence that Travis was alive and well.

If that even was him. Hard to tell from this far away.

There was an easy kind of camaraderie between the young man and his companions, as if an end-of-day beer was a very common thing amongst them. How nice that Travis got to sit here enjoying a beer with mates while his sister cried herself into an ulcer every night. Well-fed, reasonably groomed, clearly not here under any kind of duress, the kid seemed to have a pretty good gig going here in the small biker town.

Just before six, he pushed back from the table and his mates let him go easily, as if skipping out early was business as usual.

Out on the footpath, Marshall followed at a careful distance. How much better would the photo be if he could give the authorities an address to go with the covertly captured picture?

Authorities.

Not Eve.

This was about giving her back her brother, not getting back into her good books. Something he could do to help. Instead of hurt.

He was no better for Eve than she was for him. He'd finally accepted that.

The guy turned down a quiet street and then turned again almost immediately. Marshall jogged to catch up. The back of these old heritage streets were rabbit warrens of open backyards and skinny laneways. A hundred places for someone to disappear into their house. The guy turned again and Marshall turned his jog into a sprint, but as he took the corner into the quiet laneway he pulled up short.

The guy stood, facing him, dirty steel caps parted, ready to run, arms braced, ready for anything.

In a heartbeat, he recognised how badly he might have blown this for Eve. How easy it would be for Travis to just disappear again, deeper into Australia, where she'd never ever find him. And he realised, on a lurch of his stomach, that this cunning plan was maybe going to come completely unstuck.

And it would have his name all over it.

'Who sent you?' the guy challenged, dark eyes blazing in the dusk light.

Marshall took a single step forward. 'Travis?'

'Who sent you?' he repeated, stepping back. As he moved and the light shifted slightly, the facet of those blazing eyes changed and looked to him more like fear and less like threat.

And he'd know those eyes anywhere...

Marshall lifted both hands, palms outward, to show he came in peace.

'I'm a friend of your sister.'

CHAPTER TWELVE

'HEY…'

Marshall's voice was startling enough out of the silence without her also being so horribly unprepared for it. Eve's stomach twisted back on itself and washed through with queasiness.

She'd only just resigned herself to him being gone—truly gone—and now he was back? What the hell was he trying to do—snap her last remaining tendrils of emotional strength?

She managed to force some words up her tight throat. 'What are you doing here, Marshall?'

It felt as if she was forever asking him that.

Compassion from him was nearly unbearable, but it rained down on her from those grey eyes she'd thought never to see again.

'Sit down, Eve.'

Instantly her muscles tensed. Muscles that had heard a lot of bad news. 'Why?'

'I need to talk to you.'

'About…?'

'Eve. Will you just sit down?'

No. No… He was looking at her like her father had the day Travis was officially declared a missing person.

'I don't think I want to.'

As if what she wanted would, in any way, delay what she feared was to come.

'Okay, we'll do this upright, then.'

His mouth opened to suck in a deep breath but then snapped shut again in surprise. 'I don't know where to start. Despite all the trial runs I've had in my mind on the way back here…'

That threw her. Was he back to make another petition for something between them? She moved to head that off before he could begin. Hurting him once had been bad enough…

'Marshall—'

'I have news.'

News. The tightness became a strangle in her throat. Somehow she knew he wouldn't use that word lightly.

'You're freaking me out, Marshall,' she squeezed out.

The words practically blurted themselves onto his lips. 'I've found Travis.'

The rush of blood vacating her face left her suddenly nauseous and her legs started to go.

'He's alive, Eve,' he rushed to add.

That extra piece of information knocked the final support from under her and her buckling legs deposited her onto the bus's sofa.

'Eve…' Marshall dropped down next to her and enveloped her frigid hand between both of his. 'He's okay. He's not hurt. Not sick.'

Eve's lips trembled open but nothing came out and it distantly occurred to her that she might be in shock. He rubbed her frigid fingers and scanned her face, so maybe he thought so, too.

'He's living and working in a small town here in Western Australia. He has a job. A roof over his head. He's okay.'

Okay. He kept saying that, but her muddled mind refused to process it. 'If he was okay he'd have been in touch…'

And then his meaning hit her. New job and new house meant new life. They meant *voluntary.* Her heart began to hammer against her ribs. Everything around her took on an other-worldly gleam and it was only then she realised how many tears wobbled right on the edges of her lashes.

'Where is he?' she whispered.

It was then Marshall's anger finally registered and confusion battled through the chaos in her mind. Anger at her? Why? But colour was unquestionably high in his jaw and his eyes were stony.

'I can't tell you, Eve.'

Okay, her brain was seriously losing it. She waited for the actual meaning to sink in but all she was left with was his refusal to tell her where her long-lost brother was.

'But you found him…?'

'He asked me not to say.'

'What? No.' Disbelief stabbed low in her gut. And betrayal. And hurt. 'But I love him.'

'I know. *He* knows,' he hurried to add, though the anger on his face wasn't diminishing. 'He told me that he would disappear again if I exposed him. So that you'd never find him. He made me give him my word.'

Pain sliced across her midsection. 'But you don't even know him. You know me.'

You love *me.*

She might as well have said it. They both knew it to be true. Not that it changed anything.

'Eve, he's alive and safe and living a life. He's on his meds and is getting healthy. Every day. He just can't do that at home.'

The thump against her eardrums intensified. 'Okay, he doesn't have to come back to Melbourne. We could move—'

'It's not about Melbourne, Eve. He doesn't want to go *home*.'

Realisation sunk in and she whispered through the devastation, 'He doesn't want to be with his family?'

God, did she look as young and fragile as her disbelief sounded? Maybe, because Marshall looked positively sick to be having this conversation.

'He wants to be healthy, Eve. And he needed to start over for that to happen.'

Start over…

'He doesn't have to come back, I can go to him. If he likes where he is—'

'I'm so sorry.' He squeezed both his hands around both of hers and held on. And, after an endless pause, he spoke, leaning forward to hold her stinging eyes with his. 'He doesn't want you to come, Eve. Particularly you.'

Particularly you.

Anguish stacked up on top of pain on top of misery. And all of it was wrapped in razor blades.

'But I love him.'

His skin blanched. 'I know. I'm so sorry.'

'I need to see him,' she whispered. 'I've been searching for so long—'

'He wants a fresh start.'

A fissure opened up in her heart and began to tug wider. Her voice, when it came, was low and croaky. 'From me?'

'From everything.'

'Is this…' The fissure stretched painfully. 'Is this about *me*?'

Pity was like a cancer in his gaze. 'He can't be with you any more. Or your dad.'

'Why?' Her cry bounced off the Bedford's timber-lined walls.

Words seemed to fail him. He studied his feet for the barest of moments and then found her gaze again.

'Because of your mother, Eve.'

She stared at him, lost. Confused. But then something surfaced in the muddle of pain and thought. 'The accident?'

His expression confirmed it.

God, she could barely breathe, let alone carry on a conversation. 'But that was years ago.'

'Not for him, Eve. He carries it every day. The trauma. The anxiety. The depression. The guilt.'

Guilt? 'But Mum wasn't his fault.'

His fingers tightened around hers again and his gaze remained steady. 'It was, Eve. I'm so sorry.'

She shook the confusion away, annoyed to have to go back

over such old ground. But being angry at him helped. It gave all the pain somewhere to go.

'No. He was with her, but... She was driving drunk.'

But she could read Marshall like a book—even after just a few weeks together—and his book said something else was going on here. Something big. She blinked. Repeatedly.

'Wasn't she?'

'Didn't you say they were both thrown from the bike?'

She was almost too dizzy for words. So she just nodded.

'And the police determined that she was in control?'

'Travis was the only other person there. And he couldn't ride properly then. He was underage.'

Marshall crouched over further and peered right into her face. Lending her his strength. 'No. He couldn't.'

But it was all starting to be horribly, horribly clear.

Oh, God...

'Trav was driving?' she choked. Marshall just nodded. 'Because Mum had been drinking?'

No nod this time, just the pitying, horrible creasing of his eyes.

No... Not little Travis... 'And he never told anyone?'

'Imagine how terrified he must have been.'

A fourteen-year-old boy driving his drunk mother home to keep her safe and ending up killing her.

'He wouldn't have lied to protect himself.' Her certainty sounded fierce even to her.

'But what if he thought you'd all blame him? Hate him. That's a lot for someone to carry. Young or old. He can't face you.'

She sagged against the sofa back, this new pain having nowhere to go.

'He carried that all alone? All this time?' she whispered. 'Poor Trav. Poor baby...'

'No. Don't you take that on, too. He's getting treatment now. He's got support and he's getting stronger. He's doing pretty bloody well, all things considered.'

So why was Marshall still so very tense?

'But he knows what he wants. And needs. And he isn't going back to your world. And he doesn't want that world coming to him either.' He cursed silently. 'Ever.'

A tiny bit of heat bubbled up beneath her collar and she'd never been so grateful for anger. It cut like a hot knife through the butter of her numb disbelief and reminded her she could still feel something. And not a small something. The feelings she'd been suppressing for twelve months started to simmer and then boil up through the cracks of Marshall's revelation.

Ever.

'So...that's it?' she wheezed. 'I gave up a year of my life to find him—I broke my heart searching for him—and all this time he's been living comfortably across the country *starting over*?'

Marshall's lips pressed together. 'He's made his choice.'

'And you've made yours, apparently. You've taken his side pretty darned quick for a man you don't know.'

'Eve, I'm on your side—'

It was as if someone was puffing her with invisible bellows filled with hot air...making this worse and worse.

'Don't! How do I know you're not just making this all up to further your cause?'

'You can't be serious.'

'How would I know? The only evidence I have that any of this is true is your word. You might not have found him at all. You might just want me to think that. You might say anything to get me to stay with you.'

The words poured out uncontrollably.

'What the hell have I done to make you believe that of me?' But he rummaged in his pocket, pulled out his phone and opened his photo app. 'Believe this, then.'

Seeing Travis just about broke her heart.

Her baby brother. Alive. Healthy. Enjoying a beer. Even laughing. *Laughing!* She hadn't seen that in years.

She certainly hadn't done it in as long.

Tears tumbled.

'Eve—'

'What would happen, Marshall?' she asked desperately. 'If you told me where he is. How would he even know?'

She was flying through the stages of grief. At bargaining already.

'I know you, Eve…'

'So you're just going to take the choice away from me? Like some child?'

'You wouldn't be able to stay away. You know it.'

'I'm not about to *stalk him*, Marshall.'

'You already are, Eve! You're scouring the country systematically, hunting him down.'

Her gasp pinged around the little bus. 'Is that how you see it?'

'Why else would you want to know where he is? Unless you were going to keep tabs on him.'

'Because I *love* him. You have no right to keep this from me.'

'I'm not doing this to be a bastard, Eve. I don't want you in any more pain.'

'You think this doesn't hurt? Knowing he's alive and I can't get to him? Can't hold him? Or help him? You think that's kinder than letting me hear from his own lips that he doesn't want to come home?'

Just saying the words was horrible.

He took her chin in his fingers and forced her to look at him and, despite everything, her skin still thrilled at his simple touch. It had been days…

'Hear me, Eve,' he urged. 'If you go there he will disappear again. He knows what to do now, he'll be better at it and he might go off his meds to keep himself hidden. You will never see or hear from your brother again. Is that what you want?'

In all her wildest, worst dreams she'd never imagined she'd be sitting here, across from Marshall—of all people—fighting him for her brother's whereabouts.

But, dear Lord, fight she would.

'How is that any different to what I have now?'

'Because I know where he is and he's agreed to check in with me from time to time.'

The grief and hurt surged up right below her skin, preparing to boil over.

'So…what? You get to be some kind of gatekeeper to my family? Who the hell gave you that authority?'

'He has a legal right to go missing. He wasn't hurt, or forced, or under any kind of duress. He decided to leave.'

'He was sick!'

'And managing his condition.'

He had an answer for every single argument. 'Then he must have been desperate.'

'Maybe, but he's not now. He's doing okay, I swear.' He caught her eyes again and brought everything back to the simple truth. 'You've found him, Eve.'

'No, *you* found him. I have as little as I had before.' Less, really. 'And, whatever he's going through, he clearly needs some kind of psychological help. People don't just walk out on perfectly good families.'

'They do, Eve. For all kinds of reasons. He couldn't stay, not knowing what he'd done. Fearing you'd discover it. Knowing how much you'd sacrificed—'

The inquest. The random timing of his disappearance suddenly came into crystal focus. 'I can help him.'

'You're still protecting him from responsibility? He's an adult, Eve. He doesn't want your help.'

'He needs it.'

'Does he, Eve? Or do you just need to believe that?'

She stiffened where she sat.

'You were his big sister. You looked after him and your father after the accident. That became your role. And for the last twelve months you've been about nothing but him. You chucked in your job. You sold your house. What do you have if you don't have him?'

'I have…plenty, thanks very much. I'll go back to my career, reignite my friendships. Get a new place.'

Oh, such lies. There was no going back. She didn't even know how to be normal now.

'And then what? What are you if you're not all about your brother, Eve? You've been doing this since you were barely out of school.'

Furious heat sped up the back of her neck and she surged to her feet. 'Don't put this on me. You're choosing to protect him instead of me. How about we talk about that for a bit?'

He shot up right behind her and angry fists caught her upper arms. But he didn't shake her. It was more desperate and gentle than that.

'I would *never* protect him, Eve. I hate what he's done to you. I hate that I found him sitting in a pub having a relaxed beer with friends while your soul was haemorrhaging hope *every single day.* I hate that he's got himself a new life when he was gifted with *you* in his old one.'

He said 'you' as if that was something pretty darned special. The stress faults in her heart strained that tiny bit more.

'I hate that he ditched you and your father rather than find the strength to work through it and that he didn't believe in your strength and integrity more.' He sucked in a breath. 'I would never put him ahead of you. I'm choosing *you.* This is all about you.'

'Then tell me where—'

'I can't!' he cried. 'He will disappear, Eve. The first sign of someone else looking for him. The first poster he sees in a neighbouring town. The first time his phone makes a weird noise. The next stranger who looks at him sideways in the street. He's dead serious about this,' he urged. 'Please. Just let it go.'

'How can I possibly do that?' she snarled.

'You once told me that all you wanted was to know he was all right. To have an answer. And nothing else mattered. Well, now you know. He's fine. But you're shifting the goalposts.'

'So, knowing is not enough! Maybe I do want him home, safe, with us. What's wrong with that?'

'Nothing. Except it's not achievable. And you need to accept that. It will be easier.'

'On who?'

'While your head and heart are full of your brother, then no one and nothing else can get through.'

'Are we back to that, Marshall? You and me?'

'No. You've been painfully clear on that front. I just wanted…'

He couldn't finish, so she finished for him. 'To save the day? To be the hero? Guess you weren't expecting to have to come back and be the bad guy, huh?'

'I didn't *have* to be anything.'

'You preferred to have me despise you?'

His eyes flared as if her words hit him like an axe. But he let her go and she stumbled at the sudden loss of his strength.

'You bang on about your great enduring love for your brother,' he grated. 'But you don't recognise it when it's staring you in the face. I chose *you* here today, Eve. Not myself and certainly not Travis. I am critically aware that the end of your suffering means the end of any chance for you and me. Yet here I am. Begging you to come back to the real world. Before it's too late.'

'Reality?' she whispered. 'Life doesn't get much realer than having someone you love ripped from you and held away, just out of reach.'

His eyes bled grey streaks. 'Finally. Something we agree on.'

He pushed away and walked to the bus's back door. But he caught himself there with a clenched fist on each side of the doorframe. His head sagged forward and his back arched.

Everything about his posture screamed pain.

Well, that made two of them.

But he didn't step forward. Instead, he turned back.

'You know what? Yes. Maybe I did want to be the man who

took your pain away. Who ended all your suffering. Maybe I did want to see you look at me with something more heartfelt than curiosity or amusement or plain old lust.'

Haunted eyes bled.

'You're halfway to being missing yourself, emotionally speaking. And if Travis was found, then you'd have no choice but to return to the real, functional, living world. And I wanted to be the man that helped get you there.'

'Why?'

Frustrated hands flew up. 'Why do you think, Eve? Why do any of us do anything, ultimately?'

She blinked her stinging eyes, afraid to answer.

'*Love*, Eve.' So tired. So very weary. Almost a joke on himself. He made the word sound like a terminal condition. 'I love you. And I wanted to *give* you your heart's desire if I couldn't be it.'

'You barely know me,' she breathed.

'You're wrong.' He stepped up closer to her. Towered above her. 'You spend so much time stopping yourself from feeling emotion that you've forgotten to control how much of it you show. You're an open book, Eve.

'I know you're heartbroken about Travis betraying you like this,' he went on, 'and confused about loving him yet hating this thing he's done. I know you're desperate for somewhere to send all that pain, and you don't really want to throw it at me but you can't deal with it all yourself because you've closed down, emotionally, to cope with the past year. Maybe even longer. And it's easier to hate me than him.'

Tears sprang back into her eyes.

'I know it particularly hurts you that it's *me* that's withholding Travis from you because deep down you thought we had a connection even if you didn't have the heart to pursue it. You trusted me, and I've betrayed you. Maybe that's the price I had to pay for trying to rescue you.'

She curled her trembling fingers into a fist.

'I could have told you nothing, Eve. I could have simply kept driving after letting him know that you were all looking for him. Left you thinking well of me. And maybe I could have come back into your life in the future and had a chance. But here I am instead, destroying any chance of us being together by telling you the hard truth about your brother. So you hear it from me rather than from him.'

Her voice was barely more than a croak. 'What do you mean?'

'I've seen your route maps, Eve.' He sighed. 'You would have reached his town before Christmas. And *you* would have found him drinking in that pub, and *you* would have had to stand there, struggling to be strong as he told you how he'd traded up to a better new life rather than the tough old one he'd left, and as he threw everything you've sacrificed and been through back in your face.'

She reached out for something solid to hold on to and found nothing. Because he wasn't there for her any more.

'And you would have knocked on his door the next morning with takeaway coffee, only to find he'd cleared out, with not a single clue. And you would have spent the rest of your life hunting for him.

'And so, even though it hurts like death to do this to you, I would take this pain one hundred times over to spare you from it.'

She stared at him through glistening eyes—wordless—as he stepped up closer.

'I'm not fool enough to think there's a place for me here now, even if you did have some capacity in your heart. I wouldn't expect—or even want—to just slide into the emotional vacancy left by your brother. Or your mother. Or anyone else you've ever loved.

'I deserve my *own* piece of you, Eve. Just mine. I think that's all I've ever really wanted in my sorry excuse for a life. The tiniest patch of your heart to cultivate with beautiful flowering vines and tend and spoil until they can spread up your walls and through your cracks and over your trellises. Until you've forgotten what it was like to *not* have me there. In the garden of your heart.'

He leaned down and kissed her, careless of the puffy, slimy, tear-ravaged parts of her. Long, hard and deep. A farewell. Eve practically clung to the strong heat of his lips.

'But I can't do anything with the rocky, parched earth you'll have left after all this is over. Nothing will ever grow there.'

He tucked a strand of damp hair behind her ears and murmured, 'Go home, Eve. Put him behind you. Put me behind you. Just…heal.'

This time, he didn't pause at the door, he just pushed through, jumped down to the ground and strode off, leaving Eve numb, trembling and destroyed in the little bus that had become her cage.

CHAPTER THIRTEEN

Five months later

MARSHALL SPRINTED UP the valley side to the cottage, sweaty from a morning of post-hole-digging and dusting the rich dirt off his hands as he went. He snatched the phone up just before his voicemail kicked in.

Landline. Not many people called that any more.

'Hello?'

'Marshall?'

A voice familiar yet…not. Courtesy of the long-distance crackle.

'Yeah. Who's this?'

'Travis Read.'

His heart missed a beat. 'Has something happened?'

That was their agreement. Marshall would call twice a year to check in and, apart from that, Travis would only call if something was up. It had only been five months since they'd last spoken. He wasn't yet due.

'No, I'm…uh…I'm in town this afternoon and wondered if I could come and see you.'

Since Travis only had his new Victorian phone number, not his new home address, 'in town' had to mean Melbourne. That was all the area code would have told him. But what could Eve's brother possibly have to say? And why did he sound so tense? Unless it was recriminations. It occurred to him to question why he would have caught a plane anywhere since that would flag him on the Federal Police's radar and risk exposure. Unless he used a fake name. Or drove. Or maybe his family had taken him off the missing-persons register so that scarce resources weren't wasted on a man who wasn't really missing.

He'd given Travis one more go all those months ago for Eve's sake. Pointlessly tried to get him to change his mind, told him the damage it had done to his own life—in the long-term—to walk away from his family, as imperfect as they were. How it hadn't solved any of his problems at all—he'd just learned to function around them.

Or not, as the case may be.

But Travis hadn't budged. He was as stubborn as his sister, it seemed. And now he wanted to meet.

Irritation bubbled just below Marshall's surface. He was already keeping Travis's secret at the expense of his own happiness. Hadn't he done enough?

But then he remembered how important this kid was to the woman he was still struggling to get over and he reluctantly shared his new address and gave Travis a time later in the day before trundling back down the hill to the Zen meditation of punching three-dozen fenceposts into the unsuspecting earth.

About fifteen minutes before Travis was due, Marshall threw some water on his face and washed his filthy hands. The rest… Travis would have to take him as he found him.

About six minutes after their appointed time Marshall heard a knock at his front door and spied a small hire car out of one of the windows as he reached the door.

'Trav—?'

He stopped dead. Not Travis.

Eve.

In the flesh and smiling nervously on his doorstep.

His first urge was to wrap her up in his arms and never, ever let her go again. But he fought that and let himself frown instead. His quick brain ran through the facts and decided that she was obviously here in Travis's place. Which suggested Eve and Travis were in communication.

Which meant—his sinking heart realised—that everything he'd done, everything he'd given up, counted for absolutely nothing.

'How did you find him?'

'Good to see you, too,' she joked. Pretty wanly. But he wasn't in any mood for levity. Not while he was feeling this ambushed.

'I didn't find him,' she finally offered. 'He found me.'

So Travis had finally found the personal courage to pick up the phone. Good for him.

And—yeah—he'd be a hypocrite if not for the fact that he'd since taken his own advice and done the same with Rick. His brother hadn't commented on the new mobile number but Marshall felt certain he'd tried to use the old one. That was why he'd yanked out the SIM and tossed it somewhere along the Bussell Highway the same awful night he'd last seen Eve.

The whole world could just go screw itself. Travis. Eve. Rick.

Everyone.

'I was heading home,' Eve said now. 'Backtracking through Esperance. My phone rang and I thought it might be you, but... it was him.'

The flatness of her tone belied the enormity of what that moment must have meant for Eve.

'Why would you think it was me?' Hadn't they been pretty clear with each other when they'd parted?

She shrugged lightly. 'I'd tried your number several times and it was disconnected, but—you know—hope springs eternal.'

On that cryptic remark, she shuffled from left foot to right on his doorstep.

Ugh, idiot. He stepped aside. 'Sorry, come on in.'

There was something about her being here. Here, where he'd had to force himself finally to stop imagining what the cottage would be like with her in it. It felt as if he'd sprinted up the valley side and into an alternate dimension where his dreams had finally turned material.

Inside, she glanced around her and then crossed straight to the full wall window that looked out over the picturesque valley.

'Gorgeous,' she muttered almost to herself.

While she was otherwise occupied with the view, he took the opportunity to look at her. She'd changed, but he couldn't quite put his finger on how. Her hair was shorter and glossier but not that different. Her eyes at the front door had been bright but still essentially held the same wary gaze he remembered. She turned from the window and started to comment further on his view when it hit him. It was the way she carried herself; she seemed…taller. No, not taller—straighter. As if a great burden she'd been carrying around was now gone.

And maybe it was.

But having her here—in his sanctuary—wasn't good for him. It physically hurt to see her in his space, so he cut to the chase and stopped her before she offered some view-related platitude.

'What are you doing here, Eve?'

Maybe she deserved his scepticism. The way they'd left things… Certainly, Eve had known she wouldn't be walking into open arms.

'I'm sorry for the deception,' she began. 'I wasn't sure you'd see me. We didn't really leave things…open…for future contact. Your phone was dead and your infuriating Government privacy procedures meant no one in your department would give me your new one. And you moved, too.'

She caught herself before she revealed even more ways she'd tried to reach out to him. It wasn't as if she'd been short of time.

'Yet here you are.'

'I guilted Travis into hooking this up,' she confessed. 'He

wasn't very happy about betraying you when you've kept his secret in good faith.'

Which explained the tension on the phone earlier. And the long-distance hum. 'To absolutely no purpose, it seems, since you two are now talking.'

'"Talking" is probably an overstatement,' she said. 'We speak. Now and again. Just him and me at this stage but maybe Dad in the future. Trav reached out a few months ago. Said you'd called him again.'

'I did.' Though it had never occurred to him that the contents of that call might some day end up in Eve's ear.

'Talking about everything that happened is pretty hard for him,' she said flatly. 'You were right about that. And you were right that he would have bolted if I'd pushed. He was very close to it.'

'That's partly why I called him again. To make sure he hadn't already done a runner.'

But not the only reason. 'Whatever you talked about, Travis got a lot out of it. It was a real turning point for him.'

Silence fell between them and Eve struggled to know how to continue. His nerves only infected her more.

'So, you went home?' Marshall nudged.

'I was paralysed for a few days,' she admitted. 'Terrified of any forward move in case I accidentally ended up in his town and triggered another disappearance. You could hardly tell me which town not to visit, could you?'

She fought the twist of her lips so that it felt more like a grimace. Great—finally tracked him down and she was grinning like the Joker.

'So I backtracked the way I'd come,' she finished. 'That seemed safe.'

'I wondered if you might still be in Western Australia,' he murmured.

So far away. 'There wasn't anything to stay for.'

Travis in lockdown. Marshall gone. Her journey suspended. She'd never felt so lonely and lost.

'So, here you are.'

'Here I am.' She glanced around. 'And here *you* are.'

All these months he'd been here, within a single day's mountain drive of her family home. God, if only she'd known. She would have come much sooner.

'Do you know where we are?' he asked.

Not exactly warm, but not quite hostile. Just very…restrained.

'The satnav says we're near MacKenzie Falls.' A place they'd both enjoyed so much on their separate trips around the country. 'That's quite a coincidence.'

'Not really. It was somewhere I wanted to come back to.'

Okay. Not giving an inch. She supposed she deserved that.

'You gave up meteorology?'

'No. I consult now. From here, mostly. The wonder of remote technology.'

She glanced out at the carnage in his bottom paddock. 'When you're not building fences?'

'Who knew I'd be so suited to farming.'

'I think you could do pretty much anything you turned your hand to.'

'Thanks for the vote of confidence. Now why are we having this conversation, Eve?'

She sighed and crossed closer to him.

'I wanted to… I *need to* thank you.'

'For what?'

Her fingers were frozen despite the warm day. She rubbed the nerves against her jeans. 'The wake-up call.'

He crossed his arms and leaned on his kitchen island. Okay, he wasn't going to make this any easier.

'When you love a missing person,' she started, 'you can't grieve, you can't move on. You can't plan or make life decisions. So it just becomes easier to…not. It hurts less if you just shut down. And when one system goes down, they all do.

'In my case,' she went on, 'I coped by having a clear, single purpose.'

Find Travis.

'And that was all I could deal with. All I could hold in my head and my heart. I developed tunnel vision.'

Marshall studied the tips of his work boots.

'I once told you that if Travis walked in the door, healthy and alive, nothing he'd done would matter.'

He nodded. Just once.

'Me dealing with it so maturely was every bit as much a fantasy as him walking in the door unannounced. Turns out, I'm not so stoic under pressure.' She lifted her eyes. 'It matters, Marshall. It matters a lot. Even as I argued with people who warned me that he might not be alive, I secretly wanted them to be right. Rather than accept he might torture his family like this, deliberately. Leave us wondering forever. And then I hated myself for allowing those thoughts.'

Realisation dawned on his face. 'So when it turned out to be true...'

She shook her head. 'I'm very sorry for the things I said. The way I said them. I thought you were putting Travis ahead of me and that clawed at my heart. I'm sorry to say it took me days to realise that was what I did to you every single day. Put you second. The truth is, you sacrificed yourself—and any chance of us being together—for me. To help spare me pain.'

'So you came to apologise?'

Could a heart swell under pressure? Because hers felt twice its usual size. Heavy and pendulous and thumpy. And it was getting in the way of her breathing.

'You put yourself second.' After a lifetime of coming second. 'For me. Not many men would have done that.'

His voice, when it came, was not quite steady. But still a fortress wall. 'So you came to say thanks?'

She took a breath. Inside her long sleeves she twisted her fingers. Over and over. 'I came to see if I'm too late.'

Marshall didn't move. 'Too late for what?'

'For that vision you had,' she said on a sad, weak laugh.

'The timber cabin in the forest with the clear pools…and me. And you,' she finished on a rush.

And the making love twice a day part. She'd clung to that image for the many lonely nights since he'd left.

Marshall gave nothing away, simply pushed from the island bench and moved to stare out of his window.

'You stuck with me, Eve,' he admitted. 'I finished my audit and returned to Sydney, assuming that a little time was all I needed to get you out of my system. But months passed and you were still there. Under my skin like ink. I couldn't shake you. You were wedged in here.'

He tapped his chest with a closed fist.

'But it doesn't really matter what my heart thinks because my head knows better. And if my life has taught me anything, it's to listen to my head.' He turned back to her. 'I've walked away from much longer relationships than ours when they weren't good for me, Eve. Why would I set myself up to be the second most important person in your life?'

'That's not—'

'So, yes, Eve. I got the cottage in the forest surrounded by pools and, yes, I hope to be happy here. Very happy.' He expelled a long, sad breath. 'But no…there's no *you* in that plan any more.'

A rock of pain lodged in her stomach.

'At all?' she whispered.

'You don't have room for me, Eve. I'd convinced myself that you'd cast me as some kind of substitute for your brother but I no longer think that's true. I just don't think you have any emotional capacity left. And I deserve better than sorry seconds.'

She struggled to steady her breath. But it was touch and go. Every instinct she had told her to go, to flee back home. Except that when she'd come here she'd really hoped that *this* might turn out to be home.

And no home worth having came without risk. It was time to be brave.

'I wasn't out there to find Travis,' she whispered, taking

the chance. 'I think I was out there trying to find a way to let him go.'

She shuddered in a breath. 'But that was terrifying. What if I had nothing but a massive, gaping hole inside where my love and worry and pain for him used to be? What if I could never fill it? Or heal it. Who was I without him? So much of *me* was gone.'

His strong arms wrapped across his chest and all she could think about was wanting them around her.

'And what little was left around the outside was just numb.' She stepped closer to him. 'But then you came in with your ridiculous orange motorbike and your hairy face and your tattoos and you were like…an icebreaker. Shoving your stubborn way through the frost. Inch by inch.'

A tragic kind of light flickered weakly behind his eyes and it sickened her that she'd been the one to extinguish it before. The memory of him standing in her bus, appealing from the heart, in visible, tangible pain. And she'd not been able to feel a thing.

But his body language was giving nothing away now.

'I'm not a plug, Eve. I'm a person. You'll have to find someone else to fill the void.'

'I don't want you to fill it. I want you to bridge it.'

His eyes came up.

Eve picked up a cushion off his sofa and hugged it close. 'When you left, it was horrible. You gone. Travis gone. Mum gone. Dad on the other side of the country. I'd never felt so alone. Which is ridiculous, I realise, given I'd been travelling solo all year.'

His brow twitched with half a frown, so quick she almost missed it. His posture shifted. Straightened. 'What changed?'

'I couldn't stay frozen.' She shrugged. 'I tried to do what I'd done before, just…deal. But all these emotions started bubbling up out of nowhere and I realised that I'd been harbouring the same feelings Travis must have had since Mum died. Despair. Anxiety. I'd been suppressing them, just like he must have.'

'So you developed some empathy for your brother. That's great.'

'I wasn't thinking about him, Marshall,' she rushed to correct. 'God knows, I should have been, and it took me a while to notice, but eventually I thought how strange it was that I should feel such despair about my brother being *alive*. Anger, sure. Resentment, maybe. But despair…?

'Travis has been absent in my life since Mum died. Even back when he was still physically present. I'd learned how to compensate for his absence and not fall apart. But there I was, trundling up the highway, completely unable to manage my feelings about the absence of someone I'd known less than a fortnight.'

His face lifted. His eyes blazed. But he didn't say a word.

'I wasn't thinking about Travis. I wasn't weeping about Travis. I was thinking about you. Missing…you.'

He had nothing to say to that.

'Nothing felt right without you there,' she whispered.

Agony blazed from his tired eyes. 'Do you understand how hard this is to hear? Now?'

It was too late.

Something grasped at her organs and fisted deep in her gut. She gathered up her handbag. 'I don't want you thinking badly of me, Marshall. I don't want you remembering me as the outback psycho in a bus. I have years' worth of coping mechanisms that I need to unlearn. I barely know where to start. It's going to be a long work in progress.'

She stepped up to him. Determined to get one thing right in their relationship, even if that was goodbye.

'But I'm on my way. Thanks to you. I just didn't want you never knowing how much you helped me. What a difference you made. I'm just sorry I couldn't return the favour. I'm sorry I hurt you.'

She pushed up onto her toes and pressed a kiss to his face, over the corner of his mouth, and then whispered into it, 'Thank you.'

Then she dropped back onto her soles and turned for the door.

'Eve.'

His voice came just as she slid her hand onto the heritage doorknob. But she didn't turn, she only paused.

'What about that bridge?'

The one over the void where her love for Travis used to be?

'I guess I won't be needing it,' she murmured past the ache in her chest. 'It doesn't go anywhere now.'

He stepped up behind her and turned her to face him. 'Where did it go? Before?'

As she spoke, her eyes moistened and threatened to shame her. But she didn't shy away from it. She was done hiding her emotions.

'Someone once told me about a garden,' she breathed, smiling through the gathering tears. 'One which used to be barren rubble. With old stone walls and handmade trellises, and where someone had planted a beautiful, fragrant vine. That's where it went.'

He swallowed hard. 'How will you visit it with no bridge?'

'I won't,' she choked. 'But I'll imagine it. Every day. And it will grow without me—up and over the trellis, through the cracks in the wall. And eventually it will cover up all the rocky and exposed places where nothing could thrive.'

And then she'd be whole again.

Marshall glanced away, visibly composing himself. And then he spoke. 'There's something you need to see.'

He slid his fingers through hers and led her out through the front door and down the paving stones to the rear of the house where a large timber door blocked the path. He moved her in front of him and reached around her to open the door.

It swung inwards.

And Eve burst into tears.

She stepped through into the garden of her imagination. Complete with trellis, flowering vines, stone wall and even a small fishpond. All of it blurred by the tears streaming down her face.

All so much prettier than she could ever have imagined.

'Don't cry, Eve,' Marshall murmured right behind her. Closer than she'd allowed herself even to dream.

Which only escalated the sobs that racked her uncontrollably.

'It's so perfect,' she squeezed out between gasped breaths.

'I made it for you,' he confessed. 'It was the first thing I started when I came here.'

Her body jerked with weeping. 'Why?'

'Because it's yours—' he shrugged, stroking her hair '—it was always yours.'

He turned her into the circle of his arms. Warm. Hard. Sweaty from a day of work. Heartbreakingly close. One arm pulled her tighter, the other curled up behind her head so that he could press his lips there.

'You are not some outback psycho,' he soothed into her hair. 'You're passionate and warm and you feel things intensely.'

Maybe she could now that the ice inside her was starting to thaw.

'I wanted all that love you kept in reserve for your brother,' he breathed. 'I hated that Travis was hoarding it. That he'd just walked away from it as though it wasn't the most precious commodity on earth.'

She pulled back and gave him a watery smile. 'He doesn't want it.'

'Someone else does, Eve. Every single bit of it.' Grey eyes blazed down on her. 'I don't care where it comes from, or where it's been. I just care that it's here, in your garden. With me.'

She curled her hands in his shirt. 'You don't hate me?'

'I never hated you,' he soothed. 'I hated myself. I hated the world and everything in my past that stopped me from being able to just love you. And I was angry at myself for trying to be your champion and fix everything, when all I did was make things worse for you.'

'If you hadn't found Travis, I'd still be driving around the country, heartbroken.'

'If I hadn't found Travis, I'd still be driving around with you,' he avowed. 'I would never have left that easily. I would have just given you some breathing space. I was trying to protect you, not control you.'

'I couldn't face the road without you,' she admitted. 'That's why I went home.'

'I have a confession to make,' he murmured. 'This farm wasn't just about MacKenzie Falls. I picked it so that your father wouldn't have to lose you twice.'

She peered up at him and he tackled her tears with his smudged flannel shirt. 'Lose me where?'

'Lose you to here,' he said, kissing one swollen eyelid and then the other. 'To me.'

Breathless tension coiled in her belly. 'You wanted me to come here?'

'I wanted you with me.'

'Five minutes ago you said it was too late.'

'Eve…if I've learned anything from you it's that surviving is not enough. I survived by leaving my mother and brother behind but it didn't change anything—it didn't change me. I've been on emotional hold since then, just like you. And that can work to a point but it's no good forever. At some point I had to take a risk and start believing in people again. In you.'

'I let you down so badly.'

'I was expecting it. I would have found it no matter what.'

Confused joy tripped and fell over its own feet in her mind. 'You believe in me now?'

'Better, Eve. I believe in myself.'

'And you want me to stay here?'

His lips, hot and heavy, grazed hers, and it wasn't nearly enough contact after so long. She chased his touch with her own.

'I want you to *live* here,' he pledged. And then, in case her addled mind really wasn't keeping up, he added, 'With me.

And the forest. Somewhere we can retreat to when our crazy all-consuming families get too much. Somewhere we can just be us.'

A joyous blooming began somewhere just behind her heart.

'I'll always worry about him,' she warned. She wasn't simply going to be able to excise Travis from her life the way he'd done to her. Once a big sister, always a big sister.

'I know. And I'll always have the family felon to help keep tabs on him.' Then, at her quizzical expression, he added, 'Long story.'

'Everything I said—'

'*Everything* is in the past, Eve. I'm asking you to choose the future. I'm asking you to choose me.'

The last time he'd asked that of her, she'd chosen her brother. And broken Marshall's soul.

She slid her arms around his gorgeous, hard middle and peered up at him from the heart of their fantasy garden.

'No,' she said breathlessly, and then squeezed him reassuringly as he flinched. 'This time *I choose us*.'

* * * * *